Privacy Preservation and Secured Data Storage in Cloud Computing

Lakshmi D.
VIT Bhopal University, India

Amit Kumar Tyagi
National Institute of Fashion Technology, New Delhi, India

A volume in the Advances in Information Security, Privacy, and Ethics (AISPE) Book Series

IGI Global
PUBLISHER of TIMELY KNOWLEDGE

Published in the United States of America by
IGI Global
Engineering Science Reference (an imprint of IGI Global)
701 E. Chocolate Avenue
Hershey PA, USA 17033
Tel: 717-533-8845
Fax: 717-533-8661
E-mail: cust@igi-global.com
Web site: http://www.igi-global.com

Library of Congress Cataloging-in-Publication Data

Names: D., Lakshmi (Dhandabani, Lakshmi), editor. | Tyagi, Amit Kumar, 1988- editor.
Title: Privacy preservation and secured data storage in cloud computing / edited by Lakshmi D, Amit Kumar Tyagi.
Description: Hershey, PA : Engineering Science Reference, 2024. | Includes bibliographical references and index. | Summary: "This book delves into the pressing issues related to privacy and secured data storage in cloud computing. It explores the threats and vulnerabilities that cloud computing faces and discuss various techniques and strategies that can be used to safeguard data in the cloud"-- Provided by publisher.
Identifiers: LCCN 2023034630 (print) | LCCN 2023034631 (ebook) | ISBN 9798369305935 (h/c) | ISBN 9798369305942 (ebook)
Subjects: LCSH: Cloud computing--Security measures. | Data privacy. | Data protection.
Classification: LCC QA76.585 .P754 2024 (print) | LCC QA76.585 (ebook) | DDC 005.8--dc23/eng/20231023
LC record available at https://lccn.loc.gov/2023034630
LC ebook record available at https://lccn.loc.gov/2023034631

This book is published in the IGI Global book series Advances in Information Security, Privacy, and Ethics (AISPE) (ISSN: 1948-9730; eISSN: 1948-9749)

British Cataloguing in Publication Data
A Cataloguing in Publication record for this book is available from the British Library.

Advances in Information Security, Privacy, and Ethics (AISPE) Book Series

Manish Gupta
State University of New York, USA

ISSN:1948-9730
EISSN:1948-9749

Mission

As digital technologies become more pervasive in everyday life and the Internet is utilized in ever increasing ways by both private and public entities, concern over digital threats becomes more prevalent.

The **Advances in Information Security, Privacy, & Ethics (AISPE) Book Series** provides cutting-edge research on the protection and misuse of information and technology across various industries and settings. Comprised of scholarly research on topics such as identity management, cryptography, system security, authentication, and data protection, this book series is ideal for reference by IT professionals, academicians, and upper-level students.

Coverage

- Information Security Standards
- Electronic Mail Security
- Risk Management
- Telecommunications Regulations
- IT Risk
- Cyberethics
- Network Security Services
- Technoethics
- Computer ethics
- Internet Governance

IGI Global is currently accepting manuscripts for publication within this series. To submit a proposal for a volume in this series, please contact our Acquisition Editors at Acquisitions@igi-global.com or visit: http://www.igi-global.com/publish/.

The Advances in Information Security, Privacy, and Ethics (AISPE) Book Series (ISSN 1948-9730) is published by IGI Global, 701 E. Chocolate Avenue, Hershey, PA 17033-1240, USA, www.igi-global.com. This series is composed of titles available for purchase individually; each title is edited to be contextually exclusive from any other title within the series. For pricing and ordering information please visit http://www.igi-global.com/book-series/advances-information-security-privacy-ethics/37157. Postmaster: Send all address changes to above address.

Titles in this Series

For a list of additional titles in this series, please visit: www.igi-global.com/book-series

Malware Analysis and Intrusion Detection in Cyber-Physical Systems
S.L. Shiva Darshan (Department of Information and Communication Technology, Manipal Institute of Technology, India) M.V. Manoj Kumar (Department of Information Science and Engineering, Nitte Meenakshi Institute of Technology, India) B.S. Prashanth (Department of Information Science and Engineering, Nitte Meenakshi Institute of Technology, India) and Y. Vishnu Srinivasa Murthy (Department of Computational Intelligence, Vellore Institute of Technology, India)
Information Science Reference • © 2023 • 415pp • H/C (ISBN: 9781668486665) • US $225.00

Handbook of Research on Data Science and Cybersecurity Innovations in Industry 4.0 Technologies
Thangavel Murugan (United Arab Emirates University, Al Ain, UAE) and Nirmala E. (VIT Bhopal University, ndia)
Information Science Reference • © 2023 • 620pp • H/C (ISBN: 9781668481455) • US $325.00

Perspectives on Ethical Hacking and Penetration Testing
Keshav Kaushik (University of Petroleum and Energy Studies, India) and Akashdeep Bhardwaj (University of Petroleum and Energy Studies, ndia)
Information Science Reference • © 2023 • 445pp • H/C (ISBN: 9781668482186) • US $225.00

Contemporary Challenges for Cyber Security and Data Privacy
Nuno Mateus-Coelho (Lusófona University, Portugal) and Maria Manuela Cruz-Cunha (Polytechnic Institute of Cávado and Ave, Portugal)
Information Science Reference • © 2023 • 340pp • H/C (ISBN: 9798369315286) • US $275.00

AI Tools for Protecting and Preventing Sophisticated Cyber Attacks
Eduard Babulak (National Science Foundation, USA)
Information Science Reference • © 2023 • 233pp • H/C (ISBN: 9781668471104) • US $250.00

Cyber Trafficking, Threat Behavior, and Malicious Activity Monitoring for Healthcare Organizations
Dinesh C. Dobhal (Graphic Era University (Deemed), India) Sachin Sharma (Graphic Era University (Deemed), India) Kamlesh C. Purohit (Graphic Era University (Deemed), India) Lata Nautiyal (University of Bristol, UK) and Karan Singh (Jawaharlal Nehru University, India)
Medical Information Science Reference • © 2023 • 206pp • H/C (ISBN: 9781668466469) • US $315.00

Emerging Perspectives in Systems Security Engineering, Data Science, and Artificial Intelligence
Maurice Dawson (Illinois Institute of Technology, USA)
Information Science Reference • © 2023 • 315pp • H/C (ISBN: 9781668463253) • US $250.00

IGI Global
PUBLISHER of TIMELY KNOWLEDGE

701 East Chocolate Avenue, Hershey, PA 17033, USA
Tel: 717-533-8845 x100 • Fax: 717-533-8661
E-Mail: cust@igi-global.com • www.igi-global.com

Editorial Advisory Board

Table of Contents

Detailed Table of Contents

Cloud computing has swiftly emerged as the dominant IT paradigm, revolutionizing data storage and processing with scalable, cost-effective solutions for individuals and businesses. However, concerns over data security and privacy have arisen due to the migration of sensitive data to remote servers. This chapter introduces privacy and secure data storage principles in the cloud context. It covers threats, emphasizing robust security measures like encryption, access control, and anonymization. The chapter also addresses legal frameworks, urging alignment with regulations. It presents best practices for secure data storage, including encryption and emerging tech like homomorphic encryption. Ultimately, the chapter aims to equip readers with a comprehensive understanding of privacy preservation and secure data handling in the cloud, enabling informed decisions that uphold data privacy.

The adoption of cloud-based services has been on the rise in recent years. In this study, a comparative study of three major cloud database platforms, namely Microsoft Azure, IBM DB2, and Oracle Cloud, was conducted to analyze their features, performance, and suitability for different use cases. This chapter explores the architectures of these platforms, examines their database management tools, and evaluates their support for scalability, security, and data integration. In the experiment section, Oracle performed the best with an average execution time of 3.35ms, which was the fastest of the three databases. In the survey section, the results show that MS Azure is the most available, secure, cost effective, and efficient. Oracle can be seen from the survey responses as the most reliable and also most cost effective. This chapter gives insightful information to organizations and people who want to pick the finest cloud database platform for their requirements.

The delivery of healthcare is an area where data access, processing, analysis, sharing, and storage between many parties is exceedingly important. In order to address this demand, cloud computing has gained popularity in a wide range of fields, including telemedicine, information management, and bioinformatics. The gestures of the patient were continuously captured and recorded in the cloud. The gesture recognition may be applied especially for the bed-ridden patients who cannot communicate verbally. The sample simulation of the clustering and disease identification with the gesture recognition was done to prove the efficacy of the system. In this chapter, various artifacts of cloud-based technology and the possibility of implementation in the healthcare sector is discussed briefly.

As the organization moves to cloud computing to take advantage of lower cost and higher efficiencies and availability, privacy and confidentiality concerns remain a challenge. Modern techniques to manage such challenges with careful evaluation are required to implement effective strategies for privacy protection in cloud computing. In this chapter, various needs for privacy protection of sensitive data are discussed. In turn, the fundamental principles of security protection measures in cloud computing are explored. Later in the chapter, various strategies for ensuring privacy in the cloud are compared and discussed. These methods are examined in the context of allowing authorized access. preventing unauthorized access and ensuring data integrity. Furthermore, the pitfalls and weaknesses of each technique and available workarounds to avoid such vulnerability have been discussed in detail. This chapter also covers a detailed comparative analysis of these privacy preservation and secure data storage techniques, exploring their interplay and potential effective combinations.

The integration of Blockchain-IoT presents a promising platform for enhancing security, transparency, and efficiency in various applications. This work aims to provide a detailed overview of the state of the art in blockchain-IoT-based solutions. In this work, the authors begin by introducing the basic concepts of blockchain and IoT, highlighting their key features and their individual challenges. Next, this work explains benefits of combining these technologies, such as decentralized data management, immutable records, and enhanced trust and security. Further, this work explains the architecture and components of blockchain-IoT systems, including smart contracts, consensus mechanisms, and data integrity verification techniques.

The confidentiality, integrity, and availability triad is a fundamental principle for information security. The objective of this chapter is to examine this triad where blockchain technology can be applied to enhance security in cloud computing. The current pasture of cloud security is explored to identify the gaps and approaches for using blockchain technology to reduce those gaps are discussed in this chapter. Blockchain technology is well-recognized for its ability to ensure data integrity. The largest gap that can be reduced is in this area. With the decentralized and distributed architecture of blockchain, there are ways to leverage it to improve the availability of cloud security. Confidentiality, where encryption plays a significant role, has the least gap in cloud computing; however, since the responsibility for assuring confidentiality is on the user, blockchain offers alternative and additional strengths. This chapter also covers a detailed discussion of avoiding prevalent security threats by implementing blockchain technology in cloud computing for making it more secure.

Machine learning is increasingly used for data analysis, but centralized datasets raise concerns about data privacy and security. Federated learning, a distributed method, enables multiple entities to cooperatively train a machine learning model. Clients use their local datasets to train local models, while a central aggregator aggregates updates and computes a global model. Privacy-preserving federated learning (PPFL) addresses privacy issues in sensitive and decentralized data situations. PPFL integrates federated learning with privacy-preserving approaches to achieve both privacy and model correctness.

The evolution of technology has a significant impact on health data collection, transforming the way information is gathered, stored, and utilized in the healthcare industry. The big health record contains sensitive user information like contact details, health status, demographics, vaccination details, exposure history. It's worth noting that while the collection of big health records has been crucial for monitoring the patients' health history, it also raises important privacy and security considerations. Safeguarding the privacy of individuals' health data and ensuring compliance with relevant regulations is essential to maintain public trust and protect sensitive information. Therefore, healthcare data must adhere to privacy regulations and ethical considerations. This chapter elaborates on key challenges and solutions in privacy preservation within federated learning. The key challenges include data heterogeneity, information leakage, attacks, and regulatory compliances.

Facilitated by high-speed internet connectivity, the adoption of cloud computing has surged dramatically due to its distinctive attributes such as pay-as-you-go billing, ubiquitous accessibility, and minimal support requirements in the realm of service and resource delivery. While cloud computing draws inspiration from distributed, parallel, and grid computing paradigms, it also inherits their associated complexities and concerns. Among these challenges, optimizing performance stands out prominently. Enhancing performance can be achieved through the development of efficient load balancing algorithms. Efficient algorithms satisfy users and make optimal uses of resources of the cloud and hence improve performance. Several load balancing algorithms were designed to respond to performance problems. In this chapter, three well-established load balancing algorithms, namely round robin, equally spread current execution, and throttled, underwent a comprehensive analysis. This examination sought to unveil both the strengths and weaknesses inherent to these algorithms.

Clouds contain a huge number of virtualized resources that can be made available instantaneously. Cloud technology offers a wide array of services, encompassing platforms, hardware, and software, effectively providing almost anything as a service. A single host represents a physical computer component, while a datacenter comprises numerous hosts responsible for managing virtual machines throughout their life cycles. The efficient scheduling of virtual machine requests plays a crucial role in cloud, as it ensures that requested tasks are completed within the shortest time according to user-defined preferences. This chapter introduces an optimization model based on fuzzy logic for scheduling tasks in cloud computing. The proposed model was tested and evaluated using a fuzzy logic-based scheduling algorithm. The proposed algorithms were compared against scheduling algorithms without fuzzy logic. The experimental findings undeniably establish the superiority of the proposed algorithm.

Several strategies have been put forth to efficiently assign the accessible cloud nodes to the client's request and the goal is to improve the cloud's overall performance while also giving users better services and a higher level of customer happiness. An extensive investigation and analysis are done into the idea of using a load balancing method with active monitoring as well as the modification of such an algorithm. There are several ways to accomplish this. The results of the study suggest that when adopting a load balancing method with active monitoring methodology in a cloud computing environment, a more effective active monitoring load balancing method should be used. The load balancing technique gets increasingly challenging as a virtual machine's demand increases. The authors were able to improve throughput while also streamlining the load balancing procedure by using a buffer. Using this information as a foundation, the authors enhanced the load balancing method with active monitoring technique to take into account the growing demand of a virtual machine.

Successful cloud computing (CC) lets businesses and people outsource data processing, storage, and access. CC has numerous advantages but new privacy and security risks. Data owners lose control over their data at external providers, making it subject to misuse, distribution, and access. The current data security method involves encryption. Encryption increases computing complexity, especially when data is dispersed throughout several CSP servers. Simple secrecy technologies include encryption and fragmentation. HSSOA-FEW is a hybrid sparrow search optimisation method for cloud security employing fragmentation and encryption. HSSOA-FEW holds data on CSP server with minimal encryption. HSSOA-FEW considers security and data storage. HSSOA-FEW also included sparrow search algorithm (SSA) with particle swarm optimisation. Additionally, HSSOA-FEW uses fused encryption and decryption. HSSOA-FEW controls and secures cloud servers. The suggested HSSOA-FEW system is tested extensively to improve performance. The experiments indicated HSSOA-FEW outperformed others.

Outsourcing data storage in infrastructure has been a popular solution for organizations and individual users since it offers numerous advantages over traditional on-premises storage choices. Data encryption before outsourcing data to infrastructure is a general strategy to safeguard data confidentiality. It is challenging to search for the specified keywords in encrypted datasets in cloud computing settings, and it is obviously impracticable to download all the data from the cloud and decode it locally. The focus of current search technique is on exact matches and simple pattern matching, which result in incomplete or irrelevant. The approach uses 4D hyperchaotic mapping and a powerful deoxyribonucleic acid (DNA) encryption mechanism to make it very difficult to decrypt the encrypted data without the proper key. The proposed approach helps create an effective and safe encryption. Global vector word embedding is taken into consideration while generating semantically aware search results in a semantically conscious top-k multi-keyword retrieval-supporting searchable encryption technique.

In this chapter, the authors explore the application of genetic algorithms (GAs) for key generation in cryptosystems. Cryptography plays a crucial role in securing sensitive information, and the strength of a cryptosystem lies in the robustness of its encryption keys. Traditional methods of generating cryptographic keys face challenges in finding optimal key solutions, especially as computational power increases. Genetic algorithms offer a promising alternative, leveraging evolutionary principles to optimize key generation. This chapter provides an overview of genetic algorithms, their application in cryptography, and various techniques for using GAs in key generation for secure and efficient cryptosystems.

The conceptual, technological, and enabling frameworks of the original Industry 4.0 concept have all undergone significant changes. The next generation of Industry 4.0, also known as Industry 5.0, is emerging as a result of the evolution of Industry 4.0 and will require a combination of fresh new technologies. These breakthroughs come from a range of industries, such as artificial intelligence (AI), 5G technology and 6G mobile networks, ML with quantum computing, etc. Artificial intelligence (AI), 5G and 6G, and machine learning with quantum computing are expected to influence the original Industry 4.0. As mentioned, a new era of Industry 4.0 is currently emerging. The primary emerging enabling technologies for Industry 4.0 are surveyed in this chapter. Included in the topics mentioned are artificial intelligence (AI), internet of things, blockchain, 5G wireless technologies, 3D printing, biometrics, virtual and augmented reality, digital twin in 6G technology with case scenarios.

Cloud computing revolutionized business data management yet introduced security risks. This chapter assesses blockchain's impact on cloud security, highlighting the pros and cons. It introduces blockchain's role in addressing cloud security concerns via decentralization and transparency. The chapter examines how blockchain bolsters cloud security, enhancing data integrity, privacy, and encryption. Despite benefits, deployment challenges are recognized. The chapter explores blockchain's integration with AI/ML and real-world cases, equipping readers to navigate complexities. This empowers secure and resilient cloud computing. Thus, the chapter equips readers with the necessary information to navigate the complexities of deploying blockchain-based cloud security solutions, leading to a future of secure and resilient cloud computing.

Blockchain technology has gained significant attention in recent years due to its decentralized and immutable nature, and has made itself ideal for various applications such as finance, supply chain management, and healthcare. However, privacy and trust issues have emerged as major challenges in blockchain-based systems/applications. This work provides a detailed explanation of the existing privacy-preserving and trust-building techniques in blockchain-based systems. The authors begin by discussing the fundamental concepts of blockchain technology and its features that affect privacy and trust. Further, they discuss the privacy challenges faced by blockchain systems. Various privacy-preserving techniques, such as encryption, zero-knowledge proofs, and mix-zones, are explained in detail (with highlighting their strengths and limitations). In addition to privacy, trust is an important aspect of blockchain-based systems.

The threat posed by rogue access points (RAPs) has grown significantly in importance for network security as a result of the growing use of wireless local area networks (WLANs). This work proposes a novel RAP detection method that makes use of multi-parameter dynamic WLAN properties. This chapter addresses the rising problem of rogue access points (RAPs) in wireless local area networks (WLANs) and suggests a new RAP detection approach that makes better use of multi-parameter dynamic features of WLAN. The proposed approach provides a comprehensive evaluation of each access point's unique characteristics and reduces susceptibility to RAPs. The study compared the proposed approach with four other RAP detection methods using metrics such as detection rate, false positive rate, customizability, and computational resources required. Results showed that the proposed approach achieves 98.7% detection rate with lower false positive rates and greater customizability than the other methods. The proposed RAP detection can effectively detect RAPs in wireless networks and enhance network security.

Preface

This smart era is having many evolutions of technology, in that cloud computing has fundamentally transformed many applications in terms of what we store, how access, and manage the respective data. This paradigm shift, though promising in its potential, has introduced several issues like security and privacy of our digital assets. This book presents several works on privacy preserving and cloud computing, is a culmination of extensive research and provide/ include many methods/ mechanisms of safeguarding data in the cloud. In an increasingly interconnected world, where data is the oil for many industries in this Smart era (which has our footprints of our personal lives). It is important that we need to provide innovative solutions to protect the confidentiality, integrity, and availability of this data.

This book represents the collaborative efforts of experts, scholars (around the globe) a who have experience in cloud computing, cryptography, and data privacy. This book discusses the heart of cloud security, unearthing the challenges and vulnerabilities that cloud-based data storage systems face. From data breaches to regulatory compliance, from encryption techniques to access control, every facet of preserving privacy and securing data is examined with meticulous attention to detail.

This book start about introduction and explain about cloud security, which is sufficient to gain insights into the state-of-the-art practices and cutting-edge technologies that stand as essential component against the existed threats to data in the cloud. We will be equipped with a comprehensive understanding of the legal and ethical dimensions that intertwine with data privacy.

This book is not just a compendium of knowledge; it is a call to action. It calls upon organizations, governments, and individuals to recognize the significance of privacy preservation and secured data storage as essential components of responsible data management. It underscores the need for continual research and innovation in the face of evolving threats.

We extend our gratitude to the contributors, readers and future researchers, for it is your collective curiosity and dedication that drive progress in this crucial field. Together, let us embark on this expedition to safeguard the digital foundations upon which our future is built.

Welcome to a world where privacy is fundamental right and data security is non-negotiable.

D. Lakshmi
VIT Bhopal University, India

Amit Kumar Tyagi
National Institute of Fashion Technology, New Delhi, India

Acknowledgment

First of all, we would to extend our gratitude to my Family Members, Friends, and Supervisors, which stood with us as an advisor in completing this book. Also, we would like to thanks our almighty "God" who makes us to write this book.

We would like to extend our heartfelt gratitude to the management and leadership team of VIT Bhopal University and National Institute of Fashion Technology, New Delhi, for their unwavering support and encouragement throughout my research activities. Their commitment to fostering a conducive research environment and providing essential technical support has been instrumental in the successful completion of this project.

We also thank IGI Global Publishers (who has provided their continuous support during this COVID 19 Pandemic) and my friends/colleagues with whom we have work together inside the college/ university and others outside of the college/ university who have provided their continuous support towards completing this book on Data privacy/Privacy Preserving Technologies in Cloud Computing.

Chapter 1
Introduction to Privacy Preservation and Secure Data Storage in Cloud Computing

Yadav KrishnaKumar Rajnath
Institute of Engineering and Rural Technology, Prayagraj, India

Shrikant Tiwari
https://orcid.org/0000-0001-6947-2362
Galgotias University, India

Virendra Kumar Verma
Institute of Engineering and Rural Technology, Prayagraj, India

ABSTRACT

Cloud computing has swiftly emerged as the dominant IT paradigm, revolutionizing data storage and processing with scalable, cost-effective solutions for individuals and businesses. However, concerns over data security and privacy have arisen due to the migration of sensitive data to remote servers. This chapter introduces privacy and secure data storage principles in the cloud context. It covers threats, emphasizing robust security measures like encryption, access control, and anonymization. The chapter also addresses legal frameworks, urging alignment with regulations. It presents best practices for secure data storage, including encryption and emerging tech like homomorphic encryption. Ultimately, the chapter aims to equip readers with a comprehensive understanding of privacy preservation and secure data handling in the cloud, enabling informed decisions that uphold data privacy.

INTRODUCTION

In the dynamic and ever-changing realm of cloud computing, ensuring the preservation of privacy and the security of data storage has become of paramount importance. The shift to utilizing remote servers has significantly amplified concerns regarding unauthorized access and potential data breaches. Employing

DOI: 10.4018/979-8-3693-0593-5.ch001

robust security measures is an absolute necessity to mitigate these risks. Encryption methods, including both symmetric and asymmetric encryption, play a pivotal role in upholding the confidentiality of data (Awotunde, J. B et al. 2021). Mechanisms for controlling access, such as role-based and attribute-based controls, guarantee that only authorized users can gain access to sensitive information (Khan, R. et al. 2021).

Cloud computing has emerged as a triumphant model that greatly simplifies the utilization of computing resources and data storage infrastructure for businesses of all sizes. Elevated concerns about the safeguarding of data and its confidentiality within the cloud environment have arisen due to a comprehensive assessment of vulnerabilities. A multitude of security vulnerabilities have been identified within cloud services, resulting in instances of user data leakage across a wide array of cloud-based applications. Ensuring the security of data and the privacy of users during data management and query processing submitted to the cloud has become an absolute necessity to expand and enhance the utilization of cloud services (Brown, I., & Marsden, C. T. 2023; Leonelli, S. 2014).

However, the challenge lies in the complexity of ensuring secure and privacy-preserving data services, as security issues have the potential to manifest at various levels of data services. Efforts to enhance security and privacy protection might inadvertently impact the functionality and performance of these data services (Wood, A et al. 2018). The aim is to address common security and privacy threats in the cloud while focusing on research endeavors aimed at ensuring the confidentiality of data and maintaining privacy when handling sensitive information within the cloud environment (Mather, T., Kumaraswamy, S., & Latif, S. 2009; AlZain, M. A et al. 2012).

In the era of digital transformation, cloud computing has emerged as a pivotal technology, reshaping how businesses operate, collaborate, and innovate. The adaptability, scalability, and cost-effectiveness provided by cloud services have revolutionized industries globally. However, alongside the numerous benefits of cloud computing come critical concerns related to the security and privacy of data. Organizations and individuals entrust cloud providers with their sensitive data, demanding assurance that their information remains confidential, secure, and compliant with evolving privacy regulations (Büyüközkan, G., & Göçer, F. 2018; Warner, K. S., & Wäger, M. 2019; Kushida, K. E., Murray, J., & Zysman, J. 2011).

In this landscape, the principles of upholding privacy and ensuring secure data storage have gained unprecedented significance. Privacy preservation entails safeguarding personal information against unauthorized access and guaranteeing the respect of individuals' privacy rights, even when data is processed within cloud environments (Blasimme, A., Ferretti, A., & Vayena, E. 2021). Conversely, secure data storage is centered around safeguarding data integrity, availability, and confidentiality against potential breaches and unauthorized utilization.

As cloud services continue to evolve and transform industries, delving into the fundamental aspects of privacy and security that underpin responsible cloud computing becomes imperative. This exploration not only sheds light on the challenges at hand but also emphasizes innovative solutions and best practices that empower organizations to leverage the benefits of cloud computing while prioritizing the privacy and security of their most invaluable asset: data. In the subsequent sections, we will delve into the core of privacy preservation and secure data storage within the context of cloud computing, examining their applications, challenges, and the evolving landscape of technologies that empower organizations to navigate this intricate terrain (Sheninger, E. 2019; McGonigle, D., & Mastrian, K. 2021).

The subsequent segments of this manuscript are meticulously organized, mirroring the arrangement illustrated in Fig.1. Commencing with Section 1.2, the discourse delves into the intricacies of "Data Privacy and Security Challenges in Cloud Computing." Following suit is Section 1.3, which elaborates on “Robust Security Measures in Cloud Environments.” Proceeding seamlessly, Section 1.4 undertakes an examination of the “Evaluation of Privacy-Preserving Techniques.” The subsequent segment, designated as Section 1.5, adeptly navigates the “Regulatory Landscape and Legal Implications,” offering a comprehensive analysis.

Continuing the intellectual journey, Section 1.6, denoted as the 1.6th section, rigorously dissects the subject of “Emerging Technologies for Enhanced Privacy.” Notably, Section 1.7 undertakes a visionary exploration of “Future Trends and Considerations,” charting the trajectory ahead. As the narrative elegantly draws to a close, Section 1.8 encapsulates the discourse’s essence through the lens of “Conclusion and Impact,” providing a comprehensive culmination of insights and outcomes.

Figure 1. Pivotal layout of the work
Source: Tyagi, A. et al. (2021)

Cloud Computing as a Transformative IT Paradigm

Cloud computing has emerged as a revolutionary IT framework that has transformed the approach of both businesses and individuals toward technology infrastructure, services, and applications. This inventive approach to computing offers unparalleled scalability, adaptability, cost-effectiveness, and accessibility

(Yang, C., et al. 2017; Buyya, R., Broberg, J., & Goscinski, A. M.,2010). By abstracting the intricacies of hardware and software management, cloud computing has ushered in a novel computing era that empowers organizations to prioritize innovation and strategic expansion over the complexities of IT management (Mougayar, W. 2016).

Fundamental elements that underscore the transformative essence of cloud computing encompass:

- Scalability and Adaptability: Cloud computing empowers businesses to seamlessly adjust their resources in accordance with demand. This elasticity ensures that organizations can respond to shifting workloads without substantial investments in infrastructure or operational disruptions (Manvi, S. S., & Shyam, G. K. 2014).
- Cost-Effectiveness: Conventional IT infrastructure frequently entails substantial upfront expenses for hardware, software licenses, and maintenance. Cloud computing operates on a pay-as-you-go model, enabling organizations to evade overprovisioning and solely pay for the resources they actively utilize.
- Accessibility and Remote Operations: Cloud services are accessible from any location with an internet connection. This transformation has been particularly evident in facilitating remote work and collaboration, especially during global occurrences that necessitate remote functioning (Dwivedi, Y. K., et al. 2020).
- Acceleration of Innovation: Cloud computing provides a platform for swift innovation through a variety of pre-built services and tools that developers can leverage to design, test, and deploy applications more efficiently (Gubbi, J., Buyya, R., Marusic, S., & Palaniswami, M. 2013; Vermesan, O., & Friess, P. (Eds.) 2013).
- Global Scope and Expansion: Businesses can effortlessly extend their services to new markets and regions by utilizing cloud services with data centers dispersed worldwide. This global outreach is invaluable for enterprises seeking to tap into international prospects (Gupta, A. K., Govindarajan, V., & Wang, H. 2008; Kanter, R. M. 1997).
- Optimization of Resources: Cloud platforms frequently encompass sophisticated tools for optimizing resources, assisting organizations in maximizing their computing assets, curtailing waste, and enhancing efficiency (Bughin, J., Chui, M., & Manyika, J. 2010).
- Diminished Maintenance Burden: Cloud providers manage a significant portion of infrastructure upkeep, software updates, and security fixes, liberating organizations from routine management tasks (Wu, J.et al. 2010).
- Disaster Recovery and Business Continuity: Cloud services offer resilient backup and disaster recovery solutions, ensuring data integrity and availability during unforeseen circumstances.
- Democratization of Technology: Cloud computing democratizes access to advanced technologies. Smaller enterprises and startups can now access the same potent computing resources as larger corporations, leveling the technological playing field.
- Platform for Emerging Technologies: Cloud platforms serve as a foundation for emerging technologies like artificial intelligence, machine learning, Internet of Things (IoT), and big data analytics, enabling organizations to harness these innovations without constructing complex underlying infrastructures.

To sum up, cloud computing signifies a paradigm alteration in the provisioning, management, and utilization of technology. Its transformative influence has affected every facet of IT operations, spanning from infrastructure oversight to application deployment and user experience. By leveraging the advantages of cloud computing, businesses can not only amplify their operational efficiency but also unlock novel avenues for expansion, innovation, and global outreach.

Balancing Benefits With Data Privacy and Security Concerns

Navigating the advantages of cloud computing while effectively managing data privacy and security challenges is a pivotal undertaking for contemporary organizations. Despite the manifold benefits offered by cloud computing, it's imperative to address and alleviate potential risks to guarantee the privacy, authenticity, and accessibility of confidential information (Marston, S., et al. 2011; Singh, S et al. 2016). Here's a blueprint for organizations to strike an equilibrium:

- Risk Evaluation and Adherence to Regulations: Conduct a comprehensive risk appraisal to uncover potential security and privacy susceptibilities. Comprehend pertinent data safeguarding regulations (like GDPR, HIPAA, or CCPA) and uphold adherence when handling sensitive data.
- Categorization and Encryption of Data: Classify data according to its sensitivity and stipulate suitable encryption mechanisms for distinct data categories. Implement encryption for data both during storage and transmission to avert unauthorized entry.
- Access Management and Validation: Deploy resilient access control mechanisms, encompassing role-based and attribute-based access controls. Implement potent authentication techniques, such as multi-factor authentication (MFA), to ensure solely authorized users can gain access to sensitive data.
- Assessment and Prudent Selection of Vendors: Opt for established and trustworthy cloud service providers with established security protocols and compliance validations. Execute due diligence regarding your provider's security protocols, data management practices, and ability to respond to incidents.
- Data Location and Jurisdiction: Grasp the locales where your data is housed and processed, given that distinct jurisdictions uphold diverse data protection statutes. Opt for cloud providers that accommodate specifications for data residency if required.
- Data Leakage Prevention (DLP): Set up DLP mechanisms to surveil and obstruct the unauthorized dissemination of sensitive data beyond the organizational boundaries.
- Security Auditing and Monitoring: Routinely inspect and monitor your cloud environment to pinpoint anomalous activities and potential security breaches. Leverage intrusion detection and prevention systems (IDS/IPS) to spot and counteract threats in real time.
- Management of Incidents and Recovery: Fashion a comprehensive blueprint for addressing security breaches promptly and curtailing their repercussions. Regularly evaluate and update the plan to ensure its efficiency.
- Training and Sensitization of Personnel: Enlighten personnel about optimal security practices, protocols for handling data, and the significance of preserving sensitive information.
- Hybrid Cloud or Private Cloud Solutions: Consider employing hybrid cloud or private cloud solutions for sensitive data, wherein certain data segments reside on-premises or in a private cloud environment under the direct control of your organization.

- Data Mobility and Prevention of Vendor Dependence: Envisage the potential for transitioning to alternate cloud providers in the future by ensuring data mobility and evading excessive reliance on proprietary technologies.
- Continuous Enhancement and Adaptation: Remain abreast of emerging security risks and optimal practices to perpetually enhance your cloud security strategy.

Striking equilibrium between advantages and data privacy and security concerns demands an ongoing, proactive, and comprehensive approach. Through the amalgamation of technical measures, policy frameworks, and workforce enlightenment, organizations can capitalize on the benefits of cloud computing while safeguarding their most invaluable asset: data.

DATA PRIVACY AND SECURITY CHALLENGES IN CLOUD COMPUTING

In the realm of cloud computing, the challenges associated with safeguarding data privacy and security are substantial, necessitating thoughtful deliberation and preemptive actions for resolution. As enterprises increasingly rely on cloud services to handle data storage, processing, and administration, they are tasked with surmounting these challenges to assure the safeguarding of confidential information (Zhang, Q., Cheng, L., & Boutaba, R. 2010; Jaeger, P. T., et al. 2008). Here are several pivotal data privacy and security challenges within the domain of cloud computing:

- Data Compromises: Cloud environments represent enticing targets for cybercriminals due to the vast reservoirs of stored data. Successful breaches can result in the exposure of sensitive data, leading to financial losses, reputational harm, and legal repercussions.
- Data Loss and Retrieval: The risk of data loss is an inherent aspect of all computing environments, including the cloud. Organizations must establish robust mechanisms for data backup and retrieval, ensuring the capacity to reinstate data in the event of accidental erasure, hardware failures, or other disruptions.
- Data Location and Domicile: Cloud providers commonly disperse data across numerous data centers situated in diverse geographical regions. This practice can elicit concerns regarding data jurisdiction, compliance with regional data protection regulations, and the potential for data access by governments within varying jurisdictions.
- Model of Shared Responsibility: Cloud providers generally adhere to a model of shared responsibility, where they are accountable for securing the underlying infrastructure while customers are responsible for safeguarding their data and applications. Ambiguity and security gaps can arise if roles and responsibilities are not clearly defined.
- Inadequate Encryption: Inadequate or erroneously implemented encryption protocols can render data vulnerable to unauthorized access. Organizations must ensure the robustness and currency of encryption methodologies and key management practices.
- Identity and Access Management (IAM): Inadequately managed IAM can pave the way for unauthorized access to sensitive data. Organizations must institute robust authentication mechanisms, enforce principles of least privilege, and routinely scrutinize user access.

- Threats from Insiders: Insiders possessing access to cloud systems, whether intentionally malicious or inadvertently negligent, present noteworthy threats. This encompasses employees, contractors, and third-party vendors with potential access to sensitive data.
- Navigating Compliance and Regulatory Hurdles: Distinct industries are subject to a diversity of regulatory frameworks governing data privacy and security. The transition of data to the cloud introduces intricacies in upholding compliance with these regulations.
- Data Segregation and Multi-Tenancy: Cloud providers often implement multi-tenancy models, wherein multiple customers share the same underlying infrastructure. Poor data segregation can culminate in data seepage between tenants.
- Dependence on a Single Vendor: Over-reliance on tools and services from a single cloud provider can lead to vendor lock-in, rendering it arduous to switch to an alternative provider or revert to in-house services.
- Insufficiency in Transparency: Cloud providers might not invariably provide comprehensive transparency into their security methodologies and incident response protocols, instilling uncertainty in customers regarding the protection of their data.
- Emergent Threats: The adoption of cloud computing introduces novel avenues of attack and threats that may not be as comprehensively comprehended as those in traditional on-premises settings. Organizations need to remain informed about emerging threats in the cloud arena.

Tackling these challenges mandates a comprehensive strategy that encompasses technological measures, policies, employee training, recurrent audits, and continuous monitoring. Organizations should collaborate closely with their cloud providers to establish a mutual comprehension of security responsibilities and proactively ensure the security of sensitive data.

Shifting Sensitive Data to Remote Servers

The process of shifting sensitive data to remote servers, commonly known as distant data storage or remote data hosting, has emerged as a vital component in modern approaches to data administration. This approach involves moving essential data from local, on-site storage systems to external servers overseen by third-party service providers (Mather, T., Kumaraswamy, S., & Latif, S., 2009). These distant servers can be incorporated into frameworks of cloud computing, data centers, or other substitute remote hosting setups (Snyder, L., 2012).

Transferring sensitive data to remote servers offers several possible advantages, yet it also presents noteworthy considerations pertaining to security, accessibility, and governance:

- Expandability and Versatility: Remote servers, especially those within cloud settings, deliver scalability that empowers organizations to effortlessly extend their storage capacity in alignment with burgeoning data demands. This scalability negates the necessity for recurrent hardware upgrades and encourages the judicious utilization of resources.
- Economical Efficacy: Remote data storage frequently adheres to a pay-as-you-go model, wherein organizations exclusively remunerate resources utilized. This often proves to be more cost-effective in comparison to the investment and maintenance associated with dedicated on-premises infrastructure.

- Access and Collaborative Aptitude: Storing data on remote servers facilitates the authorized users' ability to access and collaborate on data from any location endowed with internet connectivity. This quality holds pronounced significance in today's dispersed work milieu.
- Disaster Recovery and Redundancy: A multitude of remote server hosting services encompass inherent redundancy and disaster recovery provisions, thereby ensuring data availability even in the event of hardware failures or unanticipated contingencies.
- Resource Delegation: Transferring data off-site empowers organizations to delegate the responsibilities associated with data management, upkeep, and security to specialized providers. This consequently empowers them to channel their concentration towards fundamental business pursuits.

However, there exist notable challenges and considerations which organizations need to address during the process of transferring sensitive data to remote servers:

- Data Security and Privacy: Entrusting sensitive data to third-party servers induces apprehensions surrounding data security and privacy. Organizations are compelled to meticulously evaluate the security protocols enacted by the hosting provider, with the aim of ensuring the safeguarding of data against unauthorized access and breaches.
- Adherence to Regulatory Frameworks: Depending on the industry and geographic jurisdiction, organizations could be subjected to varied data protection regulations that stipulate the manner in which sensitive data must be stored, accessed, and managed. Upholding compliance with these regulations during the remote storage of data stands as a cardinal imperative.
- Data Ownership and Authority: The act of transitioning data to remote servers invariably entails relinquishing a certain measure of direct control over data management. Organizations ought to possess a crystal-clear comprehension of data ownership, access privileges, and avenues for data portability.
- Dependability of Hosting Providers: The trustworthiness and reputation of the hosting provider exert substantial influence over data accessibility and the continuity of services. Organizations should subject the provider's historical performance, support capabilities, and stipulations of service level agreements to exhaustive scrutiny.
- Data Transmission and Latency: The transfer of considerable volumes of sensitive data to remote servers might introduce hurdles connected to data transmission speeds and latency. This consideration holds especially pertinent for organizations dealing with voluminous data sets.
- Potential for Vendor Entrenchment: Excessive reliance on a particular remote hosting provider could lead to a state of vendor entrenchment, thereby heightening the complexity of transitioning to alternative providers or reverting to in-house data management.
- Data Encryption: Introducing encryption to data before its transfer to remote servers has the potential to enhance security. Nevertheless, organizations are mandated to adroitly manage encryption keys to avert unauthorized access to the data.
- Contingency Planning: Organizations must meticulously devise a contingency strategy in anticipation of scenarios where they opt to switch providers or reinstate data to on-premises storage. This strategy encompasses data migration and ensuring uninterrupted business operations throughout the transitional phase.

In summation, the act of migrating sensitive data to remote servers furnishes notable merits in the realms of scalability, cost efficiency, accessibility, and disaster recovery. Nonetheless, a meticulous approach to planning and assessment is indispensable for adroitly handling the attendant challenges correlated with security, compliance, and control. Organizations should undertake exhaustive evaluations of prospective hosting providers and implement robust security measures to uphold the confidentiality and integrity of sensitive data within the remote environment.

Threat Landscape: Unauthorized Access, Data Breaches, Insider Threats

The ever-evolving landscape of data security encompasses a multitude of significant hurdles, ranging from illicit entry and data breaches to internal hazards. Unauthorized access pertains to malevolent entities gaining entry to systems, applications, or data without valid authorization. This can lead to compromised sensitive data, unauthorized modifications, and interruptions in service (Choo, K. K. R., 2010).

Persistent concerns about data breaches involve the unwarranted exposure of confidential information. Be it due to cyber assaults, system vulnerabilities, or inadequate security practices, data breaches can result in financial setbacks, harm to reputation, and legal consequences. Vigilant defense against such breaches demands robust cybersecurity measures.

Insider threats, emerging from staff members, contractors, or associates with internal system access, present a formidable risk. Whether driven by malice or negligence, these individuals can exploit their access to compromise data integrity or pilfer sensitive information. Strategies for detection and mitigation, including employee education and stringent access controls, play a pivotal role in alleviating this risk (Jansen, W., & Grance, T., 2011).

The amalgamation of these threats necessitates a comprehensive and adaptable security approach. Routine security evaluations, employee awareness initiatives, encryption protocols, multi-factor authentication, and intrusion detection systems stand as indispensable components to safeguard against unauthorized access, data breaches, and insider threats in the contemporary digital panorama. This multifaceted strategy serves as a shield to preserve the integrity and confidentiality of invaluable data.

Vulnerabilities in Cloud Environments

Vulnerabilities within cloud environments pose notable security complexities that entities must tackle to safeguard the sanctity and confidentiality of their information. Presented below are some prevalent susceptibilities exploitable in cloud computing (Subashini, S., & Kavitha, V., 2011; Hashizume, K et al., 2013; Zissis, D., & Lekkas, D., 2012):

- Improperly Configured Cloud Services: Ill-configured cloud services can lay data bare to unauthorized entry. Poor configurations might render services exposed to the public web or inadvertently construct unauthorized entry points.
- Insufficient Identity and Access Management (IAM): Fragile IAM practices can lead to unsanctioned access. The absence of effective authentication, authorization, and access controls can culminate in data breaches.
- Data Breaches: Confidential data stashed in the cloud is susceptible to breaches owing to vulnerabilities in applications, APIs, or infrastructure. Adversaries can capitalize on these weak points to purloin or manipulate data.

- Inadequate Encryption: Absence of encryption for data at rest and during transit heightens the jeopardy of data disclosure. Shielded communication channels and robust encryption for stored data stand as indispensables.
- API Susceptibilities: Cloud services frequently hinge on APIs for interaction. Insecure APIs can be commandeered by attackers to seize illicit access to data or resources.
- Shared Resources and Multi-Tenancy Challenges: Feeble segregation between tenants in a multi-tenant milieu can culminate in illicit data access among clients cohabitating the same framework (Chong, F., et al., 2006).
- Deficiency in Security Updates: Neglecting security patches and updates for cloud services and foundational systems can leave vulnerabilities unpatched.
- Data Leakage: Inadequate reins on data movement and storage can trigger inadvertent or deliberate data leakage. This transpires via wrongly configured storage settings or insecure data transmission mechanisms.
- Denial of Service (DoS) Attacks: Cloud services remain susceptible to DoS assaults, triggering disruptions in availability and impacting service efficacy.
- Insecure APIs and Fusion Points: APIs enabling app-cloud service interaction can be manipulated if improperly designed and secured.
- Vendor Vulnerabilities: While cloud providers extend security measures, flaws in their infrastructure or services can surface, possibly affecting their clientele.
- Unprotected Management Interfaces: Flimsy security measures on management interfaces, like dashboards and consoles, can furnish attackers with opportunities to undermine the ecosystem.
- Phishing and Social Engineering: Cloud users and administrators can fall prey to phishing attacks, leading to unauthenticated access or data revelation.
- Data Residency and Compliance Trials: Storing data across diverse geographical zones might expose it to disparate regulatory frameworks, giving rise to compliance conundrums.
- Reliance on Third-Party Elements: Dependence on third-party software or libraries sans vigilant vulnerability monitoring can infuse risks into the cloud milieu.

To combat these vulnerabilities, entities should adopt a proactive stance involving routine security evaluations, vulnerability scans, staff security training, continual monitoring, and observance of best practices as imparted by cloud service providers. Sustaining a robust security stance holds paramount importance in fortifying cloud environments against plausible threats.

ROBUST SECURITY MEASURES IN CLOUD ENVIRONMENTS

In the ever-evolving realm of cloud computing, it is imperative to institute resilient security protocols to mitigate risks and guarantee the safeguarding of sensitive data and vital operations. Cloud landscapes introduce distinctive challenges, such as shared infrastructure and remote data storage, necessitating a comprehensive security strategy. Below are indispensable security measures for fortifying cloud environments (Takabi, H., et al., 2010):

- Multi-Factor Authentication (MFA): Enforce the requirement for users to present multiple forms of verification prior to accessing cloud resources. This curtails the hazard of unauthorized entry stemming from compromised credentials.
- Cryptography: Employ end-to-end cryptography for data both at rest and in transit. This ensures that intercepted data remains indecipherable without the requisite decryption keys.
- Access Management: Instate rigorous access management mechanisms, such as role-based access control (RBAC) and attribute-based access control (ABAC). These mechanisms curtail users' permissions in accordance with their roles and duties.
- Frequent Security Audits: Conduct regular security evaluations and audits to unearth vulnerabilities and shortcomings, thus facilitating preemptive remediation.
- Timely Patch Application: Maintain up-to-date software and systems by promptly applying security patches to rectify known vulnerabilities and curtail exposure to potential attacks.
- Intrusion Detection and Prevention Systems (IDPS): Monitor network traffic for anomalous patterns and activities to promptly identify and counter potential security breaches.
- Data Leakage Prevention (DLP): Employ DLP solutions to oversee, identify, and prevent unauthorized movement or dissemination of sensitive data within and beyond the cloud domain.
- Secured APIs: Ensure proper fortification of APIs employed for integrating cloud services to stave off unauthorized access and potential data disclosures.
- Employee Training: Educate staff about optimal security practices, perils of social engineering, and their role in upholding a secure cloud atmosphere.
- Incident Response Blueprint: Develop a well-structured incident response strategy outlining protocols for pinpointing, containing, and mitigating security incidents to minimize potential harm.
- Vendor Evaluation: Conduct thorough evaluations of cloud service providers' security practices, certifications, and compliance with industry benchmarks.
- Network Segmentation: Partition networks to segregate distinct cloud services, thus impeding lateral progression of threats and diminishing the impact of potential breaches.
- Data Backup and Restoration: Routinely back up pivotal data and applications to expedite swift recuperation in the event of data loss or system interruptions.
- Physical Security: Verify that data centers housing cloud infrastructure are fortified with robust physical security measures to forestall illicit access.
- Geolocation Limitations: Restrict data access and storage predicated on geographical locales to conform to data privacy regulations and mitigate exposure to legal liabilities.
- Penetration Testing: Conduct routine penetration tests to expose vulnerabilities and flaws exploitable by attackers.
- Security Information and Event Management (SIEM): Employ SIEM solutions to centralize and scrutinize security logs, thereby facilitating real-time threat identification and rapid countermeasures.
- Compliance Alignment: Remain apprised of pertinent industry regulations and compliance standards, and ascertain that your cloud setup adheres to these prerequisites.
- Continuous Surveillance: Implement practices of constant monitoring to unearth anomalies and security breaches promptly.
- Encryption Key Governance: Effectively oversee encryption keys to uphold the sanctity and soundness of encrypted data.

By assimilating these robust security measures into cloud environments, organizations can amplify their defensive mechanisms, curtail vulnerabilities, and lay the groundwork for secure operations in the digital era.

Encryption Techniques: Symmetric, Asymmetric, Homomorphic

Encryption methods play a crucial role in upholding the confidentiality and security of data, especially in the context of cloud computing environments. Various encryption approaches exist, including symmetric encryption, asymmetric encryption, and homomorphic encryption (Sun, W et al., 2018):

Symmetric Encryption: Symmetric encryption, also termed secret-key encryption, involves utilizing a single secret key for both encrypting and decrypting data. It proves efficient for encrypting large data volumes but necessitates a secure distribution mechanism for the key between communicating entities. Prominent examples of symmetric encryption algorithms encompass the Advanced Encryption Standard (AES) and the Data Encryption Standard (DES).

Asymmetric Encryption (Public-Key Encryption): Asymmetric encryption deploys a pair of keys: a public key for encryption and a private key for decryption. Public keys are disseminated broadly, while private keys remain confidential. This approach eradicates the necessity for secure key exchange, although it operates more sluggishly than symmetric encryption. Eminent asymmetric encryption algorithms encompass RSA and Elliptic Curve Cryptography (ECC).

Homomorphic Encryption: Homomorphic encryption stands as an advanced technique enabling computations on encrypted data without requiring prior decryption. This encryption type spans various levels, including partially homomorphic and fully homomorphic encryption. Despite its computational intensity, homomorphic encryption marks a groundbreaking innovation for preserving data privacy while executing operations on data stored in cloud repositories.

Each encryption method caters to distinct use cases and security prerequisites:

- Symmetric encryption fits well for data encryption and transmission within secure environments, where manageable key distribution is viable.
- Asymmetric encryption finds its ideal application in secure key exchange, digital signatures, and scenarios where assured secure communication channels are lacking.
- Homomorphic encryption emerges as revolutionary for situations prioritizing privacy, where data manipulation in its encrypted state is indispensable, as seen in secure computation and secure data sharing scenarios.

In cloud computing landscapes, the selection of an encryption method hinges on the specific organizational needs, data sensitivity, available computational resources, and the sought-after security level. The fusion of these encryption techniques with other security measures culminates in a comprehensive strategy for safeguarding data within cloud environments.

Access Control Mechanisms: Role-Based, Attribute-Based, Fine-Grained

Access control mechanisms, encompassing role-based, attribute-based, and fine-grained methods, constitute pivotal elements of data security strategies within cloud computing settings. These mechanisms govern the authorization and permissions bestowed upon users, ensuring that exclusively authorized individuals can access specific resources or undertake particular actions (Li, M., et al., 2010). The three prominent access control methods are:

Role-Based Access Control (RBAC): RBAC stands as a prevalent access control model, where permissions are linked to users based on predefined roles. Users are assigned roles mirroring their organizational responsibilities. Permissions are correlated with roles, facilitating the streamlined administration of access privileges. RBAC proves effective in handling access across extensive organizations with clearly outlined roles and duties.

Attribute-Based Access Control (ABAC): ABAC expands the realm of access control by factoring in diverse attributes and circumstances prior to granting access. Attributes encompass user traits, resource characteristics, environmental factors, and more. Policies are framed utilizing these attributes, enabling more intricate and context-sensitive access determinations. ABAC demonstrates flexibility and suits fluid environments characterized by varying access prerequisites.

Fine-Grained Access Control: Fine-grained access control transcends the broad permissions of conventional models. It empowers meticulous oversight over who can access precise resources and execute specific actions. This approach shines in scenarios where data sensitivity fluctuates significantly or when designated users necessitate access to specific segments of a resource.

Each access control method yields distinct advantages:

- RBAC simplifies access administration through permissions aligned with predefined roles, rendering it suitable for organizations boasting well-defined hierarchical structures.
- ABAC facilitates context-aware decision-making by accounting for an array of attributes, adapting well to dynamic and intricate access demands.
- Fine-grained access control epitomizes the utmost granularity, guaranteeing that users can access exclusively the precise resources and actions they require, augmenting data security.

In cloud settings, the selection of an access control mechanism hinges on variables such as organizational configuration, the intricacy of access requisites, data sensitivity, and adaptability needs. The amalgamation of these mechanisms with encryption, authentication, and other security measures culminates in a comprehensive strategy for upholding data privacy and security in the cloud.

Anonymization Methods: Data Masking, Tokenization, K-Anonymity

Anonymization techniques play a pivotal role in preserving data privacy and confidentiality, particularly in scenarios involving sensitive information within various domains. Several effective anonymization methods, such as data masking, tokenization, and k-anonymity, are employed to achieve this goal:

Data Masking: Data masking, also referred to as data obfuscation or data redaction, involves the alteration of sensitive data while retaining its original format and structure. This method ensures that the data's outward appearance remains intact, making it suitable for scenarios where realistic data representations are necessary, like in application development and testing. Through techniques such as character substitution or shuffling, data masking safeguards sensitive information from unauthorized exposure.

Tokenization: Tokenization entails substituting sensitive data elements with randomly generated tokens, which are devoid of any inherent meaning or value. These tokens act as placeholders, and the original data can only be accessed through secure tokenization systems equipped with corresponding mapping mechanisms. Tokenization is widely used in payment processing and storing credit card information, as it renders the data practically useless even if intercepted.

k-Anonymity: k-Anonymity is a privacy-preserving technique that ensures that individual data records are indistinguishable from at least k-1 other records in a dataset. In other words, it mitigates the risk of singling out specific individuals within a group. Achieving k-anonymity often involves generalizing or suppressing certain attributes in a dataset, thereby creating data sets that prevent individual re-identification while maintaining the utility of the information for analysis.

Each anonymization method offers unique advantages:

- Data Masking is ideal when maintaining the authenticity and structure of data is crucial, allowing secure testing and development environments.
- Tokenization excels in scenarios requiring high-level data security, such as payment processing, as it transforms data into cryptographically secure tokens.
- k-Anonymity offers a balance between privacy and data utility, ensuring that individuals cannot be uniquely identified while enabling meaningful analysis.

In various applications, the choice of anonymization method hinges on factors like the type of data, regulatory compliance requirements, and the desired level of privacy. These techniques contribute significantly to data protection strategies, promoting the responsible use of sensitive information and reducing the risks associated with unauthorized data exposure.

EVALUATION OF PRIVACY-PRESERVING TECHNIQUES

Maintaining privacy in the modern digital landscape is crucial to ensure the security and confidentiality of sensitive information while facilitating necessary data processing and analysis. These techniques aim to harmonize data utility with individual privacy concerns. Let's evaluate several prevalent privacy-preserving methods (Braun, T., et al., 2018):

Encryption:

- Pros: Encryption is an established method to uphold data confidentiality, permitting access only to authorized entities.
- Cons: Homomorphic encryption, which allows computations on encrypted data, can be resource-intensive and sluggish for intricate operations.

Differential Privacy:

- Pros: Differential privacy injects noise into data to prevent individual data points from standing out. It furnishes a structured framework for quantifying privacy assurances.
- Cons: Precise noise calibration is necessary to balance privacy and data usefulness. Strong privacy safeguards might lead to reduced analysis precision.

Secure Multi-Party Computation (SMPC):

- Pros: SMPC empowers multiple parties to collectively compute results while guarding their individual inputs. It holds adaptability for diverse computation types.
- Cons: The complexity of configuring and upkeeping SMPC protocols can be substantial. Communication overhead and computational slowdowns might arise.

Federated Learning:

- Pros: Federated learning trains models locally on decentralized devices, only sharing model updates. It diminishes the demand for centralized data storage, augmenting privacy.
- Cons: Ensuring uniformity and security across distributed devices presents challenges. Aggregating noisy updates from varied devices can influence model accuracy.

Secure Enclaves:

- Pros: Secure enclaves, like Intel SGX, furnish hardware-based isolated environments for secure code execution. They shield both data and code from external threats.
- Cons: Susceptibility to side-channel attacks or enclave vulnerabilities exists. Enclaves might impose limitations on certain computations.

Tokenization and Anonymization:

- Pros: Tokenization swaps sensitive data with unique tokens, while anonymization removes personally identifiable details. These techniques retain data value while curbing privacy risks.
- Cons: Skillful token mapping management is needed to dodge reverse engineering. Anonymization could still be susceptible to re-identification efforts.

Data Masking and Perturbation:

- Pros: Data masking substitutes original values with masked ones, and perturbation injects controlled noise. Both approaches safeguard individual data while preserving aggregated statistics.
- Cons: Incorrect masking or perturbation can distort data and jeopardize analysis accuracy.

Zero-Knowledge Proofs:

- Pros: Zero-knowledge proofs enable one party to verify the veracity of a statement without divulging any information beyond the statement's validity.
- Cons: Integrating zero-knowledge proofs can be intricate and might introduce computational overhead.

When assessing privacy-preserving methods, factors like data sensitivity, desired privacy level, computational impact, usability, and legal/regulatory concerns must be factored in. Technique selection often hinges on specific use cases and the trade-offs amid privacy, usefulness, and performance. Staying updated on evolving privacy-preserving technologies and best practices is essential, given the rapid progression in this field.

Advantages and Limitations of Encryption

Encryption serves as a foundational method to safeguard sensitive data by converting it into a format only decipherable by authorized entities (Denning, D. E. R., 1982). Here, we delve into the benefits and constraints of encryption:

Advantages:

- Confidentiality: Encryption ensures exclusive access to original data by authorized parties possessing the decryption key. This shields sensitive information from unauthorized entry.
- Data Integrity: Encryption methods often encompass features to detect illicit alterations or tampering with encrypted data. This upholds data integrity during transmission and storage.
- Authentication: Encryption, coupled with digital signatures, can authenticate the sender's credibility and message integrity.
- Compliance: Several sectors and regulatory frameworks mandate encryption for sensitive data protection. Employing encryption aids organizations in adhering to data safeguarding rules.
- Secure Data Sharing: Encrypted data can be securely shared across untrusted networks or platforms. Even if intercepted, encrypted data remains indecipherable sans the decryption key.
- Multi-layered Security: Encryption complements other security measures to craft a multi-tiered defense strategy, heightening the difficulty of data compromise.
- Remote Access Security: Encryption often secures remote connections, like Virtual Private Networks (VPNs), preserving data confidentiality during remote data transmission.

Limitations:

- Key Management: Encryption necessitates secure encryption key administration. Lost, compromised, or mishandled keys can lead to perpetual data inaccessibility.
- Performance Impact: Robust encryption algorithms can introduce computational overhead, affecting system performance, particularly on resource-constrained devices.
- Key Distribution: Securely disseminating encryption keys to authorized parties poses challenges, especially in extensive systems or multi-party scenarios.
- Complexity: Proper encryption implementation mandates comprehension of cryptographic principles and algorithm selection. Incorrect execution can expose vulnerabilities.
- Attack Vectors: Encryption does not shield against all attack types; for example, it is ineffective against phishing, social engineering, and attacks targeting system vulnerabilities.
- Encryption at Rest vs. In Transit: Applying encryption at rest (data stored on devices/servers) versus encryption in transit (data transmitted over networks) necessitates distinct considerations and mechanisms.
- Availability: Encryption keys' unavailability due to loss, corruption, or other reasons can render encrypted data inaccessible.
- User Experience: Encryption procedures can introduce additional steps for users, impacting user experience and usability.
- Legal and Regulatory Hurdles: In some cases, laws may demand access to encrypted data under specific conditions, creating a privacy versus law enforcement conflict.
- Cryptanalysis: Advancements in computing power may render previously robust encryption vulnerable to formerly implausible attacks.

Despite these constraints, encryption remains an indispensable asset for protecting sensitive information, preserving digital communication's security and data storage privacy. Prudent assessment of trade-offs and selection of suitable encryption methods in accordance with specific requisites and context is paramount.

Balancing Security and Usability in Access Control

Finding the delicate equilibrium between robust security protocols and user-friendly access control mechanisms is a pivotal challenge in today's data management landscape. Navigating the fine line between safeguarding sensitive information and ensuring seamless user interactions is paramount for cultivating an environment that upholds both protection and user convenience (Braun, T., et al. 2023). Here, we delve into the essential factors, strategies, and considerations associated with achieving this intricate equilibrium.

Factors Influencing the Balance:

- Security Imperatives: The inherent nature of the data at stake, coupled with regulatory and compliance mandates, dictates the requisite level of security. Data of higher sensitivity mandates stringent security measures, which could potentially impact user-friendliness.
- User Experience: Access control measures must seamlessly integrate into user workflows, without introducing friction or frequent authentication hurdles that might hinder user efficiency.
- Usability Expectations: User interactions within the digital realm have set a standard for intuitive and uncomplicated experiences. Access control solutions must harmonize with these anticipations to promote user acceptance.
- Threat Landscape: The evolving landscape of cyber threats necessitates robust security measures. Striking the balance entails addressing vulnerabilities while preserving user ease.
- Organizational Culture: The prevailing company culture influences the weighting of security against convenience. Achieving equilibrium requires aligning strategies with the existing cultural context.

Approaches to Achieving Balance:

- Role-Based Access Control (RBAC): RBAC introduces a structured framework by assigning permissions based on predefined roles. This sustains security while simplifying user oversight.
- Multi-Factor Authentication (MFA): The fusion of diverse authentication methods heightens security without unduly disrupting user experience.
- Single Sign-On (SSO): SSO streamlines user access by enabling a single authentication for multiple applications, seamlessly marrying security and convenience.
- Adaptive Authentication: This method gauges user behavior and contextual cues to determine the optimal authentication level, aligning security with user-centric needs.
- User-Centric Design: Crafting access control solutions with users at the forefront ensures usability. Clear interfaces, intuitive workflows, and minimal hindrances amplify user satisfaction.
- Contextual Access Control: Analyzing variables like location, device, and access timing empowers adaptive adjustments to security levels, preserving user convenience while fortifying protection.

Key Considerations for Striking Equilibrium:

- Thorough Risk Assessment: A comprehensive evaluation of risks aids in identifying critical assets and potential threats, enabling well-informed security decisions.
- User Education: Educating users about the gravity of security can engender cooperation with more stringent access control procedures.
- Feedback Incorporation: Consistently seeking user feedback facilitates the refinement of access control mechanisms, ensuring they remain user-friendly yet robust.
- Continuous Vigilance: Employing constant monitoring detects anomalies and potential breaches, ensuring usability is not compromised by real-time security concerns.
- User-Centric Testing: Including user feedback in early design and testing phases aligns security and usability, fostering user approval.
- Adaptive Agility: Solutions must exhibit flexibility to accommodate shifts in user preferences, organizational dynamics, and the ever-evolving security landscape.
- User Acceptance Testing (UAT): UAT validates the effectiveness of security measures without impairing usability, securing user buy-in.

Balancing security and usability within access control is an ongoing endeavor demanding a nuanced grasp of organizational requisites, user anticipations, and evolving security paradigms. By amalgamating effective strategies, fostering user involvement, and embracing adaptive approaches, organizations can adeptly traverse this intricate terrain and achieve a harmonious amalgamation of security and user-friendliness.

Effectiveness of Anonymization for Different Data Types

The assessment of the effectiveness of anonymization methods across a wide range of data types holds significant importance in modern data protection initiatives. The task of gauging the extent to which anonymization safeguards confidentiality across various data categories necessitates a thorough grasp of the inherent challenges and benefits involved (Ohm, P., 2009). In this discourse, we delve into the effectiveness of anonymization for distinct data types while illuminating its implications.

- Structured Data: Structured data, comprising organized datasets like databases and spreadsheets, presents specific challenges for anonymization. Traditional techniques like generalization and suppression are employed to de-identify structured data while retaining its utility. Anonymization proves effective in this context by obscuring direct identifiers, preserving data integrity, and enabling aggregate analyses. Yet, the balance between anonymization and data utility becomes pronounced as the granularity of data increases. Aggressive anonymization can lead to information loss, potentially impacting analytical precision.
- Textual Data: Textual data, encompassing documents, emails, and online content, poses distinct anonymization complexities. Techniques such as tokenization and redaction are utilized to mask sensitive information. Anonymization proves effective here, safeguarding private details and protecting the identities of individuals involved. However, the contextual nature of textual data can present challenges. Striking the right balance between obscuring private details and maintaining document comprehensibility requires careful consideration.

- Geospatial Data: Geospatial data, including location-based information from GPS and geographic databases, encounters unique anonymization demands. Methods like spatial obfuscation are deployed to protect location privacy. Anonymization demonstrates effectiveness by preventing direct tracing of individuals' movements. Nevertheless, preserving data usability and ensuring that spatial relationships remain meaningful is a constant challenge. Over-anonymization can lead to distorted geographic patterns and reduced analytical accuracy.
- Temporal Data: Temporal data, encompassing time-based records like timestamps and event logs, involves anonymization to mitigate privacy risks. Techniques such as time shifting are employed to obscure precise timestamps. Anonymization proves effective in securing temporal data by thwarting the re-identification of individuals based on their activities. Striking an optimal balance involves retaining the chronological order of events while obscuring the exact timing.
- Multimedia Data: Multimedia data, including images and videos, introduces anonymization complexities due to their rich content. Techniques like blurring and masking are used to protect identities. Anonymization is effective in concealing faces and personally identifiable features, ensuring privacy. However, the challenge lies in maintaining data fidelity while eliminating identifying details. Over-anonymization can render the multimedia content less informative.
- Social Network Data: Social network data, comprising connections between individuals, necessitates anonymization techniques to protect social graph privacy. Anonymization effectively obscures direct connections while preserving network structure. However, network de-identification can lead to potential privacy breaches through inference attacks. Striking the balance between privacy preservation and data utility is essential.

In evaluating the effectiveness of anonymization for diverse data types, it's vital to recognize that a one-size-fits-all approach is untenable. The suitability of anonymization techniques varies with data characteristics and privacy requirements. Striking the optimal balance between privacy preservation and data utility is an intricate task that demands careful consideration of each data type's intricacies.

REGULATORY LANDSCAPE AND LEGAL IMPLICATIONS

The examination of the regulatory framework and potential legal consequences constitutes a critical facet in the current realm of data management. Understanding how the regulatory landscape impacts various industries and the potential legal outcomes arising from non-compliance involves a comprehensive grasp of the pertinent challenges and benefits. Here, we delve into the intricate interplay between regulations and legal implications, shedding light on their significance.

- The Regulatory Landscape: The regulatory environment encompasses an array of laws, guidelines, and standards that govern data handling, privacy, and security across diverse sectors. Industries such as healthcare, finance, and telecommunications, among others, must navigate this complex web of regulations to ensure compliance. Regulatory bodies, like the General Data Protection Regulation (GDPR) in the European Union and the Health Insurance Portability and Accountability Act (HIPAA) in the healthcare sector, outline stringent requirements for data protection, usage, and disclosure. Understanding these regulations is pivotal to prevent legal entanglements and reputational damage.

- Legal Implications: Non-compliance with regulatory standards can carry significant legal consequences. Fines, penalties, legal actions, and reputational harm are potential outcomes of failing to adhere to established regulations. For instance, GDPR violations can result in substantial fines, while breaches of financial regulations can lead to legal actions and financial penalties. Moreover, data breaches or improper handling of personal information can result in lawsuits from affected individuals or regulatory authorities.
- Navigating the Landscape: Staying abreast of the regulatory landscape is crucial. Compliance measures encompass data protection policies, transparency in data usage, consent mechanisms, security protocols, and breach notification procedures. Organizations must implement robust safeguards, conduct regular audits, and establish data protection officers to ensure adherence to regulations.
- Industry-Specific Implications: Different industries face unique regulatory demands. Healthcare must ensure patient data confidentiality, financial sectors need to safeguard transactional data, and e-commerce entities must address online privacy concerns. Failure to do so can lead to severe penalties and legal actions.
- Cross-Border Challenges: In a globalized world, data flows across borders. Organizations handling international data must grapple with compliance across various jurisdictions. This entails harmonizing disparate regulations to safeguard data privacy and security.
- Vendor Management and Third Parties: The legal responsibilities extend to vendor relationships. Organizations must ensure that third-party vendors adhere to relevant regulations. Failure to do so can result in shared legal liability.
- Mitigation Strategies: Comprehensive compliance programs, including legal assessments, privacy impact assessments, and employee training, are crucial. Regular monitoring and risk assessment mitigate potential legal implications.
- Conclusion: Navigating the regulatory landscape and understanding legal implications is paramount in data management. Organizations must prioritize compliance, establish robust safeguards, and stay informed about evolving regulations to prevent legal setbacks and ensure data integrity and privacy.

Data Protection Regulations: GDPR, CCPA, HIPAA

A Synopsis of Key Features in the General Data Protection Regulation (GDPR), California Consumer Privacy Act (CCPA), and Health Insurance Portability and Accountability Act (HIPAA) (Nurgalieva, L., et al., 2020):

General Data Protection Regulation (GDPR)

Scope: The GDPR is an all-encompassing data protection directive that pertains to the processing of personal data of individuals within the European Union (EU) and the European Economic Area (EEA). It also extends to non-EU/EEA organizations providing goods, services, or monitoring behaviors of EU/EEA residents.

Primary Clauses:

- Consent: Organizations must attain clear and unequivocal consent from individuals before processing their personal data.
- Rights of Data Subjects: Individuals are endowed with rights like access, correction, erasure, and limitation of their personal data processing.
- Data Breach Reporting: Entities are required to promptly report data breaches to both relevant authorities and impacted individuals.
- Data Protection Officer (DPO): Certain entities must designate a Data Protection Officer who oversees data protection activities.
- Cross-Border Data Transfer: Cross-border transfers of personal data to non-EU/EEA nations are subjected to stringent safeguards.
- Right to Erasure ("Right to Be Forgotten"): Individuals can request the erasure of their personal data under specific circumstances.
- Accountability and Documentation: Organizations must display compliance through documentation, data protection impact assessments (DPIAs), and transparent data processing policies.

California Consumer Privacy Act (CCPA)

Scope: The CCPA applies to businesses dealing with the personal information of California residents, contingent on revenue and data processing thresholds.

Salient Aspects:

- Right to Information: Consumers possess the right to be informed about their collected personal data and its utilization.
- Right to Deletion: Consumers can demand the erasure of their personal information held by businesses, subject to specific exemptions.
- Opt-Out Right for Sale: Businesses must offer an opt-out mechanism for the sale of personal information.
- Non-Discrimination: Businesses are prohibited from discriminating against consumers who exercise their privacy rights.
- Children's Privacy: The CCPA contains dedicated clauses concerning the collection and sale of minors' personal information.

Health Insurance Portability and Accountability Act (HIPAA)

Scope: HIPAA pertains to covered entities (healthcare providers, health plans, and healthcare clearinghouses) and their business associates handling protected health information (PHI) in the United States.

Prominent Components:

- Privacy Rule: Sets standards for safeguarding PHI and individuals' privacy rights, involving patient consent for specific PHI uses and disclosures.
- Security Rule: Mandates covered entities to implement security measures for safeguarding electronic PHI (ePHI) and maintaining health information's confidentiality, integrity, and availability.

- Breach Notification Rule: Requires immediate breach notification to affected individuals, the U.S. Department of Health and Human Services (HHS), and potentially the media in case of unsecured PHI breaches.
- Minimum Necessary Rule: Stipulates limiting the use and disclosure of PHI to the minimum necessary for the intended purpose.

Note: The above abridgments offer a succinct overview of these regulations. For a comprehensive understanding of the specific requisites and implications applicable to your organization, it is advisable to consult the full regulatory text and seek legal guidance. To achieve compliance, organizations must institute appropriate technical and administrative measures to preserve personal data, uphold privacy rights, institute sound governance, and respect individuals' entitlements.

Industry Standards and Compliance Requirements and Aligning Practices With Evolving Privacy Laws

Industry standards are established benchmarks of quality, safety, and best practices within a particular field. They serve as guidelines for organizations to operate efficiently, produce reliable products/services, and ensure the well-being of stakeholders. Compliance requirements, on the other hand, are regulations imposed by authorities or industry bodies that organizations must follow to legally and ethically conduct their operations.

Examples of industry standards and compliance requirements include:

- ISO Standards: International Organization for Standardization (ISO) standards cover a wide range of areas, such as quality management (ISO 9001), information security (ISO 27001), and environmental management (ISO 14001).
- Data Protection Regulations: Regulations like the General Data Protection Regulation (GDPR) and the California Consumer Privacy Act (CCPA) mandate how organizations handle personal data, emphasizing data protection, user consent, and transparency.
- Health and Safety Standards: Industries like construction and manufacturing must adhere to safety standards to prevent workplace accidents and ensure employee well-being.
- Financial Regulations: Organizations in the financial sector must comply with regulations like the Sarbanes-Oxley Act (SOX) to ensure accurate financial reporting and prevent fraudulent activities.
- Medical Standards: Medical devices and pharmaceuticals must adhere to standards set by organizations like the Food and Drug Administration (FDA) to ensure safety and efficacy.

Aligning Practices with Evolving Privacy Laws:

Evolving privacy laws, especially in the digital age, require organizations to handle personal data responsibly. Here's how to align practices with these laws:

- Understand Applicable Laws: Stay updated on privacy laws relevant to your industry and geographic location, such as GDPR, CCPA, and the Health Insurance Portability and Accountability Act (HIPAA).
- Data Inventory: Identify and categorize the personal data you collect, process, and store. This helps in understanding the scope of data handling.

- Consent Management: Obtain explicit and informed consent from individuals before collecting their data. Allow them to opt-out and manage their preferences.
- Transparency: Clearly communicate how you collect, use, and share personal data. Provide privacy notices that are easy to understand.
- Data Security: Implement strong security measures to protect personal data from breaches. This includes encryption, access controls, and regular security assessments.
- Data Subject Rights: Respect individuals' rights, such as the right to access their data, rectify inaccuracies, and request data deletion.
- Vendor Management: Ensure that third-party vendors you work with also adhere to privacy regulations when handling personal data.
- Data Protection Officer (DPO): Appoint a DPO if required by law, especially under GDPR, to oversee data protection activities.
- Incident Response Plan: Have a plan in place to respond to data breaches and privacy incidents, including notifying affected parties and regulatory authorities.
- Employee Training: Educate your staff about privacy laws and best practices to ensure a company-wide commitment to data protection.

By aligning your practices with evolving privacy laws, you not only comply with regulations but also build trust with customers, partners, and stakeholders. It demonstrates your commitment to safeguarding sensitive information

Best Practices for Secure Data Storage

Ensuring the secure storage of data is a fundamental requirement for maintaining the confidentiality, integrity, and availability of sensitive information. To this end, adhering to best practices in secure data storage is paramount. The following guidelines offer valuable insights into establishing a robust approach to secure data storage:

Data Encryption:

- Encryption at Rest: Prioritize encrypting data before it's stored on any storage medium. By doing so, even if the storage device is compromised, unauthorized access to the data remains thwarted.
- Encryption in Transit: Utilize secure protocols like HTTPS, SFTP, and SSH to safeguard data during its transfer to and from storage systems, deterring interception and tampering.

Access Control:

- Role-Based Access Control (RBAC): Implement RBAC to ensure that solely authorized entities or processes can access and manipulate stored data.
- Principle of Least Privilege (PoLP): Adhere to PoLP by providing users and processes with the minimum necessary access levels for their tasks.
- Robust Authentication: Enforce stringent authentication methods, such as multi-factor authentication, to validate user identities seeking access to the data.

Physical Security:

- Secure Storage Location: Safeguard physical storage devices within a controlled environment to thwart unauthorized physical access or theft.
- Data Erasure: Properly eliminate storage devices no longer in use using methods that prevent data recovery, like secure erasure or physical destruction.

Data Backup and Redundancy:

- Regular Backups: Regularly back up data to mitigate potential data loss resulting from hardware failures, data corruption, or unforeseen incidents.
- Redundant Storage: Maintain redundant backups in separate locations, both on-site and off-site, to bolster availability and mitigate risks.

Patch Management:

- Up-to-Date Systems: Ensure that storage systems and software are current with the latest security patches to counter vulnerabilities that could be exploited.

Monitoring and Logging:

- Comprehensive Monitoring: Implement robust monitoring and logging mechanisms to promptly identify unauthorized access attempts, anomalous activities, or security breaches.

Data Lifecycle Management:

- Clear Data Policies: Establish precise policies governing data retention, archiving, and disposal. Dispose of unnecessary data following established procedures.

Secure Coding Practices:

- Vulnerability Prevention: Implement secure coding practices to safeguard against unintended vulnerabilities in applications interacting with the storage system.

Network Security:

- Network Segmentation: Segregate networks to isolate sensitive storage systems from less critical systems.
- Network Defenses: Deploy firewalls, intrusion detection/prevention systems, and other safeguards to ward off unauthorized access.

Vendor Security:

- Third-Party Assurance: When utilizing third-party storage solutions or cloud providers, ascertain their strict adherence to security practices and compliance standards.
- Regular Audits and Assessments:
- Routine Security Audits: Conduct regular security audits and assessments to uncover vulnerabilities or weaknesses in your data storage infrastructure.

Employee Training and Awareness:

- Security Education: Provide comprehensive training to employees and users, emphasizing security best practices, including the importance of safeguarding sensitive data throughout storage and handling.

It's imperative to recognize that security is an ongoing endeavor. Staying attuned to evolving security threats and best practices is vital, necessitating the adaptability of your storage strategy over time.

Secure Data Transfer Protocols: SSL/TLS, VPNs

Ensuring the confidentiality and integrity of data during transmission is of paramount importance. Two widely employed secure data transfer protocols are SSL/TLS and VPNs.

1. SSL/TLS (Secure Sockets Layer/Transport Layer Security):

SSL and its successor TLS are cryptographic protocols that establish an encrypted connection between a client (e.g., web browser) and a server (e.g., website). These protocols guarantee that exchanged data between the two remains shielded from prying eyes. The mechanics of SSL/TLS are as follows:

- Handshake: A client-server handshake initiates, negotiating encryption settings and authentication methods.
- Encryption: Once the handshake concludes, data passing between client and server becomes encrypted using cryptographic algorithms, thus ensuring its secrecy.
- Data Integrity: SSL/TLS also upholds data integrity by employing cryptographic hashes, flagging any unauthorized tampering during transmission.

SSL, susceptible to vulnerabilities, has given way to the more secure TLS. Different versions of TLS exist, with TLS 1.2 and 1.3 being particularly secure and extensively employed.

2. VPNs (Virtual Private Networks):

VPNs serve as an additional safeguard for secure data transfer, especially over public networks like the internet. They fabricate an encrypted tunnel between a user's device and a remote server, obfuscating the user's IP address and heightening security. The process unfolds as such:

- Encrypted Tunnel: A user connecting to a VPN triggers data encryption, channeling it through a secure tunnel to a VPN server.
- Data Forwarding: Subsequently, the VPN server redirects the encrypted data to its intended endpoint, like a website or service.
- Decryption: Upon reaching the destination server, encrypted data undergoes decryption, enabling the processing of user requests.
- Response: The response from the destination server is encrypted anew and routed back through the VPN server to the user's device.
- Anonymity: VPNs yield the added advantage of masking the user's IP address, introducing an element of anonymity and shielding against online tracking.

It's pivotal to recognize the nuanced roles of SSL/TLS and VPNs:

SSL/TLS: Principally employed for securing data between a client (e.g., web browser) and a server (e.g., website). Typically used for fortified website connections (HTTPS).

VPNs: Designed to establish secure, private connections across the internet, frequently permitting users to remotely access private network resources while encrypting their connection.

SSL/TLS and VPNs both contribute substantially to the holistic security of data transfer. The selection between the two hinges on specific usage scenarios and requirements.

Data Management: Backup and Recovery, Data Lifecycle

The principles of data management encompass critical aspects like backup and recovery, along with the orchestration of data lifecycle progression:

Backup and Recovery:

- Regular and Automated Backups: Schedule automated backups at regular intervals to guarantee the safeguarding of current and crucial data.
- Full, Incremental, and Differential Backups: Employ a blend of backup types. Complete backups encompass the entire dataset, whereas incremental and differential backups exclusively record modifications since the previous backup. This approach optimizes storage and reduces backup duration.
- Off-Site and Cloud Backups: Secure copies of backups at remote sites, ideally geographically distinct, to fortify against natural calamities or physical disruptions at the primary site.
- Leverage cloud-based backup solutions to bolster redundancy and scalability.

Versioning and Retention Policies:

- Enforce versioning to uphold historical iterations of files, a pivotal resource in cases of inadvertent data alterations or unauthorized modifications.
- Institute retention policies specifying the duration backup copies are retained, aligning with regulatory prerequisites and operational requisites.

Regular Testing and Restoration:

- Regularly assess the backup and recovery process to verify the validity of backups and their successful restoration potential.
- Educate IT personnel on proficient recovery protocols, curtailing downtime following data loss incidents.

Data Lifecycle Management:

- Data Classification: Categorize data based on sensitivity, regulatory obligations, and business significance. This classification informs decisions on storage, access controls, and retention parameters.
- Data Creation and Collection: Establish unambiguous guidelines for data creation and collection, fostering coherence and precision from the outset.
- Data Storage and Access Control: Employ pertinent access controls and encryption mechanisms according to data classification. Not all data warrants uniform accessibility.

- Data Archiving: Transfer infrequently accessed data to long-term storage or archives, freeing primary storage and mitigating costs.
- Data Deletion and Retention: Define retention and deletion policies aligning with legal and regulatory dictates. Eliminate redundant data to curtail risk.
- Data Disposal: Implement secure methodologies to dispose of data that has reached the end of its lifecycle. This encompasses data wiping, degaussing, or physical destruction of storage media.
- Audit and Review: Conduct regular audits and evaluations of data lifecycle management practices to ensure their efficacy and congruence with organizational objectives and legal responsibilities.

By adhering to these data management principles, entities can exercise mastery over their data, diminish vulnerabilities linked with data loss, and affirm compliance with pertinent regulations.

EMERGING TECHNOLOGIES FOR ENHANCED PRIVACY

Emerging technologies are ushering in a new era of privacy solutions, empowering both individuals and organizations to safeguard their sensitive information more effectively. Here are several noteworthy emerging technologies that are poised to elevate privacy protection:

- Homomorphic Encryption: Homomorphic encryption facilitates computations on encrypted data without the need for decryption, ensuring data confidentiality during processing. This technology is particularly valuable for secure data analysis and sharing.
- Federated Learning: Federated learning facilitates the training of machine learning models across decentralized devices, preserving data localization while improving model accuracy and privacy.
- Differential Privacy: By introducing controlled noise into queries or algorithms, differential privacy shields individual data while still delivering meaningful aggregate outcomes, thus maintaining the anonymity of contributors.
- Secure Multi-Party Computation (SMPC): SMPC enables collaborative computations across multiple entities' private inputs without exposing those inputs. It finds utility in confidential joint analyses.
- Zero-Knowledge Proofs: Zero-knowledge proofs ascertain the veracity of a statement without divulging underlying data, bolstering data privacy during validation and authentication procedures.
- Privacy-Preserving Cryptocurrencies: Privacy-centric cryptocurrencies harness advanced cryptographic techniques to safeguard transaction specifics, enhancing both confidentiality and anonymity.
- Decentralized Identity (DID): DID frameworks empower individuals to manage their digital identities autonomously, reducing reliance on centralized entities and enhancing privacy and consent management.
- Blockchain and Distributed Ledgers: The transparent yet tamper-proof nature of blockchain can be leveraged to grant users authority over data access and sharing, ensuring privacy and consent.
- Personal Data Vaults: Personal data vaults empower individuals to control their data, permitting selective attribute sharing with various services without exposing comprehensive data.

- Biometric Authentication: Biometric authentication methods, like fingerprint and facial recognition, deliver robust security without necessitating the storage of raw biometric data, amplifying user privacy.
- Privacy-Centric Browsers and Search Engines: Emerging privacy-oriented browsers and search engines prioritize user privacy by obstructing trackers, cookies, and personalized data collection.
- AI-Driven Privacy Solutions: AI can forecast privacy risks, automate data protection measures, and boost privacy compliance via predictive analytics.

These emerging technologies stand to reshape the data privacy landscape, providing the means for individuals and entities to maintain data control while reaping the benefits of innovative services and insights. However, their ethical deployment and meticulous implementation are essential to ensure responsible use and full respect for individuals' privacy rights.

Homomorphic Encryption: Performing Computations on Encrypted Data

Homomorphic encryption represents a leading-edge cryptographic innovation that facilitates computations to be executed on encrypted data without necessitating prior decryption of the data. This distinctive capacity to manipulate encrypted information directly constitutes a substantial stride in upholding data privacy while simultaneously allowing practical operations. The principle can be elucidated as follows:

Conventional encryption methodologies encompass the transformation of plaintext data into ciphertext utilizing an encryption algorithm and a confidential encryption key. To carry out any computations on the encrypted data, it must first undergo decryption via a corresponding decryption key. This decryption stage exposes the confidential content to potential security vulnerabilities.

However, homomorphic encryption presents a paradigm shift in this process. It empowers computations to be conducted directly on ciphertext, preserving the encrypted status throughout the entire computational sequence. Consequently, data retains its confidentiality throughout, even during the course of operations. The output of the computation likewise remains encrypted. Only when the final outcome requires presentation to the authorized recipient is decryption executed using the appropriate decryption key.

Homomorphic encryption holds exceptional significance in contexts where data privacy holds paramount importance, such as cloud computing and data analysis. Consider an instance in which a healthcare provider intends to perform analysis on medical records stored in a cloud environment. Through homomorphic encryption, the provider can execute computations on the encrypted records without necessitating a preliminary decryption step. This ensures that sensitive medical data remains confidential throughout the analytical process.

Diverse tiers of homomorphic encryption exist, encompassing partially homomorphic encryption and fully homomorphic encryption. Partially homomorphic encryption caters to specific types of computations, whereas fully homomorphic encryption empowers arbitrary computations to be undertaken on encrypted data.

It is prudent to acknowledge that, despite the groundbreaking nature of homomorphic encryption, it may entail computational intensity and potentially entail performance trade-offs. Progress in technology is driving endeavors to optimize and enhance the efficiency of these methodologies, rendering them more practical for a spectrum of applications.

Multi-Party Computation: Collaborative Data Processing Without Revealing Raw Data

Multi-party computation (MPC) stands as an advanced cryptographic strategy that empowers multiple participants to jointly process data while maintaining the confidentiality of their individual input data. At its core, MPC seeks to enable computations on disparate data sources without necessitating the exposure of raw, sensitive information to any entity, including fellow computation participants. This technological breakthrough introduces a fresh approach to conducting collective analyses while upholding the paramount aspect of data confidentiality.

The foundational premise of MPC can be succinctly outlined:

Imagine a scenario involving several distinct entities, each in possession of their own private dataset. These entities share the objective of performing a computation on the amalgamated data sans the necessity to divulge their individual data to others. MPC serves as the vehicle to realize this objective.

MPC harnesses cryptographic protocols that orchestrate multiple rounds of interaction amongst the involved parties. These protocols are adept at guiding each participant to encrypt their input data in a manner that solely they hold the decryption capability. Through a sequence of collaborative calculations, these parties collaborate to attain the desired outcome, all the while ensuring that the raw data of any participant remains undisclosed.

Of notable significance, MPC offers the distinct advantage that no solitary participant can extrapolate details about the input data of others throughout the computation journey. Instead, each participant solely acquires knowledge of the ultimate computation result, remaining oblivious to the specifics of the fellow participants' data.

The practical applications of MPC span domains where data privacy is of paramount concern, including domains like financial analysis, medical research, and secure data sharing. As an illustration, contemplate a scenario wherein multiple pharmaceutical entities aspire to collectively analyze their clinical trial data to glean insights devoid of revealing individual trial results. In this context, MPC emerges as the secure conduit enabling collaborative exploration, thereby facilitating meaningful deductions while upholding data privacy.

Diverse variations of MPC exist, encompassing two-party computation (2PC) and multi-party computation involving a larger number of participants. These protocol distinctions are meticulously designed to cater to a range of collaborative scenarios, all underpinned by the core tenet of safeguarding data confidentiality.

While MPC presents an encouraging avenue for secure cooperation, its implementation can entail complexity and potential computational demands. Nonetheless, the continuous strides witnessed in cryptography and computing hold the promise of rendering MPC more pragmatic and, in turn, capable of delivering innovative solutions for collective computations without compromising data privacy.

Potential Applications and Challenges of These Technologies

The potential applications and challenges associated with the technologies mentioned in the context of cloud security:

1. Artificial Intelligence (AI) and Machine Learning (ML)

Potential Applications:

- Threat Detection and Prediction: AI and ML can analyze extensive datasets to identify patterns of malicious behavior and predict potential threats.
- Anomaly Detection: AI and ML algorithms can recognize deviations from normal patterns in real-time, indicating possible security breaches.
- Behavioral Analysis: AI and ML can establish baselines of regular behavior and detect anomalies, aiding in the identification of insider threats.
- Automated Incident Response: AI-driven automation can accelerate incident response, mitigating the impact of attacks.
- Predictive Analysis: AI and ML models have the capacity to forecast vulnerabilities, allowing for proactive patch management.

Challenges:

- Data Privacy and Bias: AI and ML models rely on significant datasets, prompting concerns about data privacy and potential biases in training data.
- Complexity: The implementation and management of AI and ML systems can be intricate, necessitating specialized skills and resources.
- False Positives and Negatives: AI and ML algorithms might generate false alerts or miss sophisticated attacks, affecting accuracy.
- Adversarial Attacks: Attackers can manipulate AI and ML models using adversarial attacks, undermining their effectiveness.

2. Blockchain

Potential Applications:

- Data Integrity: Blockchain technology can guarantee the integrity and immutability of crucial security-related data.
- Decentralized Identity: Blockchain can facilitate secure user identity verification, reducing dependence on centralized identity providers.
- Secure Transactions: Blockchain enables secure and transparent transactions between parties without intermediaries.

Challenges:

- Scalability: Blockchain's consensus mechanisms can limit scalability, posing challenges for handling high transaction volumes.
- Energy Consumption: Numerous blockchain implementations are energy-intensive, potentially raising sustainability concerns.
- Regulatory Uncertainty: The legal and regulatory frameworks surrounding blockchain technology are still evolving, leading to uncertainties.

3. Quantum Computing

Potential Applications:

- Cryptographic Breakthroughs: Quantum computing has the potential to compromise traditional encryption algorithms, spurring the development of quantum-resistant cryptography.
- Complex Problem Solving: Quantum computers can tackle complex mathematical problems, expediting the analysis of security data.

Challenges:

- Security Risks: Quantum computers pose a threat to current encryption methods, potentially jeopardizing data security.
- Maturity: Quantum computing technology is in its infancy, and practical, scalable quantum computers are not yet widely available.
- High Costs: Establishing and maintaining quantum computers is expensive, limiting access for many organizations.

4. Edge Computing

Potential Applications:

- Reduced Latency: Edge computing enhances real-time threat detection and response by processing data closer to its source.
- Privacy Enhancement: Data processing at the edge can reduce the necessity to transmit sensitive data to centralized servers.

Challenges:

- Security Risks: Edge devices might be vulnerable to attacks due to limited resources and potential lack of security measures.
- Management Complexity: Administering a distributed edge infrastructure introduces complexity in terms of security updates and patches.
- Interoperability: Ensuring compatibility and security across various edge devices and platforms can pose challenges.

Each of these technologies presents promising applications to bolster cloud security, but they also entail distinct challenges that necessitate attention for successful integration and deployment. Organizations should thoughtfully assess the advantages and risks tied to these technologies to make informed choices regarding their incorporation into cloud security strategies.

FUTURE TRENDS AND CONSIDERATIONS

The integration of privacy preservation and secure data storage in cloud computing is poised to evolve in response to emerging technologies and evolving challenges. Here are some future trends and considerations:

- Homomorphic Encryption and Privacy-Preserving Techniques: Advancements in homomorphic encryption and other privacy-preserving techniques will enable computation on encrypted data without the need for decryption, enhancing data privacy in the cloud.
- Zero-Trust Architecture: Organizations will increasingly adopt a zero-trust approach, treating every user and device as potentially untrusted. This approach aligns with secure data storage by enforcing strict access controls and continuous monitoring.
- Blockchain and Distributed Ledgers: Blockchain's decentralized and tamper-evident nature may find applications in secure data storage, ensuring data integrity and transparency while minimizing the need for centralized control.
- AI-Driven Threat Detection and Response: AI and machine learning will play a pivotal role in identifying and responding to security threats in real-time, bolstering the defense against breaches and unauthorized access.
- Edge Computing and Data Residency: Edge computing's rise will raise questions about data residency and compliance. Organizations will need to balance the benefits of edge computing with the need for secure and compliant data storage.
- Quantum Computing Challenges: As quantum computing matures, it has the potential to break traditional encryption methods. Organizations must explore quantum-resistant encryption to safeguard data stored in the cloud.
- Hybrid and Multi-Cloud Security: Organizations will continue to adopt hybrid and multi-cloud architectures. Ensuring consistent privacy and security practices across diverse cloud environments will be crucial.
- User-Centric Privacy Controls: User-centric privacy controls will gain prominence, allowing individuals more control over how their data is stored, processed, and shared within cloud environments.
- Regulatory Landscape Evolution: The regulatory landscape will evolve, with new data protection laws impacting cloud practices. Organizations must stay informed and adapt their strategies accordingly.
- Ethical Considerations: Privacy preservation in the cloud will extend beyond compliance to include ethical considerations. Striking the right balance between data utilization and individual rights will be paramount.

In the face of these trends and considerations, organizations must remain proactive in adopting cutting-edge security measures, embracing emerging technologies, and continuously updating their privacy and security practices. By doing so, they can ensure that their cloud-based operations remain resilient, compliant, and capable of withstanding the challenges of an ever-evolving digital landscape.

Evolving Threats and Responses in Cloud Security

The persistent evolution of threats in cloud security presents ongoing challenges for organizations in a rapidly changing technological landscape. Here are notable threats along with their corresponding strategies for addressing cloud security:

Data Breaches:

- Threat: Unauthorized access leading to data leaks or theft.
- Response: Strengthen security with encryption, access controls, and multi-factor authentication. Vigilantly monitor and audit access logs to detect unusual activities.

Insider Threats:

- Threat: Malicious or negligent actions by employees or authorized users.
- Response: Enforce least privilege access, conduct comprehensive background checks, and employ behavioral analytics for identifying abnormal user behavior.

Misconfigured Cloud Services:

- Threat: Inadequate configuration exposing sensitive data or allowing unauthorized access.
- Response: Employ automated security assessments and adhere to the principle of least privilege. Regularly review and audit cloud configurations.

Distributed Denial of Service (DDoS) Attacks:

- Threat: Overwhelming cloud resources through an influx of requests, causing service disruption.
- Response: Implement DDoS protection solutions, establish traffic monitoring mechanisms, and leverage cloud-based scaling for handling traffic surges.

API Vulnerabilities:

- Threat: Insecure APIs exploited to gain unauthorized access to cloud resources.
- Response: Securely design APIs with robust authentication and authorization. Maintain updated API frameworks through regular patches.

Zero-Day Exploits:

- Threat: Attackers exploit unknown vulnerabilities in cloud services or platforms.
- Response: Stay updated with security patches and updates. Employ intrusion detection systems and anomaly detection based on behavior.

Cloud Account Hijacking:

- Threat: Attackers compromising cloud user accounts for unauthorized access.
- Response: Implement strong authentication, monitor account activity for anomalies, and establish session management controls.

Cloud Service Provider Vulnerabilities:

- Threat: Vulnerabilities within the cloud service provider's infrastructure or services.
- Response: Choose reputable providers with robust security practices. Regularly assess their security stance and compliance.

Data Loss and Deletion:

- Threat: Accidental or malicious data loss or deletion leading to data unavailability.
- Response: Develop comprehensive backup and recovery plans. Utilize versioning and proper data lifecycle management practices.

Emerging Technologies and Trends:

- Threat: The advent of new technologies like AI, edge computing, and quantum computing introduces both opportunities and security challenges.
- Response: Proactively address security concerns tied to emerging technologies. Stay informed and adapt security strategies accordingly.

To navigate evolving threats effectively, organizations must adopt a proactive and all-encompassing security strategy. This strategy should encompass robust technical measures, employee training, routine audits, well-defined incident response planning, and staying current with the latest cybersecurity developments. developments.

Integration of AI and Machine Learning in Security Measures

The incorporation of AI (Artificial Intelligence) and machine learning into security practices has brought about a significant evolution in the realm of cybersecurity. This integration has empowered the field with proactive threat detection, swift response mechanisms, and fortified defense strategies. Here's how AI and machine learning are harnessed within security contexts:

Threat Detection and Anticipation:

- AI-powered algorithms meticulously scrutinize extensive datasets to discern patterns that might signify nascent threats, often even before they are recognized as established dangers.
- Machine learning models excel in prognosticating and categorizing anomalies, behavioral shifts, and trends indicative of suspicious or malicious activities.

Behavioral Analysis:

- AI algorithms set up benchmarks for typical user behavior and network actions. Any deviation from these norms triggers alerts, prompting in-depth investigation.
- This approach is adept at identifying insider threats and intricate attacks that may circumvent traditional rule-based security systems.

Real-time Surveillance:

- Security solutions bolstered by AI capabilities provide uninterrupted real-time monitoring across diverse endpoints, networks, and cloud environments.
- This rapid, continuous monitoring facilitates the swift identification of security breaches and incidents, minimizing the gap between detection and response.

Automated Incident Handling: AI introduces automation to certain facets of incident response, encompassing actions such as isolating compromised systems, blocking malicious traffic, and activating alerts for security teams.

Threat Exploration: Machine learning plays a pivotal role in proactive threat exploration, meticulously sifting through substantial data volumes to unveil subtle indications of compromise that might elude conventional methodologies.

Identification of Phishing Attempts: AI algorithms dissect email content, sender conduct, and user interactions to swiftly flag phishing endeavors and malevolent links.

Malware Identification: AI-driven malware detection tools adeptly pinpoint novel and unfamiliar malware variants by scrutinizing their conduct, file attributes, and network engagements.

User and Entity Behavior Analytics (UEBA): UEBA solutions harness AI to establish user profiles and discern aberrant behaviors, efficaciously exposing compromised accounts and internal threats.

Network Security: AI-fueled Intrusion Detection and Prevention Systems (IDS/IPS) meticulously assess patterns in network traffic, promptly recognizing and countering potential threats in real time.

Adaptive Authentication: AI evaluates the risk quotient of login attempts based on multifaceted factors like user conduct, location, and device, culminating in adaptive and accurate authentication determinations.

Vulnerability Management: AI algorithms proficiently prioritize vulnerabilities by weighing factors such as the probability of exploitation, potential impact, and extant mitigation measures.

Security Analytics: AI-emboldened security information and event management (SIEM) systems deftly interlink and scrutinize a plethora of security data sources, yielding actionable insights.

Despite the marked enhancements AI and machine learning introduce to security landscapes, it's pivotal to recognize that they are not all-encompassing solutions. Their efficacy is best realized when amalgamated with traditional security practices. Uninterrupted vigilance, iterative refinement of AI models, and a steadfast alignment with the dynamic nature of emerging threats are imperative for sustaining an effective, AI-centric security strategy.

Ethical Considerations in Privacy Preservation

Ensuring ethical considerations in privacy preservation is vital to responsibly implement privacy-enhancing practices and technologies, respecting the rights of individuals. Key ethical aspects to take into account include:

- Transparency and Informed Consent: Individuals need to be fully informed about the collection, usage, and protection of their data. Providing clear and comprehensible explanations is crucial for obtaining informed consent.
- Purpose Limitation: Data should only be gathered and processed for specific, clearly defined, and lawful purposes. Organizations should prevent any unauthorized expansion of data use beyond its original intent.
- Data Minimization: Collect and retain the minimum amount of data necessary to achieve the intended purpose. Avoid unnecessary data collection that might compromise individual privacy.
- Anonymization and De-identification: Anonymizing data ensures that individuals cannot be directly identified. However, it's important to be cautious about the potential for re-identifying individuals using other available information.
- Granular Consent: Give individuals choices regarding how their data is used and shared. Make opt-in and opt-out mechanisms easily accessible and understandable.
- Data Portability: Individuals should have the right to access and transfer their personal data across different services, promoting their control over their own information.
- Security and Encryption: Strong security measures and encryption techniques should be in place to safeguard sensitive data from unauthorized access or breaches.
- Third-Party Sharing: If data is shared with third parties, it's essential to ensure that these parties adhere to robust privacy practices and effectively protect the data.

- Accountability and Governance: Organizations must establish internal processes to ensure compliance with privacy regulations. Appointing Data Protection Officers (DPOs) and maintaining transparency in privacy practices are vital.
- Impact Assessments: Conduct assessments to identify potential risks to individuals' privacy and take necessary actions to mitigate those risks.
- Cultural and Social Considerations: Recognize that privacy expectations can differ across cultures and societies. Respect these variations when designing privacy solutions.
- Data Retention and Deletion: Clear policies for data retention and deletion should be established and communicated to users. Data should not be stored for longer than necessary.
- Children's Privacy: Special care must be taken when dealing with data from children. Obtain proper parental consent and provide privacy protections suitable for different age groups.
- Algorithmic Bias and Fairness: Monitoring AI and machine learning models used for privacy preservation is crucial to prevent bias and ensure fairness, avoiding discrimination against specific individuals or groups.

Promoting ethical privacy practices not only protects individuals' rights but also builds trust between organizations and users. Striking the right balance between innovation and privacy preservation is fundamental for responsible data management in today's digital landscape.

CONCLUSION

Conclusively, the integration of techniques focused on preserving privacy and ensuring secure data storage within the context of cloud computing has triggered a revolutionary shift in data management, storage, and processing. This shift has engendered far-reaching implications across diverse domains.

- The reinforcement of data security, facilitated by encryption, access controls, and multi-factor authentication, has emerged as a cornerstone of confidence for both individuals and entities looking to leverage cloud services. Furthermore, the necessity of adhering to stringent data protection regulations has impelled cloud service providers to implement strategies for privacy preservation, guaranteeing that user data is handled meticulously and in accordance with legal requisites.
- The cultivation of trust, often regarded as the bedrock of cloud adoption, has been nurtured through the deployment of robust privacy and security methodologies. This has led to an increased willingness among individuals and businesses to entrust sensitive information to cloud service providers, thereby fostering the expansion of the cloud ecosystem.
- The empowerment of data owners to maintain control via methods like homomorphic encryption and differential privacy has not only redefined data sharing approaches but has also empowered data proprietors in an era that places utmost importance on data privacy. The proactive tackling of internal threats, achieved through meticulous access controls and vigilant monitoring, has raised the overall security profile of cloud environments.
- The concept of sharing data across geographical and organizational boundaries has transcended limitations, facilitating collaborative ventures without compromising the privacy of individual data. The unrelenting pursuit of privacy preservation has steered advancements in cryptography,

resulting in breakthroughs like homomorphic encryption and secure multi-party computation. These innovations redefine the horizons of data processing while preserving confidentiality.

- In tandem, the landscape of research and innovation has flourished, giving rise to novel tools and methodologies that not only benefit cloud service providers but also drive the continuous evolution of data security and privacy preservation.
- Nevertheless, this journey has not been devoid of challenges. Striking an intricate equilibrium between privacy preservation and efficient data processing, coupled with the complexities inherent in computation, remains a persistent obstacle. Additionally, the implementation of comprehensive privacy preservation measures introduces cost considerations that necessitate navigation for both service providers and users.

Fundamentally, the inception of privacy preservation and secure data storage within cloud computing has ushered in an epoch where data security and privacy are indispensable prerequisites rather than negotiable elements. This transformation lays the cornerstone for a more secure, compliant, and trustworthy digital milieu, ultimately paving the path for the ongoing expansion of cloud services while steadfastly upholding the sanctity of sensitive information.

Impact

The incorporation of techniques aimed at preserving privacy and ensuring secure data storage within the realm of cloud computing has wielded a substantial influence on the management, storage, and processing of data in the contemporary digital landscape. Several noteworthy impacts have emerged:

- Elevated Data Security: The integration of privacy preservation methodologies and secure data storage approaches has ushered in a noteworthy escalation in data security. Employing techniques such as encryption, access controls, and multi-factor authentication has effectively shielded sensitive data from unauthorized access and potential breaches. This heightened security has engendered augmented confidence among both individuals and organizations to utilize cloud platforms for data storage, free from concerns of compromise.
- Alignment with Regulatory Requirements: The proliferation of stringent data protection regulations like GDPR, HIPAA, and CCPA has mandated cloud service providers to adapt to more exacting privacy standards. The introduction of privacy preservation techniques has emerged as a supportive mechanism, enabling organizations to navigate these regulations effectively. By ensuring that user data is managed and stored in accordance with legal mandates, these techniques contribute to regulatory compliance.
- Fostering Trust: Cloud users are inclined to place greater trust in service providers who demonstrate a steadfast commitment to implementing robust privacy and security measures. This trust forms a foundational element for the expansion of cloud computing, as individuals and businesses develop an increased comfort level in entrusting sensitive data to third-party entities.
- Empowerment of Data Ownership and Control: Privacy preservation techniques confer upon data owners an elevated sense of authority over their information. Mechanisms such as homomorphic encryption and differential privacy facilitate data processing in an encrypted state, lessening the necessity to fully expose raw data to service providers. This equilibrium maintains a degree of control while simultaneously leveraging cloud-based services.

- Mitigation of Internal Threats: In conjunction with external hazards, the specter of internal threats poses a substantial risk to cloud-stored data. Privacy preservation measures, including intricate access controls and vigilant auditing mechanisms, play a pivotal role in the identification and prevention of unauthorized activities perpetrated by individuals with legitimate data access.
- Facilitating Cross-Boundary Data Sharing: The application of secure data storage and privacy preservation techniques has ushered in a safe avenue for data sharing across geographical and organizational confines. This aspect gains pronounced significance in collaborative ventures where multiple stakeholders necessitate access to shared datasets without compromising individual data privacy.
- Propelling Cryptographic Advancements: The impetus to uphold privacy standards within the cloud domain has galvanized progress in cryptographic methodologies. Leading-edge technologies like homomorphic encryption, secure multi-party computation, and zero-knowledge proofs have emerged, enabling data processing without complete exposure.
- Stimulating Innovation and Research: The pursuit of privacy preservation within cloud computing has acted as a catalyst for innovation and research in fields such as cryptography, data anonymization, and secure computation. This has yielded novel tools and methodologies that yield benefits for both cloud service providers and users.
- Navigating Challenges and Complexity: While the safeguarding of privacy is pivotal, it introduces complexities to data processing and can amplify computational overhead. Striking a harmonious balance between privacy preservation and the maintenance of efficient data processing remains an ongoing challenge necessitating continuous research and development.
- Considering Financial Implications: The incorporation of robust privacy preservation measures may entail elevated costs for both cloud service providers and users. These costs stem from the additional resources required for encryption, secure key management, and the sustainable upkeep of requisite infrastructure.

In this chapter, the integration of privacy preservation techniques and secure data storage practices into cloud computing has revolutionized data management. By effectively addressing concerns of security and privacy, this integration has ushered in a climate conducive to wider cloud service adoption. It has concurrently engendered trust while aligning with data protection regulations.

REFERENCES

AlZain, M. A., Pardede, E., Soh, B., & Thom, J. A. (2012). Cloud computing security: from single to multi-clouds. In *2012 45th Hawaii International Conference on System Sciences* (pp. 5490-5499). IEEE. 10.1109/HICSS.2012.153

Awotunde, J. B., Jimoh, R. G., Folorunso, S. O., Adeniyi, E. A., Abiodun, K. M., & Banjo, O. O. (2021). Privacy and security concerns in IoT-based healthcare systems. In *The Fusion of Internet of Things, Artificial Intelligence, and Cloud Computing in Health Care* (pp. 105–134). Springer International Publishing. doi:10.1007/978-3-030-75220-0_6

Blasimme, A., Ferretti, A., & Vayena, E. (2021). Digital contact tracing against COVID-19 in Europe: Current features and ongoing developments. *Frontiers in Digital Health*, *3*, 660823. doi:10.3389/fdgth.2021.660823 PMID:34713135

Braun, T., Fung, B. C., Iqbal, F., & Shah, B. (2018). Security and privacy challenges in smart cities. *Sustainable Cities and Society*, *39*, 499–507. doi:10.1016/j.scs.2018.02.039

Brown, I., & Marsden, C. T. (2023). *Regulating code: Good governance and better regulation in the information age*. MIT Press.

Bughin, J., Chui, M., & Manyika, J. (2010). Clouds, big data, and smart assets: Ten tech-enabled business trends to watch. *The McKinsey Quarterly*, *56*(1), 75–86.

Büyüközkan, G., & Göçer, F. (2018). Digital Supply Chain: Literature review and a proposed framework for future research. *Computers in Industry*, *97*, 157–177. doi:10.1016/j.compind.2018.02.010

Buyya, R., Broberg, J., & Goscinski, A. M. (2010). *Cloud computing: Principles and paradigms*. John Wiley & Sons.

Chong, F., Carraro, G., & Wolter, R. (2006). Multi-tenant data architecture. MSDN Library, Microsoft Corporation.

Choo, K. K. R. (2010). Cloud computing: Challenges and future directions. *Trends and Issues in Crime and Criminal Justice*, (400), 1–6.

Danezis, G., Domingo-Ferrer, J., Hansen, M., Hoepman, J. H., Metayer, D. L., Tirtea, R., & Schiffner, S. (2015). *Privacy and data protection by design-from policy to engineering*. arXiv preprint arXiv:1501.03726.

Denning, D. E. R. (1982). *Cryptography and data security* (Vol. 112). Addison-Wesley.

Dwivedi, Y. K., Hughes, D. L., Coombs, C., Constantiou, I., Duan, Y., Edwards, J. S., Gupta, B., Lal, B., Misra, S., Prashant, P., Raman, R., Rana, N. P., Sharma, S. K., & Upadhyay, N. (2020). Impact of COVID-19 pandemic on information management research and practice: Transforming education, work and life. *International Journal of Information Management*, *55*, 102211. doi:10.1016/j.ijinfomgt.2020.102211

Gubbi, J., Buyya, R., Marusic, S., & Palaniswami, M. (2013). Internet of Things (IoT): A vision, architectural elements, and future directions. *Future Generation Computer Systems*, *29*(7), 1645–1660. doi:10.1016/j.future.2013.01.010

Gupta, A. K., Govindarajan, V., & Wang, H. (2008). *The quest for global dominance: Transforming global presence into global competitive advantage*. John Wiley & Sons.

Hashizume, K., Rosado, D. G., Fernández-Medina, E., & Fernandez, E. B. (2013). An analysis of security issues for cloud computing. *Journal of Internet Services and Applications*, *4*(1), 1–13. doi:10.1186/1869-0238-4-5

Jaeger, P. T., Lin, J., & Grimes, J. M. (2008). Cloud computing and information policy: Computing in a policy cloud? *Journal of Information Technology & Politics*, *5*(3), 269–283. doi:10.1080/19331680802425479

Jansen, W., & Grance, T. (2011). *Guidelines on security and privacy in public cloud computing*. Academic Press.

Jansen, W., & Grance, T. (2011). *Guidelines on security and privacy in public cloud computing*. Academic Press.

Kanter, R. M. (1997). *World class*. Simon and Schuster.

Kayworth, T., & Whitten, D. (2010). Effective information security requires a balance of social and technology factors. *MIS Quarterly Executive*, *9*(3), 2012–2052.

Kushida, K. E., Murray, J., & Zysman, J. (2011). Diffusing the cloud: Cloud computing and implications for public policy. *Journal of Industry, Competition and Trade*, *11*(3), 209–237. doi:10.100710842-011-0106-5

Leonelli, S. (2014). What difference does quantity make? On the epistemology of Big Data in biology. *Big Data & Society*, *1*(1), 2053951714534395. doi:10.1177/2053951714534395 PMID:25729586

Li, M., Yu, S., Ren, K., & Lou, W. (2010). Securing personal health records in cloud computing: Patient-centric and fine-grained data access control in multi-owner settings. *Security and Privacy in Communication Networks: 6th Iternational ICST Conference, SecureComm 2010, Singapore, September 7-9, 2010 Proceedings*, *6*, 89–106.

Manvi, S. S., & Shyam, G. K. (2014). Resource management for Infrastructure as a Service (IaaS) in cloud computing: A survey. *Journal of Network and Computer Applications*, *41*, 424–440. doi:10.1016/j.jnca.2013.10.004

Marston, S., Li, Z., Bandyopadhyay, S., Zhang, J., & Ghalsasi, A. (2011). Cloud computing—The business perspective. *Decision Support Systems*, *51*(1), 176–189. doi:10.1016/j.dss.2010.12.006

Mather, T., Kumaraswamy, S., & Latif, S. (2009). *Cloud security and privacy: an enterprise perspective on risks and compliance*. O'Reilly Media, Inc.

McGonigle, D., & Mastrian, K. (2021). *Nursing informatics and the foundation of knowledge*. Jones & Bartlett Learning.

Mougayar, W. (2016). *The business blockchain: promise, practice, and application of the next Internet technology*. John Wiley & Sons.

Nurgalieva, L., O'Callaghan, D., & Doherty, G. (2020). Security and privacy of mHealth applications: A scoping review. *IEEE Access : Practical Innovations, Open Solutions*, *8*, 104247–104268. doi:10.1109/ACCESS.2020.2999934

Ohm, P. (2009). Broken promises of privacy: Responding to the surprising failure of anonymization. UCLA l. *Rev.*, *57*, 1701.

Sheninger, E. (2019). *Digital leadership: Changing paradigms for changing times*. Corwin Press.

Singh, S., Jeong, Y. S., & Park, J. H. (2016). A survey on cloud computing security: Issues, threats, and solutions. *Journal of Network and Computer Applications*, *75*, 200–222. doi:10.1016/j.jnca.2016.09.002

Snyder, L. (2012). American College of Physicians ethics manual. *Annals of Internal Medicine*, *156*(1_Part_2), 73–104. doi:10.7326/0003-4819-156-1-201201031-00001 PMID:22213573

Subashini, S., & Kavitha, V. (2011). A survey on security issues in service delivery models of cloud computing. *Journal of Network and Computer Applications*, *34*(1), 1–11. doi:10.1016/j.jnca.2010.07.006

Sun, W., Cai, Z., Li, Y., Liu, F., Fang, S., & Wang, G. (2018). Security and privacy in the medical internet of things: A review. *Security and Communication Networks*, *2018*, 1–9. doi:10.1155/2018/5978636

Takabi, H., Joshi, J. B., & Ahn, G. J. (2010). Security and privacy challenges in cloud computing environments. *IEEE Security and Privacy*, *8*(6), 24–31. doi:10.1109/MSP.2010.186

Tikkinen-Piri, C., Rohunen, A., & Markkula, J. (2018). EU General Data Protection Regulation: Changes and implications for personal data collecting companies. *Computer Law & Security Report*, *34*(1), 134–153. doi:10.1016/j.clsr.2017.05.015

Tyagi, A. K., & Sreenath, N. (2021). Cyber Physical Systems: Analyses, challenges and possible solutions. *Internet of Things and Cyber-Physical Systems*, *1*, 22–33. doi:10.1016/j.iotcps.2021.12.002

Vermesan, O., & Friess, P. (Eds.). (2013). *Internet of things: converging technologies for smart environments and integrated ecosystems*. River publishers.

Warner, K. S., & Wäger, M. (2019). Building dynamic capabilities for digital transformation: An ongoing process of strategic renewal. *Long Range Planning*, *52*(3), 326–349. doi:10.1016/j.lrp.2018.12.001

Wood, A., Altman, M., Bembenek, A., Bun, M., Gaboardi, M., Honaker, J., & Vadhan, S. (2018). Differential privacy: A primer for a non-technical audience. *SSRN*, *21*, 209. doi:10.2139srn.3338027

Wu, J., Ping, L., Ge, X., Wang, Y., & Fu, J. (2010). Cloud storage as the infrastructure of cloud computing. In *2010 International conference on intelligent computing and cognitive informatics* (pp. 380-383). IEEE. 10.1109/ICICCI.2010.119

Yang, C., Huang, Q., Li, Z., Liu, K., & Hu, F. (2017). Big Data and cloud computing: Innovation opportunities and challenges. *International Journal of Digital Earth*, *10*(1), 13–53. doi:10.1080/17538947.2016.1239771

Zhang, Q., Cheng, L., & Boutaba, R. (2010). Cloud computing: State-of-the-art and research challenges. *Journal of Internet Services and Applications*, *1*(1), 7–18. doi:10.100713174-010-0007-6

Zissis, D., & Lekkas, D. (2012). Addressing cloud computing security issues. *Future Generation Computer Systems*, *28*(3), 583–592. doi:10.1016/j.future.2010.12.006

Chapter 2
A Comparative Study of Cloud Databases:
Analyzing Microsoft Azure, IBM db2, and Oracle Cloud

Moses Kazeem Abiodun
https://orcid.org/0000-0002-3049-1184
Landmark University, Nigeria

ABSTRACT

The adoption of cloud-based services has been on the rise in recent years. In this study, a comparative study of three major cloud database platforms, namely Microsoft Azure, IBM DB2, and Oracle Cloud, was conducted to analyze their features, performance, and suitability for different use cases. This chapter explores the architectures of these platforms, examines their database management tools, and evaluates their support for scalability, security, and data integration. In the experiment section, Oracle performed the best with an average execution time of 3.35ms, which was the fastest of the three databases. In the survey section, the results show that MS Azure is the most available, secure, cost effective, and efficient. Oracle can be seen from the survey responses as the most reliable and also most cost effective. This chapter gives insightful information to organizations and people who want to pick the finest cloud database platform for their requirements.

1.0 INTRODUCTION

A database, according to Britannica (2023) also known as an electronic database, refers to a curated assortment of data or information that is purposefully arranged to enable quick searching and retrieval by a computer. Databases are designed in a structured manner to streamline the storage, retrieval, modification, and removal of data while working alongside different data-processing tasks. Databases have become an integral part of modern life, supporting a wide range of applications and services we use daily.

DOI: 10.4018/979-8-3693-0593-5.ch002

From online banking and e-commerce platforms to healthcare systems and transportation management, databases are the foundation for many applications that make our lives more convenient and efficient.

The concept of a database has been around for centuries, dating back to the days of clay tablets and papyrus scrolls. However, the development of electronic databases in the 1960s and 1970s marked a significant turning point in how information was stored and managed. Today, electronic databases have become the norm, with virtually every business, organization, and government agency relying on them to manage and analyze data. A database management system (DBMS) is a software package to store, retrieve, query, and manage data. User interfaces (UIs) allow data to be created, read, updated, and deleted by authorized entities.

DBMSs provide an efficient and secure way of storing, organizing, and managing large amounts of data. They enable businesses and organizations to access and manipulate data easily, allowing for improved decision-making and analysis. Some common DBMS examples include Oracle, MySQL, Microsoft SQL Server, and IBM DB2.

A critical aspect of a DBMS is the ability to enforce data integrity and security through various mechanisms such as access control and encryption. Additionally, DBMSs provide features such as backup and recovery, replication, and scalability to guarantee constant availability and accessibility of data. Several cloud service providers offer cloud database services, including Microsoft Azure, IBM DB2, and Oracle Cloud. These cloud service providers offer a range of features and capabilities to store and manage data in the Cloud.

Microsoft Azure by Microsoft provides numerous database services, including Azure SQL Database, Azure Cosmos DB, and Azure Database for MySQL, PostgreSQL, and MariaDB. These services offer high availability, built-in intelligence, and scalability for applications of any size. Azure also offers hybrid cloud capabilities, allowing organizations to integrate their existing on-premises infrastructure with the Cloud.

IBM DB2 provides a suite of cloud database services, including IBM Cloud SQL Query, IBM Cloudant, and IBM Db2 on Cloud. These services provide developers and data scientists powerful tools to ingest, store, and analyze data at scale. IBM also offers robust security and compliance features, making it an attractive option for businesses that require high levels of security and data protection.

Oracle Cloud provides many cloud database services, including Oracle Autonomous Database, Oracle Database Cloud Service, and Oracle MySQL Cloud Service. These services provide a range of deployment options, including single-node, high-availability,

and sharded database architectures, and support for various data types, such as organized, semi-organized, and unorganized data. Oracle also provides advanced analytics capabilities and tools for data integration and management (Khan et a., 2020).

While cloud databases have become increasingly popular for managing data, businesses and organizations. It still faces significant challenges in choosing the right provider. With multiple cloud database providers offering different features and capabilities, it can be challenging to determine which provider offers the best value and performance for specific use cases. In addition, concerns over data security, compliance, and vendor lock-in can complicate the decision-making process. Various other researches such as (Wankhede et al., 2020) also attempted to carry out comparative researches on Cloud Platforms.

The term "cloud computing" describes the distribution of computer facilities, like the servers, networking, storage, and applications, by a cloud service provider over the internet. Users may now access these resources whenever they need them, negating the requirement for local infrastructure. Infrastructure as a Service (IaaS), Platform as a Service (PaaS), and Software as a Service (SaaS) are the three primary categories of cloud computing (Abiodun et al., 2021; Aremu & Moses, n.d.; Chai & Bigelow, 2022). Integrating cloud computing with database management systems has led to the emergence of cloud database services. Cloud database services provide an alternative to on-premises database management systems, offering several benefits, including scalability, cost savings, and flexibility (Ranger, 2022).

Whether public, private, or hybrid, a cloud database acts as a consolidated and organized store for data inside of a cloud computing platform. A cloud database is quite similar to an on-premises database, which runs on servers in a business's data center, in terms of functionality and design (Stedman, 2022). The deployment and administration components are where there are the most differences, though. Organizations should specify their exact needs before choosing a cloud service provider, which may include a demand for software as a service (Dutta & Dutta, 2019). For instance, the same database looks to end users and apps the same way whether it is in the cloud or on-premises. Based on the specific database software being used, cloud databases, just like those on-site can store organized, un-organized, or semi-organized data (Stedman, 2022). A database on the cloud is a special kind created to be use in public cloud setting or a hybrid to help companies manage, organize, and store data. A database on the Cloud can either be established on a virtual machine (VM) accommodated in the cloud and self-administered by IT team, or they can be made accessible as administered by Database-as-a-Service (DBaaS) (Google Cloud, 2022).

Regardless of whether it is hosted on-premises or in the cloud, the database remains consistent in appearance and functionality for end users and applications. Cloud databases have the capability to store structured, unstructured, or semi-structured data, depending on the database software employed (Stedman, 2022). A cloud database helps businesses manage, organize, and store their data efficiently since it is made to function in public or hybrid cloud setting (Google Cloud, 2022). These databases can be accessed as databases-as-a-service (DBaaS) or can be administered by the IT team on a simulated machine accommodated in the cloud (Google Cloud, 2022)

1.1 Introduction to Cloud Computing

The term "cloud computing" describes the distribution of computer facilities, like the servers, networking, storage, and applications, by a cloud service provider over the internet. Users may now access these resources whenever they need them, negating the requirement for local infrastructure. Platform as a Service (PaaS), Infrastructure as a Service (IaaS) and Software as a Service (SaaS) are the three primary categories of cloud computing. Additionally, there are three types of clouds: public, private and hybrid. Private clouds are only accessible to a limited number of users with permission, but public clouds are accessible to everyone online (Abiodun et al., 2021; Chai & Bigelow, 2022). Whether it is a public, private or hybrid cloud, the main objective of cloud computing is to make IT services accessible and scalable. Utilizing cloud services, companies can stay away from upfront costs and the complexities associated with managing their own IT infrastructure, instead paying for the services they utilize (Ranger, 2022). Integrating cloud computing with database management systems has led to the emergence of cloud database services. Cloud database services provide an alternative to on-premises database management systems, offering several benefits, including scalability, cost savings, and flexibility.

1.2 Types of Cloud Computing

Cloud computing can be classified as Public, Private or Hybrid.

A. Public Cloud

The public cloud, whether it be IaaS, PaaS, or SaaS, is the standard cloud computing model where customers can access a sizable pool of computer resources online. One of the main benefits in this situation is the ability to swiftly grow a service. Cloud computing companies may divide their massive quantities of processing power across a large number of clients thanks to its "multi-tenant" design. (Bigelow et al., 2023; Ranger, 2022) suggested that the public cloud operates using a third-party provider and is made available to customers via a network connection—either the open internet or a private network. Public cloud computing is frequently seen as a form of on-demand utility computing, similar to how water, gas, and telecommunications services are provided to customers. Virtual machines for processing power, file systems, data storage systems, network devices, and other components are available in public clouds. They are frequently called infrastructure as a service. A development platform as a service is also provided by different public cloud service providers and businesses that deliver software as a service (Hofmann & Woods, 2010).

B. Private Cloud

One company is a user on a private cloud. Although there may be several departments on the cloud, they are all part of the same enterprise. To increase computer use, private clouds frequently use virtualization within an organization's current computer servers. A private cloud also has provisioning and metering tools that, when necessary, allow for quick deployment and removal. This paradigm can also be used as an organization's internal delivery model; however, it is similar to traditional IT outsourcing strategies. There are numerous private cloud implementations (Kiennert et al., 2015). This cloud platform may be reused since the organization will already have a system in place for handling the digital identities of its employees, which commonly uses a database and access federation. Within the company or organization that uses them, a private cloud houses the systems and resources that provide the service. That entity is responsible for managing and overseeing the systems used to offer the service. The corporation is also accountable for any software or client applications installed on end-user computers. Private clouds are often accessed by local area networks (LAN) or wide area networks (WAN) (Rountree & Castrillo, 2014).

In recent years, cloud database services have gained significant popularity due to the increased adoption of cloud computing. This project aims to compare and analyze three primary cloud database services - Microsoft Azure, IBM DB2, and Oracle Cloud - to identify their strengths and weaknesses and provide insight into which service may best fit different use cases.

C. Hybrid Cloud

The notion of a hybrid cloud is the integration of private and public clouds into a single system. This approach is particularly beneficial for organizations that have diverse requirements and need to leverage the advantages of both private and public clouds simultaneously.

By combining private and public clouds, organizations can create a hybrid infrastructure that allows them to address different needs effectively. The private cloud component of the hybrid system provides a secure and controlled environment within the organization's network. It enables internal communication, data storage, and processing, ensuring the confidentiality and privacy of sensitive information.

On the other hand, the public cloud component enables organizations to interact with external stakeholders, such as customers or partners, over the internet. Public cloud services are typically provided by third-party vendors and offer scalability, flexibility, and cost-effectiveness. By utilizing the public cloud, organizations can leverage resources and services on-demand, expanding their capabilities and reach.

The hybrid cloud model allows organizations to benefit from the best of both worlds.

They can maintain control over critical data and operations by utilizing the private cloud, while simultaneously benefiting from the public cloud's extensive resources and accessibility for customer interaction and collaboration. This flexibility and versatility provided by the hybrid cloud model make it an attractive choice for many organizations seeking to optimize their IT infrastructure to meet diverse requirements (Wankhede et al., 2020).

1.3 Cloud Databases

Whether public, private, or hybrid, a cloud database acts as a consolidated and organized store for data inside of a cloud computing platform. A cloud database is quite similar to an on-premises database, which runs on servers in a business's data center, in terms of functionality and design (Stedman, 2022). The deployment and administration components are where there are the most differences, though. Organizations should specify their exact needs before choosing a cloud service provider, which may include a demand for software as a service (Dutta & Dutta, 2019). The same database, for instance, appears the same to end users and apps whether it is on-premises or in the cloud. Similar to their on-premises counterparts, cloud databases can store organized, unorganized, or semi-organized data depending on the particular database software being used (Stedman, 2022). A cloud database is a special kind of database created to work in a hybrid or public cloud environment and help an organization manage, organize, and store data. For DBaaS, cloud databases can be made available, or they can be use on a virtual machine hosted in the cloud and managed by an inside IT team (GoogleCloud, 2022).

Regardless of whether it is hosted on-premises or in the cloud, the database remains consistent in appearance and functionality for end users and applications. Cloud databases have the capability to store structured, unstructured, or semi-structured data, depending on the database software employed. Intended to function within a public or a hybrid cloud setting, a cloud database assists organizations in effectively handling, organizing, and storing their data (Google Cloud, 2022). These databases can be accessed as managed DBaaS or can be managed by itself or by an internal IT team on a VM hosted in the cloud (GoogleCloud,2022)

1.3.1 Microsoft Azure

According to (Chai & Bigelow, 2022). The public cloud platform called Microsoft Azure is a Platform As A Service software (PAAS) which enables users to produce and install web apps while Microsoft Datacenters stored their data. Microsoft Azure was first introduced in October 28, 2008. The software was developed with a few programming languages such as python, C++, C# and java. Figure 1 shows the interface of Microsoft Azure.

Figure 1. Microsoft Azure interface

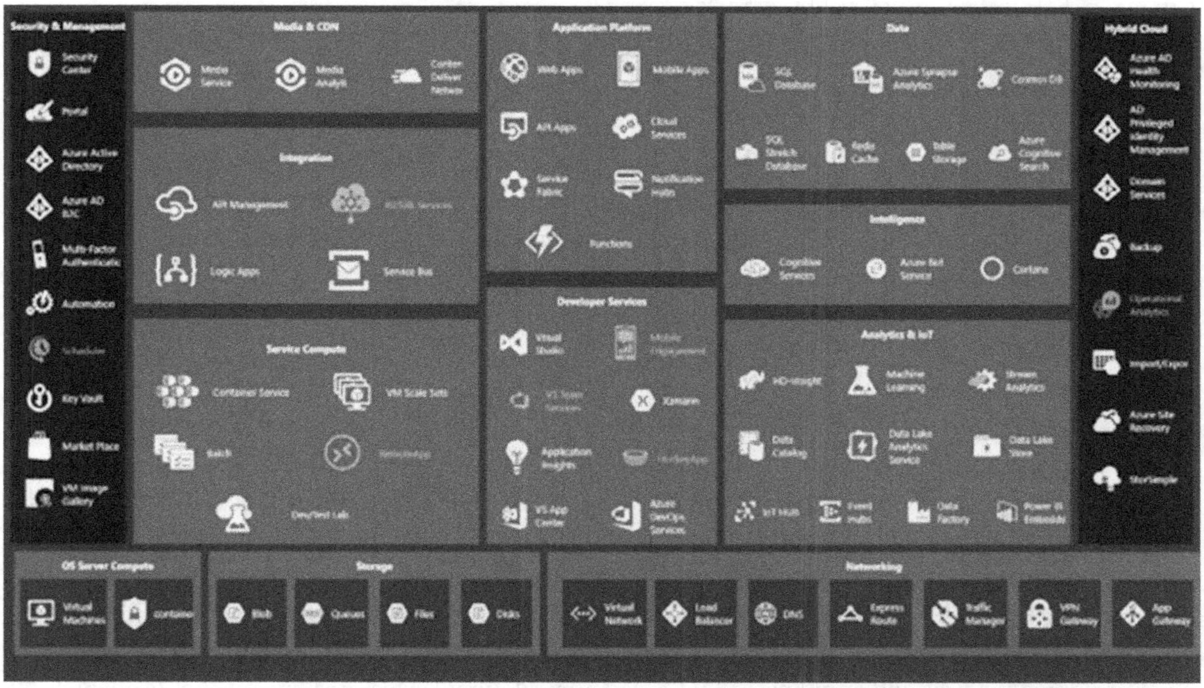

According to (Berisha et al., 2022; Hassan et al., 2022; Saif & Wazir, 2018), the software offers varieties of features such as:

i. **Hosting and Development of Web Applications**

Azure offers a scalable and adaptable platform for hosting and creating web applications. It caters for various tools, frameworks, and programming languages; enabling programmers to create and deliver applications using their favorite technologies. Azure ensures high availability and ideal performance for web applications with capabilities like load balancing and autoscaling.

ii. **Backup and Disaster Recovery**

Azure provides reliable backup and disaster recovery solutions to safeguard against data loss and guarantee business continuity. Azure Backup is a trusted resource that businesses can use to safely store and quickly restore their data from both on-premises and cloud environments. Azure Site Recovery also makes it possible for virtual machines and apps to seamlessly replicate and failover, protecting against disruptions and reducing downtime.

iii. **IoT Industry Solution Tool**

The creation and administration of IoT applications are made easier by Azure's IoT industry solution solutions. Businesses may securely connect, monitor, and control their IoT devices by using services like

IoT Hub, IoT Central, and Azure Sphere. This gives businesses the ability to create scalable and secure IoT solutions suited to the demands of their particular sectors.

iv. **Active Directory Integration**

Azure effortlessly integrates with Active Directory for identity and access management. Organizations may consolidate user management, implement single sign-on, and enforce access control across both cloud and on-premises resources by extending on-premises Active Directory architecture to Azure. Businesses can guarantee a safe and efficient user experience thanks to Azure AD's support for multiple authentication protocols and strong security features.

1.3.2 IBM DB2

Figure 2 shows the IBM interface. It is a cloud-native database called IBM Db2 has been created expressly to handle massively scalable low-latency transactions and real-time analytics. It offers a unified platform for DBAs, enterprise architects, and developers to guarantee the efficient operation of crucial applications, make it easier to store and query a variety of data types, and speed up innovation throughout the company. Db2 is a Relational Database Management System (RDBMS) that excels in effective data storage, analysis, and retrieval, according to tutorials point (2022). The Db2 solution offers support for object-oriented features and combines XML-based non-relational structures, increasing its adaptability and flexibility (Coursera, 2023).

Figure 2. IBM Db2 interface

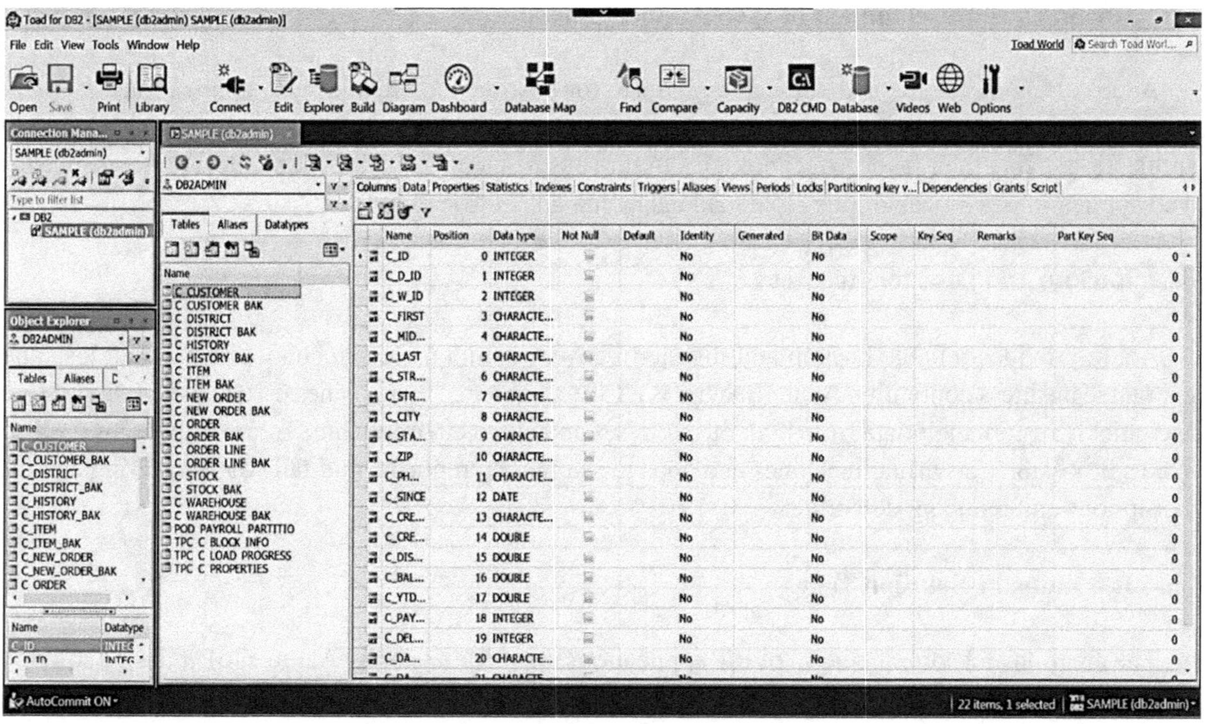

i. **AI-powered functionality**

AI-powered capability is incorporated into IBM Db2 to improve database management and performance. Db2's AI features enable it to suggest indexing plans, automatically optimize query execution plans, and offer real-time performance insights. Additionally, proactive monitoring, anomaly detection, and self-tuning are made possible by AI capabilities, allowing the database to adjust and improve itself based on workload patterns. Organizations adopting IBM Db2 can boost productivity, dependability, and overall performance by utilizing AI-powered features.

ii. **Scalability**

IBM Db2 offers scalability features that allow organizations to handle growing data volumes and increasing user loads. Db2's scalable architecture enables horizontal and vertical scaling, enabling organizations to add more computing resources or scale up their hardware infrastructure as needed. Additionally, Db2 provides built-in clustering and partitioning capabilities that distribute data and workload across multiple nodes, improving performance and scalability for large-scale deployments.

iii. **High backup, availability, and disaster recovery**

IBM Db2 prioritizes data fortification, high accessibility, and disaster recovery. It offers robust backup and recovery features, allowing organizations to create trustworthy data backups, automate backup processes, and perform point-in-time recoveries. Db2 also provides built-in high availability features, such as database mirroring, failover, and log shipping to minimize downtime and ensure continuous access to data. Additionally, Db2 integrates with IBM Tivoli Storage Manager.

iv. **Table partitioning**

Db2 incorporates table partitioning capabilities, which allow for the efficient management and querying of large datasets. Organizations may use table partitioning to separate their data into smaller segments that are simpler to handle according on predetermined criteria (such range, list, or hash). Partitioning increases query results by enabling parallel processing and data pruning, where only relevant partitions are accessed. This feature also simplifies data maintenance operations, such as data archival or deletion, by acting on specific partitions instead of the entire table.

1.3.3 Oracle Cloud

You can safely run Oracle Database workloads in Oracle Cloud Infrastructure (OCI) thanks to the low-cost, managed compute and storage platform known as Oracle Standard Database Service. Meeting application performance and availability requirements is made simpler by flexible virtual machine shapes and consumption-based pricing (Oracle, 2022). Oracle Cloud provides a wide range of services to satisfy various business demands. To automate database management duties, improve performance, and bolster security, the Oracle Autonomous Database, a key service, uses artificial intelligence and machine learning. Organizations may concentrate on data analysis and innovation because to this autonomous approach's elimination of human administration. Oracle Cloud offers a range of infrastructure services, including computation, storage, networking, and security, in addition to database services. These services give businesses the flexibility, scalability, and cost-effectiveness to create and operate their IT infrastructure in the cloud. Figure 3 shows an image of the Oracle cloud interface.

Figure 3. A generic Oracle cloud interface image

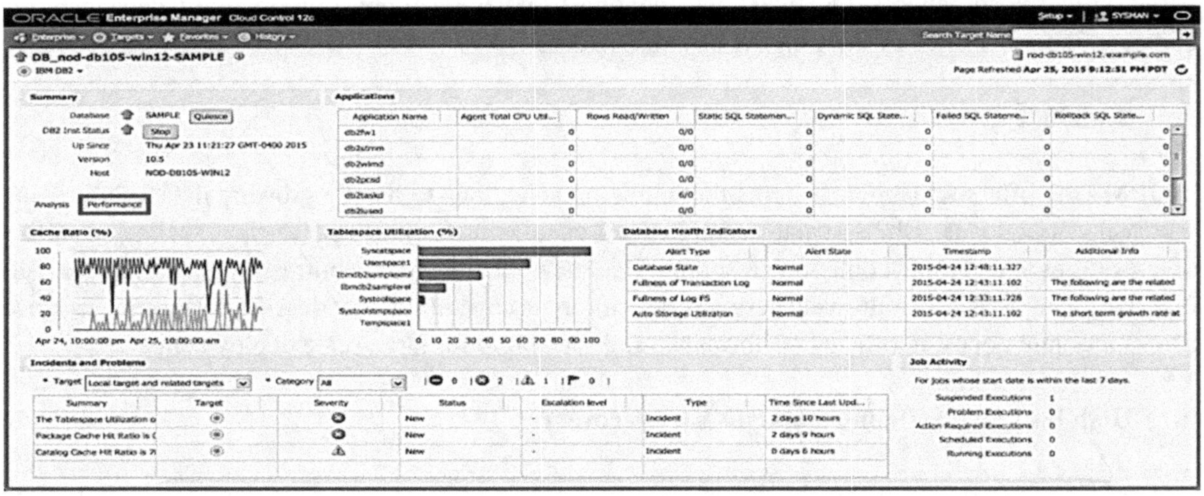

According to Oracle (2022), The Oracle cloud platform offers varieties of features such as;

i. **High Availability and Reality**

Oracle Cloud Database eliminates potential downtime and guarantees constant access to data. The database maintains a high level of availability and modernity because to its automatic backup mechanism, frequent patching, and seamless rolling upgrades. The infrastructure and redundant architecture of Oracle provide the resilience and fault tolerance needed to reduce service interruptions and prevent data loss.

ii. **Hybrid Cloud Capabilities**

The Oracle Cloud Database's hybrid cloud capabilities, which enable seamless integration and data synchronization between on-premises and cloud systems, are advantageous to organizations. Businesses may build a unified and scalable infrastructure by extending their on-premises Oracle databases to the Oracle Cloud. They gain the capacity to move workloads around, replicate data effectively, and manage data in a hybrid environment, enabling them to respond to shifting business needs.

iii. **AI Functionalities**

Oracle Cloud Database uses artificial intelligence (AI) to enhance security, improve performance, and streamline database administration. The database automatically improves query efficiency, finds and fixes performance bottlenecks, and accelerates routine administrative operations by utilizing AI-driven capabilities like Automatic Indexing and Automatic SQL Tuning. These AI capabilities enable firms to operate more efficiently and with less paperwork.

iv. **High Security**

To protect sensitive data, the Oracle Cloud Database strongly emphasizes top-notch security. It makes use of cutting-edge security tools like Transparent Data Encryption, Data Redaction, and Database Vault to protect data both in transit and at rest. Data protection is guaranteed, and Oracle's cloud infrastructure complies with strict compliance certifications and numerous levels of security controls to fulfill industry and governmental standards. Further strengthening its overall security posture are the database's powerful mechanisms for access control, thorough audit trail monitoring, and advanced threat detection.

1.4 Cloud Databases and Their Advantages

Cloud databases offer numerous advantages compared to traditional on-premises databases, which is why they are becoming increasingly popular in modern computing. These advantages are as follows:

1. **Scalability:** Cloud databases allow for seamless and cost-effective scalability, as computing resources can be quickly and easily allocated or de-allocated as needed. This is especially important for organizations with fluctuating or unpredictable workloads, as they can easily scale up or down as needed.
2. **Accessibility:** Cloud databases can be accessed from anywhere with an internet connection, making it easy for remote teams to collaborate and work on the same data. This is particularly important for organizations with distributed teams, as it eliminates the need for expensive and complex remote access solutions.
3. **Cost-effectiveness:** Cloud databases offer a pay-as-you-go pricing model, which means organizations only pay for the resources they use. This is in contrast to on-premises databases, which require significant upfront investments in hardware, software, and maintenance costs.
4. **Security:** Cloud database providers typically offer a range of security features, such as encryption, access controls, and multi-factor authentication. Additionally, cloud providers often have dedicated security teams and sophisticated security protocols to ensure the safety of the data stored in their databases.
5. **Reliability:** Cloud databases are often hosted in redundant and geographically distributed data centers, which means that even if one data center goes down, the database will still be accessible from another location. This ensures high availability and reliability for critical data.

1.5 Overview of Related Works

In the study conducted by (Lee, 2012), the emergence of Cloud Database Management Systems (DBMS) as a service rather than a product is explored. This innovative approach enables the sharing of resources, software, and information across multiple devices through network connectivity, typically over the Internet. The paper delves into the growing trend of outsourcing database management tasks to third-party providers, who can offer these services at a significantly lower cost due to economies of scale. The authors propose a scalable and elastic architecture for a DBMS in the Cloud, designed to operate as a service on a cloud infrastructure. The study highlights the potential impact of Cloud DBMSs, particularly emphasizing the cost-saving opportunities they offer for vendors seeking affordable platforms for development. This comprehensive paper provides valuable insights into the advantages and potential of Cloud DBMSs, presenting a suggested architecture for implementing a DBMS in the Cloud.

Hashem et al. (2015) provides an overview of the relationship between big data and cloud computing. The use of expensive gear, specialized space, and expensive software are not required while using cloud computing, which is acknowledged as a powerful technique for performing complicated calculations on a wide scale. The paper goes into greater detail regarding the difficulties associated with handling and analyzing large amounts of data, highlighting the need for a strong computational infrastructure to ensure effective data handling. It also offers a thorough analysis of big data's properties and classification, emphasizing how it interacts with diverse concepts like cloud computing, massive data storage systems, and Hadoop technology. The authors also discuss the problems with big data research, including scalability, availability, data integrity, data transformation, data quality, heterogeneity, privacy concerns, legal and regulatory issues, as well as governance issues.

Tsui et al. (2011) investigate the idea of Cloud Computing for Personal Knowledge Management (CBPKM) and its effects on knowledge workers adopting cloud-based enterprise apps. The authors stress how the Cloud's scalability and wide availability enable a bigger user base for traditional enterprise applications while also making it easier to allocate more resources to assist computationally demanding jobs. They introduce the idea of an integrated cloud ecosystem, seen through the perspective of knowledge management, demonstrating the Cloud's capacity to provide services that were previously unreachable using conventional methods. The study, however, largely discusses CBPKM as a conceptual service and does not go in-depth on the platform's technological or business components. Furthermore, the study ignores any potential limitations or negative aspects of the utilization of the CBPKM platform.

The authors in Singh et al. (n.d.) give a systematic appraisal and logical comparison of existing study and surveys on SLA, facilities distribution, and facilities arrangement in cloud computing. Cloud resource management is a significant challenge in efficiently allocating and scheduling resources to meet customer expectations. In a heterogeneous and dynamic cloud environment, it is tough to forecast an suitable matching, leading to performance degradation and SLA violations. The paper provides an extensive analysis of the existing research on resource management in cloud computing, including SLA, resource allocation, and resource scheduling. The authors have identified the open research issues, current status, and future research directions in cloud resource management. The paper provides valuable insights for researchers and practitioners in cloud computing, helping them comprehend the present state of the art in cloud resource management and identify the research gaps that must be addressed.

Xiong *et al.* (2020) presented a resource management solution called SmartSLA for shared cloud database systems. A system modeling module and a decision-making module for resource allocation make up the system. Machine learning techniques are used in the system modeling module to build a model that forecasts prospective profit margins for specific clients based on various resource allocations. The resource allocation decision module, on the other hand, dynamically modifies resource allocations to optimize profits. The study shows how SmartSLA can generate predictive models with different hardware resource allocations while providing intelligent service differentiation.

Cui *et al.* (2020) proposed a Software as a Service (SaaS) solution built on the Vega data model and made available through Google App Engine. This service's main objective is to effectively manage sensor data from Soyang Lake water quality monitoring. The authors succinctly show the viability of using a NoSQL cloud database method for scientific applications, particularly for processing sensor data. They thoroughly assess the cloud database service's efficiency in handling sensor data and pinpoint some processing restrictions in Datastore that could affect query speed when dealing with sophisticated queries. However, the authors suggest cost-effective ways to use Datastore services and anticipate a future decrease in cloud service costs as these services become more widely used.

The advantages of cloud computing are discussed, including reliable storage and computing, increased availability and security, quick access and adaptation, guaranteed scalability and interoperability, and effectiveness in cost and time (Tasnim et al., 2022). The three cloud computing platforms IaaS, PaaS, and SaaS as well as their unique capabilities are covered. This paper's main goal is to contrast the cloud service characteristics of three particular cloud providers: Amazon, Microsoft Azure, and Digital Ocean. It comprehensively compares cloud service features, including computing power, storage, and pricing. The comparison is based on ease of use, performance, reliability, and support. The authors have also discussed the advantages and disadvantages of each cloud provider, which can help a client, organization, or trade to choose the exemplary cloud service. However, the paper has some limitations. The authors need to provide a detailed analysis of the security features of each cloud provider, which is a crucial aspect of cloud computing.

This study will compare the three major cloud database providers: Microsoft Azure, IBM DB2, and Oracle Cloud. The comparison will cover various aspects such as features, capabilities, performance, scalability, availability, pricing, and more. By comparing these cloud database providers, we aim to provide insights to help individuals and organizations make informed decisions when selecting a cloud database provider that best meets their needs.

2.0 MATERIAL AND METHODS

This section outlines the research methodology used in the study. The study followed a descriptive research design to provide a detailed and accurate comparison of Microsoft Azure, IBM DB2, and Oracle Cloud databases. The study adopted a quantitative approach to collect and analyze data. The following are the research methods that were used:

1. Background Research was done on the three databases through literature reviews of already existing works.
2. The next step is the analysis, in this category two main methods of analysis was used namely survey collection and experiment.
    a. Surveys: An online survey was conducted to collect data on the use of cloud databases by different organizations. The survey was designed to gather information about the challenges, benefits, and best practices of using cloud databases.
    b. Experiments: These experiments were performed on a virtual based test environment, the test environment used was VMware workstation 17 virtual machines;

Figure 4 is diagram of the data flow that shows the methodology this paper will use in the comparison of the cloud databases.

Figure 4. Data flow diagram

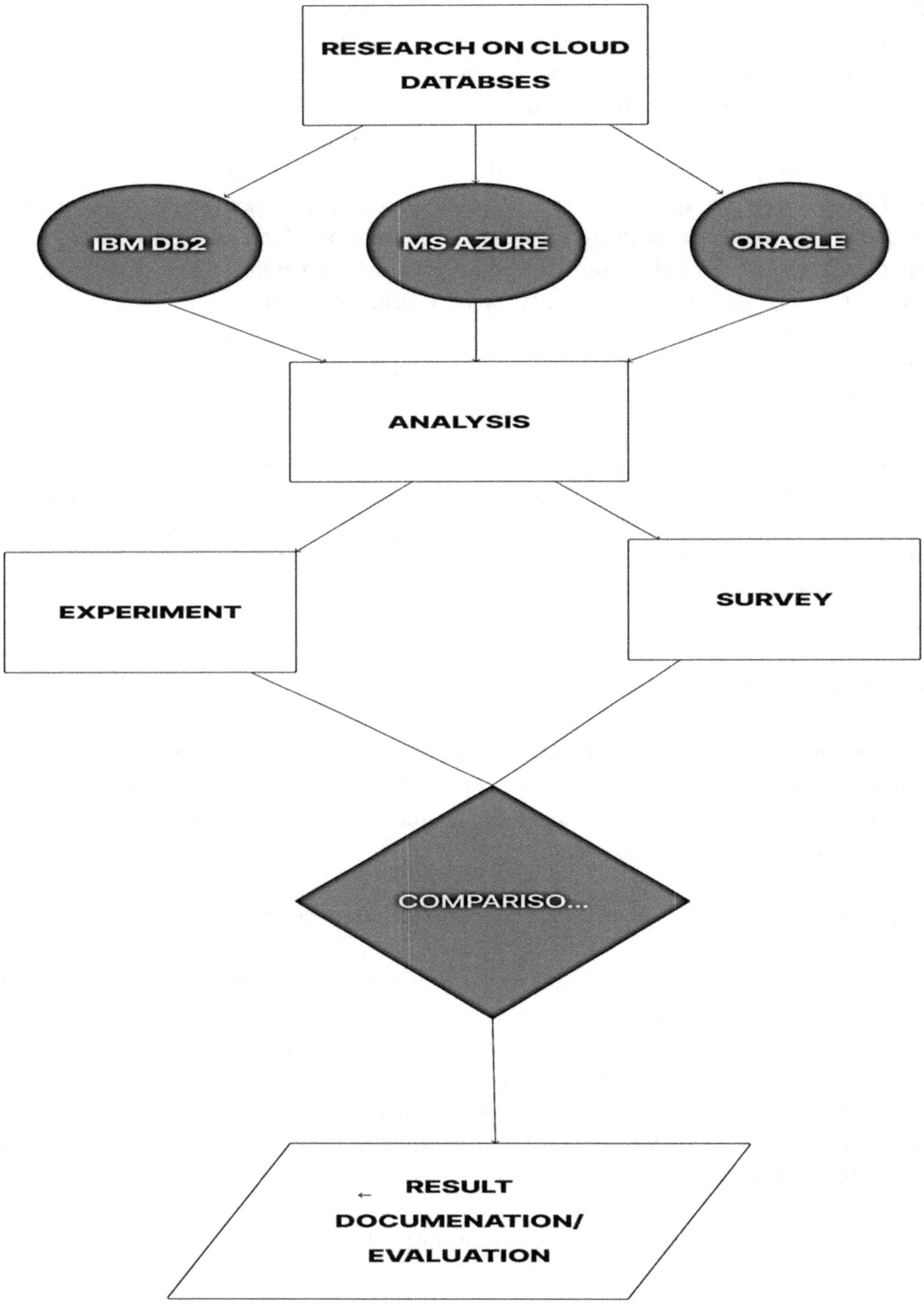

The Ubuntu server, windows server and Oracle Linux were installed on this environment for the proper simulation of Azure, IBM Db2 and Oracle cloud databases respectively. The main aim of these experiment was to test the average time it will take the various cloud databases to run the same query in 10 iterations.

3. Comparison: comparisons between the cloud databases were conducted using a tabular format with users in the field of cloud computing and database management to gain deeper insights into the strengths and weaknesses of Microsoft Azure, IBM DB2, and Oracle Cloud databases.

The above methods were used to gather and analyze data on the three cloud databases' features, performance, and pricing. The results were then used to draw meaningful conclusions and recommendations. A workflow representation of the process carried out is implemented below;

2.2 Criteria for Selection

Several factors were taken into account when selecting the three cloud databases for analysis. These criteria included:

1. Reliability and Security: The cloud database's security features are crucial as it stores confidential and critical data. The chosen database should have a high level of security and reliability to prevent data breaches and downtime.
2. Performance: The cloud database's performance is one of the most important factors to consider. It must offer efficient processing and fast response times, making it possible to manage the large amount of data.
3. Scalability: The database must have the ability to scale based on the organization's current and future data requirements.
4. Cost: The cost of the database is a significant factor that determines the selection of the cloud database provider. The provider should offer a cost-effective solution that aligns with the organization's budget.
5. Technical Support: The provider should have a responsive and helpful customer support team to address any issues that may arise.

2.3 Data Collection

Data collection is crucial to conducting a comparative study of cloud databases. The project will employ two main data collection methods: primary and secondary.

Primary data collection will involve surveys to gather information directly from users of Microsoft Azure, IBM DB2, and Oracle Cloud databases. This will provide first-hand insights into users' experiences with these cloud databases, including their strengths and weaknesses. The survey will be designed so the respondents can provide specific details about their experience with the cloud databases.

Secondary data collection will involve the use of academic journals, and other publications to gather relevant information on the three cloud databases. This method will allow for collecting a broad range of information about the databases, including their features, performance, pricing, and suitability for different use cases. The information gathered will be analyzed to draw meaningful conclusions and make informed recommendations.

Both primary and secondary data collection methods will be employed to ensure a comprehensive analysis of the cloud databases. The combination of these methods will help to provide a detailed and accurate portrayal of the capabilities of Microsoft Azure, IBM DB2, and Oracle Cloud databases.

2.4 Performance Evaluation Metrics

Performance evaluation metrics are essential in assessing the effectiveness and efficiency of cloud databases. The following are some of the criteria for evaluating performance in cloud databases:

1. Throughput: The amount of data that can be processed within a given time is a critical performance metric. It measures the speed and efficiency of data transfer and processing.
2. Latency: This is the time taken for a query or a request to be completed. Lower latency is an indication of faster response time and better performance.
3. Scalability: A cloud database can handle an increase in workload. It measures how well a cloud database can cope with more significant data volumes and concurrent requests without any degradation in performance.

There are several tools and methods used to measure the performance of cloud databases. These include:

1. Benchmarking: It involves running a series of tests on a cloud database to measure its performance under different loads.
2. Synthetic transactions: It involves simulating various transactions to measure the response time, throughput, and latency of a cloud database.

3.0 RESULT

The survey collects data from various users based on aspects such as; Security, User Friendliness, Cost, Efficiency and Reliability. This survey was filled by users with vast experience with specified cloud databases considering both personal and official use, highly experienced users who use these cloud databases mediums to store company records and information along with users who have experience with the database for educational purposes filled the survey. These users were within the age range of 21-39. A total of 53 people were invited to fill the survey online, but only 40 individuals filled it. 20 of them were filled by undergraduate students with experience of the databases, 10 were filled by undergraduate students doing remote works in cloud database and 10 filled by company technicians with over five (5) years' experience in the database administration. Table 1 highlights various questions and the responses of users from the survey.

From figure 5, it shows clearly the performances of the cloud databases in terms of availability, security, reliability, cost, ease of use and efficiency.

Table 1. Survey response analysis

	Availability %	Reliability %	Security %	Cost %	Efficiency %
MS AZURE	43	40	35	45	45
IBM Db2	20	41	18	30	20
ORACLE	30	45	30	45	35

Figure 5. Bar chart on survey results

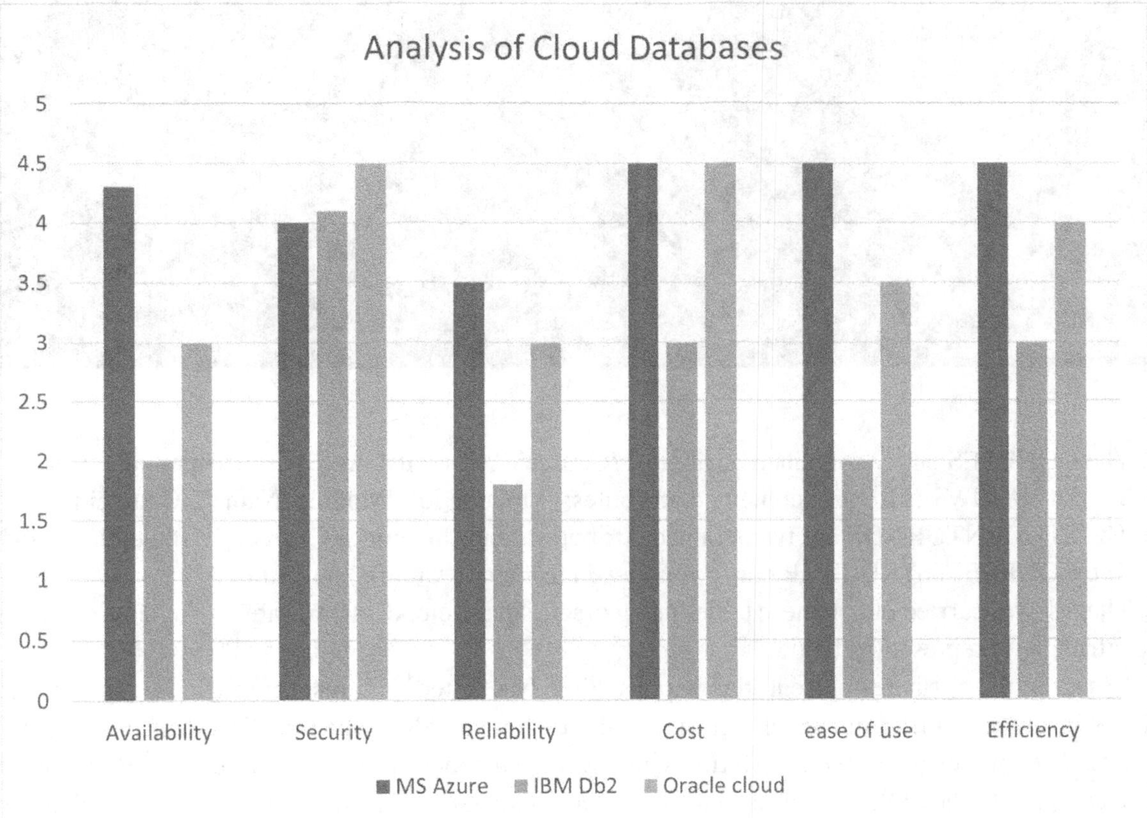

3.2 Experimental Analysis

This section comprises of methods undertaken to measure the performance of the cloud databases. the performance was measured by query response time, throughput and latency across the three cloud databases, the experiment was carried out using VMware as the test bed for the experiment. Figure 6 shows the interface of VMware.

The database created for the experiment uses STUDENT, FACULTY, COURSE all stored in DATABASE, CSC where the STUDENT entity contained attributes; 'Std_id', 'Name', 'Age', 'Level', 'Crc_code'.

The PERSON entity contained attributes; 'Personid', 'LastName', 'FirstName', 'HireDate', 'EnrollmentDate'

Figure 6. VMware workstation interface

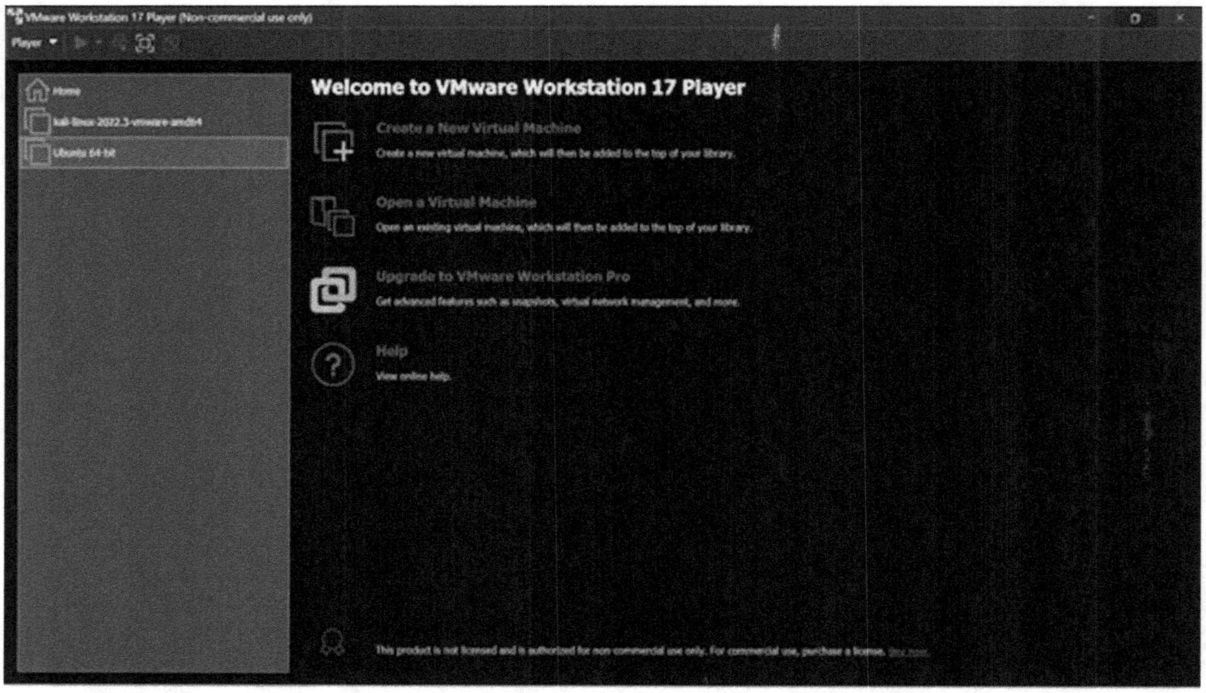

The COURSES entity contained attributes; 'Courceid', 'Credits', 'title', 'depatrmentid'.

The DEPARTMENT entity contained attributes; 'Module_id', 'Module_Name', 'Courceid'

The STUDENTGRADE entity contained attributes; 'enrollmentid', 'Courceid', 'studentid', 'grade'.

The COURSEINSTRUCTOR entity contained attributes; 'Crcid', 'personid'

The test was carried out on these tables using oracle sql developer on vmware, the schema containing the attributes is represented below;

Based on the attributes present, the response time was tested with respect to increasing number of entries in order to make inferences on the databases functionality when dealing with large amounts of data, The queries were Iterated 10 times and average response time taken to respond to the queries were computed. The SQL queries used to construct commands for the databases were assembled using DML queries such as "SELECT", the entities in the cloud databases comprises of 1,000, 100 and 150 respectively hence simple iterative queries were computed to measure the performance of the model.

3.2.1 MS Azure Query

The test was carried out on these tables using oracle SQL developer on VMware, the schema containing the attributes is represented below;

```
DECLARE @counter INT = 0;
WHILE @counter < 10
BEGIN
    SELECT Crc_code, Crc_name FROM COURSE WHERE units_no = 3
```

```
  SET @counter = @counter + 1;
END;
```

The Azure database schema used for the experiment is shown in figure 7.

Figure 7. Azure database schema

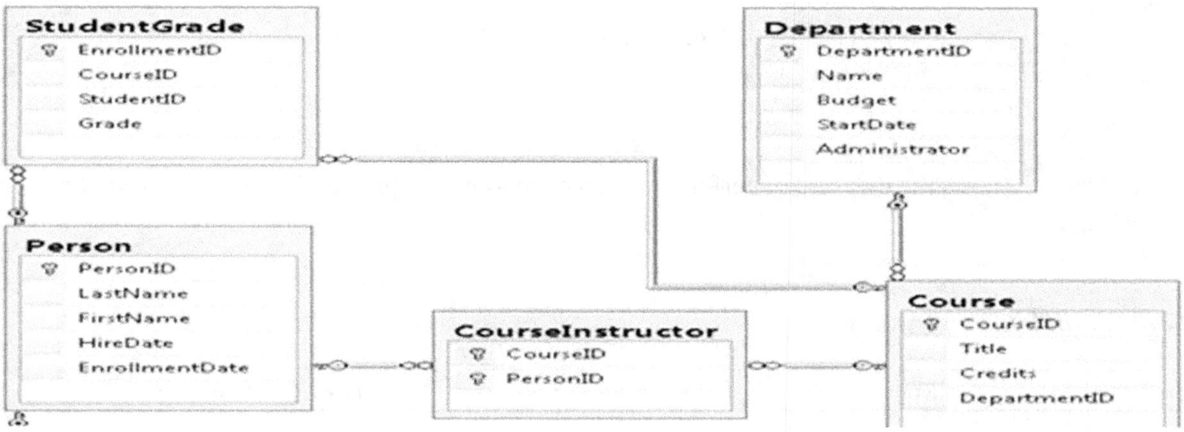

The table 2 shows the measure of performance taken to loop through the DATABASE from the query specified.

Table 2. Measure of performance

Iterations	Response Time(ms)
1	7
2	5.5
3	6
4	5
5	4
6	4
7	5.5
8	4
9	4.5
10	4.5

$$\text{Average Response Time} = \frac{7+5.5+6+5+4+4+5.5+4+4.5+4.5}{10} = 5ms$$

3.2.2 Oracle Query

The test was carried out on these tables using oracle sql developer on vmware, the schema containing the attributes is represented below;

```
DECLARE @counter INT = 0;
WHILE @counter < 10
BEGIN
    SELECT Crc_code, Crc_name FROM COURSE WHERE units_no = 3
  SET @counter = @counter + 1;
END;
```

The table 3 shows the measure of performance taken to loop through the DATABASE from the query specified.

Table 3. IBM db2 test results

Iterations	Response Time (ms)
1	4
2	3.5
3	4
4	4
5	4.5
6	3
7	3
8	3.5
9	3.5
10	3.5

$$\text{Average Response Time} = \frac{4+3.5+4+4+4+4.5+3+3.5+3.5+3.5}{10} = 3.35ms$$

4.2.3 IBM Db2 Query

The database for this service was created on a command line interface instead of a GUI interface hence, no schema is shown. Figure 8 shows a diagram of the some of the tables used in the experiment;

```
DECLARE @counter INT = 0;
WHILE @counter < 10
BEGIN
    SELECT Crc_code, Crc_name FROM COURSE WHERE units_no = 3
```

```
  SET @counter = @counter + 1;
END;
```

Figure 8. Person and column table in db2 CLI

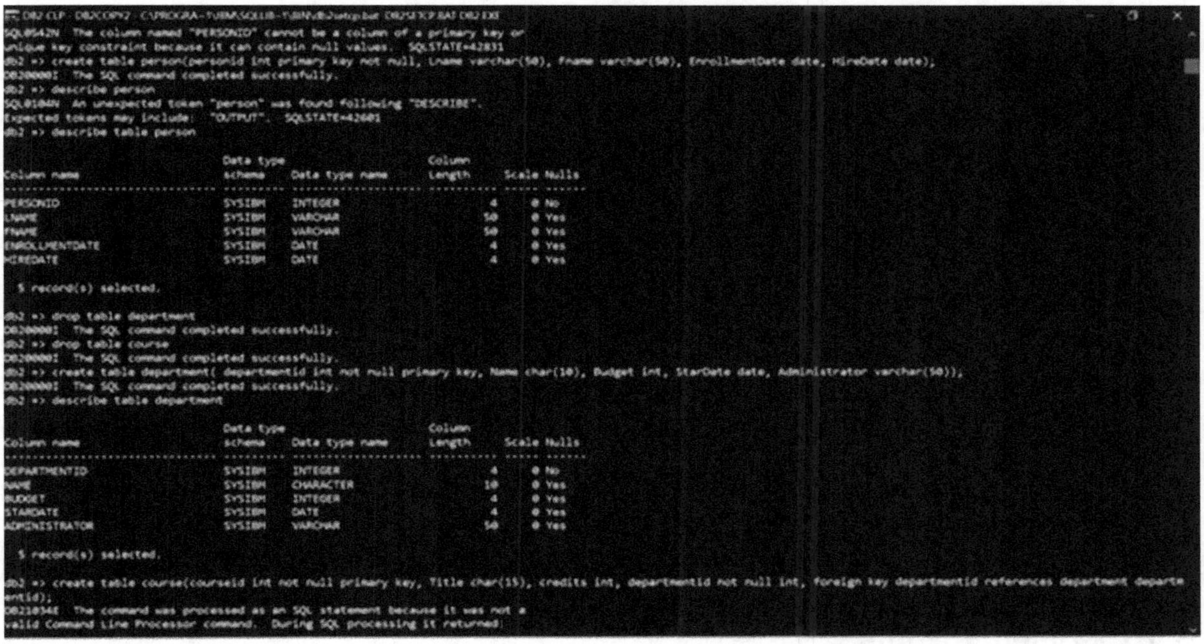

The table 4 shows the measure of performance taken to loop through the DATABASE from the query specified.

Table 4. IBM db2 Test results

Iterations	Response Time
1	7
2	6.5
3	6
4	6
5	6
6	5
7	4
8	4.5
9	4.5
10	4.5

$$\text{Average Response Time} = \frac{7+6.5+6+6+6+5+4+4.5+4.5+4.5}{10} = 5.4ms$$

N. B The IBM Db2 version used for this experiment is not the latest version and there weren't enough resources to access the latest version for this paper

4.0 DISCUSSION OF RESULT

A. Survey Result

The figure 5 highlights various questions and the responses of users from the survey.

Figure 5 and Table 1 shows the result gotten from the surveys, in terms of availability, MS Azure scored the highest with 43% followed by Oracle, 30% and IBM Db2 came last with 20%.

In terms of Reliability, Oracle scored the highest with 45% of the respondents selecting it as the most reliable, followed by IBM Db2 with 41% and MS Azure 40%.

In terms of security, MS Azure was picked by users as the most secure with 35% of users picking it, followed by Oracle 30% and IBM Db2 18%.

For Cost effectiveness, MS Azure and Oracle score the same with 45% of users picking both and 30% of users picking IBM Db2.

For Efficiency, MS Azure was the top pick with 45% followed by Oracle 35% and IBM Db2 20%.

B. Experiment Results

From the above conducted result, after 10 iterations of each experiment, MS Azure took 5ms to perform the query, Oracle took 3.35ms and IBM Db2 took 5.4ms. Oracle was the fastest with the lowest recorded time of 3.35ms.

4.1 Comparison of Cloud Databases

In this section the functionalities of these cloud databases are compared in a tabular from based on features exhibited below;

From the experiments, analysis and comparisons carried out on the cloud database mediums as this study is concerned, the following inferences can be drawn;

i. Microsoft Azure is considered a comprehensive Platform-as-a-Service (PaaS) solution due to its user-friendly interface, accessibility through web consoles and APIs. Although it may have some functional glitches, but it is an effective cloud model with efficient customer support.
ii. Oracle cloud is relatively flexible and possess various number of features with good levels of efficiency in performing tasks specified by users. It provides a graphical user interface (GUI) for comprehensive database management and command-line access interface for greater control over features and functionality. It is highly secure and reliable, but its customer support efficiency is not as good as Azure.

iii. IBM Db2 allows for identifying and addressing performance bottlenecks, resulting in quicker response times and more effective data processing. It also enables evaluating security compliance, detecting vulnerabilities, and managing user access controls, authentication procedures, and encryption. Resource usage and consumption trends can be analyzed as well.

This discussion emphasizes the importance of finding ways to reduce expenses while maintaining desired performance levels in cloud databases. The comparison and analysis provide insights into the strengths and weaknesses of each cloud database option, helping organizations make informed decisions based on their specific requirements.

Table 5. Comparison of cloud databases

Features	Microsoft Azure	IBM Db2	Oracle Cloud
Virtualization	Microsoft CLR VM	VmWare, Microsoft Hyper-V, KVM	Oracle VM (OVM)
Pricing model	Pay-as-you-go	Subscription	Pay-as-you-go
Access Interface	Web-based, API, console	Command-line, API, GUI, IDE	Web-based, API, Command-line
Availability (%)	90%	70%	85%
Reliability	93%	95%	98%
Security	90%	80%	87%
Scalability	Basic	Basic	Basic
Cost Effectiveness	99%	85%	99%
Efficiency	95%	80%	93%
Technical Support	Good	Basic	Good
Tools / Frameworks	Java, PHP, Python, Basic	IBM Data studio, Infosphere OPTIM	APEX, C#, ODT(VS)

5.0 CONCLUSION

The performance of cloud databases like IBM Db2, Oracle, and Microsoft Azure is compared using a variety of approaches such as Survey and an Experiment. These methods give users useful information about the performance characteristics of the databases, enabling them to make wise selections. Experiments are essential for objective assessments. Therefore, the study evaluates the efficiency of the databases using query execution time as a performance metric. In the Experiment section, Oracle performed the best with an average execution time of 3.35ms which was the fastest of the three databases.

In the survey section, the results shows that MS Azure is the most available, Secure, cost effective, and efficient. Oracle can be seen from the survey responses as the most reliable and also most cost effective.

Using this information, making informed decisions is made possible by these methods, which provide users with important information on the performance characteristics of the databases.

Both Oracle and Microsoft Azure have extensive scalability options, enabling users to extend resources both horizontally and vertically as necessary if scalability is a crucial component of your application.

Although IBM Db2 has scalability options as well, it's important to consider whether they meet your particular scalability needs. When selecting a database, security should come first. Oracle enjoys a strong reputation for having strong security features and adhering to industry standards. To guarantee the protection of your data, Microsoft Azure provides a variety of security measures and compliance certifications. Although IBM Db2 has security features as well, it's best to determine whether they meet your particular security needs. It is also important to look over the support options and pricing strategies each database vendor offers. Oracle and Microsoft Azure provide thorough assistance, satisfying various needs. However, it's worth looking into the cost to make sure it suits your budget and support needs. IBM Db2 offers support and affordable solutions. Consider how each database can be integrated with your current setup. Microsoft Azure provides a unified user experience. Oracle offers a variety of integration possibilities and has good support from third-party tools. Although IBM Db2 also has integration capabilities, it's important to determine whether they are compatible with your particular integration requirements. Keep in mind that the final decision will depend on your particular needs, preferences, and restrictions. Examine Oracle, IBM Db2, and other database systems' performance characteristics, scalability choices, security features, and pricing policies in detail.

REFERENCES

Abiodun, M. K., Awotunde, J. B., Ogundokun, R. O., Misra, S., Adeniyi, E. A., Arowolo, M. O., & Jaglan, V. (2021, February). Cloud and big data: A mutual benefit for organization development. *Journal of Physics: Conference Series, 1767*(1), 012020. doi:10.1088/1742-6596/1767/1/012020

Aremu, D. R., & Moses, A. K. (n.d.). Grid, cloud, and big data: Technologies overlaps. *International Journal of Information Processing and Communication.*

Berisha, B., Mëziu, E., & Shabani, I. (2022) Big data analytics in Cloud computing: an overview. *Journal of Cloud Computing, 11*, 24.

Bigelow, S. J., Neenan, S., Casey, K., & Earls, A. R. (2023, May 17). *What is public cloud? Everything you need to know.* Cloud Computing. https://www.techtarget.com/searchcloudcomputing/definition/public-cloud

Britannica. (2023, March 3). Information retrieval. In *Encyclopedia Britannica*. https://www.britannica.com/technology/information-retrieval

Chai, W., & Bigelow, S. J. (2022, November 10). *Cloud computing*. https://www.techtarget.com/searchcloudcomputing/definition/cloud-computing

Cui, Z., Jiang, M., Jeong, K., & Kim, B. (2014, May). A Cloud Database Service Approach to the Management of Sensor Data. *2014 International Conference on Information Science & Applications (ICISA).* 10.1109/ICISA.2014.6847327

Dutta, P., & Dutta, P. (2019, April 30). Comparative Study of Cloud Services Offered by Amazon, Microsoft and Google. *International Journal of Trend in Scientific Research and Development, 3*(3), 981–985. doi:10.31142/ijtsrd23170

Hashem, I. A. T., Yaqoob, I., Anuar, N. B., Mokhtar, S., Gani, A., & Ullah Khan, S. (2015, January). The rise of "big data" on cloud computing: Review and open research issues. *Information Systems, 47*, 98–115. doi:10.1016/j.is.2014.07.006

Hassan, M., Obazu, D., Zmij, K., Azhygulov, K., & Sitaula, S. (2022). Microsoft Azure's Leading Edge in Cloud Computing Services. *IUP Journal of Computer Sciences, 16*(2).

Hofmann, P., & Woods, D. (2010, November). Cloud Computing: The Limits of Public Clouds for Business Applications. *IEEE Internet Computing*, *14*(6), 90–93. doi:10.1109/MIC.2010.136

Khan, I., Dewangan, B., Meena, A., & Birthare, M. (2020). Study of Various Cloud Service Providers: A Comparative Analysis. SSRN *Electronic Journal*. doi:10.2139/ssrn.3672950

Kiennert, C., Bouzefrane, S., & Benkara Mostefa, A. F. (2015). Digital Identity in Cloud Computing. *Digital Identity Management*, 207–244. doi:10.1016/B978-1-78548-004-1.50005-5

Lee, S. (2012). Database management system as a cloud service. *International Journal of Future Generation Communication and Networking*, *5*(2).

Ranger, S. (2022, February 25). *What is cloud computing? Everything you need to know about the cloud explained.* ZDNET. https://www.zdnet.com/article/what-is-cloud-computing-everything-you-need-to-know-about-the-cloud/

Rountree, D., & Castrillo, I. (2014). Introduction to the Cloud. *The Basics of Cloud Computing*, 1–17. doi:10.1016/B978-0-12-405932-0.00001-3

Saif, S., & Wazir, S. (2018). Performance Analysis of Big Data and Cloud Computing Techniques: A Survey. *Procedia Computer Science*, *32*, 118-127, ISSN 1877-0509.

Singh, H., Bhasin, A., Kaveri, P. R., & Chavan, V. (n.d.). Cloud Resource Management: Comparative Analysis and Research Issues. *International Journal of Scientific & Technology Research.* www.ijstr.org

Stedman, C. (2022, July 26). *What is a cloud database? An in-depth cloud DBMS guide*. Cloud Computing. https://www.techtarget.com/searchcloudcomputing/definition/cloud-database

Tasnim, R., Mim, A. A., Mim, S. H., & Jabiullah, M. I. (2022). A Comparative Study on Three Selective Cloud Providers. *International Journal on Cybernetics & Informatics*. https://www.ijcionline.com/paper/11/11422ijci13.pdf doi:10.5121/ijci.2022.110413

Tsui, E., Cheong, R. K., & Sabetzadeh, F. (2011, June). Cloud-Based Personal Knowledge Management as a service (PKMaaS). *2011 International Conference on Computer Science and Service System (CSSS)*. 10.1109/CSSS.2011.5975019

Wankhede, P., Talati, M., & Chinchamalatpure, R. (2020, April 2). Comparative study of cloud platforms - microsoft azure, google cloud platform and amazon EC2. *International Journal of Research in Engineering and Applied Sciences, 5*(2).

Xiong, P., Chi, Y., Zhu, S., Moon, H. J., Pu, C., & Hacigumus, H. (2011, April). Intelligent management of virtualized resources for database systems in cloud environment. *2011 IEEE 27th International Conference on Data Engineering*. 10.1109/ICDE.2011.5767928

Chapter 3
Cloud-Enhanced Real-Time Disease Classification With Vital Sign Monitoring:
Role of Cloud in Healthcare

Lakshmi Kanthan Narayanan
https://orcid.org/0000-0002-1221-2268
Saveetha University, India

P. Selvaraj
SRM Institute of Science and Technology, India

ABSTRACT

The delivery of healthcare is an area where data access, processing, analysis, sharing, and storage between many parties is exceedingly important. In order to address this demand, cloud computing has gained popularity in a wide range of fields, including telemedicine, information management, and bioinformatics. The gestures of the patient were continuously captured and recorded in the cloud. The gesture recognition may be applied especially for the bed-ridden patients who cannot communicate verbally. The sample simulation of the clustering and disease identification with the gesture recognition was done to prove the efficacy of the system. In this chapter, various artifacts of cloud-based technology and the possibility of implementation in the healthcare sector is discussed briefly.

1. INTRODUCTION

The IoT (Internet of Things) and Machine Learning have been widely applied to evaluate a patient's condition in the area of health diagnosis and personalized medical care. Moreover, the computing capability of the cloud computing drives the IoT applications to the level applicable in the real time based use cases, with the support of more immersive and conducive UI based interactions. The cloud computing provides the distributed computing environment for an on-request based accessibility of infrastructural

DOI: 10.4018/979-8-3693-0593-5.ch003

assets, especially data storage and computing requirements, without the necessity of the human administration. This work focuses on the patient sign monitoring with gesture recognition to identify the disease and the condition of the patient. The system consisted of Raspberry Pi with camera module and was programmed with python programming language as bolstered by the Open Source Computer Vision library. The model would contain resistant HDMI screen of size 800*480 would be included in the device for data input and output. The Raspberry Pi includes the hand-gesture image processing technology. The Raspberry Pi has an image-processing algorithm embedded named hand-gesture recognition that aims to recognize and differentiate between the diverse hand gestures of the patient and alert the medical staff if required. The collected features were extracted and classified based on the SVM (Support Vector Machine) algorithm. The primary aim of the health care workers is to monitor the patients remotely and get immediate alerts whenever the patients are in need of any urgent medical emergency. The finger gestures were used to train the system and to trigger certain alerts with respect to a specific signal. The vital signs of the healthy human were used to set a range to be followed by the temperature sensor and other sensors. Anything beyond the limit has been made to set an alert signal. The normal high and low values of the vital signs were used to set the thresholds. Anything beyond that was trained to set an alert signal. Eye area ratio change was used to send an alert in response to irregular eye movements. The different facial features were used for eye recognition.

The rest of the paper is organized as follows: Section 2 narrates the relevant concepts available in the literatures, Section 3 critically analyzes the drawbacks of the existing system, Section 4 explains the objectives and the notable aspects of the proposed approach, Section 5 proposes the various modules in the proposed system architecture, Section 6 demonstrates the implementation methodology, Section 7 explains the results, and Section 8 concludes the overall system.

2. LITERATURE SURVEY

2.1 ML Algorithms in Disease Prediction

Naive Bayes algorithm is used to classify the heart beat data set (Palagan et al., 2022). K-Means Clustering was used to partition information into various informational indexes without class labels (Adeniyi et al., 2021). They have used K-Means Clustering technique for disease identification at H. A Malik Hospital located in Medan.

2.2 Advanced Healthcare Frameworks

A large number of wireless networks have been utilized in the healthcare industry. We were inspired by the valuable research work done on the design and working of those wireless communication systems for health monitoring systems (de Oliveira et al., 2021). The bioelectric records were grouped for each patient based on the output from ECG and blood pressure sensors. The significant work done portrays the remote sensor based framework for health care applications (Hady, 2020). The principle results were recorded within 2ms in 80% of the cases with clustering precision as high as 90%. (Barsocchi et al., 2020) deployed a trustworthy and error-free system that can help to monitor the health of the elders. One of the many advantages was carrying out data analysis on the cloud instead of the gateway server.

The usage of GSM modules with the microcontroller device was proposed (ShayestehTabatabaei, 2020). The principal objective was to develop a usable system that will be able to assist the doctors via means of tele-monitoring. To figure out a solution for the above problem, a solution has been proposed (Shrestha et al., 2019) stating another design utilizing IoT to store and process varied sensor information for medicinal services applications.

From the contributions of the it was evident that the health monitoring system can be coupled with Zigbee, web services and various other technologies (Bhola et al., 2019). It has been have explored various aspects of healthcare and gesture recognition (Moqadam & Kazemi, 2019). They have used gesture recognition using gloves for accurate gesture recognition. This however was not feasible due to an increased cost overhead. For a lot of hospitals in remote areas it was not feasible for healthcare faculties to purchase SLR gloves. Also this limits the recognition to merely the hand whereas patients often indicate signs of consciousness or urgency by other means such as the movement of the eye or other organs of the body. Therefore we zeroed down on the camera recognition technologies.

Moreover, in (Wang, Gao, Yin et al, 2018) they built up a Data Acquisition and Control (DAC) framework that makes an interpretation of the communication via gestures into content can be perused by anybody. They called their framework as Sign Language Translator and Gesture Recognition. They had built up a keen glove that catches the motion of the hand and deciphers these gestures into lucid content. This content has been sent remotely to an advanced mobile phone or appeared in an inserted LCD show. It is clear from the test results that motions can be caught by set of modest sensors, which measure the positions and the direction of the fingers. The present rendition of the framework can decipher 20 out of 26 letters with an acknowledgment precision of 96%. But in our application, using Raspberry pi the speed of the response was improved.

In (Wang, Ju, Gao et al, 2018) it is recognized that the problem that our society faces nowadays is that people with disability are finding hard to grapple with the fast growing technology. In this situation they are two clients, one client utilizes eye flicker sensor to convey a sentence or word through EOG innovation and the other client utilizes flex sensor their by correspondence between one another happens. Additionally the inspiration for adding an audio output to the project came from their work. Their proposed device architecture converts sign language to audio interpretations that enabled people to understand the deaf and dumb even better.

3. DRAWBACKS OF THE EXISTING SYSTEM

The major drawbacks of the existing disease surveillance system are listed below:

1. The physical diagnosis requires visit to hospital and the doctor prescribes medicines without the aid of any automated system.
2. The conventional devices can only measure a particular parameter and making a contextual understanding requires expertise.
3. The wearable smart watches are too expensive and not specifically made for disease identification with alerting system.
4. The smart watches don't upload data on the cloud. This limits the usage of the collected data.
5. There is no functionality exists to predict diseases only by analyzing the obtained sensor data and movements of the patient.

4. PROPOSED SYSTEM

In this work, a cost effective 24/7 health surveillance system was proposed. The Arduino board was used for collecting and processing the sensor data. The various sensor data were simultaneously uploaded on the ThingSpeak cloud platform for remote analysis. An ESP8266 module was utilized for interfacing with the web. The SMS and Email notifications were generated whenever the sensor value crosses beyond the critical threshold. The proposed system has integrated machine learning algorithms for disease identification and early prediction. We trained the SVM algorithm on the raw data set to predict eight different types of commonly occurring disease conditions.

The proposed system consisted of pulse rate sensing unit, temperature sensing unit, blood pressure measurement unit and adaptive gesture detection unit for continuously monitoring the patients in real time using raspberry pi module. With this system the daily vitals and the gestures are recorded in the cloud platform. The camera attached with the system provides 360 degree patient monitoring by capturing the eye movements and feeble hand gestures of the patients so as to alert the doctor/health care personal regarding the state of wakefulness or need. Moreover, a mobile based application was created to communicate via Wi-Fi to the system that consists of Raspberry Pi and sensors. This proposed system is used to safeguard the lives of patients in case of emergency. The collected dataset will be kept in the cloud to understand the patient's behavior. Hence the patients need not waste money on tests that are not required and optimize their checkup cycles at lower cost.

The proposed approach is energy efficient and scalable as we can scale up with more sensors to the raspberry pi unit as and when sensor technologies emerge. The required cloud computing power can also be availed in an ala-carte basis. The raspberry pi unit contains wifi and Bluetooth modules to ease communication. We have used the best practices of digital image processing to extract gestures with enhanced image acquisition and preprocessing. We achieved this with background removal and final marking with distance between image vectors of the finger open and finger close image. Whenever the distance crosses another higher threshold the system will trigger the suitable audio alert.

4.1 Objectives

In order to provide a patient with efficient health monitoring, this effort intends to merge the concepts of IoT and automated learning. The objectives of the proposed approach are given below:

1. To have the option to screen the vitals of the patient through an easy and cheaper means.
2. To design a health monitoring system that monitors the patient's vitals temperature, heartbeat, & spo2 is easier.
3. To generate an email, SMS or voice alerts to the peers of the patient and the doctor, by providing the values obtained through sensors.
4. This system can detect the status of the patient if the patient is going through any abnormality.
5. To provide the ability to the doctor to monitor the person's health from anywhere in the world through the Thingspeak cloud platform.

4.2 Proposed Method

A cloud database will receive the data from the IoT sensors connected to the PIC microcontroller with the help of the Wi-Fi module. With the mix of sensors, such as heart rate, temperature, spo2, and a camera an Arduino-based system can be conceived as a mini home health care center. The parameters like the BP, heartbeat, and glucose level were continuously monitored. The utilization of these affordable medical systems could diminish the clinical expenses of the country over a period and make the country as self-sustained in combating and controlling commonly occurring diseases.

The set of functionalities provided by the proposed system as follows:

1. Collection of information from the patient through three sensor devices.
2. Uploading the real-time information onto the Thingspeak cloud platform.
3. In case of any abnormalities the doctor and patient's peer will be alerted using Email/SMS Notification module.
4. Appropriate ML algorithms were used to perform an analysis of the values of the sensors and initiate the necessary medical prescriptions.

The wearable device's test information has been incorporated into the trained cloud-based model. The model for classifying the sick individual and the healthy person was the SVM algorithm. The data collected from the sensors was analyzed and checked on serial monitor in arduino. The sensor values were compared to the threshold levels. Whenever the live value exceeds threshold, a notification will be generated. Following this, all the values are stored in a file that can later passed to the SVM algorithm to perform classification and prediction of the health condition. Moreover, to incorporate remote monitoring, the values were uploaded on a cloud channel and can be accessed by the doctor anywhere and anytime. The values are obtained and shown visually in form of graphs on the screen. The fluctuations in the reading along with timestamp can be observed.

This system altogether helps in saving the patient from any sort of critical situation and to keep a remote watch on patient's health in an effective manner.

4.2.1 SVM (Support Vector Machine)-Based Disease Classification

Support Vectors are termed as the vectors or the particulars of data that are located closely to the hyperplane and they have the ability to influence the scene of the particular hyperplane. In other words, the hyperplane is supported by the presence of these vectors and hence they are being referred to as Support Vectors. The SVM classifier can be discovered in certain ways by different types of algorithms. The latest algorithms make use of sub angle plunge and organize drop in order to explore the SVM classifier. When there is a need to manage large, complex and low quality sets of data, the above-said methods have shown relevant points of interest as compared to the on-going and old traditional methods. The productivity of the sub-inclination methods is directly proportional to the number of models of preparation. They also provide a dropping facility in case of high value of the component of the element space.

4.2.2 Parameter Selection

There are certain factors that affect the efficiency and performance of SVM. They are listed as follows:

1. The selection of the kernel.
2. The parameters of the Kernel.
3. The parameter "C" of the soft margin.

One of the commonly used kernal is a Gaussian kernel and it has a uni-parameter . A grid search is responsible to select the best fusion of C and The sequences of C and are incrementing exponentially.

4.2.3 Issues With SVM-Based Classification

The potential drawbacks of the SVM include the following aspects:

- It requires the information to be completely named.
- Unstandardized class participation probabilities restrict SVM to calculate class labels with limited data since it is stocked from Vapnik's theory.
- If given 2 class allotments then SVM proves to be the only conceptually correct strategy. In this similar way, Multi class SVM can be utilized to resolve the issues emanating from algorithms declining multi class work.
- The process of streamlining the parameters that are required to develop an illuminated model is hard to perform.

5. PROPOSED SYSTEM DESIGN

5.1 Cloud System Architecture

The cloud computing includes many cloud parts, which are inexactly coupled. We can extensively separate cloud engineering into two sections namely Cloud Front End and Cloud Back End. The constituent elements of the cloud computing was associated through an internet backbone. The accompanying Figure.1 shows the graphical perspective of cloud computing and its major components.

The front end alludes to the patient part of cloud computing framework. It comprises of interfaces and web based applications to get connected with the cloud computing phases. The back End alludes to the cloud itself. It comprises of the considerable number of assets required to give cloud computing administrations. It involves gigantic information stockpiling, virtual machines, security system, administrations, arrangement models, servers, and so forth.

Figure 1. Cloud computing framework with front end and back end

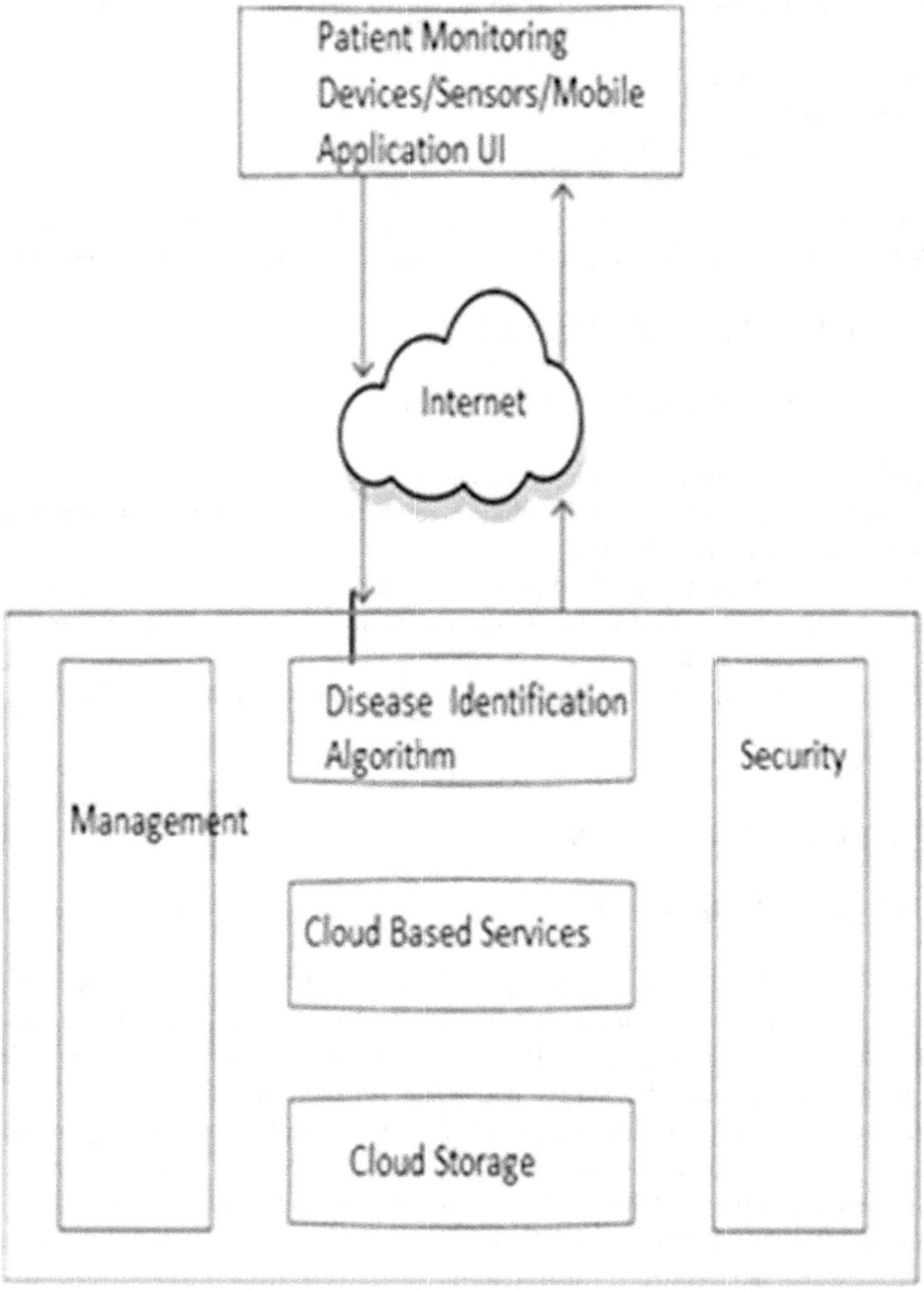

5.2 Proposed System Architecture

The above Figure 2 depicts the various components that make up the architecture of the healthcare monitoring system. The various components are- Cloud, Arduino, SVM algorithm and the 3 sensors namely- Pulse, Temperature and SPO2. Through the 3 sensors the vital sign of the person was observed and those values were compared with the threshold values. Further, the SVM algorithm analyses these values and classifies them in order to predict whether the person is fit or not by analyzing the symptoms of diseases. The webpage was designed to display the final output i.e. the condition of the patient.

Figure 2. Disease classification and gesture recognition architecture

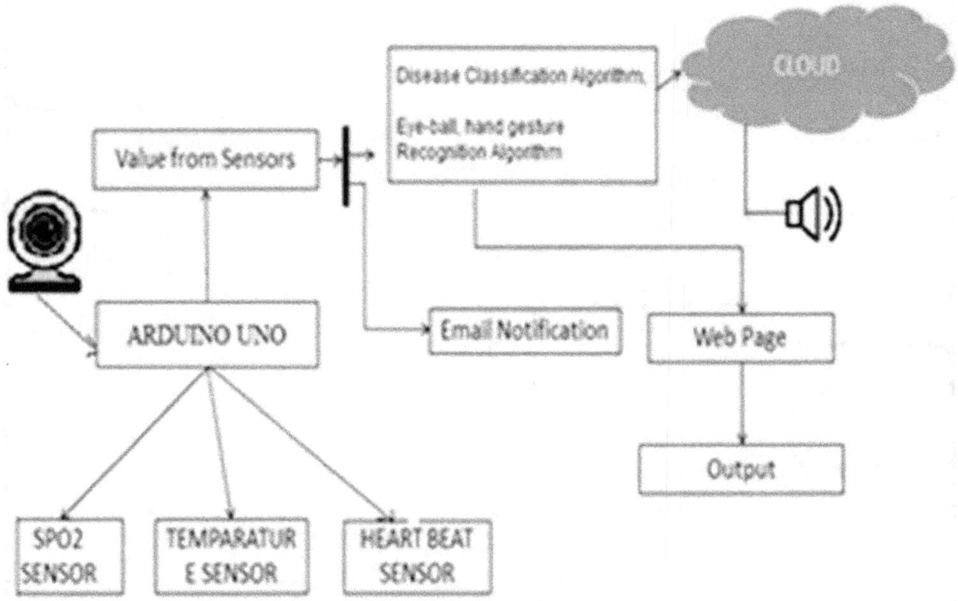

The proposed eye-lid recognition module (Figure.3) captured the data points of temperature and pulse of a patient and with the aid of two different OpenCV modules.

- The data points of temperature and pulse helps the nurse to remotely monitor the patients
- The Second Part of OpenCV uses image pre processing and thresholding to remove the background from the image and single out the object of interest.
- After removing the object by the subtraction of running averages, the gestures are recognized and given meaning for the same.
- The patient merely needs to put up their fingers if they require any assistance. Our system comprises of two frames; one for gesture recognition and the other for the capturing of eye movements.
- An alert system will begin to initiate the alert if the patient is in comatose state and making gestures to denote his/her wakefulness or need.

The various components in the framework are Thingspeak cloud module, Arduino, SVM and the 3 sensors namely- Pulse, Temperature and SPO2. The 3 sensors obtain values from the person and those values are compared to the threshold values and if they exceed them, notification is sent to the doctor as well as patient. Further, the SVM algorithm analyses these values and classifies them in order to predict whether the person is fit or is showing symptoms of any type of disease.

Figure 3. Eye-lid movement recognition module

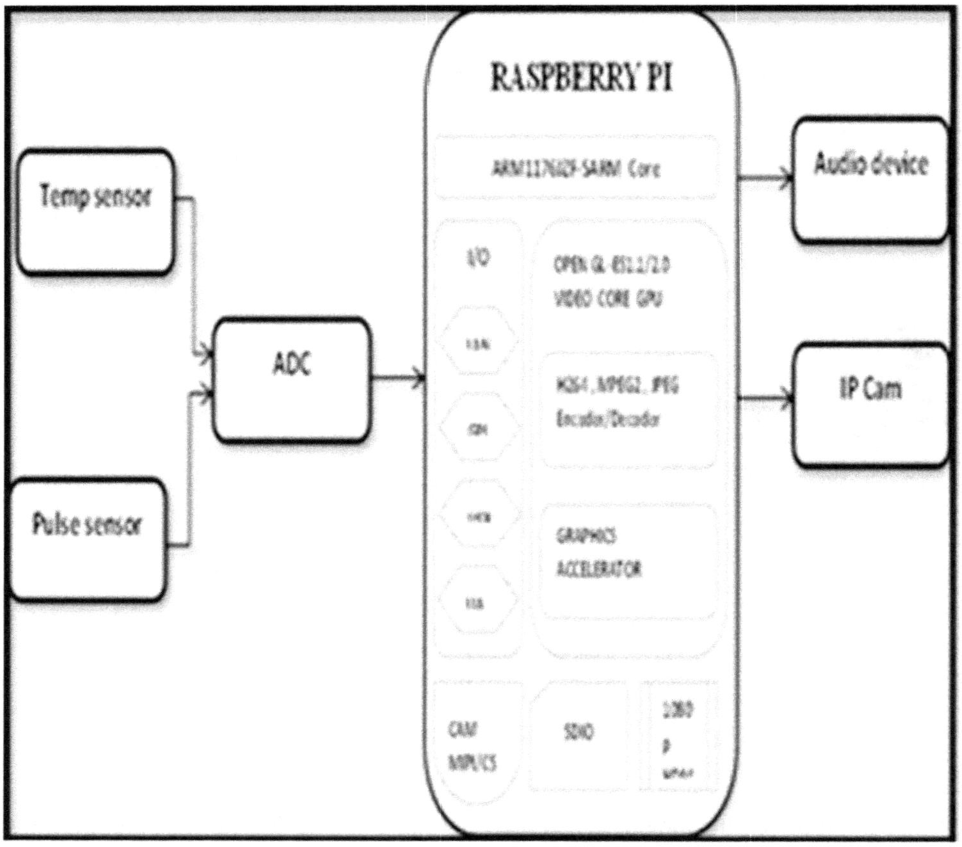

Virtualization is an innovative upheaval that isolates capacities from hidden equipment and enables us to make helpful conditions from dynamic assets. Virtualization innovation has been focused on users to understand their needs in a more viable technological perspective. Users could bargain custom VM frameworks, enabling them to get to different VMs on a similar framework and even the host. This work underscores on the appraisal of virtualization explicit issues, and potential arrangements. The idea to store API on an external cloud is to maintain the integrity of API even if the primary cloud is compromised during the attack.

This proposed system has exploited the cloud based IoT and machine learning algorithms. The controlling of sensors and information processing tasks were accomplished with help of Arduino. Through this system, the temperature, Heartbeat and spo2 levels were continuously monitored. Through different sensors, it was possible to gauge the life sign quantities in real-time. As the temperature sensor functions with analog signals it was connected to Arduino through the ADC unit whereas the rest of the sensors were directly connected with the board. This work has incorporated machine learning algorithms for the prediction of the various virus based diseases. We trained machine learning algorithm on the raw data set to increase the prediction accuracy.

A sequence diagram is one of the interaction diagrams because it describes how a group of objects works together along with the order they follow. Software developers and business professionals generally use sequence diagrams to understand requirements for a new system or for the documentation purpose of an existing process. The specific focus is on lifelines, or the processes and objects that live/ operate simultaneously, and the messages exchanged between them to perform a function before the end of a lifeline.

Building blocks of sequence diagram are given as below: "Messages, written with horizontal arrows with the message name written above them, display interaction. If a caller sends a synchronous message, it must wait until the message is done, such as invoking a subroutine. If a caller sends an asynchronous message, it can continue processing and doesn't have to wait for a response.

The patient makes a specific gesture to the system and the system replies with appropriate result like raising the bed or calling the nurse. If the the doctor is called the system alerts the doctor. The second part where machines reads the pulse ans temperature and sends an alert if the value is not normal. Everything is stored in database which can be accessed by the doctor (Figure 4).

Figure 4. Sequence diagram of the proposed approach

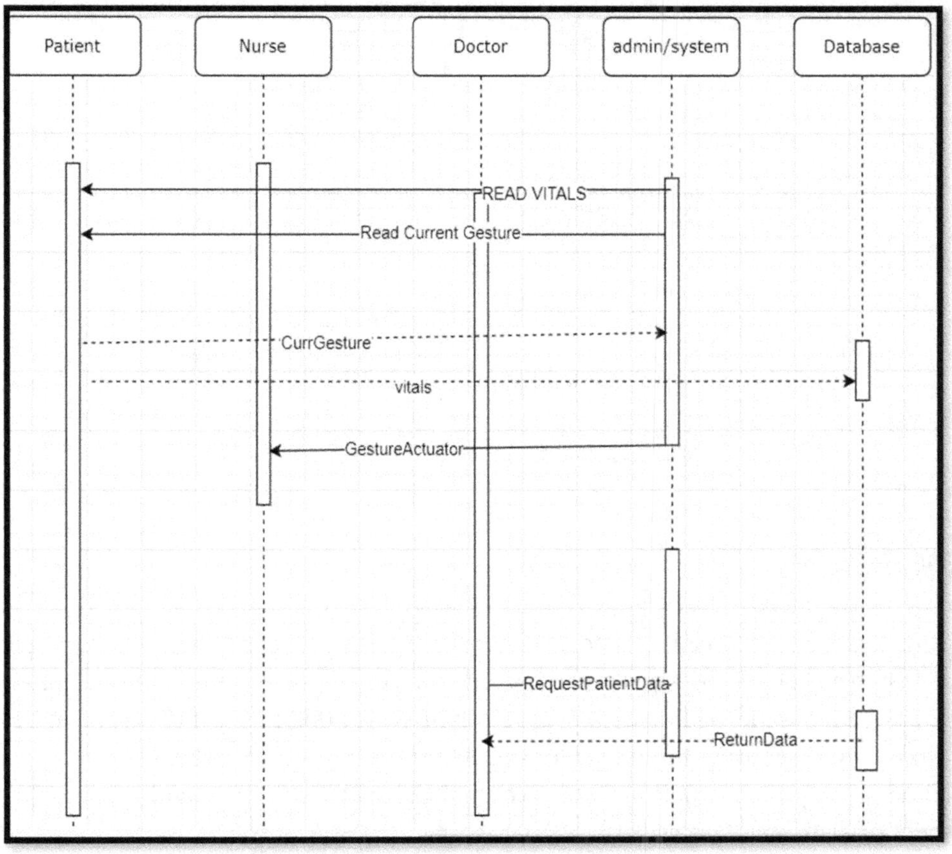

This system mainly depends on two actors. The Patient and the Doctor. There are a set of operations to be performed by these 2 actors individually. The equipment or the sensors collect the live data from the patient. These sensor readings are then pre-processed and features are extracted from them in order to carry out the analysis. The readings are classified and disease prediction is done based on the classification. The doctor receives an email notification alert in case of any abnormality in the readings. Moreover, these readings are further stored on a cloud platform named ThingSpeak.

The above class diagram (Figure 5) comprises 6 different classes. The Arduino and Cloud classes are associated with the Healthcare Setup. The Arduino class is used by the healthcare system. The patient class holds the attributes like age, email-id, and any medical history. It comprises the healthcare class. There is a direct association between the doctor and patient class with a multiplicity of 1 and 1..n.

Figure 5. Class diagram of the proposed approach

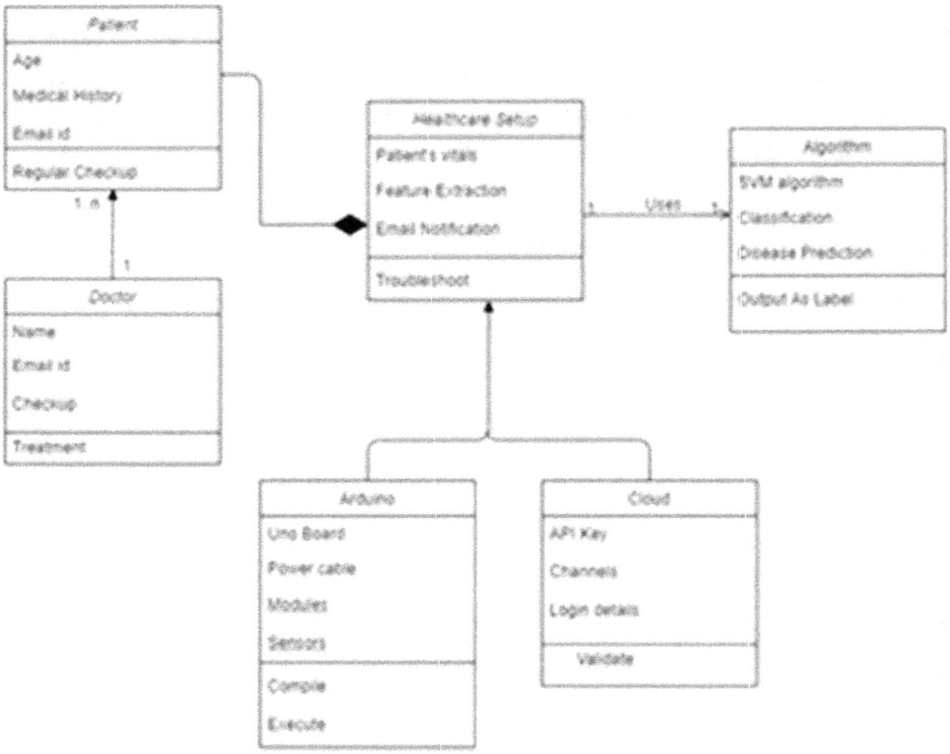

6. IMPLEMENTATION

Understanding of the advancement is a necessary requirement in order to determine the parameters of the largest side hyperplane. SVM also acts as a source for a quadratic programming issue. Although this issue can be solved by some arithmetic's particularly used for this issue. It depends on heuristics and resolves the issue by separating it into smaller and incrementing sensible chunks.

This method is the perfect solution to resolve this pertinent issue again and again instead of facing an arrangement of distributed issues.

A low placed guess to the grid needs to be daily utilized in the portion stunt to cease from illuminating a direct along with the large piece lattice. One more technique on the list to solve the issue is Platt's continuous negligible improvisation (SMO) calculation. It dispenses the need of a numerical up gradation calculation and lattice stockpiling and works by separating the problem into 2d sub-problems that are properly described and explained. There are certain advantages of making use of this algorithm such as:

1. It is conceptually very simple.
2. Easy application.
3. Fast process most of the time.
4. Possess even better calculating properties for complex SVM issues.

In order to effectively solve linear SVM, we need to utilize the calculations that are considered correct and result oriented in optimizing logistic fixation that is its close pair. Sub gradient Descent and Coordinate Descent are included in this class of measurements. LIBLINEAR which is a type of Coordinate Descent has some effective training-time characteristics. The Q-direct interconnecting property of the cycles is highly effective in lowering the calculation time. Also, an investment is needed by all assembly emphasis in the time taken in order to obtain train information.

In case of permissible parallelization, the illumination of the general portion SVMs can be carried out more effectively by utilizing sub-inclination plummet.

6.1 Dataset

The illness-detection dataset was collected from the kaggle datastore (Figure.6) and the model was trained using SVM and Naïve Baye's algorithms.

Figure 6. Kaggle dataset view

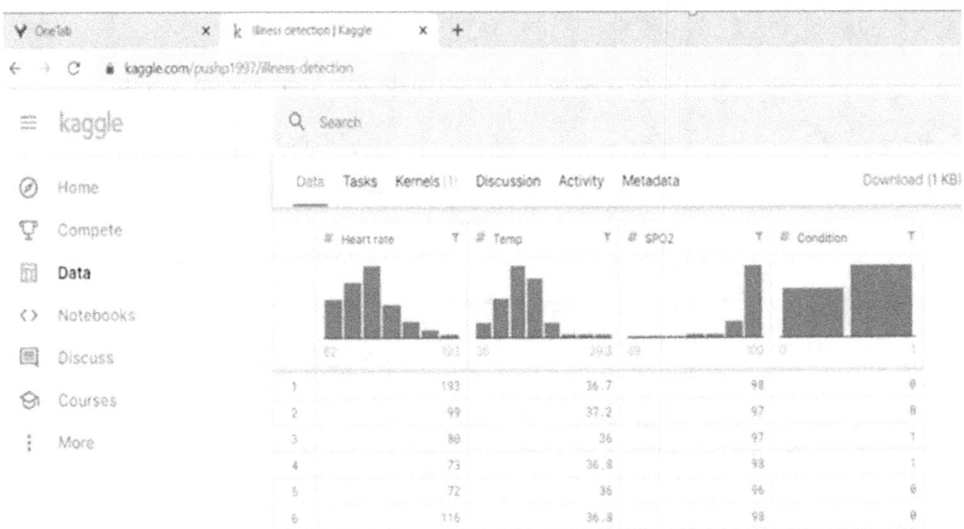

In the below Table.1 the various diseases were numbered between zero to seven. The ML based model was a trained to predict the various diseases like fever, arrhythmia, tachycardia, stroke, hypoxia, pneumonia and Sleep Apnea. This table basically indicates the condition state that corresponds to a particular disease or symptoms. For instance, if the condition or the output of the algorithm is zero then it means the patient is in normal condition or having some other particular disease otherwise.

Table 1. Various flags and their related diseases

S.No	Condition	Disease
1.	0	Normal condition
2.	1	Fever
3.	2	Arrhythmia
4.	3	Tachycardia
5.	4	Stroke
6.	5	Hypoxia
7.	6	Pneumonia
8.	7	Sleep apnea

6.2 Procedure of the Proposed Framework

The steps followed in the proposed approach are given below:

1. The data from the temperature sensor was fed into ADC and in turn connected to Arduino in the appropriate pins. Similarly the different sensors were also connected to the arduino. Through the arduino interface, the board option was selected from the arduino tools and the com5 port was selected. This is the port through which any desktop connects to the Arduino.
2. After the successful compilation of code the same was uploaded on the Arduino. In the serial monitor the baud rate of 9600 was set and the sensor values were received from the Arduino.
3. The sensors were mounted on the body of the patient and the values collected. If case of abnormal condition an email notification will be sent to the registered mail ids.
4. In the thingspeak cloud platform the private channels were created and the key was fed into the python code. The python code will create a .csv file on the thingspeak cloud platform.
5. Simultaneously the pre-trained machine learning model will perform the prediction on the data being fetched from the sensors.
6. This prediction will indicate any early warning symptoms of certain diseases without going to the clinic.

7. RESULTS

The data were fetched from the Arduino unit while set the baud rate of 9600 in the serial port. Figure 7 is showing the results fetched by the hardware unit. At rare occasions there may be a possibility of short circuits in the wearable device's sensors that can cause hardware issues.

Whenever the threshold values reaching its threshold and email notification will be sent to the registered mail ids of the patient (Figure 8).

After the data of the patient was fetched by the hardware it got transferred to the ThingSpeak cloud for further analysis with the aid of ML algorithms. The cloud module enables the doctors and patients to login and check the data anytime from anywhere in the world. The view of the mail notification sent to the doctor is shown in Figure 9.

In the Figures from 10 to 15 the various vital sign readings over a period of time is shown. The eyelid movement detection and the gesture recognition is also shown in the above figures.

The image above shows the results of the temperature and pulse reading of the user with- out sounding an alarm for they are in the specified normal range. The above image indicates the different outputs based on the different gestures recognized such as "I need to life my bed" and "I need to go to the Restroom."

Using the algorithm of calculating the distance from the ear, the eye movement is detected by virtue of there being any change in the calculated distance.

In the below Table 2 the comparison of the output of the two different algorithms (SVM and Naive Bayes) is given. By comparing the result it is evident that SVM is more accurate than the Naive Bayes algorithm for the synergy of the problem. Also, we can conclude from the table that SVM draws a wider gap between two sets of classification which helps us to achieve better classification while Naive Bayes sometimes fails to judge the boundary conditions and gives the wrong classification.

Figure 7. Arduino reading

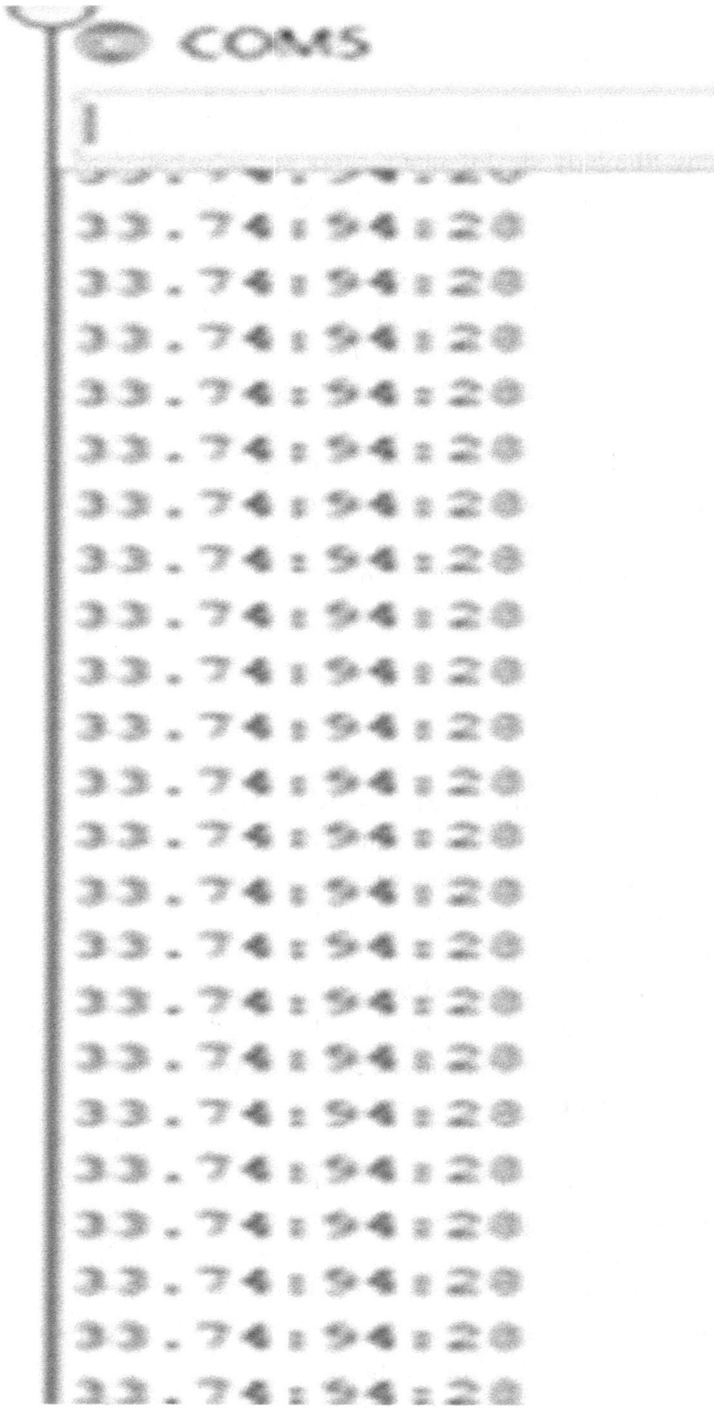

The results of the model based on machine learning that uses the learned information and the input from the dashboard along with the SVM Classifier method are displayed in the above table. Here, it can be seen that the model depicts the patient as being in a normal state, which is accurate given that the patient's vital signs are all within normal limits.

Figure 8. Web interface for the patient

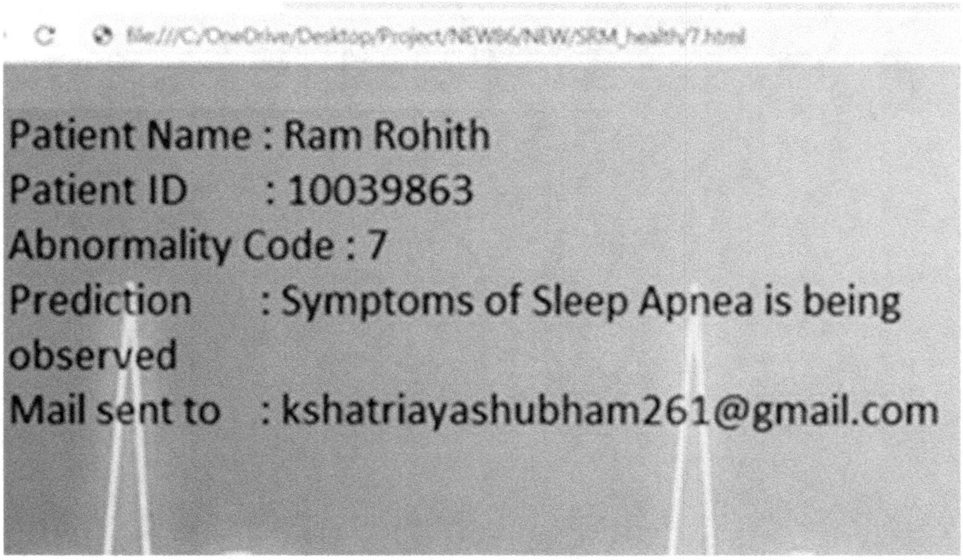

Figure 9. View of email notification

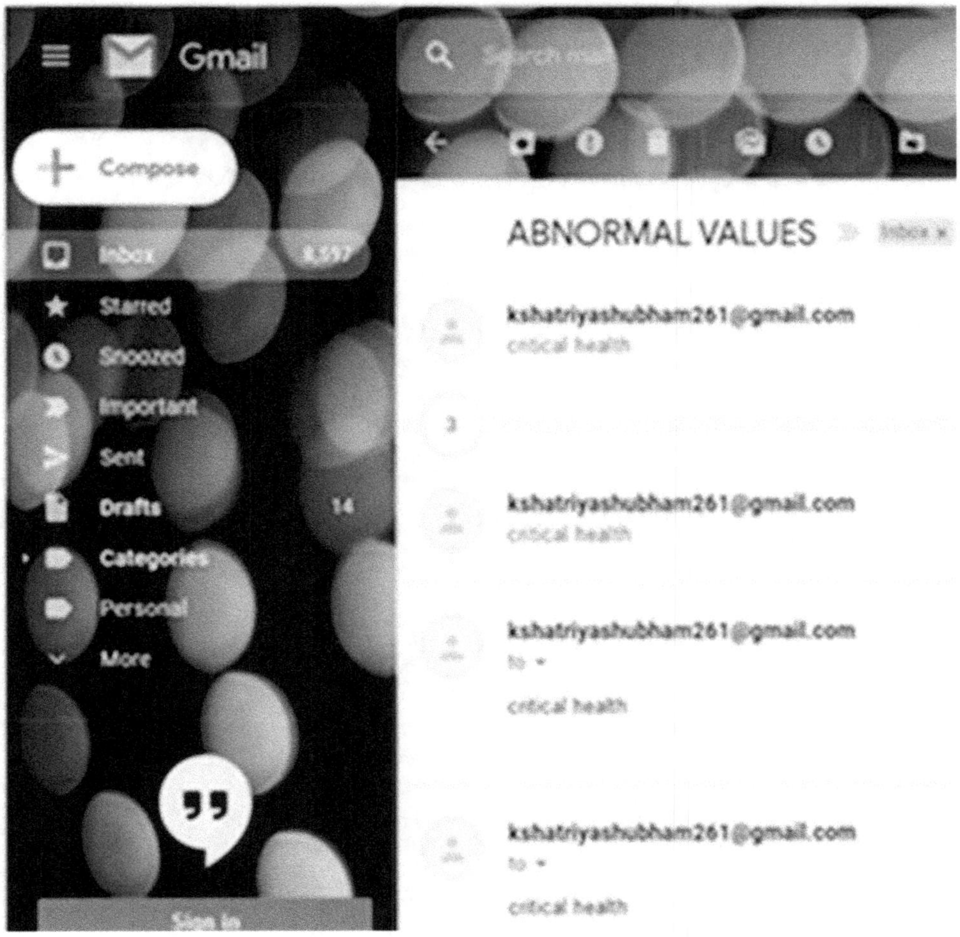

Figure 10. Variation in pulse readings over days

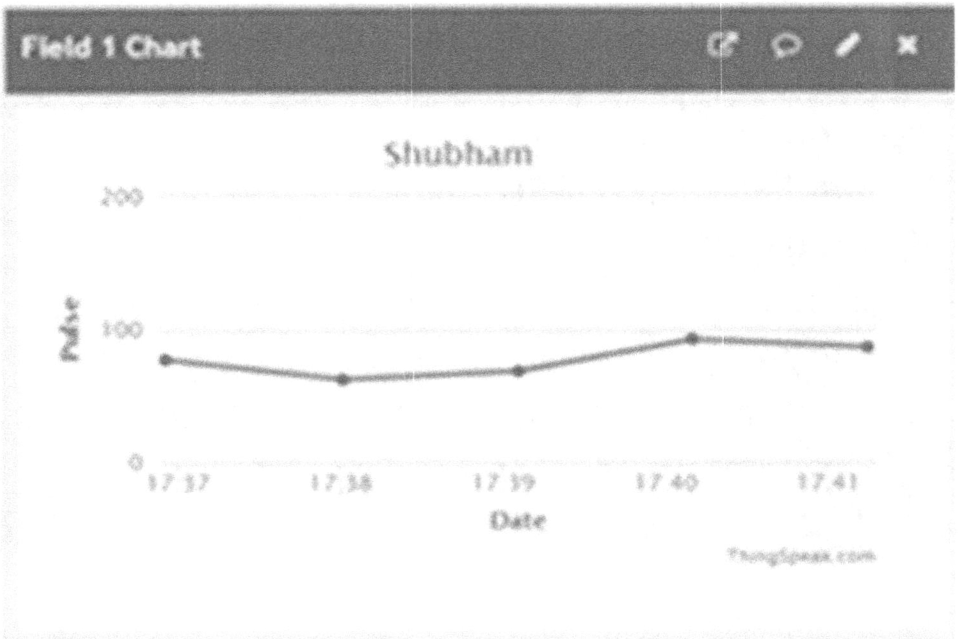

Figure 11. Variation in temperature readings over days

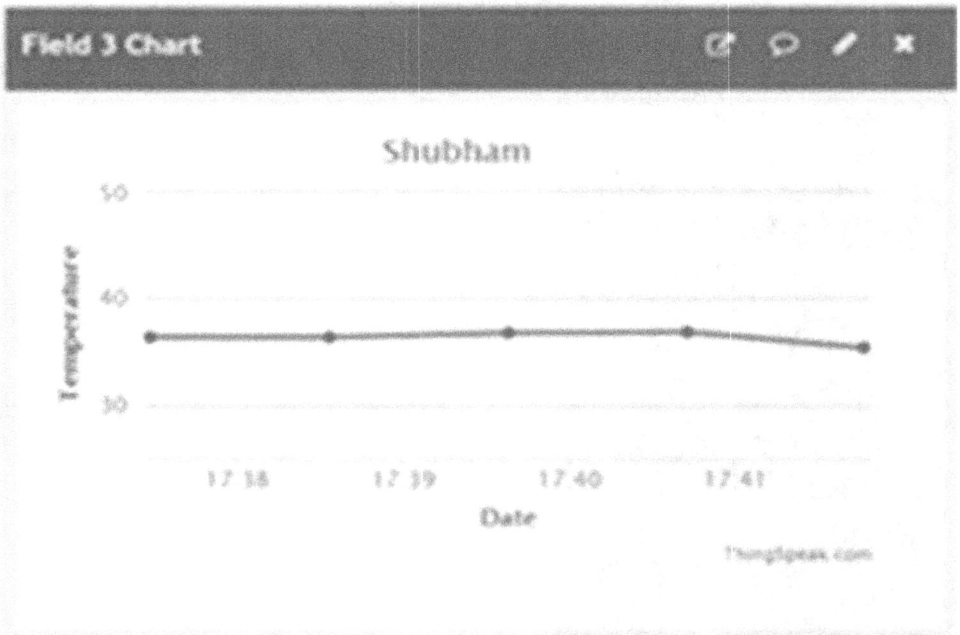

Figure 12. Variation in pulse readings over days

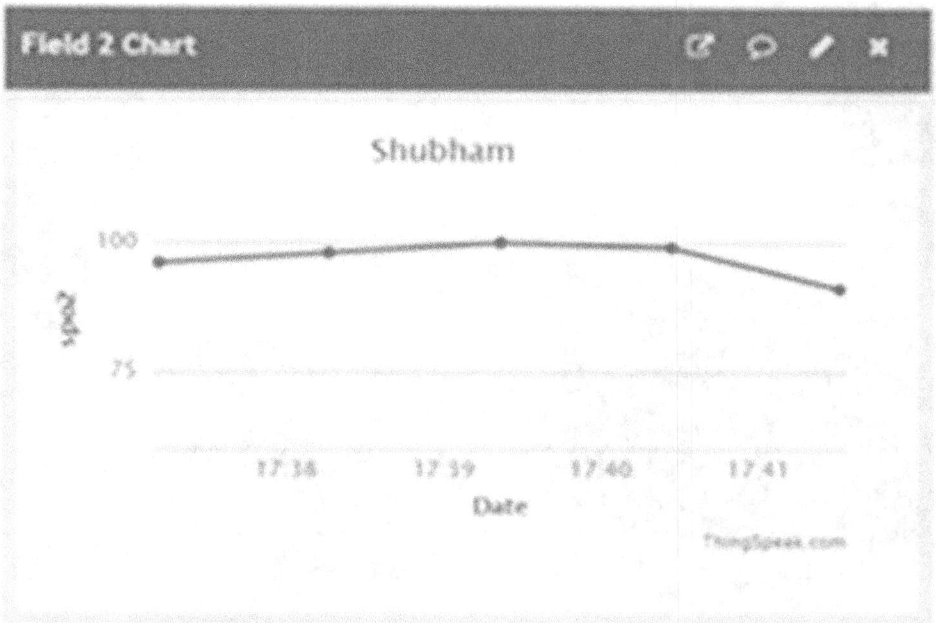

Figure 13. Gesture recognition with eye-lid movement

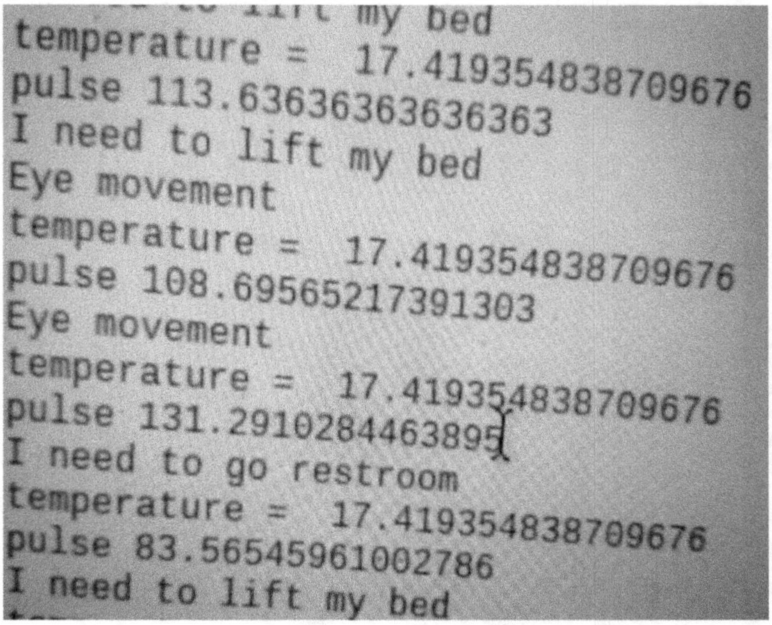

Figure 14. Eye movement recognition

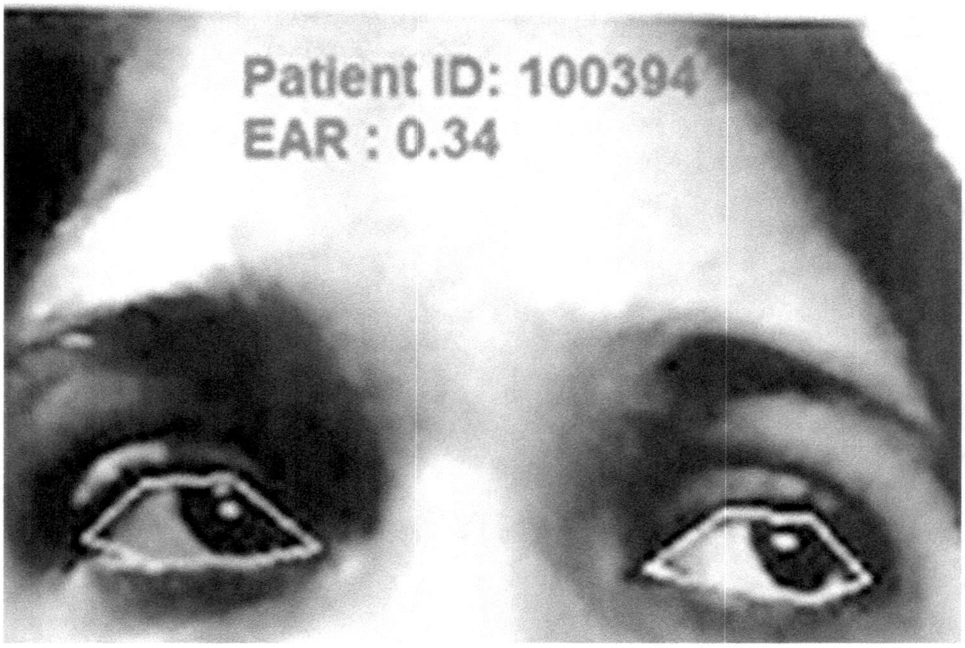

Figure 15. View of vital signs and gesture recognition

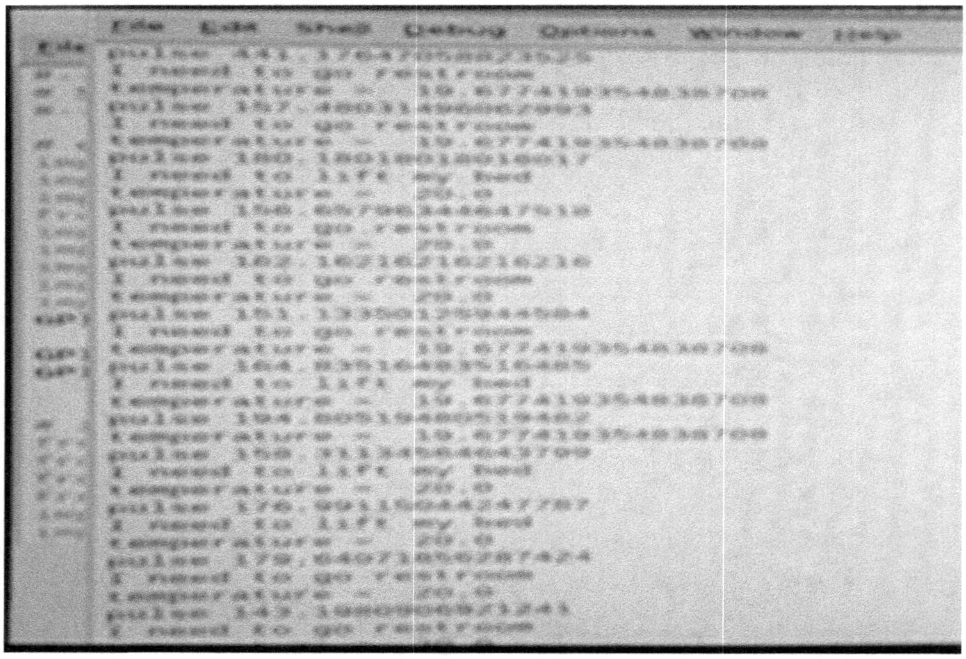

Table 2. Output of the disease prediction using Naive Bayes and SVM algorithms

S.no	pulse	spo2	temp	Expected output	Naive Bayes	SVM
1.	95	94	36.9	0	0	0
2.	99	97	36.5	0	0	0
3.	86	98	38.6	1	1	1
4.	99	97	42.3	1	1	1
5.	103	80	36.7	7	7	7
6.	114	98	37.3	3	3	3
7.	100	99	37.3	0	0	0
8.	120	73	42.5	6	6	6
9.	101	67	37.1	7	5	7
10.	122	78	36.7	7	7	7
11.	154	98	37	4	4	4
12.	91	88	36.5	5	5	5
13.	108	88	42.3	6	6	6
14.	114	56	36.7	7	7	7
15.	79	98	38.1	1	0	1
16.	198	97	37	4	4	4
17.	103	80	42.5	6	6	6
18.	89	95	42.5	1	1	1
19.	63	96	40.2	1	1	1
20.	83	78	36.7	5	5	5

8. CONCLUSION

Hence the proposed disease surveillance system has exploited the cloud-assisted IoT and machine learning-based architecture. The controlling of sensors and information processing tasks were accomplished with help of Arduino. Through this system, the temperature, Heartbeat, and spo2 levels were continuously monitored. Through different sensors, it was possible to gauge the life sign quantities in real time. This work has incorporated machine learning algorithms for the prediction of various virus-based diseases. We trained a machine learning algorithm on the raw data set to increase the prediction accuracy. The utilization of SVM and NN algorithm-based calculations made the systems progressively precise and powerful. In cases where the information changes, due to live transmission an emergency alert was sounded if the specifications of the patient go above or beyond a threshold data. Their movement and gestures are also monitored to make communication easy or alert the doctors if attention is required. The current system aims to equip healthcare facilities with being the ability to provide effective diagnosis and prompt attention. The aforementioned collection of patient data and monitoring will enable world- class consultation and assistance possible for patients in remote areas which will therefore increases chance of recovery with enhanced medical care and facilities at a relatively lower cost. All these systems together helped in saving the patients from the critical situation and kept a watch on a patient's health in an effective manner. As a continuation of this work, the GSM and IR sensors would be used to overcome the range limitations of Wifi devices. Smartphones can also become a health monitoring node and interact between multiple sensors. The various other algorithms and datasets may be used accordingly to make the systems more accurate. To improve the visual appeal of the results, raspberry pi may be used for the easy presentation of the monitoring information.

REFERENCES

Adeniyi, E. A., Ogundokun, R. O., & Awotunde, J. B. (2021). IoMT-Based Wearable Body Sensors Network Healthcare Monitoring System. In IoT in Healthcare and Ambient Assisted Living. Studies in Computational Intelligence (vol. 933). Springer. doi:10.1007/978-981-15-9897-5_6

Barsocchi, P., Bartoli, G., Betti, M., Girardi, M., Mammolito, S., Pellegrini, D., & Zini, G. (2020). Wireless Sensor Networks for Continuous Structural Health Monitoring of Historic Masonry Towers. *International Journal of Architectural Heritage*. Advance online publication. doi:10.1080/15583058.2020.1719229

Bhola, J., Soni, S., & Kakarla, J. (2019). A scalable and energy-efficient MAC protocol for sensor and actor networks. *International Journal of Communication Systems*, *32*(13), e4057. doi:10.1002/dac.4057

de Oliveira, B. C. F., Marció, B. S., & Flesch, R. C. C. (2021). Enhanced damage measurement in a metal specimen through the image fusion of tone-burst vibro-acoustography and pulse-echo ultrasound data. *Measurement, 167*. doi:10.1016/j.measurement.2020.108445

Hady, A. A. (2020). Duty cycling centralized hierarchical routing protocol with content analysis duty cycling mechanism for wireless sensor networks. *Computer Systems Science and Engineering*, *35*(5), 347–355. doi:10.32604/csse.2020.35.347

Moqadam, A. N., & Kazemi, R. (2019). A novel triple-band microwave chip-less sensor tag for structural health monitoring applications. *Electromagnetics*, *39*(7), 524–535. doi:10.1080/02726343.2019.1658168

Palagan, C.A., Gupta, S., & Dhas, A.J. (2022). An IoT scheme based on wireless body area sensors for healthcare applications. *SIViP*. doi:10.1007/s11760-022-02294-0

ShayestehTabatabaei. (2020). A novel fault tolerance energy-aware clustering method via social spider optimization (SSO) and fuzzy logic and mobile sink in wireless sensor networks (WSNs). *Computer Systems Science and Engineering*, *35*(6), 477–494. doi:10.32604/csse.2020.35.477

Shrestha, K., Alsadoon, A., Prasad, P. W. C., Maag, A., Thu Hang, P. D., & Elchouemi, A. (2019). Health Monitoring based on Wireless Sensor Networks: A Comprehensive Framework. *2019 11th International Conference on Knowledge and Systems Engineering (KSE)*, 1-6. 10.1109/KSE.2019.8919390

Wang, J., Gao, Y., Yin, X., Li, F., & Kim, H.-J. (2018). An enhanced PEGASIS algorithm with mobile sink support for wireless sensor networks. *Wireless Communications and Mobile Computing*, *2018*, 9472075. doi:10.1155/2018/9472075

Wang, J., Ju, C., Gao, Y., Sangaiah, A. K., & Kim, G. J. (2018). A PSO based energy efficient coverage control algorithm for wireless sensor networks. *Computers, Materials & Continua*, *56*(3), 433–446.

Chapter 4
Privacy Preservation and Cloud Computing

Rahul K. Patel
https://orcid.org/0000-0003-1175-0635
Illinois Institute of Technology, Chicago, USA

Piyush Gidwani
Sikkim Manipal University, India

Nikunj R. Patel
University of Wisconsin-Madison, Madison, USA

ABSTRACT

As the organization moves to cloud computing to take advantage of lower cost and higher efficiencies and availability, privacy and confidentiality concerns remain a challenge. Modern techniques to manage such challenges with careful evaluation are required to implement effective strategies for privacy protection in cloud computing. In this chapter, various needs for privacy protection of sensitive data are discussed. In turn, the fundamental principles of security protection measures in cloud computing are explored. Later in the chapter, various strategies for ensuring privacy in the cloud are compared and discussed. These methods are examined in the context of allowing authorized access. preventing unauthorized access and ensuring data integrity. Furthermore, the pitfalls and weaknesses of each technique and available workarounds to avoid such vulnerability have been discussed in detail. This chapter also covers a detailed comparative analysis of these privacy preservation and secure data storage techniques, exploring their interplay and potential effective combinations.

PRIVACY RIGHTS AND HISTORICAL BACKGROUND

The concept of privacy is deeply embedded in the fabric of human society with its rich and complex history. The delineation of private and public spaces was a fundamental aspect of societal structure even in ancient civilizations. Over time, the understanding and the importance of privacy have evolved,

DOI: 10.4018/979-8-3693-0593-5.ch004

shaped by cultural, social, and technological changes and the digital age has brought about a significant shift in the perception of privacy. The ease with which personal information can be collected, stored, and shared using information technology and the Internet has created new challenges and complexities, and has raised profound questions about the nature and extent of privacy rights.

The Universal Declaration of Human Rights (UDHR) by the United Nations General Assembly defined and acknowledged that privacy is one of the essential human rights and sought protection for it. Article 12 of the UDHR states that "No individual shall be subject to random or capricious infringement of their privacy, family, home, or correspondence, or assaults on their honor and reputation. Everyone is entitled to the defense of the law against such infringements or assaults" (Woods, 2019). The UN Privacy Law is also rooted in the principles outlined in the UDHR and sets out a comprehensive framework for the protection of personal data and includes evolving technological landscapes and the new challenges they present to privacy rights protection.

Privacy is a necessity and not a luxury, for the functioning of a free and democratic society. It serves as a bulwark against unwarranted intrusion into personal life and provides personal space free from scrutiny. Privacy also underpins many other fundamental rights, including freedom of speech, freedom of thought, and freedom of association (Rothstein & Tovino, 2019). In the context of the digital age, various frameworks and guidelines have been developed to help organizations protect personal data and manage privacy risks emphasizing the importance of privacy by design and encourage organizations to consider privacy risks from the outset providing a systematic and structured approach to managing information security risks and protecting personal data.

PRIVACY PRESERVATION ENVIRONMENT AND REQUIREMENTS

The cloud environment, characterized by the storage and processing of vast amounts of data, presents unique challenges to privacy preservation and necessitates robust privacy protection measures. Various strategies and techniques are implemented to preserve privacy in the cloud environment such as data anonymization, where personal identifiers are removed from data before it is stored in the cloud; encryption, where data is transformed into a format that can only be read by those with the necessary decryption key; and access control, where measures are put in place to ensure that only authorized individuals can access certain data. Furthermore, privacy-by-design approaches are increasingly being adopted where implementing privacy protection measures from the outset of system design and development are required.

In the United States, the absence of federal regulation due to lack of support from political partied (Iqbal, 2020) on privacy has led to individual states crafting their own privacy regulations. These regulations are primarily focused on two aspects, consumer rights, and business obligations. Consumer Rights encompass the rights of consumers to control their personal data including the right to make decisions for data movement, opt-out or opt-in, and against automated decision-making. Business Obligations, on the other hand, refer to the responsibilities that businesses have in relation to handling consumer data including the obligation to provide notice, be transparent about data handling practices, ensure privacy in operational programs and conduct formal risk assessments for privacy concerns and implement security projects or procedures to protect privacy. They are prohibited from discriminating against consumers who exercise their privacy rights. Many US States have already enacted comprehensive consumer privacy laws. For example, California enacted the California Consumer Privacy Act of 2018 (CCPA). These laws vary in their specifics, but they all aim to protect the privacy rights of consumers and place obligations on businesses to handle personal data responsibly.

In conclusion, privacy preservation requirements and measures are complex in nature, and it is an even more complex and multifaceted issue in the cloud environment. This challenge requires a combination of timely technical, procedural, and regulatory measures. As cloud computing continues to evolve and becomes increasingly prevalent, the importance of privacy preservation will only continue to grow. It is therefore crucial for both individuals and organizations to understand consumer privacy rights and business obligations under the various privacy regulations, and to effectively respond to protect sensitive data.

Categories of Personally Identifiable Information (PII)

In privacy and data protection, the categorization of Personally Identifiable Information (PII) is especially important to decide the scope of obligations and requirements. PII is any information about an individual that can be used to distinguish or trace an identity of individuals identity, such as name, social security number, date and place of birth, mother's maiden name, or biometric records; and any other information that is linked or linkable to an individual, such as medical, educational, financial, and employment information (McCallister et al., 2010). Direct identifiers are pieces of information that can independently identify an individual. These include:

Personal identification number: Personal identification numbers (PIN) such as social security, passport, driver's license, taxpayer identification, financial account, or credit card number.

Name: This includes first name, last name, middle name, or any combination thereof. Names, especially when combined with other pieces of information like a date of birth, can uniquely identify individuals.

Address: This includes both physical address and electronic address that can be used to locate individuals and, in some cases, infer additional information about them.

Phone number: This includes both landline and mobile numbers that can be used to contact and locate individuals.

Indirect identifiers are pieces of information that may not independently identify an individual but can do so when combined with other pieces of information.

Date of birth: While there may be many people with the same date of birth when combined with information like a name or address, it can be used to uniquely identify individuals.

Place of birth: The place of birth can be a useful identifier when combined with other pieces of information.

Mother's maiden name: This piece of information is often used as a security question in various systems and, when combined with other identifiers, can be used to identify individuals.

PII can also include any other information linked or linkable to an individual, such as medical, educational, financial, and employment information (McCallister et al., 2010). This information can be used to distinguish or trace an individual's identity, either alone or when combined with other information that is linked or linkable to a specific individual (FAR 52.224-3 Privacy Training 2023).

Each type of PII carries with it a certain level of risk if it were to be compromised, and as such, requires a corresponding level of protection. Due to the distributed nature of cloud computing, PII data can be stored and processed in multiple locations and may cross national borders making the task of ensuring that all PII is adequately protected challenging. Organizations can implement effective data protection strategies including encryption, access controls, and other security measures by understanding the categories of PII and the risks associated with them. Furthermore, the categorization of PII can assist organizations in complying with various data protection regulations that require organizations to take specific measures to protect certain types of PII.

Analyzing Consumer Rights and Business Obligations

An understanding of the progression of privacy measures can be gained by examining the critical fundamental elements and related roles and responsibilities for preserving the privacy of the data in the cloud environment. These elements are typically classified into two categories — those concerning protections afforded to consumers, and those detailing the obligations imposed on businesses.

Consumer Rights: Broad Categories in Data Privacy

Consumer rights include the decision-making capabilities for many different actions for the PII related to themselves.

Access rights: Access rights denote a consumer's ability to retrieve information about what specific personal data is collected, information shared or disclosed with third parties from a data handler. Access rights, in the context of data privacy, refer to a consumer's entitlement to not only access and retrieve their personal data collected by a business or data custodian but also to understand if and how this data has been shared with third parties. The identities or categories of these third parties should also be disclosed whenever the consumer wishes if the business or data handler still possesses the data. Different authorities might stipulate specific timelines for businesses to adhere to such requests. This right is universally applicable. However, its extent and mode of implementation could vary based on specific data protection laws and regulations prevalent in different authorities. The objective of access rights is ensuring greater transparency and empower individuals with more control over their personal data and provides consumers with insights into what personal data is held about them and how it is used. Access Right enables consumers to verify the accuracy of their data and request amendments, if necessary and aids them in making more informed decisions about giving further consent for data usage. Access to information allows individuals to scrutinize and evaluate their activities and guarantees the ability to monitor the realization of basic and human rights and other rights guaranteed to individuals (Tiilikka, 2013).

The exercise of the Access Rights begins with the consumer submitting a formal request to the business or data handler often in writing and businesses must respond within a specific time limit as per the specific applicable regulations for the process. Upon receiving the request, the business or data handler needs to provide a copy of the personal data they have about the consumer including the categories of personal data, any third parties to whom the data has been disclosed, the purpose of the data usage, and any other relevant information in a common, easily readable format.

Correction rights: This pertains to a consumer's power to demand the correction of incorrect or outdated personal data. Consumer rights include the request to rectify, erase, or restrict the processing of their data if the information is incorrect, outdated, or used illegitimately. The timeline for exercising these rights is flexible, extending if the data remains under the custodianship of the business or data handler. The exercise and enforcement of these rights may vary, as they are subject to data protection laws specific to different authorities. Correction rights are aimed at guaranteeing the accuracy of personal data managed by businesses or data handlers that is instrumental in maintaining the integrity of personal data and mitigating the risks of potential harm or misunderstandings stemming from incorrect or outdated information. By empowering consumers to amend their personal data, correction rights enhance transparency and bolster data reliability, thereby fostering a sense of trust between consumers and businesses.

The process for exercising correction rights begins with the consumer recognizing an error or outdated information in their personal data held by a business or data handler and submitting the correction request to the respective business or data handler in writing if required by local regulation. Upon receiving the request, the business or data handler must address it by correcting, updating the data, and informing the third-party business associates for such corrections within a specified time limit determined by the relevant data protection laws to ensure that any decisions or actions taken based on inaccurate or outdated data can be revised or corrected, as necessary.

Deletion rights: In the context of data privacy, deletion rights represent the entitlement of a consumer to demand the removal of their personal data that is held by a business or data handler. The application of deletion rights can be set in motion at any time the consumer decides typically when they no longer want their personal data in the possession of the business or data handler, or if they perceive the data processing to be inappropriate or illicit. Deletion rights have universal relevance, applying to all businesses and data handlers operating across both physical and digital realms. However, their enforcement and scope often depend on the local data protection regulations. The objective of deletion rights is to provide consumers with a certain level of control over their personal data to allow consumers to demand data removal thereby helping to protect individual privacy and reduce the risk of unauthorized data use, abuse, or disclosure. Enabling consumers to request data deletion adds an additional layer of transparency to data handling procedures and practices, thus cultivating a relationship of trust between businesses and consumers.

The exercise of deletion rights typically commences when a consumer decides they no longer want their personal data to be retained by a business or data handler, or when they believe that the data has been handled improperly or unlawfully with a formal request for deletion is usually submitted by the consumer typically in writing to the organization in question. The business must then proceed with the deletion of the consumer's personal data, given that certain conditions are met, and no legitimate reasons exist for retaining it. The business or data handler is responsible for processing the consumer's request within a stipulated time limit defined by the applicable data protection laws. Business or data handler is obligated to inform their third-party business associates about the deletion request so that the data can be removed from their databases as well. This process ensures a comprehensive execution of the consumer's deletion rights and prevents any further use or disclosure of the deleted data.

Processing opt-out rights: In the context of data privacy, processing opt-out rights are fundamentally about empowering consumers to limit a business's authority to process their personal data and can be invoked at any point when a consumer has concerns about how their data is being processed or used. These rights remain valid and applicable if the personal data remains within the business's possession. The application of these opt-out rights spans the globe, affecting businesses operating in every sector and space, be it physical or digital. However, the practical application and scope of these rights might differ owing to the distinct data protection laws of different authorities. Opt-out rights aim to fortify individuals' control over their personal data, bestowing upon them the power to limit its processing and enabling consumers to protect their privacy and curb potential misuse of their personal data by bring a level of transparency to the data processing activities of businesses and in turn fostering a strengthened bond of trust between consumers and businesses.

The exercise of processing opt-out rights begins when a consumer decides they want to limit how a business uses or processes their personal data. Request starts with the consumer submitting a formal opt-out request to the business and intern the business responding and complying within a defined time limit, as determined by the applicable regulations. In the absence of any legal exceptions or reasons for continued processing, the business is expected to cease or limit the processing of the consumer's personal data in accordance with the request. Businesses may be required to notify third parties, with whom they have shared the consumer's data, about the opt-out request. This process, in its entirety, affirms the consumer's control over their personal data and helps maintain a level of transparency about how businesses handle and process personal data.

Portability rights: This refers to a consumer's right to demand that personal data about them be disclosed and recognized as the consumer's authority to demand that their personal data, which is retained by a business, be provided in a universally understood file format. Consumers can assert these rights whenever they desire to obtain their personal data in a format that simplifies its transfer to different service providers. Portability rights hold a global significance and affect businesses operating across both digital and physical platforms depending on the individual data protection laws enforced by various authorities. The underlying objective of portability rights is to boost consumer control over personal data by enabling consumers to transition between service providers without the loss of their personal data. These rights foster competition and provide flexibility.

To invoke portability rights, consumers must first submit a formal request to the business that holds their data by specifying widely recognized and machine-readable data format, such as CSV or XML according to the specific applicable regulations. Upon receipt of this request, the business is obligated to respond unless there are legally valid reasons for the business to refuse the request. In some situations, businesses may be required to assist in the direct transfer of the data to a new service provider. This aspect of portability rights is particularly valuable for consumers who wish to switch service providers without losing their personal data.

Sales opt-out rights: This represents a consumer's right to refuse the sale of their personal data to third parties and embodied in a consumer's privilege to prohibit the sale of their personal data to third parties by a business. These rights hold no specified time constraints, empowering consumers to exercise them at any point they deem necessary. This privilege extends universally, affecting businesses and data handlers across the globe, irrespective of whether they operate in physical or digital landscapes as per the applicable regulations. The fundamental purpose of sales opt-out rights is to increase individuals' control over their personal data acting as deterrent against the potential misuse by third parties. By enabling consumers to exercise these rights, businesses can enhance the transparency of their data practices and help reinforce the trust between them and their consumers.

The execution of sales opt-out rights typically involves a formal request made by the consumer to the business or data handler in writing, specifying that the consumer does not consent to the sale of their personal data to third parties. The business is usually required to acknowledge and respond to such requests within a stipulated period. Compliance mechanisms and procedures can vary, depending on the specific privacy regulations of the district in which the business operates. Some businesses provide easily accessible 'opt-out' options in their privacy settings, thereby streamlining the process for consumers to exercise this right.

Sensitive data processing opt-in rights: This involves a consumer's right to provide consent prior to a business processing their sensitive data. Sensitive data processing opt-in rights alludes to the prerogative of a consumer to grant explicit permission prior to the processing of their sensitive personal data by a business. These rights come into effect any time a business intends to process such data, with no pre-determined timeline, making them continuously applicable if the data is held by the business. These rights impact businesses across many physical or digital platforms. However, differences in data protection laws across diverse authorities may result in variations in the application and enforcement of these rights. The fundamental objective of sensitive data processing opt-in rights is to bolster safeguards surrounding a consumer's sensitive data. These rights allow consumers to exert significant control over their personal information, ensuring that sensitive data is only processed upon obtaining the consumer's explicit consent.

To exercise sensitive data processing opt-in rights, the consumer must first be informed about the intended processing of their sensitive data by the business. The business is obligated to provide explicit, clear, and comprehensive information about why and how the sensitive data will be processed. Once informed, the consumer can provide or withhold their clear affirmative consent so that it cannot be assumed through inaction. If consent is provided, the business can then proceed with the processing of the consumer's sensitive data. Withdrawal of the consumer consent should be easy to request at any point and businesses are required to cease processing the sensitive data from that point onwards. The rights and processes for withdrawal of consent should be clearly communicated to consumers and may vary according to specific local regulatory requirements.

Rights against automated decision-making: Rights against automated decision-making restricts a business from making decisions about a consumer solely based on an automated process without human intervention and denote a consumer's privilege to challenge decisions about them, which are derived from automated operations devoid of human intervention. These rights become applicable when a business employs an automated process to make significant decisions concerning a consumer unrestricted by definitive timelines and applicable worldwide operating in physical and digital landscapes. Yet, the precise implementation and scope of these rights may diverge owing to the distinctive data protection legislation prevalent in various authorities. The essence of these rights against automated decision-making lies in safeguarding consumers from potential inaccuracies, biases, or unfair outcomes that could emanate from decisions solely dictated by automated processes. They emphasize the indispensable role of human intervention in decision-making processes involving personal data, thereby nurturing an environment of fairness, transparency, and trust in data practices between businesses and consumers.

To exercise the rights against automated decision-making, consumers can communicate their requests to the business with clear objection of decisions made purely based on automated processes. Following such a request, businesses are required to review the decision-making process including re-evaluating the decision using a method that includes human intervention. The consumer should be provided with a platform to express their point of view and contest the decision. It is essential for businesses to respond to these requests within a reasonable time limit, ensuring they comply with the relevant data protection regulations.

Private right of action: Private right of action stands as a right allowing consumers to pursue civil damages from businesses for contravention of a statute. These rights are invoked when a consumer perceives that a breach of statutory duty related to their personal data has occurred by a business. These rights remain effective if the breach persists. The private right of action impacts businesses and data handlers operating in both physical and online domains. However, the specific implementation and extent of these rights may be influenced by the data protection regulations. The fundamental goal of the private right of action is to offer a legal channel for consumers to seek restitution for any violation of their data rights and stands as an effective deterrent against negligent or improper handling of personal data by businesses, ensuring a level of accountability underscoring the importance of transparent and lawful data practices.

The private right of action can be executed by a consumer through the initiation of a lawsuit against the business that they believe has violated a data privacy statute related to their personal information. This often involves the engagement of legal counsel, the accumulation of substantial evidence supporting their claim, and the submission of the case to the relevant court. Depending on the area and specific nature of the case, the court procedure may vary, but it includes stages such as pleadings, discovery, trial, and an appeal. If the consumer successfully proves the violation, the court can order the business to pay civil damages as a form of redress. Thus, through this mechanism, the private right of action serves as a potent tool for consumers to protect their data privacy rights.

Business Obligations: Key Requirements in Data Privacy

Several obligations and restrictions are imposed on businesses concerning data privacy and protection. Common requirements are typically grouped into the following categories:

Age-based opt-in requirements: Age-based opt-in requirements constraints businesses, obligating them to implement an opt-in default for the sale of personal data pertaining to consumers below a specified age. Grounded in the broad spectrum of data privacy regulations, age-based opt-in requirements serve as constraints mandating businesses to establish an opt-in default for selling personal data pertaining to consumers below a certain age threshold. These provisions come into play when a business intends to transact personal data concerning underage consumers and remain pertinent till it handles data. These age-based opt-in requirements are instituted to provide an additional layer of safeguarding for young consumers, who may not fully comprehend the implications of their personal data being sold. By compelling an opt-in default, these requirements transfer the power of controlling the sale of their children's personal data to the guardians encouraging a responsible utilization of personal data. Such requirements are universal regardless of business locations or data format. Nevertheless, their actual enforcement and extent might differ owing to the local data protection regulations.

Implementation of age-based opt-in requirements necessitates businesses to adopt systems that accurately verify the age of their consumers. This implies that explicit consent must be obtained, typically from a parent or guardian, prior to the sale of personal data. The actual mechanics of implementing these requirements may involve the integration of age-verification software or other stringent identification checks. Compliance with these requirements promotes responsible data practices and ensures adherence to data privacy laws and regulations.

Notice and transparency mandates: Businesses must keep consumers informed about specific data practices, privacy activities, and/or privacy programs. The obligation to notify of a data breach forms a particularly powerful incentive for strengthening security and avoiding data breaches (Selvadurai et al., 2017).

Risk assessment duties: This entails the obligation for businesses to carry out formal evaluations of risks associated with privacy and/or security initiatives or procedures. Within the expansive realm of data privacy regulations, the term 'risk assessment duties' is employed to represent the obligation entrusted to businesses. This obligation entails conducting formal assessments that evaluate potential risks associated with privacy and/or security initiatives or procedures. Businesses find themselves faced with these duties when they launch new initiatives or significantly alter existing ones that have a bearing on privacy or security. Importantly, these duties do not cease to exist post-implementation, but continue to be relevant for as long as business operations can potentially influence personal data privacy or security.

Risk assessment duties have a universal impact, reaching businesses across all spheres, regardless of whether they operate in physical or digital spaces. However, the specifics of these duties, including their interpretation and scope, are likely to diverge across different districts. This divergence can be attributed to the unique data protection laws and regulations prevalent in each district. At its core, the concept of risk assessment duties has been instituted with the intent to identify proactively any potential threats to personal data. Once these threats have been identified, businesses are expected to devise strategies to alleviate these risks. The ripple effect of these actions leads to enhanced security of personal data, fortifying the trust and confidence that consumers place in businesses. The actualization of these duties involves systematic identification, analysis, and evaluation of potential risks associated with privacy and security initiatives. Businesses are expected to develop and implement risk management strategies, encompassing steps such as risk identification, assessment, mitigation, and ongoing monitoring. This process should be transparent and iterative, capable of adapting to evolving risks and legislative landscapes.

Discrimination prohibition: This signifies a restriction against businesses behaving differently towards consumers who exercise their rights compared to those who do not. Enshrined in the expansive domain of data privacy laws, 'discrimination prohibition (in the context of exercising rights)' is a restrictive principle that bars businesses from treating consumers who exercise their data privacy rights differently from those who do not. This notion swings into action when consumers exercise their privacy rights, its relevancy stretching indefinitely to all such instances. This principle exhibits a global reach, impacting businesses operating across physical and digital realms alike. However, one must bear in mind that the enforcement and scope of this prohibition could exhibit variations due to the diverse data protection laws and regulations implemented across different districts.

At its core, the rationale for discrimination prohibition lies in emboldening consumers to assert their rights without the trepidation of differential treatment. It strives to maintain a level playing field for all consumers, thus cultivating an atmosphere of respect for consumer rights, and solidifying the trust inherent in business practices. Businesses are bound by this prohibition and are expected to respect it under all circumstances, contributing to an ecosystem where privacy rights are valued, and discrimination is eschewed. To uphold the principle of discrimination prohibition, businesses are required to implement policies and procedures that ensure consumers are treated equitably regardless of their decision to exercise their privacy rights. This can include regular training for employees on non-discriminatory practices, monitoring, and auditing of business operations to identify and address potential discriminatory practices, and maintaining transparency with consumers about their privacy rights and how they are upheld by the business.

Purpose or processing limitations: Drawing from the model of the EU General Data Protection Regulation, this restrictive framework prevents the collection or processing of personal data unless it is for a well-defined purpose. Under the umbrella of data privacy regulations, 'Purpose or processing limitations' emerge as a restrictive construct, taking cues from the EU General Data Protection Regulation (GDPR). This construct restricts businesses from collecting or processing personal data unless there exists a well-articulated purpose for doing so. These limitations come into play right from the instance a business initiates the collection or processing of personal data. Their relevance persists throughout the entire life cycle of the data, as long as the data remains within custody or under the control of the business.

Despite these limitations having their roots in the European Union's data protection framework, their impact extends to businesses around the globe, encompassing all sectors and platforms, irrespective of whether they operate in physical or digital domains. However, the practical implementation and the extent to which these limitations are enforced can vary. Such variations are often a result of the distinct data protection laws and regulations that are in effect within different districts. At its core, the principal intent of these purposes or processing limitations is to safeguard personal data from unnecessary collection or processing. This framework of limitations fosters a culture of respect for individual privacy rights by encouraging businesses to restrict their data collection and processing to well-defined purposes. It thereby enhances the culture of trust and promotes compliance with data privacy norms.

Businesses are required to clearly define the purpose for which they are collecting and processing the consumer's personal data. They should ensure that the data is not used beyond this specified purpose, and this should be communicated clearly to the consumers. The data collected must be adequate, relevant, and limited to what is necessary for the intended purpose. Any deviation from the stated purpose could lead to legal consequences, making it incumbent upon businesses to strictly adhere to these limitations.

In summary, consumer rights and business obligations ensure that data protection principles are followed. Data protection principles are geared towards making sure that the collected information is used fairly, lawfully, and transparently, used for specified, explicit purposes, used in a way that is adequate, relevant, and limited to only what is necessary, accurate, and, kept up to date, kept for no longer than necessary and handled in a way that ensures appropriate security, including protection against unlawful or unauthorized processing, access, loss, destruction, or damage (Rachur, Putman, & Fisher, 2022).

DATA PROTECTION IN CLOUD ENVIRONMENT

Cloud computing offers many benefits from IT operations and management perspectives such as scalability and efficiency, and cost management. As more IT systems are created or migrated to the cloud environment, data protection in a cloud environment is becoming a more critical aspect. As a result, the task of continuously preserving the privacy of data stored and processed in the cloud is becoming a unique challenge and imposing privacy risks related to data protection. Cloud Environment provides some new and unique capabilities that can be implemented to handle the challenges related to data privacy requirements. Cloud implementations can offer the ability to self-manage confidential information. Self-management can include granting users the ability to opt in, opt-out, delete, download, correct, and manage their data (Bannerman & Orasch, 2020).

Data Classification

Data classification is an essential step and a prerequisite in managing data security and protection on only in the cloud but in any environment. A well-architected and implemented data classification approach based on its sensitivity, criticality, and regulatory requirements. In turn, it helps identify and implement appropriate privacy protection control and resources in the most effective manner to ensure compliance with privacy-related regulations. The following steps must be taken to be prepared for efficient and effective control implementations in cloud environments.

Data Classification Indicators: The cloud environment provides fundamental classification capabilities for well-known data related to privacy regulation for all major regulatory frameworks around the world. This includes personally identifiable information (PII), Protected Health Information (PHI), financial data, intellectual property (IP), confidential business information (CBI), Controlled Unrestricted Information (CUI) and many more. Most of the cloud capabilities include machine learning (ML) and artificial intelligence (AI) capabilities that understand relations among various data fragments and provide automated classification mechanism for clusters of related data fragments. Organizations can use these prepackaged cloud capabilities to tag or label the data with a classification indicator with various levels to represent the sensitivity and criticality of data. For example, you can use labels like "Extremely Confidential," "Confidential," "For Internal Use Only," "Non-Confidential" or "Public" to denote distinct levels of data classification.

Data Handling Criteria: Organizations must use the data classification indicators, tags, and labels to decide the criteria that should be used for handling the classified data while storing, in transit, or while processing it. Information handling decisions should be taken considering the factors such as the potential financial and reputational impact on the organization if the data is compromised or lost, regulatory requirements, contractual obligations, privacy considerations, and requirements for complying with internal policies. The security and privacy of cloud data are important, as regulators, individuals and organizations are concerned that sensitive data might fall into the hands of third parties who can use them for their own purposes (Razaque et al., 2022).

Automated Processes in the Cloud: Leveraging cloud technology solutions supporting matured privacy controls to automate the classification and handling process provides access to the advanced capability without expert skill sets that saves time and money while providing better security and privacy controls. These tools can analyze elements, metadata, standardized formats, and information content to assign appropriate classification labels and invoke handling controls automatically. Matured and global Cloud service providers prepackage the capabilities required for the compliance requirements relevant to the industry, region, and information that the organization is required to handle as a part of their business operation. Such advanced cloud-based tools ensure that organizations and their stakeholder's data are classified and handled in alignment with the requirements for regulatory frameworks such as the Payment Card Industry Data Security Standard (PCI DSS), Health Insurance Portability and Accountability Act (HIPAA) in the USA and General Data Protection Regulation (GDPR) in EU Region.

Regular Review and Updates: Periodic reviews and updates of data classification and handling framework to account for any changes in data sensitivity, business needs, or regulatory requirements is required in the cloud environment to ensure the implementation aligned with requirements as well as reduce the false positives and false negatives. Conduct regular audits and realignments not only to ensure data is appropriately classified and security controls are effective but additionally to direct and steer the cloud-based machine learning and artificial intelligent tools to reduce future errors and anomalies.

Privacy protection framework is an ongoing and evolving process and hence there are many regulations and requirements that are changing. In addition, over time, organizations generate and handle many new and distinct types of data, and hence the data classification must be treated as an ongoing process that requires continuous monitoring, assessment, and revision to changing business and regulatory frameworks. Many aspects of information classification and handling requirements are available as an automated process in cloud environments however many decision points require additional oversights from experts in the field for the correct interpretation of requirements and necessary handling capability to meet these requirements.

Securing Access to the Data

Cloud environment offers matured implementation of access control mechanisms to allow access based on a need-to-know basis. It also offers advanced technological implementation of data encryption for data at rest and in transit to avoid unauthorized access to the data. Encryption helps safeguard data from unauthorized access even if there is a breach or unauthorized disclosure. Security and privacy of data stored, processed, and transmitted to the cloud can be warranted with the use of role-based access and strong encryption algorithms. This approach helps fulfill the consumers' access rights and aids in fulfilling the risk assessment and transparency business obligations.

Authentication for the Data Access

Authentication is an essential security and privacy control in cloud computing for verifying the identity of users or entities attempting to access data and resources hosted on cloud servers. Proper authentication ensures that only authorized personnel can access sensitive information, reducing the risk of data breaches and unauthorized access. Cloud computing supports many traditional as well as modern authentication mechanisms. This approach helps fulfill the consumers' access rights and correction rights, as well as aids in fulfilling the risk assessment and transparency business obligations.

Username and Password: This is the most generic form of authentication, where users provide a unique username and a corresponding password. However, it is essential to enforce strong password policies and encourage users to use two-factor authentication (2FA) for added security. This approach helps fulfill the consumers' access rights and aids in fulfilling the risk assessment obligation.

Multi-Factor Authentication (MFA): Three factors that can be used to authenticate users are the ones that can verify who you are such as retina scans, fingerprints, what you have such as OTP sent to the device that you have, or what you know such as passwords. MFA requires users to provide more than one factor, typically, additional forms of authentication beyond the standard username and password. This can include one-time passwords (OTP) sent to a registered mobile device, fingerprint scans, smart cards, or other biometric methods. MFA enhances authentication security by adding an extra layer of verification. This approach helps fulfill the consumers' access rights and aids in fulfilling the risk assessment obligation.

Single Sign-On (SSO): SSO allows users to log in once and gain access to multiple applications or services without re-entering their credentials each time. SSO is often used to simplify access management and improve user experience while maintaining security. However, SSO authentication schemes are insecure and vulnerable to a wide range of attacks (Manzoor et al., 2019) unless used with other methods to improve security such as MFA. This approach helps fulfill the consumers' access rights and aids in fulfilling the risk assessment obligation.

Public Key Infrastructure (PKI): PKI utilizes cryptographic keys, including public and private keys, for authentication. Users possess a private key known only to them, while the public key is available to anyone for verification. PKI is commonly used for secure communication and user authentication. The security of PKI depends on the trustworthiness and security of the central certificate authority CA which could be a single point of failure hence as an alternative, a blockchain PKI solution can be used which adopts a distributed solution to reduce trust placed in any single party (Khan et al., 2020). This approach helps fulfill the consumers' access rights and aids in fulfilling the risk assessment obligation.

OAuth: OAuth is an authorization framework that allows third-party applications to access resources on behalf of a user. It is an indirect authentication method that enables secure authorization and controlled access to cloud data for the third-party. The OAuth protocol allows users to authenticate using an existing authentication method and eliminates the need to maintain separate user accounts for different applications so that users can use the same credentials across different applications without having to provide their login credentials multiple times (Munonye & Péter, 2021). This approach helps fulfill the consumers' access rights and aids in fulfilling the risk assessment obligation.

Blockchain-Based Authentication: As mentioned in the previous answer, blockchain technology can be utilized to manage user identities securely. Blockchain's tamper-proof nature and decentralized approach offer enhanced security for authentication and access control. Combining the cloud and the blockchain can result in a verifiable, permanent, and unmodified file in terms of data sharing between a private chain, eliminating the primary issue of supervision by allowing anybody permitted to join the network to observe and evaluate the activities transparently (Li, 2022). This approach helps fulfill the consumers' access rights and aids in fulfilling the risk assessment obligation.

Certificate-Based Authentication: This method uses digital certificates issued by a trusted authority. Certificates are used to verify the authenticity of users, devices, or applications before granting access. This approach helps fulfill the consumers' access rights and aids in fulfilling the risk assessment obligation.

It is widespread practice for cloud service customer organizations to use hybrid strategies to implement a combination of these authentication mechanisms offered by the cloud service providers based on their specific security and privacy requirements and the sensitivity of the data being accessed.

Encryption for Data in Transit

Encryption for data in transit is one of the critical security and privacy measures in a cloud environment. It ensures that data remains protected while it is exchanged between the machines. Encrypting data in transit safeguards against unauthorized interception and ensures the confidentiality, integrity, and authenticity of the data. Cloud environments do not offer any new mechanisms compared to traditional environments, however, implementation of the technology in the cloud environment is mostly of a higher level of maturity.

Transport Layer Security (TLS)/Secure Sockets Layer (SSL): TLS and SSL are cryptographic protocols that establish a secure and encrypted connection between a client (e.g., a web browser) and a server (e.g., a cloud server). This encryption ensures that data transmitted over the network remains confidential and cannot be easily intercepted or modified by attackers. This approach helps fulfill the consumers' access rights and aids in fulfilling the risk assessment obligation.

HTTPS (HTTP Secure): HTTPS is an extension of the HTTP protocol that uses TLS/SSL encryption for secure communication between web browsers and servers. It is widely used to protect sensitive data transmitted over the internet, such as login credentials, personal information, and financial data. This approach helps fulfill the consumers' access rights and aids in fulfilling the risk assessment obligation.

IPsec (Internet Protocol Security): IPsec is a suite of protocols that encrypts data at the IP layer. It provides secure communication between devices over an untrusted network, such as the Internet, by encrypting the data packets and verifying their integrity. This approach helps fulfill the consumers' access rights and aids in fulfilling the risk assessment obligation.

VPN (Virtual Private Network): VPNs create a secure and encrypted tunnel between the user's device and the cloud server, allowing remote users to access cloud resources securely over the internet. All data passing through the VPN tunnel is encrypted, preventing eavesdropping and unauthorized access. This approach helps fulfill the consumers' access rights and aids in fulfilling the risk assessment obligation.

SSH (Secure Shell) and SFTP: Secure Shell is a cryptographic network protocol for secure remote access and file transfers. It encrypts data exchanged between the client and the server, protecting sensitive information from interception. Secure shell file transfer protocol (SFTP) is a secure version of the File Transfer Protocol (FTP). It uses SSH for encryption and provides secure and encrypted file transfers between the user's device and the cloud server. This approach helps fulfill the consumers' access rights and aids in fulfilling the risk assessment obligation.

Cloud servers use secure communication protocols like Transport Layer Security (TLS). This ensures that data transmitted between the user's devices and the cloud remains confidential and tamper-proof. Secure file transfer protocols (e.g., SFTP) and virtual private networks (VPNs) can also be employed for secure data transfer in the cloud environment, adding an extra layer of protection to sensitive information (Maheswari et al., 2023). It is essential for cloud service providers and users to implement strong encryption protocols and regularly update them to address any known vulnerabilities. Additionally, organizations should follow best practices for key management to protect encryption keys from unauthorized access, as the security of encrypted data relies heavily on the secrecy of the encryption keys. By employing robust encryption methods for data in transit, cloud environments can significantly enhance their security posture and protect sensitive information from potential unauthorized access-related threats.

Managing Authorization for the Data Access

Authorization mechanisms in the cloud refer to the methods and techniques used to provide authorization to the user, applications, and services for allowing operations such as read, write, execute, modify, or delete access, to cloud resources and services. These mechanisms ensure that only allowed operations are performed by authorized users, applications, or services can interact with specific resources, while unauthorized access is prevented.

Role Based Authorization

Implement robust access controls to ensure that only authorized users and processes that have a specific role in the workflow can access and manipulate data. Role-based Authentication uses strong authentication mechanisms, such as multi-factor authentication, and enforces the principle of least privilege, granting users the minimum privileges required to perform their tasks. A primary limitation of Role-based systems is their significant dependence on user and object identity for mapping it to a set of roles (Batra et al., 2019).

Attribute-Based Authorization

ABAC is a more flexible authorization model where access decisions are based on attributes associated with users, resources, and environmental conditions. ABAC evaluates multiple attributes to determine if access should be granted. Attribute-based access control's flexibility, portability, and identity-less access control make it an attractive choice to be employed in many application domains (Batra et al., 2019).

Role-based access control (RBAC) and attribute-based access control (ABAC) models can be employed to assign appropriate access privileges to users based on roles, and responsibilities, and as a result, such fine-grained access control policies enable organizations to enforce the principle of least privilege, granting only necessary permissions to individuals and reducing the risk of data exposure (Maheswari et al., 2023). Each cloud provider may have its own implementation of these authorization mechanisms, but the core principles are mostly consistent across different platforms. It is essential to understand and configure these mechanisms appropriately to ensure the security and privacy of cloud-based resources.

Securing Processing and Storage Infrastructure for the Data

Securing the processing and storage infrastructure for data in the cloud is critical to ensuring the confidentiality, integrity, and availability of sensitive information. Cloud computing environments typically offer various security features and tools to help protect data.

Data Backup and Recovery

Implement a robust data backup and recovery strategy. Regularly back up your data and test the restoration process to ensure data availability in case of accidental deletion, hardware failures, or other incidents. Data backups in cloud computing seek to reduce existing security and privacy concerns, such as data loss, data manipulation, and data theft (Adee & Mouratidis, 2022), and offers solutions such as offsite backups at a different location within the cloud, snapshots which is the point in time backup, and write-once backups which cannot be modified but only accessed as it is.

Data Residency and Compliance

Cross-border data flows are a vital component of international trade. However, for several reasons, restrictions on the transfer of personal data and data localization requirements have sprung up (Voss, 2022). Understanding the data residency requirements and legal regulations applicable to the data is required to ensure that your cloud service provider complies with relevant data protection regulations, such as the General Data Protection Regulation (GDPR) or the Health Insurance Portability and Accountability Act (HIPAA). Cloud computing makes data transfer easy and hence introduces a higher risk to compliance. However, it also provides a control framework to avoid or monitor cross border data movements with checks and balance mechanisms.

Encryption for Data at Rest

Encryption for data at rest is a fundamental security measure in a cloud environment. Data at rest refers to data stored and not actively being accessed, processed, or transmitted. Encrypting data at rest ensures that the data remains unintelligible without the appropriate decryption key even if an unauthorized entity gains access to the physical storage medium on the cloud infrastructure. To overcome security issues related to data storage, cloud service providers are required to use strong security measures to secure their storage and protect cloud data from unauthorized access (Mohammed & Abed, 2020). The following are some of the encryption algorithms, methods, and solutions supported and used in cloud environments.

AES (Advanced Encryption Standard): AES encryption is a widely used encryption algorithm. It is symmetric meaning both nodes have same key for encryption and decryption. It is highly secure and efficient, making it suitable for encrypting large volumes of data stored in the cloud. AES encrypts and decrypts data using a secret encryption key, which must be kept secure to ensure data confidentiality. This approach helps fulfill the consumers' access rights and aids in fulfilling the risk assessment obligation.

TDE (Transparent Data Encryption): TDE is a database-level encryption solution provided by many cloud database platforms. It encrypts the entire database, including backups and transaction logs, transparently without requiring changes to the application code. This approach helps fulfill the consumers' access rights and aids in fulfilling the risk assessment obligation.

File-Level Encryption: File-level encryption encrypts individual files before they are stored in the cloud. Each file is encrypted with its own unique encryption key. This approach allows for selective encryption of specific files and provides an added layer of security. This approach helps fulfill the consumers' access rights and aids in fulfilling the risk assessment obligation.

Disk-Level Encryption: Disk-level encryption, also known as full disk encryption (FDE), encrypts the entire storage disk or volume where data is stored. This encryption ensures that all data written on the disk is automatically encrypted, and all read data is decrypted on-the-fly. This approach helps fulfill the consumers' access rights and aids in fulfilling the risk assessment obligation.

Key Management Services: Proper key management is essential for data at-rest encryption. Key management services help generate, store, rotate, and revoke encryption keys securely. Cloud providers often offer key management services to help organizations manage their encryption keys effectively. Hardware Security Modules (HSM) are specialized hardware devices that securely store encryption keys and perform cryptographic operations. They offer an added layer of protection for encryption keys, making it harder for attackers to access the keys and decrypt the data. This approach helps fulfill the consumers' access rights and aids in fulfilling the risk assessment obligation.

Encrypted Cloud Storage Services: Some cloud storage providers offer built-in encryption services that automatically encrypt data before storing it on their servers. This ensures that data is encrypted at rest. Some cloud storage providers offer end-to-end encryption for data stored on their servers. In such cases, data is encrypted on the user's device before being uploaded to the cloud. This ensures that even if there is a breach on the cloud server, the data remains unreadable without the decryption key. This approach helps fulfill the consumers' access rights and aids in fulfilling the risk assessment obligation.

Cloud service providers offer many different traditional encryption methodologies for data at-rest services however it is imperative for customers to implement a strategy using a combination of strong encryption algorithms and key lengths that align with industry best practices and compliance requirements. Additionally, organizations must implement access controls and strong authentication mechanisms to control who can access the encrypted data and manage encryption keys.

Protecting the Integrity of the Data

data integrity is data accuracy and continuity in the cloud without modification by any unauthorized party and guarantees data resource reliability (Karagozlu et al., 2020). The data integrity protection measures in the cloud ensure that the data remains accurate, unaltered, complete, and consistent throughout its lifecycle. Here are some best practices to help safeguard the integrity of data in a cloud environment. Some of the processes that ensure data integrity in cloud computing are as follows.

Data Validation and Verification

In cloud storage, clients outsource data storage to save local resources, and, in the process, they lose the controllability to manage data and hence validation system is needed to verify the correctness of data (Guo & Ye, 2020). Robust data validation mechanisms to ensure that data is accurate and consistent using techniques such as checksums, hash functions, and digital signatures to verify the integrity of data both at rest and in transit can be implemented more efficiently in cloud environments.

Encryption in Transit: Utilize encryption techniques to protect data integrity. Encrypt data at rest using technologies like disk encryption or database-level encryption. Additionally, encrypt data in transit using secure communication protocols like TLS/SSL to prevent unauthorized modifications during transmission. This approach helps fulfill the consumers' access rights and aids in fulfilling the risk assessment obligation.

Secure Data Transfer: Ensure secure data transfer between different components of your cloud environment. Use secure file transfer protocols (SFTP), secure APIs, or virtual private networks (VPNs) to maintain data integrity during data exchanges. This approach helps fulfill the consumers' access rights and aids in fulfilling the risk assessment obligation.

Immutable Storage: Leverage immutable storage capabilities offered by your cloud provider. Immutable storage prevents data from being modified or deleted for a specified period, ensuring the integrity and non-repudiation of data. This approach helps fulfill the consumers' access rights and aids in fulfilling the risk assessment obligation.

Data Versioning and Auditing: Implement version control mechanisms and maintain an audit trail of changes to data. Regularly monitor and review logs, access records, and activity reports to detect any unauthorized modifications and ensure data integrity. This approach helps fulfill the consumers' access rights and aids in fulfilling the risk assessment obligation.

Intrusion Detection and Prevention Systems (IDPS): Deploy IDPS solutions that monitor network traffic and system activities to detect and prevent unauthorized modifications or tampering with data. These systems can provide real-time alerts and automated responses to mitigate potential integrity threats. This approach helps fulfill the consumers' access rights and aids in fulfilling the risk assessment obligation.

By implementing these practices, you can enhance the integrity of your data in the cloud and minimize the risk of unauthorized modifications or tampering. Regularly review and update your security measures to stay abreast of evolving threats and vulnerabilities.

Monitoring and Logging in Cloud Environment

Security Monitoring and Logging: Implement comprehensive security monitoring and logging mechanisms to detect and respond to security incidents promptly. Monitor access logs, network traffic, and system logs to identify any suspicious activities or potential security breaches. IDS and security information and event management (SIEM) solutions tools analyze system logs, network traffic, and behavior patterns to identify potential security threats and anomalies and trigger automated alerts, and initiate incident response procedures to mitigate risks and ensure prompt remediation by detecting suspicious activities can be taken (Maheswari et al., 2023).

Vendor Due Diligence: Before selecting a cloud service provider, conduct thorough due diligence to assess their security practices, certifications, and compliance measures. Review their data protection policies, data breach notification processes, and service level agreements (SLAs). Organizations should implement the process for conducting due diligence on vendors, including reviewing their security and compliance policies, performing on-site inspections, and obtaining references from other organizations (Teppler, 2023).

Incident Response and Business Continuity: Organizations must develop and regularly test an incident response plan to handle data breaches or other security incidents effectively. They also must ensure that they have a robust business continuity plan in place to mitigate disruptions or downtime.

Employee Awareness and Training: Organization must train their staff on data protection best practices, cloud security risks, and their responsibilities in safeguarding data. Creating a culture of security awareness lowers the risk of human errors or insider threats.

Data Loss Prevention: Organizations can deploy DLP solutions to prevent the unauthorized exfiltration or leakage of sensitive data. DLP tools can monitor data flows within the cloud environment, identify sensitive data, and enforce policies to prevent data breaches.

SUMMARY

Many regulations around the world collectively recognized that privacy is one of the fundamental human rights and its protection includes digital and data privacy for all sensitive information stored processed, transmitted, and used in digital environments. As organizations increasingly rely on the cloud computing environment for their data processing, concerns related to data privacy protection need to be addressed. Hence data privacy and security are critical concerns in the cloud computing environment. The main goals for security in the cloud are protecting data against unauthorized access, disclosure, and modification of information, protecting against unauthorized access to cloud resources, ensuring efficient management, control, and compliance with established processes and ensuring incidents, detecting incidents and action (Iovan & Iovan, 2016). In this chapter, specific privacy requirements have been discussed earlier and available security measures in cloud environment are discussed later in the chapter. Robust security measures, adherence to privacy regulations, and ongoing monitoring and risk assessment are essential to protect sensitive information (Maheswari et al., 2023).

REFERENCES

Adee, R., & Mouratidis, H. (2022). A dynamic four-step data security model for data in cloud computing based on cryptography and Steganography. *Sensors (Basel)*, *22*(3), 1109. doi:10.339022031109 PMID:35161853

Bannerman, S., & Orasch, A. (2020). Privacy and smart cities: A Canadian survey. *Canadian Journal of Urban Research*, *29*(1), 17–38.

Batra, G., Atluri, V., Vaidya, J., & Sural, S. (2019). Deploying ABAC policies using RBAC Systems. *Journal of Computer Security*, *27*(4), 483–506. doi:10.3233/JCS-191315 PMID:31929684

FAR 52.224-3 Privacy Training. (2023). *Acquisition.GOV*. https://www.acquisition.gov/far/52.224-3

Guo, Z., & Ye, J. (2020). Improved Algorithm for Management of Outsourced Database. *Neural Computing & Applications*, *33*(2), 647–653. doi:10.100700521-020-05047-7

Iovan, Ş., & Iovan, A. A. (2016). Cloud Computing Security. *Fiability & Durability / Fiabilitate Si Durabilitate, 1,* 206–212.

Iqbal, A. (2020). Protecting Digital Privacy: Why the United States Should Follow Europe's Lead and Pass Federal Legislation. *Harvard Kennedy School Review*, *20*, 87–91.

Karagozlu, D., Ajamu, J., & Mbombo, A. B. (2020). Adaptation and effects of cloud computing on small businesses. *Brain. Broad Research in Artificial Intelligence and Neuroscience*, *11*(4), 149–167. doi:10.18662/brain/11.4/146

Khan, S., Zhang, Z., Zhu, L., Rahim, M. A., Ahmad, S., & Chen, R. (2020). SCM: Secure and accountable TLS Certificate Management. *International Journal of Communication Systems*, *33*(15), e4503. Advance online publication. doi:10.1002/dac.4503

Li, X. (2022). A blockchain-based verifiable user data access control policy for secured cloud data storage. *Computational Intelligence and Neuroscience*, *2022*, 1–12. doi:10.1155/2022/7498025 PMID:35528363

Maheswari, J. U., Vijayalakshmi, S., N, R. G., Alzubaidi, L. H., Anvar, K., & Elangovan, R. (2023). Data Privacy and Security in Cloud Computing Environments. *E3S Web of Conferences, 399*, 04040. doi:10.1051/e3sconf/202339904040

Manzoor, A., Shah, M. A., Khattak, H. A., Din, I. U., & Khan, M. K. (2019). Multi-tier authentication schemes for Fog computing: Architecture, security perspective, and challenges. *International Journal of Communication Systems*, *35*(12), e4033. Advance online publication. doi:10.1002/dac.4033

McCallister, E., Grance, T., & Scarfone, K. (2010, April). *Identifiable information (PII)*. Guide to Protecting the Confidentiality of Personally Identifiable Information (PII). doi:10.6028/NIST.SP.800-122

Mohammed, M. A., & Abed, F. S. (2020). A symmetric-based framework for securing cloud data at rest. *Turkish Journal of Electrical Engineering and Computer Sciences*, *28*(1), 347–361. doi:10.3906/elk-1902-114

Munonye, K., & Péter, M. (2021). Machine learning approach to vulnerability detection in OAUTH 2.0 authentication and authorization flow. *International Journal of Information Security*, *21*(2), 223–237. doi:10.100710207-021-00551-w

Rachur, A., Putman, J., & Fisher, C. (2022). What did the digital age mean for privacy in the United States? *Journal of Business &amp. The Journal of Business and Retail Management Research*, *17*(01). Advance online publication. doi:10.24052/JBRMR/V17IS01/ART-08

Razaque, A., Shaldanbayeva, N., Alotaibi, B., Alotaibi, M., Murat, A., & Alotaibi, A. (2022). Big Data Handling Approach for unauthorized cloud computing access. *Electronics (Basel)*, *11*(1), 137. doi:10.3390/electronics11010137

Rothstein, M. A., & Tovino, S. A. (2019). California takes the lead on Data Privacy Law. *The Hastings Center Report*, *49*(5), 4–5. doi:10.1002/hast.1042 PMID:31581323

Selvadurai, N., Kisswani, N., & Khalaileh, Y. (2017). Strengthening data privacy: The obligation of organizations to notify affected individuals of data breaches. *International Review of Law, Computers &amp. Technology*, *33*(3), 271–284. doi:10.1080/13600869.2017.1379368

Teppler, S. W. (2023). Attorney Cybersecurity and Supply Chain Risk. *The Florida Bar Journal*, *97*(3), 14–16.

Tiilikka, P. (2013). Access to information as a human right in the case law of the European Court of Human Rights. *Journal of Medicine and Law*, *5*(1), 79–103. doi:10.5235/17577632.5.1.79

Voss, W. G. (2022). Cross-border data flows, the GDPR, and Data Governance. *International Organisations Research Journal*, *17*(1), 56–95. doi:10.17323/1996-7845-2022-01-03

Woods, L. (2019). Digital Privacy and Article 12 of the Universal Declaration of Human Rights. *The Political Quarterly*, *90*(3), 422–429. doi:10.1111/1467-923X.12740

Chapter 5
A Survey on Blockchain-Internet of Things-Based Solutions

R. Hariharan
https://orcid.org/0000-0001-5958-8185
St. Joseph's University, India

Amit Kumar Tyagi
https://orcid.org/0000-0003-2657-8700
National Institute of Fashion Technology, New Delhi, India

Gulshan Soni
https://orcid.org/0000-0001-7279-2981
MSEIT, MATS University, India

ABSTRACT

The integration of Blockchain-IoT presents a promising platform for enhancing security, transparency, and efficiency in various applications. This work aims to provide a detailed overview of the state of the art in blockchain-IoT-based solutions. In this work, the authors begin by introducing the basic concepts of blockchain and IoT, highlighting their key features and their individual challenges. Next, this work explains benefits of combining these technologies, such as decentralized data management, immutable records, and enhanced trust and security. Further, this work explains the architecture and components of blockchain-IoT systems, including smart contracts, consensus mechanisms, and data integrity verification techniques.

1. INTRODUCTION

Blockchain and Internet of Things (IoT) integration refers to the merging of these two transformative technologies to create a secure, transparent, and efficient ecosystem for managing and exchanging data and value in the context of IoT devices. The IoT involves a network of interconnected physical devices, sensors, and machines that collect and exchange data over the internet. These devices generate vast

DOI: 10.4018/979-8-3693-0593-5.ch005

amounts of data, enabling real-time monitoring, automation, and decision-making in various industries such as healthcare, logistics, manufacturing, and smart cities. On the other hand, blockchain technology provides a decentralized and tamper-resistant ledger that records and verifies transactions in a transparent and secure manner. It operates on a peer-to-peer network where multiple participants validate and maintain the integrity of the data stored on the blockchain. Note that integrating blockchain with IoT can address several challenges associated with the current IoT infrastructure, including data security, privacy, trust, and interoperability. Here are some key aspects of blockchain-IoT integration:

- Data Integrity and Security: Blockchain's distributed ledger ensures the integrity of IoT data by providing a transparent and immutable record of all transactions and data exchanges. Any attempt to tamper with the data would require consensus from a majority of participants, making it extremely difficult to compromise the system.
- Identity and Access Management: Blockchain can enable secure identity management and access control for IoT devices. Each device can have a unique identity stored on the blockchain, allowing for secure authentication and authorization processes. This ensures that only authorized devices can interact with the network, reducing the risk of unauthorized access and potential attacks.
- Smart Contracts and Automation: Smart contracts are self-executing contracts with predefined rules encoded on the blockchain. By integrating smart contracts with IoT devices, automated actions can be triggered based on predefined conditions. For example, in a supply chain, a smart contract can automatically initiate payment or trigger a shipment when certain conditions, such as temperature or location, are met.
- Supply Chain Management: Blockchain-IoT integration can enhance transparency and traceability in supply chains. By recording every transaction and data exchange on the blockchain, stakeholders can track and verify the movement of goods, ensuring authenticity, quality, and compliance. This can help mitigate fraud, counterfeiting, and improve efficiency in supply chain operations.
- Data Monetization and Ownership: With blockchain, individuals and organizations can have better control over their IoT-generated data. Blockchain-based platforms can enable secure data sharing and monetization, allowing individuals to retain ownership of their data and have more control over its usage and value.
- Decentralized Infrastructure: Traditional IoT architectures often rely on centralized servers or cloud platforms for data storage and processing. By considering blockchain's decentralized nature, IoT systems can distribute data processing and storage across the network, reducing the reliance on central authorities and improving system resilience and fault tolerance.

In summary, the integration of blockchain and IoT has the potential to revolutionize various industries by providing a secure, transparent, and efficient infrastructure for managing IoT devices, data, and transactions. It addresses critical challenges associated with data security, privacy, and trust, while enabling new business models and opportunities in the rapidly expanding IoT ecosystem.

1.1 Convergence of Blockchain and IoT

The convergence of blockchain and the IoT brings together two transformative technologies to create new possibilities and address challenges in various industries. Here are some key aspects of the convergence of blockchain and IoT:

- Data Integrity and Security: The integration of blockchain with IoT can enhance data integrity and security. Blockchain's decentralized and tamper-resistant nature ensures that the data generated by IoT devices remains immutable and trustworthy. Each data transaction is recorded on the blockchain, providing a transparent and auditable history of data exchanges. This feature is especially essential in sensitive/ important applications such as healthcare, supply chain management, and smart cities, where data accuracy and security are paramount.
- Trusted Identity and Access Management: Blockchain can provide a secure and decentralized identity management system for IoT devices. Each device can have a unique identity stored on the blockchain, enabling secure authentication and access control. This ensures that only authorized devices can interact with the IoT network, mitigating the risk of unauthorized access and potential security breaches.
- Smart Contracts for Automation: The combination of blockchain and IoT can add smart contracts to automate processes and transactions. Smart contracts are self-executing contracts with predefined rules and conditions encoded on the blockchain. They can facilitate automated actions triggered by IoT device data or events. For example, a smart contract can automatically execute a payment when a certain condition is met, such as a sensor detecting a specific temperature or humidity level.
- Decentralized Data Marketplaces: Blockchain-IoT integration can enable decentralized data marketplaces, where IoT-generated data can be securely shared and monetized. Blockchain provides a transparent and trusted platform for data owners to directly sell or share their data with interested parties. This allows for more efficient data transactions and empowers individuals and organizations to retain ownership and control over their data.
- Supply Chain Traceability: Blockchain can enhance supply chain management by providing end-to-end traceability and transparency. IoT devices equipped with sensors can collect and record data at each stage of the supply chain. This data, combined with blockchain's immutable and transparent nature, enables stakeholders to track and verify the origin, authenticity, and condition of goods as they move through the supply chain.
- Peer-to-Peer Energy Trading: Blockchain-IoT integration can revolutionize the energy sector by enabling peer-to-peer energy trading. IoT devices, such as solar panels and smart meters, can generate and track energy production and consumption data. Blockchain can facilitate direct energy trading between producers and consumers, eliminating intermediaries and allowing for more efficient and decentralized energy markets.
- Scalability and Interoperability: As the number of IoT devices and transactions grows, scalability and interoperability become critical. Blockchain solutions are continuously evolving to address these challenges. New consensus algorithms, such as Proof of Stake (PoS), and layer-2 scaling solutions are being developed to improve blockchain's scalability and efficiency, making it more suitable for large-scale IoT deployments.

The convergence of blockchain and IoT holds great promise for transforming industries by addressing security, data integrity, automation, and trust challenges. However, it also presents complexities and requires careful consideration of factors such as scalability, interoperability, privacy, and regulatory compliance. As both technologies continue to advance, their integration will likely drive innovation and shape the future of various sectors.

1.2 Significance and Potential Benefits of Blockchain-IoT Solutions in This Smart Era

Blockchain-IoT solutions have significant significance and potential benefits in the smart era. Here are some key reasons why the integration of blockchain and IoT is important:

- Data Security and Integrity: The combination of blockchain and IoT enhances data security and integrity. The decentralized and tamper-resistant nature of blockchain ensures that IoT-generated data remains immutable and trustworthy. This is particularly important in applications where data accuracy and security are critical, such as healthcare, supply chain management, and smart cities.
- Trust and Transparency: Blockchain-IoT solutions provide a transparent and auditable platform for data exchange and transactions. The decentralized nature of blockchain eliminates the need for intermediaries, fostering trust among participants. This transparency increases accountability and reduces the risk of fraud, as all transactions can be traced and verified by multiple parties.
- Efficient and Automated Processes: Smart contracts, enabled by blockchain, automate processes and transactions in the IoT ecosystem. These self-executing contracts enforce predefined rules and conditions, eliminating the need for manual intervention. This automation improves efficiency, reduces costs, and enables real-time decision-making based on IoT device data.
- Secure Identity and Access Management: Blockchain enhances identity and access management in IoT networks. Each IoT device can have a unique identity stored on the blockchain, ensuring secure authentication and access control. This helps mitigate the risk of unauthorized access and potential security breaches.
- Decentralized Data Marketplaces: The integration of blockchain and IoT enables decentralized data marketplaces. IoT-generated data can be securely shared and monetized, empowering individuals and organizations to retain ownership and control over their data. This opens up new opportunities for data-driven businesses and innovation.
- Supply Chain Transparency and Traceability: Blockchain-IoT solutions enhance supply chain management by providing transparency and traceability. IoT devices equipped with sensors collect and record data at each stage of the supply chain, which is then securely stored on the blockchain. This enables stakeholders to track and verify the origin, authenticity, and condition of goods, improving efficiency, trust, and accountability in supply chain operations.
- Energy Efficiency and Peer-to-Peer Energy Trading: Blockchain-IoT integration has the potential to revolutionize the energy sector. IoT devices, such as smart meters and renewable energy sources, can generate and track energy production and consumption data. Blockchain facilitates direct peer-to-peer energy trading, eliminating intermediaries and enabling more efficient, decentralized energy markets. This can lead to increased energy efficiency, cost savings, and a transition to cleaner and more sustainable energy sources.
- Interoperability and Standardization: Blockchain-IoT solutions can address interoperability challenges in the IoT ecosystem. Blockchain provides a standardized framework for data exchange and communication among different IoT devices and platforms. This promotes seamless integration and interoperability, enabling diverse IoT systems to work together efficiently.

In summary, the integration of blockchain and IoT offers a range of benefits in terms of data security, trust, automation, transparency, and efficiency. It has the potential to transform industries and sectors, improving processes, enabling new business models, and driving innovation in the smart era.

2. LITERATURE SURVEY

With the purpose of transforming into smart healthcare ecosystems, traditional healthcare institutions are drastically embracing contemporary technologies. The main forces behind this transformation are user convenience and ease of usage. There are several difficulties and problems relating to the security, openness, and privacy of the data and users, even with smart healthcare systems (SHS). The study provided by (Tripathi et al., 2020) examines the social and technological impediments to the adoption of SHS by examining user perception and cutting-edge expert opinions. It also suggests a SHS architecture built on a blockchain to ensure the system's integrity and inherent security. The discussion concludes with future research paths and blockchain use cases in the healthcare sector. Numerous scientific disciplines have adopted the idea of blockchain, and its application is predicted to increase significantly soon. The use of intermediaries can be eliminated, and the number of contracts that can be executed at once increased, by executing short scripts of predetermined code known as smart contracts on Blockchain. (Sharma et al., 2020) address the idea of blockchain and smart contracts and how they may be applied to the Internet of Medical Things (IoMT) in the field of electronic healthcare. In addition to outlining a novel architecture, the article analyses the directions that decentralization and the usage of smart contracts will take the IoMT in e-healthcare as well as the benefits, difficulties, and upcoming trends associated with their combination.

One of the important conditions with the fastest rate of growth in the global death rate is diabetes. The framework for detecting diabetes disease using Blockchain is presented by (Chen et al., 2021). It uses a variety of machine learning classification algorithms to detect the disease sooner and secures patient EHRs. Our EHRs sharing platform integrates symptom-based disease prediction, Blockchain, and the interplanetary file system (IPFS), and wearable sensor devices are used to gather patient health data. The EHRs manager receives this data and uses an ML model to process it further and get the appropriate findings. In the study presented by (Xu et al., 2019) Healthchain, a broad-based blockchain-based system for maintaining the privacy of health data, where health data are encrypted to carry out fine-grained access control. Users can use user transactions for key management to efficiently cancel or add authorized doctors. In addition, Healthchain makes it impossible to alter or delete doctor diagnoses or IoT data, preventing medical conflicts. Experimental data and security analyses demonstrate the proposed Healthchain's suitability for use in smart healthcare systems. An intelligent Blockchain Manager (BM) based on DRL, primarily Deep Q-Learning and its modifications, was presented by (Al-Marridi et al., 2021) to optimize the behavior of the Blockchain network in real-time while considering the needs of medical data, such as urgency and security levels. The suggested BM aims to optimize the trade-off between security, latency, and cost while intelligently modifying the blockchain setup. The optimization model is described as a Markov Decision Process (MDP), and three RL-based strategies are used to successfully solve it. Deep Q-Networks (DQN), Double Deep Q-Networks (DDQN), and Dueling Double Deep Q-Networks are these three approaches (D3QN). Finally, a thorough comparison between the suggested methodologies and two heuristic approaches is made.

In the work proposed by (Khatoon, 2020) current research and blockchain-based applications for the healthcare sector is examined. Additionally, for better data management, this paper also suggests a number of workflows for the healthcare sector using blockchain technology. The ethereum blockchain platform has been used to develop and implement a variety of medical processes, including complicated surgical and clinical trial procedures. Accessing and controlling a sizable amount of medical data are also included. The cost of this system has been estimated as part of a feasibility study that has been extensively reported in this article. This cost is related with the deployment of the workflows of the medical smart contract system for healthcare management. By 2020, the volume of healthcare data is expected to be about 2314 exabyte thanks to improvements in data collection and connected technology (Mikulic, 2019). The cybercriminals are investing a lot of time, effort, and money into utilizing and profiting from healthcare data. Considering this threat, the healthcare industry's cybersecurity market is predicted to increase and reach USD 27.10 billion by 2026 (Healthcare Cybersecurity Market to Reach USD 27.10 Billion by 2026, 2019). In order to collect data for clinical studies and ensure patient privacy, a single database might be created with the use of the blockchain. In order to guarantee the security of healthcare data, (Quasim et al., 2020) suggest a safe framework based on blockchain. The suggested paradigm considers processing power, IoT devices, and wearable sensors. (Pham et al., 2018) suggest using blockchain-based smart contracts to manage patient data and medical devices in order to safeguard personally identifiable information and information generated by devices. They develop a remote healthcare system including patients, doctors, and healthcare providers (such as hospitals) using blockchain technology based on the Ethereum protocol. Sensors measure a patient's health, and this data is automatically entered into a blockchain. A processing method for efficiently and sparingly storing patient health-related information from medical devices.

64 articles on blockchain-based healthcare systems that were published between 2016 and January 2020 in 21 conferences, 33 journals, and 10 internet sources are critically reviewed by (Soltanisehat et al., 2020). Three major questions will be addressed in this article. What are the applications of blockchain in healthcare systems, as well as the structures and difficulties involved in implementing blockchain to a particular area of healthcare? What are the technical, temporal, and spatial features of the blockchain applications that are now being developed for various healthcare domains? What are the third and fourth potential research trajectories for developing and deploying blockchain-based healthcare systems? We also talk about possible future directions for study, like incorporating blockchain technology into AI-based solutions, cloud computing-based solutions, and parallel blockchain architecture. Protecting sensitive patient data from possible enemies is one of the key criteria for today's smart healthcare systems. Thus, having secure data access methods that can guarantee that only authorized parties can access the patients' medical information is important. As a result, this research views blockchain technology as a distributed strategy to safeguard patient data. In a particular healthcare system, (Ramani et al., 2018) suggests a blockchain-based secure and effective data accessible mechanism for patients and doctors. The proposed technology is also capable of preserving patient privacy. Our plan's security study demonstrates that it can withstand well-known attacks while still preserving the system's integrity.

Blockchain is a revolution in the healthcare industry that could significantly alter the services that are currently provided. It addresses the problem of constructing and adjusting a healthcare system in the healthcare sector, the pharmaceutical business, and insurance firms. The base for protecting healthcare data is presented in (Khubrani, 2021). The core tenets of the proposed framework are public ledger, private ledger, smart contracts, and context-based access control. Additionally, this suggested approach offers dependable patient data access, secure storage, and interoperability. A large-scale scheme for preserving the privacy of health data that is built on blockchain technology and uses encryption to carry out fine-grained access control (Xu et al., 2019). By utilizing user transactions for key management, users can specifically add or revoke authorized doctors with ease. Also, by introducing Health chain, it is impossible to delete or tamper with doctor diagnoses or IoT data, preventing medical disputes. To safeguard the patient data, an emergency access control management system is suggested in (Son et al., 2021). This solution is based on the Hyperledger fabric for permissioned Blockchain. Many rules and regulations will be defined in the proposed system employing smart contracts and time duration to handle emergencies. In such urgent situations, the patients also set time limits on when they can view the data. To help readers comprehend the suggested management system, several algorithms that explain how the system functions are also offered.

In Healthcare 4.0, wearable sensors can be used for remote patient monitoring (RPM), which is a more effective and flexible method of patient observation. RPM's most narrowly targeted application field enables clinicians to obtain real-time patient data from a distance through a wireless communication technology. RPM therefore cuts down on the patient's time and expense. Also, it offers the patient high-quality care. (Hathaliya et al., 2019) describe a Permissioned blockchain-based healthcare architecture to improve patient data security and privacy. We have also talked about the problems and their fixes. The applications of blockchain have been discussed. We also discussed how blockchain technology and machine learning can affect the healthcare sector. In the research provided by (Wu et al., 2021), a blockchain-based smart healthcare system with granular privacy protection for trustworthy data sharing and exchange between various users. To provide attribute-based privacy protection in transaction processing, a blockchain-enabled dynamic access control framework is build integrated with Local Differential Privacy (LDP) techniques. To satisfy the demands of anonymous transaction, dynamic access control, advantageous matching decision, and evaluation of public data in an open network, four types of smart contracts in the framework is developed. To enhance privacy preservation in the intelligent healthcare system, a permissioned blockchain-based private information retrieval mechanism called Ring Signature is presented (Ali et al., 2022). The suggested scheme uses a better multi-transaction mode consortium block-chain initially to maximize appointment offers based on accessibility, transparency, and security by making varying amounts of requests to the healthcare providers. Information retrieval from several domains can benefit from our proposed System. The simulation results demonstrate the suggested Scheme's superior performance in maximizing patient privacy while minimizing processing and communication costs.

The article (Sharma et al., 2022) suggests an Identity-Based Encryption (IBE) algorithm-based blockchain-based IoT architecture to provide improved security for healthcare data. Here, the smart contract outlines all the basic functions of the healthcare system, which is advantageous for all parties involved. To determine the effectiveness of the suggested plan, numerous experiments are conducted. The findings indicate that the suggested system is superior to the well-known current schemes. Among other important application areas, healthcare is one where blockchain is expected to have a significant impact. In the current healthcare systems, it is creating a wide range of options and possibilities. Consequently, the focus of (Kumar et al., 2018) is on examining the possible uses of blockchain technology in present healthcare systems and highlighting the key conditions that must be met for such systems to function, such as transparent and trustless healthcare systems. The work also discusses the difficulties and barriers that must be removed before blockchain technology can be successfully implemented in healthcare systems. Also, they introduce the smart contract, which is essential for defining the pre-defined agreements among the numerous involved stakeholders, for blockchain-based healthcare systems. In order to preserve patient data, the study (Nair & Tyagi, 2023) suggests a control and management system called the Patient-Chain platform, which is a patient-centered healthcare system that uses Blockchain technology (). The Patient-Chain system is constructed using the authorized Blockchain Hyperledger Fabric, establishes various rules and regulations using smart contracts, and specifies a time period to handle emergencies. In such urgent circumstances, the patients also place time restrictions on when they can access the data. To help readers comprehend the proposed management system, numerous algorithms that explain how the system functions are also presented.

3. BLOCKCHAIN-IOT ARCHITECTURE AND FRAMEWORKS

3.1 Architectural Models for Blockchain-IoT Integration

Several architectural models can be used to integrate blockchain and IoT effectively. Here are three commonly used models for Blockchain-IoT integration:

- Blockchain as a Service (BaaS) Model: In this model, a third-party blockchain platform provides blockchain services to IoT devices and applications. The BaaS provider manages the underlying blockchain infrastructure, including security, scalability, and consensus mechanisms. IoT devices connect to the BaaS platform to store and retrieve data on the blockchain. This model simplifies the integration process for IoT applications, as developers can add the ready-to-use blockchain services without having to manage the blockchain infrastructure themselves.
- Hybrid Architecture Model: The hybrid architecture model combines both centralized and decentralized components to achieve the integration of blockchain and IoT. In this model, a central authority or intermediary is responsible for managing and authenticating IoT devices. The IoT devices collect data and send it to the central authority, which then validates and records the data on the blockchain. This approach considers the decentralization and immutability of blockchain while still maintaining a central authority for managing device identities and access control.
- Peer-to-Peer (P2P) Model: In the P2P model, IoT devices directly interact with each other through blockchain technology, without the need for a centralized authority. Each IoT device becomes a node in the blockchain network, maintaining a copy of the distributed ledger. The devices communicate and exchange data using smart contracts deployed on the blockchain. This model offers increased decentralization, transparency, and resilience, as there is no single point of failure or control. However, it may face scalability challenges due to the resource constraints of IoT devices.

Note that the choice of architectural model depends on the specific requirements, use case, and constraints of the Blockchain-IoT integration. Factors such as scalability, security, privacy, interoperability, and the resources available to IoT devices should be considered when selecting an architectural model. Additionally, ongoing research and development efforts are exploring new architectural models and protocols tailored specifically for Blockchain-IoT integration to address the unique challenges and requirements of this combination.

3.2 Blockchain Platforms and Protocols for IoT Applications

There are several blockchain platforms and protocols that can be used for IoT applications. Here are some popular ones:

- Ethereum: Ethereum is one of the most widely adopted blockchain platforms and supports the development of decentralized applications (DApps) through smart contracts. It provides a robust ecosystem for IoT applications, allowing developers to create secure and transparent IoT solutions using the Solidity programming language. Ethereum's flexibility and large developer community make it a popular choice for IoT integration.
- Hyperledger Fabric: Hyperledger Fabric is an open-source blockchain framework hosted by the Linux Foundation. It offers a modular architecture that enables organizations to build private, permissioned blockchains for enterprise-grade IoT solutions. Fabric provides features such as privacy, scalability, and fine-grained access control, making it suitable for IoT use cases that require stringent data governance and confidentiality.
- IOTA: IOTA is a distributed ledger technology specifically designed for the Internet of Things. It employs a Directed Acyclic Graph (DAG) structure called the Tangle, which allows for secure and feeless micro-transactions between IoT devices. IOTA aims to address scalability and transaction fee challenges commonly associated with traditional blockchains, making it suitable for IoT applications involving a large number of devices.
- Stellar:Stellar is an open-source blockchain platform that focuses on cross-border payments and financial transactions. It offers fast transaction settlement times and low transaction fees, making it suitable for IoT applications requiring efficient and cost-effective micro-payments. Stellar's consensus protocol, the Stellar Consensus Protocol (SCP), provides decentralized control and fault tolerance.
- R3 Corda: R3 Corda is a blockchain platform designed for enterprise use cases. It offers a permissioned blockchain network that focuses on privacy and confidentiality. Corda's unique architecture enables secure data sharing and smart contract execution between trusted parties. It is well-suited for IoT applications that require data privacy and compliance with regulatory requirements.
- VeChain: VeChain is a blockchain platform that focuses on supply chain management and product authenticity. It provides a decentralized platform for tracking and verifying the origin, quality, and movement of products throughout the supply chain. VeChain's IoT integration allows for real-time data collection and validation, ensuring transparency and trust in supply chain processes.
- IoT-specific Protocols: In addition to blockchain platforms, there are also IoT-specific protocols that incorporate blockchain elements. Some notable examples include IoT Chain (ITC), Waltonchain (WTC), and IoTeX. These protocols aim to address scalability, security, and interoperability challenges specific to IoT environments while considering blockchain technology for data integrity and trust.

Note that the choice of blockchain platform or protocol depends on factors such as the specific IoT use case, scalability requirements, data privacy needs, and the level of decentralization desired. Hence, we need to evaluate the features, capabilities, and community support of each platform or protocol to ensure it aligns with the requirements of the IoT application.

3.3 Integration Approaches and Communication Protocols

Integration approaches and communication protocols play an important role in the successful integration of blockchain and IoT. Here are some common approaches and protocols used for integrating blockchain and IoT:

- Gateway-Based Integration: In this approach, a gateway device acts as an intermediary between the IoT devices and the blockchain network. The gateway collects data from IoT devices, performs necessary data transformations or preprocessing, and communicates with the blockchain network to store or retrieve data. This approach enables compatibility between IoT devices and the blockchain network by handling the necessary protocol translations and data formatting.
- Direct Integration: Direct integration involves IoT devices connecting directly to the blockchain network. IoT devices can communicate with the blockchain using protocols such as HTTP(S), MQTT, CoAP, or WebSockets. These protocols facilitate data transmission and interaction between the devices and the blockchain network, enabling direct storage of IoT-generated data on the blockchain or execution of smart contracts.
- Off-Chain Data Integration: In some cases, it may be more efficient or practical to store IoT data off-chain while utilizing the blockchain for specific operations, such as data validation or triggering smart contracts. Off-chain storage solutions, such as distributed databases or cloud storage, can be used to store large volumes of IoT data, while important data hashes or summarized data are stored on the blockchain for verification purposes. This approach balances the scalability requirements of IoT data with the immutability and integrity benefits of the blockchain.
- Communication Protocols: Communication protocols are essential for establishing seamless and secure communication between IoT devices and the blockchain network. Some commonly used protocols in blockchain-IoT integration include:
  - MQTT (Message Queuing Telemetry Transport): A lightweight publish/subscribe messaging protocol suitable for resource-constrained IoT devices. MQTT facilitates efficient and real-time communication between devices and the blockchain network.
  - CoAP (Constrained Application Protocol): Designed for low-power and limited-resource devices, CoAP enables simple and efficient communication between IoT devices and the blockchain network. It is often used in IoT applications where energy efficiency and bandwidth optimization are critical.
  - HTTP(S) (Hypertext Transfer Protocol/Secure): HTTP(S) is a widely used protocol for communication between web-based applications and services. It can be employed for communication between IoT devices and blockchain platforms, especially when compatibility with existing web infrastructure is necessary.
  - WebSockets: WebSockets is a bidirectional communication protocol that allows for full-duplex communication between IoT devices and the blockchain network. It provides real-time data streaming and facilitates interactive and responsive applications.

Note that we need to select the appropriate integration approach and communication protocol based on factors such as the specific use case, scalability requirements, security needs, and the capabilities of the IoT devices and blockchain network. Additionally, interoperability standards and protocols, such as the InterPlanetary File System (IPFS) or the Hyperledger Caliper, can also be considered to ensure seamless integration and compatibility across different blockchain and IoT platforms.

4. SECURITY AND PRIVACY IN BLOCKCHAIN-IOT SOLUTIONS

4.1 Security Challenges in Blockchain-IoT Systems

While the integration of blockchain and IoT brings numerous benefits, it also introduces unique security challenges that need to be addressed. Here are some key security challenges in Blockchain-IoT systems:

- Device Vulnerabilities: IoT devices often have limited computing resources, which can make them susceptible to security vulnerabilities. Weak or default passwords, outdated firmware, and lack of security updates make IoT devices attractive targets for hackers. Compromised devices can be used to launch attacks or gain unauthorized access to the blockchain network, compromising the integrity and security of the system.
- Data Integrity and Authenticity: Ensuring the integrity and authenticity of IoT data is important in a Blockchain-IoT system. However, IoT devices can be compromised, leading to the injection of false data or manipulation of data transactions. Maintaining the integrity and authenticity of IoT data on the blockchain requires robust device authentication mechanisms and secure data transmission protocols.
- Scalability and Performance: Blockchain technology, especially public blockchains, may face scalability and performance challenges when handling a massive number of IoT devices and their data. The need for all nodes to validate and store every transaction can lead to increased latency and reduced transaction throughput. Scaling blockchain networks to handle the volume of IoT data without sacrificing security and performance remains a challenge.
- Privacy and Confidentiality: IoT systems generate vast amounts of data, often including sensitive or personal information. Ensuring privacy and confidentiality of this data is essential. Blockchain's transparent nature, where data is visible to all participants, can pose privacy challenges. Techniques such as encryption, off-chain data storage, and selective disclosure mechanisms are needed to protect sensitive IoT data while considering the benefits of blockchain technology.
- Consensus Mechanisms: Consensus mechanisms in blockchain determine how transactions are validated and added to the blockchain. Traditional consensus algorithms like Proof of Work (PoW) and Proof of Stake (PoS) may not be well-suited for resource-constrained IoT devices due to their energy and computational requirements. Designing lightweight and energy-efficient consensus mechanisms that can accommodate IoT devices while maintaining security and decentralization is a research challenge.
- Network and Communication Security: IoT devices often communicate over untrusted networks, increasing the risk of eavesdropping, data interception, and man-in-the-middle attacks. Securing IoT device communication channels using encryption, secure protocols, and mutual authentication mechanisms is important to protect the integrity and confidentiality of data transmitted to and from the blockchain network.
- Governance and Standardization: Establishing governance models and standards for secure Blockchain-IoT systems is an ongoing challenge. Consistent security practices, guidelines, and

interoperability standards need to be developed to ensure secure integration and communication between blockchain and IoT components.

Hence, these security challenges require a multi-layered approach that combines secure IoT device design, robust network and communication security, secure blockchain protocols, and ongoing monitoring and updates. Collaboration between IoT, cybersecurity, and blockchain experts is essential to develop comprehensive security frameworks that mitigate risks and protect the integrity and privacy of data in Blockchain-IoT systems.

5. SCALABILITY AND PERFORMANCE OPTIMIZATION

Scalability is a significant challenge in Blockchain-IoT solutions due to the large volume of data generated by IoT devices and the resource-intensive nature of blockchain technology. Here are some scalability issues and potential solutions in Blockchain-IoT solutions (see Figure 1).

Figure 1. Scalability and performance optimization

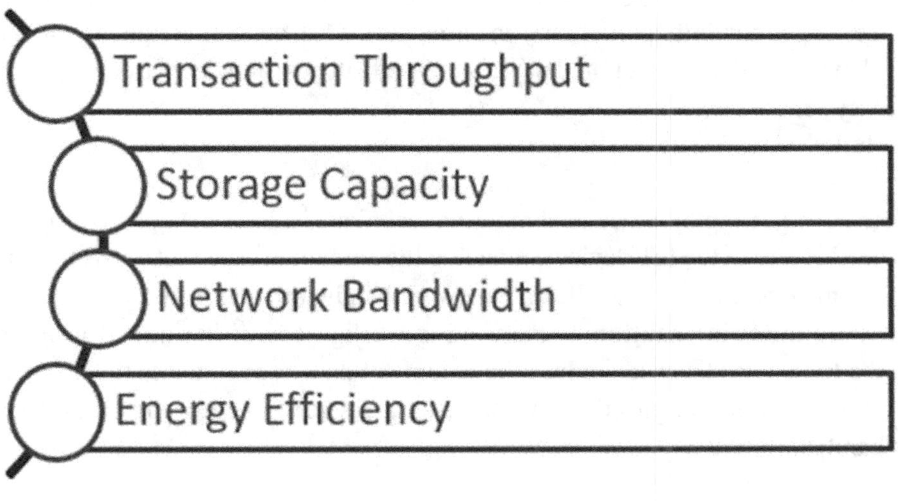

A. Transaction Throughput: Blockchain networks typically have limited transaction throughput, which can become a bottleneck when dealing with many IoT devices generating a high volume of transactions. As IoT devices generate real-time data, the blockchain network may struggle to process and confirm transactions in a timely manner.

Potential solutions:

a. **Sharding**: Sharding involves dividing the blockchain network into smaller partitions called shards, allowing parallel processing of transactions. Each shard processes a subset of transactions, improving the overall transaction throughput.

b. **Off-Chain Transactions:** Off-chain solutions, such as state channels or sidechains, enable certain transactions to be conducted off the main blockchain. Only the final settlement is recorded on the blockchain, reducing the overall transaction load and increasing scalability.

B. Storage Capacity: IoT devices generate a massive amount of data, and storing all the data on the blockchain can be impractical due to the limited storage capacity of blockchain networks. Storing large volumes of IoT data on-chain may increase the size of the blockchain significantly, leading to scalability and performance issues.

Potential solutions:

a. **Data Compression and Aggregation**: IoT data can be compressed or aggregated before storing it on the blockchain. This reduces the amount of data that needs to be stored while preserving essential information.
b. **Distributed File Systems:** Storing IoT data in distributed file systems, such as IPFS (InterPlanetary File System), allows for decentralized and efficient storage of large files associated with IoT devices. Only the file hash or reference is stored on the blockchain, while the actual data resides in the distributed file system.

C. Network Bandwidth: The continuous transmission of IoT data to the blockchain network can strain the available network bandwidth, particularly in cases where IoT devices are geographically dispersed. Limited network bandwidth can result in delays, increased latency, and decreased responsiveness in the Blockchain-IoT system.

Potential solutions:

a. **Edge Computing**: Employing edge computing techniques allows data processing and analysis to be performed closer to the IoT devices, reducing the amount of data that needs to be transmitted to the blockchain network. This can alleviate network bandwidth constraints and improve scalability.
b. **Data Filtering and Prioritization**: Implementing intelligent data filtering and prioritization mechanisms at the IoT device level can reduce the volume of data transmitted to the blockchain network. Only essential data or data meeting certain criteria are forwarded to the blockchain, optimizing network bandwidth usage.

D. Energy Efficiency: Blockchain mining, consensus mechanisms, and cryptographic operations can be resource-intensive, consuming significant computational power and energy. In the context of IoT devices, which often have limited power sources, this energy consumption can become a scalability issues.

Potential solutions:

a. **Proof of Stake (PoS):** Utilizing PoS consensus mechanisms instead of energy-intensive PoW (Proof of Work) can significantly reduce the energy consumption of the blockchain network.
b. **Offloading Computational Tasks**: Offloading computationally intensive tasks to more powerful devices or specialized nodes can alleviate the energy burden on resource-constrained IoT devices.

Hence, scalability issues in Blockchain-IoT solutions requires a combination of architectural design, consensus mechanism optimization, off-chain solutions, edge computing, and efficient data management techniques. It is important to strike a balance between the decentralized nature of blockchain and the scalability requirements of IoT systems to enable efficient and scalable integration.

6. OPEN ISSUES TOWARDS BLOCKCHAIN-IOT-BASED SYSTEMS

While the integration of blockchain and the IoT holds great potential, there are several open issues and challenges that need to be addressed:

- Scalability: Both blockchain and IoT generate vast amounts of data, and scaling the systems to handle high transaction volumes and data throughput can be challenging. Blockchain networks need to ensure fast transaction processing and confirmation times, while IoT devices must handle large-scale data collection and transmission. Finding scalable solutions that can accommodate the growing number of devices and transactions is important.
- Data Privacy and Security: IoT devices collect sensitive data, and ensuring data privacy and security is of utmost importance. While blockchain provides a secure and immutable record, ensuring the privacy of IoT data on the blockchain and during transmission is critical. Encryption techniques, data anonymization, and access control mechanisms need to be implemented to protect sensitive information.
- Interoperability: IoT devices come from various manufacturers and operate on different protocols, making interoperability a challenge. Blockchain-IoT systems need to address the issue of integrating heterogeneous devices and standardizing communication protocols to ensure seamless data exchange and interaction between devices and the blockchain.
- Energy Efficiency: IoT devices often operate on limited power sources, and blockchain networks require significant computational resources and energy consumption for consensus mechanisms. Developing energy-efficient consensus algorithms and optimizing the energy consumption of both blockchain and IoT devices is important to ensure the longevity and sustainability of blockchain-IoT systems.
- Governance and Regulatory Frameworks: Blockchain and IoT technologies raise regulatory and governance issues. Defining legal frameworks, data ownership, liability, and compliance standards for blockchain-IoT systems is necessary to build trust among stakeholders and ensure compliance with existing regulations.
- Integration Complexity: Integrating blockchain and IoT requires expertise in both domains, which can pose challenges for organizations. There is a need for specialized knowledge and skills to develop and deploy blockchain-IoT solutions effectively. Collaboration between blockchain and IoT experts is important to overcome integration complexities and develop robust and secure systems.
- Cost and Infrastructure: Implementing blockchain-IoT systems can involve significant upfront costs for hardware, software, and infrastructure. Upgrading existing IoT devices or deploying new ones to support blockchain integration can be expensive. Additionally, maintaining blockchain networks and ensuring their reliability and availability require a robust infrastructure and investment in ongoing maintenance.
- User Experience: Blockchain-IoT systems need to provide a seamless and intuitive user experience for both end-users and developers. User interfaces and developer tools should be designed to

simplify interactions with blockchain and IoT components, ensuring that the technology is accessible and user-friendly.

Hence, these challenges require collaborative efforts from industry stakeholders, researchers, and policymakers. Ongoing research and innovation are important to overcome these open issues and unlock the full potential of blockchain-IoT integration.

7 TECHNICAL, NON-TECHNICAL, AND RESEARCH CHALLENGES TOWARDS BLOCKCHAIN-IOT SYSTEMS

Blockchain-IoT systems face a range of challenges across technical, non-technical, and research domains. Here are- some of the key challenges in each category (see Figure 2).

Figure 2. Technical, non- technical and research challenges towards blockchain-IoT systems

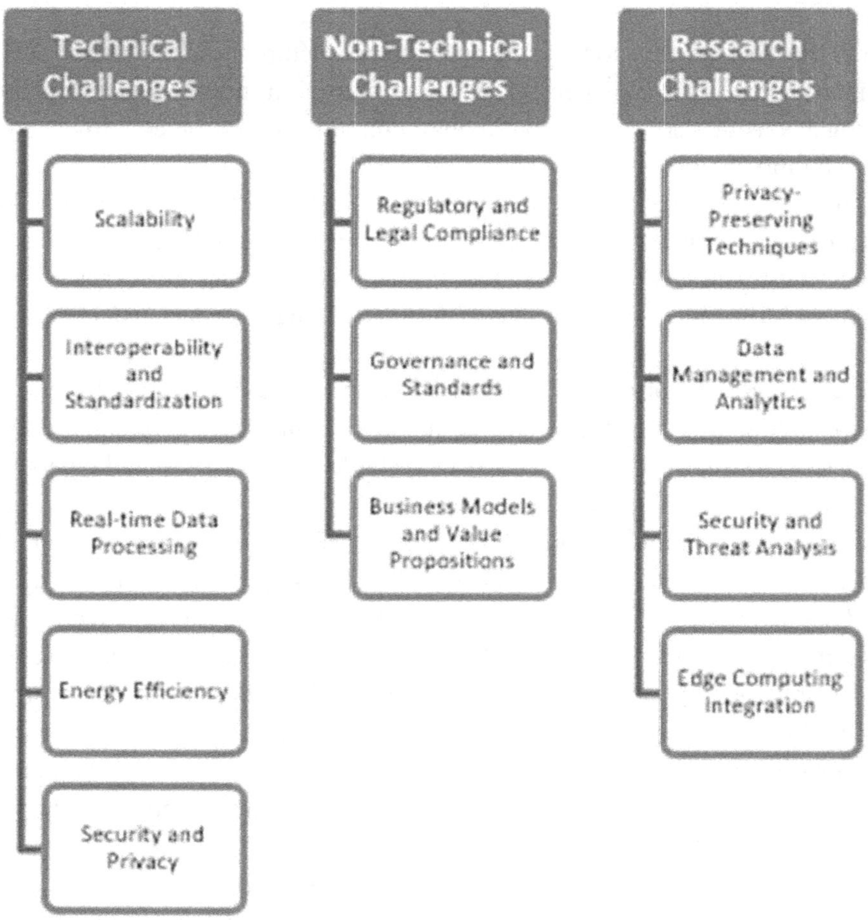

7.1. Technical Challenges

- Scalability: As mentioned earlier, scaling blockchain networks to handle the massive influx of IoT data and transactions is a major technical challenge. Increasing transaction throughput, optimizing storage requirements, and improving consensus algorithms are critical to achieving scalability.
- Interoperability: Integrating diverse IoT devices and platforms with different protocols into a unified blockchain ecosystem poses interoperability challenges. Developing standardized interfaces, common data formats, and communication protocols is essential to ensure seamless interoperability.
- Security and Privacy: Ensuring the security and privacy of data in Blockchain-IoT systems is a complex task. Addressing vulnerabilities, implementing secure communication protocols, protecting against cyber threats, and developing privacy-preserving mechanisms are key technical challenges.
- Energy Efficiency: Blockchain networks, particularly those using energy-intensive consensus algorithms like Proof of Work, consume substantial amounts of energy. Enhancing the energy efficiency of blockchain networks, optimizing resource usage, and exploring alternative consensus algorithms are important technical issues.
- Real-Time Data Processing: Many IoT applications require real-time data processing and decision-making. Developing efficient mechanisms for real-time data processing within blockchain networks is a technical challenge that involves optimizing transaction confirmation times and ensuring timely data availability.

7.2 Non-Technical Challenges

- Regulatory and Legal Compliance: Adhering to existing regulations, navigating legal frameworks, and addressing compliance requirements pose non-technical challenges. Complying with data protection, privacy, intellectual property, and cross-border data transfer regulations is critical.
- Governance and Standards: Establishing effective governance models, decision-making processes, and industry-wide standards is essential for the successful adoption and interoperability of Blockchain-IoT systems. Defining roles and responsibilities, addressing disputes, and creating governance frameworks are non-technical challenges.
- Business Models and Value Propositions: Identifying compelling use cases, developing viable business models, and demonstrating the value proposition of Blockchain-IoT systems can be non-technical challenges. Convincing stakeholders, securing funding, and ensuring a return on investment are important issues.

7.3 Research Challenges

Consensus Algorithms and Performance: Researching and developing new consensus algorithms or optimizing existing ones to achieve better scalability, energy efficiency, and performance is a key research challenge. Consensus protocols that cater specifically to the requirements of IoT environments need further exploration.

- Privacy-Preserving Techniques: Researching advanced cryptographic techniques, zero-knowledge proofs, and privacy-enhancing technologies to address privacy issues in Blockchain-IoT systems is a research challenge. Developing methods for preserving privacy while enabling data transparency is critical.
- Data Management and Analytics: Researching efficient data management and analytics techniques that can handle the massive volume, velocity, and variety of IoT data is important. Developing scalable and distributed data processing frameworks, real-time analytics algorithms, and predictive modeling techniques is a research challenge.
- Edge Computing Integration: Investigating the integration of edge computing capabilities with Blockchain-IoT systems to address latency, bandwidth, and data processing challenges is a research focus. Developing efficient edge-to-blockchain integration mechanisms and exploring distributed computing frameworks are important areas of research.
- Security and Threat Analysis: Conducting research on potential security vulnerabilities, attack vectors, and threat models specific to Blockchain-IoT systems is important. Analyzing the security implications of different consensus algorithms, communication protocols, and smart contract vulnerabilities is an ongoing research challenge.

Hence addressing these technical, non-technical, and research challenges requires collaboration among academia, industry, policymakers, and standardization bodies. Continuous research, innovation, and iterative development are necessary to overcome these challenges and unlock the full potential of Blockchain-IoT systems.

8. EMERGING TRENDS AND RESEARCH OPPORTUNITIES FOR BLOCKCHAIN-IOT SYSTEMS

Emerging trends and research opportunities in the field of Blockchain-IoT systems offer exciting possibilities for innovation and advancement. Here are some key areas that hold promise for future exploration:

- Scalability and Performance Optimization: Developing scalable and high-performance blockchain architectures specifically designed for IoT environments remains an important research focus. Optimizing consensus algorithms, exploring sharding techniques, and investigating off-chain solutions can enhance the scalability and efficiency of Blockchain-IoT systems.
- Privacy and Security Enhancements: Addressing privacy and security issues in Blockchain-IoT systems continues to be a critical research area. Novel cryptographic techniques, privacy-preserving mechanisms, and secure communication protocols can enhance data protection, confidentiality, and integrity within the ecosystem.
- Edge Computing Integration: Integrating edge computing capabilities with Blockchain-IoT systems offers opportunities for real-time data processing, reduced latency, and bandwidth optimization. Exploring edge-to-blockchain integration, distributed computing frameworks, and resource management techniques can improve the performance and efficiency of these systems.
- Hybrid Architectures: Investigating hybrid architectures that combine both public and private blockchains can provide flexibility and scalability while ensuring data privacy and regulatory

compliance. Researching mechanisms for interoperability and seamless data exchange between different blockchain types is an important area of exploration.

- Energy Efficiency and Sustainability: Designing energy-efficient blockchain consensus algorithms and exploring alternative consensus mechanisms can address the energy consumption challenges associated with blockchain networks. Researching sustainable deployment models and investigating green energy integration in Blockchain-IoT systems can contribute to a more environmentally friendly approach.
- AI and Machine Learning Integration: Further integrating AI and machine learning techniques with Blockchain-IoT systems offers opportunities for enhanced data analytics, autonomous decision-making, and optimization. Research in this area can focus on developing advanced algorithms, federated learning techniques, and intelligent automation for improved system performance.
- Governance and Incentive Mechanisms: Designing robust governance models and incentive mechanisms for decentralized Blockchain-IoT systems is a research opportunity. Investigating decentralized decision-making, consensus on rule enforcement, and mechanisms for stakeholder participation can contribute to the development of effective governance frameworks.
- Interoperability and Standardization: Advancing interoperability and standardization efforts for seamless integration of diverse IoT devices and blockchain networks is important. Research can focus on developing common data formats, communication protocols, and semantic interoperability standards to enable efficient data exchange and collaboration.
- Real-World Use Cases: Exploring and evaluating the practical implementation of Blockchain-IoT systems in various domains such as healthcare, supply chain, energy management, and smart cities presents important research opportunities. Investigating real-world challenges, assessing the impact of these systems, and identifying best practices can guide future deployments.
- Ethical and Legal Implications: Investigating the ethical and legal implications of Blockchain-IoT systems, including issues related to data ownership, accountability, and transparency, is an important research area. Examining the societal impact and implications for privacy, fairness, and bias can contribute to responsible and ethical system development.

Hence, these emerging trends and research opportunities highlight the ongoing evolution of Blockchain-IoT systems. By addressing these areas, researchers can advance the capabilities, efficiency, and security of these systems, enabling their widespread adoption and unlocking their full potential in transforming industries and society as a whole.

9. COMPARISON AND EVALUATION OF BLOCKCHAIN-IOT SOLUTIONS

9.1 Simulation Tools for Blockchain-IoT Systems

There are several simulation tools available that can be used to simulate and evaluate Blockchain-IoT systems. These tools help in understanding the behavior, performance, and scalability of such systems before actual implementation. Here are a few commonly used simulation tools for Blockchain-IoT systems:

- Ethereum Simulation Tool (Ethereum-Sim): Ethereum-Sim is a simulation framework specifically designed for simulating Ethereum-based blockchain networks. It allows users to model and simulate various aspects of Ethereum-based systems, including smart contracts, transactions, and network behavior.

- Hyperledger Caliper: Hyperledger Caliper is a benchmarking and performance measurement tool developed by the Hyperledger project. It supports benchmarking various blockchain platforms, including Hyperledger Fabric, for evaluating their performance in terms of throughput, latency, and resource utilization.
- OMNeT++: OMNeT++ is a widely used discrete event simulation framework that provides support for modeling and simulating complex systems, including Blockchain-IoT systems. It offers a modular and extensible architecture, allowing users to build custom simulation models for blockchain and IoT components.
- Cooja: Cooja is a simulator specifically designed for Wireless Sensor Networks (WSNs) and IoT applications. It can be used to simulate IoT devices and their interactions with blockchain networks. Cooja supports various IoT protocols, such as IEEE 802.15.4, and can be extended to incorporate blockchain-specific functionalities.
- NetSim: NetSim is a comprehensive network simulation tool that supports the modeling and simulation of various network technologies, including IoT and blockchain. It offers a visual interface for designing network topologies and allows users to simulate different network applications to evaluate the performance of Blockchain-IoT systems.
- BlockSim: BlockSim is a blockchain simulation tool that focuses on the performance evaluation of blockchain systems. It supports modeling and simulating different blockchain consensus algorithms, network topologies, and transactional workloads to analyze the scalability, throughput, and latency of blockchain networks.

Note that these simulation tools provide researchers and developers with the means to evaluate the performance, scalability, and behavior of Blockchain-IoT systems in a controlled environment. They can help in identifying potential bottlenecks, optimizing system parameters, and understanding the impact of different factors on the overall system performance before deploying the system in real-world applications.

9.2 Evaluation Criteria and Metrics for Blockchain-IoT Systems

When evaluating Blockchain-IoT systems, it is important to consider various criteria and metrics that assess the performance, efficiency, security, and overall effectiveness of the system. Here are some key evaluation criteria and metrics for Blockchain-IoT systems:

9.2.1 Scalability

- Transaction Throughput: Measures the number of transactions processed per unit of time, indicating the system's capacity to handle a high volume of transactions.
- Network Scalability: Assesses the system's ability to handle a growing number of participants and devices while maintaining performance and efficiency.

9.2.2 Performance

- Transaction Latency: Measures the time taken for a transaction to be processed and validated on the blockchain, indicating the system's responsiveness.
- Network Latency: Measures the time it takes for data to travel between IoT devices and the blockchain network, reflecting the system's efficiency in real-time data transmission.

9.2.3 Security

- Data Integrity: Ensures the immutability and tamper-resistance of data stored on the blockchain, indicating the system's ability to maintain the integrity of IoT-generated data.
- Consensus Mechanism Security: Evaluates the security guarantees provided by the chosen consensus mechanism to prevent malicious attacks and ensure the validity of transactions.

9.2.4 Privacy and Confidentiality

- Identity Management: Assesses the system's ability to manage and protect the identities of participants, ensuring privacy and preventing unauthorized access to sensitive data.
- Data Encryption: Evaluates the encryption mechanisms employed to secure data transmission and storage, protecting the confidentiality of IoT-generated data.

9.2.5 Interoperability

- Data Standardization: Assesses the use of standardized data formats and communication protocols to enable seamless data exchange between IoT devices and the blockchain network.
- Integration with Existing Systems: Measures the system's ability to add with legacy systems and other technologies, ensuring interoperability and compatibility.

9.2.6 Resource Efficiency

- Energy Efficiency: Evaluates the energy consumption of IoT devices and the blockchain network, ensuring resource-efficient operation.
- Storage Efficiency: Measures the storage requirements of the blockchain network and data compression techniques employed to optimize storage capacity.

9.2.7 Reliability and Availability

- System Uptime: Measures the system's availability and uptime, indicating its reliability and ability to provide continuous service.
- Fault Tolerance: Evaluates the system's ability to withstand failures, ensuring the availability and integrity of data in the event of network or device failures.

9.2.8 User Experience

- Ease of Use: Assesses the user-friendliness of the system, considering the user interface, interaction design, and accessibility of functionalities.
- Accessibility: Evaluates the system's accessibility for users with disabilities, ensuring inclusivity and equal access to the system.

These evaluation criteria and metrics provide a comprehensive framework for assessing the performance, security, privacy, and usability of Blockchain-IoT systems. Organizations and researchers can use these criteria and metrics to evaluate and compare different systems, identify areas for improvement, and make informed decisions regarding the adoption and deployment of Blockchain-IoT solutions.

9.3 Comparative Analysis of Existing Solutions for Blockchain-IoT Systems

To provide a comparative analysis of existing solutions for Blockchain-IoT systems, let's consider several prominent platforms and frameworks:

9.3.1 Hyperledger Fabric

- Scalability: Hyperledger Fabric supports a scalable network architecture, enabling high throughput and parallel transaction processing.
- Performance: Fabric add its modular architecture to optimize performance, allowing for customizable consensus algorithms and pluggable smart contract execution engines.
- Security: Fabric provides robust security features, including fine-grained access control, private data collections, and channel-based data isolation.
- Interoperability: Fabric offers interoperability through its pluggable consensus mechanism and support for various programming languages and smart contract platforms.
- Privacy and Confidentiality: Fabric incorporates private channels and confidential smart contracts to ensure privacy and confidentiality of data.
- Reliability and Availability: Fabric provides fault tolerance and high availability through its consensus protocols and support for multiple endorsing peers.

9.3.2 Ethereum

- Scalability: Ethereum faces scalability challenges due to its Proof of Work consensus mechanism, but ongoing research and development aim to improve scalability with the introduction of Ethereum 2.0 and its transition to Proof of Stake.
- Performance: Ethereum's transaction processing speed and latency are influenced by network congestion and gas fees.
- Security: Ethereum has a strong security focus, with its large developer community actively discovering and addressing vulnerabilities.
- Interoperability: Ethereum offers interoperability through its standardized smart contract language, Solidity, and its support for token standards like ERC-20 and ERC-721.

- Privacy and Confidentiality: Ethereum's privacy features are being enhanced through solutions like zero-knowledge proofs and off-chain transactions.
- Reliability and Availability: Ethereum's reliability and availability depend on the decentralized network of nodes that maintain the blockchain.

9.3.3 IOTA

- Scalability: IOTA's unique Tangle architecture is designed to scale horizontally as the number of transactions and participants increase.
- Performance: IOTA aims for high transaction throughput and low latency by adding its directed acyclic graph (DAG) structure.
- Security: IOTA employs cryptographic algorithms to secure transactions and prevent tampering or double-spending.
- Interoperability: IOTA focuses on machine-to-machine (M2M) interactions and aims to enable interoperability between IoT devices using its protocol.
- Privacy and Confidentiality: IOTA addresses privacy issues by implementing transaction pseudonymity and exploring techniques like maskable authentication.
- Reliability and Availability: IOTA's reliability relies on the integrity and consensus of the Tangle, which is continuously validated by participating nodes.

9.3.4 R3 Corda

- Scalability: Corda employs a unique shared ledger architecture that allows for scalability and privacy among participants.
- Performance: Corda's performance is optimized for financial and enterprise use cases, with a focus on achieving high throughput and low latency.
- Security: Corda enables secure coding practices and provides fine-grained access controls to protect data and ensure transaction integrity.
- Interoperability: Corda supports interoperability through its ability to integrate with existing enterprise systems and facilitate data exchange between different networks.
- Privacy and Confidentiality: Corda's design emphasizes privacy by only sharing necessary data with involved parties and utilizing secure key management.
- Reliability and Availability: Corda ensures reliability through its consensus algorithm and consensus notary services, enabling non-repudiation and fault tolerance.

Note that each solution has its strengths and weaknesses, and the choice of platform depends on specific use cases, requirements, and the trade-offs that organizations are willing to make. Further research and evaluation are necessary to select the most suitable solution for a particular Blockchain-IoT application.

9.4 Strengths and Limitations of Different Approaches for Blockchain-IoT Systems

Different approaches for Blockchain-IoT systems have their own strengths and limitations. Here are some common approaches and their associated strengths and limitations:

9.4.1 Public Blockchain Approach

Strengths:

- Decentralization: Public blockchains provide a decentralized network, ensuring transparency and resilience against single points of failure.
- Security: Public blockchains utilize consensus mechanisms and cryptographic algorithms to ensure data integrity and prevent tampering.
- Trust: Public blockchains eliminate the need for trust between participants, as the trust is placed in the consensus protocol and the blockchain itself.

Limitations:

- Scalability: Public blockchains often face scalability challenges due to the large number of participants and the computational overhead of consensus mechanisms.
- Privacy: Public blockchains typically have limited privacy features, as all transactions and data are publicly visible, compromising the confidentiality of sensitive IoT data.
- Governance: Public blockchains may face challenges related to governance, decision-making processes, and regulatory compliance due to their decentralized nature.

9.4.2 Private/Consortium Blockchain Approach

Strengths:

- Scalability: Private/consortium blockchains can achieve higher scalability compared to public blockchains by limiting the number of participating nodes.
- Privacy: Private/consortium blockchains provide stronger privacy features by restricting data visibility to authorized participants, ensuring confidentiality.
- Governance: Private/consortium blockchains offer more centralized governance structures, making decision-making processes and regulatory compliance more manageable.

Limitations:

- Centralization Issues: Private/consortium blockchains introduce centralization issues, as decision-making authority is concentrated among a limited number of participants.
- Trust Requirements: Private/consortium blockchains rely on trust among the participating entities, which may be a limitation if trust is not established or maintained.
- Reduced Security: Private/consortium blockchains may have a lower level of security compared to public blockchains, as they are not subject to the same level of consensus and validation from a large network.

9.4.3 Hybrid Approaches

Strengths:

- Scalability and Performance: Hybrid approaches combine the benefits of public and private blockchains, allowing for scalable and performant solutions.
- Privacy and Confidentiality: Hybrid approaches can offer a balance between data privacy and transparency by utilizing public and private blockchain components appropriately.

- Flexibility: Hybrid approaches provide flexibility in terms of data sharing, allowing organizations to determine the level of data visibility based on their specific requirements.

Limitations:

- Complexity: Hybrid approaches can introduce additional complexity in terms of system design, implementation, and interoperability between public and private blockchain components.
- Governance Challenges: Hybrid approaches may face challenges related to governance and coordination between public and private blockchain networks.

9.4.4 Off-Chain Solutions

Strengths:

- Scalability: Off-chain solutions, such as sidechains or state channels, offer scalability by moving some transactions and data off the main blockchain.
- Performance: Off-chain solutions can provide faster transaction processing and lower fees compared to on-chain transactions.
- Privacy: Off-chain solutions can enhance privacy by keeping sensitive data off the main blockchain, reducing public visibility.

Limitations:

- Trusted Third Parties: Off-chain solutions often require trust in third-party intermediaries to handle off-chain transactions, raising issues about centralization and security.
- Complexity: Off-chain solutions add complexity to system architecture and require additional development and maintenance efforts.

Hence, we need to assess the strengths and limitations of different approaches for Blockchain-IoT systems based on specific use cases, requirements, and trade-offs. Organizations should carefully consider these factors when selecting an approach that best aligns with their needs and objectives.

10. CONCLUSION

This chapter explains about Blockchain-IoT solutions which have the potential to revolutionize various industries by addressing critical issues of security, trust, and automation. However, challenges related to interoperability, scalability, and energy efficiency must be addressed to unlock the full potential of this technology convergence. As the technology continues to evolve, continued research, development, and collaboration are crucial to drive innovation and harness the benefits of Blockchain-IoT solutions.

REFERENCES

Al-Marridi, A. Z., Mohamed, A., & Erbad, A. (2021). Reinforcement learning approaches for efficient and secure blockchain-powered smart health systems. *Computer Networks*, *197*, 108279. doi:10.1016/j.comnet.2021.108279

Ali, A., Pasha, M. F., Fang, O. H., Khan, R., Almaiah, M. A., & Al Hwaitat, A. K. (2022). Big Data Based Smart Blockchain for Information Retrieval in Privacy-Preserving Healthcare System. In *Big Data Intelligence for Smart Applications* (pp. 279–296). Springer International Publishing. doi:10.1007/978-3-030-87954-9_13

Chen, M., Malook, T., Rehman, A. U., Muhammad, Y., Alshehri, M. D., Akbar, A., Bilal, M., & Khan, M. A. (2021). Blockchain-Enabled healthcare system for detection of diabetes. *Journal of Information Security and Applications*, *58*, 102771. doi:10.1016/j.jisa.2021.102771

Deshmukh, A., Sreenath, N., Tyagi, A. K., & Eswara Abhichandan, U. V. (2022). Blockchain Enabled Cyber Security: A Comprehensive Survey. *2022 International Conference on Computer Communication and Informatics (ICCCI)*, 1-6. 10.1109/ICCCI54379.2022.9740843

Hathaliya, J., Sharma, P., Tanwar, S., & Gupta, R. (2019). Blockchain-based remote patient monitoring in healthcare 4.0. In *2019 IEEE 9th international conference on advanced computing (IACC)* (pp. 87-91). IEEE. 10.1109/IACC48062.2019.8971593

Healthcare Cybersecurity Market to Reach USD 27.10 Billion by 2026. (2019). *Reports and Data.*

Jayaprakash, V., & Tyagi, A. K. (n.d.). The Security Optimization of Resource-Constrained Internet of Healthcare Things (IoHT) Devices Using Lightweight Cryptography. Information Security Practices for the Internet of Things, 5G, and Next-Generation Wireless Networks. doi:10.4018/978-1-6684-3921-0.ch009

Khatoon, A. (2020). A blockchain-based smart contract system for healthcare management. *Electronics (Basel)*, *9*(1), 94. doi:10.3390/electronics9010094

Khubrani, M. M. (2021). A framework for blockchain-based smart health system. *Turkish Journal of Computer and Mathematics Education*, *12*(9), 2609–2614.

Kumar, T., Ramani, V., Ahmad, I., Braeken, A., Harjula, E., & Ylianttila, M. (2018). Blockchain utilization in healthcare: Key requirements and challenges. In *2018 IEEE 20th International conference on e-health networking, applications and services (Healthcom)* (pp. 1-7). IEEE. 10.1109/HealthCom.2018.8531136

Mikulic, M. (2019). *Projected growth in global healthcare data* (Vol. 2020). Statista.

Nair & Tyagi. (2023). Blockchain technology for next-generation society: current trends and future opportunities for smart era. In *Blockchain Technology for Secure Social Media Computing*. doi:10.1049/PBSE019E_ch11

Nair, M. M., & Tyagi, A. K. (2021). Privacy: History, Statistics, Policy, Laws, Preservation and Threat Analysis. Journal of Information Assurance & Security, 16(1), 24-34.

Pandey, A. A., Fernandez, T. F., Bansal, R., & Tyagi, A. K. (2022). Maintaining Scalability in Blockchain. In A. Abraham, N. Gandhi, T. Hanne, T. P. Hong, T. Nogueira Rios, & W. Ding (Eds.), *Intelligent Systems Design and Applications. ISDA 2021. Lecture Notes in Networks and Systems* (Vol. 418). Springer. doi:10.1007/978-3-030-96308-8_4

Pham, H. L., Tran, T. H., & Nakashima, Y. (2018). A secure remote healthcare system for hospital using blockchain smart contract. In 2018 IEEE GLOBECOM workshops (GC Wkshps) (pp. 1-6). IEEE. doi:10.1109/GLOCOMW.2018.8644164

Quasim, M. T., Algarni, F., Abd Elhamid Radwan, A., & Goram Mufareh, M. A. (2020). A blockchain based secured healthcare framework. In *2020 International Conference on Computational Performance Evaluation (ComPE)* (pp. 386-391). IEEE. 10.1109/ComPE49325.2020.9200024

Ramani, V., Kumar, T., Bracken, A., Liyanage, M., & Ylianttila, M. (2018). Secure and efficient data accessibility in blockchain based healthcare systems. In *2018 IEEE Global Communications Conference (GLOBECOM)* (pp. 206-212). IEEE. 10.1109/GLOCOM.2018.8647221

Sharma, A., Tomar, R., Chilamkurti, N., & Kim, B.-G. (2020). Blockchain based smart contracts for internet of medical things in e-healthcare. *Electronics (Basel)*, *9*(10), 1609. doi:10.3390/electronics9101609

Sharma, P., Moparthi, N. R., Namasudra, S., Shanmuganathan, V., & Hsu, C.-H. (2022). Blockchain-based IoT architecture to secure healthcare system using identity-based encryption. *Expert Systems: International Journal of Knowledge Engineering and Neural Networks*, *39*(10), e12915. doi:10.1111/exsy.12915

Sheth, & Tyagi. (2022). Deep Learning, Blockchain based Multi-layered Authentication and Security Architectures. *2022 International Conference on Applied Artificial Intelligence and Computing (ICAAIC)*, 476-485. 10.1109/ICAAIC53929.2022.9793179

Soltanisehat, L., Alizadeh, R., Hao, H., & Choo, K.-K. R. (2020). Technical, temporal, and spatial research challenges and opportunities in blockchain-based healthcare: A systematic literature review. *IEEE Transactions on Engineering Management.*

Son, H. X., Le, T. H., Nga, T. T. Q., Hung, N. D. H., Duong-Trung, N., & Luong, H. H. (2021). Toward a blockchain-based technology in dealing with emergencies in patient-centered healthcare systems. In *Mobile, Secure, and Programmable Networking: 6th International Conference, MSPN 2020, Paris, France, October 28–29, 2020, Revised Selected Papers 6* (pp. 44-56). Springer International Publishing. 10.1007/978-3-030-67550-9_4

Srivastava, Anshu, Bansal, Soni, & Tyagi. (2023). Blockchain Enabled Internet of Things: Current Scenario and Open Challenges for Future. In Innovations in Bio-Inspired Computing and Applications. IBICA 2022. Lecture Notes in Networks and Systems (vol. 649). Springer. doi:10.1007/978-3-031-27499-2_59

Tripathi, G., Ahad, M. A., & Paiva, S. (2020). S2HS-A blockchain based approach for smart healthcare system. Healthcare, 8(1). doi:10.1016/j.hjdsi.2019.100391

Tyagi, A. K. (2021). *Analysis of Security and Privacy Aspects of Blockchain Technologies from Smart Era' Perspective: The Challenges and a Way Forward. In Recent Trends in Blockchain for Information Systems Security and Privacy*. CRC Press.

Tyagi, A. K. (2023). Decentralized everything: Practical use of blockchain technology in future applications. In Distributed Computing to Blockchain. Academic Press. doi:10.1016/B978-0-323-96146-2.00010-3

Tyagi, A. K., & Aswathy, S. U. (2021, October). AARIN: Affordable, Accurate, Reliable and INnovative Mechanism to Protect a Medical Cyber-Physical System using Blockchain Technology. *IJIN*, *2*, 175–183.

Tyagi, A. K., Chandrasekaran, S., & Sreenath, N. (2022). Blockchain Technology:– A New Technology for Creating Distributed and Trusted Computing Environment. *2022 International Conference on Applied Artificial Intelligence and Computing (ICAAIC)*, 1348-1354. 10.1109/ICAAIC53929.2022.9792702

Tyagi, A. K., Dananjayan, S., Agarwal, D., & Thariq Ahmed, H. F. (2023). Blockchain—Internet of Things Applications: Opportunities and Challenges for Industry 4.0 and Society 5.0. *Sensors (Basel), 23*(2), 947. doi:10.339023020947 PMID:36679743

Varsha, R. (2020, January 1). Deep Learning Based Blockchain Solution for Preserving Privacy in Future Vehicles. *International Journal of Hybrid Intelligent Systems, 16*(4), 223–236.

Wu, G., Wang, S., Ning, Z., & Zhu, B. (2021). Privacy-preserved electronic medical record exchanging and sharing: A blockchain-based smart healthcare system. *IEEE Journal of Biomedical and Health Informatics, 26*(5), 1917–1927. doi:10.1109/JBHI.2021.3123643 PMID:34714757

Xu, J., Xue, K., Li, S., Tian, H., Hong, J., Hong, P., & Yu, N. (2019). Healthchain: A blockchain-based privacy preserving scheme for large-scale health data. *IEEE Internet of Things Journal, 6*(5), 8770–8781. doi:10.1109/JIOT.2019.2923525

Chapter 6
Improving Cloud Security Using Distributed Ledger Technology

Rahul K. Patel
https://orcid.org/0000-0003-1175-0635
Illinois Institute of Technology, Chicago, USA

Deekshitha Somanahalli Umesh
Illinois Institute of Technology, Chicago, USA

Nikunj R. Patel
University of Wisconsin-Madison, Madison, USA

ABSTRACT

The confidentiality, integrity, and availability triad is a fundamental principle for information security. The objective of this chapter is to examine this triad where blockchain technology can be applied to enhance security in cloud computing. The current pasture of cloud security is explored to identify the gaps and approaches for using blockchain technology to reduce those gaps are discussed in this chapter. Blockchain technology is well-recognized for its ability to ensure data integrity. The largest gap that can be reduced is in this area. With the decentralized and distributed architecture of blockchain, there are ways to leverage it to improve the availability of cloud security. Confidentiality, where encryption plays a significant role, has the least gap in cloud computing; however, since the responsibility for assuring confidentiality is on the user, blockchain offers alternative and additional strengths. This chapter also covers a detailed discussion of avoiding prevalent security threats by implementing blockchain technology in cloud computing for making it more secure.

Ensuring the security of cloud computing is crucial to safeguard the data, applications, and infrastructure involved in cloud computing. This protection is achieved through the implementation of policies and various security technologies. Cloud computing plays a significant role in network and information security. Organizations utilize the cloud environment, employing diverse cloud service models and deployment options. Cloud security concerns can be classified into two categories: issues faced by the cloud provider and issues faced by the consumer of the cloud.

DOI: 10.4018/979-8-3693-0593-5.ch006

The provider is responsible for securing their infrastructure, data, and applications of their clients. Meanwhile, users employ robust passwords and authentication methods. Therefore, it is essential to have an effective cloud security architecture that offers control to protect applications and minimize potential attacks. Blockchain emerges as a novel technology in the era of information, offering exceptional security through peer authentication, encryption, and hash value mechanisms. Due to its efficiency and availability, cloud computing finds applications across various IT environments (Pavithra et al., 2019).

Cloud users request services from the Cloud Service Providers (CSP) (Gupta et al., 2019). A cloud service provider (CSP) is an Information technology organization that provides scalable, on-demand computing resources including computing power, data storage, applications, and middleware over the internet on subscription. Typically cloud resources are provided as the SaaS (software-as-a-service) or the "on-demand software" as a service, the PaaS (platform-as-a-service), where the customer organization maintains the applications and requires the cloud as the running platform for these applications, or the IaaS (infrastructure-as-a-service), where the CSP provides and maintains the IT infrastructure systems such as servers, storage, backup, network (Lahouij, Hamel, & Graiet, 2022). Additional third-party service providers in the cloud include the Third-Party Auditor (TPA) and Attribute Authority (AA), both of which are responsible for delivering various security functionalities (Gupta, Siddiqui, Alam., & Shuaib, 2019).

Blockchain technology offers superior security when compared to traditional centralized database security. The members of the gadgets within the blockchain are known as hubs. Blockchain enables a decentralized system in which all the coordinating hubs have an active stake in approving and validating the information. To ensure data integrity, the information stored on the blockchain is encrypted using encryption techniques. The blocks in the blockchain are interconnected using encrypted hashes, timestamps, and hashes of their immediate predecessors. This design guarantees the immutability of the stored information, as no one can tamper with it. There is no need for consumers to worry about their data being compromised because blockchain technology ensures that all participants are verified across the network (Rani et al., 2022).

It is crucial to acknowledge that although blockchain technology presents numerous security advantages, its implementation and integration with the current cloud infrastructure must be meticulously planned and assessed. Blockchain is not a universal solution for all cloud security issues, and organizations should consider factors like scalability, performance, and privacy considerations when considering its adoption for cloud security purposes.

CURRENT STATE OF CLOUD SECURITY

In recent years, numerous surveys have been concentrated on exploring security challenges in cloud computing. A comprehensive review of cloud security is provided by delving into distinct aspects while addressing the issues and challenges in this chapter's cloud security. A cloud service provider (CSP) refers to an entity or organization that provides services to cloud consumers. To enhance the security capabilities, cloud service providers are dedicating considerable resources however there are still challenges remaining. Their responsibilities encompass procuring and managing cloud infrastructure, as well as structuring and arranging cloud infrastructure.

CSPs offer cloud services that are generally aligned to three different models. In the software as a service (SaaS) model, services are delivered by the cloud provider at specified levels by configuring, maintaining, deploying, and updating the various software applications. The SaaS provider manages and controls the infrastructure and applications due to the limited administrative applications of cloud. In the Platform as a Service (PaaS) model, the cloud provider manages the computing infrastructure of the platform, whereas cloud software supplies the platform elements such as runtime software, databases, and middleware components. In the Infrastructure as a Service (IaaS) model, the cloud provider provides computing resources encompassing networks, storage, servers, and hosting infrastructure (Tabrizchi & Rafsanjani, 2020).

All cloud vendors provide security services under a Shared Responsibility model where responsibility for security is shared by CSPs and Customer organizations at varying degrees. The Shared Responsibility Model stands as a security and compliance framework outlining the responsibilities of both cloud service providers (CSPs) and customers in ensuring the security of distinct aspects of the cloud environment. These responsibilities encompass infrastructure, hardware, endpoints, settings, data, configuration, network controls, operating system (OS), and access rights. As per the Shared Responsibility Model, the cloud provider is responsible for supervising and addressing security risks related to the cloud platform and its underlying infrastructure.

On the other hand, end users, whether they are individuals or organizations, bear the responsibility of protecting their data and other resources stored in any cloud environment. To ensure the adherence to security standards, Cloud security practices are influenced by compliance requirements and regulations. Compliance with industry standards and data privacy regulations such as General Data Protection Regulation (GDPR) in the EU, Health Insurance Portability and Accountability Act (HIPAA) in the USA, and California Consumer Privacy Acts (CCPA) remain a top concern, and cloud providers are working to ensure compliance with the services. There are more such regulations in development that will become regulatory requirements worldwide. Encryption plays a significant role in ensuring the security of data stored in the cloud. Organizations are implementing encryption methods to protect data while it is at rest, in motion, and being processed in the cloud. In addition, strategies such as data loss prevention (DLP) and data classification are used to protect sensitive information.

To ensure compliance with security standards, Cloud security practices are influenced by compliance requirements and regulations. Compliance with industry benchmarks and privacy regulations for data (such as GDPR, HIPAA, and CCPA) remains a top concern, and cloud providers are striving to guarantee compliance in their services. Encryption serves a pivotal function in upholding the security of data stored in the cloud. Enterprises are integrating encryption techniques to protect data throughout its static, transit, and processing phases in the cloud. Additionally, strategies like data loss prevention (DLP) and data classification are employed to protect sensitive information.

Cloud Security Principles

A safer environment to do business and hence cybersecurity concerns are acute for cloud computing and hence cloud security is becoming increasingly prominent, showing a trend of diversification and complexity. Meanwhile, it is also imperative to select guiding principles to focus the effort on the most prominent needs. Multifaced hacking attacks warrant that cloud computing services must be deployed with safe and effective network protection and monitoring mechanisms (Fu, 2022). The architecture of a cloud security system considers the tools, policies, and procedures needed to protect cloud resources from security threats. Among its fundamentals, it includes:

Security by Design and Visibility: Built-in protection against cybersecurity threats must be considered in the architecture and design phase of the cloud infrastructure components according to the principle of security by design. The cloud architecture's design should integrate security measures that are resistant to security misconfigurations. For example, when the cloud storage container holds sensitive information, external access will be restricted, and the administrator will have no way of opening access to the public internet. Numerous organizations employ hybrid and multi-cloud deployments that conventional security solutions struggle to protect. A successful approach considers both tools and methodologies to sustain visibility throughout an organization's cloud infrastructure.

Cybersecurity and Unified Management Interface: Cloud computing requires shared responsibility for the security of cloud resources. The customer organization is responsible for ensuring the security of traffic flows to and from cloud resources; and between the public cloud and the on-premises network. CSP is responsible for ensuring the cybersecurity capabilities available as a part of services. Customer organizations need to leverage the capability offered by CSP and implement those in an effective way for their needs. Effective network segmentation also plays a key role in limiting attackers' ability to move sideways once they gain access to the network. Security teams frequently face heavy workloads and limited staffing; hence cloud security solutions must offer unified management interfaces. Teams should be able to centrally administer multiple cloud security solutions from a single screen.

Agility and Automation: Cloud computing facilitates the development and deployment of innovative solutions by seamlessly integrating various capabilities in a logical way. It is important that security does not hinder this agility. Organizations can adopt cloud-native security solutions that seamlessly integrate into agile development extending the software development operation from DevOps to DevSecOps. Automation is required to deliver and update security controls in a cloud environment. In addition, it helps to detect and correct misconfigurations and other security vulnerabilities in real-time. Cloud Computing makes automation easier with modern machine learning (ML) and artificial intelligence (AI) services as an integrated offering.

Compliance: Many Cloud Computing services provide automated checks for the regulations and standards such as GDPR, CCPA, and PCI/DSS for verifying the effectiveness of technical and procedural controls in the cloud by providing self-monitoring and auditing tools. While organizations can take advantage of such solutions offered by a cloud provider, the solution may not provide visibility across multiple clouds and hybrid implementations. Customer organizations often need to implement third-party solutions to effectively protect, monitor, and manage compliance needs across multiple cloud providers.

Shared Security Model

The shared security model is a fundamental concept in cloud security that outlines the division of responsibilities between cloud service providers (CSPs) and their customers (users) when it comes to securing data, applications, and resources in the cloud environment. This model is especially relevant in Infrastructure as a Service (IaaS), Platform as a Service (PaaS), and Software as a Service (SaaS) deployments. It aims to create a clear understanding of who is responsible for various aspects of security, ensuring a collaborative approach to maintaining a secure cloud ecosystem. In the shared security model, the distribution of security responsibilities is typically divided into two main categories: the "security of the cloud" and the "security in the cloud."

Security "of" the Cloud: Responsibilities of the CSP

Physical premises security: Cloud infrastructure is hosted in the CSP's datacenters except on-premises cloud implementations. The cloud service provider (CSP) bears the responsibility of protecting the physical nodes, including the data center, as well as other presence points like the edge locations within the provider's content delivery network. CSP ensures the security and fault tolerance of all supporting systems. This involves maintaining dependable power, HVAC systems, and protection against natural disasters. CSPs also carry the responsibility for automated failover to another physical location in disastrous situations.

Hosted infrastructure: CSP protects the internal network, storage, and computing infrastructure. In a multi-tenant architecture, they ensure that the customer organization's assets, using common infrastructure sub-systems for transmission, processing, and storing customer information, are segregated from each other. Communication service providers are also subjected to a variety of compliance tests to ensure that the services they deliver to customers are legal. Furthermore, they maintain infrastructure in multiple geographic areas to meet regulations that require data to be held in specific regions.

Security "in" the Cloud: Customer Responsibility in the Cloud

Operating System and Network: The security of the operating system (OS) that customers install on their instances is their responsibility when using the cloud services under SaaS model. Customers manage operating system security as well as configurations, updates, and security patches. Customer is also responsible for the security of virtualized networks that customer deploys for communication between customer's resources and the outside world, including all network-enabled services such as identity and access management (IAM), firewalls, access control lists (ACLs), gateway configuration, domain name services (DNS) server and distributed denial of service (DDoS) protections.

Application and Data Protection: Customers are responsible for safeguarding their applications against attacks such as SQL injection, cross-site scripting, and brute-force intrusion attempts. Customers must secure the data they put into the cloud, both in storage (hosted in the cloud) and in transit, using encryption and IAM controls. Companies must protect their data from both external and internal threats. All groups must follow a least privileged access policy, and user activity must be monitored using machine learning models to detect unusual activities. By combining IAM policies and audit logs, customers can audit events related to data access and data leaks that occurred in the environment.

Security Mechanisms in Cloud Computing

Cloud computing services providers offer many traditional and cloud specific security capabilities in cloud environments. Typically, these capabilities are available to the customer and require further configuration and implementation. Customers usually harden controls using these functionalities based on the threats, vulnerabilities, and required data protection. A threat is a potential cause of a problem that can harm a system or organization, while a vulnerability can be defined as a weakness in a system that is exploited by a threat. A threat actor exploits one or more vulnerabilities to execute a threat.

Encryption

By default, data is encrypted in plain text, which is readable. When transmitted over a network, the risk is unauthorized access and potential danger. Encryption technology works by converting plaintext data into encrypted data, known as ciphertext, using a standard process called cryptography. Except for other sorts of metadata such as message length and creation date, access to the ciphertext does not reveal the exact specifics of the text. When using encryption to listen to data, the data is linked to a string of characters known as an encryption key. The encryption key is used to decrypt the ciphertext and convert it back to its original written format.

Hashing

Hashing is a one-way cryptographic conversion of a string of characters (data) into a restricted number of short lengths or a key that reflects the original string. Hashing provides a unique string for unique content. Since the hash value is shorter and it is a standard length, it provides faster identify, search, and retrieve capabilities that can be used to verify the integrity of data in large databases. Some of the commonly used hashing algorithms in the cloud environment include Secure Hash Algorithm 256 (SHA-256, Secure Hash Algorithm 3 (SHA-3) for various purposes, including data integrity verification and digital signatures.

Digital Signatures

A digital signature scheme is an effective approach to achieve non-repudiation and verifying the integrity of a file or a message (Fang, Chen, Zhang, Pei, Gao, & Wang, 2020). Prior to transmission, a message is granted a digital signature, and any subsequent, unauthorized modifications render the message invalid. A digital signature verifies that the message received is identical to the original message provided by the proper sender.

A digital signature is created using hashing and asymmetrical encryption. It exists as a message digest that was encrypted using a private key and attached to the original message. The recipient verifies the signature validity by using the corresponding public key, which generates the message digest, to decrypt the digital signature's encrypted hash. The hashing mechanism is applied to the original message to produce the message digest. Identical results from two distinct methods indicate that the message's integrity was preserved.

Single Sign-On

Single sign-on (SSO) systems strengthen the authentication while retaining most of the benefits of traditional password-based authentication techniques. SSO allows users to rely on a single master credential to access a multitude of accounts using federated identity systems (FIS) allows user to authenticate with primary identity provider which in turn relays approval/denial decision to relaying parties or using credential managers (CM) where central CM entity provides authentication services to all subscribing parties (Alaca & Oorschot, 2020). Without SSO the service consumer would have to re-authenticate themselves with each subsequent request. The SSO systems allow independent FIS or CM to generate and distribute operational authorization that are typically one-time tokens avoiding requirement for password transmissions every time user authenticates to new system.

Public Key Infrastructure

PKI is a framework for the secured data exchanges using a private key and a public key in an insecure public network (Park, Kim & Ryou, 2018). PKI enables large-scale systems to safely use public-key cryptography, is a standard way for managing the issue of asymmetric keys. This approach is used to associate public keys with their respective key owners (known as public-key identification) while also allowing key validity to be verified. PKIs use digitally signed data structures that rely on digital certificates to bind public keys to the identities of certificate owners and relevant information such as validity periods. The digital certificates are digitally signed by a third-party certificate authority (CA).

A PKI's components include a certificate authority (CA) that provides certificates, a registration authority (RA) that approves certificate issuance, a public directory storing the issued certificates, and a certificate revocation list (CRL).

Identity and Access Management

With the accumulation of sensitive and confidential data files and applications in the cloud, it is important to take all necessary precautions to protect our cloud resources, preventing breaches and possible loss of systems and data. Identity and access management (IAM) stands out as one of the most effective ways to ensure cloud security. This chapter aims to examine the rationale behind the importance of the identity and access management domain as the center of control for data security in a cloud environment.

Aspects of identity and access management include authentication, authorization, federated identity, and compliance. This integrated approach ensures that only authorized users are effectively included in the cloud environment.

Authentication

Authentication is important for cloud security as it helps to verify and prove the identity of the user. A similar process exists in the real world as an ID card or other identification document. IAM systems provide an elevated level of security in the cloud through several secure authentication mechanisms.

Common authentication mechanisms in a cloud system include "login credential, multi-factor authentication, third-party authentication, plain text password, 3D password object, password graphics, biometric authentication, and digital device authentication". To improve security controls, some cloud service providers (CSPs) use physical security mechanisms, such as access tokens or biometrics, to deny unauthorized access to information via authentication. In addition, identity and access management may include some sort of digital mechanism, ensuring security in a cloud environment.

Authorization

The concept of delegation ensures that the entities identified are only capable of performing the tasks for which they are authorized to perform. Authorization is used to check the access rights an entity is entitled to. To avoid compromising data security, the cloud environment determines the authorization levels of different entities. After successful authentication, authorization management determines if the authenticated entity can perform any function in each application. The cloud offers many granular levels of authorization mechanisms based on applicable service role and user role. These can be further controlled based on process, location, time, and behavior-based policies.

Federated Identity Management

Federated identity management ensures trust between the web application and the identity provider through a public key infrastructure (PKI) and certified public key exchange. In Federated Identity Management implementation, cloud services authenticate using the organization's identity provider which acts as a primary authentication provider.

In conclusion, IAM systems are essential to providing security in cloud environments through complex authentication and authorization management mechanisms. These mechanisms may include physical methods or digital methods such as public key infrastructure. Privacy is considered vital in protecting the cloud environment and can be achieved through identity and access management, ensuring the highest level of data security (IMI, 2021).

Data Protection

Cloud data protection is accomplished by developing a third-party proxy that users trust. A trusted proxy is not a physical entity. It is a logical entity that can be developed on the user's side (such as on the user's personal computer) or where the user can trust it. Most of the time, all local proxies are used as an additional service or as an additional module (like a browser plugin). To fulfill the purpose of data protection of agents, certain requirements must be met. The requirements are given below:

There are several goals of user privilege or user empowerment, however, the main goal is to increase user trust in the data protection proxies used by the cloud. Another important goal is that when users outsource their sensitive data to trusted proxies, their data stays intact and unaltered. Cloud computing provides great computing power and saves resources. However, one concern is that if we increase data security, the computational cost will not increase. We want to minimize the computational overhead on the proxy.

Maintain the functionality of the cloud. Maintaining cloud functionality is the most important goal. Users encrypt their sensitive data on personal computers by applying different encryption techniques to increase the protection of their data, however, by applying different encryption techniques to each other, they may not be able to enjoy some of the cloud features due to compatibility issues (Hassan, Shehzad, Habib, Aftab, Ahmad, Kuleev & Mazzara, 2022).

Security Logging and Monitoring

A security log is a record of the events occurring on the systems and networks that contain information related to computer security. Computer security logs are generated by multiple sources including various security software, operating systems, networking equipment, middleware, and applications (Kent & Souppaya, 2006). Threat logging and detection includes cloud threat detection controls, and enables, collects, and stores audit logs for cloud services, including enabling detect, investigate, and remediate with controls to generate high-quality alerts with native threat detection in cloud services; it also includes log collection using cloud monitoring service, centralized security analysis using security information and event management system (SIEM), time synchronization and log retention.

Cloud security monitoring is the continuous monitoring of virtual and physical servers to scan data for threats and vulnerabilities using the automation techniques such as AI or ML to measure and evaluate behaviors related to data, applications, and infrastructure. Like SIEM, cloud security monitoring works by collecting log data from a server. Advanced cloud monitoring solutions analyze and collate collected data for anomalous activity, then send alerts and trigger incident response. Cloud security monitoring services typically provide:

Visibility and ability to correlate: Migrating to the cloud inherently reduces an organization's visibility into its infrastructure, so cloud monitoring security tools must provide a single window to monitor their behavior. applications, users, and files to identify potential attacks. Cloud security monitoring tools must be able to monitor enormous amounts of data across multiple distributed locations.

Auditability, reconciliation, and continuous monitoring: Cloud security monitoring tools provide powerful auditing and monitoring capabilities that can be reconciliation based on timestamps, user IDs, machine IDs, and other contexts. Advanced cloud security monitoring solutions must continuously monitor real-time behavior to quickly identify malicious activity and prevent an attack. Integration. To maximize visibility, ideally, the cloud monitoring solution should integrate with the organization's existing services, such as productivity suites, endpoint security solutions, identity services, and authentication.

CURRENT STATE OF BLOCKCHAIN TECHNOLOGY

Blockchain, also called digital ledger, is a decentralized technology that allows multiple stakeholders to maintain a shared database without the need for a central authority. While blockchain was originally proposed as a mechanism for trustless digital currency, the proposed uses have expanded well beyond that particular use case where a need is a general mechanism for recording and ordering transactions (Waldo, 2018). It provides a transparent, secure, and tamper-resistant way of recording and verifying transactions. Blockchain's foremost attributes include resiliency and data integrity, which are well-suited for various applications in government, supply chain management, healthcare, and decentralized finance (DeFi). Most blockchain protocols have become platforms for developing distributed applications (Lee, Kang, Ko, Woo & Hong, 2023). Blockchain technology is rapidly evolving and advancing and hence has potential use in more fields where data integrity, trust, resiliency, security, and availability are of prime importance. Since these aspects are some of the fundamental requirements in security implementation, it provides valuable benefits. While cloud computing offers many native security controls as discussed earlier, its main goal is to make IT operations efficient and cost-effective, and hence, Blockchain technology compliments or extends security capability in a cloud environment when implemented strategically.

Basics of Blockchain Technology

Organizations that are considering the implementation of blockchain technology need to understand the fundamental aspects of the technology because blockchain implementations are often designed with a specific purpose, application, or function (Yaga & Mell, 2018). Blockchain technology consists of several key components that are interdependent and work together to create a decentralized, autonomous, and secure blockchain system. These components include blocks that hold information and block rules that include qualification criteria for the new block to be added to the blockchain, and the chain rules that include criteria for encryption, hashing, linking, sequencing, and timestamping.

Blocks

A block is a unit of data that contains a set of transactions or information. Blocks are data structures on which each transaction is recorded (López-Sorribes, Rius-Torrentó, & Solsona-Tehàs, 2023). Block serves as an envelope for storing a collection of related information. Each block in the blockchain carries a unique serial number, its hash value the hash value of the previous block and the root block, a timestamp, the size of the current block, the nonce value, which is a number manipulated by the mining node to solve the hash puzzle that gives them the right to publish the block, and a list of transactions included within the current block (Yaga & Mell, 2018). Each block in the blockchain is linked to the previous and the next block, forming a chain of blocks that is constantly growing as new transactions or information are added.

Cryptography

Each block in the blockchain has a unique mathematical hash value generated by using a specific cryptographic algorithm to maintain the integrity of the block. Each block in the chain has a unique hash value that represents a unique digital fingerprint and hence data integrity for that block. Hashing is a method of calculating a practically unique fixed-size output for any block size. The cryptographic hash of a block ensures that the smallest change in the block will result in a completely different output digest thus ensuring the detection of the integrity issues.

To maintain the confidentiality of the information contained in the block, asymmetric-key cryptography is used where a pair of public and private keys are used for securing the confidential information in the block. This process ensures that the private key can be used to create cryptographic protection for the information and the public key can be used for audit and verification without compromising the confidentiality of confidential information.

Chaining (Consensus) Mechanism

Each block needs to be a part of a chain to form a blockchain in a sorted structure. The chain is a chronological link that connects blocks in the order in which they were created based on timestamps. For chaining the block in sequential order, each block contains a hash value of the previous block in the chain, creating a chronological order of blocks. The Chaining mechanism also consists of Consensus mechanisms for the agreement on the qualification criteria to allow the new blocks to be added to the system. There needs to be a system for an agreement to validate or invalidate the new addition when the new block needs to be added to the chain. In addition, due to distribution in nature, there needs to be a mechanism for deciding the order in which blocks need to be added to the chain. Consensus mechanisms, using the preset rules, ensure that all nodes in the blockchain network agree on (a) the validity of transactions by making sure that the transaction has occurred by following the preset blockchain ruleset and (b) the order in which they are added to the blockchain based on the timestamp created. Most consensus algorithms used in public blockchains are Proof of Work (PoW), Proof of Stake (PoS) or the Round Robin Consensus Model (Yaga & Mell, 2018). Many private blockchain implementations use Proof of

Authority (PoA). These consensus mechanisms ensure the accuracy and consistency of the blockchain. Chaining and consensus-building mechanism ensures the immutability and integrity of the blockchain.

Time Stamping

Timestamping of each block in the blockchain serves as a record to verify the exact time at which a particular block was created or added to the chain. Timestamps provide the basis for making the decision to maintain the chronological order and immutability of the blockchain and the data it contains. It also helps make sure that the cryptographic hash is unique for each block even if all other information is identical. When a transaction is initiated or data is added to the blockchain as a new block, the timestamp is bundled into the block along with other transactional information or data. Timestamps can be used to verify the sequence of events, ensure data integrity, provide proof of existence, and enable an audit trail. It can also be used for auditing recorded events within specific time ranges.

Security Benefits of Blockchain Technology

The architectures of blockchain and cloud computing are vastly different, so their security advantages are also different. Both blockchain and cloud computing technologies have their own advantages and disadvantages.

There are three types of integration model between blockchain and cloud; Cloud as a Blockchain Service where the blockchain is used to manage cloud computing environment, Blockchain as a Cloud Service where blockchain services are provided in cloud computing platforms and lastly blockchain and cloud computing are used as two independent networks for their complementary strengths (Zou et al., 2021) - for example, data processing and storage are in a cloud computing platform but they are encrypted, audited and, monitored by Blockchain. The following attributes of Blockchain technology provide specific benefits that are not available natively in cloud computing.

Decentralization

In traditional centralized systems, data is stored, transmitted, and processed on a single server or a limited number of servers. In a cloud environment, data is stored, transferred, and processed in a similar but large and multi-tenant data center that is geographically clustered. In contrast, blockchains run on a network of nodes distributed around the world. Every node in the network has a copy of the entire blockchain, making it highly resistant to single points of failure or attacks. The decentralization property of the blockchain helps cloud computing to further extend the availability and reduces susceptibility to natural disasters and cyberattacks such as DDoS.

Immutability

Each block in the blockchain contains a cryptographic hash of the previous block. Blocks are linked in chronological order to create a sequential chain of linked blocks. Any attempt to modify data in any block within the blockchain would require changes to subsequent blocks, which is computationally infeasible and obvious to the network. It is almost impossible to change or delete the data in any block once the data is recorded on the blockchain since the hash values will become inconsistent and hence the change will be detected and blocked. This immutability enhances data integrity and prevents unauthorized tampering, identity theft, and white-collar crimes such as forgery.

Transparency

Blockchain technology ensures that all transactions registered in each block are visible and auditable, ensuring transparency and accountability. While metadata related to transactions is transparently visible, the collection of information (private transactions) can be encrypted to protect privacy and data, especially sensitive information. The transparent nature of the blockchain makes it exceedingly difficult for anyone to manipulate the data. Blockchain's transparent nature allows for an easy audit of transactions. Every action on the blockchain is recorded and timestamped, creating an auditable trail of activities. This traceability is beneficial for regulatory compliance and investigating suspicious activities. Due to the transparency of the blockchain any discrepancies and be avoided or detected and resolved quickly which helps reduce data integrity-related cyberattacks such as ransomware, man-in -the-middle and data tampering. Due to the access to auditable information, many detective measures such as SEIM, Log analysis, and continuous monitoring and alerting measures, can be implemented more efficiently and effectively.

While blockchain technology provides several security benefits, it is essential to remember that no system is entirely invulnerable. Potential security risks can still arise from vulnerabilities in the implementation, smart contract bugs, social engineering attacks, and more. Hence, adopting best practices in blockchain development and regularly updating security measures are crucial to maintaining a robust and secure blockchain ecosystem.

CONFIDENTIALITY IMPROVEMENT USING BLOCKCHAIN IN THE CLOUD

Blockchain data are cryptographically secure using verified identity authenticity using public-private key pairs for encryption partnered with decryption and mathematical-based digital signatures (Church et al., 2020). Blockchain technology can offer confidentiality improvements in cloud computing environments by introducing decentralized and cryptographic mechanisms.

Data Encryption

Blockchain networks can integrate strong encryption techniques to secure data stored and transmitted in the cloud. Data encryption ensures that only authorized parties with the appropriate decryption keys can access and view the data. Even if a malicious actor gains unauthorized access to cloud storage; the encrypted data remains incomprehensible without the decryption keys. Such blockchain-based data encryption can be offered by CSPs for security applications in the form of SaaS or it can be offered by CSPs as IaaS or PaaS for customer organizations to use for cyber security management efforts such as security log management, monitoring, or performing security audits.

Private and Permissioned Blockchains

In public blockchains, all data and transactions are visible to everyone. However, private, or permissioned blockchains can be utilized to limit access to sensitive data within a closed group of participants. This way, only authorized entities have access to specific data, improving confidentiality. Unlike public blockchains where the participants have anonymous identities, using which they can make transactions, and take part in a consensus mechanism, permissioned blockchains maintain the identity of participants and regulate the role of participants, which provides more trackability and efficiency allowing the organization controls the read or write access to the blockchain (Zafar et al., 2022). For security improvement in the cloud infrastructure private or permissioned blockchain are more appropriate where you get most of the benefits of public blockchain while maintaining control.

Zero-Knowledge Proofs

Zero-knowledge proofs (ZKPs) are cryptographic methods that can be used by independent auditors to verify the integrity of the data. ZKP methods do not require prior knowledge, and an audit can be performed without revealing any additional information beyond the statement's validity. ZKP is well suited for the identification and signing within a network system (Chain et al., 2015) and can be used in blockchain-based cloud systems to validate the integrity of data without disclosing the data itself, ensuring confidentiality. Zero-knowledge proofs and protocols are frontier in blockchain technology with potential in a variety of applications such as identity management where sensitive information exchange is required without fully disclosing it. Since sensitive information is not required to be disclosed, ZKP is well suited for public cloud environments that are susceptible to the information disclosure.

Secure Identity Management

Cloud services have provided several mechanisms based on traditional solutions for access management however the need for new grounds for robust access management in cloud services is still urgently needed and permissioned blockchain can provide such a solution (Ghorbel, Ghorbel & Jmaiel, 2021). Blockchain-based identity management systems can enhance the security and confidentiality of user identities in the cloud. Users can control their identity information without relying on a central authority using decentralized identity management solutions. Blockchain-based decentralized solutions for fine-grained and privacy- preserving access control in the cloud environment (Ghorbel et al., 2021) can reduce or eliminate the risk of data breaches due to identity theft.

Encrypted Communication

Blockchain can facilitate secure and encrypted communication between cloud-based services, ensuring that sensitive information exchanged between different components of the cloud infrastructure remains confidential and protected from eavesdropping. Frequent attacks on the certificate authority (CA) have exposed the trust problem of the traditional public key infrastructure (PKI) for the web service and blockchain-based distributed and encrypted communication channels can resist the attacks such as domain name preemption attacks (Zhai et al., 2022). Due to scalability and efficiency requirements many cloud implementations such as virtualization solutions based on Docker Containers provide a more lightweight and efficient virtual environment for Edge and cloud-based applications (Kaliappan et al., 2022). However, such implementations are exposed to existing vulnerabilities in PKI and CA. Blockchain-based encrypted PKI solutions can reduce such vulnerabilities.

It is important to note that while blockchain technology can enhance confidentiality in cloud computing, it is not a one-size-fits-all solution. The implementation of blockchain in the cloud should be carefully planned, considering the specific use case, security requirements, and potential trade-offs, such as scalability and performance. Hybrid solutions that combine blockchain's confidentiality features with traditional cloud security measures may be beneficial in some scenarios.

INTEGRITY IMPROVEMENT USING BLOCKCHAIN IN THE CLOUD

Cloud computing introduces new security challenges related to data integrity protection and blockchain can be leveraged to address these challenges, partly due to the underlying characteristics such as transparency, traceability, decentralization, security, immutability, and automation (Zou et al., 2021). Blockchain technology can significantly improve data integrity in cloud computing environments by leveraging its inherent features.

Immutable Record

Blockchain's primary strength is its immutability providing the guarantee that data cannot be altered or deleted once it is recorded on the blockchain. In blockchains, data are verified and approved by the network, validated via consensus, and immune to manipulation using fixed-length digest hash functions (Church et al., 2020). By storing critical data and transaction records on the blockchain, cloud providers can ensure the integrity of the data, preventing unauthorized modifications and ensuring that historical data remains unchanged.

Time Stamped Records

Every transaction or data entry on the blockchain is timestamped and linked to the previous block using cryptographic hashes. This timestamping mechanism provides an accurate and irrefutable record of when specific data was added to the blockchain, making it easier to detect any unauthorized changes or tampering. Timestamping provides basic building blocks in many cloud-security applications including authentication, data protection, and security logging and monitoring.

Digitally Signed Block

In blockchain networks, transactions are secured using digital signatures. Each participant has a unique private key to sign transactions, proving their authenticity. This cryptographic mechanism ensures that only authorized parties can initiate and approve transactions, preventing unauthorized changes and maintaining data integrity.

Data Validation and Verification

Data Integrity Verification and Validation: Before data is added to the blockchain, it undergoes a verification and validation process by the network nodes. This process ensures that data meets predefined criteria and conforms to the rules of the system. Predefined rules can be utilized to verify the correctness of data or outcomes before executing actions. In turn, invalid or erroneous data is rejected, promoting data integrity in the blockchain. This response ensures that the data integrity conditions are met preemptively, maintaining data integrity throughout the execution process.

By incorporating blockchain technology into cloud computing, data integrity is reinforced through proactive verification and validation and open and transparent validation processes. However, it comes at the cost of computing and storage overhead, which may negatively impact in terms of scalability and performance.

AVAILABILITY IMPROVEMENT USING BLOCKCHAIN IN THE CLOUD

Blockchain technology utilizes a decentralized consensus mechanism delivering in a secured and high-availability environment with complex computations and verifiable methods (Church et al., 2020). Blockchain technology can contribute to improved availability in cloud computing environments by providing enhanced fault tolerance, redundancy, and decentralized architecture.

Decentralization

blockchain offers a progressive solution to address present-day technology concerns and overcome the limitation of cloud computing with solutions such as decentralization for identity, trust, ownership of data, and information-driven choices (Sharma et al., 2020). Blockchain technology works on the network of participating computing devices that are distributed on the network and holds a copy of the entire blockchain. Blockchain technology is not prone to single points of failure due to the decentralization architecture. Such architecture ensures that the data and services are available, even if some nodes are not available or become inaccessible. The redundancy of data across multiple nodes improves the overall availability of the system.

Distributed Data Storage

Blockchain can be implemented as a distributed database solution for maintaining continuously growing data records confirmed and verified by the participating nodes where the data is recorded in a public ledger containing entire historical data with the metadata related to every transaction ever completed (Yli-Huumo et al., 2016). Blockchain networks often use distributed data storage mechanisms to store transactional data across multiple nodes. This distribution of data enhances availability, as the data remains accessible even if some nodes experience temporary outages or hardware failures.

It is important to note that while blockchain can enhance availability, it also has its limitations. Implementing blockchain in cloud computing introduces some overhead and requires careful consideration of scalability, performance, and resource requirements. In some cases, a hybrid solution that combines traditional cloud computing with blockchain elements may be more suitable to balance the need for availability, security, and performance.

FUTURE DIRECTIONS

There are many opportunities for using block-chain technology in the cloud computing environment for offering security solutions. Many applications of blockchain technology discussed here are still in the proof of concept and prototype stages. Further research and demonstration of blockchain technology at mainstream scales is yet to come. In addition, there are many new avenues that require additional research and exploration.

One of the promising applications could be large-scale blockchain-based independent Identity Provider Services. Many governments are offering such solutions for their local citizens but many of them lack scalability and efficiency because they may not be cloud hosted nor may not use blockchain technology currently. Efficient blockchain and cloud-based identity provider independent solutions can be created by nation-state governments that can be used by many critical service providers in the private sector.

One of the current constraints is that it is challenging to coordinate transactions from different blockchains to support cross-chain distributed applications as different blockchains have different properties such as architecture, protocols, and services (Belchior et al., 2021). Hence there is a need to develop a public blockchain cross-connect framework for removing this roadblock and allowing distributed applications to support multiple blockchains seamlessly.

One of the newer requirements beyond confidentiality, integrity, availability is privacy. Regarding privacy requirements, one of the General Data Protection Regulation (GDPR) requirements is the right-to-forget, in which users can request their data to be removed from the blockchain (Belchior et al., 2021). Practically, to fulfill such a requirement requires full or partial reconstruction of blocks in the chain which could be time and resource-consuming and hence not practical. In the future, blockchain technology researchers need to figure out an efficient and effective way to achieve this goal without compromising the benefits of all other properties of the blockchain.

Some of the work that is at the research and PoC stage targets the application for enhancing integrity and privacy of security logs, certificate management for encryption with better blockchain-based PKI, digital signature management, ensuring data integrity and data management, and detecting violations of identity and access control policies in cloud environments.

SUMMARY

Blockchain technology offers significant potential for enhancing security in the cloud computing environment. It is a distributed, decentralized, and immutable ledger system that allows secure and transparent record-keeping of transactions. By leveraging blockchain's unique characteristics, cloud providers and users can enjoy enhanced security and privacy measures. Attributes of blockchain technology such as data Integrity, decentralization, and encryption makes it a complementary technology for improving the security and privacy of cloud applications such as access control, identity management, auditing, and data encryption at rest, in transit, and while processing.

It is essential to consider that blockchain technology is not a one-size-fits-all solution for all cloud security challenges. Implementing blockchain in a cloud environment can come with its own set of complexities and overheads. It requires careful planning, proper accord mechanisms, and integration with existing cloud infrastructure. Moreover, blockchain's public nature might not be suitable for all sensitive data applications, making private or permissioned blockchains a more suitable choice in such cases. As technology evolves, blockchain's role in enhancing cloud security is likely to become more prominent, but it should be combined with other security measures to provide a comprehensive and robust security framework.

REFERENCES

Alaca, F., & Oorschot, P. C. (2020). Comparative analysis and framework evaluating Web single sign-on systems. *ACM Computing Surveys*, *53*(5), 1–34. doi:10.1145/3409452

Belchior, R., Vasconcelos, A., Guerreiro, S., & Correia, M. (2021). A survey on blockchain interoperability: Past, present, and future trends. *ACM Computing Surveys*, *54*(8), 1–41. doi:10.1145/3471140

Chain, K., Chang, K.-H., Kuo, W.-C., & Yang, J.-F. (2015). Enhancement authentication protocol using zero-knowledge proofs and chaotic maps. *International Journal of Communication Systems*, *30*(1), e2945. Advance online publication. doi:10.1002/dac.2945

Church, K. S., Schmidt, P. J., & Ajayi, K. (2020). Forecast Cloudy—Fair or Stormy weather: Cloud computing insights and issues. *Journal of Information Systems*, *34*(2), 23–46. doi:10.2308/isys-18-037

Fang, W., Chen, W., Zhang, W., Pei, J., Gao, W., & Wang, G. (2020). Digital Signature Scheme for information non-repudiation in Blockchain: A state of the art review. *EURASIP Journal on Wireless Communications and Networking, 2020*(1). doi:10.1186/s13638-020-01665-w

Fu, Z. (2022). Computer Cyberspace Security mechanism supported by cloud computing. *PLoS One*, *17*(10), e0271546. Advance online publication. doi:10.1371/journal.pone.0271546 PMID:36206264

Ghorbel, A., Ghorbel, M., & Jmaiel, M. (2021). Accountable privacy preserving attribute-based access control for cloud services enforced using blockchain. *International Journal of Information Security*, *21*(3), 489–508. doi:10.100710207-021-00565-4

Gupta, A., Siddiqui, S. T., Alam, S., & Shuaib, M. (2019). Cloud Computing Security using Blockchain. *International Journal of Emerging Technologies and Innovative Research*, *6*(6), 791–794.

Hassan, J., Shehzad, D., Habib, U., Aftab, M. U., Ahmad, M., Kuleev, R., & Mazzara, M. (2022). The Rise of Cloud Computing: Data Protection, Privacy, and open research challenges—a systematic literature review (SLR). *Computational Intelligence and Neuroscience*, *2022*, 1–26. doi:10.1155/2022/8303504 PMID:35712069

IMI. (2021, April 22). *Identity and Access Management for Cloud Security*. Identity Management Institute. https://identitymanagementinstitute.org/identity-and-access-management-for-cloud-security/

Kaliappan, V., Yu, S., Soundararajan, R., Jeon, S., Min, D., & Choi, E. (2022). High-secured data communication for cloud enabled secure Docker image sharing technique using blockchain-based homomorphic encryption. *Energies*, *15*(15), 5544. doi:10.3390/en15155544

Kent, K., & Souppaya, M. (2006). *Guide to Computer Security Log Management*. National Institute of Standards and Technology. doi:10.6028/NIST.SP.800-92

Lahouij, A., Hamel, L., & Graiet, M. (2022). Formal reconfiguration model for cloud resources. *Software & Systems Modeling*, *22*(1), 225–245. doi:10.100710270-022-00990-6

Lee, C., Kang, C., Ko, H., Woo, J., & Hong, J. W.-K. (2023). A comprehensive and quantitative evaluation method for Blockchain Protocols. *2023 IEEE International Conference on Blockchain and Cryptocurrency (ICBC)*. 10.1109/ICBC56567.2023.10174935

López-Sorribes, S., Rius-Torrentó, J., & Solsona-Tehàs, F. (2023). A Bibliometric Review of the Evolution of Blockchain Technologies. *Sensors, 23*(6), 3167. . doi:10.3390/s23063167

Park, S., Kim, H., & Ryou, J. (2018). Utilizing a lightweight PKI mechanism to guarantee secure service in a cloud environment. *The Journal of Supercomputing*, *74*(12), 6988–7002. doi:10.100711227-018-2506-3

Pavithra, S., Ramya, S., & Prathibha, S. (2019). A survey on cloud security issues and blockchain. *2019 3rd International Conference on Computing and Communications Technologies (ICCCT)*. 10.1109/ICCCT2.2019.8824891

Rani, M., Guleria, K., & Panda, S. N. (2022). Blockchain technology novel prospective for cloud security. *2022 10th International Conference on Reliability, Infocom Technologies and Optimization (Trends and Future Directions) (ICRITO)*. 10.1109/ICRITO56286.2022.9964666

Sharma, P., Jindal, R., & Borah, M. D. (2020). Blockchain technology for Cloud Storage. *ACM Computing Surveys*, *53*(4), 1–32. doi:10.1145/3403954

Tabrizchi, H., & Kuchaki Rafsanjani, M. (2020). A survey on security challenges in cloud computing: Issues, threats, and solutions. *The Journal of Supercomputing*, *76*(12), 9493–9532. doi:10.100711227-020-03213-1

Waldo, J. (2018). A hitchhiker's guide to the blockchain universe. *ACM Queue; Tomorrow's Computing Today*, *16*(6), 21–35. doi:10.1145/3305263.3305265

Yaga, D., & Mell, P. (2018). *Blockchain Technology Overview*. National Institute of Standards and Technology. doi:10.6028/NIST.IR.8202

Yli-Huumo, J., Ko, D., Choi, S., Park, S., & Smolander, K. (2016). Where is current research on blockchain technology?—A systematic review. *PLoS One*, *11*(10), e0163477. Advance online publication. doi:10.1371/journal.pone.0163477 PMID:27695049

Zafar, S., Hassan, S. F., Mohammad, A., Al-Ahmadi, A. A., & Ullah, N. (2022). Implementation of a distributed framework for permissioned blockchain-based Secure Automotive Supply Chain Management. *Sensors (Basel)*, *22*(19), 7367. doi:10.339022197367 PMID:36236466

Zhai, Z., Shen, S., & Mao, Y. (2022). BPKI: A secure and scalable blockchain-based public key infrastructure system for web services. *Journal of Information Security and Applications*, *68*, 103226. doi:10.1016/j.jisa.2022.103226

Zou, J., He, D., Zeadally, S., Kumar, N., Wang, H., & Choo, K. R. (2021). Integrated Blockchain and cloud computing systems: A systematic survey, solutions, and challenges. *ACM Computing Surveys*, *54*(8), 1–36. doi:10.1145/3456628

Zyuzin, V. D., Vdovenko, D. V., Bolshakov, V. N., Busenkov, A. A., & Krivdin, A. D. (2020). Attack on hash functions. *EurAsian Journal of Biosciences*, *14*(1), 907–913.

Chapter 7
Privacy-Preserving Federated Machine Learning Techniques

Gobinath Subramaniam
https://orcid.org/0009-0009-0024-4164
Builders Engineering College, India

Santhiya Palanisamy
https://orcid.org/0009-0008-0963-9827
Builders Engineering College, India

ABSTRACT

Machine learning is increasingly used for data analysis, but centralized datasets raise concerns about data privacy and security. Federated learning, a distributed method, enables multiple entities to cooperatively train a machine learning model. Clients use their local datasets to train local models, while a central aggregator aggregates updates and computes a global model. Privacy-preserving federated learning (PPFL) addresses privacy issues in sensitive and decentralized data situations. PPFL integrates federated learning with privacy-preserving approaches to achieve both privacy and model correctness.

1. INTRODUCTION

1.1. Information Security in Machine Learning

The growing privacy concerns in machine learning applications are a reflection of how much AI and data-driven technologies have impacted our lives. The sensitive nature of the data being processed is a rising source for concern as machine learning algorithms become indispensable to many facets of society, from individualized suggestions to healthcare diagnoses (Truong, 2021). People are understandably concerned about the possible misuse or improper treatment of their personal information. Public trust has been eroded by high-profile data breaches and scandals that have brought to light the true dangers of data privacy infractions.

DOI: 10.4018/979-8-3693-0593-5.ch007

Data privacy issues are heightened in the context of machine learning since models frequently need access to large and varied datasets. Questions concerning data ownership, permission, and the possibility of prejudice and discrimination are raised by this. The difficulty is in using machine learning effectively while upholding the autonomy and rights of each person (Tan et al., 2022). In the end, the growing privacy concerns highlight the necessity of responsible and moral AI development. It demands openness, responsibility, and the inclusion of privacy-protecting methods in machine learning procedures. Only by solving these issues can make sure that machine learning advantages are achieved while maintaining the security and privacy of people and their data.

1.2. Risks of Revealing Private Information for Model Training

There are various inherent dangers when sharing sensitive data for model training, thus they should be carefully considered. The possibility of data breaches or unauthorized access is one of the main worries (Yin, 2021). There is a higher risk of cyber assaults and data leaks when sensitive information, such as personal identifiers, medical records, or financial details, are exchanged. These hacks have the potential to seriously hurt both people and companies by exposing highly personal data, facilitating identity theft, fraud, and other crimes.

The potential of privacy infringement is another. Sharing sensitive information without strong privacy safeguards may violate people's right to privacy control. When users or data subjects have not given their explicit agreement to the sharing or use of their data for model training, this can lead to a breach of trust.

Additionally, when sensitive data is involved, the danger of prejudice and discrimination is increased. Unfair or biased outcomes may result from models trained on such data in a variety of applications, including lending, hiring, and criminal justice.

1.3. Privacy Needs in Machine Learning

In our increasingly data-driven society, the requirement for privacy in machine learning has emerged as a crucial factor (Di Chai et al., n.d.). The safety of personal data has assumed center stage as machine learning algorithms become more interwoven into all facets of our life, from tailored recommendations to healthcare diagnoses. Machine learning applications frequently revolve around sensitive data, such as user activity data, financial information, and medical records (Di Chai et al., n.d.; Pramod et al., 2020). As a result, protecting sensitive data from dangers like identity theft, fraud, and illegal access has become crucial.

In order to apply machine learning responsibly and ethically, it is imperative to uphold user trust, respect consent, and maintain data security. The machine learning community can create more reliable, safe, and fair AI systems that advance society while upholding the autonomy and rights of individuals by placing a higher priority on privacy (Di Chai et al., n.d.).

Here are a few major arguments for why privacy is crucial in the context of machine learning:

(i) Protection of Personal Data: Machine learning frequently makes use of sensitive and private data, including user behavior data, financial data, and medical records.

(ii) User Consent and Trust: It's important to keep users' and data subjects' consent. Users must be confident that their privacy rights are upheld and that their data is managed appropriately. The building blocks of user trust are openness and getting informed permission. Machine learning models and data repositories are appealing targets for cyberattacks, thus security against data breaches is important. Sensitive information may be exposed, a company may suffer financial losses, and its reputation may be harmed. Protections against these dangers are provided by privacy measures.

(iii) International Data Sharing: In today's globalized society, data sharing across national boundaries is frequently necessary for applications, research, and partnerships. Cross-border data transfer can be challenging; however, privacy safeguards might aid while still adhering to multiple regulatory frameworks.

2. AUTOMATED FEDERATED LEARNING

FedML tackles the major issues of data privacy, security, and scalability in the digital age when data is a valuable commodity. It enables businesses and people to take use of machine learning while safeguarding the privacy of sensitive data. Additionally, it promotes data-driven partnerships, allowing businesses to enhance their models together without having to share raw data.

Models are trained using a central dataset in classical machine learning, where data is normally collected, stored, and retrieved. Federated machine learning, in contrast, spreads the model-training process to the data sources themselves, protecting the confidentiality and privacy of the individual data while yet enabling aggregate model improvements (Gu et al., 2023). Without the need to centralize data, it enables the cooperative training of models across several devices or servers, each retaining its own local data. In response to the increasing significance of data-driven applications across numerous sectors, this ground-breaking idea has evolved.

Federated Machine Learning (FedML) is a decentralized and ground-breaking method to machine learning that eliminates the need to consolidate local data by conducting model training across numerous edge devices or servers that contain local data. In industries like healthcare, banking, and edge computing, where data is sensitive and dispersed, FedML is especially pertinent. The emergence of laws like GDPR, the necessity for privacy-preserving machine learning algorithms, and the moral obligation to uphold individuals' data rights all serve to highlight its importance (Truong, 2021). Federated machine learning is emerging as a disruptive paradigm, giving a way to harness the potential of data while protecting data privacy and security a critical tenet of responsible AI development as data-driven applications continue to impact our society.

2.1. Federated Machine Learning's Main Traits Are

2.1.1. Decentralized Data

Federated Machine Learning (FML), data remains distributed across individual devices or servers where it is originally created or stored. This decentralized approach contrasts with traditional methods where data is centralized on a single server. This has significant privacy implications because sensitive or private data remains localized and doesn't need to be moved to a central location. This reduces the risk of data breaches or unauthorized access to sensitive information.

2.1.2. Collaborative Model Training

Instead of a single central server handling all the data for model training, multiple edge devices or servers collaborate to train a global machine learning model. Each device trains its local model using its own data and then contributes by sharing updates to the central server. These updates are used to refine the global model. This approach allows a broader range of data sources to contribute to the model's development, leading to a more comprehensive and robust model.

2.1.3. Protection of Privacy

One of the key advantages of FML is its privacy-preserving nature. Individual devices or servers do not need to expose their raw data to a central server or other participants. Instead, they share model updates or gradients, which are mathematical representations of how the model should change to improve its performance. This way, private data remains secure and isolated, and the global model benefits without directly accessing personal information.

2.1.4. Communication Overhead Reduction

In traditional machine learning, transmitting large datasets for central processing can lead to high communication costs and slow down the training process. In FML, only model updates are exchanged, and these updates are usually much smaller in size compared to raw data. This greatly reduces communication overhead and the amount of data that needs to be transmitted over the network, making the process more efficient.

2.1.5. Edge and IoT Compatibility

Federated Machine Learning is well-suited for scenarios where data is generated at the edge, such as in Internet of Things (IoT) devices. These devices often have limited resources and cannot easily send large amounts of data to a central server. By training models directly on these devices using local data and then aggregating updates, FML enables efficient model improvement without the need for extensive data transfer.

2.1.6. Customization and Personalization

FML allows for a dual benefit of customization and global model improvement. Each device can customize its local model based on specific hardware constraints or user preferences. Despite these customizations, the aggregated model retains the collective knowledge from all devices. This balance between personalization and collective learning is a significant advantage of FML.

2.2. Federated Machine Learning Goals

The goal of "Privacy-Preserving Federated Machine Learning Techniques" is to investigate, comprehend, and successfully use privacy-preserving methods within the framework of federated machine learning (Behnia et al., 2023; Elhussein & Gursoy, 2023). Among the key goals are:

(i) Define Federated Machine Learning (FedML) with respect to privacy
(ii) Emphasize the value of privacy protection
(iii) Describe the fundamental privacy-preserving methods
(iv) Describe FedML's workflow
(v) Deal with ethical issues
(vi) Discuss the difficulties and compromises

2.3. GDPR's Stance on Privacy Protection in Federated Learning

One of the most extensive and significant data protection laws in the world is the General Data Protection Regulation (GDPR). Since May 2018, the European Union (EU) has been enforcing GDPR, which establishes strict guidelines for the gathering, handling, and protection of personal data. Its guiding principles place a strong emphasis on openness, equity, and responsibility in the processing of data, guaranteeing that people have more control over their personal information (Di Chai et al., n.d.). The GDPR has an influence outside of the EU since it applies to any company processing data of EU citizens anywhere in the globe. Businesses and organizations must abide by its standards since non-compliance might result in hefty fines.

Figure 1. GDPR principles

The GDPR has been essential in changing how personal data is handled in the digital era, elevating privacy rights to the fore, and requiring ethical and responsible data practices from businesses all over the world. Protecting personal data is of utmost importance under GDPR, and Federated Learning takes this into consideration. In order to minimize data and confine processing for a particular, specified purpose collaborative model training raw data never leaves the local devices or entities. The GDPR's emphasis on purpose restriction and data protection by design and default is met by this method. Additionally, because people retain ownership of their information throughout the Federated Learning process, the rights of individuals about their data are protected. Encryption, strong security protocols, and open accountability all help to further protect user privacy. Federated Learning, which enables collaborative machine learning while protecting data privacy and abiding with the strict data protection laws and privacy standards of the EU, essentially encapsulates the spirit of the GDPR.

2.4. Workflow of Client-Server Architecture for Federated Learning

Federated Learning revolutionizes machine learning while addressing data privacy and decentralized data sources with a unique workflow and client-server architecture. A central server first distributes a global model to involved clients or devices in this procedure. These customers train the model locally using their unique datasets and update it depending on their local knowledge. Importantly, sensitive data is protected during the model update calculation by using privacy-preserving approaches (Yin, 2021). The central server will then receive the securely anonymised model changes for aggregation. In order to enhance the overall model, the server accumulates these changes. Until convergence is reached and the entire model is deemed appropriately trained, this iterative procedure is continued.

Figure 2. Working process of federated learning

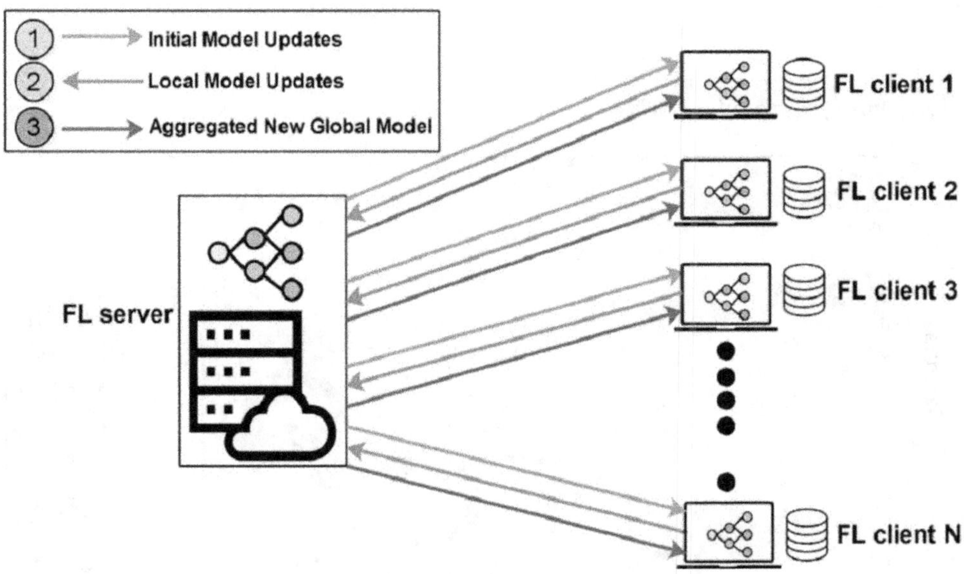

In collaborative and privacy-conscious machine learning applications, the federated learning strategy guarantees that sensitive data is decentralized, protecting privacy, while yet reaping the benefits of pooled model improvements. Federated learning has several advantageous features, especially in terms of scalability and privacy. This strategy distinguishes out in terms of privacy by design. Decentralized data storage protects data privacy by avoiding central repositories that can be valuable targets for data breaches. Individual data is kept private throughout model changes thanks to privacy-preserving mechanisms, giving data owners trust and facilitating safe cooperation.

Another outstanding feature of federated learning is scalability. Its architecture allows for an increasing number of participants, which qualifies it for applications on a broad scale. The IoT and edge computing settings, where data is produced locally, benefit from the same scalability. When used in this situation, federated learning allows devices to improve models without disclosing private information, protecting both privacy and processing speed.

2.5. Federated Learning Models

Federated learning comes in a variety of forms, each of which is intended to meet certain data distribution scenarios and privacy issues.

2.5.1. Federated Horizontal Learning

A particular method under the federated learning paradigm called horizontal federated learning (homogenous federated learning) is designed for situations in which various parties or entities have datasets with the same attributes but different data samples. It allows these organizations to jointly train a machine learning model while maintaining the confidentiality and privacy of their data (Saha & Ahmad, n.d.). Each participant builds its own local model on its own set of data, autonomously, to gain insights without transferring raw data.

Figure 3. Horizontal federated learning

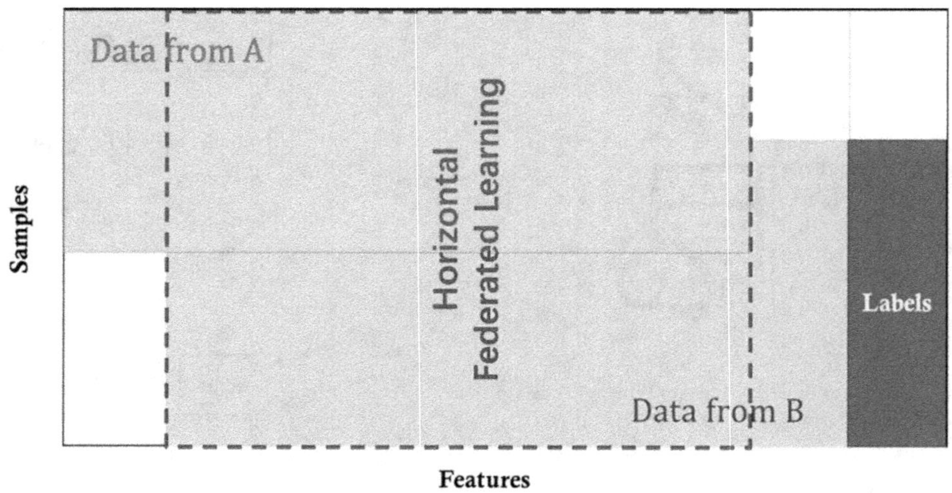

A central server then compiles these local model changes, collectively enhancing a global model. It is a strong solution for applications spanning healthcare, finance, and more where data segregation and security are crucial since it enables collaborative machine learning while keeping sensitive information decentralized and distinct (Dayan et al., 2021; Prayitno et al., 2021). This kind is appropriate when the parties desire to work together on a shared prediction goal while maintaining the privacy of their respective data sets owing to legal or privacy considerations.

2.5.2. Federated Vertical Learning

A particular method inside the Federated Learning framework called Vertical Federated Learning was created for cases when numerous parties or entities have datasets with various sets of characteristics but some overlap. These organizations may work together to jointly train a machine learning model using vertical federated learning without disclosing their whole datasets, protecting data privacy (Liu, 2022). Instead of exchanging raw data, each participant trains a local model using their own set of characteristics.

The changes are then collected by a central server, allowing for the development of a global model that utilizes the complementing data from all parties. When data sharing is constrained and multiple entities possess important but separate data components, combining them can considerably improve the performance and insights of machine learning models, this strategy is beneficial. Applications for vertical federated learning may be found in a variety of industries, including banking, healthcare, and collaborative research, where feature segregation and data protection are crucial factors.

Figure 4. Vertical federated learning

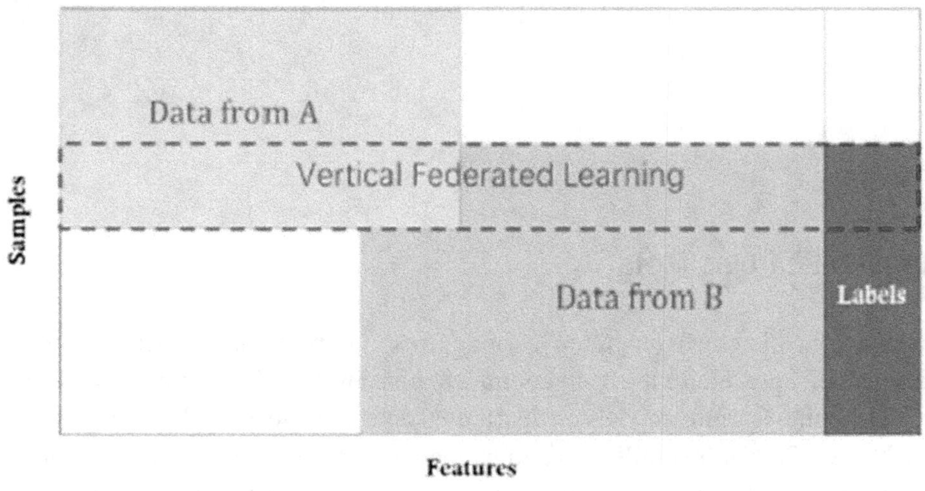

2.5.3. Federated Transfer of Learning

A novel strategy inside the Federated Learning framework called Transfer Federated Learning concentrates on the transfer of knowledge from one FL context or area to another. In essence, it enables the adaptation and refinement of knowledge and pre-trained models obtained from a source domain for use in a related target domain (Saha & Ahmad, n.d.). This strategy speeds up learning, which is particularly useful when the target domain has few or expensive data sources.

Transfer Federated Learning efficiently improves the performance of machine learning models in the target domain by utilizing the knowledge from the source domain, enabling businesses and entities to gain from shared insights and experiences across many data contexts. Building on existing information may considerably increase the efficiency and efficacy of machine learning solutions, making it more important in a variety of applications, such as healthcare, finance, and industry.

Figure 5. Transfer federated learning

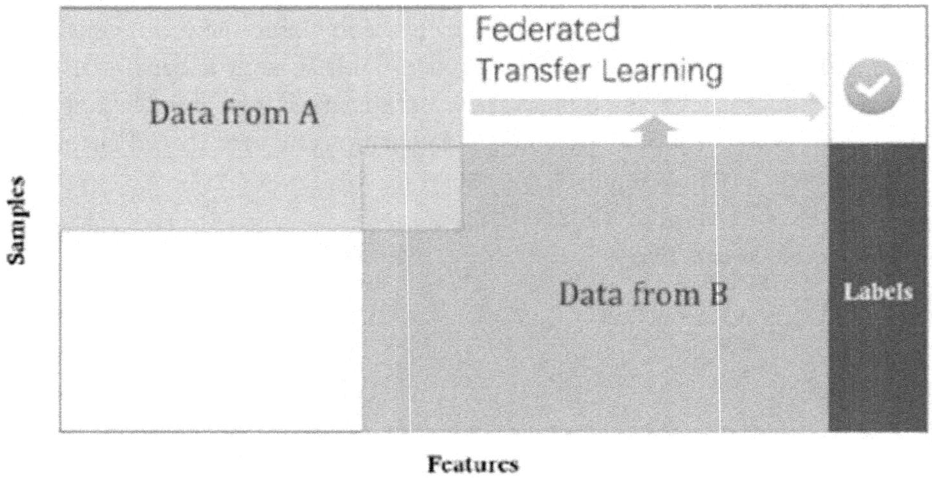

2.5.4. Federated Learning Meta

An advanced strategy called meta federated learning tries to improve and maximize the efficacy of the federated learning (FL) procedure itself. In contrast to conventional FL, which involves users working together to train machine learning models on distributed data, meta federated learning emphasizes meta-learning (Fallah et al., 2020). It entails educating a meta model to make wise choices about crucial FL issues including hyperparameter tuning, communication tactics, algorithm selection, model initialization, and even robustness-boosting tactics.

A more effective and efficient FL system is produced by this meta model, which iteratively learns to enhance the FL procedure. Meta Federated Learning is an essential tool in many data-driven fields since it is especially useful in large-scale FL settings where scaling and model performance may be considerably impacted by improving the FL process.

Figure 6. Meta federated learning

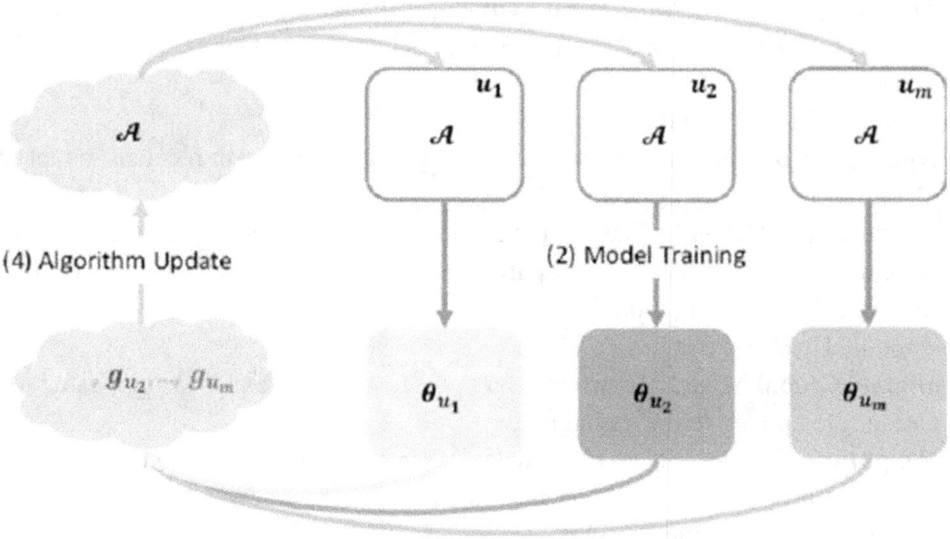

2.6. Federated Learning Lifecycle

The training and deployment of machine learning models across decentralized data sources is governed by the Federated Learning lifecycle, a methodical procedure that protects the security and privacy of the data (Di Chai et al., n.d.; Truong, 2021; Yin, 2021). The identification of participating devices or entities and the setup of a global model are the first steps. On their own data, these participants run local model training and produce model updates that incorporate their own insights. The global model is then improved as a result of these updates being combined by a central server or aggregator. Until convergence is reached, this process iterates over several communication cycles. The performance of the resultant federated model is assessed, and if suitable, it is implemented for use in practical applications. For the approach to remain functional, regular monitoring, upkeep, and re-federation are required.

In industries like healthcare and finance where data decentralization is crucial, the federated learning lifecycle is essential because it fosters cooperative machine learning while upholding data confidentiality and privacy.

(i) Initialization:
  - **Global Model Initialization:** The procedure starts with the initialization of a global model. This model is frequently a neural network that has already been trained or is randomly initialized and will be enhanced by all participants.
  - **Participant Selection:** Select the systems, businesses, or other entities that will take part in the federated learning process. Sometimes, these participants are referred to as "parties."

(ii) Local Model Development:
  - **Data on Local Devices:** Each participant uses its own data to train local models; no external data is ever shared.
  - **Iterative Training:** Participants put their nearby models through a series of iterations. Usually, each cycle includes many training epochs on the local data.

(iii) Update Generation for Models:
- **Model Updates:** Each participant computes model updates following local training. The variation between the participant's local model and the global model is represented by these updates.

(iv) Aggregation of Model Updates:
- **Aggregator or Central Server:** A central aggregator or server receives model changes from all participants.
- **Aggregation Method:** The aggregator uses a variety of aggregation methods, such as weighted averaging, secure multi-party computing, or other privacy-preserving strategies, to integrate the incoming model changes.

(v) Global model Update:
- **Update Global Model:** To produce an updated global model, the aggregated model modifications are applied to the global model.
- **Weighting:** The weights of the updates are frequently determined by variables like the accuracy of the local model, the accessibility of processing power, or other pertinent standards.

(vi) Synchronization and communication:
- **Communication Rounds:** Each communication round includes a repetition of steps 3 through 5. Participants update their local models, create model updates, submit them to the aggregator, and update the global model during each cycle.
- **Convergence:** Up until the global model converges or hits a predetermined stopping threshold, the procedure is continued.

(vii) Evaluation:
- **Performance Evaluation:** Using a validation dataset or other evaluation metrics, the federated model's performance is evaluated. This aids in determining if the model satisfies other performance requirements and the necessary accuracy.

(viii) Deployment:
- **Model Deployment:** After the federated model has been evaluated as suitable, it may be used to make forecasts or choices in practical applications.
- **Inference:** Using the deployed federated model on fresh, unused data, inferences are drawn.

(ix) Upkeep and Inspection:
- **Continuous Monitoring:** To guarantee that the federated model operates well in production, continuous monitoring is essential. As they happen, data drift and model drift must be handled.
- **Periodic Re-federation:** Depending on the use case, federated learning could be restarted frequently to include fresh information or adjust to shifting conditions.

3. TECHNIQUES FOR PROTECTING PRIVACY IN FEDERATED LEARNING

In Federated Learning, privacy preserving strategies are crucial because they fulfil the urgent requirement to safeguard personal data privacy while gaining the advantages of collaborative model training. Homomorphic encryption, Differential Privacy (Aono & Hayashi, 2017), Secure Multi-Party Computation (SMPC) (Gu et al., 2023), and other techniques are included in these methods. While Homomorphic Encryption allows calculations to be done on encrypted data, maintaining secrecy throughout the process,

SMPC enables clients to jointly calculate model changes without disclosing their local data. Contrarily, Differential Privacy introduces controlled noise to the model updates, making it extremely difficult to determine a specific person's contribution to the training. Together, these methods guarantee that private information stays private even during model updates and aggregation, promoting confidence, adherence to privacy laws, and ethical data practices in Federated Learning applications.

3.1. Secure Multi-Party Computation

A wonder of cryptography known as Secure Multi-Party Computation (SMPC) enables several parties to jointly calculate functions over their secret inputs without disclosing those inputs to one another (Behnia et al., 2023). When sensitive information needs to be processed collectively, this ground-breaking method assures data privacy and confidentiality. Parties start with private data they want to remain private, calculate a desired function's output without disclosing their underlying data via a secure protocol comprising sophisticated cryptographic procedures.

SMPC uses cryptographic primitives like encryption and secret sharing to make sure that no participant can see what the inputs of another participant are. Its numerous uses in federated learning, secure auctions, private data analysis, and group decision-making make it an essential tool for preserving privacy and fostering fruitful partnerships in today's data-driven society.

3.2. Homomorphic Encryption

An innovative cryptographic method called homomorphic encryption enables data to stay encrypted even when calculations are being done on it. Homomorphic encryption enables calculations to be performed directly on the encrypted data, maintaining its secrecy throughout, in contrast to conventional encryption techniques that demand data be decrypted before processing (Aono & Hayashi, 2017; Luo et al., 2023). In applications where privacy is crucial, such cloud computing, healthcare, and safe data sharing, this breakthrough has enormous potential for secure data processing. There are many types of homomorphic encryption, such as somewhat homomorphic, slightly homomorphic, and fully homomorphic encryption, each of which offers a different amount of computing power while protecting data privacy (Jin et al., 2023). Homomorphic encryption is advancing secure data analysis and collaborative research while protecting individual privacy rights by providing secure and private computing on sensitive data.

3.3. Differential Privacy

Differential Privacy is a key idea in the field of data privacy and security, providing a strong framework to safeguard private data while still gaining insightful knowledge (Luo et al., 2023). Differential privacy fundamentally makes it extremely challenging to ascertain whether any specific individual's data was included in the dataset by introducing controlled noise or randomness into data searches or statistical studies. This method prevents the possibility of re-identification or data breaches, even when an attacker has extensive prior information. Differential Privacy is not simply a theoretical idea; it also has real-world uses in the social sciences, finance, and healthcare industries. It enables enterprises to exchange data for research and analytics while upholding privacy rights and complying with data protection laws like the GDPR by quantifying and guaranteeing a mathematical guarantee of privacy (Ficek et al., 2021; Truong, 2021). Differential Privacy, which serves as a cornerstone for responsible and ethical data activities, is becoming more and more essential in our data-driven society as worries about data privacy continue to grow.

3.4. Local Differential Privacy

A cutting-edge method for protecting personal data privacy in the era of data sharing and analysis is called local differential privacy. Local differential privacy acts at the individual level as opposed to classic differential privacy, which introduces noise to data in the data center or during analysis. In this model, data owners add noise directly to their data before sharing it or using it for calculations, making it difficult to tell how any one person contributed to the dataset. Individuals may participate in cooperative data-driven efforts while still maintaining control over their data and protecting their privacy rights thanks to this decentralized method. When data is created locally and transferred for analysis in settings like mobile applications and IoT devices, local differential privacy is very important. It guarantees the confidentiality of sensitive data even when centralized data protection measures may not be possible or feasible. Local Differential Privacy is a crucial tool for responsible and safe data sharing at a time when privacy concerns are growing, allowing people to contribute to communal understandings without jeopardizing their private.

3.5. Federated Averaging With Differential Privacy

Federated Averaging with Differential Privacy combines two cutting-edge machine learning and privacy-preserving approaches in a potent way. By aggregating model updates from several clients or devices, federated averaging is a technique used in federated learning to enhance a global model. Federated Averaging with Differential Privacy, which combines these two methods, guarantees that model updates contributed by each client are private. Differential Privacy, on the other hand, is a privacy-preserving mechanism that adds controlled noise to data or computations to protect individual privacy (Ficek et al., 2021; Tan et al., 2022). This implies that participant privacy is maintained even when numerous people work together to build a machine learning model. The outcome is a worldwide model that has been enhanced by the contributions of several clients together while upholding stringent privacy rules. This strategy enables enterprises to collaborate on machine learning projects without jeopardizing the security of sensitive data, which is especially relevant in industries where data privacy is crucial, like healthcare or finance. Federated Averaging with Differential Privacy advances responsible and safe collaborative machine learning by combining the advantages of shared insights with strong data security.

3.6. Secure Aggregation

In the field of safe and privacy-preserving computing, secure aggregation is a fundamental approach that is frequently used in collaborative contexts where numerous participants must aggregate their data or computations without disclosing individual contributions (Behnia et al., 2023). Through the use of this approach, sensitive data is kept private throughout the aggregate process. To do this, Secure Aggregation uses cutting-edge cryptography protocols and methods. In reality, Secure Aggregation allows parties to make machine learning model upgrades, compute statistics, or get aggregated results without revealing their personal information. To enable the aggregate while prohibiting any member from obtaining access to other participants' data, cryptographic primitives like encryption and secret sharing are utilized. Application areas for Secure Aggregation include secure multi-party computation, where parties jointly compute functions over their data while maintaining privacy, and federated learning, where clients or devices work together to train machine learning models without centralizing data. safe Aggregation is essential in allowing safe and privacy-preserving collaborations, promoting insights and decision-making across businesses and entities without jeopardizing sensitive information as data privacy concerns continue to rise.

3.7. Proofs of Zero Knowledge

An intriguing notion in cryptography called Zero-Knowledge Proofs (ZKPs) allows one party to demonstrate to another that they have certain knowledge without disclosing any details about that knowledge itself. ZKPs essentially provide people or organizations the ability to prove a claim is true without revealing the supporting information or specifics. This unique capacity has several uses in terms of security and privacy (Xing et al., 2023). Identity verification and authentication are two of ZKPs' most famous uses. For instance, a user can demonstrate to a service provider that they are familiar with a valid password via a cryptographic protocol without actually disclosing the password. By lowering the chance of password leakage, this improves security.

ZKPs are essential in blockchain and cryptocurrency technologies, where transactions must be confirmed without revealing the sender, receiver, or transaction amount. This is in addition to authentication. In privacy-preserving data analysis, ZKPs are also employed so that parties may demonstrate the characteristics of their datasets (such as the totality of their data) without revealing the data itself.

3.8. Homomorphic Information Sharing

With the help of the complex cryptographic approach known as homomorphic secret sharing, safe collaborative computations may be performed without disclosing private information (Aono & Hayashi, 2017; Behnia et al., 2023). In this method, shares of a piece of confidential information are divided and sent to several people. This method is extremely effective since calculations may be done on these shares while they are still encrypted, maintaining secrecy all the time (Aono & Hayashi, 2017).

Each side can change their respective portions of the data, and when the portions are added together, the outcome is the same as if the calculations were performed on the original data without disclosing it. Homomorphic Secret Sharing is incredibly useful in situations where confidentiality and safe data processing are crucial, such collaborative research, secure data analysis, and private financial transactions, because to its characteristic.

Homomorphic Secret Sharing permits groups and individuals to work together while maintaining the privacy of their sensitive data by enabling secure computations on shared secrets. It serves as an illustration of how crucial cryptographic methods are becoming to preserving data security and privacy in our increasingly linked digital world. Best in Class.

3.9. Primitives of Cryptography

Modern cryptography's core building elements, known as cryptographic primitives, offer the fundamental methods and tools for protecting digital communication, data storage, and information sharing. Building blocks for specialized cryptographic processes like encryption, decryption, hashing, and digital signatures include algorithms, protocols, and mathematical functions (Di Chai et al., n.d.; Yin, 2021). The secrecy, integrity, and validity of digital data are ensured by increasingly sophisticated cryptographic systems and protocols, which are built on top of cryptographic primitives.

Symmetric-key encryption for safe data transmission, public-key encryption for key exchange and digital signatures, cryptographic hash functions for data verification, and random number generators for making safe keys and tokens are some of the most used cryptographic primitives. These elements cooperate to secure sensitive data in a number of applications, including online communications security, financial transaction protection, and digital document integrity.

4. PROBLEMS AND RESTRICTIONS WITH PPFL TECHNIQUES

The complexity of establishing privacy-preserving techniques is one of the major challenges. Secure multi-party computing, homomorphic encryption, and differential privacy are three examples of techniques that might be computationally demanding and may need specialist knowledge to perform successfully. The cost and resource demands of federated learning programs may rise due to this complexity. The trade-off between privacy and model performance presents another difficulty. Techniques for protecting privacy frequently contribute noise or encryption that might reduce the model's accuracy. Finding the ideal balance between model accuracy and privacy is a tricky undertaking, and it might not always be feasible to do both at once.

Scalability is also another drawback. A federated learning system's management and guaranteeing safe connection become more challenging as the number of users or devices grows. In some applications, this may restrict the scalability of privacy-preserving federated learning.

4.1 Privacy and Model Performance Concessions

The trade-offs between privacy and model performance are a key factor in federated learning and other privacy-preserving machine learning techniques (Yin, 2021). These trade-offs result from the use of privacy-enhancing techniques that incorporate noise, encryption, or other privacy measures to safeguard sensitive data, such as differential privacy, secure multi-party computing, and homomorphic encryption. The main trade-offs are as follows:

(i) Accuracy vs. Privacy
(ii) Privacy vs. Communication Overhead
(iii) Privacy vs. Complexity
(iv) Model Utility vs. Individual Privacy
(v) Sharing of Data vs. Privacy

4.1.1 Privacy Concessions

- **Noise Addition:** Techniques like differential privacy involve adding noise to data or model updates to protect individual privacy. However, this noise can impact the accuracy and utility of the trained model. The higher the noise added, the better the privacy, but at the cost of reduced model quality.

- **Data Aggregation:** Aggregating data from multiple sources inherently compromises individual-level privacy. While aggregation reduces the risk of exposing specific data points, the aggregated information might still reveal patterns or trends that could be considered sensitive.
- **Limited Data Sharing:** In some cases, privacy requirements might limit the amount of data that can be shared among devices or with a central server. This limited data sharing can hinder the model's ability to generalize and might lead to overfitting.
- **Centralized Parameters:** Sharing model parameters or architectures can inadvertently reveal information about the training data. Careful design is required to prevent such leaks while still allowing collaboration.

4.1.2 Model Performance Concessions

- **Model Accuracy:** Applying privacy-preserving techniques like noise addition or data perturbation can negatively impact the model's accuracy. This might result in predictions that are less reliable for critical tasks.
- **Convergence Speed:** Introducing privacy mechanisms can slow down the convergence of the learning process, requiring more iterations to achieve a satisfactory model. This can extend training times and increase resource requirements.
- **Bias and Fairness:** Privacy-preserving techniques might introduce bias into the model, which can lead to unfair predictions, especially for underrepresented groups. Balancing privacy and fairness is a complex challenge.
- **Generalization:** With limited access to individual data, the trained model might have difficulty generalizing to new and diverse data points, potentially reducing its overall usefulness.
- **Resource Intensiveness:** More complex privacy techniques can demand greater computational resources for encryption, decryption, secure aggregation, and noise generation. This can strain edge devices or central servers.

5. PPFL APPLICATION

In many real-world situations where data privacy is crucial, privacy-preserving federated learning approaches have found effective uses. Here are a few noteworthy instances:

5.1. Healthcare and Medical Research:

Predictive models have been trained using federated learning on medical (Ficek et al., 2021) data spread across many healthcare organizations (Dayan et al., 2021). Without disclosing sensitive patient information, hospitals can work together to enhance illness diagnosis and treatment recommendations. A great example is Google's "Federated Learning of Cohorts" for online advertising, which allows for customized ad targeting while retaining user data on individual devices (Prayitno et al., 2021).

5.2. Financial Services

Fraud detection and risk assessment are carried out in the financial sector via federated learning. In order to improve the accuracy of fraud detection algorithms while protecting client privacy, banks and credit card firms can work together to train models on transaction data without disclosing specific customer information.

5.3. Telecommunications

To enhance network efficiency and service quality, telecom operators adopt federated learning. Mobile devices gather network data and distribute it for analysis, which enables service providers to make changes without having access to particular user location or identification data.

5.4. Agriculture

Federated learning in precision agriculture helps farmers to jointly enhance crop yield forecasting and disease detection models. Data from each farmer is kept private while also adding to the body of knowledge, which eventually helps the whole agricultural industry.

5.5. IoT and Edge Devices

Because local data generation occurs with IoT and edge computing, federated learning is perfect for these applications (Liu et al., 2022). Smart cameras, sensors, and wearable technologies are examples of devices that can help with model training without sending private data to a central server.

Example application Review-1: Healthcare Diagnostics and Disease Prediction

Description:

In the field of healthcare, PPFL plays a crucial role in improving diagnostic accuracy and predicting diseases while safeguarding patients' sensitive medical information. Consider a scenario where multiple hospitals and medical centers want to collaborate on building a robust disease prediction model using patient data. However, due to regulatory compliance and patient privacy concerns, sharing raw medical data is not feasible.

How PPFL is applied?

(i) **Data Distribution:** Each hospital possesses patient data, including medical history, diagnostic tests, and treatment records. To maintain privacy, hospitals retain their data locally.
(ii) Collaborative Model Training:

Local Model Training: Each hospital trains a local machine learning model on its own patient data to predict diseases based on various features and parameters.

Model Update Sharing: Instead of sharing raw data, hospitals share encrypted and privacy-preserving model updates (gradients) with a central aggregator.

(iii) Aggregation and Model Refinement:

Aggregation: The central aggregator receives the encrypted model updates from all hospitals and aggregates them to create a global model that benefits from the collective knowledge of the participating hospitals.

Privacy-Preserving Aggregation: Techniques like secure aggregation ensure that the central server doesn't learn specifics about any individual hospital's data.

(iv) Improved Disease Prediction:

Global Model Deployment: The aggregated global model is deployed to hospitals and medical centers, enabling accurate disease prediction based on the combined insights from diverse patient populations.

Privacy-Preserving Predictions: When a new patient's data needs to be evaluated, only the encrypted model parameters are used to make predictions, without exposing individual patient information.

Benefits:

Data Privacy: Raw patient data remains decentralized and confidential within each hospital, complying with healthcare data protection regulations like HIPAA.

Collaborative Learning: Hospitals collectively contribute to building a more accurate disease prediction model by pooling their insights without compromising data privacy.

Improved Diagnostics: The global model benefits from diverse datasets, leading to more robust disease predictions.

Secure Predictions: Patient-specific predictions are made using the global model's encrypted parameters, preserving privacy.

Challenges and Considerations:

- Ensuring data quality and consistency across hospitals.
- Addressing heterogeneity in data distributions and hospital practices.
- Optimizing privacy-preserving techniques to balance privacy and model accuracy.
- Handling differences in hospital resources and technical capabilities.

Example application Review-2: Healthcare Diagnostics and Disease Prediction

Description:

The Internet of Things (IoT) involves a network of interconnected devices, sensors, and systems that exchange data for various applications. Privacy-Preserving Federated Learning (PPFL) plays a significant role in enabling efficient and secure model training for anomaly detection in IoT devices while preserving the privacy of users' data.

How PPFL is applied?

(i) Distributed IoT Devices:

Scenario: Consider a network of IoT devices deployed in a smart home environment, each collecting data on temperature, humidity, occupancy, and more.

Data ***Localization***: Raw data from each IoT device remains localized on the device itself, ensuring privacy and compliance with data protection regulations.

(ii) Collaborative Anomaly Detection:

Local Model Training: Each IoT device trains a local machine learning model to identify anomalies and unusual patterns in the data it collects.

Model Update Sharing: Instead of sharing raw data, IoT devices share encrypted and privacy-preserving model updates with a central aggregator.

(iii) Aggregation and Model Enhancement:

Aggregation: The central aggregator receives the encrypted model updates from all IoT devices and aggregates them into a global anomaly detection model.

Privacy-Preserving Aggregation: Techniques like federated averaging ensure that the central server gains insights without accessing the individual device data.

(iv) Secure Anomaly Detection:

Global Model Deployment: The aggregated global model is deployed back to the IoT devices, enabling them to detect anomalies based on the collective learnings from the network.

Privacy-Preserving Analysis: IoT devices use the encrypted model parameters to detect anomalies in their own data without sharing raw data externally.

Benefits:

Data Privacy: Raw data from IoT devices remains on the devices themselves, ensuring users' data privacy and addressing concerns about data breaches.

Collaborative Learning: IoT devices collectively contribute to building a robust anomaly detection model by sharing knowledge without revealing data.

Efficient Anomaly Detection: By training models locally and sharing updates, devices can identify anomalies efficiently without centralizing data.

Edge Computing: IoT devices themselves are capable of performing anomaly detection, reducing the need for sending data to a centralized server.

Challenges and Considerations:

- ***Resource Constraints:*** IoT devices often have limited computational power and memory, requiring efficient model architectures.
- ***Communication Overhead:*** Sending model updates can introduce communication overhead, which needs to be minimized in resource constrained environments.
- ***Data Heterogeneity:*** Different IoT devices might have varied data distributions and quality, necessitating techniques to handle diversity.

6. CASE STUDY: PPFL IN VARIOUS DOMAINS

6.1. "FedPass: Privacy-Preserving Vertical Federated Deep Learning With Adaptive Obfuscation" (Gu et al., 2023)

In this research paper, a ground-breaking method for privacy-preserving vertical federated deep learning is presented under the name "FedPass." This ground-breaking framework incorporates the idea of adaptive obfuscation, which has the dual function of protecting both the data labels and the data itself. The technique entails the deft incorporation of private passports into passive as well as active models, improving deep learning models' adaptability while guaranteeing their performance is unaffected. This study convincingly shows that FedPass outperforms other privacy protection methods, excelling in terms of both model performance and its capacity to maintain data privacy. This is accomplished through a series of extensive experiments carried out across multiple datasets, coupled with rigorous theoretical analysis.

6.2. "Efficient Secure Aggregation for Privacy-Preserving Federated Machine Learning" (Behnia et al., 2023)

This research work presents e-SeaFL, a very efficient secure aggregation protocol that provides verifiability with just one communication cycle during the aggregation process. A special feature of e-SeaFL allows the aggregation server to show that the participants' aggregation was sincere. The main idea entails using a number of supporting nodes to aid the aggregation server, agreeing with prior works' assumptions on the reliability of participating users. e-SeaFL makes use of authenticated homomorphic vector promises to provide verifiability. Extensive experimentation reveals that users may achieve efficiency benefits on the order of five orders of magnitudes, outperforming the state-of-the-art approach (PPML 2022), when working with gradient vectors with high dimensions, even those with 100,000 dimensions.

6.3. "Privacy-Preserving Patient Clustering for Personalized Federated Learning" (Elhussein & Gursoy, 2023)

In this research project, the idea of "Privacy-Preserving Community-Based Federated Machine Learning" (PCBFL). Utilizing Secure Multi-Party Computation (SMPC), PCBFL skillfully computes patient-level embedding similarities across various sites, all while steadfastly safeguarding the privacy of this data. This ground-breaking framework seamlessly integrates a preprocessing step involving clustering into the domain of federated learning, appropriately named "Clustered FL." In order to ensure that the participating entities continue to be unable to distinguish the input from the hidden secrets and have no intention of cooperating to reveal this information, our study considers the situation of a "honest-but-curious" opponent. Our main goal is to improve the performance of the next task by using individual patient embedding similarity scores to classify patients into various groups. In the context of a downstream goal centered on mortality prediction, carefully evaluate the PCBFL algorithm in contrast to two key federated analogues. Two well-known comparators are "Community-Based Federated Machine Learning" (CBFL) and "FedAvg."

6.4. "Practical Privacy-Preserving Gaussian Process Regression via Secret Sharing" (Luo et al., 2023)

This study presents a unique SS-based GPR model that effectively addresses both horizontal and vertical data-sharing scenarios. It outlines a thorough procedure for carrying out PP-GPR's model development and prediction stages. In order to build a safe and effective GPR model suggest two additive SS-based operations, namely PP-Exp and PP-MI, which can be smoothly merged with current SS-based operations. Due to additional interactions between the two computing servers and a few additional processing steps, PP-GPR does need a little longer computation time, but it still provides a noteworthy degree of efficiency. Importantly, it offers strong security assurances while doing GPR duties in a reasonable amount of time. In comparison to current Federated Learning (FL) and Differential Privacy (DP)-based privacy-preserving GPR techniques, it is therefore a better option, especially when working with datasets of moderate size.

6.5. FedML-HE: An Efficient Homomorphic-Encryption-Based Privacy-Preserving Federated Learning System" (Jin et al., 2023)

This paper introduces a simplified system for privacy-preserving federated learning that makes use of homomorphic encryption. This system is intended to be user- and device-friendly, and it has a flexible and user-friendly deployment platform. Additionally, it included a general optimization strategy that works well when applied to a network of distributed edge devices. With an emphasis on minimizing computational and communication overheads throughout the deployment process, this optimization strategy was created to support the realistic deployment of secure aggregation applications. It also provides dynamic privacy assurances that may be customized to meet certain requirements and preferences.

6.6. "Zero-Knowledge Proof-based Practical Federated Learning on Blockchain" (Xing et al., 2023)

In this paper, we present the ZKP-FL framework, a cutting-edge strategy created to protect privacy while maintaining the correctness of federated learning tasks. Our approach uses secure multi-party computing and Zero-Knowledge Proofs (ZKPs) to check the accuracy of local computations and global model parameters while concealing local data and model parameters from view. The Practical ZKP-FL (PZKP-FL) framework is also shown, which expands support for non-linear and fractional operations. This is accomplished by using Taylor expansion and creating a Fraction-Integer mapping. With a specific focus on proving the PZKP-FL scheme's efficacy, we thoroughly assess both the security and performance elements of these suggested frameworks. The developed federated learning (FL) system built on a foundation of blockchain, Zero-Knowledge Proofs (ZKPs), and Local Differential Privacy (LDP) offers a practical solution that simultaneously accomplishes verifiability, privacy, and streamlined communication, all while maintaining practicality and scalability.

6.7. "Falcon: A Privacy-Preserving and Interpretable Vertical Federated Learning System" (Wu et al., 2023)

In this paper, Falcon presents a novel VFL system that prioritizes both privacy protection and interpretability. Falcon's skills include VFL training and prediction while maintaining strong and effective privacy protection across a wide range of ML models, including logistic regression, multi-layer perceptrons, and linear regression. This degree of security is made feasible via a special hybrid strategy that combines additive secret sharing with threshold partly homomorphic encryption (PHE), which ensures that no intermediate information is exposed.

Falcon excels in making it easier to understand VFL model predictions. It does this by integrating cutting-edge interpretable techniques into a decentralized setting using a flexible and privacy-preserving interpretability framework. Falcon also fine-tunes parallelism factors to reduce overall execution time and optimizes data parallelism for VFL operations. Six real-world datasets and several synthetic datasets were used in our lengthy tests, which were effectively implemented using Falcon. The findings clearly show that Falcon outperforms three secure baseline approaches in terms of performance while achieving accuracy levels comparable to non-private algorithms.

REFERENCES

Aono, Y., & Hayashi, T. (2017). *Privacy-preserving deep learning via additively homomorphic encryption*. IEEE TIFS.

Behnia, R., Ebrahimi, M., & Riasi, A. (2023, July). Efficient Secure Aggregation for Privacy-Preserving Federated. *Machine Learning*, *19*. arXiv2304.03841v4 [cs.CR]

Briggs, Z. F., & Andras, P. (2021). *A review of privacy-preserving federated learning for the internet-of-things*. Federated Learning Systems. doi:10.1007/978-3-030-70604-3_2

Cao, X., & Fang, M. (2020). *Fltrust: Byzantine-robust federated learning via trust bootstrapping*. arXiv preprint arXiv:2012.13995.

Cho, Jhunjhunwala, Li, & Smith. (2022). *To federate or not to federate: Incentivizing client participation in federated learning*. arXiv preprint arXiv.

Dayan, I., Roth, H. R., Zhong, A., Harouni, A., Gentili, A., Abidin, A. Z., Liu, A., Costa, A. B., Wood, B. J., Tsai, C.-S., Wang, C.-H., Hsu, C.-N., Lee, C. K., Ruan, P., Xu, D., Wu, D., Huang, E., Kitamura, F. C., Lacey, G., ... Li, Q. (2021, September). Zhong. Federated learning for predicting clinical outcomes in patients with COVID-19. *Nature Medicine*, *27*(10), 1735–1743. doi:10.103841591-021-01506-3 PMID:34526699

Di Chai, L. W., Yang, L., Junxue, Z. J., Chen, K., & Yang, Q. (n.d.). *A Survey for Federated Learning Evaluations: Goals and Measures*. https://www.researchgate.net/publication/373333429_A_Survey_for_Federated_Learning_Evaluations_Goals_and_Measures

ElhusseinA.GursoyG. (2023). Privacy-preserving patient clustering for personalized federated learning. arXiv:2307.08847v1 [cs.LG].

Fallah, A., Mokhtari, A., & Ozdaglar, A. (2020). *Personalized federated learning: A meta-learning approach*. arXiv preprint arXiv:2002.07948.

Ficek, J., Wang, W., Chen, H., Dagne, G., & Daley, E. (2021, September). Differential privacy in health research: A scoping review. *Journal of the American Medical Informatics Association : JAMIA*, *28*(10), 2269–2276. doi:10.1093/jamia/ocab135 PMID:34333623

GuH.LuoJ.KangY.FanyL.WebankQ. Y. (2023). HKUST, FedPass: Privacy-Preserving Vertical Federated Deep Learning with Adaptive Obfuscation. arXiv:2301.12623v2 [cs.DC].

Huang, W., Li, T., Wang, D., Du, S., Zhang, J., & Huang, T. (2022, April). Fairness and accuracy in horizontal federated learning. *Information Sciences*, *589*, 170–185. doi:10.1016/j.ins.2021.12.102

JinW.YaoY.HanS.CarleeJ. (2023). *FedML-HE: An Efficient Homomorphic-Encryption-Based Privacy-Preserving Federated Learning System*. arXiv:2303.10837v1 [cs.LG].

Kostiainen. (2012). *On-board credentials: An open credential platform for mobile devices*. Academic Press.

Li, X., Cheng, L., Sun, C., Lam, K.-Y., Wang, X., & Li, F. (2021). Federated learning- empowered collaborative data sharing for vehicular edge networks. *IEEE Network*, *35*(3), 116–124. doi:10.1109/MNET.011.2000558

LiuY. (2022). *Vertical Federated Learning*. arXiv:2211.12814v2 [cs.LG].

Liu, Z., Chen, Y., Zhao, Y., Yu, H., Liu, Y., Bao, R., Jiang, J., Nie, Z., Xu, Q., & Yang, Q. (2022). Contribution-aware federated learning for smart healthcare. *Proceedings of the 34th Annual Conference on Innovative Applications of Artificial Intelligence (IAAI-22).*

LuoJ.ZhangY.ZhangJ.QinS.WangH.YuY.XuZ. (2023). Practical Privacy-Preserving Gaussian Process Regression via Secret Sharing. arXiv:2306.14498v1 [cs.CR].

Pramod, A., Naicker, H. S., & Tyagi, A. K. (2020). *Machine Learning and Deep Learning: Open Issues and Future Research Directions for Next Ten Years. In Computational Analysis and Understanding of Deep Learning for Medical Care: Principles, Methods, and Applications.* Wiley Scrivener.

Prayitno, C.-R. S., Putra, K. T., Chen, H.-C., & Tsai, Y.-Y. (2021, November). A systematic review of federated learning in the healthcare area: From the perspective of data properties and applications. *NATO Adv. Sci. Inst. Ser. E. Applied Sciences (Basel, Switzerland)*, *11*(23), 11191. doi:10.3390/app112311191

Saha & Ahmad. (n.d.). *Federated Transfer Learning: concept and applications*. Academic Press.

Tan, Z., Yu, H., Cui, L., & Yang, Q. (2022). *Towards personalized federated learning*. IEEE Transactions on Neural Networks and Learning Systems. doi:10.1109/TNNLS.2022.3160699

Truong, N. (2021). *Privacy preservation in federated learning: An insightful survey from the GDPR perspective.* Elsevier Ltd. https://creativecommons.org/licenses/by/4.0/

Wu, Y., Xing, N., Chen, G., Tien, T. A. D., & Luo, Z. (2023). Falcon: A Privacy-Preserving and Interpretable Vertical Federated Learning System. *Proceedings of the VLDB Endowment, 16*(10). 10.14778/3603581.3603588

XingZ.ZhangZ.LiM.LiuJ.ZhuL.RusselloG.AsgharM. R. (2023). Zero-Knowledge Proof-based Practical Federated Learning on Blockchain. arXiv:2304.05590v2 [cs.CR].

Yin. (2021, July). A Comprehensive Survey of Privacy-preserving Federated Learning: A Taxonomy, Review, and Future Directions. *ACM Computing Surveys*, *54*(6), 131.

Chapter 8
Privacy-Preserving Federated Learning for Healthcare Data

S. Sangeetha
https://orcid.org/0000-0003-2513-5502
Kumaraguru College of Technology, India

ABSTRACT

The evolution of technology has a significant impact on health data collection, transforming the way information is gathered, stored, and utilized in the healthcare industry. The big health record contains sensitive user information like contact details, health status, demographics, vaccination details, exposure history. It's worth noting that while the collection of big health records has been crucial for monitoring the patients' health history, it also raises important privacy and security considerations. Safeguarding the privacy of individuals' health data and ensuring compliance with relevant regulations is essential to maintain public trust and protect sensitive information. Therefore, healthcare data must adhere to privacy regulations and ethical considerations. This chapter elaborates on key challenges and solutions in privacy preservation within federated learning. The key challenges include data heterogeneity, information leakage, attacks, and regulatory compliances.

1. INTRODUCTION

In the era of the digital world, healthcare is being digitalized at an increasingly rapid pace. The advancements in technology have revolutionized the healthcare industry, transforming the way healthcare services are delivered, accessed, and managed. The digitalization uses digital technologies and information systems to improve patient care, the delivery of healthcare, and administrative processes. It involves the use of various technologies, such as electronic health records (EHRs), telemedicine, health apps, wearable devices, artificial intelligence (AI), data analytics, Virtual Reality (VR) and Blockchain.

The key aspects and benefits of healthcare digitalization includes Electronic Health Records (EHRs), Telemedicine, Health Apps and Wearable devices, Artificial Intelligence and Data Analytics, Virtual Reality and Augmented Reality, and Blockchain. Electronic Health Records (EHRs): EHRs replace tra-

DOI: 10.4018/979-8-3693-0593-5.ch008

ditional paper-based records with electronic systems that store and manage patient health information. They enable efficient and secure sharing of medical records among healthcare providers, reducing errors, improving coordination, and enhancing patient safety. Telemedicine: Telemedicine allows patients to receive medical consultations and treatments remotely using digital communication tools. It improves access to healthcare, particularly for individuals in rural or underserved areas, reduces travel time and costs, and enables remote monitoring of patients' health conditions. Health Apps and Wearable Devices: Mobile health applications and wearable devices enable individuals to monitor their health, track fitness levels, and manage chronic conditions. These tools provide real-time data, encourage self-care, and empower patients to take an active role in their healthcare.

Artificial Intelligence (AI) and Data Analytics: AI technologies can analyze vast amounts of healthcare data, identify patterns, and generate insights for clinical decision-making. AI-powered algorithms can help in diagnosing diseases, predicting outcomes, and recommending personalized treatment plans. Data analytics can also be utilized to improve operational efficiency, identify trends, and enhance population health management. Virtual Reality (VR) and Augmented Reality (AR): VR and AR technologies have applications in medical training, patient education, and surgical planning. They offer immersive and interactive experiences, allowing medical professionals to practice complex procedures in a realistic virtual environment. Blockchain: Blockchain technology has the potential to improve data security, privacy, and interoperability in healthcare. It can enhance the integrity of medical records, enable secure sharing of sensitive data, and facilitate streamlined processes, such as insurance claims and supply chain management.

The benefits of healthcare digitalization include:

- Improved access to healthcare services, especially for underserved populations.
- Enhanced patient engagement and empowerment.
- Enhanced communication and collaboration among healthcare providers.
- Increased efficiency and accuracy of medical records and administrative processes.
- More personalized and precise treatment plans.
- Early detection and prevention of diseases.
- Cost savings through streamlined operations and reduced hospital readmissions.

It is to be noted that healthcare organizations collect and generate a significant amount of data on a daily basis. This data comes from various sources such as electronic health records (EHRs), medical imaging, wearable devices, genomics, clinical trials, administrative systems, and more. The volume and complexity of healthcare data have grown exponentially with the digitalization of healthcare. However, it's important to address challenges related to data security, privacy, interoperability, and the digital divide to ensure equitable access to digital healthcare solutions for all individuals.

2. FEDERATED LEARNING IN HEALTHCARE

Federated learning is a machine learning technique that enables a model to be trained across numerous decentralized servers or devices while maintaining the data on those servers or devices. When training machine learning models on sensitive data, concerns about privacy and data security were addressed by the emergence of federated learning.

For model training, data from several sources or devices are collected onto a single server or data centre in typical machine learning settings. However, when dealing with sensitive or private information, this centralized method may give lead to privacy concerns. On the other hand, federated learning enables model training on the device without transferring raw data to a centralized server.

Federated learning operates as follows:

1. **Initialization:** On a global server, a global machine learning model is generated and set to zero.
2. **Distribution:** Individual devices with their own local datasets, such as smartphones, IoT devices, or edge servers, are delivered the first model. Without sharing the data itself, each device locally trains the model using its own data.
3. **Model Update**: Following local training, the individual devices send back model updates (not raw data) to the central server.
4. **Aggregation:** To build a more accurate global model, the central server combines the model updates it has received from all devices. The devices then receive this updated global model once again.
5. **Iterative Process**: To improve the global model, the local training, model update, and aggregation processes are repeatedly iterated.

Federated Learning has a number of benefits, including individual users' privacy is protected because only model changes are sent, leaving the raw data on the local devices. Federated Learning eliminates the need to send massive datasets to a single server, conserving bandwidth and cutting down on communication expenses. Decentralization allows for the training of models on edge hardware, lowering latency and enabling real-time inference without the need for a centralised cloud infrastructure. Because individual devices can continue training even when some are offline or unavailable, federated learning is more resilient to failures.

Figure 1. Federated learning architecture

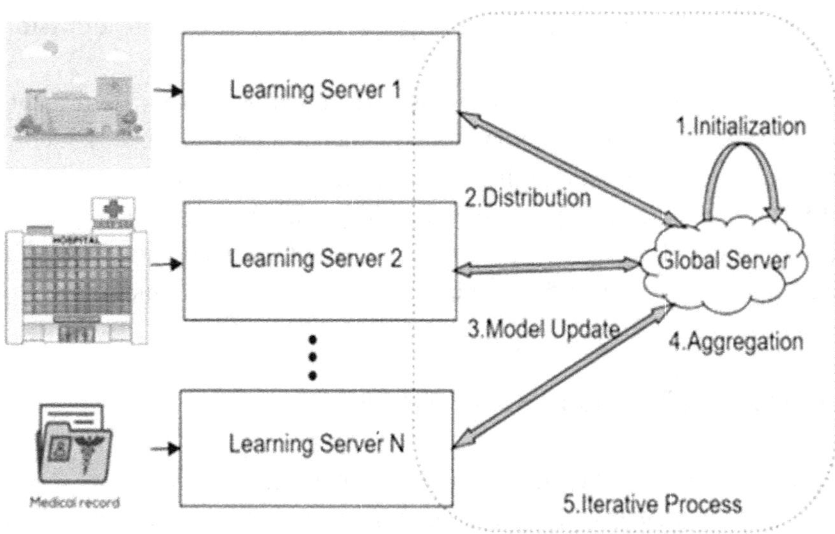

Figure 1 depicts the architecture and steps in federated learning system. As explained in federated learning steps the global model is initialized. Every learning server collects data from respective hospital. Using the data that is collected from multiple devices local model training is initiated in each learning server. The learned model is aggregated in global sever using model updates collected from multiple learning servers to create a global model.

Federated learning is especially helpful in situations when data is delicate or difficult to transfer because of privacy laws, or widely dispersed datasets. It can be used in numerous applications such as healthcare, finance, smart homes, and Internet of Things (IoT) gadgets. The handling of heterogeneous devices, dealing with connectivity and security issues, and managing concept drift as a result of different data distributions among devices are the challenges in Federated Learning. Federated learning mechanisms provide the advantage of ensuring user privacy in spite of these limitations in healthcare domains.

3. BENEFITS OF PRIVACY PRESERVING FEDERATED LEARNING

Federated learning provides a lot of potential and benefits for the healthcare sector. Due to the sensitive nature of patient information, data privacy and security are crucial in the healthcare industry. A way to use remote healthcare data without compromising patient privacy is offered by federated learning. It leverages the power of machine learning while ensuring the privacy and security of sensitive patient data. In traditional machine learning, data from multiple sources are centralized to build a model, which can raise privacy concerns when dealing with sensitive healthcare information.

Federated learning addresses this issue by decentralizing the model training process. Instead of sending patient data to a central server, federated learning enables model training to occur locally at each data source (e.g., hospitals, clinics, or individual devices). The central server only coordinates the training process by aggregating the locally trained models' updates. This way, the actual patient data remains within the local environment, and only the model's weight updates are shared.

The following are some key benefits of federated learning in healthcare:

- Patient privacy protection: Federated Learning enables collaboration and model training between healthcare organizations without disclosing private patient information. Instead, of protecting patient privacy, models are trained locally using the data from each institution, and only the model updates are aggregated centrally.
- Data Security and Compliance: Healthcare organisations frequently have to adhere to strict data security laws, including HIPAA in the US. As data stays inside the local institutions, Federated Learning assists with compliance with these requirements by lowering the danger of data breaches.
- Improved Generalization: Federated Learning can build a more robust and universal model by training on a variety of datasets from various hospitals and clinics. Accuracy and performance may be enhanced as a result of this more inclusive data representation.
- Federated Learning makes it possible for numerous healthcare institutions to work together on research initiatives without disclosing sensitive information. This makes it possible to combine data from diverse sources, producing analyses and insights that are more substantial.
- Real-time personalized medicine: Federated learning can be used to create models for personalized medicine that are trained on patient-specific data from many sources. Better therapy suggestions based on the particular traits of each patient is obtained with real time personalized medicine.

- Distributed healthcare devices: As wearable medical devices and Internet of Things (IoT) sensors proliferate, federated learning can be used to train models on these dispersed devices to track and forecast patient health problems.

4. CHALLENGES IN HEALTHCARE DATA SHARING

Healthcare data is available in a variety of formats across numerous systems, which makes it difficult to share and integrate it. The inability to aggregate and analyse data from many sources is hampered by the lack of uniform data formats, which affects the effectiveness and quality of collective healthcare initiatives. Obstacles to interoperability also limit the possibilities for cross-institutional research and analysis and the creation of unified, comprehensive patient data. To overcome these obstacles, thoughtful efforts must be made to create data standards and protocols that provide secure and effective data transmission while protecting patient privacy. The following outlines the challenges associated with healthcare data sharing:

- Patient Privacy and Confidentiality: Protecting patient privacy and maintaining the confidentiality of sensitive medical information is of utmost importance while sharing healthcare data.
- Data Security and Breach Risks: Healthcare data breaches can result in identity theft, fraud, and compromised patient records, underscoring the necessity for strong cybersecurity safeguards.
- Legal and Regulatory Compliance: Healthcare data sharing is subject to strict regulations such as HIPAA (in the U.S.) and GDPR (in the EU), which require adherence to specific standards and protocols.
- Consent and Ethical Considerations: Obtaining informed consent from patients for sharing their medical data can be challenging, and ethical considerations about data usage and patient autonomy arise.
- Data Standardization and Interoperability: Due to the lack of standardisation, healthcare data is available in a variety of formats and systems, making integration and exchange between organizations challenging.
- Data Quality and Accuracy: Patient care can be adversely affected by incorrect inferences and medical decisions resulting from inaccurate or inadequate healthcare data.
- Data Governance and Ownership: Governance and ownership issues arise when determining who owns the data, who has the authority to share it, and how data should be managed.
- Technical Integration Hurdles: It can be extremely difficult to integrate data from numerous sources using various technologies, formats, and systems.
- Lack of Incentives for Sharing: Healthcare organisations might not have strong incentives to exchange data, especially if doing so would not directly benefit them.
- Data Fragmentation and Dispersal: It might be challenging to put together a complete view for analysis because patient data is frequently dispersed throughout numerous providers and systems.
- Data Bias and Fairness: When employed in analysis and decision-making, bias existing in healthcare data, either originating from demographic differences or medical history, can create imbalances.
- Complexity of Data Sharing Agreements: Legal, technical, and privacy factors must be taken into account when negotiating and creating data sharing agreements between healthcare organisations.

- Data Management Costs: Healthcare businesses may find it expensive to implement secure data sharing mechanisms and maintain data quality.
- Data Access Control and Granularity: It might be difficult to grant proper access with several stakeholders while controlling access to sensitive data.

From the above challenges it is clearly evident that informed consent is required and ethical issues must be taken into account, to protect patient privacy in healthcare data exchange. Clear communication, streamlined consent procedures, and transparency are necessary in order to strike a balance between patients' rights to control their data and the potential benefits of sharing for research and care. The difficulty lies in creating consent systems that protect moral norms and preserve trust in the healthcare ecosystem while enabling patients to make informed decisions without impeding data exchange.

5. ATTACKS IN FEDERATED LEARNING ENVIRONMENT

Although federated learning has inherent privacy protection due to the localization of data and reduction in data exchange, it still has limitations. Table 1 summarizes the vulnerable attacks in federated learning environment.

Table 1. Vulnerable attacks in federated learning environment

S.No.	Attack Type	Attacker Target	Attacker Intention
1	Model Poisoning (Yang et al., 2023)	Model	Attackers modify the local training datasets of participating devices with malicious data or biased samples to affect the performance of the global model.
2	Data Poisoning	Model	Attackers manipulate the input data present in the participating devices in a way that affects the training process and reduces the accuracy of the overall model.
3	Backdoor Attacks (Naseri, M., Hayes, J., & De Cristofaro, 2020)	Privacy	Attackers introduce subtle patterns or triggers into the local data, causing the global model to behave incorrectly when exposed to specific inputs.
4	Membership Inference	Model	By taking advantage of information leakage in model updates or outputs, attackers try to ascertain whether a certain piece of data was included in the training dataset.
5	Model Inversion	Model	Attackers rebuild portions of the original training data using the information provided by the model's outputs, potentially disclosing sensitive information.
6	Sybil Attacks	Privacy	Attackers fabricate several false identities or devices to artificially influence the model aggregation procedure.
7	Model Inference Attacks	Model	Attackers might presumably compromise privacy by using the global model to infer details about the local data used for training.
8	Gradient Leakage (Hatamizadeh et al., 2023)	Privacy	Attackers deduce sensitive details about local data by analysing gradients shared during federated learning.

It's important to note that federated learning environments can be vulnerable to these attacks due to their distributed nature and reliance on data sharing and model aggregation. Researchers are continuously working to develop techniques and strategies to mitigate these threats and enhance the security and privacy of federated learning systems.

6. OVERVIEW OF PRIVACY-PRESERVING TECHNIQUES

(Sangeetha & Sudha Sadasivam, 2019) present a comprehensive survey on the various privacy preservation mechanisms. Privacy preserving data mining (PPDM) (Shreyas Madhav, A.V., Ilavarasi, A.K., Tyagi, 2022) which is explained in this section can be categorised as shown in Figure 2.

Figure 2. Privacy preservation techniques

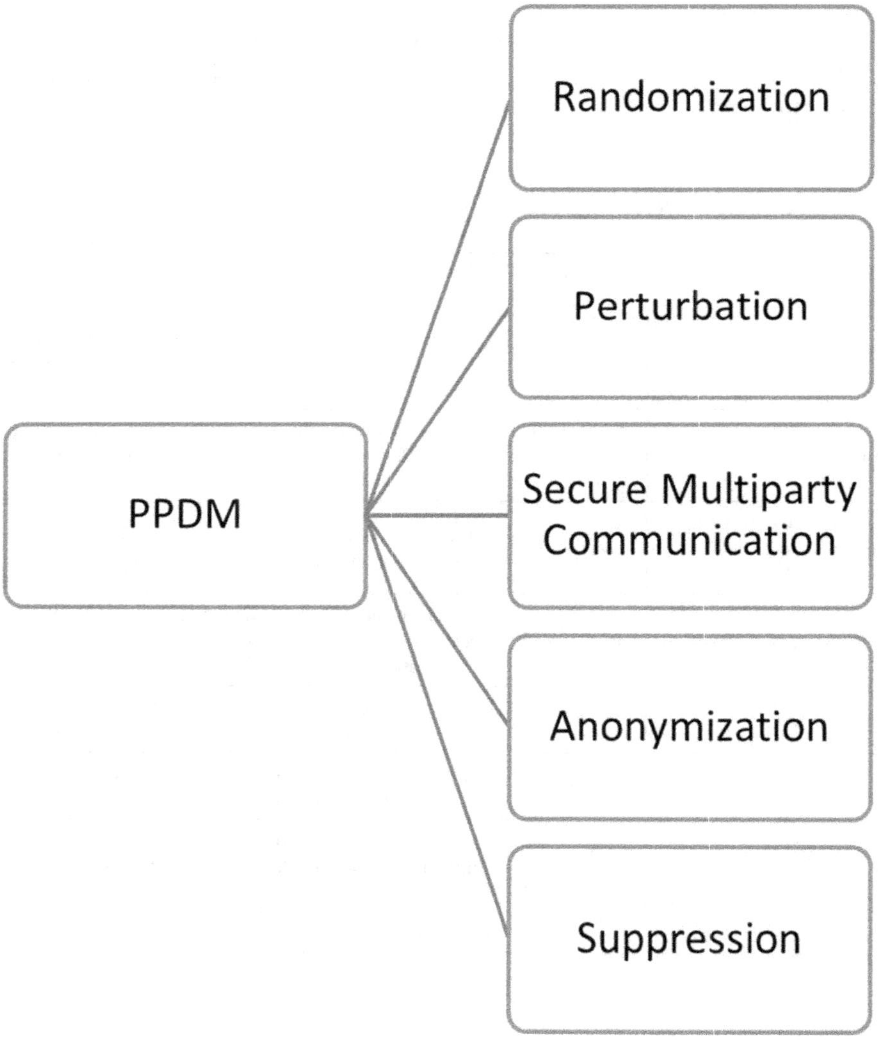

6.1 Randomization

Historically, randomization strategies have been employed to generate accurate responses to sensitive yes/no questions in surveys. Respondents may be reluctant to provide truthful answers to these questions if the data collector (surveyor) is unreliable. A seminal work on randomized response, randomizes each individual i independently and answer as follows: i answers truthfully with probability , and lies with probability (1-) (Warner, 1965). An anonymous response is ensured by a randomised response because the users do not reveal the true value. For instance: Google Chrome uses a random response system called RAPPOR (Randomized Aggregatable Privacy Preserving Ordinal Responses) to gather usage data. A SulQ (SubLinear Queries) system based on randomised answer was proposed by Microsoft researchers. SulQ is primarily a statistical database with a reliable administrator.

6.2 Perturbation

Before publishing the original data, the perturbation approach alters the data (Chen et al., n.d.). The data pattern must be preserved, and sensitive information must be hidden when using such a transformation. The major challenge in the perturbation technique is to strike a balance between data privacy and utility. The following perturbation techniques can be used to enforce user privacy: rotation, projection from high dimension to low dimensional space, sketch-based approach, and geometric perturbation (Chamikara et al., 2018; Chen et al., 2011).Other perturbation methods add noise to the data to protect privacy It is true that adding noise to a small dataset renders it useless, but doing so for a huge dataset is beneficial. This method works well with datasets that have enormous amounts of data because most real-world applications do. The user's presence or absence is concealed by the noise addition, and the aggregate distribution reveals the underlying pattern. The matrix factorization framework, for instance, can be perturbed to assure privacy preservation (Hu et al., 2020).

6.3 Secure Multiparty Communication

A cryptography-based method called Secure Multiparty Communication (SMC) enables learning from private data. The user can find the joint function from private data with the aid of SMC (Javed et al., 2023). To gain the benefit of collaboration with confidentiality, end-to-end computation is performed on the encrypted data (Jia & Lei, 2021; Kumari et al., 2023). The requirement for a reliable third party is removed by Secure Multiparty Computation. For instance, a secure multiparty protocol can be used for feature selection, a vital pre-processing step in the majority of machine learning algorithms (Myrzashova et al., 2023). Third parties are not given information about the feature value or the features they have chosen.

6.4 Anonymization

Anonymization hides or modifies the dataset so that the individual user in the dataset cannot be identified. The following are the most well-known anonymization techniques.

The ground-breaking work that suggested user privacy protection is K anonymity (Naseri et al., 2020). Date of birth, sex, and zipcode are used as quasi-identifiers to identify the users who are present in the dataset. Sweeney demonstrated that it is possible to identify the unique persons involved in the data by mapping the quasi-identifiers from the medical database with the voter id information. K-anonymity was subsequently proposed to safeguard the user. For the purpose of maintaining privacy, K anonymity (Naseri et al., n.d.; Sai et al., 2023; Sangeetha et al., 2019, 2022, 2023) required that each record in the dataset be represented by k groups of records.

However, homogeneity and background knowledge attacks can weaken anonymity. As a result, diversity was proposed (Sangeetha et al., 2022). diversity protects the user from attacks based on background knowledge and uniformity. When more than k anonymous users possess the same sensitive attribute, a homogeneity attack takes place. When the attacker attempts to interpret the sensitive attribute while having some prior information about the neighbours, a background knowledge attack is produced.

Skewness and similarity attacks are the attacks in diversity. Because there are fewer samples in the training record, skewness attack happens. When the same category of the sensitive property is found in the detected records, a similarity attack takes place. t – closeness (Selvaraj et al., 2021), which leverages earth movers distance between the data records to guarantee privacy, was presented as a solution to these attacks.

6.5 Suppression

To protect privacy, suppression substitutes an asterisk "*" for the actual values. However, this affects the usefulness of the data. It is challenging to train the model with such input data since values are not available. As a result, very few studies (Shi et al., 2021) in the literature use suppression and generalisation to protect privacy. Suppression can be used for extremely sensitive information like a person's name, customer ID number, or personal identification number. For instance, banks hold client credit card information more securely. Customer id and CVV (card verification value) attributes are suppressed and maintained on the banking server.

7. PRIVACY-PRESERVING FEDERATED LEARNING IN HEALTHCARE

The concept of privacy-preserving federated learning is evolving rapidly, and numerous current research projects and developments are underway. In this section three popular privacy preservation techniques using federated learning for healthcare is discussed Figure 3.

7.1 Differential Privacy Federated Learning

By enabling collaborative data analysis while adhering to strong privacy rules, differential privacy federated learning in healthcare has the potential to revolutionise medical research and enhance patient care. However, overcoming the technical obstacles and making sure that all legal requirements are met continue to be essential components of its creation and acceptance. This section outlines healthcare data privacy protection using differential privacy.

Differential privacy noise is applied in federated learning to protect the privacy of individual data contributions while still enabling model training across decentralized data sources (Sangeetha Selvaraj et al., 20211 Sangeetha, Sudha Sadasivam, & Srikanth, 2022). Here are key application points where differential privacy noise is commonly used in federated learning:

Figure 3. Privacy preservation with federated learning

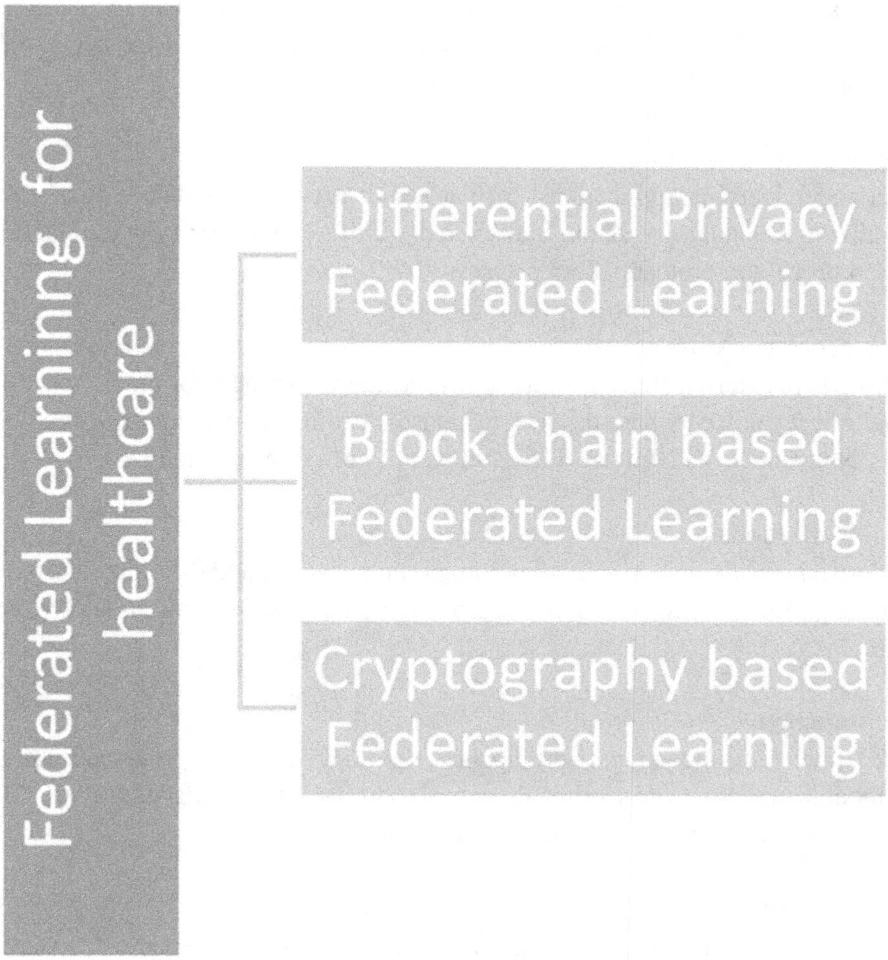

1. Gradient Perturbation:

In federated learning, participants (e.g., devices or institutions) compute gradients based on their local data and share these gradients for model updates (Hatamizadeh et al., 2023; Tyagi et al., n.d.; Wu et al., 2022). To protect privacy, participants add differential privacy noise to their gradients before sharing them. This ensures that individual data points cannot be reconstructed from the gradients.

2. Model Updates:

Instead of sharing raw model updates, participants add differential privacy noise to the updates before sending them to the central server (Javed et al., 2023; Shi et al., 2021). This protects the individual contributions to the model while still allowing the global model to improve.

3. Aggregation of Model Updates:

When the central server receives model updates from participants, it aggregates these updates to compute the new global model. Adding noise during the aggregation process helps ensure that no participant's contribution is exposed, even indirectly.

4. Query Responses:
   In some federated learning scenarios, the central server may need to query the participants for information about their local data. When responding to queries, participants can add noise to their responses to preserve privacy while still providing useful information.

5. Data Aggregation for Analysis:
   In some federated learning applications, such as healthcare research, data is aggregated for analysis without centralizing it (Chuanxin, Zhou, Sun Yi, n.d.). Differential privacy noise can be added during this aggregation process to protect patient privacy.

6. Querying Federated Models:
   In scenarios where external entities want to query a federated model for predictions or insights, adding differential privacy noise to these queries' responses ensures that sensitive information is not leaked (Van Dijk, M., Nguyen, N. V., Nguyen, T. N., Nguyen, L. M., & Nguyen, 2020).

7. Weight Initialization:
   During federated learning model initialization, participants can add differential privacy noise to the initial weights to protect against potential privacy leaks during the training process (Sun, L., Qian, J., & Chen, 2020).

8. Input Perturbation:
   In some federated learning setups, participants (e.g., mobile devices) may add noise to their local data or local model updates before sending them to the central server Sangeetha et al., 2022; Selvaraj et al., 2021). This can be a form of client-side privacy protection.

9. Learning Rate Adjustment:
   The learning rate in federated learning can be dynamically adjusted based on privacy requirements. Higher privacy demands may lead to lower learning rates to accommodate the added noise.

It's important to note that the choice of where and how to apply differential privacy noise in federated learning depends on the specific use case, privacy requirements, and the nature of the data and participants. Proper parameter tuning, noise levels, and privacy guarantees are essential to balance privacy protection with model utility. Additionally, differential privacy is a nuanced field, and its application in federated learning should be guided by experts in both privacy and machine learning. Various perturbation points using differential privacy is demonstrated in the following Figure 4.

By enabling collaborative data analysis while adhering to strong privacy rules, differential privacy federated learning in healthcare has the potential to revolutionise medical research and enhance patient care. However, overcoming the technical obstacles and making sure that all legal requirements are met continue to be essential components of its creation and acceptance.

7.2 Blockchain-Based Federated Learning

A potential solution to handle privacy issues while maintaining the collaborative benefits of federated learning is blockchain-based privacy protection.

Figure 4. Differential privacy perturbation in federated learning

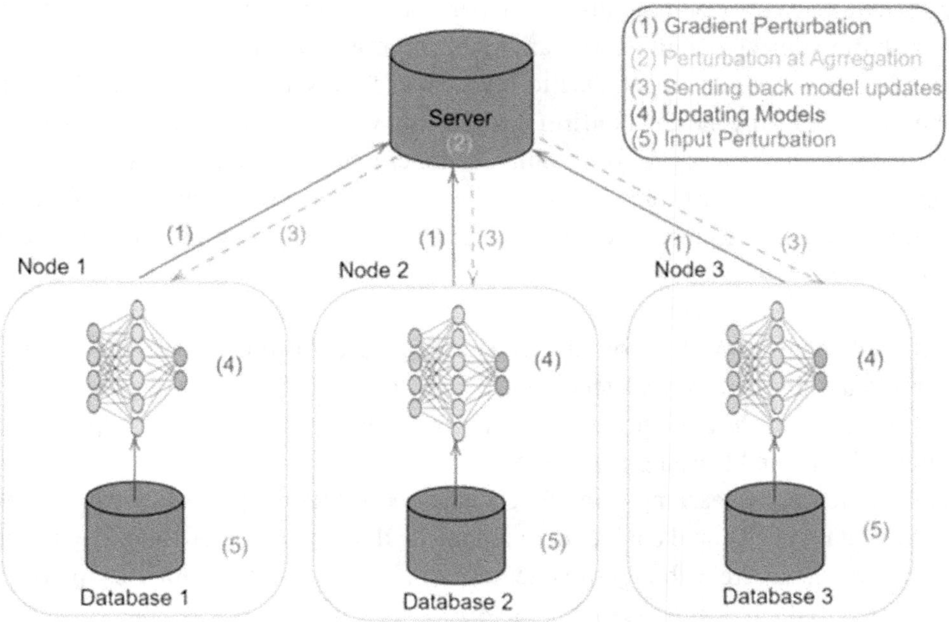

A machine learning technique called federated learning enables several parties to train a framework without revealing their raw data. However, protecting privacy in federated learning is complicated because models could accidentally reveal private information about the training data. There are numerous approaches to use blockchain technology to improve privacy in federated learning (Sh8 et al., 2021; Madhave et al., 2022; Kumari et al., 2023; Sangeetha et al., 2023; Myrzashova et al., 2023; Amit Kumar Tyagi, Aswathy S U, G Aghila, n.d.l H. S. K. Sheth, 2022):

1. Data Ownership and Control: A decentralised ledger that tracks data ownership and access rights can be created using blockchain technology. Owners of data can continue to oversee their information and give authorization for participation in federated learning. These rights can be enforced by smart contracts on the blockchain, ensuring that only authorized parties can access and use the data.
2. Data Provenance: Blockchain provides a transparent and immutable record of all data transactions. This can help preventing data poisoning attacks, guaranteeing the use of only high-quality data, and ensuring the validity and integrity of data used in federated learning.
3. Privacy Preserving Aggregation: In federated learning, blockchain can be used to safely aggregate model updates from participating devices or nodes. Blockchain can be linked with privacy-preserving approaches to ensure that model updates are aggregated without revealing individual contributions, such as homomorphic encryption or zero-knowledge proofs.
4. Incentive Mechanisms: Blockchain can enable token-based incentive mechanisms feasible without sacrificing data privacy, rewarding players for their contributions to federated learning. Tokens can be automatically distributed to participants based on their contributions to the model while maintaining anonymity thanks to smart contracts.

5. Decentralized Identity: With the help of blockchain, participants in federated learning can demonstrate their legitimacy without disclosing personal information. By eliminating the requirement for data sharing during identity verification, this improves privacy.
6. Auditability and Accountability: Due to blockchain's transparency, federated learning processes may be examined. Anyone can confirm that the data was utilised and updated in accordance with the terms set forth, fostering accountability, and increasing participant trust.
7. Consensus & Security: By preventing hostile actors from manipulating the federated learning process, blockchain consensus techniques like proof-of-work and proof-of-stake can improve the security of federated learning.

It's important to note that while blockchain can improve federated learning's privacy and security, it also poses problems with scalability, latency, and energy use. In addition, the selection of the blockchain platform, consensus algorithm, and privacy-preserving methods must consider the specific requirements and limitations of federated learning applications.

In conclusion, federated learning using blockchain-based privacy protection can help with privacy issues, improve data security, and enable more reliable and trustworthy collaborative machine learning processes. However, it requires a thoughtful integration of blockchain technology and privacy-preserving techniques tailored to the federated learning context.

7.3 Cryptography-Based Federated Learning

In federated learning, it's essential to use cryptography-based privacy protection measures to keep sensitive information private while permitting model training across several dispersed parties (Sangeetha, Sudha Sadasivam, Nithesh, et al., 2022). Here are several methods for federated learning privacy protection based on cryptography:

1. Homomorphic Encryption:

Homomorphic Encryption: Use partial homomorphic encryption to allow computations on encrypted data using ElGamal or Paillier encryption methods. Participants in federated learning can compute updates on locally stored encrypted data without disclosing the original data. The central aggregator can complete the aggregate while the data is still encrypted after receiving the encrypted updates.

2. Secure Multi-Party Computation SMPC:

SMPC protocols should be used to enable several parties to cooperatively compute on their private data without disclosing it, such as secure addition and secure multiplication. This makes it possible to jointly train federated learning models while maintaining the privacy of the data.

3. Zero Knowledge Proofs:

Proof of Knowledge: Use zero-knowledge proofs (like zk-SNARKs) to demonstrate knowledge of specific facts without disclosing the facts directly. Without disclosing the data or preliminary results, this can be used to validate individual circumstances or examine model improvements.

4. Proxy Re-encryption

Re-encryption Schemes: Proxy re-encryption methods can be used to safely transform and assign access to encrypted data. Data confidentiality is ensured by the ability of data owners to assign access permissions to federated learning participants without disclosing the decryption key.

5. Federated Learning with Secure Aggregation:

Secure Aggregation Protocols: Implement secure aggregation methods, such as secure enclaves or secure hardware, to carry out the aggregate of model updates in a trusted setting. This prevents individual updates from being exposed in the aggregated model.

6. Threshold Cryptography:

Threshold Encryption and Decryption: Utilize threshold encryption and decryption to spread encryption and decryption keys among numerous parties. The data must be decrypted by a specific number of parties working together, improving security and privacy.

7. Ring Signatures:

Anonymous Authentication: Utilize ring signatures for anonymous authentication to make sure that contributions to federated learning cannot be traced back to particular users. This makes it impossible to trace contributions back to specific data sources.

8. Secure Hash Functions:

Data Anonymization: Apply secure hash methods to data to make it anonymous before sharing it with other federated learning participants. This makes sure that the hashes cannot be used to recreate the original data.

9. Post processing of model updates:

Applying cryptographic methods to the post-processing of model outputs will ensure that private data is kept private, even in the final forecasts.

It's crucial to remember that the choice of privacy protection methods based on encryption relies on the demands and limitations of your federated learning application. Every technique has advantages and disadvantages; therefore the choice should be made depending on things like security, processing complexity, and the level of privacy desired.

When applying these methods in federated learning systems, significant thought should also be given to key management, cryptographic protocol integration, and performance optimization.

8. FUTURE DIRECTIONS AND RESEARCH CHALLENGES

As researchers and practitioners work to find solutions to the problems posed by privacy, security, and scalability in collaborative machine learning, emerging trends in privacy-preserving federated learning are continually evolving (Sai, G.H., Tripathi, K., Tyagi, 2023). Here is a summary of some of the major new trends in this area:

1. Differential Privacy Enhancements

Advanced Differential Privacy: To lessen the trade-off between privacy and model accuracy, researchers are creating more advanced differential privacy techniques. This features enhanced noise injection methods and more stringent privacy protections.

2. Homomorphic encryption advancements

Enhancements to Efficiency: Ongoing research is aimed at improving the efficiency of homomorphic encryption, allowing faster computations on encrypted data and lowering the computational overhead.

3. Secure Multi-Party Computation (SMPC) and Zero-Knowledge Proofs:

Integration: To strengthen privacy guarantees and enable complicated calculations on encrypted data, zero-knowledge proofs (such zk-SNARKs) and SMPC are being integrated into federated learning.

4. Hybrid strategies

Combining Techniques: A new concept involves layering privacy protection by combining diverse privacy-preserving techniques, like differential privacy and federated learning.

5. Federated Learning and the Edge:

Edge Devices: It is increasingly common to extend federated learning to edge devices, such as smartphones and Internet of Things (IoT) gadgets. On-device training is made possible while data privacy is maintained.

6. Blockchain Integration:

Secure Record-keeping: Integrating blockchain technology will provide secure and open record-keeping of participant contributions, data exchanges, and federated learning processes.

7. Secure Aggregation Techniques:

Improving Trustworthiness: To increase trustworthiness, more secure aggregation methods could be created using trusted execution environments (TEEs), secure multi-party computation, or secure hardware.

8. Privacy Preserving Transfer Learning:

Transferable Knowledge: Methods for securely transferring information from one federated learning model to another, allowing transfer learning that is more effective and secure.

9. Federated learning with AutoML:

Automated Model Selection: Research is being done on automating the selection of suitable machine learning models for federated learning tasks in order to maximise performance and privacy.

10. Frameworks and standardised practises:

Privacy Standards: The creation of frameworks and standards for federated learning that protect privacy in order to encourage adoption and interoperability.

Safe Federated Learning in Finance and Healthcare:

11. Secure Federated Learning in Healthcare and Finance:

Vertical-Specific Solutions: Increased focus on privacy-preserving federated learning applications in highly regulated domains like healthcare and finance, with specific privacy-preserving techniques tailored to these sectors.

12. Ethical Consideration:

The ethical concerns of federated learning, including as fairness, bias, and accountability in privacy-preserving models, are becoming more and more well-known and the subject of research.

13. Privacy Preserving AI Regulations:

Governmental and industry regulations: anticipating and adapting to changing norms and privacy laws relating to federated learning and AI.

These new patterns demonstrate how adaptable privacy-preserving federated learning is as it changes to satisfy the changing requirements of privacy-conscious applications and legal frameworks. To be at the forefront of this rapidly growing field, companies and academics working on privacy-preserving federated learning must keep up with these trends.

9. CONCLUSION

Federated learning that protects patient privacy is crucial to the advancement of healthcare because it makes it possible to enhance healthcare results and enhances patient privacy. In order to interact and train AI models without jeopardising patient privacy, medical institutions, academics, and healthcare providers must adopt privacy-preserving federated learning.

This strategy makes it easier for many entities to share crucial medical data, which has a number of important advantages: Improved Healthcare Outcomes: By combining data from many sources, federated learning makes it possible to construct AI models that are more reliable and accurate. These models can help with disease prediction, diagnosis, suggested treatments, and outcome predictions, which will ultimately result in better patient care and better healthcare outcomes.

Collaboration among institutions: Healthcare organisations can work together and pool their data without really disclosing it. This is essential for analysing patient groups dispersed across several sites and conducting epidemiological research on rare diseases. Federated learning makes collaboration easier while protecting the privacy of data.

Data about specific patients is secured with privacy-preserving techniques like differential privacy, secured multi-party computation, and homomorphic encryption. Patients can have complete confidence that their sensitive health information is secure, allaying worries about data breaches and unauthorised access.

Compliance with Regulations: In the United States and Europe, strong privacy laws like HIPAA and GDPR apply to the healthcare industry. By reducing the risks connected with data sharing and guaranteeing patient consent is recognized, privacy-preserving federated learning aids healthcare companies in adhering to these rules.

Reduced Data Centralization: Sensitive data is frequently centralised via traditional methods of data sharing in healthcare, making it an ideal target for hackers. Using federated learning Data is dispersed across several sites, which also improves data security by lowering the possibility of a single point of failure.

Ethical Research: By limiting the exploitation of patient data and addressing concerns with prejudice and discrimination in data, federated learning supports ethical research techniques. This guarantees that recommendations and predictions made by AI models are impartial and fair.

Patient Empowerment: When patients are certain that their privacy is safeguarded, they are more inclined to contribute to medical research and share their data. Federated learning that protects privacy fosters trust and promotes patient involvement in healthcare projects.

In conclusion, privacy-preserving federated learning in healthcare is of paramount importance since it fosters interdisciplinary research, enhances patient outcomes, and fosters the creation of AI models while adhering to high patient privacy requirements. It strikes a balance between data sharing and privacy protection, making it a key enabler of advancements in medical research and patient care.

REFERENCES

Abaoud, M., Almuqrin, M. A., & Khan, M. F. (2023). Advancing Federated Learning Through Novel Mechanism for Privacy Preservation in Healthcare Applications. *IEEE Access : Practical Innovations, Open Solutions*, *11*, 83562–83579. doi:10.1109/ACCESS.2023.3301162

Chamikara, M. A. P., Bertok, P., Liu, D., Camtepe, S., & Khalil, I. (2018). Efficient data perturbation for privacy preserving and accurate data stream mining. *Pervasive and Mobile Computing*, *48*, 1–19. doi:10.1016/j.pmcj.2018.05.003

Chen, K., Liu, L., Chen, K., & Liu, L. (2011). Geometric data perturbation for privacy preserving outsourced data mining. *Knowledge and Information Systems*, *29*(3), 657–695. doi:10.100710115-010-0362-4

Chen, W. N., Choquette-Choo, C. A., & Kairouz, P. (n.d.). Communication efficient federated learning with secure aggregation and differential privacy. NeurIPS 2021 Workshop Privacy in Machine Learning.

Chuanxin, Zhou, Sun Yi, & W. D. (n.d.). Federated learning with Gaussian differential privacy. *Proceedings of the 2020 2nd International Conference on Robotics, Intelligent Control and Artificial Intelligence*, 296-301.

Hatamizadeh, A., Yin, H., Molchanov, P., Myronenko, A., Li, W., Dogra, P., Feng, A., Flores, M. G., Kautz, J., Xu, D., & Roth, H. R. (2023). Do Gradient Inversion Attacks Make Federated Learning Unsafe? *IEEE Transactions on Medical Imaging*, *42*(7), 2044–2056. doi:10.1109/TMI.2023.3239391 PMID:37021996

Hu, R., Guo, Y., Li, H., Pei, Q., & Gong, Y. (2020). Personalized Federated Learning With Differential Privacy. *IEEE Internet of Things Journal*, *7*(10), 9530–9539. doi:10.1109/JIOT.2020.2991416

Javed, L., Anjum, A., Yakubu, B. M., Iqbal, M., Moqurrab, S. A., & Srivastava, G. (2023). ShareChain: Blockchain-enabled model for sharing patient data using federated learning and differential privacy. *Expert Systems: International Journal of Knowledge Engineering and Neural Networks*, *40*(5), e13131. doi:10.1111/exsy.13131

Jia, J., & Lei, Z. (2021). Article. *Journal of Physics*. Advance online publication. doi:10.1088/1742-6596/1802/3/032021

Kumari, K. A., Sangeetha, S., Rajeevan, V., Dharshini, M. D., & Haritha, T. (2023). Trade Management System Using R3 Corda Blockchain BT - Intelligent Systems Design and Applications. Springer Nature Switzerland.

Myrzashova, R., Alsamhi, S. H., Shvetsov, A. V., Hawbani, A., & Wei, X. (2023). Blockchain Meets Federated Learning in Healthcare: A Systematic Review With Challenges and Opportunities. *IEEE Internet of Things Journal, 10*(16), 14418–14437. doi:10.1109/JIOT.2023.3263598

NaseriM.HayesJ.De CristofaroE. (2020). *Local and Central Differential Privacy for Robustness and Privacy in Federated Learning*. https://doi.org/https://doi.org/10.48550/arXiv.2009.03561

Naseri, M., Hayes, J., & De Cristofaro, E. (n.d.). *Toward Robustness and Privacy in Federated Learning: Experimenting with Local and Central Differential Privacy*. Academic Press.

Sai, G. H., Tripathi, K., & Tyagi, A. K. (2023). Internet of Things-Based e-Health Care: Key Challenges and Recommended Solutions for Future. *Proceedings of Third International Conference on Computing, Communications, and Cyber-Security. Lecture Notes in Networks and Systems.* https://doi.org/https://doi.org/10.1007/978-981-19-1142-2_37

Sangeetha, S., Kumari, K. A., Shrinika, M., Sujaybharath, P., Varsini, S. M., & Kumar, K. A. (2023). Ensuring Location Privacy in Crowdsensing System Using Blockchain BT - Futuristic Communication and Network Technologies. Springer Nature Singapore.

Sangeetha, S., & Sudha Sadasivam, G. (2019). Privacy of Big Data: A Review. In A. Dehghantanha & K. K. Choo (Eds.), *Handbook of Big Data and IoT Security*. Springer. doi:10.1007/978-3-030-10543-3_2

Sangeetha, S., Sudha Sadasivam, G., Nithesh, V., & Mounish, K. (2022). *Confluence of Cryptography and Differential Privacy: A Hybrid Approach for Privacy Preserving Collaborative Filtering BT - Proceedings of the International Conference on Paradigms of Communication, Computing and Data Sciences*. Springer Singapore. 10.1007/978-981-16-5747-4_29

Sangeetha, S., Sudha Sadasivam, G., & Srikanth, A. (2022). Differentially private model release for healthcare applications. *International Journal of Computers and Applications, 44*(10), 953–958. doi:10.1080/1206212X.2021.2024958

Selvaraj, S. (2021, June 1). Utility-Based Differentially Private Recommendation System. *Big Data, 9*(3), 203–218. Advance online publication. doi:10.1089/big.2020.0038

Selvaraj, S., Sadasivam, G. S., Goutham, D. T., Srikanth, A., & Vinith, J. (2021). Privacy Preserving Bloom Recommender System. *2021 International Conference on Computer Communication and Informatics (ICCCI)*, 1–6. 10.1109/ICCCI50826.2021.9402528

Sheth, H. S. K. I. A. K., & A. K. T. (2022). Deep Learning, Blockchain based Multi-layered Authentication and Security Architectures. *2022 International Conference on Applied Artificial Intelligence and Computing (ICAAIC),* 476-485. doi:10.1109/ICAAIC53929.2022.9793179

Shi, L., Shu, J., Zhang, W., & Liu, Y. (2021). HFL-DP: Hierarchical Federated Learning with Differential Privacy. *2021 IEEE Global Communications Conference (GLOBECOM)*, 1–7. 10.1109/GLOBECOM46510.2021.9685644

Shreyas Madhav, A. V., Ilavarasi, A. K., & Tyagi, A. K. (2022). (2022). The Heroes and Villains of the Mix Zone: The Preservation and Leaking of User's Privacy in Future Vehicles. *Arunachalam, V., Sivasankaran, K. (Eds) Microelectronic Devices, Circuits and Systems. ICMDCS 2022. Communications in Computer and Information Science*. https://doi.org/https://doi.org/10.1007/978-3-031-23973-1_12

Singh, S., Rathore, S., Alfarraj, O., Tolba, A., & Yoon, B. (2022). A framework for privacy-preservation of IoT healthcare data using Federated Learning and blockchain technology. *Future Generation Computer Systems*, *129*, 380–388. doi:10.1016/j.future.2021.11.028

Sun, L., Qian, J., & Chen, X. (2020). LDP-FL: Practical Private Aggregation in Federated Learning with Local Differential Privacy. *ArXiv. Abs*, *2007*, 15789.

Tyagi, Aswathy, & Aghila. (n.d.). *AARIN: Affordable, Accurate, Reliable and INnovative Mechanism to Protect a Medical Cyber-Physical System using Blockchain Technology*. Academic Press.

Tyagi, A. K., Nair, M. M., & Niladhuri, S. (2020). Security, Privacy Research issues in Various Computing Platforms: A Survey and the Road Ahead. Journal of Information Assurance & Security, 15(1), 1-16.

Van Dijk, M., Nguyen, N. V., Nguyen, T. N., Nguyen, L. M., & Nguyen, P. H. (2020). Asynchronous Federated Learning with Reduced Number of Rounds and with Differential Privacy from Less Aggregated Gaussian Noise. *ArXiv. Abs*, *2007*, 09208.

Warner, S. L. (1965). Randomized Response: A Survey Technique for Eliminating Evasive Answer Bias. *Journal of the American Statistical Association*, *60*(309), 63–69. doi:10.1080/01621459.1965.10480775 PMID:12261830

Wei, K., Li, J., Ding, M., Ma, C., Yang, H. H., Farokhi, F., Jin, S., Quek, T. Q. S., & Poor, H. V. (2020). Federated Learning With Differential Privacy: Algorithms and Performance Analysis. *IEEE Transactions on Information Forensics and Security*, *15*, 3454–3469. doi:10.1109/TIFS.2020.2988575

Wu, X., Zhang, Y., Shi, M., Li, P., Li, R., & Xiong, N. N. (2022). An adaptive federated learning scheme with differential privacy preserving. *Future Generation Computer Systems*, *127*, 362–372. doi:10.1016/j.future.2021.09.015

Yang, M., Cheng, H., Chen, F., Liu, X., Wang, M., & Li, X. (2023). Model poisoning attack in differential privacy-based federated learning. *Information Sciences*, *630*, 158–172. doi:10.1016/j.ins.2023.02.025

Zhang, H., Li, G., Zhang, Y., & Gai, K. (n.d.). Blockchain-based privacy-preserving medical data sharing scheme using federated learning. *Knowledge Science, Engineering and Management: 14th International Conference, KSEM 2021, Tokyo, Japan, Proceedings, Springer International Publishing,* 634–646.

Chapter 9
Enhanced Throttled Load Balancing Algorithm for Optimizing Cloud Computing Efficiency

Sudhir Kumar Mohapatra
https://orcid.org/0000-0003-3065-3881
Sri Sri University, India

Tarikwa Tesfa
Addis Ababa Science and Technology University, Ethiopia

Srinivas Prasad
GITAM University, India

Natnael Tilahun Tilahun
Addis Ababa Science and Technology University, Ethiopia

ABSTRACT

Facilitated by high-speed internet connectivity, the adoption of cloud computing has surged dramatically due to its distinctive attributes such as pay-as-you-go billing, ubiquitous accessibility, and minimal support requirements in the realm of service and resource delivery. While cloud computing draws inspiration from distributed, parallel, and grid computing paradigms, it also inherits their associated complexities and concerns. Among these challenges, optimizing performance stands out prominently. Enhancing performance can be achieved through the development of efficient load balancing algorithms. Efficient algorithms satisfy users and make optimal uses of resources of the cloud and hence improve performance. Several load balancing algorithms were designed to respond to performance problems. In this chapter, three well-established load balancing algorithms, namely round robin, equally spread current execution, and throttled, underwent a comprehensive analysis. This examination sought to unveil both the strengths and weaknesses inherent to these algorithms.

DOI: 10.4018/979-8-3693-0593-5.ch009

INTRODUCTION

Cloud computing is akin to the electricity grid, with computing resources connected centrally rather than each entity generating their own (Kashyap & Viradiya, 2014). This arrangement offers advantages in terms of cost-efficiency and time savings. Modern cloud computing shares similarities with traditional mainframe computing but distinguishes itself through its remarkable advancements in speed, storage capacity, memory capabilities, and cost-effectiveness. Despite these advantages, direct access to cloud resources introduces security concerns, representing a primary challenge in cloud computing (Kashyap & Viradiya, 2014). Furthermore, performance optimization and load balancing pose additional hurdles in ensuring equitable distribution of millions of user requests to data centers while maximizing resource utilization and user satisfaction (Qi & Boutaba, 2010). Researchers are actively addressing these issues by devising frameworks and strategies, with particular emphasis on mitigating vulnerabilities that may expose vulnerabilities to potential attackers. The cloud continues to experience sustained growth within the business community, primarily due to its ability to offer cost-effective solutions to customers. This expansion prompts cloud service providers to reevaluate their resource management strategies. Efficient resource management is crucial in accommodating the increasing number of customer requests without the necessity of expanding physical infrastructure. Additionally, there arises a need for equitable distribution of customer requests across available resources to ensure optimal utilization. In the realm of Cloud computing, providers are dedicated to enhancing overall performance. Various strategies are employed to achieve this goal, and among them, load balancing stands out as a pivotal technique. Load balancing has garnered significant attention in recent years within the Cloud computing landscape (Reddy & Reddy, 2014). Its importance cannot be overstated, as it brings a multitude of benefits, including improved revenue, heightened user satisfaction, enhanced performance characterized by reduced response times, increased acceptance rates, and more efficient resource utilization. But to obtain all these services providers should use efficient virtual machine (VM) load balancing policy.

In the contemporary cloud computing environment, a diverse range of VM load balancing policies has gained prominence. Among these, the Throttled load balancing algorithm, Equally Spread Current Execution, and Round-robin are widely recognized. These algorithms play a crucial role in optimizing resource allocation and ensuring efficient performance within cloud-based systems.

Operating in a circular fashion, the Round-Robin load balancing algorithm distributes tasks evenly among virtual machines. When a request enters the data center, it randomly selects the first available virtual machine to handle the assignment. Subsequent requests are then allocated to virtual machines in a cyclical manner. Notably, this algorithm efficiently utilizes available resources without considering the current status of the virtual machines, such as whether they are busy, available, or their current load. Consequently, this approach evenly distributes requests across all virtual machines but may result in longer wait times for most requests before execution, in addition to their actual execution time. This leads to a higher overall response time for requests, making the Round-Robin algorithm susceptible to having a maximum response time (T. S. S. K. S. M. & Ramasubbareddy, 2019).

The Equally Spread Current Execution (ESCE) load balancing algorithm utilizes an index table to store information about virtual machines, including their current workload. When a request enters the data center, the data center controller (DCC) instructs the load balancer to identify the most appropriate VM for task assignment. The load balancer then systematically scans the index table, starting from the beginning and proceeding sequentially to the end, in search of the VM with the lowest current workload. Subsequently, the load balancer communicates the identifier of the selected VM back to the DCC, which proceeds to assign the request to that specific VM. After the assignment, the DCC acknowledges the allocation to the load balancer, which increments the current workload of the chosen VM by 1. Once the request processing is complete, the VM sends the response back to the DCC. The DCC, in turn, signals the load balancer with an acknowledgment of de-allocation, leading the load balancer to reduce the current workload of that VM by 1. However, it's worth noting that a drawback of this algorithm lies in its scanning process, which occurs each time a request arrives. As a consequence, the waiting time for requests can be relatively high due to the sequential scanning process, which may impact overall system efficiency (T. S. S. K. S. M. & Ramasubbareddy, 2019). In addition, one VM may be allocated continuously if it is least loaded (Zhang et al., 2010). This will degrade performance of the Cloud.

The Throttled load balancing algorithm relies on an index table managed by the load balancer to monitor VM details and their status, which can be categorized as either "BUSY" or "AVAILABLE." When a request enters the data center, the Data Center Controller (DCC) prompts the load balancer to identify the most suitable VM for task assignment. The load balancer subsequently scans the index table to locate the first available VM. Once an available VM is identified, it returns the VM's identifier (ID) to the DCC, enabling the DCC to assign the request to the designated VM. Following the assignment, the DCC acknowledges the allocation to the load balancer, which then updates the status of the VM to "BUSY." Upon completion of the request processing, the VM transmits the response back to the DCC. In response, the DCC sends an acknowledgment of de-allocation to the load balancer, which proceeds to update the status of the VM identified by the ID to "AVAILABLE." This approach effectively manages VM allocation and ensures that each VM is assigned tasks only when it is available, which can contribute to efficient resource utilization within the cloud computing environment. In this algorithm also performance of the Cloud is not efficient as required as the index table is scanned repeatedly for every request. So, there is a huge gap between efficient use of resources and efficiency of algorithm for effective load balancing (Al-Rayis & Kurdi, 2013).

While the existing load balancing algorithms in the realm of cloud computing effectively tackle certain challenges, they still exhibit limitations that warrant improvement, particularly in terms of achieving better response times and optimizing resource utilization. In a comprehensive analysis conducted by Govinda et al., as documented in (R, 2015), Round Robin, ESCE, and Throttled load balancing algorithms were scrutinized with a specific focus on response time. Their research findings highlighted the Throttled load balancing algorithm's superior performance when compared to the other two alternatives. Drawing inspiration from this study, this thesis endeavors to address the challenges associated with response time and resource utilization inherent in the Throttled load balancing algorithm framework within the context of Cloud computing. The primary objective of this thesis is to contribute to the development of an optimized load balancing algorithm and facilitate a comparative analysis between the modified algorithm and the original Throttled algorithm. Through this research effort, the overarching goal is to enhance the overall performance of Cloud computing, ultimately enabling cloud service providers to more effectively cater to the needs of their users. Through improved response times and resource utilization, service users will gain swifter access to their requested services, resulting in an enhanced overall experience within the Cloud computing environment.

Cloud Computing, as elucidated in (Jadeja & Modi, 2012), represents a continually evolving, large-scale model designed to deliver on-demand IT resources encompassing computing power, storage, networks, platforms, and applications as a service accessible via the Internet. This paradigm shift has been made possible through the advancement of virtualization, widespread high-speed Internet access, and crucial support from leading IT software providers. The concept of "computing as a utility" has materialized, establishing Cloud Computing as one of the most rapidly expanding disciplines within the IT industry (O. B, 2013). The burgeoning appeal of Cloud Cloud computing derives its strength from its core attributes, encompassing flexibility, efficiency, and the capacity to empower users through on-demand resource provisioning and ubiquitous access, all within a pay-as-you-go framework. By externalizing hardware and software management to a scalable environment, cloud computing liberates users from the complexities of installation and upkeep, promoting both high availability and cost-efficiency.

To harness the full potential of this technology, it is imperative for cloud stakeholders to grasp the key characteristics of Cloud services, recognize their advantages, and acknowledge their limitations. This foundational understanding equips them to make informed decisions and derive maximum benefits from the Cloud Computing ecosystem.

Cloud computing architecture consists of two primary layers: the front-end and the back-end. The front-end, which users directly interact with, serves as the interface through which individuals engage with the cloud environment. An example of this is when users access their Facebook accounts, employing front-end software such as web browsers to communicate with the cloud (Outsideinmarketing, 2012).

Conversely, the back-end of cloud computing encompasses the hardware and software infrastructure tasked with handling incoming requests and facilitating the delivery of cloud services. This intricate system coordinates tasks crucial for maintaining the cloud's functionality. To enable connectivity, cloud computing relies on a network layer that links users' devices, like computers and smartphones, to centralized resources located within data centers. Users can access these data centers through the Internet or corporate networks, granting them the flexibility to interact with cloud resources from anywhere, supporting the accessibility needs of mobile workers and reinforcing the convenience and versatility of cloud computing.

Figure 1. Cloud computing system model (Outsideinmarketing, 2012)

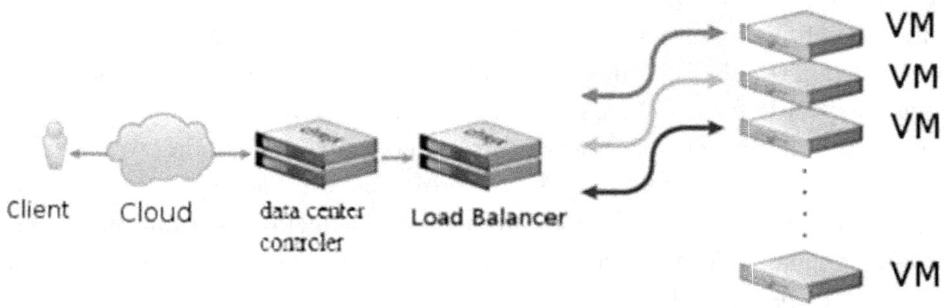

Applications hosted on the cloud harness the inherent flexibility of available computing power. Through the configuration of computers to function harmoniously, these applications seamlessly operate as if they were running on a singular, dedicated machine. This adaptability stands as a key benefit of cloud computing, allowing users to promptly harness cloud resources when required, without the need for advance allocation of specific hardware resources. This dynamic allocation empowers users to scale their computing resources up or down based on demand, offering a high degree of adaptability and cost-efficiency (Outsideinmarketing, 2012).

Numerous technologies underpin the concept of cloud computing, with virtualization playing a pivotal role. Virtualization, along with technologies like distributed file systems, abstracts and isolates resources and services from the underlying physical infrastructure (Tiwari & Katare, 2014). It is regarded as a cornerstone of cloud computing, facilitating the creation of multiple virtual environments on a single physical server, each capable of running distinct operating systems and applications simultaneously (Padhy, 2011; Srikanth et al., 2014). The abstraction of physical attributes from users and the underlying hardware fosters the portability of higher-level functions and efficient sharing and consolidation of physical resources. Essentially, virtualization serves as a bridge connecting the virtual realm of cloud computing with the underlying physical infrastructure, facilitating dynamic resource allocation to users and the simultaneous execution of multiple operating systems and applications (Agarwal, 2014; Chandra & Bahuguna, 2017; Taylor, 2015).

In cloud computing, memory and space are virtually allocated to users within servers, typically requiring a host platform that runs a hypervisor. Hypervisors play a pivotal role as essential software tools responsible for the creation of virtual machines (VMs) and the facilitation of hardware resource virtualization, encompassing CPU, storage, and networking devices. This architectural approach enables multiple VMs to operate on a single physical machine simultaneously, efficiently utilizing available resources within a cloud computing environment (Berwal & Kant, 2015).

Figure 2. Virtualization architecture (Panghal & S. R., 2015)

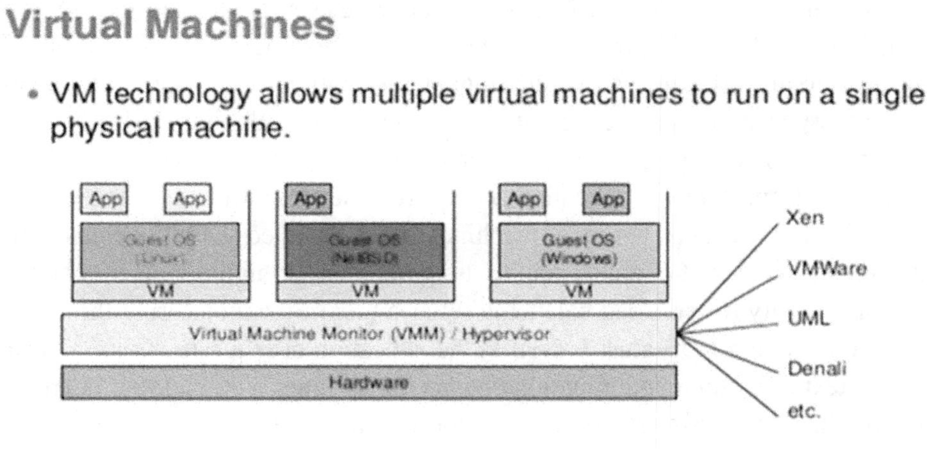

Load balancing stands as a pivotal concern within the domain of cloud computing, functioning as a mechanism designed to equitably distribute workloads across all nodes within the cloud infrastructure. This balancing act is essential to avoid situations where some nodes are overwhelmed while others remain underutilized, especially given the escalating web traffic and the proliferation of data-generating web applications. Load balancing extends its reach to aspects like CPU load, memory capacity, and network resources. In the event of a host system failure, load balancing becomes paramount to prevent the isolation of web resources in the digital landscape. Effective load balancing systems should ensure both availability and scalability, facilitating uninterrupted access to web resources while efficiently handling the ever-increasing workload demands (Jadeja & Modi, 2012).

Figure 3. Cloud computing load balancing (Bala et al., 2014)

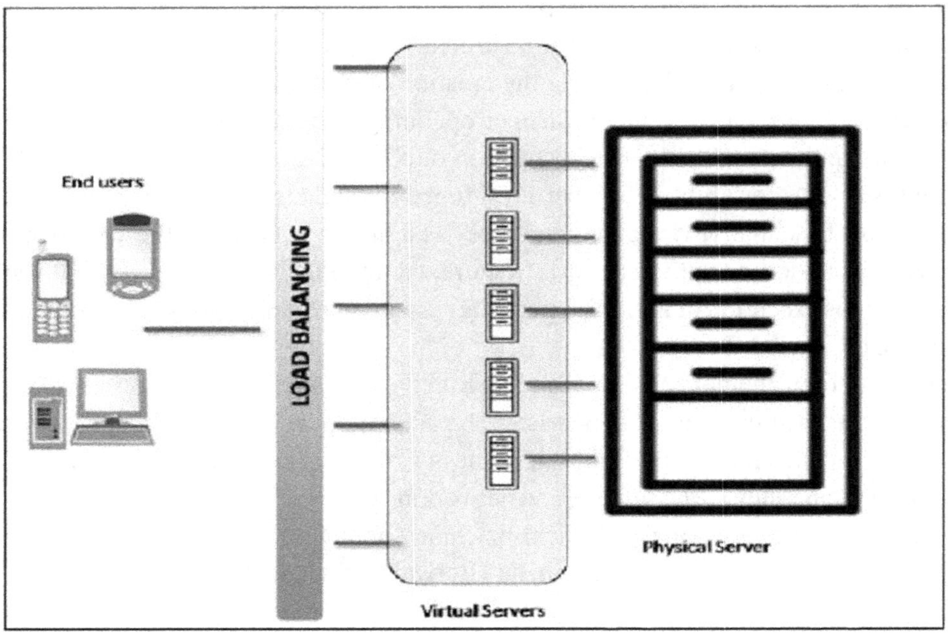

Load balancing serves as a crucial mechanism in enhancing user satisfaction and optimizing resource utilization, ultimately leading to improved overall system performance. This process involves the equitable distribution of total workloads across individual nodes within a collective system, with the aim of achieving optimal response times and efficient resource utilization (Shobha, 2018).

Load balancing serves a dual purpose: firstly, it efficiently assigns a high volume of incoming requests or data traffic to multiple machines for execution, thereby reducing user wait times for responses. Secondly, it redistributes the load from heavily burdened machines to less occupied ones, thus enhancing the resource utilization of each data center. It operates akin to assigning tasks to individuals to maintain a dynamic equilibrium, akin to a duty roster. Load balancing relies on real-time monitoring through various tools to assess CPU, memory, and I/O status, as well as the allocation of requested tasks (Bikramjit, 2017).

Within the context of cloud computing, load balancing assumes a crucial role in enhancing performance by directing incoming requests to the most appropriate virtual machines. This assignment technique is instrumental in achieving minimal response times, efficient processing, and cost minimization. Load balancing algorithms primarily aim to optimize the utilization of system resources, consequently boosting system throughput and diminishing the average response time for requests. The attainment of a balanced load distribution among virtual machines ensures that no single machine remains idle or experiences underutilization while others bear heavy loads.

Effective allocation of incoming requests is a critical challenge in cloud computing, one that demands both efficiency and effective resource utilization (Bikramjit, 2017).

Challenges of Load Balancing

Notwithstanding their benefits, load balancing algorithms in cloud computing introduce several noteworthy challenges that require resolution before fully realizing the potential of this technology. These challenges encompass performance issues, quality of service concerns, security considerations, legal and compliance issues, interoperability challenges, and data management complexities. While existing load balancing techniques mitigate some of these challenges, there remains a need for continuous improvement to ensure proper and effective resource utilization. Implementing load balancing systems can introduce overhead due to task movement and execution, which necessitates optimization for effective load balancing techniques. Evaluating the efficacy of load balancing methods can be accomplished using various metrics to determine whether they successfully distribute workloads evenly and efficiently (Mahalle et al., 2013; Sidhu & Kinger, 2013).

Related Works

The Throttled load balancing algorithm, proposed by author Mahalle, operates by maintaining an index table that stores essential information such as VM identifiers and their current state (either "Available" or "Busy"). When a request reaches the data center, the data center controller communicates with the load balancer to determine the most suitable virtual machine for the task. The load balancer performs a sequential scan of the index table, commencing from the beginning and continuing until it identifies the first available VM. Once an available VM is located, its identifier is returned to the data center controller, which then assigns the request to that specific VM and acknowledges the load balancer for the successful allocation. Following this, the load balancer updates the state of the selected VM in the index table. However, a notable limitation of this algorithm is that it does not take into account the current load on the VM when allocating a request, potentially resulting in increased response times for tasks. Furthermore, the algorithm's repetitive scanning of the index table for every incoming request may introduce inefficiencies in terms of computational overhead and response time (Bagwaiya & Raghuwanshi, n.d.).

The authors Shridhar et al. introduce the Modified Throttled algorithm as an alteration of the traditional Throttled algorithm, specifically tailored for load balancing purposes. This algorithm relies on an index table that stores pertinent information about virtual machines (VMs) and their operational states, categorized as either "Available" or "Busy." Upon the arrival of a request, the data center controller calls upon the Modified Throttled load balancer to identify the most suitable VM for the task. The load balancer initially selects a VM at the first index, taking into account its state, and if the VM is available, its identifier is returned to the data center controller. Subsequently, the data center controller proceeds to assign the request, acknowledges the load balancer, and updates the VM's state in the index table. However, when no available VM is found, the load balancer returns -1. For subsequent requests, the load balancer selects the VM adjacent to the previously assigned one, considering its state, and follows the same process (Tiwari & Katare, 2014). A limitation of this algorithm is that starting the search from the next index to the already assigned VM may not always be optimal, as VM states can change due to allocation and de-allocation processes.

The author Yodit introduces a hybrid load balancing algorithm which is called the Randomized Weighted Throttled Load Balancing Algorithm (RWTLBA), that combines elements of the Random and Throttled algorithms and incorporates a weighting concept to enhance response time and resource utilization parameters. RWTLBA operates by maintaining an index table containing VM status information (either "Busy" or "Available"). The algorithm selects two virtual machines from this index table, then identifies the one with the highest weight and checks its availability. If the chosen VM is available, the request is allocated to it; otherwise, the incoming request is directed to the next VM in line. In situations where both VMs are engaged, the algorithm proceeds to randomly select two additional VMs and repeats the process (Hussien et al., 2015). However, a notable drawback of RWTLBA is its method of selecting random VMs, which may occasionally result in the same VMs being chosen in consecutive rounds. This can lead to reduced resource utilization and prolonged response times.

Manan et al. introduce a modified version of the traditional Throttled load balancing algorithm, which they break down into three distinct phases. In the initial phase, the algorithm computes the expected response time for each virtual machine. The second phase entails identifying the most optimal VM to handle the incoming request, and the final step involves returning the identifier of the selected VM. When a request arrives at the data center, the data center controller engages the modified load balancer to search for a suitable VM. The load balancer initiates the process by determining the expected response time for each VM through the use of a resource information program. Subsequently, it selects the most efficient VM, taking into account both the load and response time criteria, and then returns the VM's identifier to the data center controller. The data center controller proceeds with request allocation and notifies the load balancer of the allocation (Ghosh & Banerjee, 2016). However, it's important to note that this algorithm introduces additional overhead due to the utilization of the resource information program for identifying the efficient VM.

Bagwaiyal et al. introduce a hybrid load balancing algorithm that amalgamates aspects of both the Equally Spread Current Execution and Throttled load balancing algorithms. This algorithm manages two separate index tables: the first table maintains VM allocation states (either busy or available), while the second table monitors the current count of allocated requests. Upon the arrival of a request at the data center, the data center controller calls upon the hybrid load balancer to determine a suitable VM for allocation. The load balancer initiates the process by comparing the size of the VM state list with a Hashmap. If the size of the VM state list surpasses the size of the Hashmap, signifying the presence of available VMs, the load balancer proceeds with request allocation based on VM availability (VibhoreTyagi & Kumar, 2015). It's important to note, however, that this algorithm introduces additional overhead due to the need to compare index table sizes for each incoming request.

Hussein et al. present the weighted Throttled virtual machine load balancing algorithm, a alteration of the traditional Throttled load balancing algorithm that incorporates the concept of weight. In this algorithm, VMs are endowed with varying amounts of available processing power from the server or physical host, which is allocated to individual application services. The central principle of this algorithm is to direct requests to the most powerful VM available, thus avoiding queuing. Instead of queuing, requests are assigned to a busy VM with a higher weight compared to others, giving priority to computational power (T. W. P. & Ramadhan, 2018). However, it's important to note that this algorithm introduces additional overhead in terms of assigning and managing weights for each virtual machine.

Ghosh et al. introduced an algorithm that modifies traditional Throttled load balancing by incorporating a priority-based approach. When a request arrives, the Dynamic Capacity Controller (DCC) employs the priority-based modified Throttled algorithm to determine an appropriate VM for request allocation. If a virtual machine is available, the request is promptly allocated to it. However, in cases where all VMs are currently occupied, the load balancer evaluates the executing VMs to pinpoint the one with the lowest priority. It then proceeds to temporarily halt its execution, redirecting the request to the Switching Queue for future processing. This queue temporarily stores requests displaced by higher-priority arrivals. While this prioritization scheme benefits high-priority requests, it may lead to lower-priority jobs experiencing extended waiting times, potentially resulting in starvation. To address this issue, the algorithm elevates the priority of waiting requests, and when a VM becomes available, it selects the request with the highest priority from both new and waiting requests for VM allocation (Bedi & Singh, 2014). Nonetheless, a drawback of this approach is that requests with the lowest priority may endure prolonged waiting periods, and some VMs might be excessively utilized.

Tyagi et al. conducted an experimental evaluation to gauge the performance of the Throttled load balancing algorithm in contrast to Round Robin and ESCE. Their assessment focused on critical metrics, including overall response time, data center processing time, and the total cost encompassing VM and data transfer expenses. The findings highlighted the Throttled load balancing policy's superiority, especially when combined with the Optimized Response Time service broker policy and specific parameter optimizations. This configuration yielded enhanced overall response times, minimized data center processing times, and cost-effective processing, surpassing the performance of alternative load balancing algorithms (Internet World Stats, n.d.).

In an independent investigation, Govinda et al. conducted a thorough examination of load balancing algorithms, encompassing Round Robin, Throttled, and ESCE. Their analysis focused on response time and cost of utilization, with the intention of offering insights into the selection of the most suitable load balancing algorithm for various scenarios. Employing the CloudAnalyst simulator, their results consistently demonstrated that the Throttled load balancing algorithm surpassed Round Robin and Equally Spread Current Execution (ESCE) in terms of both performance and cost-related factors (R, 2015).

Ramadhan et al. conducted an experiment to evaluate the effectiveness and efficiency of existing load balancing algorithms in cloud computing, specifically Round Robin, ESCE, and Throttled. Their assessment encompassed key metrics such as overall response time, request servicing, data center loading, and detailed cost analysis related to virtual machines. The outcomes of their investigation consistently demonstrated the Throttled load balancing algorithm's superior performance compared to Round Robin and ESCE. Furthermore, the authors introduced an enhanced version of the Throttled load balancing algorithm tailored to meet the demands of cloud computing (Mulat et al., 2022). Furthermore, in the broader context of cloud resource management and security, researchers have explored machine learning-based approaches for task scheduling and resource allocation, as highlighted in reference (Bal et al., 2022). This innovative research avenue aims to enhance the efficiency and security of cloud computing systems by leveraging machine learning techniques to optimize resource allocation and task scheduling.

Proposed Algorithm

Cloud computing, at its core, relies heavily on the functionality of the load balancer within its infrastructure. Its primary function is to evenly distribute incoming user requests through various load balancing algorithms. However, the available algorithms vary in terms of efficiency and are not uniformly effective, each carrying its unique set of limitations. The core motivation behind this research stems from the imperative to tackle inefficiency, notably concerning response time and resource utilization. This is achieved through the introduction of an innovative and efficient load balancing algorithm. There exists a specific slot within the cloud architecture where this proposed algorithm can be seamlessly integrated, potentially revolutionizing the performance of cloud environments as illustrated in the following Figure 4.

Table 1. Comparison on various load balancing algorithms

Techniques	Advantages	Limitations
Modified Throttled Algorithm	Improved resource Utilization as compared with the Throttled algorithm.	This method does not take into consideration the priority of the work.
Randomized weighted Throttled algorithm	Avoid scanning of the index table again and again from its first index to find the available VM	Resource utilization and response time is not good since the same VM may be selected again and again
Throttled Algorithm	Assign the workload on the virtual machines for effective resource utilization	Response time is high because of scanning the index table again and again.
A Weighted Throttled Algorithm	Request is not queued	Involves additional overhead in assigning weight to each VM
Round Robin	Distribute workload uniformly to the available VMs	Some nodes might be heavily loaded and some are not. Since the running time of any process is not known in advance, there is a possibility that nodes may get heavily loaded.
ESCE	Preserve equal load to all virtual machines	High response time because of repeated scanning of index table

Figure 4. Position of proposed algorithm in the architecture of cloud computing

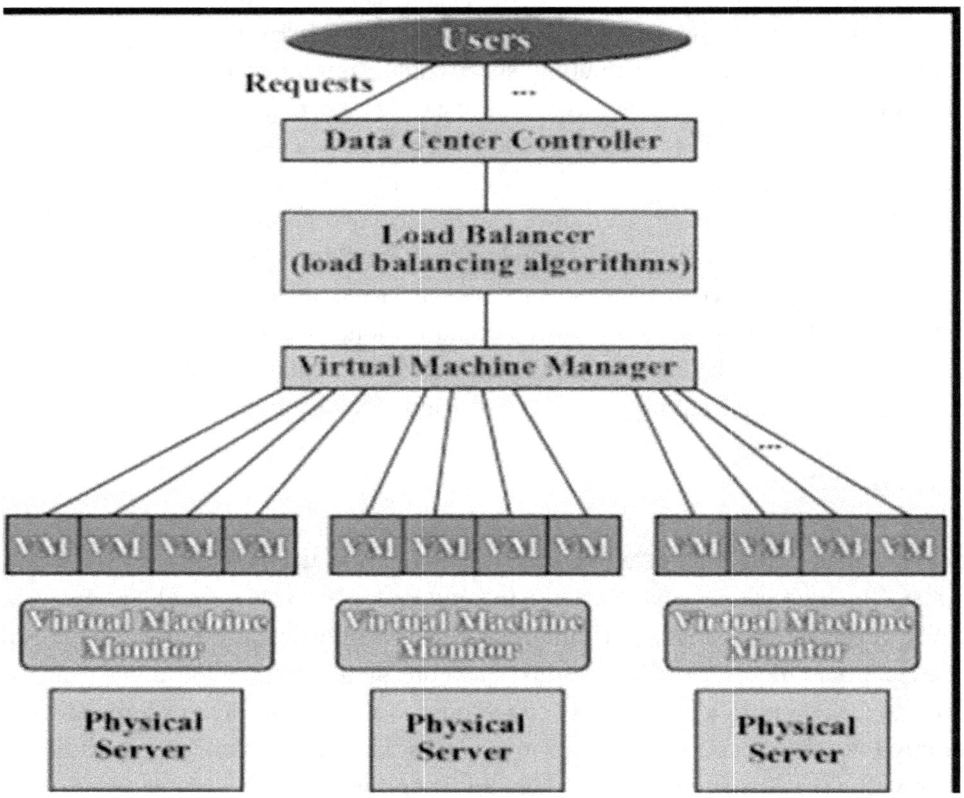

Improved Throttled Algorithm Description

At the heart of this research lies the introduction of a novel load balancing algorithm achieved through the refinement of the existing Throttled load balancing algorithm. While the traditional Throttled load balancing algorithm has showcased commendable performance in comparison to its counterparts, it harbors a significant limitation. This limitation pertains to the necessity for the load balancer to conduct repetitive scans of the index table for every incoming request directed to the data center. This repetitive scanning, unfortunately, leads to increased response times, as the response time calculation includes both the operational time and the duration required for index table scanning. Furthermore, an additional challenge emerges in the form of certain virtual machines (VMs) being frequently employed, particularly if they are marked as available and occupy positions near the beginning of the index table.

Within the framework of the proposed load balancing algorithm, a dual-queue system is employed. The initial queue, denoted as VmAvailableQueue, serves as the repository for virtual machine statuses, specifically those marked as AVAILABLE, paired with their respective IDs. The secondary queue, known as VmBusyQueue, is exclusively designated for housing the IDs of virtual machines that are currently in use or occupied, signifying a BUSY status.

Upon the arrival of a request at the data center, a series of orchestrated actions ensue. Initially, the data center controller takes charge by directing the request to the load balancer. The load balancer commences its evaluation by conducting a thorough examination of the VmAvailableQueue. Should an available virtual machine reside within this queue, the load balancer promptly retrieves and returns the corresponding ID to the data center controller. Subsequently, the data center controller seamlessly allocates the request to the designated virtual machine and swiftly dispatches an acknowledgment to the load balancer. In parallel, the load balancer efficiently performs a series of queue operations, specifically dequeuing (removing) the virtual machine identified by the given ID from VmAvailableQueue and subsequently enqueuing (inserting) it into VmBusyQueue, hereby marking it as "busy."

In the scenario where VmAvailableQueue does not harbor any available virtual machines, the load balancer adeptly responds by returning a designated code, -1, to the data center controller. Subsequently, the request seamlessly proceeds to be queued in a waiting queue. Notably, at this juncture, the proposed load balancing algorithm strategically leverages the pre-existing Throttled load balancing algorithm. This utilization allows the algorithm to efficiently store the request within the waiting queue, effectively handling the situation when all virtual machines are preoccupied or busy.

Upon the completion of their assigned tasks, the virtual machines dutifully return the results to the data center controller, which perceives these results as cloudlets. In response, the data center controller promptly issues an acknowledgment to the load balancer, expressing its appreciation for the successful deallocation of the virtual machine. Subsequently, the load balancer proceeds with precision, executing a sequence of queue operations. Specifically, it initiates by dequeuing (removing) the virtual machine identified by its unique ID from the VmBusyQueue. Following this, the load balancer efficiently enqueues (inserts) the aforementioned virtual machine back into the VmAvailableQueue, thereby reestablishing its status as "available" for future assignments.

The utilization of these two queues within the proposed algorithm serves as a pivotal strategy to accomplish two primary objectives. Initially, it significantly diminishes the waiting period for incoming requests by effectively curtailing the time required for scanning the index table. Consequently, this meticulous optimization leads to a noteworthy reduction in the system's response time. Subsequently, the algorithm ensures equitable distribution of tasks among the virtual machines by adhering to a round-robin allocation method. Each virtual machine is accorded the opportunity to process requests in a fair and balanced manner, thanks to the queue's adherence to a First Come First Serve (FIFO) protocol. This approach distinctly contributes to the overall enhancement of resource utilization within the system.

Figure 5. Flowchart of the proposed algorithm

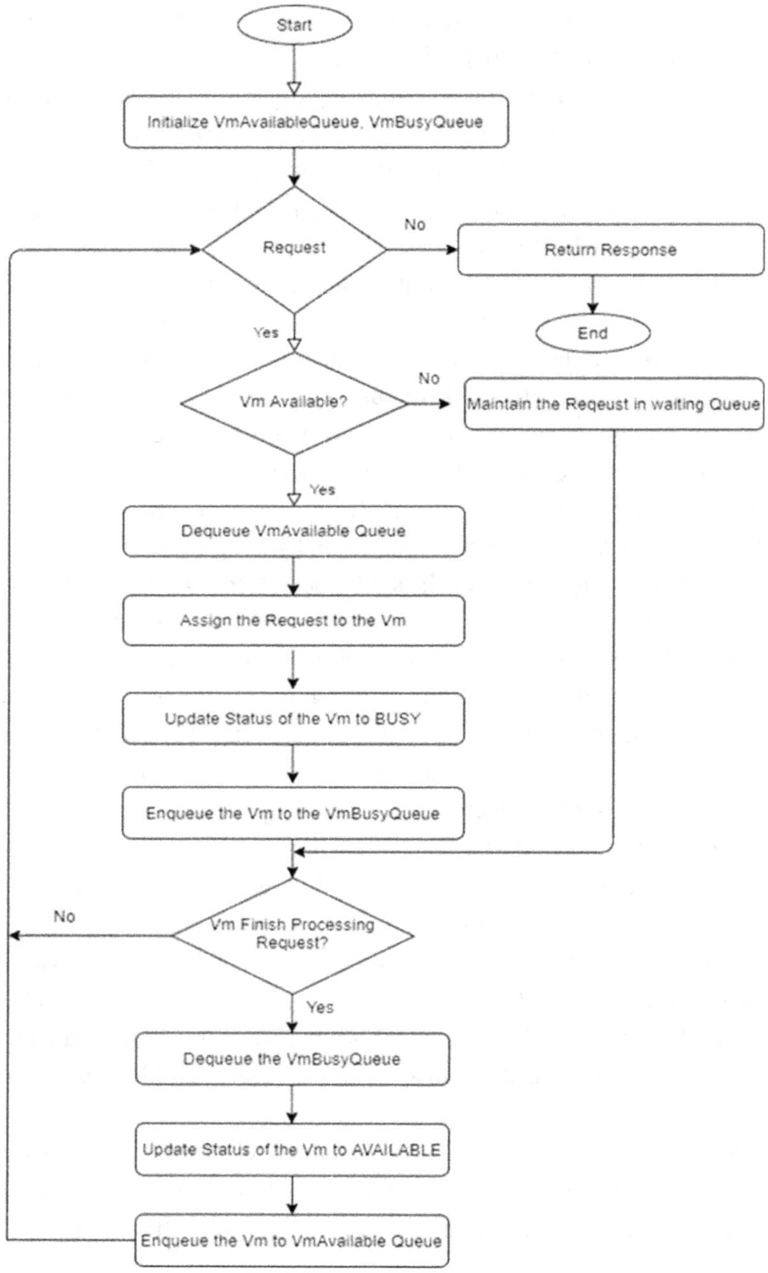

FLOWCHART OF THE PROPOSED ALGORITHM

Experimentations and Results

This section delves into a comprehensive series of experiments designed to evaluate and compare the performance of the innovative load balancing algorithm against three established counterparts: Round Robin, Equally Spread Current Execution, and the Throttled load balancing algorithms. The scrutiny of these algorithms is executed through a rigorous assessment encompassing essential evaluation metrics. These metrics encompass response time, data center processing time, and resource utilization, collectively serving as pivotal parameters for comparison. The achievement of results was arranged by subjecting the simulator to multiple iterations, each tailored to the specific scenario under consideration, thereby yielding a robust and well-rounded assessment.

Experiment 1

The primary objective of this experiment centers on an in-depth performance evaluation of the Improved Throttled load balancing algorithm. It specifically targets scenarios characterized by a relatively modest volume of requests originating from individual users.

Configuration of Experiment 1 Scenario 1

In this specific scenario, the experimental configuration revolves around a solitary data center configuration. This data center is furnished with a total of 10 virtual machines (VMs), and its operational scope extends to accommodating and managing a substantial influx of 300 requests originating from each distinct user base. It's worth noting that these individual requests are characterized by a data payload, with each request carrying a load of 300 bytes. The simulation protocol extends over an average timespan of 30 minutes. Within this well-defined context, a comprehensive performance assessment unfolds, placing a particular emphasis on scrutinizing and evaluating the response time and data center processing time exhibited by the four load balancing algorithms when confronted with the intricacies of processing relatively petite user requests. Configuration of the experiment is shown in Figure 6 and Figure 7, 7a, 7b.

Figure 6. User base configuration for Experiment 1 Scenario 1

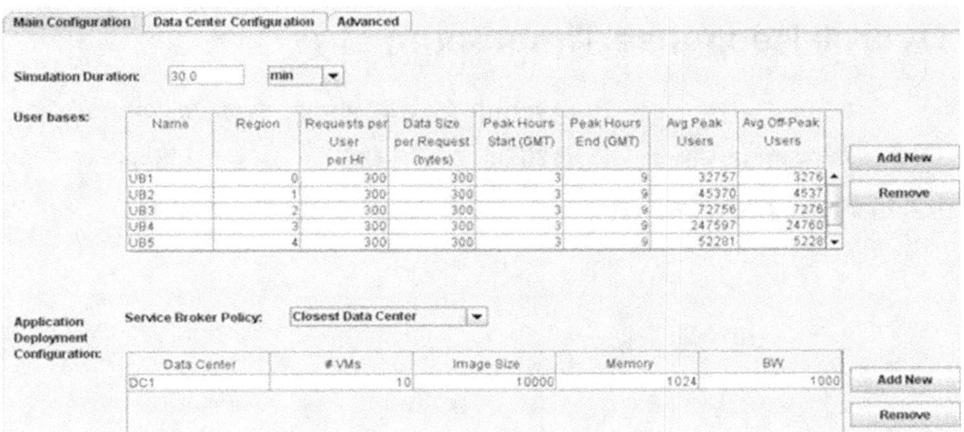

Figure 7. Data center configuration for Experiment 1 Scenario 1

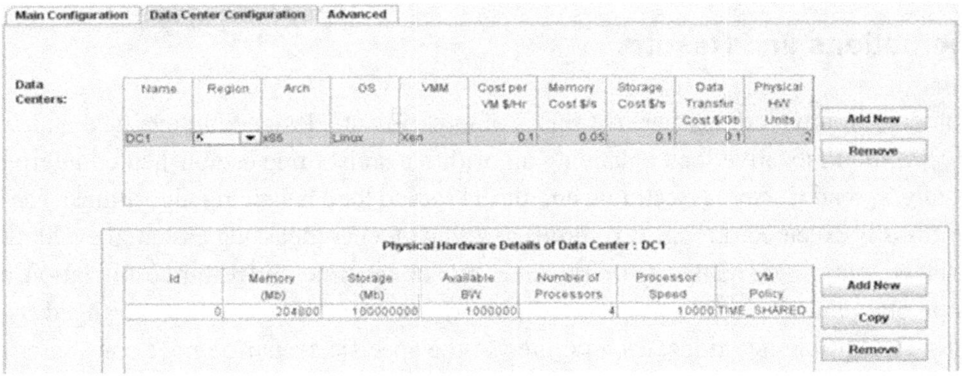

Result of Experiment 1 Scenario 1

In this experimental setup, a solitary data center boasting a complement of 10 virtual machines (VMs) takes center stage. The simulation is rigorously executed, encompassing iterative runs that span a gamut of load balancing algorithms, including Round Robin, ESCE, Throttled, and ITLBA. Subsequent to multiple iterations of the simulation process, a comprehensive summary of the overall response times emerges, offering valuable insights into the performance dynamics of these four distinct algorithms.

Figure 8. Round robin simulation result of Experiment 1 Scenario 1

Overall Response Time Summary

	Average (ms)	Minimum (ms)	Maximum (ms)
Overall Response Time:	786.44	42.82	1309.96
Data Center Processing Time:	3.08	0.04	11.24

Figure 9. ESCE simulation result of Experiment 1 Scenario 1

Overall Response Time Summary

	Average (ms)	Minimum (ms)	Maximum (ms)
Overall Response Time:	786.35	42.33	1304.65
Data Center Processing Time:	2.97	0.04	5.97

Figure 10. Throttled simulation result of Experiment 1 Scenario 1

Overall Response Time Summary

	Average (ms)	Minimum (ms)	Maximum (ms)
Overall Response Time:	786.33	42.32	1304.65
Data Center Processing Time:	2.96	0.04	5.01

Figure 11. ITLBA simulation result of Experiment 1 Scenario 1

Overall Response Time Summary

	Average (ms)	Minimum (ms)	Maximum (ms)
Overall Response Time:	786.20	38.10	1330.11
Data Center Processing Time:	2.96	0.03	4.77

Figure 12. Response time in Experiment 1 Scenario 1

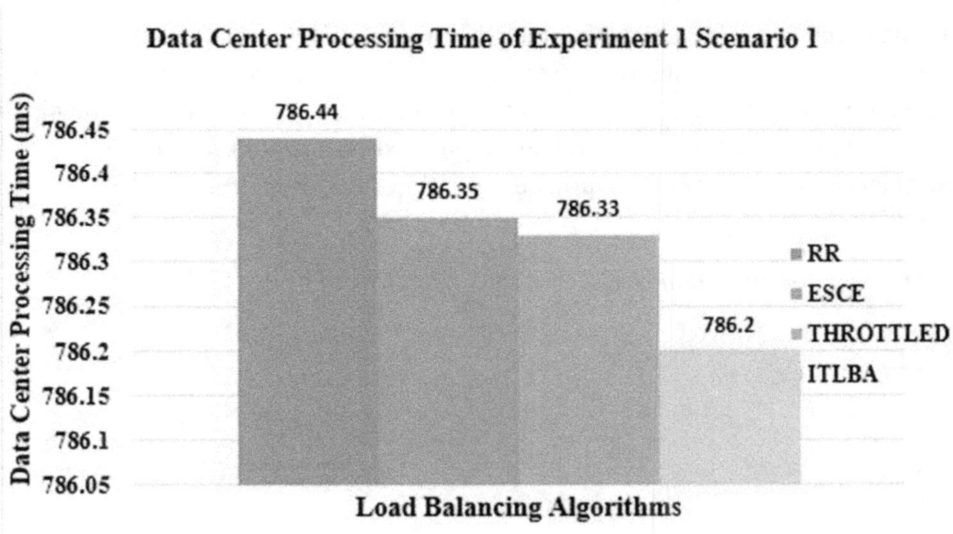

Experiment 2

This experiment delves into the performance evaluation of the Improved Throttled algorithm, mirroring the conditions of the initial experiment. Here, the focus is once again on scenarios characterized by a relatively limited volume of requests originating from individual users. However, in this case, the quantity of requests has been increased from the previous experiment for further evaluation.

Figure 13. Data center processing time in Experiment 1 Scenario 1

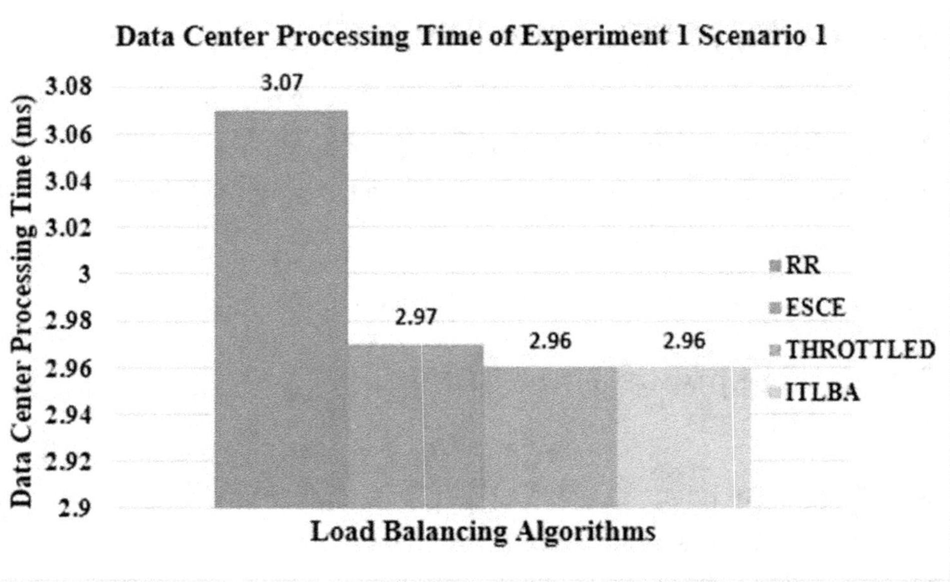

Configuration of Experiment 2 Scenario 1

In this experiment, the focus is on assessing the performance of the Improved Throttled algorithm under conditions similar to those in the first scenario of the first experiment. Nonetheless, in this specific iteration, the experiment introduces a significant augmentation by expanding both the number of VMs and data centers into the equation. This strategic augmentation aims to provide a more comprehensive and robust evaluation of the Improved Throttled algorithm's performance.

Figure 14. User base configuration of Experiment 2 Scenario 1

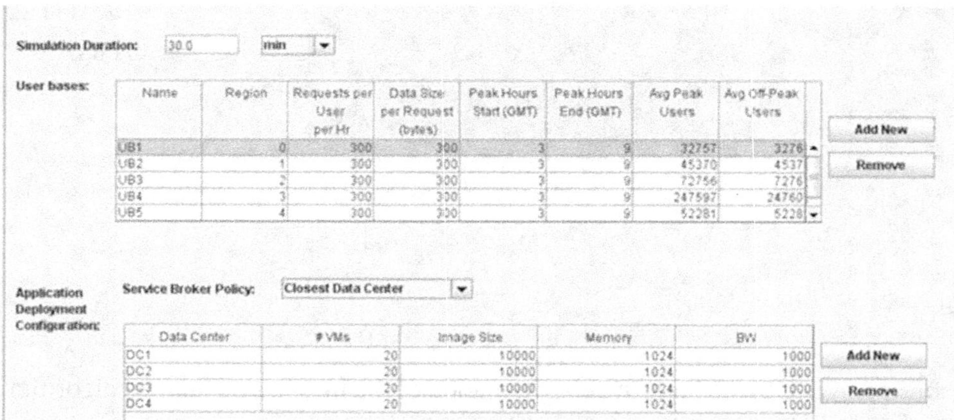

Name	Region	Requests per User per Hr	Data Size per Request (bytes)	Peak Hours Start (GMT)	Peak Hours End (GMT)	Avg Peak Users	Avg Off-Peak Users
UB1	0	300	300	3	9	32757	3276
UB2	1	300	300	3	9	45370	4537
UB3	2	300	300	3	9	72756	7276
UB4	3	300	300	3	9	247597	24760
UB5	4	300	300	3	9	52281	5228

Data Center	# VMs	Image Size	Memory	BW
DC1	20	10000	1024	1000
DC2	20	10000	1024	1000
DC3	20	10000	1024	1000
DC4	20	10000	1024	1000

In this scenario, four data centers are employed, with each data center equipped with 20 virtual machines VMs. The designated VMs in this setup shoulder the responsibility of overseeing 300 requests originating from each user base. Each of these individual requests carries a payload of 300 bytes of data. The simulation unfolds over a span of 30 minutes on average, providing ample time for an in-depth analysis of the load balancing algorithms' performance within the specified parameters.

Figure 15. Data center configuration of Experiment 2 Scenario 1

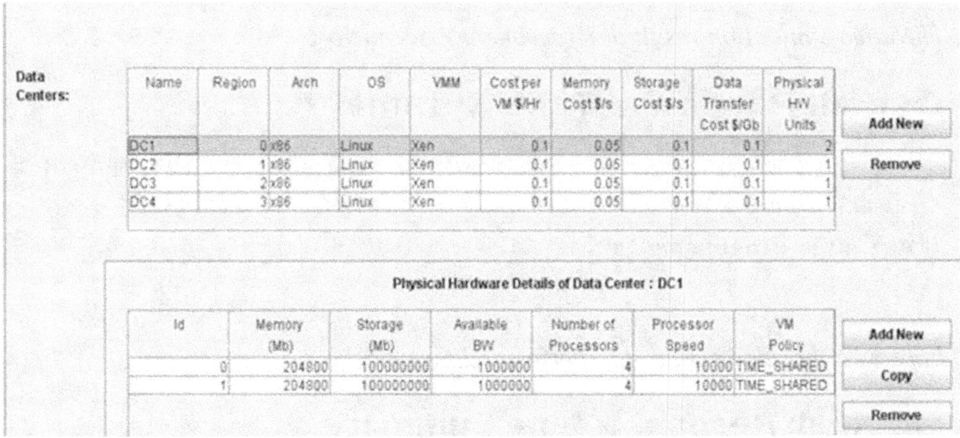

Data Centers:

Name	Region	Arch	OS	VMM	Cost per VM $/Hr	Memory Cost $/s	Storage Cost $/s	Data Transfer Cost $/Gb	Physical HW Units
DC1	0	x86	Linux	Xen	0.1	0.05	0.1	0.1	2
DC2	1	x86	Linux	Xen	0.1	0.05	0.1	0.1	1
DC3	2	x86	Linux	Xen	0.1	0.05	0.1	0.1	1
DC4	3	x86	Linux	Xen	0.1	0.05	0.1	0.1	1

Physical Hardware Details of Data Center : DC1

Id	Memory (Mb)	Storage (Mb)	Available BW	Number of Processors	Processor Speed	VM Policy
0	204800	100000000	1000000	4	10000	TIME_SHARED
1	204800	100000000	1000000	4	10000	TIME_SHARED

Result of Experiment 2 Scenario 1

This simulation scenario is based on the utilization of four data centers, each of which was equipped with 80 virtual machines, meticulously orchestrated to manage a collective influx of 300 requests originating from distinct user bases. The simulation was meticulously replicated across four load balancing algorithms: Round Robin, ESCE, Throttled, and the proposed Improved Throttled algorithm. The resounding outcome of the simulation unequivocally affirmed the superior performance of the proposed Improved Throttled algorithm over its counterparts within this specific scenario.

Figure 16. Round robin simulation result of Experiment 2 Scenario 1

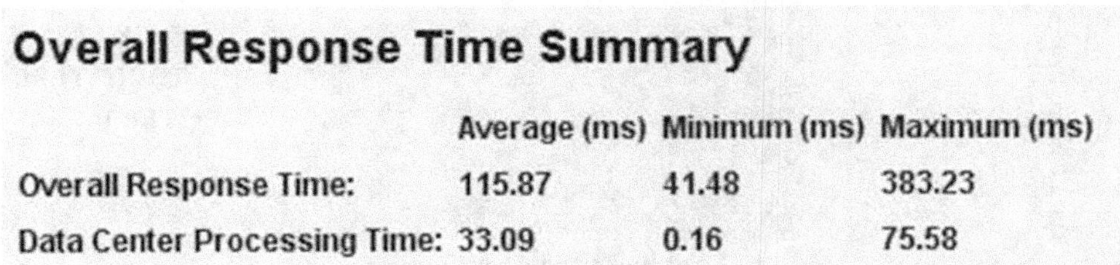

Overall Response Time Summary

	Average (ms)	Minimum (ms)	Maximum (ms)
Overall Response Time:	115.87	41.48	383.23
Data Center Processing Time:	33.09	0.16	75.58

Figure 17. ESCE simulation result of Experiment 2 Scenario 1

Overall Response Time Summary

	Average (ms)	Minimum (ms)	Maximum (ms)
Overall Response Time:	116.04	41.48	383.23
Data Center Processing Time:	33.25	0.16	80.07

Figure 18. Throttled simulation result of Experiment 2 Scenario 1

Overall Response Time Summary

	Average (ms)	Minimum (ms)	Maximum (ms)
Overall Response Time:	100.78	41.48	383.23
Data Center Processing Time:	18.42	0.16	66.08

Figure 19. Improved throttled result of Experiment 2 Scenario 1

Overall Response Time Summary

	Average (ms)	Minimum (ms)	Maximum (ms)
Overall Response Time:	100.56	42.08	401.66
Data Center Processing Time:	18.42	0.08	67.20

Figure 20. Chart of response time of Experiment 2 Scenario 1

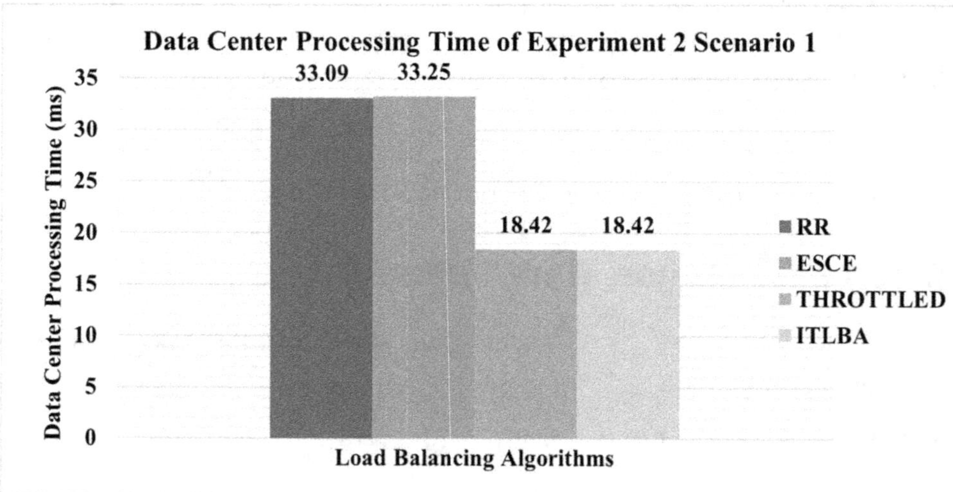

Figure 21. Chart of data center processing time of Experiment 2 Scenario 1

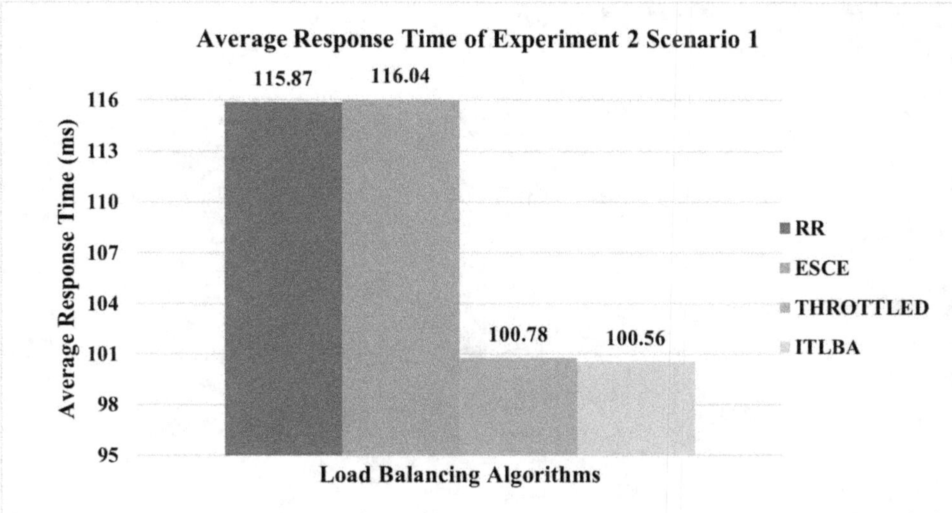

Experiment 3

This specific experiment observes the performance of Improved Throttled algorithm by maximizing the number of data centers, virtual machines, user requests and data size from each user bases on experiment 2 scenario 1. The remaining configuration were the same.

Configuration of Experiment 3 Scenario 1

To configure the CloudAnalyst simulation, six data centers are established, with each data center housing 20 virtual machines (VMs). These VMs take the responsibility of efficiently managing a substantial deluge of 1000 requests originating from diverse user bases. Each individual request handles a data payload weighing in at 1000 bytes, a factor critical to the evaluation of system performance. It's worth noting that these data centers are distributed across different regions. The simulation is conducted over an average duration of 40 minutes to comprehensively evaluate the performance of the system under these conditions.

Figure 22. User base configuration of Experiment 3 Scenario 1

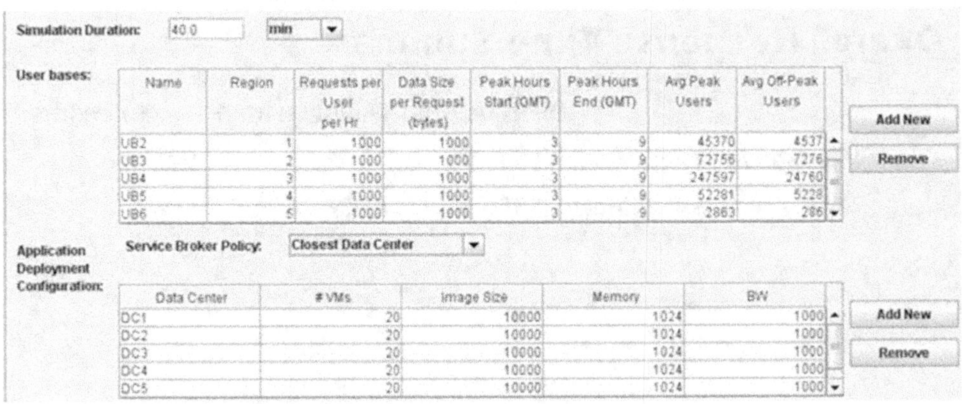

Simulation Duration: 40.0 min

User bases:

Name	Region	Requests per User per Hr	Data Size per Request (bytes)	Peak Hours Start (GMT)	Peak Hours End (GMT)	Avg Peak Users	Avg Off-Peak Users
UB2	1	1000	1000	3	9	45370	4537
UB3	2	1000	1000	3	9	72756	7276
UB4	3	1000	1000	3	9	247597	24760
UB5	4	1000	1000	3	9	52281	5228
UB6	5	1000	1000	3	9	2863	286

Add New
Remove

Application Deployment Configuration: Service Broker Policy: Closest Data Center

Data Center	# VMs	Image Size	Memory	BW
DC1	20	10000	1024	1000
DC2	20	10000	1024	1000
DC3	20	10000	1024	1000
DC4	20	10000	1024	1000
DC5	20	10000	1024	1000

Add New
Remove

Figure 23. Data center configuration of Experiment 3 Scenario 1

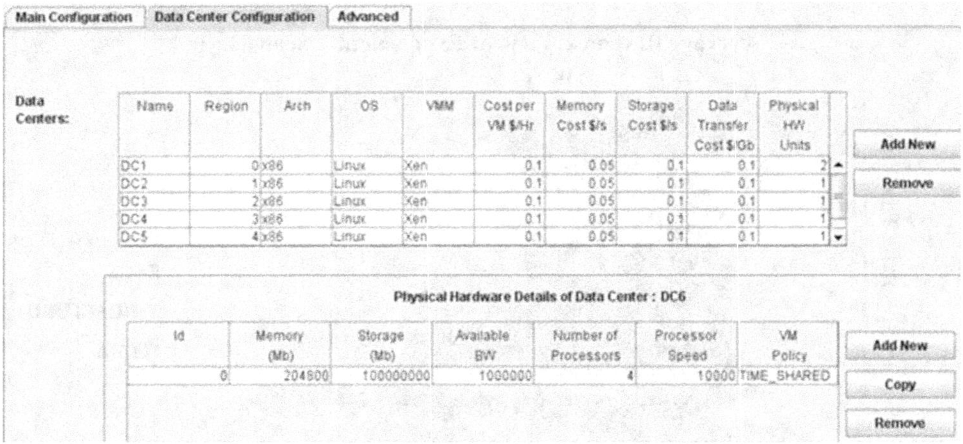

Result of Experiment 3 Scenario 1

In this simulation setup, six data centers are employed, each equipped with 120 virtual machines, to efficiently manage 1000 requests originating from various user bases. The experiment was replicated for the Round Robin, ESCE, Throttled, and Improved Throttled algorithms. The results of the simulation consistently demonstrated that the proposed Improved Throttled algorithm surpassed the other load balancing algorithms in this specific context.

Figure 24. Round robin simulation result of Experiment 3 Scenario 1

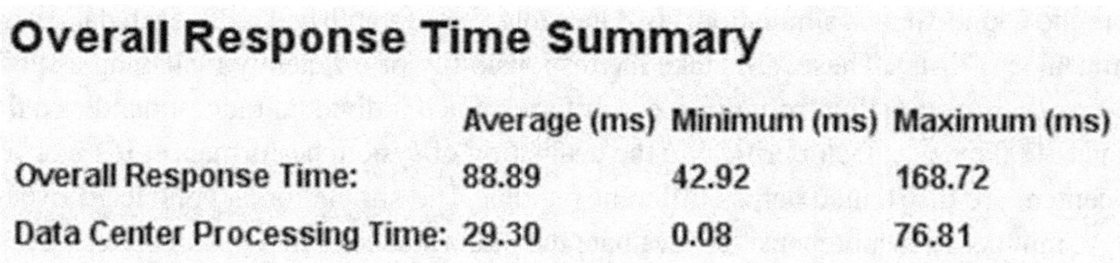

Figure 25. ESCE simulation result of Experiment 3 Scenario 1

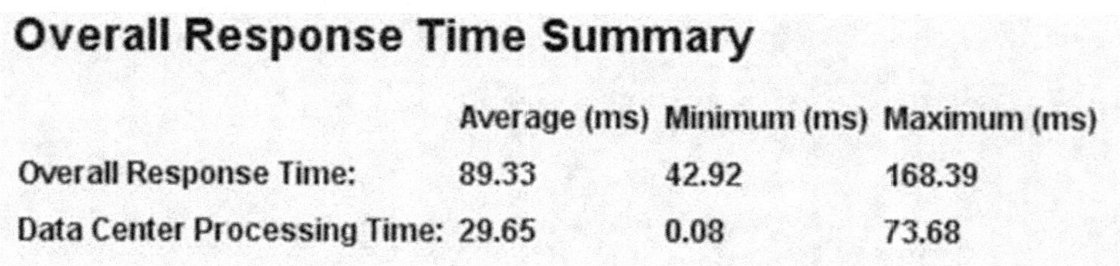

Figure 26. Throttled simulation result of Experiment 3 Scenario 1

Overall Response Time Summary

	Average (ms)	Minimum (ms)	Maximum (ms)
Overall Response Time:	76.67	42.92	144.14
Data Center Processing Time:	16.82	0.08	62.32

Figure 27. ITLBA simulation result of Experiment 3 Scenario 1

Overall Response Time Summary

	Average (ms)	Minimum (ms)	Maximum (ms)
Overall Response Time:	76.23	38.46	139.31
Data Center Processing Time:	16.82	0.06	61.55

Figure 28. Chart of response time of Experiment 3 Scenario 1

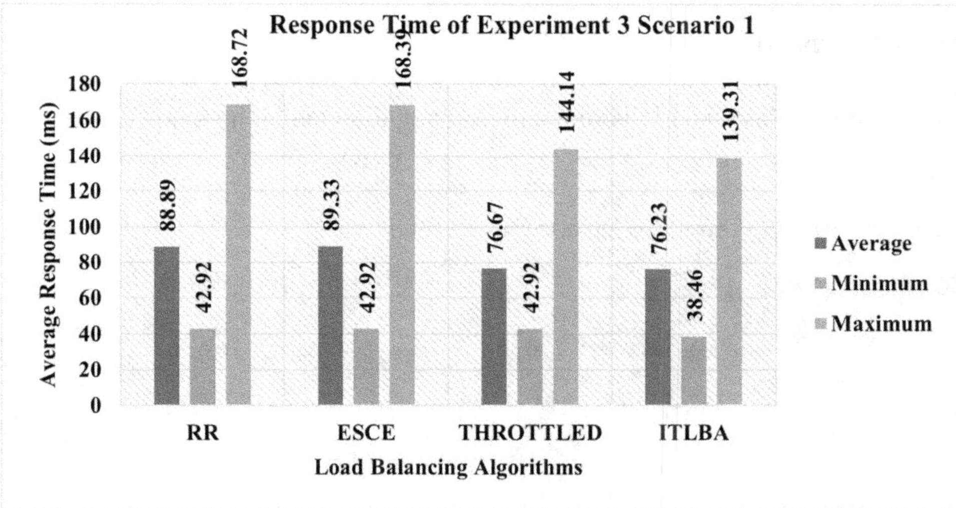

Experiment to measure the performance of Improved Throttled algorithm and the others in heterogeneous environment In this part of the experiment heterogeneous environment is used.

Configuration of Experiment

In this scenario, the CloudAnalyst simulator is configured with two data centers, each equipped with 20 virtual machines tasked with handling requests of varying sizes. These requests include differences in the number of requests per user and the data size per request, reflecting the dynamic nature of user demands from different regions. The simulation extends over an average duration of 40 minutes, facilitating a thorough assessment of how load balancing algorithms perform when faced with such diverse and variable conditions.

Figure 29. Chart of data processing time of Experiment 3 Scenario 1

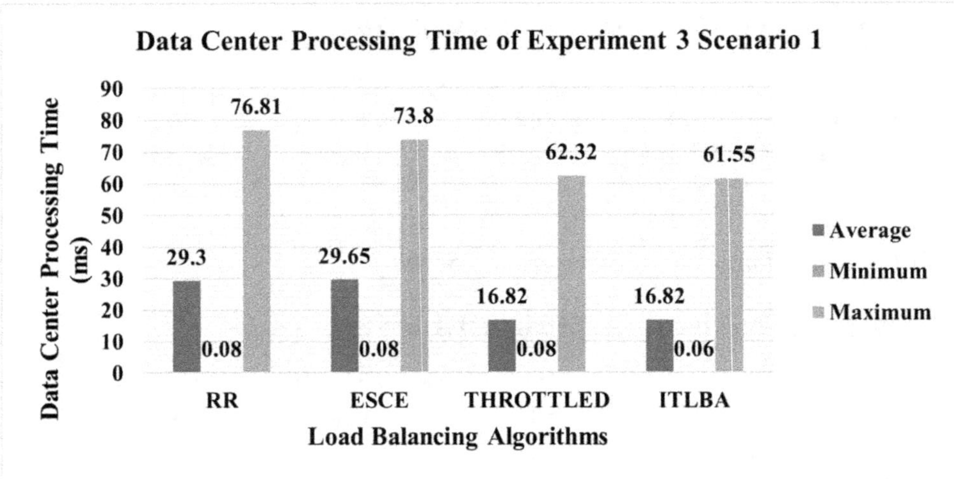

Figure 30 and Figure 31 shows user base and data center configuration of Experiment 1 Scenario 1.

Result of Experiment

The simulation result of this scenario is summarized and presented in the following way.

Figure 30. User base configuration of Experiment 1 Scenario 1

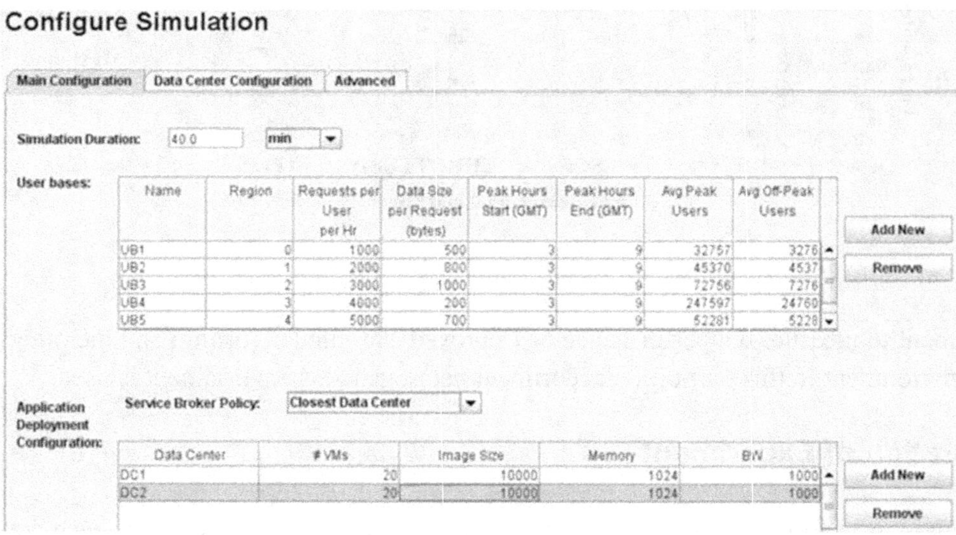

Configure Simulation

Main Configuration | Data Center Configuration | Advanced

Simulation Duration: 40.0 min

User bases:

Name	Region	Requests per User per Hr	Data Size per Request (bytes)	Peak Hours Start (GMT)	Peak Hours End (GMT)	Avg Peak Users	Avg Off-Peak Users
UB1	0	1000	500	3	9	32757	3276
UB2	1	2000	800	3	9	45370	4537
UB3	2	3000	1000	3	9	72756	7276
UB4	3	4000	200	3	9	247597	24760
UB5	4	5000	700	3	9	52281	5228

Add New
Remove

Application Deployment Configuration: Service Broker Policy: Closest Data Center

Data Center	# VMs	Image Size	Memory	BW
DC1	20	10000	1024	1000
DC2	20	10000	1024	1000

Add New
Remove

Figure 31. Data center configuration of Experiment 1 Scenario 1

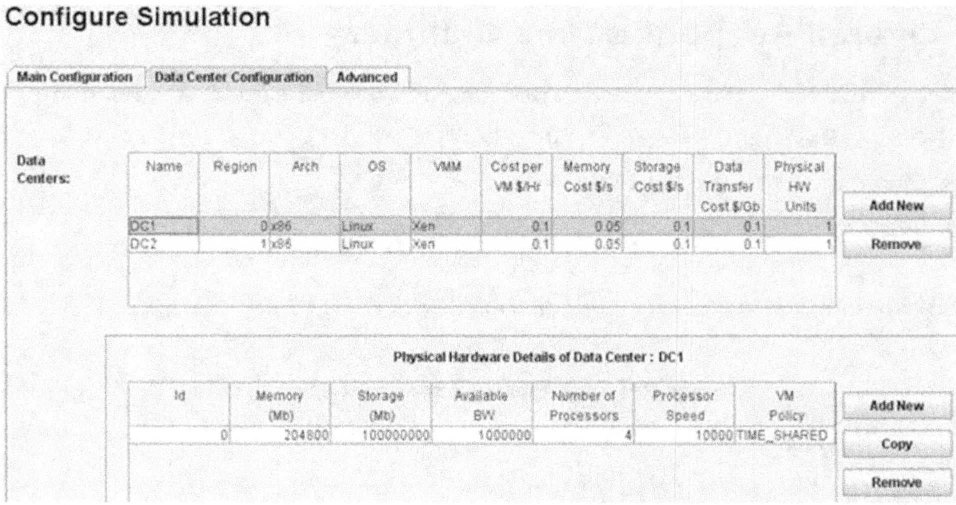

Figure 32. Round robin response time of Experiment 1 Scenario 1

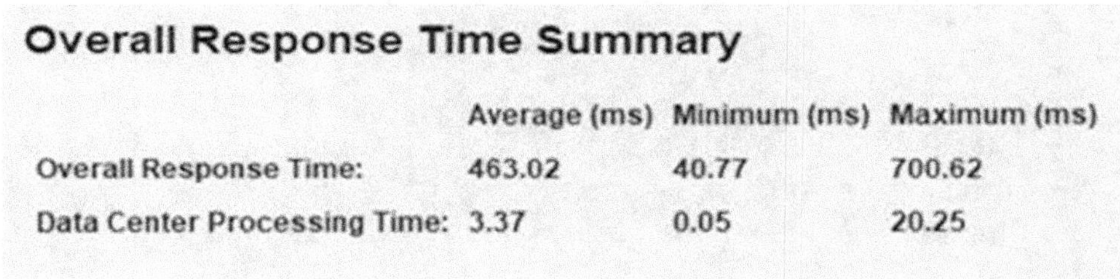

Overall Response Time Summary

	Average (ms)	Minimum (ms)	Maximum (ms)
Overall Response Time:	463.02	40.77	700.62
Data Center Processing Time:	3.37	0.05	20.25

Figure 33. ESCE response time of Experiment 1 Scenario 1

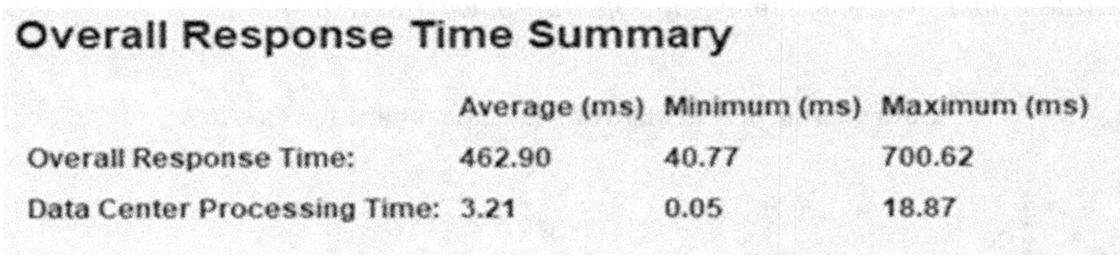

Overall Response Time Summary

	Average (ms)	Minimum (ms)	Maximum (ms)
Overall Response Time:	462.90	40.77	700.62
Data Center Processing Time:	3.21	0.05	18.87

Figure 34. Throttled response time of Experiment 1 Scenario 1

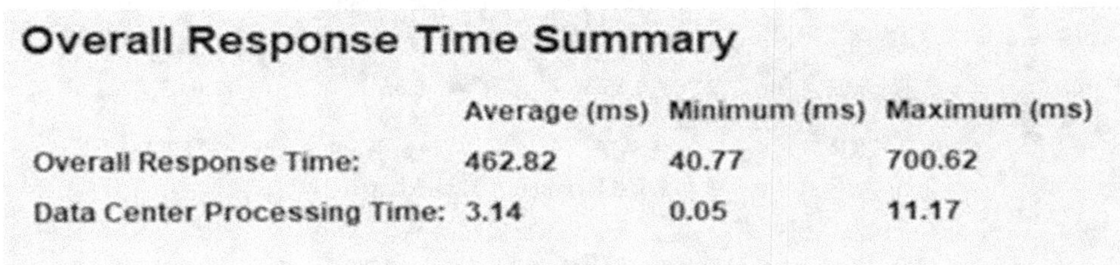

Overall Response Time Summary

	Average (ms)	Minimum (ms)	Maximum (ms)
Overall Response Time:	462.82	40.77	700.62
Data Center Processing Time:	3.14	0.05	11.17

Figure 35. ITLBA response time of Experiment 1 Scenario 1

Overall Response Time Summary

	Average (ms)	Minimum (ms)	Maximum (ms)
Overall Response Time:	462.72	40.61	700.62
Data Center Processing Time:	3.14	0.05	11.17

Figure 36. Average response time chart of Experiment 1 Scenario 1

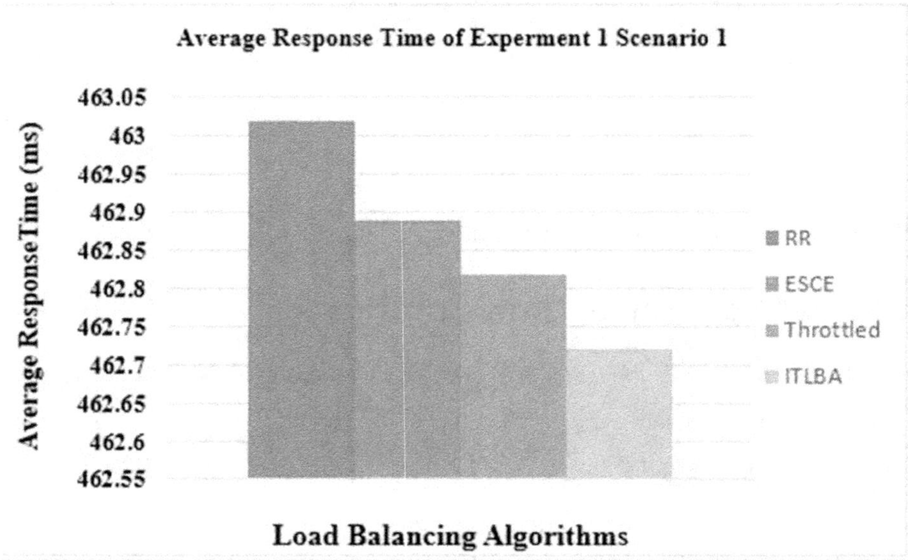

Figure 37. Data center processing time chart of Experiment 1 Scenario 1

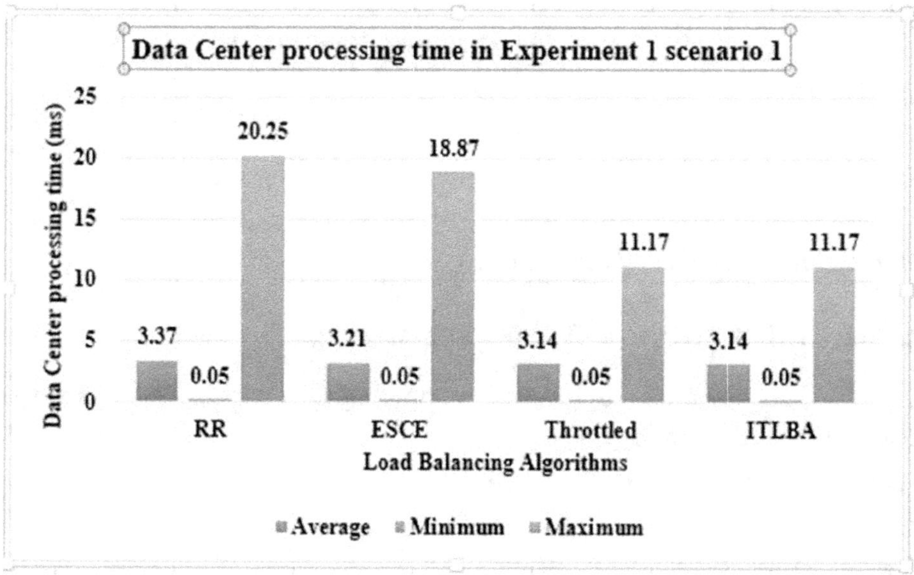

Experiment to Measure and Compare Resource Utilization

In this part of the experiment the objective is to measure and compare resource utilization of the four algorithms.

Configuration of Experiment

This experiment was conducted using a single data center, which housed 5 virtual machines in total. The user base and data center configuration for this experiment is visually depicted in the following figures.

Userbase Configuration

Figure 38. User base configuration of Experiment 1 Scenario 1

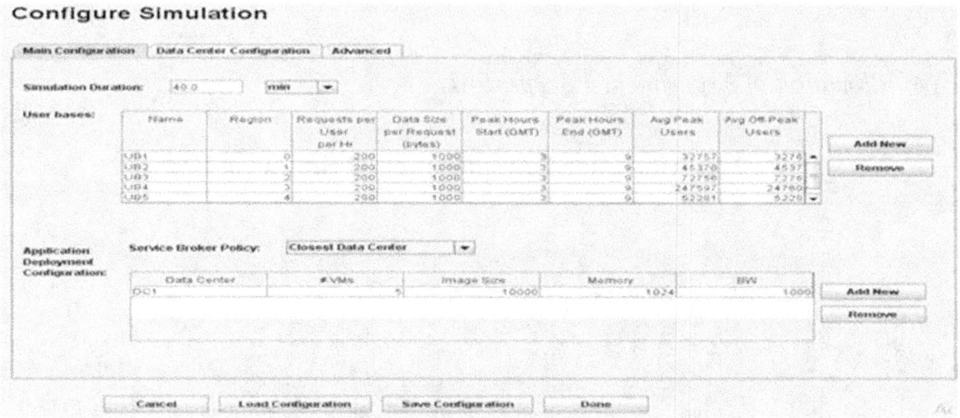

Result of Experiment

The simulation for this scenario were conducted with five virtual machines to test resource utilization and load distribution of the four algorithms. The simulation is executed repeatedly for the four algorithms, and the resulting data is summarized and presented in the following tables and charts.

Table 2. VM allocation count for experiment 1 scenario 1 for 5VMs

3.1.1 List of VM	3.1.2 RR	3.1.3 ESCE	3.1.4 Throttled	3.1.5 ITLBA
3.1.6 VM1	3.1.7 24415	3.1.8 53551	3.1.9 50059	3.1.10 42314
3.1.11 VM2	3.1.12 24415	3.1.13 28246	3.1.14 24244	3.1.15 21652
3.1.16 VM3	3.1.17 24414	3.1.18 18104	3.1.19 14307	3.1.20 13026
3.1.21 VM4	3.1.22 24414	3.1.23 12915	3.1.24 9502	3.1.25 9208
3.1.26 VM5	3.1.27 24414	3.1.28 9256	3.1.29 6617	3.1.30 8714

Figure 39. Data center configuration of Experiment 1 Scenario 1

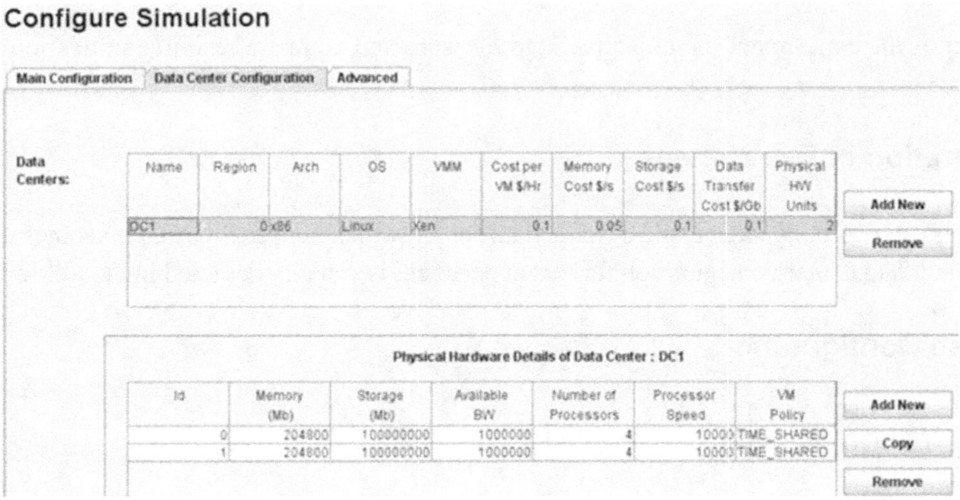

Figure 40. VM allocation of Experiment 1 Scenario 1

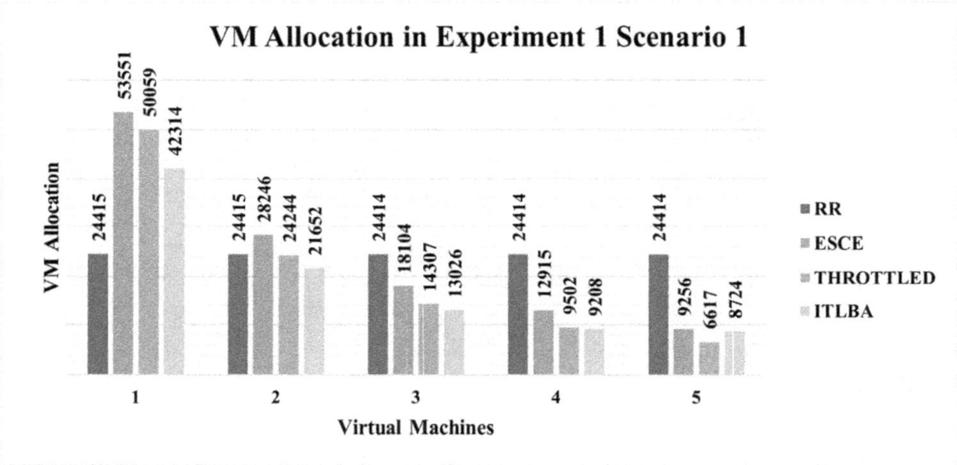

CONCLUSION

The proposed algorithm is intricately designed to address a critical issue in the Throttled algorithm by eliminating the necessity for repetitive scanning of the index table. In this novel approach, two queues have been introduced. One of these queues is designated to store available VMs, while the other queue is designated to store busy VMs. When a request arrives, the load balancer first examines the queue containing available VMs and allocates the request to the foremost VM, if one is available. This will avoid scanning the index table repeatedly for every request. As a result, waiting time of requests will decrease. When a VM finishes its task, it will be added to the end of the available queue. This approach ensures that VMs are utilized in a circular fashion, promoting equitable and balanced resource allocation. To evaluate the performance of the proposed algorithm, three distinct experiments were conducted. The first two experiments encompassed scenarios within both homogenous and heterogeneous environments. These experiments sought to assess the performance of the proposed algorithm in comparison to the other three algorithms while manipulating parameters such as the quantity and size of data centers, virtual machines, and requests. In the third experiment resource utilization of the algorithms were compared by varying the number of resources. The experiments were executed, and performance evaluations were conducted using the CloudAnalyst simulator. The outcomes unequivocally indicated that the proposed algorithm consistently outperformed the other three algorithms in terms of response times. Additionally, it exhibited fair and balanced resource utilization, ranking closely behind Round Robin in this aspect. This is because of avoiding scanning of the index table and circular utilization of VMs. The experiment was repeated with the same input parameter for each algorithms several times. Since the experimentation tool is simulator, which is pre-defined sequence of steps and controlled, the result obtained were the same when the experiment repeated with the same input. The result of the experiments the proposed algorithm recorded better performance in all scenarios. Hence, the proposed algorithm signifies a noteworthy enhancement of the Throttled load balancing algorithm, effectively tackling its limitations and markedly enhancing its performance across diverse scenarios.

REFERENCES

Agarwal. (2014). Virtualization in Cloud Computing. *Information Technology and Software Eng, 4*(2).

Al-Rayis, E., & Kurdi, H. A. (2013). Performance Analysis of Load Balancing Architectures in Cloud Computing. *IEEE Proc. of European Modeling Symposium (EMS),* 520-524. 10.1109/EMS.2013.10

Bagwaiya & Raghuwanshi. (n.d.). *Hybrid approach using Throttled and ESCE Load Balancing Algorithm in Cloud Computing*. Academic Press.

Bal, P. K., Mohapatra, S. K., Das, T. K., Srinivasan, K., & Hu, Y. C. (2022). A joint resource allocation, security with efficient task scheduling in cloud computing using hybrid machine learning techniques. *Sensors (Basel), 22*(3), 1242. doi:10.339022031242 PMID:35161987

Bala, K., Vashist, S., Singh, R., & Singh, G. (2014). A Review of the Load Balancing Techniques. *International Journal of Advances in Computer Science and Communication Engineering, 2*(I).

Bedi, & Singh. (2014). *An Efficient Load Balancing based on Resource Utilization in Cloud Computing*. Computer Science and Engineering Department of Thapar University.

Berwal & Kant. (2015). Load Balancing in Cloud Computing. *International Journal of Computer Science and Computing, 6*(2).

Bikramjit, A. (2017). Survey on Various Load Balancing Techniques in Cloud Computing. *Advances in Computers, 2*, 28–34.

Chandra, H., & Bahuguna, H. (2017). A survey of load balancing algorithms in cloud computing. *International Journal of Computer Engineering and Applications, 11*(12).

Ghosh & Banerjee. (2016). *Priority Based Modified Throttled Algorithm in Cloud Computing*. Academic Press.

Hussien, W., Peng, T., & Wang, G. (2015). A Weighted Throttled Load Balancing Approach for Virtual Machines in Cloud Environment. *International Journal on Computer Science and Engineering*, *11*(4).

Internet World Stats. (n.d.). https://www.internetworldstats.com/stats.htm

Jadeja, Y., & Modi, K. (2012). Cloud Computing - Concepts, Architecture and Challenges. *International Conference on Computing, Electronics and Electrical Technologies (ICCEET),* 877-880. 10.1109/ICCEET.2012.6203873

Kashyap & Viradiya. (2014). A Survey of Various Load Balancing Algorithms in Cloud Computing. *International Journal of Scientific & Technology Research, 3*(11).

Mahalle, S., Kaveri, R., & Chavan, V. (2013). Load Balancing on Cloud Data Centers. *International Journal of Advanced Research in Computer Science and Software Engineering*, 1–4.

Mulat, W. W., Mohapatra, S. K., Sathpathy, R., & Dhal, S. K. (2022, May). Improving Throttled Load Balancing Algorithm in Cloud Computing. In *Proceedings of International Joint Conference on Advances in Computational Intelligence: IJCACI 2021* (pp. 369-377). Singapore: Springer Nature Singapore. 10.1007/978-981-19-0332-8_27

O. B. (2013). *SATW White Paper Cloud Computing*. Swiss Academy of Engineering Science.

Outsideinmarketing. (2012). http://outsideinmarketing.files.wordpress. com/2012/02/cloud_difference_aas.jpg

Padhy, R. (2011). Load Balancing in Cloud Computing Systems. Academic Press.

Panghal, & S. R. (2015). A Parametric Weighted Approach to Perform Load Balancing in Load Balancing. *IJCSC, 6*, 45–52.

Qi, Z., & Boutaba, L. C. R. (2010). Cloud Computing: State-of-the-Art and Research Challenges. *Journal of Internet Services and Applications*, *1*(1), 7–18. doi:10.100713174-010-0007-6

R. (2015). *An Analytical Model to Efficiently Assess Data Centre Performance and QOS in Cloud.* International Journal of Multidisciplinary Research Development.

Reddy, S. G., & Reddy, G. R. M. (2014). *Optimal Load Balancing in Cloud Computing By Efficient Utilization of Virtual Machines*. IEEE.

Shobha. (2018). *A Novel Load Balancing Algorithm Based on the Capacity of the Virtual Machine.* Academic Press.

Sidhu, A. K., & Kinger, S. (2013). Analysis of Load Balancing Techniques in Cloud Computing. *International Journal of Computers and Technology*, *4*(2), 737–741. doi:10.24297/ijct.v4i2C2.4194

Srikanth, K., Reddy, S. R., & Swathil, T. (2014, May). Virtualization in cloud. *International Journal of Computer Science and Mobile Computing*, *3*(15), 540–546.

T. S. S. K. S. M. & Ramasubbareddy. (2019). Analysis of Load Balancing Algorithm using Cloud Analyst. *International Journal of Recent Technology and Engineering, 7*(6).

T. W. P.; Ramadhan. (2018). Experimental Model for Load Balancing in Cloud Computing Using Throttled Algorithm. *International Journal of Applied Engineering Research, 13*(2), 1139-1143.

Taylor. (2015). *Inessential of Cloud Computing*. CRC Press.

Tiwari & Katare. (2014). Analysis of Public Cloud Load Balancing using Partitioning Method and Game Theory. *International Journal of Advanced Research in Computer Science and Software Engineering, 4*(2), 807-812.

VibhoreTyagi & Kumar. (2015). ORT Broker Policy: Reduce Cost and Response time using Throttled Load Balancing Algorithm. *International Conference on Intelligent Computing, Communication ,and Convergence, 48*, 217-221.

Zhang, Q., Cheng, L., & Boutaba, R. (2010). Cloud Computing: State-of-the-art and research challenge. *Journal of Internet Services and Applications, 1*(1), 7–18. doi:10.100713174-010-0007-6

Chapter 10
Effective Cloudlet Scheduling Algorithm for Load Balancing in Cloud Computing Using Fuzzy Logic

Ali Wided
https://orcid.org/0000-0002-3530-7884
Echahid Cheikh Larbi Tebessi University, Algeria

Numan Çelebi
Sakarya University, Turkey

Bouakkaz Fatima
Echahid Cheikh Larbi Tebessi University, Algeria

ABSTRACT

Clouds contain a huge number of virtualized resources that can be made available instantaneously. Cloud technology offers a wide array of services, encompassing platforms, hardware, and software, effectively providing almost anything as a service. A single host represents a physical computer component, while a datacenter comprises numerous hosts responsible for managing virtual machines throughout their life cycles. The efficient scheduling of virtual machine requests plays a crucial role in cloud, as it ensures that requested tasks are completed within the shortest time according to user-defined preferences. This chapter introduces an optimization model based on fuzzy logic for scheduling tasks in cloud computing. The proposed model was tested and evaluated using a fuzzy logic-based scheduling algorithm. The proposed algorithms were compared against scheduling algorithms without fuzzy logic. The experimental findings undeniably establish the superiority of the proposed algorithm.

DOI: 10.4018/979-8-3693-0593-5.ch010

INTRODUCTION

The scheduling issue arises across various fields and continuously evolves alongside industry and technology advancements. Particularly in computer processors, scheduling has garnered significant attention due to the expanding use of computers. The primary objective often revolves around minimizing task execution times, which is commonly referred to as Makespan.

Cloud computing has become a popular service in recent years, providing customers with computer resources, frequently in a virtualized manner, and alleviating them from the burdens of resource management. Consequently, cloud computing infrastructures, including clusters and grids, have become integral parts of datacenters, necessitating the establishment of novel optimization objectives and variables that align with green computing and utility computing principles.

In 1999, Kwok and Ahmad acknowledged that incorporating heterogeneous platforms presented a challenging path for developing scheduling algorithms. However, with the rise in popularity of these platforms in grids and cloud computing, the literature has since witnessed the emergence of new scheduling concepts (SunilKumar, 2021).

In their book, Thomas Erl et al. (Thomas et al., 2013) assert that scheduling remains an unresolved issue as persistent challenges continue. They argue that scheduling techniques must effectively address uncertainty, facilitate controlled solution modifications, and enable swift constraint negotiation and refinement, as these factors are crucial for successful scheduling. Additionally, they emphasize that operating within the context of multiple interested agents is an unavoidable requirement in the scheduling domain.

While cloud computing has gained popularity for its convenience and resource management benefits, it has also introduced complexities in scheduling tasks across heterogeneous platforms within cloud infrastructures, such as clusters and grids. These complexities align with green and utility computing principles, calling for innovative optimization approaches.

This study addresses the pressing need for efficient cloudlet scheduling on cloud computing virtual machines (VMs) using fuzzy logic, a concept introduced by Zadeh in 1965 (Zadeh, 1965).Unlike binary logic, fuzzy logic allows for flexible membership assignments between elements and sets, represented by values between 0 and 1. Our proposed fuzzy controller leverages this flexibility to enhance cloud services by optimizing Makespan, a crucial metric for task scheduling.

The following is the format of the study's succeeding sections: A review of pertinent studies is given in Section 2. The concept for the model is presented in Section 3, and the recommended approaches are explained in Section 4. Section 6 provides the study's conclusion, whereas Section 5 details the simulation results.

BACKGROUND

In this section, we introduce several relevant works to our research. These studies address the challenges and issues associated with scheduling techniques and task scheduling in an academic context. They propose optimization solutions incorporating hybrid algorithms, with the latter approach utilizing fuzzy logic to attain optimal scheduling.

k-means clustering and Fuzzy logic are used in the work by Hamdani (Hamdani,2021) to present an improved Active VM load balancing solution that lowers datacenter transfer costs, total virtual machine expenses, datacenter processing times, and response times. The approach efficiently divides the load and improves CPU efficiency. The Cloud Analyst simulator is used to implement the algorithms. They are then compared against some load balancing strategies, such as Particle Swarm Optimisation (PSO), Round Robin (RRB), Active VM Load Balancing (ESP), Throttled algorithms (THR), Ant Colony Optimisation (ANT), Honey Bees load balancer (BEE), and Throttled algorithms (THR). The proposed algorithm clearly outperforms the competition in terms of overall performance, load balancing, and throughput capability. But, because bandwidth and other relevant aspects aren't considered, the study can't improve load balancing. An issue is that fuzzy sets and weights are computed so that when VMs operate equally well, the method converges to an equally distributed form.

The paper's authors (Sagar, 2021) suggest a fuzzy-based randomised load balancing (FRLB) model to solve the drawbacks of throttled load balancing. Using fuzzy logic, the FRLB gets around the limitations of the throttled load balancing method by efficiently using system resources and determining which virtual machine is least burdened. According to simulation testing, using FRLB improves about 8% over throttled load balancing and about 18% more bandwidth utilisation than round-robin. Moreover, the fuzzy nature of FRLB offers advantages in memory utilisation of roughly 16% and 7%, respectively, compared to throttled and round-robin algorithms. It is crucial to remember that FRLB does not consider fault tolerance in cloud systems.

Their study (Hind & Sanaa, 2021) presented a hybrid algorithm to schedule jobs and effectively balance workloads in cloud systems. It blends fuzzy logic with the benefits of the honeybee behaviour algorithm. This study's main objective was to examine how much power virtual machines (VMs) use while selecting the best hosts and VMs for a given task by considering important Quality of Service (QoS) factors. To simulate the proposed method, ILBA-HB, CloudSim was utilised. Concerning makespan, average reaction time, and workload imbalance, the ILBA-HB algorithm's performance was assessed and contrasted with the LBA-HB and HBB-LB algorithms. It would be helpful to investigate novel nature-inspired meta-heuristic load-balancing techniques in future research, with an emphasis on energy efficiency and quality of service. Furthermore, real-time implementation of the suggested approach is urged to ease result comparisons.

The authors of the study (Ragmani,2020) introduced a hybrid fuzzy ant colony algorithm (FACO) that computes pheromone values using a fuzzy logic module and the Taguchi concept to optimise the ant colony optimisation (ACO)'s parameters. With this method, scheduling virtual machines in a cloud environment should be quite efficient. The fuzzy module that has been suggested makes use of past data to determine the pheromone value and choose a suitable server while preserving the best computing time. An excellent way to overcome load balancing issues is to use the ant colony optimisation approach, which efficiently manages many nodes. The primary contributions of the suggested method are the shorter computation time obtained from the use of fuzzy logic in the calculation of pheromone probability and the Taguchi experience design in selecting the optimal ACO parameters, which determines the optimal parameter combination. The suggested method showed appreciable gains in load balancing inside the cloud architecture through simulations run on the CloudSim and Cloud Analyst libraries. Based on the applied scenario, the acquired results revealed savings in response time of up to 82%, processing time of up to 90%, and overall cost of up to 9%. It's also critical to remember that the suggested method is applicable in real-time scenarios.

The objective of the proposed approach by Ebadifard (Ebadifard, 2021) was to establish a dynamic scheduling technique for effectively distributing requests among virtual machines (VMs). To achieve this, a new dynamic scheduling system was introduced, considering the available resources for each VM, the resource requirements of individual requests, and the dynamic allocation of requests to VMs. Dynamic load balancing techniques often suffer from significant communication overhead. To address this challenge, a combination of autonomy and prediction was employed. By utilizing forecasting, the selection of future overloaded VMs could be avoided, thereby reducing the overhead associated with relocating requests from overloaded to underloaded VMs. To accomplish this, ANFIS (Adaptive Neuro-Fuzzy Inference System) was employed to forecast the future condition of virtual machines. ANFIS serves as the foundation for the adaptive fuzzy interface. The real workload simulations demonstrated that the suggested strategy, which evenly splits requests among VMs, maximizes resource utilization and, reduces response time and makespan, especially with increasing demands, their variability, and the presence of heterogeneous VMs. The study's limitation lies in the absence of an evaluation or a comparison between the suggested algorithm and the most advanced load-balancing methods available, which could affect the paper's overall credibility and relevance in cloud computing.

This research (Gardie, 2021) proposed a hybrid approach combining genetic algorithms and fuzzy set theory. This technique aims to maximise resource utilisation, minimise execution time, and reduce makespan in order to achieve optimal load balancing. The study presents a hybrid genetic algorithm that efficiently combines the benefits of both algorithms, taking into account variables like the processing speed of virtual machines (VMs), the bandwidth of VMs, and the variable memory usage of cloudlets. The algorithm allocates computing resources to cloudlets based on their varying lengths by incorporating these parameters. The simulation was conducted using the CloudSim simulator, and the results indicate that the execution time of cloudlets is shorter compared to the classical genetic method. The limitation of this study lies in the need for extensive experimental evaluation or real-world implementation to substantiate the effectiveness and efficiency of the proposed hybrid fuzzy-genetic load balancing scheme.

The authors (Mou De & kundu, 2020) introduced a cloud architecture that employs fuzzy reasoning to predict datacenter load. This method estimates the availability of datacenters with dynamically shifting task loads using fuzzy-based datacenter prediction analysis. Scheduling algorithms efficiently distribute the load among datacenters, virtual computers, and physical resources. By leveraging fuzzy-based datacenter prediction analysis, the execution response times of datacenters are improved, and dynamic job load management becomes more feasible. To ensure optimal task handling, the size and number of virtual machines are carefully evaluated before assigning tasks, thereby reducing task waiting times. Moreover, the system optimizes energy consumption and stabilizes the dynamic load in virtual machines. The study's experimental results are examined to ensure efficient system accuracy. The limitation of this study is the need for a comprehensive comparison with alternative datacenter selection techniques. A more extensive comparison would enhance the credibility and applicability of the study's findings.

The authors (Chraibi et al, 2022) aimed to enhance task scheduling by formulating it as a bin packing problem. They presented three modified bin packing techniques as part of a project called MBPTS (Minimization of Makespan-based Bin Packing Task Scheduling). with the express goal of minimising makespan. The study's findings, which were obtained using the open-source simulator CloudSim, showed that, in comparison to other scheduling algorithms like first come first serve (FCF). Particle swarm optimisation (PSO), the suggested MBPTS approach successfully optimised balance results, decreased waiting times and makespan, and improved resource utilisation. Moreover, the proposed algorithms have an advantage over the PSO and FCFS approaches since they incorporate load balancing while allocating cloudlets to available resources. But, because it was limited to metrics like makespan, waiting time, resource usage, and degree of imbalance, the research had some drawbacks. To provide a more thorough assessment of the suggested MBPTS strategy, further study might include more optimisation approaches and investigate other quality criteria, such as job migration between queues, VM migration concepts, and energy consumption.

After a thorough examination of the previous research, the following observations can be made:

- Fuzzy Logic Integration: Numerous studies have incorporated fuzzy logic to handle uncertainties and vagueness in load balancing decisions, leading to improved utilization of system resources and more effective load distribution.
- Hybrid Algorithm Proposals: Many research works have introduced hybrid algorithms that combine various techniques, including fuzzy logic, genetic algorithms, k-means clustering, ant colony optimization, among others, to enhance load balancing efficiency and overall performance.
- Simulation-Based Evaluations: The studies commonly utilize simulation tools like CloudSim and Cloud Analyst to assess the performance of proposed load-balancing algorithms and compare them with existing approaches.
- Performance Evaluation Metrics: The evaluation of these algorithms is based on multiple metrics, including overall performance, throughput, load balancing ability, response time, makespan, resource utilization, and cost.
- Resource Optimization Focus: A primary emphasis in these studies is to optimize resource utilization, reduce processing times, and minimize datacenter transfer costs.

  The preceding studies lack these concepts:
- Fault Tolerance Consideration: Most studies do not explicitly address fault tolerance, a critical aspect in cloud systems to ensure high availability and reliability.
- Practical Implementation Validation: Although some research suggests feasibility in real-time settings, there is a lack of practical implementation and validation of the proposed algorithms in real-world cloud environments.
- Comprehensive Comparative Analysis: Some studies lack comprehensive comparisons with state-of-the-art load balancing techniques, which limits the assessment of the proposed approaches' superiority.
- Additional Quality Measures: While some studies explore multiple metrics, others could benefit from considering additional quality measures, such as energy consumption and job migration between virtual machines (VMs).

PROPOSED MODEL

The cloud provider aims to minimize waiting times, optimize VM (Virtual Machine) utilization, and reduce the makespan (time taken to complete all tasks). When a cloud broker receives multiple user tasks (as illustrated in Figure 1), they are initially sorted based on their submission order, and a first-come, first-First-Serve (FCFS) queue is employed for task execution.

Major cloud providers like Amazon, Azure, and App Engine offer datacenters as critical infrastructure services. A datacenter comprises a collection of host instances, which may vary in hardware configurations, including memory, processing capacity, and storage. Alternatively, they may be homogeneous, resembling a standard server model. Each component within the datacenter is responsible for general application provisioning, which adheres to specific policies governing memory allocation, bandwidth, and peripheral storage for hosts and their associated virtual machines.

The Cloud Broker facilitates the mediation between software-as-a-service (SaaS) providers and cloud providers. Quality of Service (QoS) requirements is the guiding principles behind these negotiations. Applications fall under the purview of the Broker class, responsible for searching the Cloud Information System (CIS) for relevant resources and services. It negotiates their allocation to meet the application's QoS demands. Enhancements are required to expand this class to explore customized negotiation tactics.

A host represents a physical resource, such as a server or computer, and includes information like storage size, memory capacity, CPU details (in the case of systems with multiple processors), and provisioning policies for computation, memory, and bandwidth allocation to virtual machines.

Cloud hosts manage and host virtual machines, each with its own attributes, including internal provisioning policies, CPU specifications, memory capacity, and storage.

'Cloudlet' (or 'task') refers to cloud-based application services typically deployed in data centers, encompassing activities like social networking, content distribution, and business process management.

Figure 1. The proposed task scheduling model for cloud computing

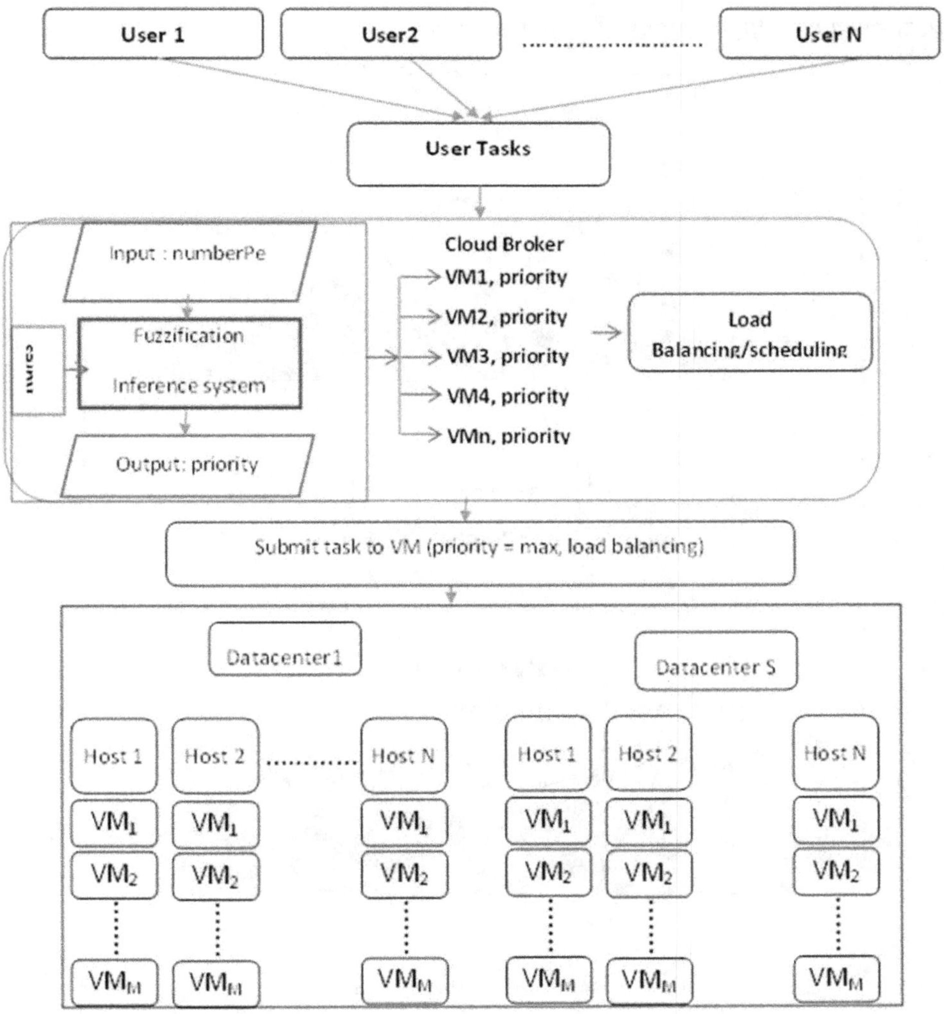

Fuzzy Logic Controller

A fuzzy logic controller (FLC) comprises three key components: an inference engine, a fuzzifier, and a defuzzifier. FLC is a methodology employed to mitigate measurement uncertainty. It operates on two input variables: RAM and numberPe. In a fuzzy logic system, input variables are mapped using a set of membership functions. The process of converting an input value into a fuzzy value is referred to as fuzzification.

To establish linguistic rules governing the relationship between inputs and outputs, fuzzy membership functions are essential. Each of the input variables is categorized into three states, and triangular-shaped membership functions (MF) are utilized for handling these input variables. Additionally, the output variable is defined within three state ranges.

Defuzzification is the process of extracting a precise numerical value from the fuzzy output. This process is associated with three linguistic variables describing the performance of each virtual machine (VM) node: medium, high, and low."

Figure 2. Fuzzy membership functions for input variables

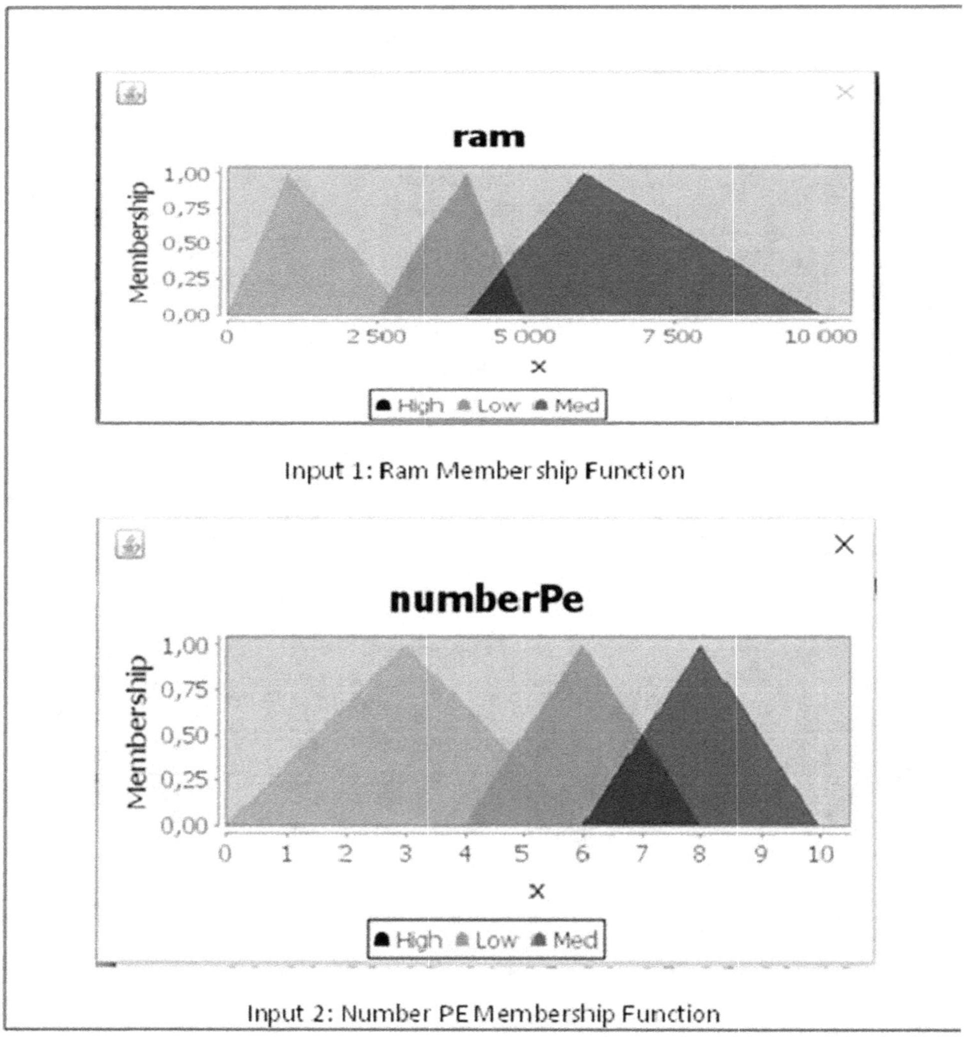

Figure 2 represents the membership functions of inputs of the fuzzy control system.

Fuzzy logic system output: The fuzzy logic system determines the virtual machine priority. Table 1 lists the rules that the fuzzy system uses.

Table 1. Rules used in the fuzzy logic system

Rules Base	Input Variables		Output Variable
	RAM	**NumberPE**	**Priority**
1	Low	Low	Low
2	Low	Med	Low
3	Low	High	Med
4	Med	Low	Low
5	Med	Med	Med
6	Med	High	High
7	High	Low	Med
8	High	Med	High
9	High	High	High

Proposed Cloudlet Scheduling Algorithm

In this section, we introduce the proposed cloudlet scheduling algorithm using Fuzzy Logic. This algorithm represents a key contribution to our research, addressing the challenges associated with cloudlet scheduling on virtual machines (VMs) in cloud computing environments. Through the integration of fuzzy logic, we have developed a novel approach to optimize cloudlet scheduling, enhancing the efficiency and adaptability of cloud computing systems.

Algorithm 1 outlines the fundamental processes of fuzzy logic:

1. Fuzzification: Initially, a crisp set of input data is transformed into a fuzzy set using linguistic terms, linguistic variables, and membership functions. This step is known as fuzzification.
2. Inference Construction: The next phase involves constructing an inference using predefined rules. These rules define how fuzzy inputs are processed to derive fuzzy outputs.
3. Defuzzification: Finally, the fuzzy output is converted back into a crisp output using the membership functions. This process, known as defuzzification, maps the fuzzy results to precise numerical values.

Algorithm 1: Fuzzy Controller (FCL Language): Pseudo-Code

```
String fcl= "FUNCTION_BLOCK Test     + //
"VAR_INPUT      // input variables\n" +
                                    "    ram: real;\n" + //
                                    "    numberPe: REAL ;\n" + //
```

```
                                    "END_VAR\n" + //
"VAR_OUTPUT      // output variable\n" + //
                                     "   Priority: REAL;\n" + //
                                     "END_VAR\n" + //
"FUZZIFY numberPe\n" + //
"   TERM Low:= (0,0)(3,1) (6, 0) ; \n" + //
"   TERM Med:= (4, 0) (6,1) (8,0);\n" + //
"   TERM High:= (6,0)(8,1) (10,0);\n" + //
"END_FUZZIFY \n" + //
"FUZZIFY ram \n" + //
"   TERM Low:= (0,0) (1000, 1) (3000,0) ;\n" + //
"   TERM Med:= (2500, 0) (4000, 1) (5000,0) ;\n" + //
"   TERM High:= (4000,0)(6000, 1)(10000,0);\n" + //
"END_FUZZIFY \n" + //
"DEFUZZIFY Priority \n" + //
"   TERM Low:= (0,0)(3,1) (6, 0) ; \n" + //
"   TERM Med:= (4, 0) (6,1) (8,0);\n" + //
"   TERM High:= (6,0)(8,1) (10,0);\n" + //
"   METHOD: COG;       // Use 'Center Of Gravity' defuzzification method\n" +
// "   DEFAULT:= 0;
 "END_DEFUZZIFY\n" + //
"RULEBLOCK No1\n" + //
 "   ACCU: MAX;          // accumulation method\n" + //              "   AND:
MIN;          + //
"   ACT: MIN;           //  activation method\n" + //
"    RULE 1: IF numberPe IS Low AND ram IS Low THEN Priority IS Low;\n" + //
"    RULE 2: IF numberPe IS Low AND ram IS Med THEN Priority IS Low;\n" + //
"    RULE 3: IF numberPe IS Low AND ram IS High THEN Priority IS Med;\n" +//
"    RULE 4: IF numberPe IS Med AND ram IS Low THEN Priority IS Low;\n" + //
"   RULE 5: IF numberPe IS Med AND ram IS Med THEN Priority IS Med;\n" + //
"   RULE 6: IF numberPe IS Med AND ram IS High THEN Priority IS High;\n" +//
"   RULE 7:  IF numberPe IS High AND ram IS Low THEN Priority IS Med ;\n" +//
"  RULE 8:  IF numberPe IS High AND ram IS Med THEN Priority IS High ;\n" +//
" RULE 9:  IF numberPe IS High AND ram IS High THEN Priority IS High ;\n"+ //
"END_RULEBLOCK\n" + //
"END_FUNCTION_BLOCK\n";
```

'High,' 'Medium,' and 'Low' are the output variables representing VM priorities. Based on the assigned VM priority of 'High,' 'Medium,' or 'Low,' the VM is placed into the corresponding priority list (High priority list, Medium priority list, or Low priority list) as outlined in Algorithm 2.

Algorithm 2: VM Classification

```
Input: VM-priority
Begin
If (VM-priority = 'High') Then
VM Î High-priority-list
end If
If (VM-priority = 'Medium') Then
VM Î Medium-priority-list
end If
If (VM-priority = 'Low') Then
VM Î Low-priority-list
end If
End.
Cutput: High-priority-list, Medium-priority-list,Low-priority-list
```

The next step entails the cloud broker identifying the 'Higher-VM' and the 'Lower-VM.' The 'Higher-VM' corresponds to the first virtual machine in the High-priority list, while the 'Lower-VM' corresponds to the first virtual machine in the Low-priority list (refer to Algorithm 3)

Algorithm 3: Decision Making

```
Input: High-priority-list, Low-priority-list, Medium-priority-list
Begin
Sort High-priority-list by descending order according
    to VM priority.
Sort Low-priority-list by ascending order according
    to VM priority.
While (High-priority-list ¹ ϕ. AND.  Low-priority-list ¹ ϕ) do
Higher-VM = the first VM Î to High-priority-list
Lower-VM = the first VM Î to Low-priority-list
Update High-priority-list, Medium-priority-list and Low-priority-list
 End While
End
Output: Higher-VM, Lower-VM
```

The cloud broker then decides to submit the cloudlet to Higher-VM, and it applies Algorithm 4:

Algorithm 4: Pseudo-Code: Cloudlet Assignment

```
 {
for (Cloudlet cloudlet: getCloudletList()) {
Vm vm;
if (cloudlet.getVmId() == -1) {
```

```
vm = getVmsCreatedList().get(vmIndex);
if (vm.priority ==High) {
cloudlet.setVmId(vm.getId());
} else {
if (vm.priority ==Low)
System.out.println("priority of vm is Low.......next vm"
}else {
if (vm.priority ==Medium)
cloudlet.setVmId(vm.getId());
}
Continue;
} }
```

SIMULATION RESULTS

To showcase the effectiveness of the proposed approach, we conducted a comparative analysis between the results obtained using our technique and those generated by a scheduling algorithm that did not utilize fuzzy logic. Fuzzy logic was utilized to assess and assign priorities to multiple virtual machines based on their respective attributes.

Simulation Platform and Programming Language

We utilized the following software tools:

- CloudSim: Developed by the CLOUDS Laboratory in Melbourne, Australia (Rodrigo et al., 2011), CloudSim is a stand-alone framework designed for simulating and modeling large-scale cloud computing infrastructures. It extends the basic functionalities of GridSim and includes features such as support for scheduling, allocation policies, and service brokers. CloudSim is particularly suitable for modeling virtualized cloud-based datacenter infrastructures and provides specialized management interfaces for memory, storage, bandwidth, and virtual machines (VMs).
- jFuzzyLogic: Cingolani (Cingolani,2013) created this open-source Java package that enables the creation and development of fuzzy logic controllers that adhere to the IEC 61131-7 Fuzzy Control Language standard. jFuzzyLogic uses a Block of Function (FB) structure comprising multiple components forming a FIS (Fuzzy Inference System) inference system. Each FB contains one or more rule blocks, input and output variables, and additional elements. Programmers seeking to incorporate fuzzy logic into their Java projects will find jFuzzyLogic a valuable tool. It provides a means to address ambiguity and approximation reasoning, making it suitable for situations where precise conclusions may be challenging due to inherent ambiguity in requirements or data.

Metrics Used

In our evaluation, we focus on the following key metrics:

Makespan: In CloudSim, makespan is a measure of the overall duration of a simulation. It can be calculated by determining the total time required for all cloudlets in a simulation to complete their execution. Makespan represents the time taken from the start of the first cloudlet to the completion of the last cloudlet and is expressed as:

makespan = Completion Time of Last cloudlet - Start Time

Total Cloudlet Cost: Calculating the total cost of cloudlets in CloudSim involves aggregating the costs associated with the execution of individual cloudlets. Cloudlet costs typically encompass expenses related to resource usage (e.g., CPU and memory), execution time, and any other resource-specific costs. This implementation computes the processing cost by considering the cloudlet's execution time and the cost rate associated with CPU resource usage. The cost rate is typically specified as a parameter during VM or cloudlet setup.

Resource Utilization: This metric assesses how efficiently cloud resources (CPU, memory, storage, etc.) are utilized. Higher resource utilization generally signifies better operational efficiency and is calculated as a percentage:

Resource Utilization (%) = (Resource Usage / Total Resource Capacity) * 100

Scalability: Scalability pertains to the scheduling algorithm's capacity to manage an increasing number of cloudlets and resources while maintaining performance levels.

Experimental Results

We evaluated the performance of the proposed algorithms in an experimental context using CloudSim as our cloud simulation platform. Additionally, we utilized jFuzzyLogic, the Java FuzzyLogic library, for creating and implementing fuzzy logic controllers.

Simulation 1

In the initial simulation, we opted for the First Come, First Served scheduling algorithm (FCFS). This scenario involved 10 cloudlets, and the outcomes are summarized in Table 2.

Table 2 illustrates a simulation in which a set of cloudlets was allocated to specific virtual machines within a datacenter. All cloudlets successfully completed their execution.

- Cloudlet ID: Represents the unique identifier for each cloudlet in the simulation.
- STATUS: "SUCCESS" indicates that all cloudlets were successfully processed.
- Datacenter ID: Identifies the data center where each cloudlet was processed.
- VM ID: Each cloudlet has a unique virtual machine (VM) assigned to it, identified by "VM ID."
- Execution Time: The time it took for each cloudlet to complete its execution on the respective VM, with values falling within a relatively narrow range.
- Start Time: Indicates when each cloudlet started its execution on the VM.
- Finish Time: Represents when each cloudlet completed its execution on the VM.

Table 2. Simulation 1 results

Cloudlet ID	STATUS Data	Datacenter ID	VM ID	Execution Time	Start Time	Finish Time
0	SUCCESS	2	9	1.74	2.66	4.4
1	SUCCESS	2	8	1.74	2.66	4.4
2	SUCCESS	2	7	1.74	2.66	4.4
3	SUCCESS	2	6	1.74	2.66	4.4
4	SUCCESS	2	5	1.74	2.66	4.4
5	SUCCESS	2	4	1.74	2.66	4.4
6	SUCCESS	2	3	1.74	2.66	4.4
7	SUCCESS	2	2	1.63	2.66	4.29
8	SUCCESS	2	1	1.62	2.55	4.17
9	SUCCESS	2	0	1.62	2.44	4.06
10	SUCCESS	2	14	1.44	1.34	2.77
11	SUCCESS	2	13	1.44	1.34	2.77
12	SUCCESS	2	12	1.44	1.23	2.66
13	SUCCESS	2	11	1.44	1.23	2.66
14	SUCCESS	2	10	1.44	1.23	2.66
15	SUCCESS	2	9	1.44	1.23	2.66
16	SUCCESS	2	8	1.44	1.23	2.66
17	SUCCESS	2	7	1.44	1.23	2.66
18	SUCCESS	2	6	1.44	1.23	2.66
19	SUCCESS	2	5	1.44	1.23	2.66
20	SUCCESS	2	4	1.44	1.23	2.66

Simulation 2

In the second simulation, we implemented the suggested fuzzy logic algorithm to allocate a set of cloudlets to specific virtual machines within a datacenter. The outcomes of Simulation 2 are presented in Table 3.

From table 3, which employed fuzzy logic for cloudlet allocation, demonstrated more uniform and efficient execution compared to Simulation 1, which used a simple FCFS scheduling algorithm. Fuzzy logic appears to have contributed to improved cloudlet allocation and execution consistency

Simulation 3

In this simulation, we evaluated two distinct approaches: one employing fuzzy logic and the other without it. The primary focus of this comparison revolves around assessing 'makespan,' and this evaluation encompasses various numbers of cloudlets.

From Figure 3 we can observe:

Number of Cloudlets vs. Makespan:

- As the cloudlets number increases, both the makespan with and without fuzzy logic also increase. This is expected, as more cloudlets generally require more time to complete.
- The makespan with fuzzy logic is consistently lower than the makespan without fuzzy logic for each number of cloudlets. This suggests that the fuzzy logic approach is more efficient in terms of reducing the makespan.

Rate of Increase:

- The rate of increase in makespan appears to be roughly linear for both approaches. In other words, as the number of cloudlets doubles, the makespan roughly doubles as well. This linear relationship is a common characteristic in certain types of scheduling problems.

Table 3. Simulation 2 results

Cloudlet ID	STATUS Data	Data Center ID	VM ID	Execution Time	Start Time	Finish Time
0	SUCCESS	2	0	1	0.1	1.1
1	SUCCESS	2	2	1	0.1	1.1
2	SUCCESS	2	4	1	0.1	1.1
3	SUCCESS	2	8	1	0.1	1.1
4	SUCCESS	2	12	1	0.1	1.1
5	SUCCESS	2	6	1	0.1	1.1
6	SUCCESS	2	10	1	0.1	1.1
7	SUCCESS	2	14	1	0.1	1.1
8	SUCCESS	3	13	1.13	0.1	1.23
9	SUCCESS	3	1	1.24	0.1	1.34
10	SUCCESS	3	3	1.24	0.1	1.34
11	SUCCESS	3	5	1.24	0.1	1.34
12	SUCCESS	3	9	1.24	0.1	1.34
13	SUCCESS	3	7	1.24	0.1	1.34
14	SUCCESS	3	11	1.24	0.1	1.34
15	SUCCESS	2	14	1.26	1.1	2.36
16	SUCCESS	2	0	1.37	1.1	2.47
17	SUCCESS	2	2	1.37	1.1	2.47
18	SUCCESS	2	4	1.37	1.1	2.47
19	SUCCESS	2	8	1.37	1.1	2.47
20	SUCCESS	2	12	1.37	1.1	2.47

Figure 3. Number of cloudlets vs. makespan

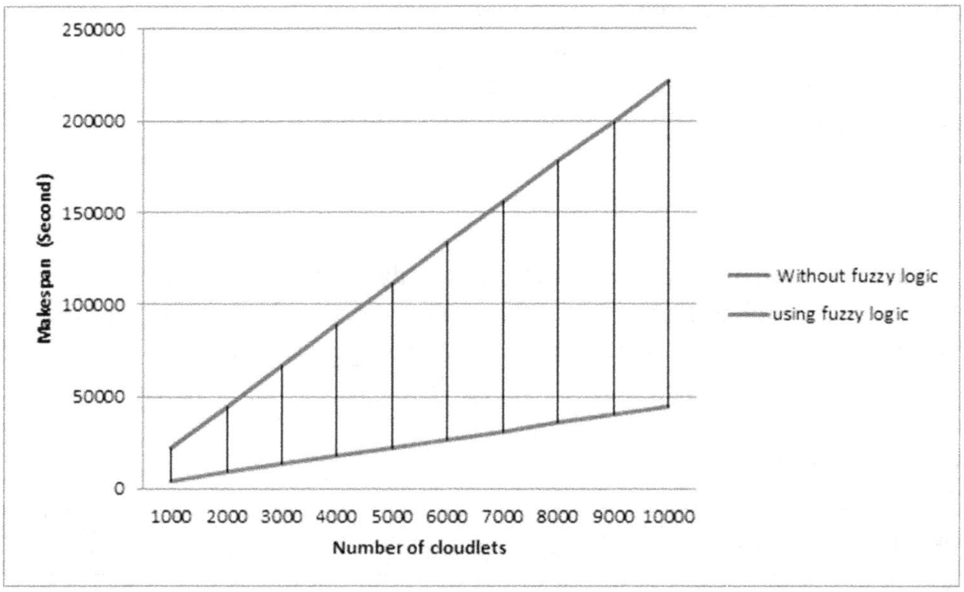

Efficiency of Fuzzy Logic:

- The most noticeable difference between the two approaches is the efficiency gained from using fuzzy logic. In some cases, the difference in makespan between the two approaches is quite substantial. For instance, when there are 1,000 cloudlets, the makespan with fuzzy logic is approximately one-quarter of the makespan without fuzzy logic.

In conclusion, the figure 3 demonstrates that using fuzzy logic in the cloudlet scheduling process can significantly improve the efficiency and reduce the makespan when compared to a non-fuzzy logic approach. As the number of cloudlets rises, so does the makespan, which are expected due to the increased workload. However, even with this increase, the fuzzy logic approach consistently outperforms the non-fuzzy logic approach in terms of makespan, indicating its effectiveness in optimizing task scheduling in this context.

Simulation 4

This simulation compares the total cost of processing cloudlets using two different approaches: one with fuzzy logic and the other without it, considering various numbers of cloudlets.

From Figure 4 we can observe the total cost of processing cloudlets increases with an increasing number of cloudlets due to higher resource usage and processing time. The most significant observation is that, in each case, the total cost using fuzzy logic is notably lower than the total cost without fuzzy logic, indicating the cost-effectiveness of the fuzzy logic approach.

In conclusion, these results demonstrate that using fuzzy logic in the cloudlet processing approach not only significantly improves efficiency and makespan reduction but also leads to lower total costs, making it a more efficient and cost-effective approach, regardless of the number of cloudlets.

Figure 4. Number of cloudlets vs. total cost

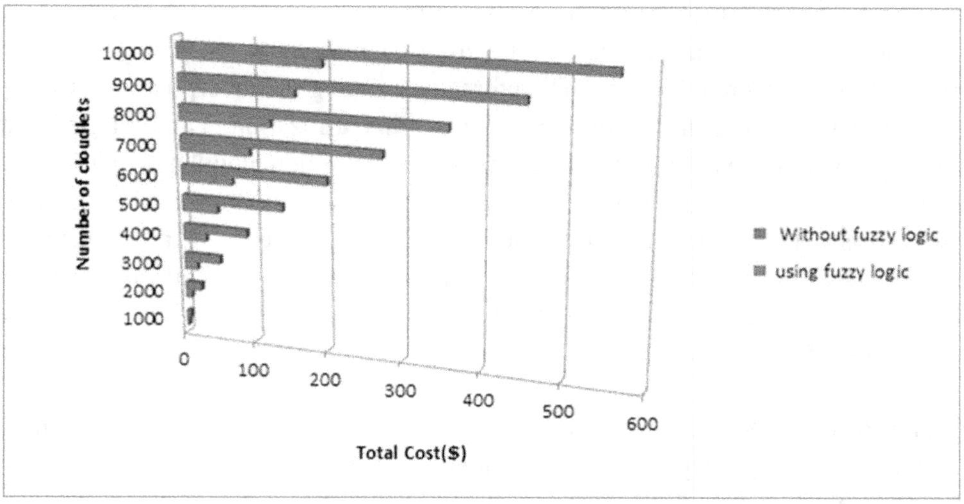

CONCLUSION

One of the significant challenges in cloud computing is determining the optimal timing for task scheduling. Scheduling involves defining the order in which tasks from different processes should be executed and allocating the necessary resources for each task. Additionally, users must decide which resources (providers) to utilize.

In this chapter, we have addressed the optimization of cloud performance specifically in the realm of cloudlet scheduling, aiming to provide users with faster access to cloud services.

To achieve these objectives, we introduced and evaluated a novel fuzzy logic-based scheduling algorithm as an effective method for allocating virtual machines across data centers to prioritize cloudlets according to user demands.

The simulation results presented in this study offer strong evidence for the effectiveness of integrating fuzzy logic into cloudlet scheduling algorithms in cloud computing. The key findings can be summarized as follows:

Efficiency in Makespan: A comparison between fuzzy logic and non-fuzzy logic scheduling algorithms consistently demonstrated the superiority of the fuzzy logic approach in terms of makespan. As the number of cloudlets increased, both approaches experienced an expected rise in makespan due to the increased workload. However, the fuzzy logic approach consistently exhibited a significantly lower makespan, highlighting its efficiency in optimizing cloudlet scheduling.

Cost Savings: An analysis of the total cost for processing cloudlets consistently showed that the fuzzy logic approach incurred lower costs compared to the non-fuzzy logic approach, regardless of the number of cloudlets. This cost-effectiveness became more pronounced as the number of cloudlets increased, emphasizing the economic advantages of incorporating fuzzy logic in cloudlet scheduling.

Linear Rate of Increase: Both approaches demonstrated a roughly linear relationship between the number of cloudlets and makespan or total cost. This linear rate of increase is a common characteristic in scheduling problems and provides insights into the scalability of the proposed fuzzy logic approach.

The utilization of fuzzy logic in cloudlet scheduling clearly offers advantages in terms of both efficiency and cost-effectiveness. These findings suggest that fuzzy logic is a valuable tool for optimizing cloudlet allocation and scheduling in cloud computing environments, especially when dealing with varying workloads and resource demands. Therefore, considering the incorporation of fuzzy logic is a promising approach to enhance the performance and resource utilization in cloud-based systems.

In concluding our study on optimizing cloud performance through cloudlet scheduling, it's essential to acknowledge not only the achievements but also the limitations that are intrinsic to the CloudSim simulator, which served as the foundation for our experimentation. One of the significant challenges faced during our research was the reliance on CloudSim as the simulation platform. While CloudSim is a valuable tool for modeling and simulating cloud computing environments, it has its own set of drawbacks. These limitations include:

- Simplified Resource Models: CloudSim employs simplified resource models, which might not fully capture the complexity of real-world cloud infrastructures. Real cloud environments often involve diverse and dynamic resource provisioning, which CloudSim may not precisely replicate.
- Limited Real-time Factors: CloudSim primarily focuses on batch processing and scheduling. Real-time considerations and intricate performance variations, often seen in actual cloud environments, might not be effectively modeled in CloudSim.
- Assumptions and Simplifications: Like any simulation tool, CloudSim relies on certain assumptions and simplifications. These assumptions can affect the fidelity of the results, especially when applied to complex scenarios.

REFERENCES

Buyya, R., & Murshed, M. (2002). Gridsim: A toolkit for the modeling and simulation of distributed resource management and scheduling for grid computing. *Concurrency and Computation*, *14*(13-15), 1175–1220. doi:10.1002/cpe.710

Chraibi, A., Alla, S. B., & Ezzati, A. (2022). An efficient cloudlet scheduling via bin packing in cloud computing. *Iranian Journal of Electrical and Computer Engineering*, *12*(3), 3226–3226. doi:10.11591/ijece.v12i3.pp3226-3237

Cingolani, P., & Alcalá, F. J. (2013). jFuzzyLogic: A java library to design fuzzy logic controllers according to the standard for fuzzy control programming. *International Journal of Computational Intelligence Systems*, *6*(1), 61–75. doi:10.1080/18756891.2013.818190

Comer, D. E. (2021). The Cloud Computing. CRC Press.

De, M., & Kundu, A. (2020, October). *Datacenter Selection in Cloud Framework for Efficient Load Distribution Using a Fuzzy Approach. Mexican International Conference on Artificial Intelligence*, Mexico City, Mexico. 10.1007/978-3-030-60884-2_32

Ebadifard, F., & Babamir, S. M. (2021). Autonomic task scheduling algorithm for dynamic workloads through a load balancing technique for the cloud-computing environment. *Cluster Computing*, *24*(2), 1075–1101. doi:10.100710586-020-03177-0

Gardie, B., Azezew, K., & Bitew, H. (2021). Hybrid Fuzzy-Genetic Load Balancing Scheme for Cloud Computing. *International Journal of Research in Engineering and Science*, *9*(3), 82–89.

Hamdani, M., & Youcef, A. (2021). Enhanced active VM load balancing algorithm using fuzzy logic and K-means clustering. *Multiagent and Grid Systems*, *17*(1), 59–82. doi:10.3233/MGS-210343

Hind, S. A., & Sanaa, A. S. (2021). Hybrid Load Balancing Approach based on the Integration of QoS and Power Consumption in Cloud Computing. *International Journal of Advanced Trends in Computer Science and Engineering*, *10*(2), 1079–1090. doi:10.30534/ijatcse/2021/841022021

Ragmani, A., Elomri, A., Abghour, N., Moussaid, K., & Rida, M. (2020). FACO: A hybrid fuzzy ant colony optimization algorithm for virtual machine scheduling in high-performance cloud computing. *Journal of Ambient Intelligence and Humanized Computing*, *11*(10), 3975–3987. doi:10.100712652-019-01631-5

Rodrigo, N. C., Rajiv, R., Anton, B., Cesar, A. F. D., & Rajkumar, B. (2011). CloudSim: A Toolkit for Modeling and Simulation of Cloud Computing Environments and Evaluation of Resource Provisioning Algorithms. *Software, Practice & Experience*, *41*(1), 23–50. doi:10.1002pe.995

Sagar, S., Ahmed, M., & Husain, M. Y. (2021). Fuzzy Randomized Load Balancing for Cloud Computing. In *Advances on P2P, Parallel, Grid, Cloud and Internet Computing-Proceedings of the 16th International Conference on P2P, Parallel, Grid, Cloud and Internet Computing, PGCIC 2021* (vol. 343, pp. 18-29). Academic Press.

Sunilkumar, M., & Gopal, S. K. (2021). *Cloud Computing concepts and technologies*. CRC Press.

Thomas, E., Zaigham, M., & Ricardo, P. (2013). *Cloud Computing Concepts, Technology & Architecture*. Prentice Hall/Pearson PTR.

Zadeh, L. A. (1965). Fuzzy sets. *Information and Control*, *8*(3), 338–353. doi:10.1016/S0019-9958(65)90241-X

Chapter 11

A Load Balancing Algorithm for Enhanced Active Monitoring in a Cloud Environment

Sudhir Kumar Mohapatra
https://orcid.org/0000-0003-3065-3881
Sri Sri University, India

Tegegn Dita
Adama Science and Technology University, Ethiopia

Mesfin Abebe
Adama Science and Technology University, Ethiopia

Jasobanta Laha
Sri Sri University, India

Biswajit Tripathy
Einstein College of Computer Application and Management, India

ABSTRACT

Several strategies have been put forth to efficiently assign the accessible cloud nodes to the client's request and the goal is to improve the cloud's overall performance while also giving users better services and a higher level of customer happiness. An extensive investigation and analysis are done into the idea of using a load balancing method with active monitoring as well as the modification of such an algorithm. There are several ways to accomplish this. The results of the study suggest that when adopting a load balancing method with active monitoring methodology in a cloud computing environment, a more effective active monitoring load balancing method should be used. The load balancing technique gets increasingly challenging as a virtual machine's demand increases. The authors were able to improve throughput while also streamlining the load balancing procedure by using a buffer. Using this information as a foundation, the authors enhanced the load balancing method with active monitoring technique to take into account the growing demand of a virtual machine.

DOI: 10.4018/979-8-3693-0593-5.ch011

1. INTRODUCTION

Clients from all around the world want for a wide range of cloud computing services. Currently, load balancing techniques are created to intelligently and efficiently distribute user requests and tasks across cloud resources (Bhaskar et al., 2012). The cloud computing infrastructure supports every aspect of our lives. But there are some obstacles it must go over in order to satisfy some of our wishes. Additionally, it calls for our attention to be directed at problems like availability, security, load balancing, fault tolerance, and security (Bhaskar et al., 2012). Effective load balancing will improve a computer system's overall cloud performance.

Numerous techniques have been devised to enhance the current solutions in order to address new issues because there is no universal mechanism that can adapt to all conceivable varied conditions (Bhaskar et al., 2012). Each technique, though, offers a benefit in a certain context, not in all others. The load balancing method with active monitoring solution has been developed to reduce overall response time and data center processing time (Amit & Kariyani, 2013).

In this work, a load balancing method with active monitoring was suggested to optimally distribute requests and tasks to all of the virtual machines while taking into account how much CPU each virtual machine uses.

2. LITERATURE REVIEW

"Current global trends in computing include the cloud computing. It is a contemporary method of remotely accessing resources by using the power of the internet and WAN. It is a cutting-edge method and solution that seeks to offer high availability, adaptability, cost savings, and on-demand scaling (Doddini Probhuling, 2013; Kaur, 2012).

According to (Kashyap & Viradiya, 2014), cloud computing is a widely used technique that has given rise to new technology. And that promises higher scalability, better availability, and lower administration and maintenance expenses while offering its consumers a lot of computation and data storage capacity. According to (Kaur, 2012)'s explanation of cloud computing, this dynamic stability and wide range of resource support are also meant to be made possible.

The core idea behind cloud computing at the moment is to provide resources, such virtual machines, as services on demand (Ahmed, 2012; Soumya, 2013).

Cloud Computing and Virtualization

The three (three) fundamental components of a cloud computing system are clients, datacenters, and distributed servers, each of which has a certain function and behaves in a particular way (Bhaskar et al., 2012).

Load Balancing Algorithm in Cloud Computing

To achieve the greatest resource usage, the quickest reaction time, the fastest throughput, and to minimize overload, load balancing "often distributes duty among a number of computers or other devices across network links" (Amandeep et al., 2014; Panwar, 2015; Rastogi et al., 2014).

Figure 1. The environment of a simple cloud

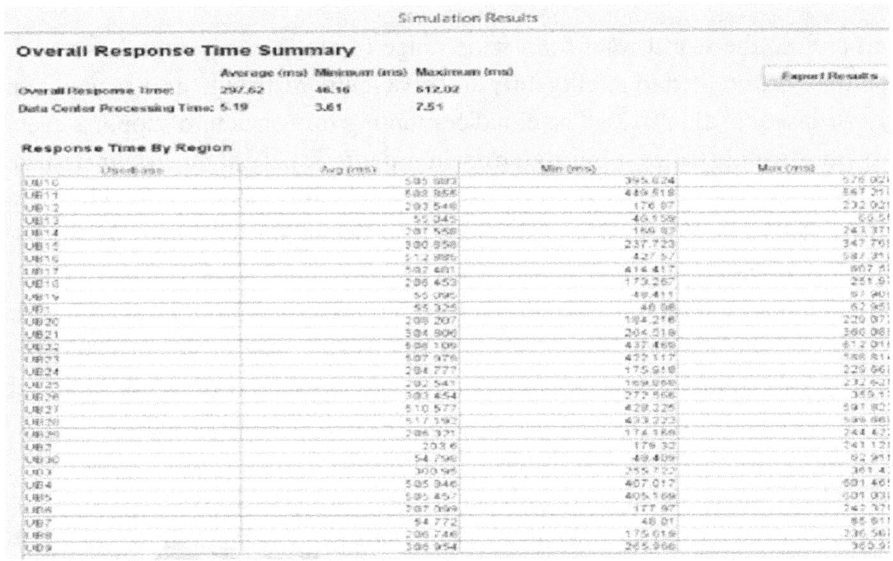

Figure 2. Architecture for cloud computing (Zaouch & Benabbou, 2015)

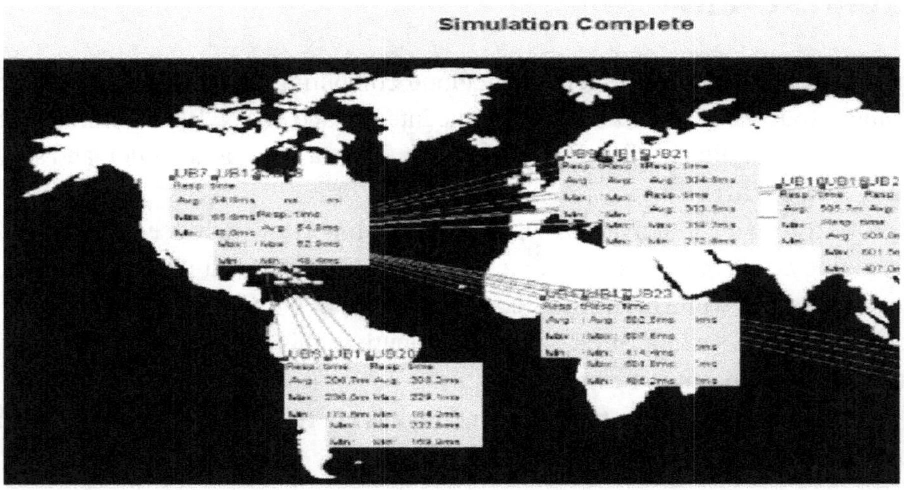

According to (Zaouch & Benabbou, 2015), "Load balancing is a crucial and useful concept in cloud computing, and it helps to make the best use of the resources." It is therefore used to lower resource utilization. According to Figure 4 (Bhaskar et al., 2012), a cloud computing system consists of three parts.

Round Robin Scheduling Algorithm

Before directing the initial request to that virtual machine, the data center controller randomly selected one of the virtual machines in the round robin load balancer (Sharma et al., 2012). circulates the requests to the VMs in a circle as well. The selected virtual machine is then moved to the bottom of the virtual machine list after receiving the request assigned to it.

Figure 3. A cloud computing system is made up of three parts

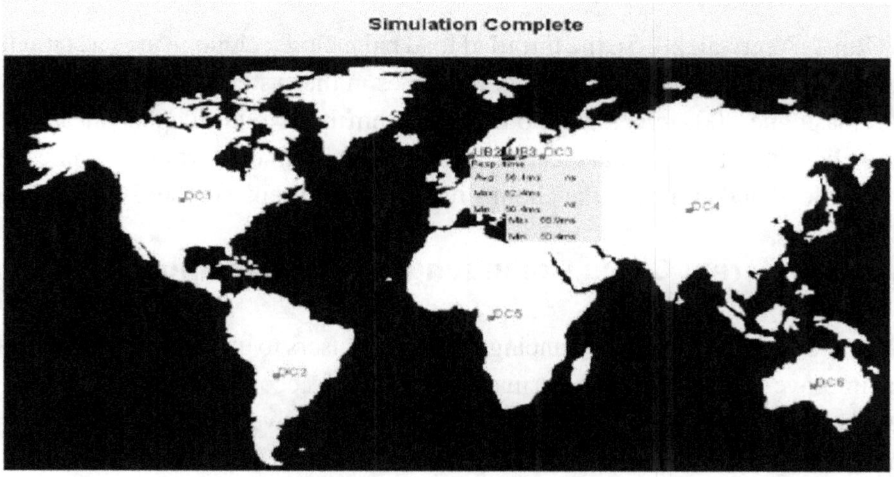

Figure 4. A cloud computing solution is made up of three elements (Bhaskar et al., 2012)

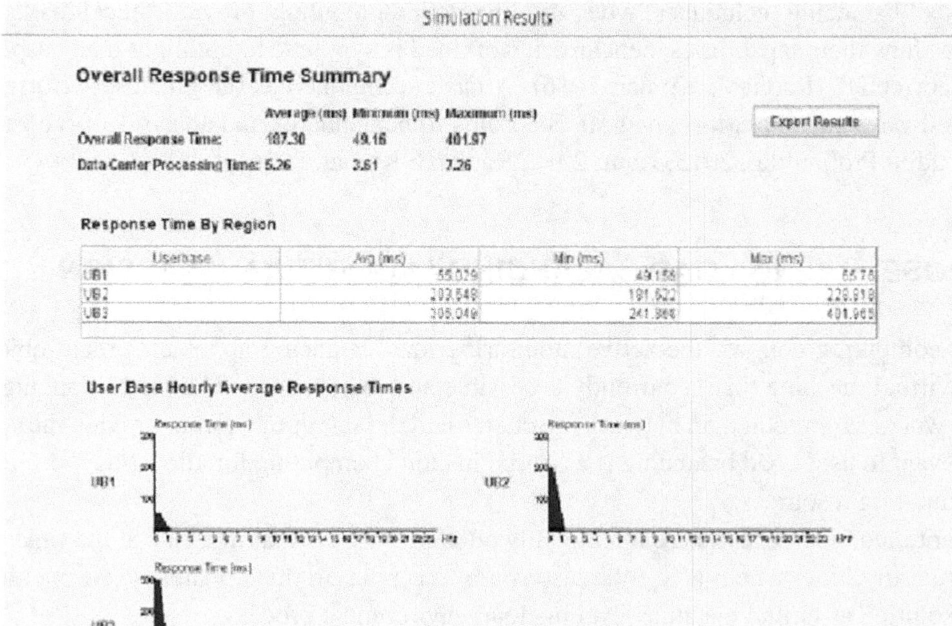

Algorithm for (Optimal) Active Monitoring Load Balancing

Dynamic load balancing is used for active monitoring. The number of requests presently assigned to each virtual machine is one of the data that are logged when a request to allocate a new virtual machine is received. The amount of requests that are now being distributed across the VMs is tracked using the active monitoring load balancing approach, which was created by the (Berwa, 2015).

Algorithm for Throttling Load Balancing

According to (Raj & Agarwal, 2015), the throttled load balancing technique uses a static load balancing algorithm. Here, the index values of the virtual machines in the system are first analyzed.

The (Wickremasinghe, 2009) created a throttled algorithm that is totally dependent on virtual machines. In this case, the client asks the load balancer to check out the pertinent virtual machine first since it can readily access that load and carry out the client's requests (Wickremasinghe, 2009).

An Analysis of Different Cloud Computing Load Balancing Algorithms

(Mallick, 2015) asserts that good load balancing encourages users to utilize resources wisely in response to demand and improves overall cloud performance. The cloud, according (Mallick, 2015), is "the fastest developing technology in the IT industry and a new method of delivery for the services on a pay-per-use basis." Understanding the various load balancing algorithms is vital (Mallick, 2015).

An Effective Load Balancing Method in a Cloud Environment

Effective load balancing techniques, when used to cloud computing, provide "benchmarks for the algorithms to show their capabilities, benchmark workload is synthetic to highlight many aspects of load balancing correctly" (Radha & Kumar, 2016). A basic technique has the greatest performance of all implemented ways and is platform neutral, according to benchmarks and analyses of the various algorithms (Doddini Probhuling, 2013; Kaur, 2012; Radha & Kumar, 2016).

3. PROPOSED USING LOAD BALANCING ALGORITHM VM-ASSIGN

In a cloud computing context, the active monitoring load balancing approach's main objective is to locate the virtual machine that is currently accessible and least loaded. The load balancing algorithm essentially works as a middleman between the clients and the server in order to provide the services that the clients want to use. Load balancing is essential in cloud computing for allocating workloads among diverse computing resources.

The client incoming requests are intelligently allotted at the virtual machine at the time of the least loaded virtual machine, which is not the last virtual machine, in this updated active monitoring load balancing solution at virtual machine level in cloud environment process.

The picture below shows the key designs of the enhanced active monitoring load balancing method. How to maximize the usage of your computer's resources by using the load balancing strategy. to show how to utilize the load balancing system at the virtual machine level in a cloud environment and to have easy access to resources.

The following table shows how many users are seeking to access cloud computing resources using the enhanced a load balancing method with active monitoring approach at the virtual machine level: Before making a request to the virtual machine, a client must submit it to the data center controller. In this case, the data center controller will also send the request to the load balancing method with active monitoring. After that, the virtual machine table is kept up to date using a load balancing method with active monitoring.

Figure 5. The proposed VM-assign algorithm's flow

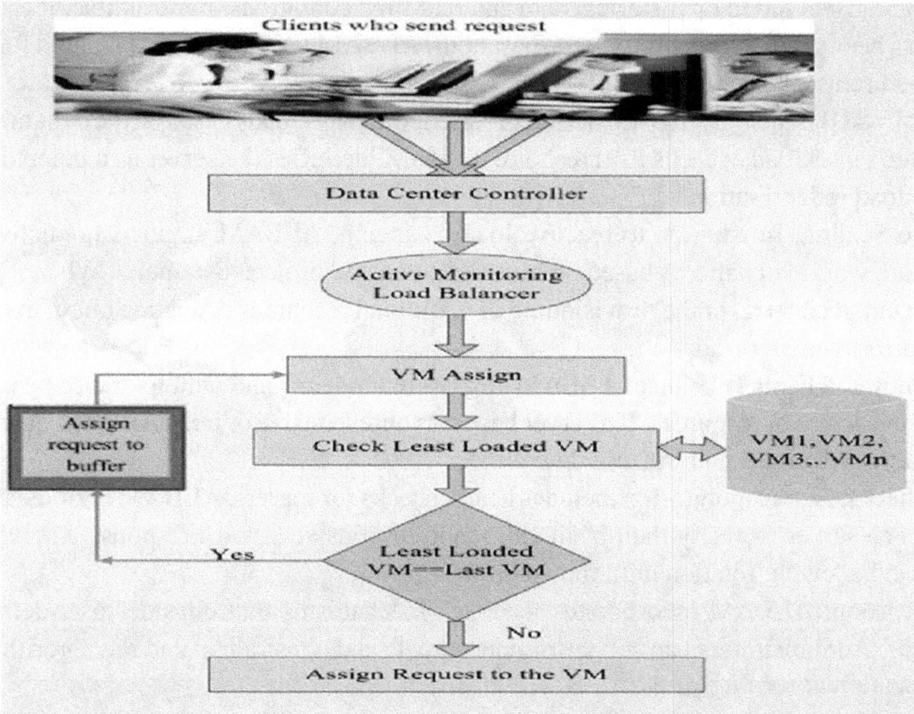

The virtual machine with the lowest load is chosen for execution. The virtual machine that was available in this instance with the lowest load was chosen. If the chosen virtual machine was not utilized in the previous iteration, assign it to the tasks or requests; otherwise, store them in a buffer until the next virtual machine with the least amount of load is identified. The author proposed improved throttled load balancing in cloud computing (Mulat et al., 2022). The researchers used machine learning for task scheduling in cloud computing for resource allocation and security (Bal et al., 2022).

Load balancing is a crucial component in cloud environments to ensure that resources are distributed efficiently among servers or virtual machines to optimize performance, minimize downtime, and enhance active monitoring. Several load balancing algorithms are employed in cloud environments, each with its own advantages and use cases. In this context, I'll describe a load balancing algorithm that enhances active monitoring in a cloud environment.

Algorithm Name: Adaptive Load Balancing with Active Monitoring (ALBAM)

Objective: The ALBAM algorithm aims to improve resource allocation and enhance active monitoring in a cloud environment to ensure high availability, efficient resource utilization, and responsiveness to changing workloads.

Algorithm Description

Workload Monitoring: ALBAM continuously monitors the workload of each server or virtual machine in the cloud environment. This monitoring includes metrics such as CPU utilization, memory usage, network traffic, and response times.

Dynamic Thresholds: ALBAM uses dynamic thresholds for workload metrics. These thresholds are continuously adjusted based on historical data and real-time conditions. For example, if a server's CPU utilization has been consistently high for the past hour, ALBAM will lower the threshold for that metric, triggering load redistribution sooner.

Proactive Load Balancing: ALBAM actively redistributes workloads based on the dynamic thresholds. When a server's workload exceeds its threshold, ALBAM identifies the server as a potential bottleneck and initiates load redistribution.

Predictive Scaling: In addition to reactive load balancing, ALBAM employs predictive scaling. It forecasts future workload patterns based on historical data and projected demand. When it anticipates a surge in demand, it can trigger the provisioning of additional resources or scaling out of existing servers to prevent performance degradation.

Redundancy and Fault Tolerance: ALBAM ensures redundancy and fault tolerance by maintaining a reserve pool of servers or resources. If a server becomes unresponsive or fails, ALBAM quickly redirects traffic to healthy resources, minimizing downtime.

Health Checks: Active monitoring includes health checks for servers. ALBAM periodically sends test requests to each server to verify their availability and responsiveness. Unresponsive servers are taken out of the load balancing rotation until they recover.

Feedback Loop: ALBAM incorporates feedback mechanisms that consider user-defined policies and objectives. Administrators can set performance goals and constraints, and the algorithm optimizes resource allocation accordingly.

Benefits of ALBAM

Improved Performance: ALBAM ensures that resources are allocated optimally, preventing overutilization or underutilization of servers, which leads to improved application performance.

Enhanced Active Monitoring: By continuously adjusting thresholds and proactively redistributing workloads, ALBAM enhances the cloud environment's active monitoring capabilities, enabling early detection of performance issues.

Scalability: The predictive scaling feature allows the cloud environment to adapt to changing workloads efficiently.

High Availability: ALBAM's redundancy and fault tolerance mechanisms minimize downtime and ensure high availability of services.

Customization: Administrators can customize ALBAM to align with specific performance objectives and policies.

4. RESULT AND DISCUSSION

We can calculate the total response time and the overall data center processing time of the various load balancing strategies after several successful trials using the CloudAnalystsimulator tool and settings.

We used a variety of instances to better understand how the load balancing algorithms worked:

Figure 6. Simulation result for case one

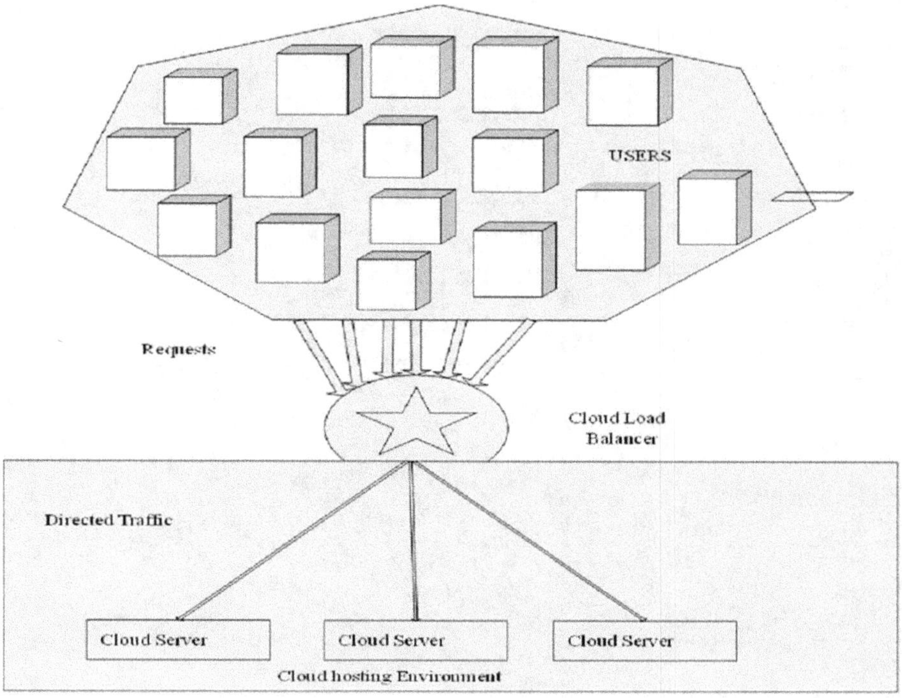

Figure 7. Results of the simulation with 3 UBs and 6 DC

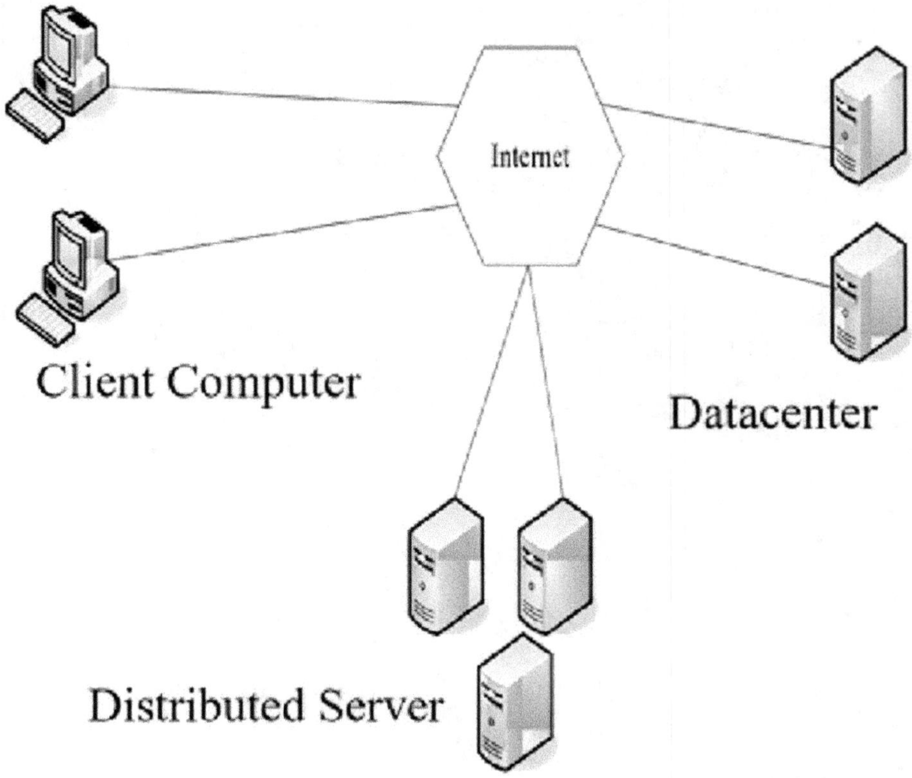

Figure 8. Simulation result for 30 UBs

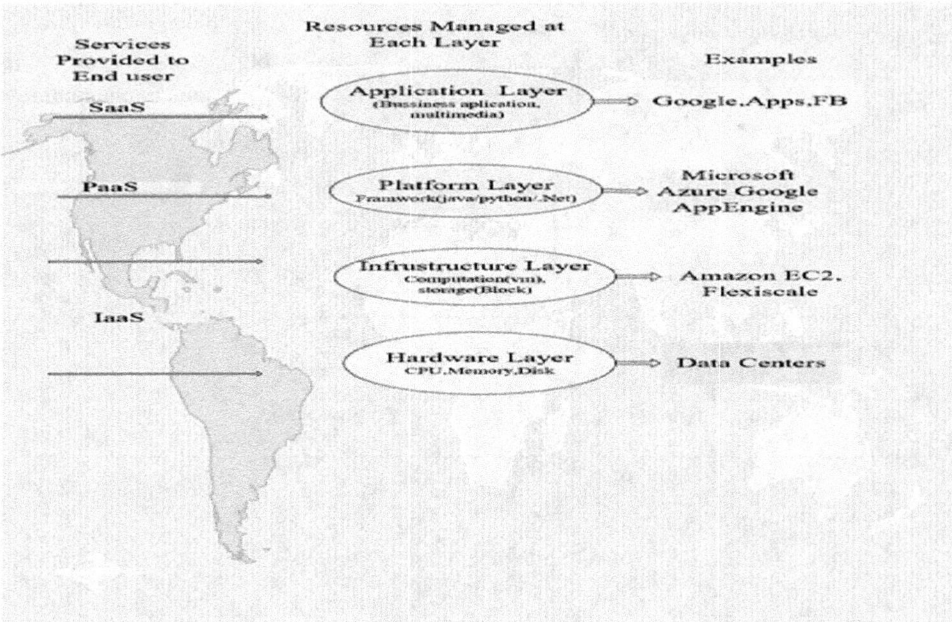

Figure 9. Overall response time analysis 30 UBs

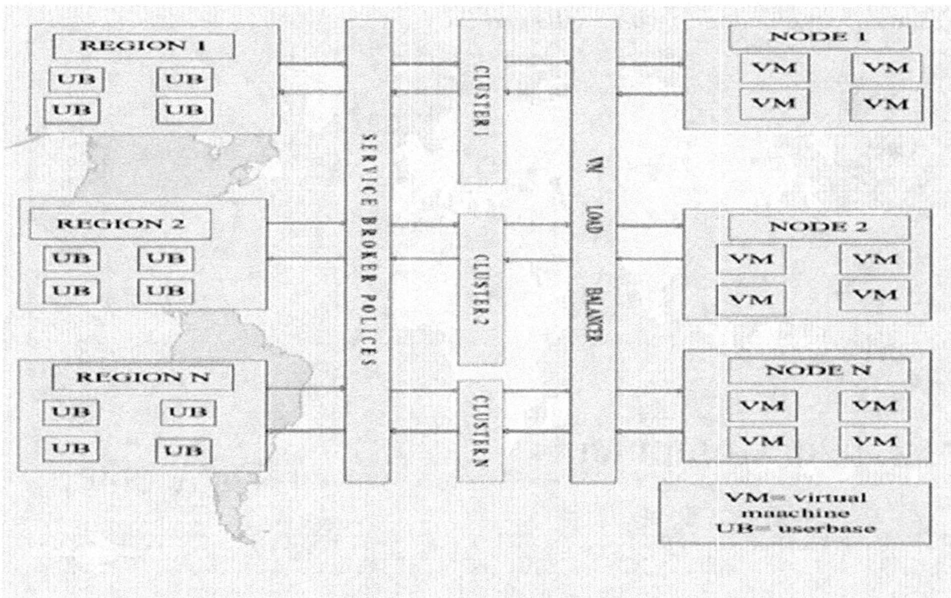

5. CONCLUSION

In this study, we began by defining the specific research question and arguing that a literature evaluation was necessary to ascertain whether a load balancing approach will be used in a cloud computing context. It looked at how load balancing strategies are now being used in the context of cloud computing.

Results are produced by analyzing different load balancing strategies using the CloudAnalyst simulator application. By avoiding the complexity of the load balancing method with active monitoring strategy at the time that the amount of requests or tasks on a virtual machine increases, it is feasible to assess the effective usage of virtual machines. Requests from users are then forwarded to the least-loaded virtual machine among those that are reachable utilizing the cloudsim simulator. If the virtual machine's capacity to receive requests had been achieved, the cloudsim simulation utilized to assign requests to a buffer.

The study used qualitative evaluation and analytic methodologies. which contrast the features of the existing load balancing method, the suggested load balancing algorithm, and the intended result. Two indices of qualitative performance are the size of the entire response time and the data center's overall processing time. Theoretically, this kind of analysis may include any relevant logical support.

In general, the active monitoring load balancing method becomes more difficult as the number of requests and actions on a virtual machine rises. We want to offer a straightforward, effective active monitoring load balancing solution in a cloud computing environment by providing the modification and usage notion of this approach.

This research study is crucial given the benefits of using cloud computing resources for us. In a cloud environment, we all require load balancing techniques at the virtual machine level in order to access the resources. It also gave us our first introduction to load balancing methods and the cloud computing environment.

REFERENCES

Ahmed, T. Y. (2012). Analytic Study of Load Balancing Techniques Using Tool Cloud Analyst. *International Journal of Engineering Research and Applications, 2*(2). www.ijera.com

Amandeep, Yadav, & Mohammad. (2014). Different Strategies for Load Balancing in Cloud Computing Environment: A Critical Study. *International Journal of Scientific Research Engineering & Technology, 3*(1).

Amit & Kariyani. (2013). Allocation Of Virtual Machines In Cloud Computing Using Load Balancing Algorithm. *International Journal of Computer Science and Information Technology & Security, 3*(1).

Bal, P. K., Mohapatra, S. K., Das, T. K., Srinivasan, K., & Hu, Y. C. (2022). A joint resource allocation, security with efficient task scheduling in cloud computing using hybrid machine learning techniques. *Sensors (Basel), 22*(3), 1242. doi:10.339022031242 PMID:35161987

Benabbou, F. (2015). Load Balancing for Improved Quality of Service in the Cloud. *International Journal of Advanced Computer Science and Applications, 6*(7).

Berwa. (2015). *Load Balancing in Cloud Computing*. Department of Computer Science and Application, K.U., Kurukshetra, India.

Bhaskar, Deepu, & Shylaja. (2012). Dynamic Allocation Method For Efficient Load Balancing In Virtual Machines For Cloud Computing Environment. *Advanced Computing: An International Journal, 3*(5).

Calheiros, Ranjan, De Rose, & Buyya. (2009). *CloudSim: A Novel Framework for Modeling and Simulation of Cloud Computing Infrastructures and Services*. Academic Press.

Chaudhary, D., & Chhillar, R. S. (2013). A New Load Balancing Technique for Virtual Machine Cloud Computing Environment. Department of Computer Science and applications, M.D. University, Rohtak, Haryana, India. doi:10.5120/12114-8498

Daryapurkar, A. (2013). Efficient Load Balancing Algorithm in Cloud Environment. International Journal of Computer Science and Applications, 6(2).

Doddini Probhuling, L. (2013). Load Balancing Algorithms In Cloud Computing. *International Journal of Advanced Computer and Mathematical Sciences, 4*.

Faraahi & Goudarzi. (2014). Effective load balancing in cloud computing. *International Journal of Intelligent Information Systems*.

Gnanasundaram & Suresh. (2015). Optimal load balancing in cloud computing by efficient utilization of virtual machines. *International Journal of Advanced Technology in Engineering and Science, 3*(2).

Kashyap & Viradiya. (2014). A Survey of Various Load Balancing Algorithms In Cloud Computing. *International Journal of Scientific & Technology Research, 3*.

Kaur, J. (2012). Comparison of load balancing algorithms in a Cloud. *International Journal of Engineering Research and Applications*.

Ladani & Gupta. (2013). A Framework for Performance Analysis of Computing Clouds. *International Journal of Innovative Technology and Exploring Engineering, 2*(6).

Mahalle, Kaveri, & Chavan. (2013). Load Balancing on Cloud Data Centres. *Advanced Research in Computer Science and Software Engineering, 3*.

Mallick. (2015). A Comparative Study of Load Balancing Algorithms in Cloud Computing. *International Journal of Computer Applications, 117*(24).

Mulat, W. W., Mohapatra, S. K., Sathpathy, R., & Dhal, S. K. (2022, May). Improving Throttled Load Balancing Algorithm in Cloud Computing. In Proceedings of International Joint Conference on Advances in Computational Intelligence: IJCACI 2021 (pp. 369-377). Singapore: Springer Nature Singapore. 10.1007/978-981-19-0332-8_27

Panwar. (2015). A Comparative Study of Load Balancing Algorithms in Cloud Computing. *International Journal of Computer Applications, 117*(24).

Pasha, & Agarwal. (2014). Round Robin Approach for VM Load Balancing Algorithm in Cloud Computing Environment. *International Journal of Advanced Research in Computer Science and Software Engineering, 4*(5).

Preethi, B. (2014). Optimization of Resources in Cloud Computing Using Effective Load Balancing Algorithms. International Advanced Research Journal in Science, Engineering and Technology, 1(1).

Radha & Kumar. (2016). Efficient VM Load Balancing Algorithm for Dynamic Allocation of Resources in Cloud Computing Environment. *International Journal of Innovative Research in Computer and Communication Engineering, 4*(6).

Raj & Agarwal. (2015). Load Balancing Algorithm in Cloud Computing. *International Journal of Computer Applications, 132*(2).

Rastogi, Pasha, & Agarwal. (2014). Round Robin Approach for VM Load Balancing Algorithm in Cloud Computing Environment. *International Journal of Advanced Research in Computer Science and Software Engineering, 4*(5).

Sandip Patel. (2015). *CloudAnalyst A Survey of Load Balancing Policies*. Patel Department of Computer Engineering, Charusat University Changa, Gujarat, India.

Sharma, Sharma, & Sharma. (2012). *Efficient Load Balancing Algorithm in VM Cloud Environment*. Dept. of CSE Sri Sai College of Engineering & Technology, Badhani, Pathankot, Punjab, India.

Soumya. (2013). Response Time Minimization of Different Load Balancing Algorithms in Cloud Computing Environment. *Computer Applications, 69*(17).

Wickremasinghe, B. (2009). CloudAnalyst: A CloudSim-based Tool for Modelling and Analysis of Large Scale Cloud Computing Environments. Distributed Computing Project, Csse Dept., University of Melbourne.

Younis, H. J. (2015). *Efficient Load Balancing Algorithm in Cloud Computing*. Gaza Deanery of Post Graduate Studies Faculty of Information Technology.

Zaouch, A., & Benabbou, F. (2015). Load Balancing for Improved Quality of Service in the Cloud. *International Journal of Advanced Computer Science and Applications, 6*(7). doi:10.14569/IJACSA.2015.060724

Chapter 12
Implementation and Deployment of Privacy Preservation and Secure Data Storage Techniques in Cloud Computing

Priyanga Subbiah
https://orcid.org/0000-0002-2395-7492
SRM Institute of Science and Technology, India

Krishnaraj Nagappan
SRM Institute of Science and Technology, India

Kiran Bellam
Prairie View A&M University, USA

Preethiya Thandapani
https://orcid.org/0000-0003-3504-1884
SRM Institute of Science and Technology, India

ABSTRACT

Successful cloud computing (CC) lets businesses and people outsource data processing, storage, and access. CC has numerous advantages but new privacy and security risks. Data owners lose control over their data at external providers, making it subject to misuse, distribution, and access. The current data security method involves encryption. Encryption increases computing complexity, especially when data is dispersed throughout several CSP servers. Simple secrecy technologies include encryption and fragmentation. HSSOA-FEW is a hybrid sparrow search optimisation method for cloud security employing fragmentation and encryption. HSSOA-FEW holds data on CSP server with minimal encryption. HSSOA-FEW considers security and data storage. HSSOA-FEW also included sparrow search algorithm (SSA) with particle swarm optimisation. Additionally, HSSOA-FEW uses fused encryption and decryption. HSSOA-FEW controls and secures cloud servers. The suggested HSSOA-FEW system is tested extensively to improve performance. The experiments indicated HSSOA-FEW outperformed others.

DOI: 10.4018/979-8-3693-0593-5.ch012

INTRODUCTION

Cloud computing (CC) provides cloud users with a flexible resource that could be acquired and released on demand (Xie et al., 2021). Cloud users pay for the leased resource on a pay-as-you-go basis. Such pay-as-you-go strategy elastic and resource provisioning attracts research institutes or enterprises for running their workflow application on cloud at lower cost without the need of maintaining and purchasing any framework (Zhou et al., 2021). In CC, IT resource is frequently encapsulated as virtual machines (VMs). The running VM is named VM instances. Usually, cloud user wants to achieve the computational outcome of the workflow within a provided deadline at low implementation cost (Fattahi & Hasanipanah, 2021). In general, the more computational power a VM has, the high its price. To balance the runtime of a workflow and execution cost, task scheduling of a workflow onto VM instance is highly crucial for CC. But the flexible management of cloud resources and the complicated workflow structure makes them more challenging (Siddiqui & Raza, 2021). In CC platform, customers of cloud services don't need anything means not going into details about the execution and they access the data and complete the computing task with an Internet connection (Murlidhar et al., 2020). Throughout the access to the data and computing, the users don't know the location of the data or where the information is put away. Therefore, here the security issue stands up quickly. Data security in the CC is challenging when compared to the conventional data system (Rodríguez-Mazahua et al., 2021). Figure 1 defines the general overview of fragmentation process.

Figure 1. General overview of fragmentation process

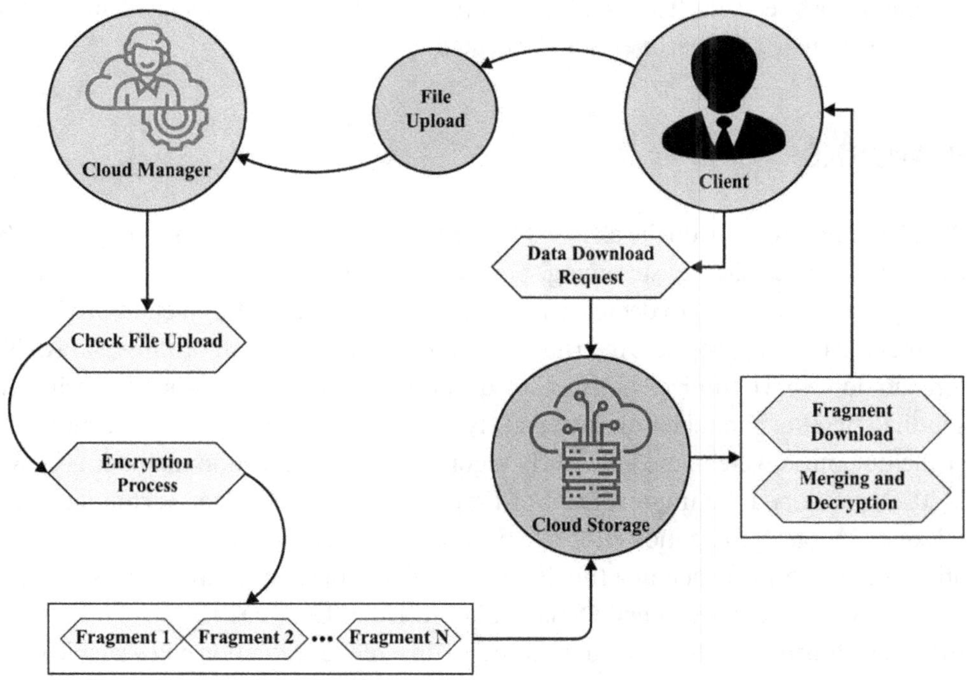

Two natural protection approaches were developed for satisfying confidentiality requirements fragmentation and encryption (Bhatawdekar et al., 2021). Encryption contains in encrypting the information beforehand outsourcing them to external provider for making them intelligible to the users who hold the decryption keys and protect them from unauthorized eyes (involving the provider itself). Even though symmetric and asymmetric encryption schemes are adopted for performance reason, most proposal assumes the adoption of symmetric encryption (Bahache, 2018). Encryption can be imposed at distinct levels of granularity: column, table, individual cell, and tuple. Encrypting at the level of table indicates that the entire relationship should be returned to the user for access, which requires substantial transmission and leaves the entire query processing work to the user (Zeng et al., 2021). Fragmentation comprises splitting the attribute of relation R producing dissimilar vertical views (fragments) so the sensitive relation is characterized by a relation constraint c once the attribute in c doesn't appear in the fragments, and same (openly accessible) fragment could not be combined via nonauthorized user. It should be noted that singleton constraint is enforced properly only if the corresponding attribute doesn't appear in any fragment (Singh & Choudhary, 2021). However, Fragmentation could be considered the case of potential relation amongst attributes (that can enable linking or present inferences).

This paper presents a hybrid sparrow search optimization algorithm based on fragmentation with encryption (HSSOA-FEW) technique for cloud security. The presented HSSOA-FEW technique effectually saves the data on CSP server with minimal quantity of encryption. The presented HSSOA-FEW technique considered the security and data storage aspects. In addition, the HSSOA-FEW system was mainly dependent upon the hybridization of sparrow search algorithm (SSA) with particle swarm optimization (PSO) algorithm. Moreover, the HSSOA-FEW technique employs a fused approach for encryption and decryption processes. The presented HSSOA-FEW technique can manage the cloud server and accomplishes security. To ensure the improved performance of the presented HSSOA-FEW system, an extensive range of experiments are executed.

RELATED WORKS

Asl et al. (2018) attempts to develop the efficient factor for Tajareh limestone mine explosion (viz., blasthole, burden, hole length, spacing, stemming, powder factor, sub-drilling, Geological Strength Index (GSI), and charge in every delay) to decrease flyrock and inappropriate fragmentation. Meanwhile, the experimental method is not appropriate interms of accuracy, using firefly algorithms and ANN, rock, and flyrock fragmentation were optimized and predicted, correspondingly. Afterward gathering information and choosing the effecting parameter on rock and flyrock fragmentation, an ANN technique was introduced, later the outcomes were named as firefly algorithm for optimization method. Issa, M. and Abd Elaziz, M., 2020, developed the improvement of Fragmented Local Aligner Technique (FLAT) based on improved Ions Motion Optimization (IMO) to produce the longest common consecutive subsequence (LCCS) with effective performance in a timely manner. The projected technique was tested to find the LCCS amongst surface glycoprotein and Orflab poly-protein of COVID19.

Lotfi (2019) developed a new hybrid model based on differential evolution and variable neighborhood search (DEVNS) mechanisms for resolving DAP problems. The presented model's aim is to surge the performance of DE by employing crossover operators and effective selection. Furthermore, the presented method aims to enhance the solution by means of VNS approach. Through VNS, a more promising part of search space is removed. Finally, the presented DEVNS discovers the searching space through

DE and satisfies exploitation via neighborhood searching model. Huang et al. provide an auto tuning mechanism, named cat swarm optimization (CSO), to forecast rock fragmentation. CSO is a powerful and robust metaheuristic approach stimulated by the behavior of cats; it can be made up of two search techniques: tracing and seeking that is combined using mixture ratio parameter. To assess the efficacy of the presented algorithm, its attained outcomes are compared to the PSO approach. In this work, two forms of PSO and CSO models, involving linear and power forms, have been proposed.

Halim (2020) introduced a hybrid model based on Overlap Layout Consensus for the DNA fragment assembly, whereby Recentering and Restarting GA (RRGA) with incorporated PALS are exploited as evolutionary operators. The quality of the presented study is measured by means of the count of contigs and overlap scores. Selvakumar and Manivannan developed a novel technique for overcoming the disadvantages and enhancement in the quality of service. The presented technique holds the technique of reactive and proactive along with the metaheuristic nature inspired optimization method named Jellyfish Search Optimization (JSO). Mehrdanesh et al. (2021) attempts to perform effective technologies for forecasting rock fragmentation because of blasting in open pit mines through the efficient parameter. Since rock, fragmentation prediction is complicated and very difficult, and because of that different AI-based technologies like SVM, ANN classification, and regression tree have been preferred for the modeling.

THE PROPOSED MODEL

In this study, a new HSSOA-FEW techniques have been developed for effective cloud storage and security. The presented HSSOA-FEW techniques effectually save the data on CSP server with minimal quantity of encryption. The presented HSSOA-FEW techniques considered the security and data storage aspects.

Design of HSSOA

The HSSOA-FEW techniques is mainly based on the hybridization of SSA with PSO algorithm. For addressing the problems of present hyperparameter optimization method that simply get trapped in local optima solution, we integrate SSA to PSO, called HSSOA, by using displacement and velocity equation in PSO according to SSA and it is further explained in Xue and Shen (2020). Amongst them, individuals with higher fitness values act as discoverers and other individuals act as followers. Simultaneously, a specific proportion of individuals in the population is chosen for early warning and detection. Once they found any danger, it searches for alternatives as follows:

$$X = \begin{Bmatrix} x_1^1 & x_1^2 & \cdots & x_1^m \\ x_2^1 & x_2^2 & \cdots & x_2^m \\ \cdots & \cdots & \cdots & \cdots \\ x_n^1 & x_n^2 & \cdots & x_n^m \end{Bmatrix} \tag{1}$$

In Eq. (1), m characterizes the dimension of the variable to be enhanced, and n indicates the individual count. m depending on the dimension of the search space. n characterizes the size of the population. Generally, a larger n results in higher optimization accuracy and population diversity however, the iteration speed is slower. The fitness value of each sparrow is formulated by Eq. (2):

$$F = \begin{Bmatrix} f(x_1^1 & x_1^2 & \cdots & x_1^m) \\ f(x_2^1 & x_2^2 & \cdots & x_2^m) \\ \cdots & \cdots & \cdots & \cdots \\ f(x_n^1 & x_n^2 & \cdots & x_n^m) \end{Bmatrix} \tag{2}$$

Now, f indicates the fitness values. F comprises the fitness of each individual in the whole population. Generally, the discoverer has higher energy reserve and are accountable to search for food-rich area. They offer foraging region and direction for every follower. The levels of energy reserves depend on fitness values of all the individuals.

Once the predator is identified, sparrow begins to chirp for sending alarm signal. When the alarm values are larger than the safer value, discoverer takes follower to new safer region. Discoverer and follower dynamically change. If the best source of food is found, sparrow becomes discoverers, however, the percentage of discoverer and follower in the whole population remains same. In another word, when a sparrow becomes a discoverer, other sparrows become followers.

Followers with lesser food have inadequate foraging positions among the whole population. The hungry follower is highly possible for flying towards another place for getting food.

In the foraging process, followers could often seek the discoverer who gives the better food or forage nearby the discoverers. Simultaneously, to rise the food reserve, some followers might continuously monitor discoverer for the food resource. If they are aware of danger, individuals at the edge of population rapidly move towards the safe region for best position. Individuals positioned in the middle of population would arbitrarily fly to another sparrow.

Discoverer is accountable for 1020% of the whole population. Position update of the discoverer is provided in the following:

$$X_{i,j}^{s+1} = \begin{cases} X_{i,j}^{s}.\exp\left(-\dfrac{i}{\alpha \cdot s_{\max}}\right), & R < T \\ X_{i,j}^{s} + g \cdot L, & R \geq T \end{cases} \tag{3}$$

Whereas j and s indicate the *i-th* sparrow, *j-th* dimension, and s-ith iteration, correspondingly, X characterizes position data. $s$max indicates the maximal amount of iterations. $\alpha(\alpha \in (0,1])$ represents a random value. $R(R \in [0,1])$ and $T(T \in [0.5,1])$ characterize the warning and safety values, correspondingly, g denotes an arbitrary value of uniform distribution. l characterizes a $1 \times m$ matrixes, and every component in the matrix is 1. Commonly the large the value of s, the best the optimization effects; but more time was required. The probability of individuals being scared is based on T.

Each sparrow accepts discoverer as are follower. The new position updating equation in SSA is shown below:

$$X_{i,j}^{s+1} = \begin{cases} g \cdot \exp\left(\dfrac{x_w^s - x_{i_j}^{s_i}}{i^2}\right), & i > n/2 \\ X_P^{s+1} + \left|X_{i,j} - X_P^{s+1}\right| \cdot A^+ \cdot L, & i \le n/2 \end{cases} \tag{4}$$

Now, X_w indicates the worst location. The study shows that Eq. (4) has information overflow problem created by extreme exponent if $i>n/2$ the solution values are larger. For instance, when X_{sw}=5000, $X_{i,j}^s = 1000$, i=4, $X_{i,j}^s = g \times \exp(250)$.

To resolve these problems and increase the global searching capability, we integrate Eq. (4) with the displacement and velocity equation in PSO. The novel position upgrades of followers are given below:

$$V_{i,j}^{s+1} = \omega \cdot V_{i,j}^s + c_1 \cdot r_1 \cdot \left(B_{i,j}^s - X_{i,j}^s\right) + c_2 \cdot r_2 \cdot \left(B_{g,j}^s - X_{i,j}^s\right) \tag{5}$$

$$X_{i,j}^{s+1} = \begin{cases} X_{i,j}^s + V_{i,j}^{s+1}, & i > n/2 \\ X_P^{s+1} + \left|X_{i,j} - X_P^{s+1}\right| \cdot A^+ \cdot L, & i \le n/2 \end{cases} \tag{6}$$

Now V refers to the speed. $\omega(\omega \in [0,1])$ indicates inertia weight. c_1 and c_2 specifies learning factor that usually takes value of 04. r_1 and r_2 indicates random number within [0,1]. Bi $_i$ndicate the past optimum solution of *i-th* sparrows. B_g represents the global optimum solution for whole population. X_p denotes the optimal location taken by the discoverer. A *c*haracterizes a 1×m *m*atrixes, and every component in the matrixes is 1 or -1, and $A^+ = A^T(AA^T)^{-1}$. ω shows non-negative. Generally, if it is larger, the global searching capability becomes stronger; if it is smaller, the local searching capability becomes stronger. c_1 and c_2 indicates the individual and social learning factors, correspondingly. Nandar's study shows that suitable solution is attained while c_1 and c_2 are constant; generally, c_1=c_2=2. Figure 2 depicts the steps involved in SSOA.

Eq. (5) refers to the speed updating equation. Eq. (6) is generated by adding the speed updating equation to the location updating equation of follower. This development resolves the overflow dataset problems and enhances the search speed. It allows HSSOA to seek hyperparameter optimization in a satisfactory time.

The position updating of vigilante is given below:

$$X_{i,j}^{s+1} = \begin{cases} B_{g,j}^s + \beta \cdot | X_{i,j}^s - B_{g,j}^s |, f_i > f_g \\ X_{i,j}^s + k \cdot \left(\dfrac{\left|X_{i,j}^{s_i} - X_w^s\right|}{(f_i - f_w) + \varepsilon}\right), f_i \le f_g \end{cases} \tag{7}$$

In Eq. (7), X_w indicates the worst location. β denotes the variables to control step length. It is an arbitrary value which follows the uniform distribution. k represents a random value within [0,1]. f_i denotes the fitness values of present sparrow f_g and h indicates global best and worst fitness values, correspondingly, ε represents constant to prevent zero from the denominator. The SSA part involves the location computation of vigilantes, discoverers, and followers. The PSO part evaluates the location of follower if i>$n/2$. The phases of HSSOA are given below.

Initially, the early population is arbitrarily produced. Next, a fitness function is defined for evaluating the fitness of all the individuals and upgrading the better solution. Next, the population is classified into discoverer and follower according to the fitness for updating the position of discoverer and follower. When i>n/2, the PSO part is utilized for calculating the location of follower. Then, vigilantes are arbitrarily produced for updating the location. Lastly, the global optimum solution is evaluated for determining whether the ending criteria are satisfied. The abovementioned steps are iterated until an individual meets the end criteria. The individual who meets the end criteria is regarded as the better solution for HSSOA.

Figure 2. Steps involved in SSOA

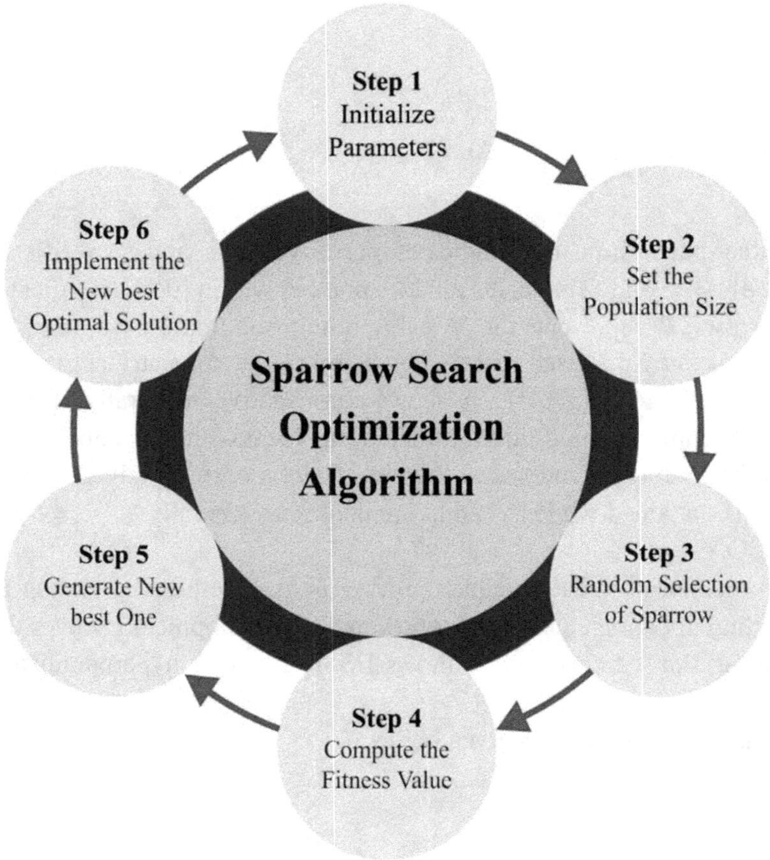

Process Involved in HSSOA-Based Fragmentation

The presented HSSOA-FEW technique considered the security and data storage aspects. In addition, the HSSOA-FEW technique is mainly based on the hybridization of SSA with PSO algorithm. The storage approaches are frequently constrained by many real limitations or restrictions namely data integrity, storage capacity off-site backup, influences of storage devices, and storage security. Such limitations must be inevitably taken into consideration, Liu, Fan, et al., 2016. The constraint is briefly discussed in the following:

1. During storing, novel data and backup files were preserved that were similar. In a realistic storage method, every inseparable data file (involving the backup file) must be allocated to single server.
2. To inseparable data files f_i, the count of backups shouldn't be lesser than the number $L(f_i)$ to backup with similar security level. These constraints are formulated by $\sum_{j=1}^{N} sign(Y_{ij}) \geq L(f_i)$.
3. The data files f_i and backups must be allocated that are saved at multiple servers in various locations betwixt one another. Such constraints are reflected through the inequality $\sum_{j=1}^{N} sign(Y_{ij}) \geq L(f_i)$.
4. If data files f_i was allocated that saved from the server s_j, the presented storage space in s_j must be sufficient for storing the allocated data file with reliability. These constraints are formulated by $(f_i) \leq R(Y_{ij})$.

From the abovementioned, the multi-objective optimization technique for enormous data storage is expressed in the following:

$$\min \zeta(F,S,t) = \zeta_s(F,t) + \zeta_m(F) + \zeta_c(F)$$

$$= \sum_{i=1}^{M} \sum_{j=1}^{N} C(s_j, L(f_i)) X(f_i, s_j) \cdot t$$

$$+ \sum_{k=1}^{M} \sum_{j=1}^{N} C_m X(f_k, s_j) d(s_u, s_j) + \sum_{k=1}^{M} \sum_{i=1}^{N} [X(f_k, s_i) \omega(s_i, s_m) d(s_i, s_m)]$$

$$\max \xi(F,S) = \prod_{i=1}^{M} \xi_r(f_i, s_j, s_b) = \prod_{i=1}^{M} (\sum_{j=1}^{N} R_t(s_j, s_b) \times R_E(s_j, s_b) \times R_S(s_j, s_b) \times P(Y_{ij}))$$

s.t. $L(f_i) \leq R(Y_{ij})$, $i=1,2,\ldots,M$; (8)

$f_i \leq A_{Y_{ij}}(s_j)$, $i=1,2,\ldots,M$;

$\sum_{j=1}^{N} \text{sign}(Y_{ij}) \geq L(f_i)$, $i=1,2,\ldots,M$;

$R(s_i) \in [0,1)$, $i=1,2,\ldots,M$;

$P(h) \in [0,1)$, $h=1,2,\ldots,K$.

The presented multi-objective optimization technique for reliable cloud storage is a constraint multi-objective group optimized problem that is too challenging to be resolved by conventional optimization techniques. Therefore, the HSSOA-FEW technique is employed in this study.

Encryption and Decryption

In this study, the HSSOA-FEW technique employs a fused approach for encryption and decryption processes. Afterward finishing the HSSOA, the fused encryption and decryption systems are performed for the enhancement of data security from the clouds. In the FED method, firstly the procedure of encrypts can be performed that converts the original information of plaintext to respective ASCII code values and later produces a key to encrypt cipher texts. In order to decryption technique, it can be vice versa of encrypting that recovers the original information from the cipher text via created key.

RESULTS AND DISCUSSION

This section inspects the fragmentation and security performance of the HSSOA-FEW model under different aspects.

Table 1 and Figure 3 provide an average replication cost (ARC) saving of the HSSOA-FEW model for increase in number of nodes. The results denoted that the HSSOA-FEW model has attained better performance with lower ARC values under all architectures. For instance, on three tier architecture, the HSSOA-FEW model has attained reduced ARC of 21.70% whereas the greedy, DROPS, and APSDRDO models have reached increased ARC of 69.75%, 25.39%, and 23.27% respectively. At the same time, on D-cell architecture, the HSSOA-FEW technique has gained lesser ARC of 19.62% whereas the greedy, DROPS, and APSDRDO systems have obtained superior ARC of 74.45%, 21.74%, and 20.57% correspondingly.

Figure 3. ARC analysis of HSSOA-FEW approach under distinct count of nodes

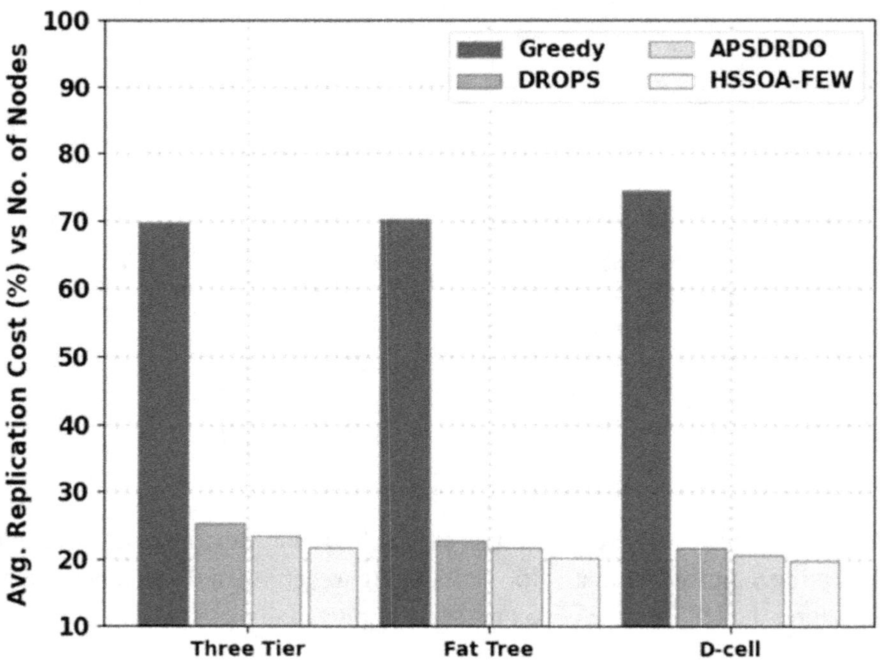

Table 1. ARC analysis of HSSOA-FEW approach under distinct count of nodes

Architecture	Greedy	DROPS	APSDRDO	HSSOA-FEW
Three Tier	69.75	25.39	23.27	21.70
Fat Tree	70.21	22.63	21.74	20.13
D-cell	74.45	21.74	20.57	19.62

Table 2 and Figure 4 give an ARC saving of the HSSOA-FEW systems for increase in distinct storage capacity. The outcome demonstrated that the HSSOA-FEW techniques has achieved better performance with reduced ARC values under all architectures. For sample, on three-tier architecture, the HSSOA-FEW systems has attained reduced ARC of 16.85% whereas the greedy, DROPS, and APSDRDO techniques have achieved enhanced ARC of 72.81%, 20.29%, and 17.88% correspondingly. Also, on D-cell architecture, the HSSOA-FEW model has accomplished lesser ARC of 18.25% whereas the greedy, DROPS, and APSDRDO methodology have gained maximal ARC of 70.73%, 22.19%, and 19.05% respectively.

Table 2. ARC analysis of HSSOA-FEW approach under distinct storage capacity

Architecture	Greedy	DROPS	APSDRDO	HSSOA-FEW
Three Tier	72.81	20.29	17.88	16.85
Fat Tree	69.73	21.39	20.63	18.94
D-cell	70.73	22.19	19.05	18.25

Figure 4. ARC analysis of HSSOA-FEW approach under distinct storage capacity

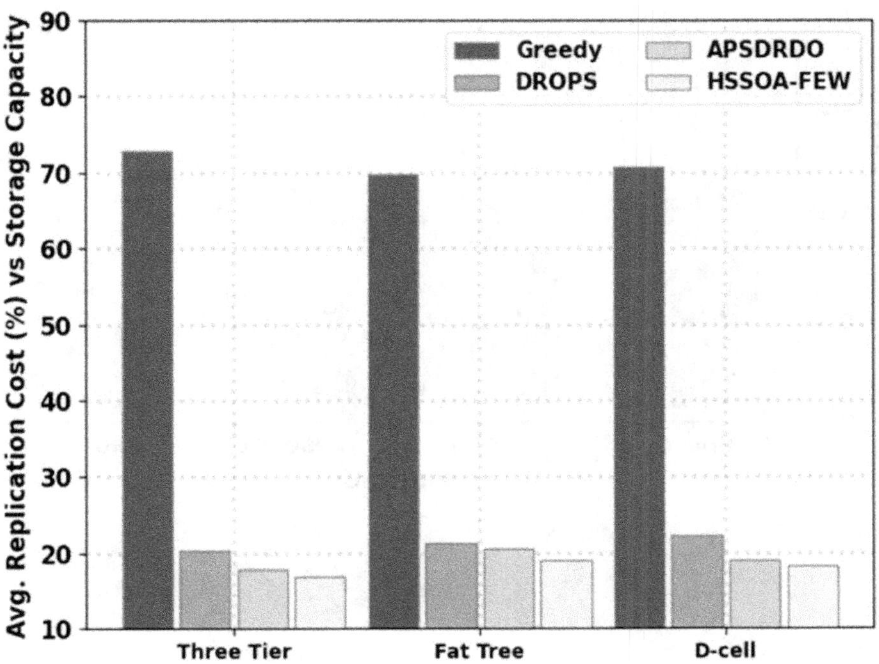

Table 3 and Figure 5 provides a comparative data access delay (DACD) examination of the HSSOA-FEW model with recent models. The experimental outcomes implied that the HSSOA-FEW model has shown effective performance with minimal DACD values under all files. For instance, with 30MB data, the HSSOA-FEW model has offered reduced DACD of 0.39ms whereas the greedy, DROPS, and APSDRDO models have obtained increased DACD of 0.66ms, 0.54ms, and 0.46ms respectively. Moreover, with 80MB data, the HSSOA-FEW technique has obtainable decreased DACD of 0.61ms whereas the greedy, DROPS, and APSDRDO techniques have acquired higher DACD of 1.09ms, 0.82ms, and 0.74ms correspondingly.

Table 3. DACD analysis of HSSOA-FEW algorithms with recent methodologies

Methods	30 (MB)	60 (MB)	80 (MB)
Greedy	0.66	0.82	1.09
DROPS	0.54	0.63	0.82
APSDRDO	0.46	0.57	0.74
HSSOA-FEW	0.39	0.48	0.61

Figure 5. DACD analysis of HSSOA-FEW algorithms with recent methodologies

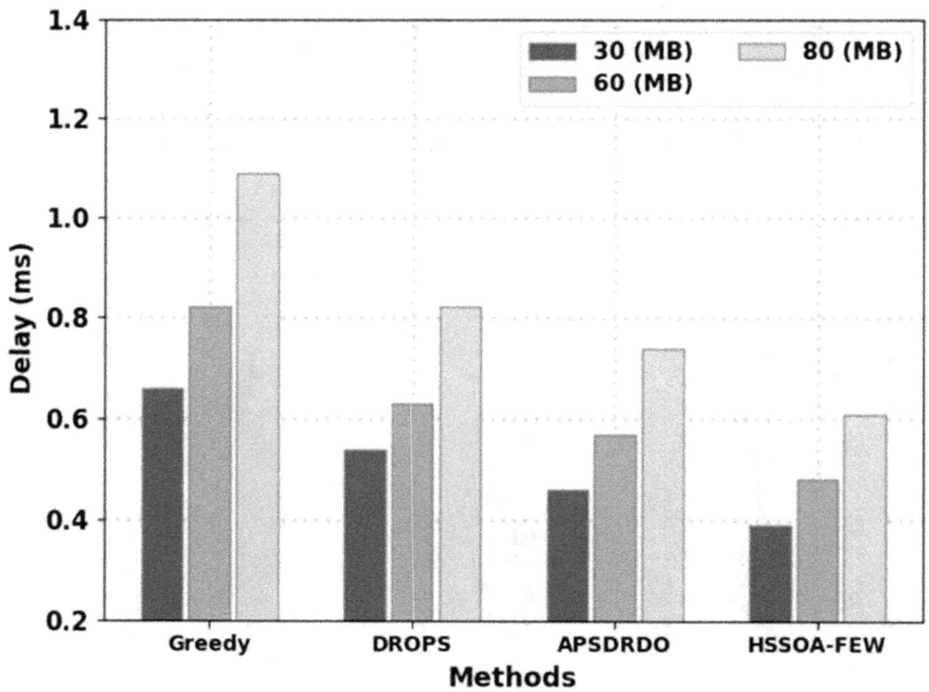

With respect to ET, the HSSOA-FEW model has obtained lower ET of 1159ms whereas the AES, RSA, Diffie Hellman, and Blowfish models have attained higher ET of 2566ms, 3973ms, 2109ms, and 1363ms respectively. In addition, interms of DT, the HSSOA-FEW approach has attained lesser DT of 2192ms whereas the AES, RSA, Diffie Hellman, and Blowfish techniques have obtained greater DT of 3348ms, 3678ms, 3411ms, and 2424ms correspondingly.

Therefore, these results affirmed that the HSSOA-FEW model has shown better results compared to recent models.

CONCLUSION

In this study, a novel HSSOA-FEW systems were established for effective cloud storage and security. The presented HSSOA-FEW techniques effectually save the data on CSP server with minimal quantity of encryption. The presented HSSOA-FEW techniques considered the security and data storage aspects. In addition, the HSSOA-FEW techniques is mainly based on the hybridization of SSA with PSO algorithm. Moreover, the HSSOA-FEW techniques employ a fused approach for encryption and decryption processes. The presented HSSOA-FEW techniques can manage the cloud server and accomplishes security. To ensure the enhanced performance of the projected HSSOA-FEW systems, an extensive range of experiments are implemented. The experimental outcomes stated enhancements of the HSSOA-FEW systems over other existing algorithms. In future, lightweight cryptographic solutions can be derived to enhance security in the cloud environment.

REFERENCES

Asl, P. F., Monjezi, M., Hamidi, J. K., & Armaghani, D. J. (2018). Optimization of flyrock and rock fragmentation in the Tajareh limestone mine using metaheuristics method of firefly algorithm. *Engineering with Computers*, *34*(2), 241–251. doi:10.100700366-017-0535-9

Bahache, A. N. E. (2018). *A Metaheuristic Based Approach for Solving the Index Selection Problem in Data Warehouses* [Doctoral dissertation]. FACULTE Mathématique et Informatique Departement D'Informatique.

Bhatawdekar, R. M., Armaghani, D. J., & Azizi, A. (2021). Review of Empirical and Intelligent Techniques for Evaluating Rock Fragmentation Induced by Blasting. In *Environmental Issues of Blasting* (pp. 21–39). Springer. doi:10.1007/978-981-16-8237-7_2

Fattahi, H., & Hasanipanah, M. (2021). Prediction of blast-induced ground vibration in a mine using relevance vector regression optimized by metaheuristic algorithms. *Natural Resources Research*, *30*(2), 1849–1863. doi:10.100711053-020-09764-7

Halim, Z. (2020). Optimizing the DNA fragment assembly using metaheuristic-based overlap layout consensus approach. *Applied Soft Computing*, *92*, 106256. doi:10.1016/j.asoc.2020.106256

Huang, J., Asteris, P. G., Manafi Khajeh Pasha, S., Mohammed, A. S., & Hasanipanah, M. (2020). A new auto-tuning model for predicting the rock fragmentation: A cat swarm optimization algorithm. *Engineering with Computers*, 1–12.

Issa, M., & Abd Elaziz, M. (2020). Analyzing COVID-19 virus based on enhanced fragmented biological local aligner using improved ions motion optimization algorithm. *Applied Soft Computing*, *96*, 106683. doi:10.1016/j.asoc.2020.106683 PMID:32901204

Liu, X., Fan, L., Wang, L., & Meng, S. (2016). Multiobjective reliable cloud storage with its particle swarm optimization algorithm. *Mathematical Problems in Engineering*, *2016*, 2016. doi:10.1155/2016/9529526

Lotfi, N. (2019). Data allocation in distributed database systems: A novel hybrid method based on differential evolution and variable neighborhood search. *SN Applied Sciences*, *1*(12), 1–10. doi:10.100742452-019-1787-3

Mehrdanesh, A., Monjezi, M., Khandelwal, M., & Bayat, P. (2021). Application of various robust techniques to study and evaluate the role of effective parameters on rock fragmentation. *Engineering with Computers*, 1–11.

Murlidhar, B. R., Armaghani, D. J., & Mohamad, E. T. (2020). Intelligence prediction of some selected environmental issues of blasting: A review. *The Open Construction & Building Technology Journal*, *14*(1), 298–308. doi:10.2174/1874836802014010298

Rodríguez-Mazahua, N., Rodríguez-Mazahua, L., López-Chau, A., Alor-Hernández, G., & Peláez-Camarena, S. G. (2021). Comparative Analysis of Decision Tree Algorithms for Data Warehouse Fragmentation. In *New Perspectives on Enterprise Decision-Making Applying Artificial Intelligence Techniques* (pp. 337–363). Springer. doi:10.1007/978-3-030-71115-3_15

Selvakumar, S., & Manivannan, S. S. (2021). A spectrum defragmentation algorithm using jellyfish optimization technique in elastic optical network (EON). *Wireless Personal Communications*, •••, 1–19.

Siddiqui, A. W., & Raza, S. A. (2021). A general ontological timetabling-model driven metaheuristics approach based on elite solutions. *Expert Systems with Applications*, *170*, 114268. doi:10.1016/j.eswa.2020.114268

Singh, A. P., & Choudhary, A. (2021). Approach for Ensuring Fragmentation and Integrity of Data in SEDuLOUS. In *Proceedings of Second International Conference on Computing, Communications, and Cyber-Security* (pp. 857-869). Springer. 10.1007/978-981-16-0733-2_61

Xie, C., Nguyen, H., Bui, X. N., Choi, Y., Zhou, J., & Nguyen-Trang, T. (2021). Predicting rock size distribution in mine blasting using various novel soft computing models based on meta-heuristics and machine learning algorithms. *Geoscience Frontiers*, *12*(3), 101108. doi:10.1016/j.gsf.2020.11.005

Xue, J., & Shen, B. (2020). A novel swarm intelligence optimization approach: Sparrow search algorithm. *Systems Science & Control Engineering*, *8*(1), 22–34. doi:10.1080/21642583.2019.1708830

Zeng, H., Zhang, C., Yi, X., & Xiong, R. (2021). Heuristic fragmentation-aware scheduling for a multicluster time-sensitive passive optical LAN. *Optical Fiber Technology*, *66*, 102662. doi:10.1016/j.yofte.2021.102662

Zhou, J., Qiu, Y., Armaghani, D. J., Zhang, W., Li, C., Zhu, S., & Tarinejad, R. (2021). Predicting TBM penetration rate in hard rock condition: A comparative study among six XGB-based metaheuristic techniques. *Geoscience Frontiers*, *12*(3), 101091. doi:10.1016/j.gsf.2020.09.020

Chapter 13
Semantic-Aware Efficient Multi-Keyword Top K-Similarity Search Over Encrypted Cloud Data

S. Muthurajkumar
https://orcid.org/0000-0003-3960-6926
Anna University, India

R. Shangeeth
Anna University, India

S. Anika Lakshmi
Anna University, India

R. Gaythrisri
Anna University, India

ABSTRACT

Outsourcing data storage in infrastructure has been a popular solution for organizations and individual users since it offers numerous advantages over traditional on-premises storage choices. Data encryption before outsourcing data to infrastructure is a general strategy to safeguard data confidentiality. It is challenging to search for the specified keywords in encrypted datasets in cloud computing settings, and it is obviously impracticable to download all the data from the cloud and decode it locally. The focus of current search technique is on exact matches and simple pattern matching, which result in incomplete or irrelevant. The approach uses 4D hyperchaotic mapping and a powerful deoxyribonucleic acid (DNA) encryption mechanism to make it very difficult to decrypt the encrypted data without the proper key. The proposed approach helps create an effective and safe encryption. Global vector word embedding is taken into consideration while generating semantically aware search results in a semantically conscious top-k multi-keyword retrieval-supporting searchable encryption technique.

DOI: 10.4018/979-8-3693-0593-5.ch013

1. INTRODUCTION

As cloud computing technology develops, more and more documents are encrypted before being transferred to the cloud for both convenience and economic reasons. As a result, security and privacy concerns are emerging in the cloud environment. A possible method to provide secure information retrieval without affecting data privacy is a keyword search over encrypted data. The existing search algorithms, however, do not take into account the semantic retrieval information of users and are therefore unable to fully satisfy users' search intentions.

The semantic and syntactic connections between words are captured using global vector word embedding. Global vector word embedding includes local and global information regarding the word vector presentation. Each word is represented as a vector of real numbers that accurately represents its meaning and context in a global vector word embedding. The vectors are intended to be distinct for unrelated and comparable terms for words with similar meanings and are used in similar circumstances. Word embedding is used to identify entities and determine similarity by analyzing the statistics of word-to-word co-occurrences in a corpus (i.e., Collection of documents). Instead of only matching keywords, semantic search seeks to return items or information relevant to a query's meaning. The embedding of the words in the documents or information we want to retrieve is then compared to these embedded values. The most appropriate outcomes for the query in terms of its meaning is obtained by rating the documents or information based on their cosine similarity scores with the query embedding.

The word embedding matrix is factorized using Singular Value Decomposition (SVD). Factorization reduces the matrix's dimensions and space's sparseness. A GloVe can produce high-quality word embedding by factorizing the matrix with SVD in order to capture the underlying relationships between words. The purpose of dimensionality reduction is to highlight the relationships between the words and reduce the impact of the words' frequent repetition.

Deoxyribonucleic Acid (DNA) Encryption converts each letter of the alphabet into a complex combination of the four bases that make up DNA adenine (A), cytosine (C), guanine (G), and thymine (T). Whereas DNA contains the genetic code of information. Information is concealed using DNA computing cryptography by first being converted to ASCII code (decimal format), then to binary format. The binary sequence is then divided into groups of two digits. A represents 00, T represents 11, G represents 01, and C represents 10 when these groupings are finally transformed into DNA code.

For each session, the plaintext is divided into two equal parts and translated to DNA sequences using a different set of encoding tables. The cipher text is generated after implementing the given technique measures. Any type of digital data is binarized in encryption, then it is transformed into DNA by sequencing, reshaping, encrypting, crossing over, mutating, and finally reshaping. The primary steps of DNA encryption are repeated three times or more. Text files are used for transmitting encrypted data.

DNA encryption may produce a great number of potential DNA sequences by applying genetic operators including reshaping, crossover, and mutation, making it challenging for attackers to crack the encryption and recover the original data. The chromosomal population sequence is created through the reshaping process. DNA encryption uses crossover and mutation to create new DNA sequences from existing ones. Considering the following cross-over operations: rotate crossover to produce a new offspring sequence, the operator combines the DNA sequences of two parents through a series of rotational and crossover operations and single-point crossover. A DNA sequence can become mutated by randomly altering one or more nucleotides. The first form of mutation is done by flipping the bits from 0 to 1 or vice versa. In the second form of mutation, the DNA base tables are also changed arbitrarily.

Binarization, transformation into DNA sequence, reshaping, encryption, crossing across, mutating, and reshaping again are all processes in the DNA encryption process. As a result, the decryption process will include performing these procedures the other way around. Restoring the DNA sequence to its original shape requires decrypting it. Then the crossover and mutation operations are reversed, and finally the encryption procedure. The plaintext can then be extracted from the encrypted binary data by reversing the transformation. However, the chaotic sequence produced by the 4D hyperchaotic system, which serves as the decryption key, must also be known in order to effectively decrypt the DNA sequence. It would be difficult to undo the encryption process and get back the original plaintext without the decryption key.

When a chaotic system has two or more positive Lyapunov exponents, the system is said to be hyper-chaotic. The rate of divergence of neighboring trajectories in a dynamical system is quantified by the Lyapunov exponent. Positive Lyapunov exponents show sensitive beginning condition dependency, a feature of chaotic systems. It is very challenging for an attacker to predict the encryption key or decipher the encrypted message without the accompanying decryption key because of the randomness. Due to the encryption process's sensitivity to the initial conditions and parameters, even little changes will result in drastically different cipher messages. A hyper-chaotic system's trajectory can diverge dramatically, making long-term behavior prediction nearly impossible.

We have used 4D Hyper Chaotic key generation in current instance. Precise beginning conditions and control parameters are used to initialize the 4D Hyper Chaotic system in order to generate the secure key. The beginning conditions are kept a secret, and the system behavior is determined by the control settings. The system is then repeatedly iterated to create a set of values that exhibit chaotic behavior. The cryptographic key is built on the foundation of these values. Data security will be increased by encrypting the data with the generated key after converting binary data to DNA sequences. The equations for a four-dimensional hyper-chaotic system are as follows:

$$x1 = a(y - x) + yz; \tag{1}$$

$$y1 = cx - y0xz + w; \tag{2}$$

$$z1 = xy - bz; \tag{3}$$

$$q1 = dy - xz; \tag{4}$$

Where a, b, c, and d are the system parameters and are set with random initial parameter values, which makes the system to perform in chaotic state.

2. LITERATURE SURVEY

This section explains the literature survey of the proposed work is done by various researcher in this direction is explained.

The publications which offered ground-breaking solutions to safeguard data integrity, enable secure data sharing, and solve user privilege issues in the field of data security and encryption techniques were demonstrated. Systems with improved security features and control over data access and usage were presented by A. Wu et al. (2022) and C. Hahn et al. (2023). In order to ensure data integrity and to enable secure data sharing between a data owner and several users, the first study focused on a multi-user FSSE scenario by protecting data integrity, which also verified the search results provided by a public cloud server. The owner obtained the hash value from both the public and private cloud servers after a data user submits a search request, evaluates the two outcomes, and decides whether to trust the public cloud server's result. By addressing potential weaknesses and limiting user privileges, the second study (Hahn et al., 2023) investigated a data-sharing model that emphasizes the secrecy of data and inquiries as well as the dependability of the underlying payment system. The current MKSE systems gave authorized users too much authority so they may let unauthorized users submit legitimate queries without damaging their credit. In the context of secure data sharing and user permission, both publications advance encryption methods and data security.

Techniques for encryption are essential for protecting privacy and safeguarding data. These publications discuss various facets of encryption techniques. Public key encryption was the main emphasis of L. Xu et al. (2020), which employs a pair of keys for encryption and decryption. They suggested a searchable encryption strategy that permits safe and reliable keyword searches on encrypted data, maintaining the material's secrecy. Authorized users can access the data during predetermined time windows with time-controlled access. The concealing of the client's access pattern in encrypted data was addressed by S. Oya and F. Kerschbaum et al. (2021). They provided an access and search pattern leak-based query recovery mechanism that made use of the maximum likelihood estimation technique. They attack privacy-preserving SSE strategies that try to conceal the access pattern data. At last, Sun, Shi-Feng et al. (2021) presented DSSE, a backward-private searchable encryption method. It made sure that later search queries cannot be linked to older documents that had been removed and that earlier search queries cannot be related to updates in the future. Their strategy used the Bloom filter, a multi-puncturable pseudorandom function, and the innovative cryptographic primitive known as Symmetric Revocable Encryption. By tackling a variety of topics like public key encryption, access pattern concealment, and backward privacy in searchable encryption schemes, these publications together developed encryption approaches.

The publications provided insights into effective and secure searchable encryption algorithms and promoted attribute-based search, verified SE, and optimized route finding. By employing multiplication operations to create encrypted keyword indices, Y. Cui et al. (2020) demonstrated attribute-based multiple keyword searches. The index for each encrypted term was produced by multiplying the attribute sets associated with that keyword. By encrypting every shared record with a different encryption key, Y. Miao et al. (2022) Verifiable SE system provided record privacy in multi-user scenarios. In VKSF, the fundamental VSEF accomplished both correctness and soundness. In order to provide optimized routes within a preset distance, Z. Feng et al. (2020) presented a technique that combines keyword relevance with geographic distance. IKRQ shrinked the search space by employing pruning rules to build bi-directional mapping structures and compute ranking scores for routes with indoor partitions.

In the realm of information retrieval, various techniques were employed to enhance search efficiency and accuracy. Relevant techniques using vector space model were proposed by D. Das and S. Kalra (2020), J. Li et al. (2022), V. Sharma and S. Ramamoorthy (2023), W. Yang and Y. Zhu (2021). G. Liu et al. (2022) introduced a secure index-based method that leveraged homomorphic ordered encryption to protect index and query vectors, ensuring the confidentiality of pertinent encrypted data. Meanwhile, Handa R et al. (2020) proposed a system facilitating disjunctive searches, which allowed users to seek data matching any of the query's keywords. To filter out irrelevant documents and improve retrieval precision, a vector space model based on the TF-IDF rule was applied (Liu et al., 2022). The approach effectively eliminated a significant number of pointless documents using diverse strategies to identify documents that align with the query vector. The ranking technique employed in (Handa et al., 2020) by TF-IDF, arranged search results based on their relevance to the query, although the inability to handle complex search queries might lead to increased search time and communication overhead. It was worth noting that the bag of words paradigm adopted in these models overlooked the contextual and sequential nature of words within documents, potentially compromising the accuracy of search outcomes.

In the field of information retrieval, the vector space model explored various studies to improve keyword search systems. Y. Miao et al. (2023) introduced a machine learning-based ranked keyword search system, utilizing the k-means clustering algorithm. On the other hand, Z. Xia et al. (2020) presented a secure multi-keyword ranked search system called unencrypted dynamic multi-keyword ranked search. The system combined both the vector space model and the TF-IDF model, employing tree-based indexing. The creation of secret key and the file vectors were constructed based on keywords and TF-IDF values in (Miao et al., 2023). The relevance score between the encrypted file vector and encrypted query vector were calculated using secure kNN computation. The Data Owner was allowed to perform operations such as editing, deleting, and modifying data while ensuring system security through dynamic updates (Xia et al., 2020). The advancements made in machine learning-based ranked keyword search systems, showcasing techniques such as clustering algorithms, secure computation, dynamic updates, and the utilization of the vector space and TF-IDF model were highlighted.

Search techniques were used to retrieve the information on developments in the optimization and security of search operations on encrypted data. These papers addressed a variety of privacy, verifiability, and index management issues while advancing secure and effective search methods for encrypted data. Fuzzy matching strategies were proposed by H. Zhang et al. (2023), M. Zhang et al. (2021), and X. Li et al. (2023) using various methodologies. Other search techniques were proposed by Li, Feng et al. (2023), C. Guo et al. (2020), D. Wang et al. (2015). The study (Zhang et al., 2023) suggested building an index for encrypted data using a variety of indexing methods to facilitate effective keyword or phrase searches. In order to accept partial or approximate matches in search queries, fuzzy keyword-matching algorithms were used.

In (Zhang et al., 2021), privacy problems were addressed by letting cloud users search for encrypted data using numerous keywords and fuzzy matching methods. Search operations on the index created from the encrypted data and keywords were made easier by the TF-IDF-based computation of keyword correlation scores. The fuzzy keyword search feature of VRFMS, which enabled imprecise keyword matching in cloud-based document retrieval, in (Li, Tong, Zhao et al, 2023). The cloud server retrieved the majority of pertinent documents because of TF-IDF. Each keyword in the query was splitted into two bi-grams in order to build a binary keyword vector, which simplifies search operations. Additionally, VRFMS had limitations when it comes to handling more intricate questions requiring semantic search.

These publications made innovative contributions to search strategies by addressing problems in dynamic, wildcard, and symmetric search contexts. Dynamic searchable encryption algorithms were effective in enabling changes to outsourced databases, as demonstrated by J. G. Chamani et al. in their study (2022). An inner product encryption technique was the foundation of the wildcard searchable encryption system proposed by Y. Li et al. (2022). The approach created a two-dimensional inner-product relationship, eliminating wildcard constraints. An effective update method in distributed key-value stores, ZW. Lin et al. (2021) provided a framework for privacy-preserving similarity searches. To guarantee data privacy, a number of cryptographic approaches were used, including homomorphic encryption, secure multi-party computing.

In (Chamani et al., 2022), dynamic search used forward-backward private DMUSSE systems, the first DMUSSE scheme that had been demonstrated to be secure and implemented in two variations with trade-offs in performance. The distribution of fresh secret keys to the remaining participants were made necessary due to the convoluted revocation process. The wildcard search in (Li, Ning, & Chen, 2022) stops the cloud server from learning information from search trapdoors containing wildcard-containing phrases provided by data users by improving adaptive simulation-based security through trapdoor privacy. By using trapdoor privacy, which prevented the cloud server from learning anything from the search trapdoors formed by the wildcard-containing phrases that data users had uploaded, adaptive simulation-based security was improved. The proposed framework (Lin et al., 2021) used a distributed key-value store to store the encrypted data. The key-value store was distributed across multiple nodes to provide fault tolerance, scalability, and high availability.

3. SYSTEM ARCHITECTURE

This section describes the proposed work system architecture and explains the workflow of the proposed work. The objective is to provide an advanced search method that allows multi-keyword semantic search, and cloud-stored encrypted data. The main goal is to increase the security of the outsourced data by using a powerful encryption. The suggested system acts as a search engine with enhanced relevancy for document retrieval. In order to create a secret key with great randomness, the proposed method uses the concepts of Chaos theory. The key supports the system's use of encryption, bolstering security measures and protects sensitive data.

The application's system model is depicted in Figure 1. Three entities, a data owner, a data user authorized by the data owner, and an external server make up the system in our application environment. An uncertain and delicate data collection belongs to the data owner. Before being sent to a cloud server, the data must be encrypted for security and privacy reasons. When the data owner uploads the document to the cloud server, it is pre-processed. After pre-processing, the document's textual data is converted into numerical data using the global vector word embedding model. The GloVe is enhanced by the usage of singular value decomposition. The document is simultaneously encrypted using DNA encryption and a 4D hyper-chaotic map. The steps of DNA encryption, such as binarizing, reshaping, crossing, and mutation processes, are carried out.

The query request is made by the data user. When a data user conducts a multi-keyword query to find documents. Each query is converted into numerical data using word embedding before being sent to the cloud server. The user's search word is then used to search the document. The document with the highest score is the one that is most relevant. The top k documents are listed for the user. To request access to a certain file, the user contacts the owner. The user can view the documents by inputting the secret key and nonce that were sent to them through email by the data owner.

We have developed a system that enables the user to conduct a semantic search query on server data without revealing private information. The data user and the server will be interacting while the keyword search query is processed. A search on encrypted data can only be done by users who have been given permission by the data owner. Global word-embedded vector values will be created for the query. The global word-embedded document collection will then be compared using the cosine similarity metric based on the search query.

Figure 1. Architecture of semantic search over encrypted data

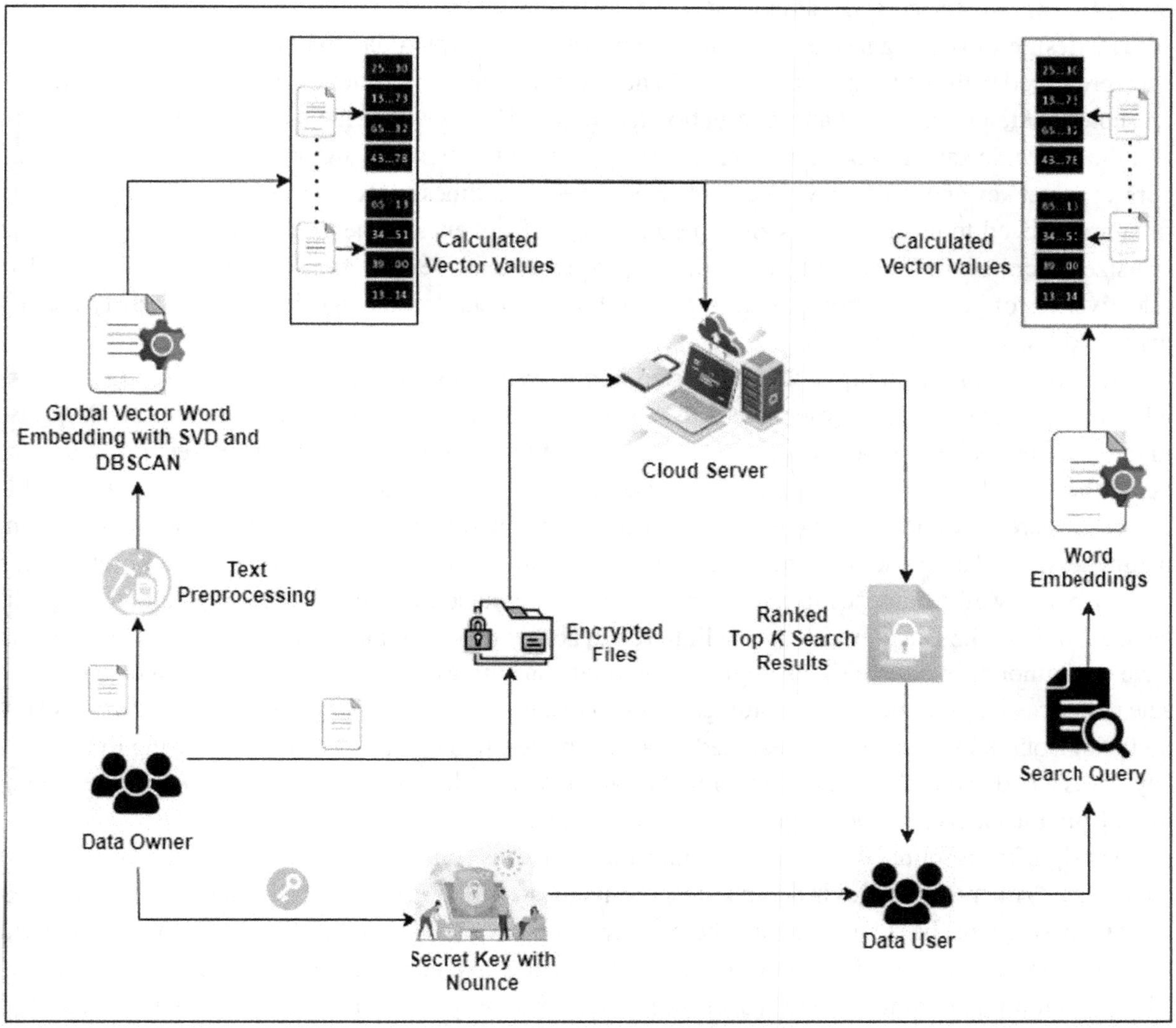

To find the documents that are most pertinent, the collected similarity scores will be sorted in descending order. Based on the top-k search results, a data user may send a request for access to the document. The owner will analyze the request and decide in accordance with their own standards and criteria. The owner often has administrative rights or greater authority. An email notification alerting the data owner to the access request for a specific document will be sent. By requesting access to private information, the owner is able to assess the request and decide in accordance with their own standards. By employing this strategy, the owner can make sure that only people with the appropriate authorization have access to confidential data.

The secret key and the nonce will be sent to the Data User's email once the Data Owner has granted access. The user will only be permitted to see the document after receiving permission from the data owner and completing the credentials section. By asking the user for a secret key and nonce credentials and encrypting the document, the credentials section for decryption technology helps to ensure the security and integrity of the data. The system will help to keep the server and the data it hosts to be secure by restricting illicit access and alteration.

The design of our suggested semantic search over an encrypted data while protecting the data has been presented in the corresponding section. The data owner accessibilities over the entire workplace are presented first, and then the DNA encryption technique. Then we describe the data user accessibilities and the semantic search procedure over the encrypted data. The decoding process will begin after the correct secret key and nonce have been uploaded. Execution times based on file size and key generation time are utilized to evaluate a system's performance effectiveness. The execution time dependent on file size describes the length of time needed to process or execute operations on various file sizes. The effectiveness of key generation has an impact on how well encryption algorithms and security mechanisms work overall.

Building the master setup is the initial step in our system's process. It entails developing a system with three key parts: a data owner, a data user, and an external server. While the data user needs access to the data for analysis, processing, or other purposes, the data owner is in charge of keeping and managing the data. The outsourced server is in charge of giving the data storage and processing capabilities. The secret key and system parameters must be generated by the data owner. According to system parameters, the data owner uses searchable encryption to encrypt documents. Then it sends encrypted documents as well as indexes to the external server. The outsourced server's encrypted database will be accessible to the Data Owner, who will have the ability to add and remove documents. Data owners have the authority to revoke rights, register, and retain an authorized user for a specific amount of time. The resources for computation and storage on the outsourced server are boundless. The documents kept on the outsourced server may be searched by a search user. It generates search tokens using the desired keywords and delivers them to the server that is outsourced. It decrypts the search results after receiving them from the external server to get the target document indexes.

One significant source of unstructured information that is equally significant is textual data. Textual data presents many challenges in deciphering grammatical structure, semantics, format, and content. Text pre-processing must be properly treated before any feature extraction is done. Various strategies are used in the pre-processing stage to convert the raw text data into an analysis-ready format as follows: Lowercasing, Stemming, Lemmatization, Tokenization, Removal of special characters and Stop word removal.

In the module, a random key is created utilizing a hyperchaotic system, and the final result depends on the parameters that have been passed in as well as the initial conditions. The chaotic sequence produced by the hyperchaotic system iterates with the values of the beginning conditions and control parameters to create the cipher text, which is the first stage of encryption. We develop an algorithm based on Watson and Crick's DNA principles for the encryption of textual data; the sender considers a file with an input of the .txt extension. Through a number of subsequent stages, the data will be encrypted.

Table 1. DNA and representation of bits

DNA Component	Binary Coded Form
Adenine(A)	00
Cytosine(C)	01
Guanine(G)	10
Thymine(T)	11

In DNA genetic encryption, the 4D hyper chaotic key generation method is utilized to generate a chaotic sequence that is used as a key to encrypt plain text and generate cipher text. The 4D hyperchaotic system generates an unpredictable and apparently random series of values. To make sure that the plain text cannot be easily decoded by unauthorized persons, the sequence is employed as the encryption key. In order to make the sequence complex, the chaotic system is iterated numerous times to generate the key. In terms of complexity and security, it offers a high level of encryption. It is challenging for unauthorized users to decipher the plain text when a chaotic sequence is used as the encryption key. Table. 1 shows the list of all possible two-bit binary values mapped to the four DNA bases.

Algorithm. 1: DNA Encryption

```
Input: Plain text (M)
Output: Encrypted text (D_enc)
    BEGIN
        DNA Encoding Scheme: S={A,C,G,T}
        B1 = binarized_data(M)
        D_seq = bits_to_dna (B1, 2B_to_dna_base_table)
        enc_key(data, key)
        while (round > 0) do
            (a) B2=bits_to_dna (group_bits (enc_key (dna_to_bits ((D_seq,
              dna_base_to_2B_table), key)),2B_to_dna_base_table)
            (b) Offspring = crossover(B2)
            (c) new_pop = mutation(Offspring)
           round - = 1
        End while
        D_enc = new_pop
        Return D_enc
END
```

The DNA base table is used in the encryption process to encode the plaintext message. Initially, it converts plain text to binary data. The DNA sequence is created through the transformation of each bit's associated DNA base value from two bits to the DNA base table. For the associated textual data, a 4d hyper chaotic key is produced. A chromosomal population of DNA sequences is created through several rounds of encryption, crossover, and mutation on the DNA sequence. Rotate and single point crossover are two crossover techniques in DNA encryption. To make new offspring sequences, two DNA sequences are split into two distinct parts and rotated before combining, known as a "rotate crossover". The rotational distance is determined at random. Single-point crossover is the process of exchanging the DNA segments that follow a random point in two DNA sequences to produce new offspring sequences. The mutation is the process of adding random deviations to an individual's genetic information to produce new genetic information. Bitwise flipping and changing the DNA base table are two mutation techniques. Random bits in a DNA sequence are flipped from 0 to 1 or vice-versa. Changing the DNA base table entails randomly choosing one DNA base from a sequence and swapping it for another base or two bases. The concatenated chromosomal sequences form a DNA population that serves as the encrypted text.

Table 2 shows the list of all possible four-bit binary values mapped to the four DNA bases. The list is used to map four-bit binary numbers to pairs of DNA bases in the encryption process. These lists are used in the DNA encryption process to encode and decode the plaintext message using DNA strands.

Table 2. DNA bases and representation of bits

DNA	Bits	DNA	Bits	DNA	Bits	DNA	Bits
TA	0000	GA	0100	CA	1000	AA	1100
TC	0001	GC	0101	CC	1001	AC	1101
TG	0010	GG	0110	CG	1010	AG	1110
TT	0011	GT	0111	CT	1011	AT	1111

The proposed system is a search engine for document retrieval that employs an effective search approach that will recognize synonyms, related terms, and contextually relevant results, producing a more accurate and relevant search result in less computing time. The system will paraphrase the pertinent information that fits the semantics to produce a summary that contains all of the real points from the source document. Words that share semantic or syntactic links will be represented by vectors and be mapped in close proximity to one another by using a word embedding as opposed to the lexical-based syntactic parsers. With the word's co-occurrence throughout the entire corpus in mind, the words are incorporated in a global contextual manner.

Here, we employed semantic search with pre-trained GloVe embedding. By looking up the matching embedding vectors in the pre-trained GloVe model, one may find the GloVe embedding for each token in the documents. Singular value decomposition (SVD), which divides a matrix into three matrices: a left singular matrix, a diagonal matrix, and a right singular matrix, is then used by GloVe to factorize the matrix. The associations between the words in the corpus can be captured by these matrices and used to recreate the original matrix. The general meaning of the text will remain intact if the mean is applied to the resulting vectors.

Algorithm 2. Global Vector Representation

```
Input: Document (d), Query (q)
Output: Top k documents.
BEGIN
     glove_vec= load_glove ()
    def get_em (d)
          For each doc in d:
                tokenizer.word_index (doc)
            For word, i in tokenizer.word.index.items ():
                 em_vec= glove_vec.get (word)
                if em_vec is not none:
                    em_matrix[i] = em_vec
               End if
```

```
                End For
            End For
    return em_matrix
    For each doc in d:    // Document embedding
        avg_vec =np.mean (np.array (get_em (d)))
    End For
    For each word in the q:   // Query Embedding
         q_avg_vec=np.mean (np.array (get_em (word)))
    End For
    For doc_id in avg_vec.items ():
            sim [doc_id]  = cosine_similarity (q_avg_vec, avg_vec)
     End For
    return sim[:k]
END
```

The GloVe embeddings are used to convert a user query into a vector representation during retrieval. Measures like cosine similarity are used to calculate how similar the document vectors in the collection are to the query vector. The retrieval results consist of the documents with the highest similarity scores, which are thought to be the most pertinent. The algorithm has the pre-trained glove loaded at the beginning. By breaking the pre-trained glove up into a list of sub-strings, it can be loaded. Each list contains a word and the embedded values that relate to it. Each word has its matching vectors listed after it. The text is cleaned up and tokenized into individual words for each document in the collection. The matching word-embedded vectors for each word are retrieved. The complete meaning of the document will be reserved by averaging out the words. Likewise, each word in a search query entered by a data user corresponding glove vectors are collected. After obtaining the GloVe embeddings for the documents and query, the similarity between the query and each corpus document can be determined using a similarity metric like cosine similarity. Search results will be returned for documents with higher similarity scores since they are thought to be more pertinent to the query.

Algorithm 3. DNA Decryption

```
Input: Encrypted data (text), secret key (key)
Output: Decrypted data (D_enc)
BEGIN
    B1= text
    r_no = int (get_pattern (round_no_del, key))
    round = get_pattern (round_del, key)
    while (r_no > 0) do
        round_info = round [r_no - 1]
        B1 = reshape (B1, get_pattern (reshape_del, round_info)
        Offspring = mutation (B1, get_pattern (mutation_del, round_info)
        new_pop= crossover (Offspring, round_info)
       enc_key = get_pattern (sec_key_del, key)
       r_no - = 1
```

```
        End while
        D_enc = bin_to_str (dna_bits (B1, dna_base_to_2B_table))
        Return D_enc
    END
```

DNA decryption begins when the user correctly matches the secret key and nonce generated. The encrypted text is first entered into the DNA decryption procedure. Once the secret key's round number and round information have been obtained. For each round, the decryption procedure is repeated in a loop. The encrypted text is first modified using the round information in each round. Then the encrypted data is subjected to a mutation procedure. After mutating the altered DNA Base table, bitwise flipping will be performed. To create a new population, a crossover operation is applied to the altered sequence. The secret key is then used to decrypt the fresh population. Using a conversion table derived from the key, the binary sequence is first converted into DNA sequences, and then back into binary as part of the decryption process. The data is then decrypted by converting the encrypted binary sequence into a plaintext string.

The similarity score between a query and each document in a collection is computed using the spatial distance measure. The query is tokenized and the embedding for each word in the query is computed using the Global word vectors. These embeddings are then averaged to obtain an embedding for the entire query. The similarity score between the query embedding and the document embeddings in a collection is then computed using the cosine similarity measure. The documents are then ranked in descending order based on their similarity score, and the top most similar documents are returned.

4. IMPLEMENTATION

The data owner can safely share their data with the data user by granting access to the outsourced server. The data owner maintains control over the data and has the ability to define access restrictions that control who have access to and may make use of the data. The outsourced server does not have access to the raw data itself; instead, it processes the data in accordance with the instructions given by the data user. It guarantees that the data is secure and secret during the whole processing procedure. The encrypted results can then be provided back to the data user after the data processing is finished. The information remains secure even during transmission because it can only be accessed by persons with the required access rights and authorization keys.

Under the master setup, the system parameters typically include user and role listing. A list of all users who have permission to access the system, along with their corresponding user roles, is referred to as a "User listing". The actions a user is permitted to take within the system are often determined by user roles that are set based on access criteria. A list of all the roles that are defined within the system, along with their related permissions and access levels, is referred to as a "Role listing". Depending on the organizational structure, roles may be specified. The master setup offers a flexible and scalable architecture for managing access to sensitive data by establishing user roles and role permissions. It makes sure that only authorized users have access to data and that access privileges are determined by predetermined standards. It is possible for effective data sharing and cooperation within the system while also reducing the risk of unauthorized access and data breaches.

The Owner of the role listing part has control over how different users can access the features of the other section and can give them various roles. The document uploading role allows the users who have been given the document uploading role are able to add new documents to the area that lists available documents. Users with the position have the ability to upload documents, articles, and any other pertinent content that may be useful for the system's repository. They increase the number of resources that are available for other users to search, access, and use by uploading documents. Users who have been given the keyword search role can search the system using the role's capabilities. To get pertinent documents from the document listing area, users can enter particular terms or phrases in the search field. Users can search the system's database using the role to identify content that interest them or meet their information needs. Users who have been given the user page access role will be able to access the system's user management page. They can interact with user-related data on the page and carry out a number of operations, including reading user details, adding new users, editing already-existing user profiles, and deleting user records.

In order to ensure proper administration and control over user accounts, the position gives users the ability to manage user-related issues. The system's role management page is accessible to users with the role page access role provided to them. They can supervise and control user responsibilities and access levels using the page. Users who have the ability can view the current roles, create new roles, change the settings for existing roles, and delete any roles that are superfluous. Users can define and maintain the hierarchical structure of user roles and access privileges within the system by having access to the role management page. Operations included are creation, modification, and deletion.

Figure 2 shows the list of newly created roles. The owner of the listing webpage will control what actions each user is permitted to take on the webpage by giving each user a separate role. For instance, if the owner limits the keyword search role to a specific group of users who are only permitted to search for documents not upload them and gives the document uploading position to a trusted user who is responsible for adding new documents to the document area.

Figure 2. Role listing

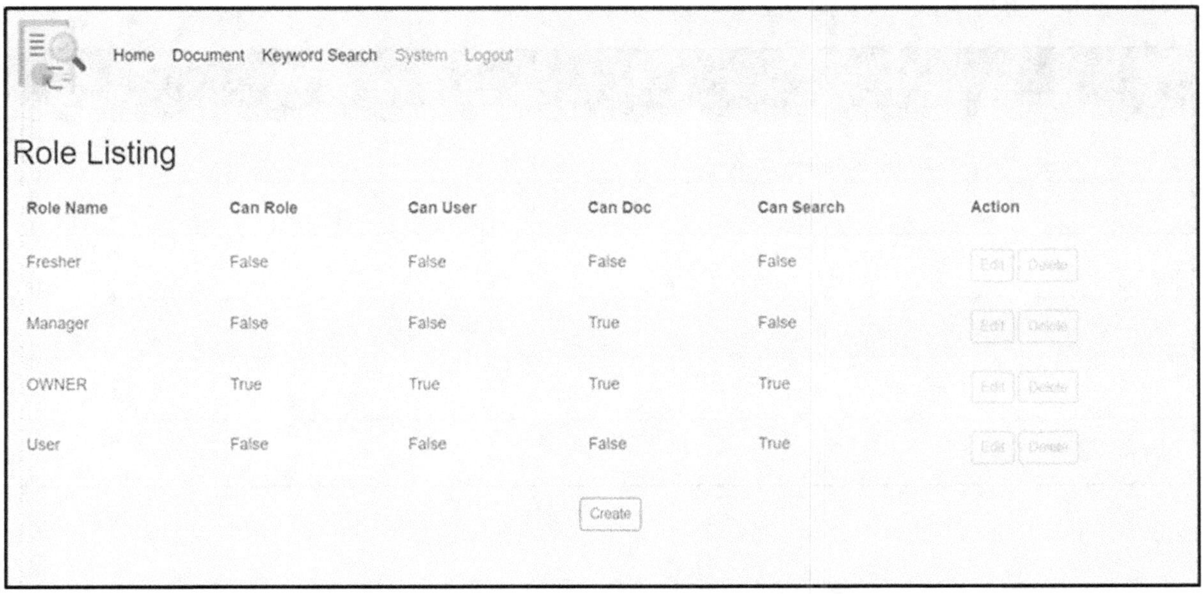

Role creation demonstrates the primary function of the role listing section. The form allows the administrator to create new roles by providing pertinent information such as the role name and access rights. As soon as a role is successfully created, a role ID is generated. Role editing section, which normally provides the current information about the role that the administrator wants to change, such as the name and access rights at the time of display. By choosing or deselecting particular items from a list, the administrator can change the access permissions for the role. Typically, the administrator must choose the role they wish to delete from a list of available roles before using the Delete Role functionality.

An administrator can examine and manage a list of users who have access to the system or application using the User Listing section's abilities. The system administrator can create new users and add them to the system using the Create User feature. The administrator can enter pertinent data about the new user, such as their name, email address, and password, using the feature's user-friendly interface. The administrator starts the process of setting up a user account within the system by filling out these details. The function is essential for growing the user base and allowing access to new people who require the system's features. The administrator can change the information on an existing user account using the Edit user function. With the use of the feature, the administrator can update the user's name, email address, or any other pertinent information as needed. By using the capability, the administrator can reset a user's password, assuring system security and password management.

The administrator can modify the user's role or active status using the Edit user tool. For instance, the administrator can modify a user's active status to change their role or temporarily revoke their access. With the help of the function, user accounts may be managed more freely, and the system can continue to include correct user data. The administrator has the option to completely delete a user from the system using the Delete User feature. When a person has to have their access, privileges removed or when they are no longer authorized to use the system or are a member of the organization, the capability is crucial. The administrator can permanently deactivate a user's account, ending their access to the system and all of its resources, by using the deactivate User feature. By erasing all traces of a user who is no longer affiliated with the system, it helps to preserve system security, user management, and data privacy.

Figure 3. User listing

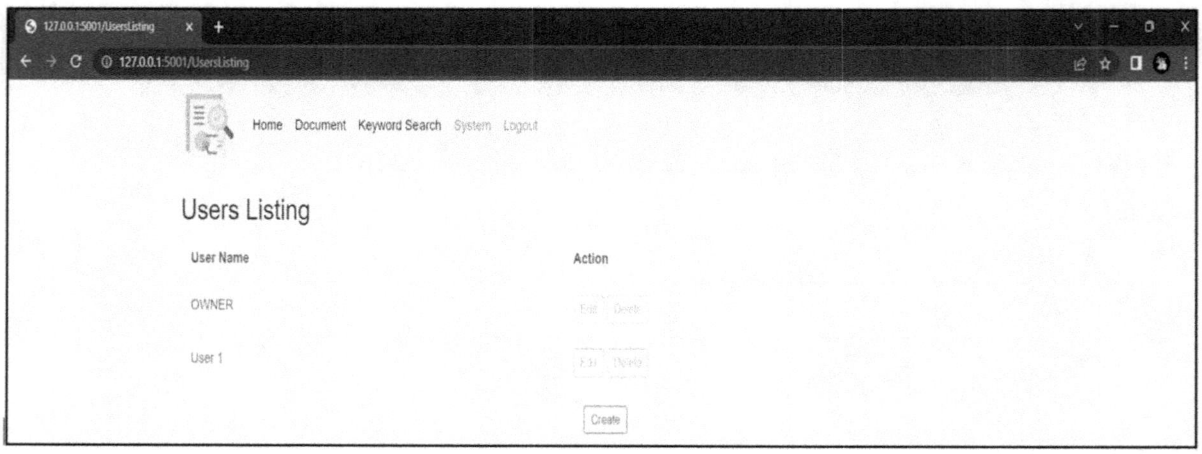

Figure 3 displays user listing page, which lists all of the users that have been created on the system. The list contains information about each user, such as name, email address, contact information, assigned role, and active status.

The management of the documents that have been posted using the document listing portal is completely at the authority of the system owner. The owner is given the authority to carry out a number of document management tasks, ensuring that the uploaded documents are accessible. The owner's capacity to add new documents to the system is one of his or her most important talents. The owner can start the construction of a new document using the document listing webpage. The owner can upload a new document to the system after it has been created. In order to do so, the file must be chosen from local storage and uploaded to the system's storage infrastructure. The system then securely stores the uploaded documents, guaranteeing their accessibility to authorized users. The owner is also in charge of restricting authorized users' access to documents. It includes giving certain users the necessary permissions to see the documents. The textual data in a new document undergoes a number of pre-processing procedures when an owner uploads it, including lowercasing, tokenization, removal of special characters, and stop words.

Figure 4. Document listing

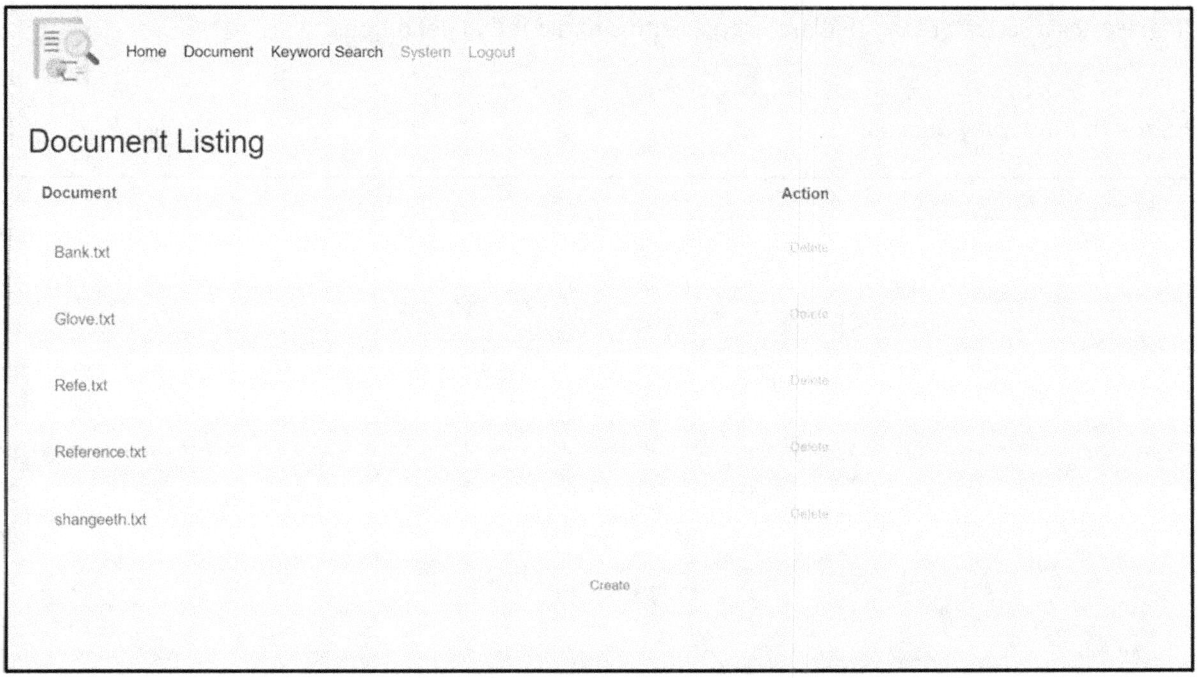

The Document Listing Page, a user interface element that offers a summary of all the documents uploaded by their respective owners in the system, is shown in Figure 4. Users can see a tabular representation of the document's essential details when they reach the Document Listing Page. Within the system, these features promote controlled access, enabling effective information sharing and upholding proper document ownership and access management.

Figure 5. Pre-processing

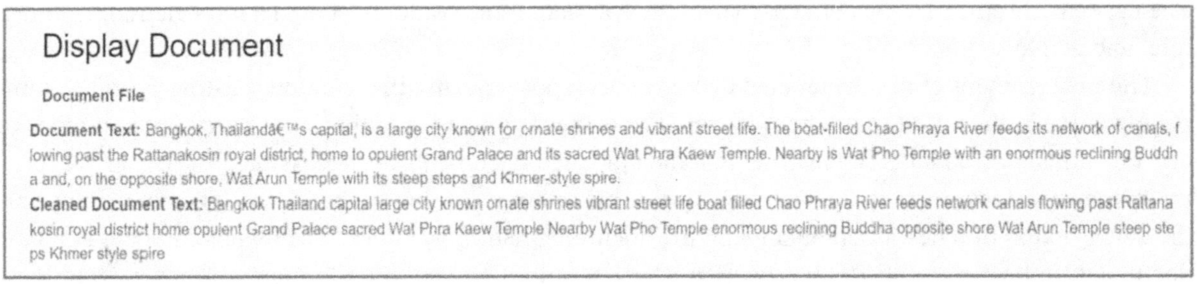

Document Text and Cleaned Document Text, two separate areas of the uploaded document, are shown in Figure 5. The raw text that was directly taken from the uploaded document is shown in the Document Text section. The section titled “Cleaned Document Text” displays the document’s text in its processed state following text pre-processing.

A chaotic dynamical system that can be utilized for key creation in DNA encryption is the 4D hyper chaotic map. By repeatedly iterating the chaotic map with various initial conditions and control parameters, the key is created. As a result, it becomes incredibly challenging for an attacker to predict the key. It generates a series of keys that are very sensitive to the initial conditions.

Figure 6. Encrypted document

Figure 6 illustrates how the cleaned text is encrypted using DNA encryption. DNA Encryption is then used to convert the text into an encrypted form after the cleaned text has been extracted from the uploaded document. The modified text is contained in the encrypted file, which cannot be opened without the accompanying decryption key. When the user log into a session and use their credentials to access the document listing system. The user could occasionally come upon a document they would like to examine but don't have the secret key needed to decrypt it. Without the particular secret key linked with each document, even if a user has access to the document listing system, they are unable to directly view or decrypt encrypted documents. It makes sure that only people with the right decryption keys and authorization may access the sensitive information in the documents.

Figure 7. User requesting access from owner

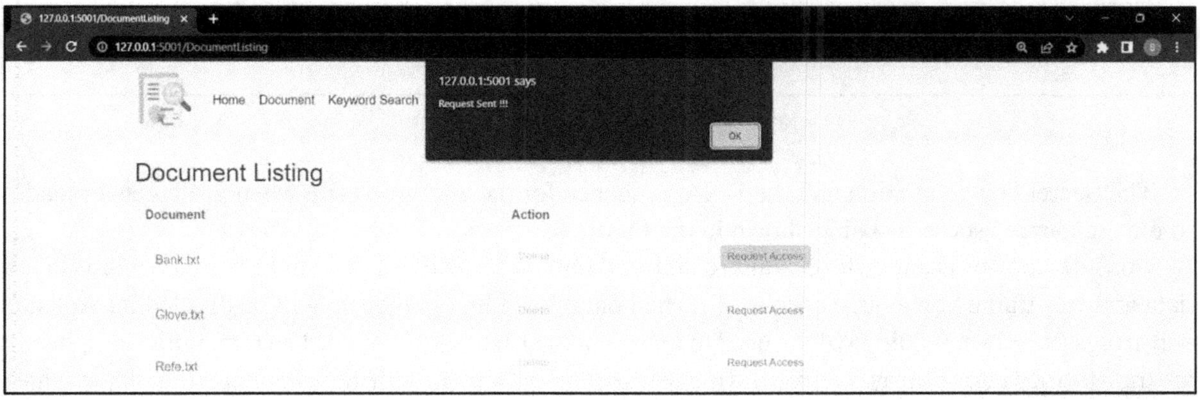

Figure 7 demonstrates the raising of a document request. When a user selects the "Request Access" button next to the document they want to access. The system sends a notification email, as seen in Figure 8, to the owner's email address informing them that access has been requested for that specific email. After reading the notification email, the owner decides whether to allow the user access or not. If the owner agrees to the request, they can choose from the document listing to provide the user the necessary access permissions.

Figure 8. Email notification sent to owner

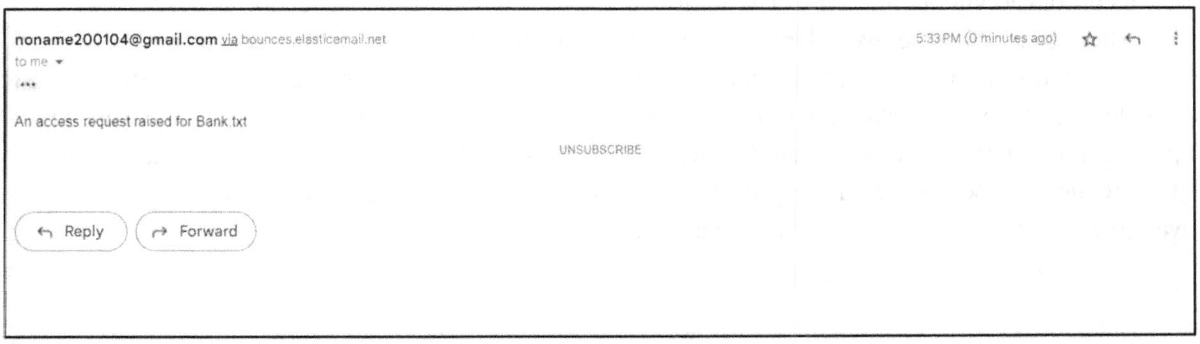

Figure 9. Secret key with encrypted sequence

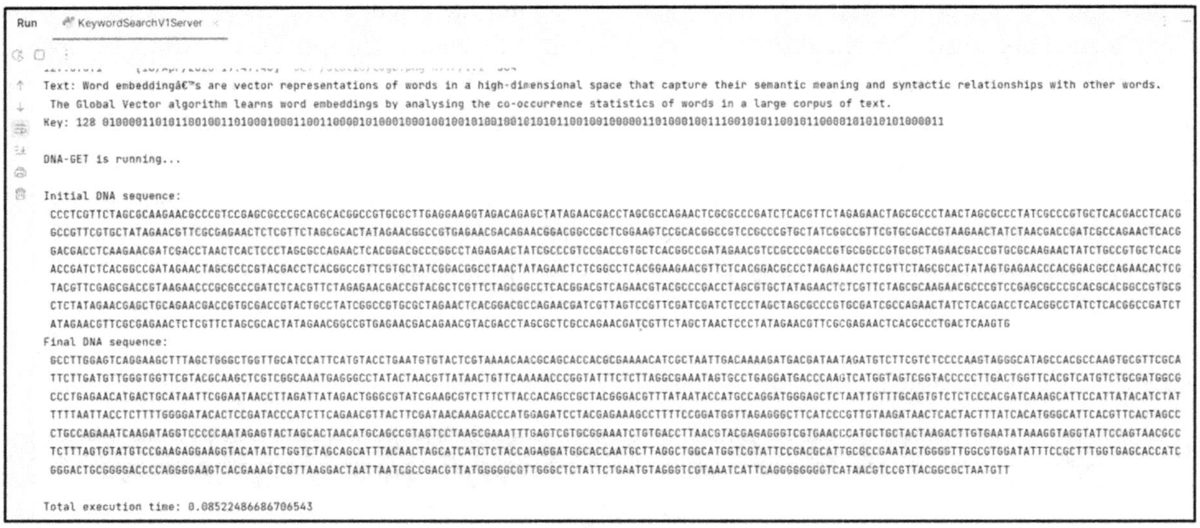

The Secret key generation and the DNA Sequence for the encrypted file when a file gets uploaded to the outsourced server is being shown in the Figure 9.

Consider the pre-trained glove, which captures the semantic and syntactic links between words in text data and was trained on a huge corpus of textual data. Each line in the file will be divided into a list of substrings. Word embedding will be used to represent the first index's word. The remaining components are transformed into an array. The word is mapped as key-value pairs with the accompanying vector values.

Word embedding is used to represent the position vectors of words that have semantic meanings or grammatical connections close to each other, instead of relying on lexical-based syntactic parsers. The entire document's textual information is retrieved by preprocessing and tokenization, each word in the document receives a word embedding. By connecting each phrase's word embedding to its matching sentence, a dictionary is kept up to date.

Visualizations of the effects of factorization on the matrix are shown in Figure 10. The original matrix is divided into two or more lower-rank matrices during the factorization process. The Decomposition effectively lessens the matrix's sparsity. Factorization can assist in revealing hidden patterns and relationships in the data by lowering the dimensionality. The matrix's dimensions are shrunk, and its sparsity is diminished. The data may become more manageable and easier to analyze as a result of the reduction in dimensionality. On the other hand, Figure 11 illustrates the impact of averaging over the condensed vectors produced via factorization. The vectors used to represent the data get shorter when the matrix's dimension is shrunk. The overall meaning of these sentences is kept intact throughout the procedure.

Users will only have a limited amount of access to the workspace, but they can ask the owner to provide them access to certain documents there. The owner can evaluate the request and approve or disapprove it based on their own standards, such as the user's function, level of clearance, or the sensitivity of the requested documents. The approach of requesting access aids in ensuring that private data is only available to those with the proper authorization.

Figure 10. Reduced vector after applying SVD

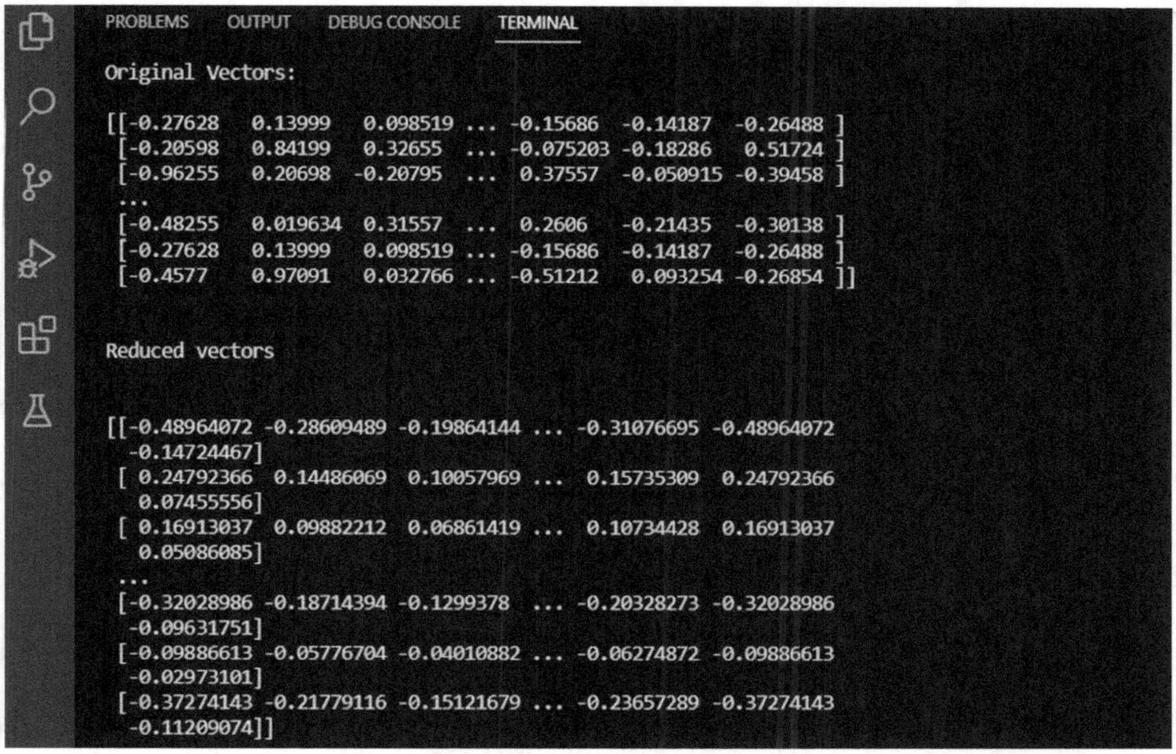

Figure 11. Obtained average vectors

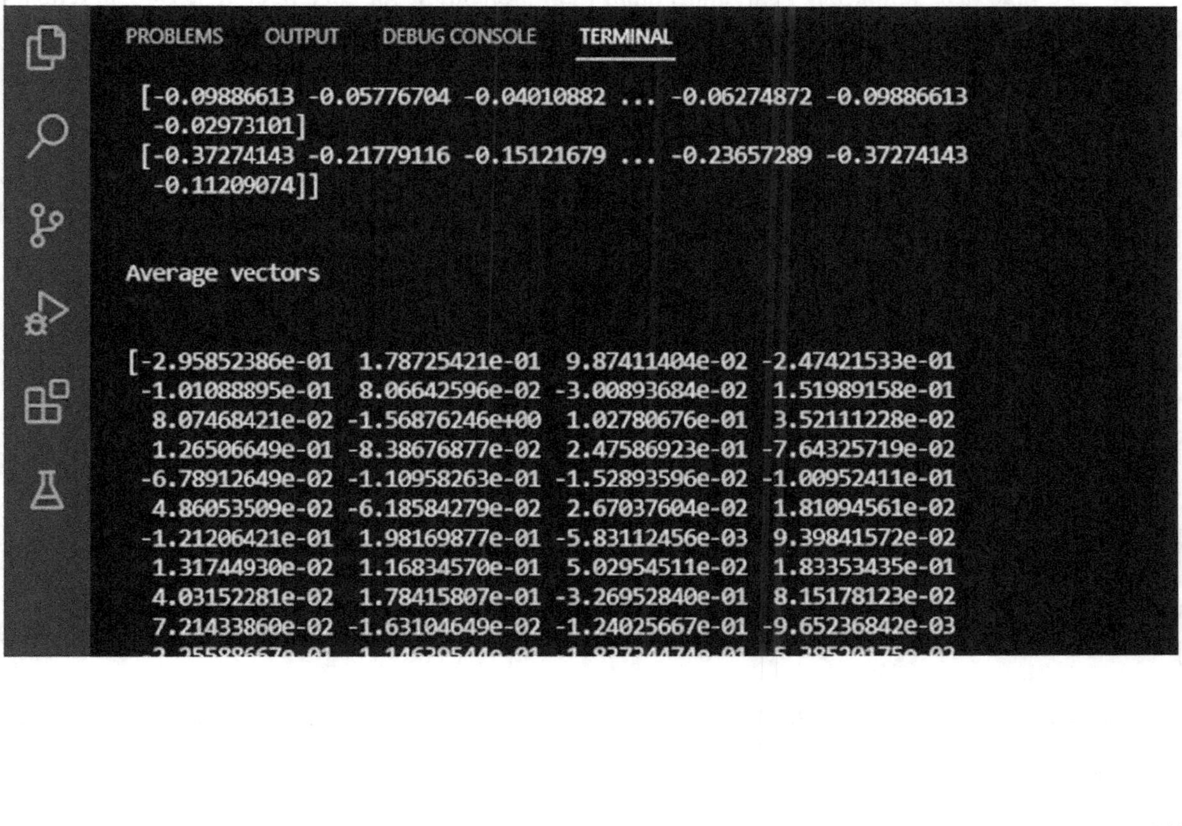

Figure 12. Owner's dashboard

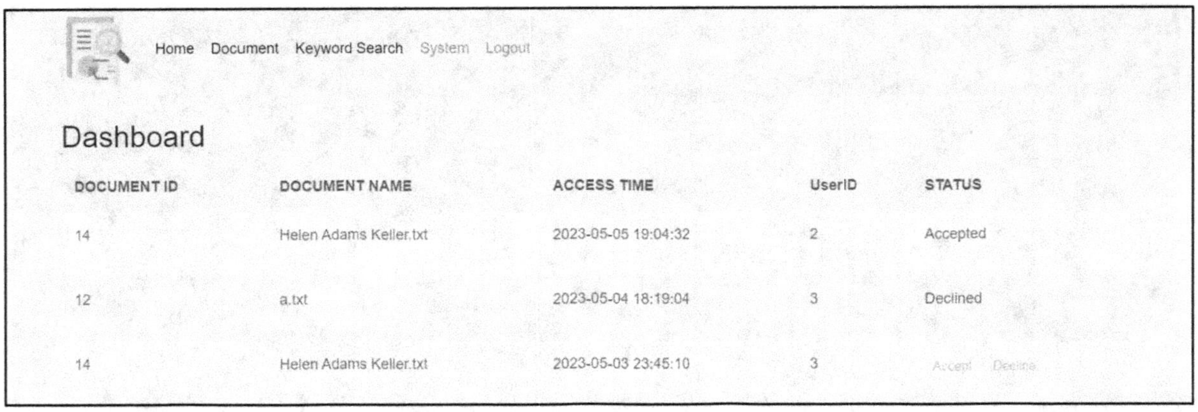

The owner has the choice to approve or deny an access request sent by a user. According to Figure 12, if the request is allowed, the user will have access to the desired documents; if it is denied, it will not be available. It also enhances openness and accountability in the request process to ensure that users are aware of the status of their requests and can take further action if needed.

The status will be shown as "accepted," "declined," or "pending" based on whether the owner has approved the request or not as shown in Figure 13. If the status is "accepted", the user will be allowed to read the requested content, providing the necessary access permissions. The user won't be allowed to read the requested document if the status is "declined". If the status is "pending", the user must wait while the owner answers to their request. The Data user can use the secret key credential to decrypt the file and read the plain text data. On request, the user will receive a letter with the secret key. To access the content, they have requested, users must enter their credentials on the Credentials screen, which is depicted in Figure 14.

Figure 13. User's dashboard

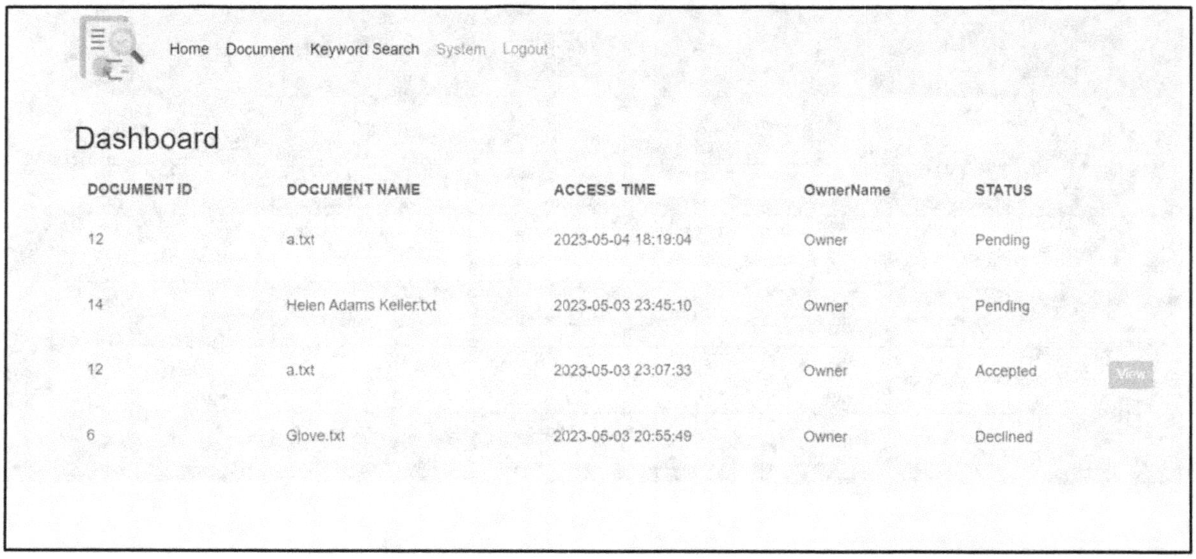

Figure 14. Credentials page

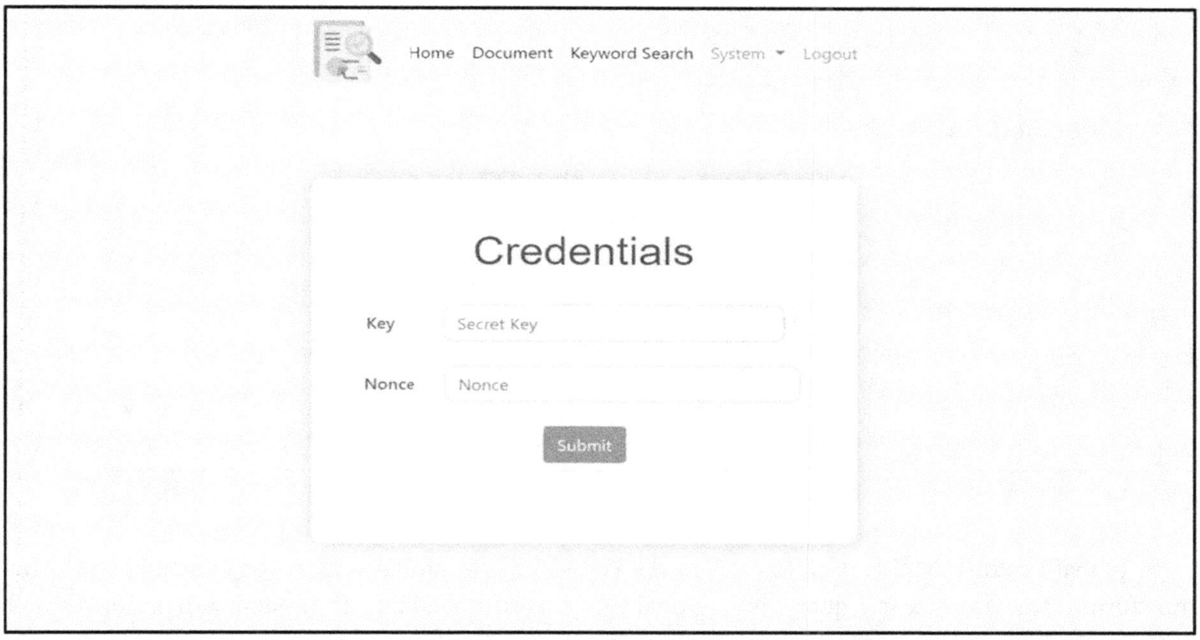

Asking the user for a secret key credential and encrypting the document, technology helps to ensure the security and integrity of the data. Limiting unauthorized access helps to maintain the security of the documents it contains. The document that the user has requested to view is the encrypted data, and the textual data that makes up the document is the original form. If the wrong key is entered, the document won't be properly decrypted and the user won't be able to view the original text. It enables the assurance that the sensitive data in the database can only be accessed by approved users. When the credentials match, the decryption process will begin as shown in Figure 15, enabling the user to view the document text as shown in Figure 16.

Figure 15. Decryption of the encrypted data

Figure 16. Decrypted document

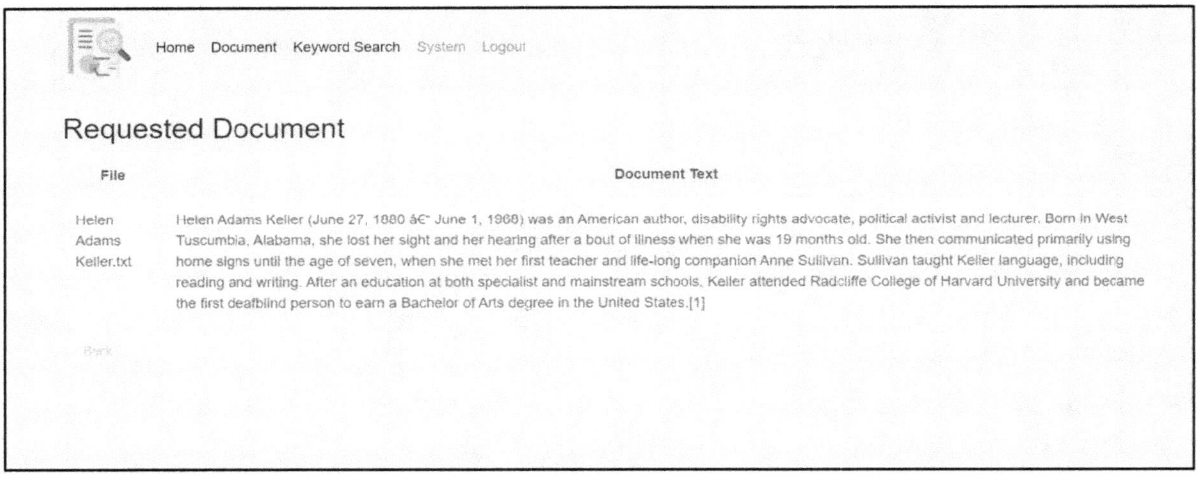

A global vector model is used to convert the keywords into global vector word embeddings. After transforming the user's search query into a global vector word embedding, the system will perform search in the collection of documents having similar embeddings. The user's search query is used to discover and display the documents with material that is related to it. The system will generate embeddings using a global vector model and compare them to document embeddings to do a semantic search, which has the potential to be more effective than simple keyword matching. It helps the system to comprehend the meaning of the user's search query rather than just matching terms in a document. The search query can be entered by the user in the search area field. A list of keywords can be used to run word-embedded searches on a number of encrypted documents in the workspace. The degree to which the returned documents match the user's query determines their ranking. The documents will be ranked in descending order based on their similarity scores once the similarity scores have been computed. The user is shown a list of relevant documents, with the documents with the greatest similarity appearing at the top of the list.

Figure 17. Retrieval of relevant documents for the query

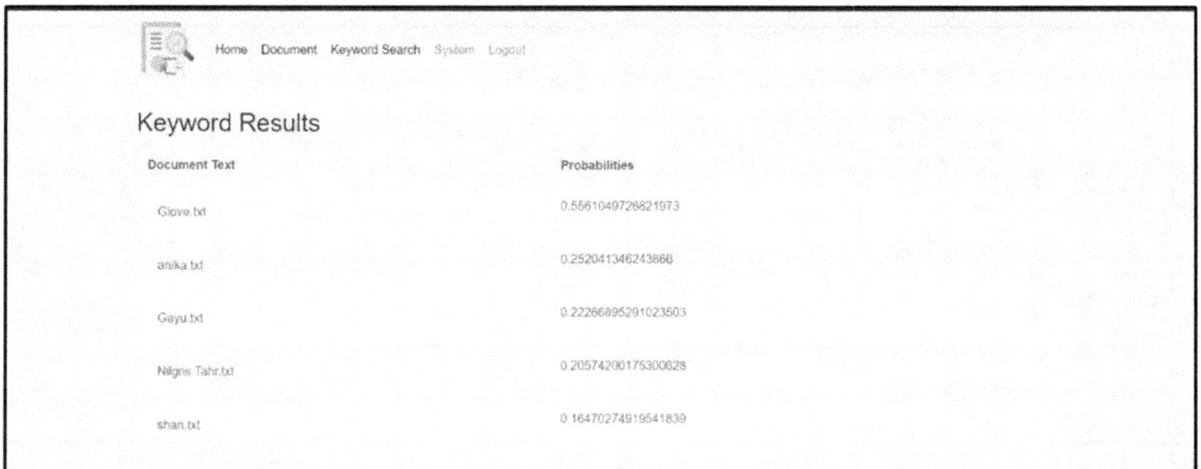

The arrangement shown visually in Figure 17 provides a list of documents with the most relevant ones at the top. Users can concentrate their attention on the top-ranked documents, which are likely to have the most important information, due to the prioritization. Users can save time by being presented with the most important documentation first by organizing the list of documents according to relevancy. It eliminates the need for users to manually sort through a large number of possibly irrelevant. Information retrieval operations are more productive when using these techniques.

5. RESULT ANALYSIS

The results illustrated are obtained for the proposed system during encryption time and key generation time. Potential processing bottlenecks or inefficiencies in the system are identified by evaluating execution times for various file sizes. A graph comparing the encryption times of the three-encryption methods AES, Chens, and the proposed method is shown in Figure 18. The file size in kilobytes is represented by the y-axis, while the various encryption methods are represented by the x-axis. The four equal parts of the y-axis on the graph stand for the following file sizes: 20 KB, 25 KB, 50 KB, and 100 KB. Four bars on the graph, one for each encryption method, indicate the encryption time for each file size. The first bar under "Proposed encryption method" for instance shows how long it takes to encrypt a 20 KB file. A visual depiction of the encryption time is provided by the height of each bar, which displays the encryption time in seconds.

Figure 18. File size vs encryption time

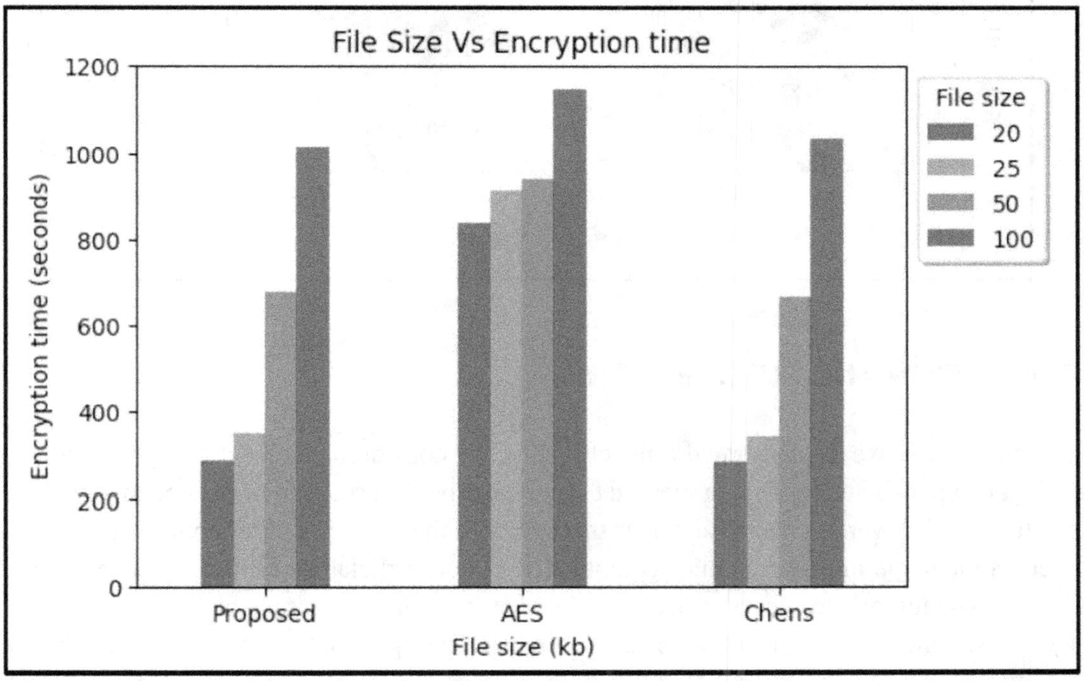

The effectiveness of key generation has an impact on how well encryption algorithms and security mechanisms work overall. Faster key generation speeds are preferred as they enable more efficient data transfer or secure communication by reducing delays in cryptographic procedures. A graph comparing the key generation timings of two key generation methods for various key lengths is shown in Figure 19. Each algorithm's key generation time is clearly visualized in the graph, making it simple to compare and evaluate each algorithm's effectiveness. Understanding the trade-offs between key generation techniques in terms of processing performance is made easier by the graphical representation. The key length in bits is represented by the y-axis, while the key generation algorithms are represented by the x-axis. Key generation time is calculated using the key length as a numerical scale. Three distinct key lengths are represented on the y-axis: 56 bits, 128 bits, and 1024 bits. Three bars on the graph, one for each key generation algorithm, show how long it takes to generate a key for a given key length.

Figure 19. Key length vs key generation time

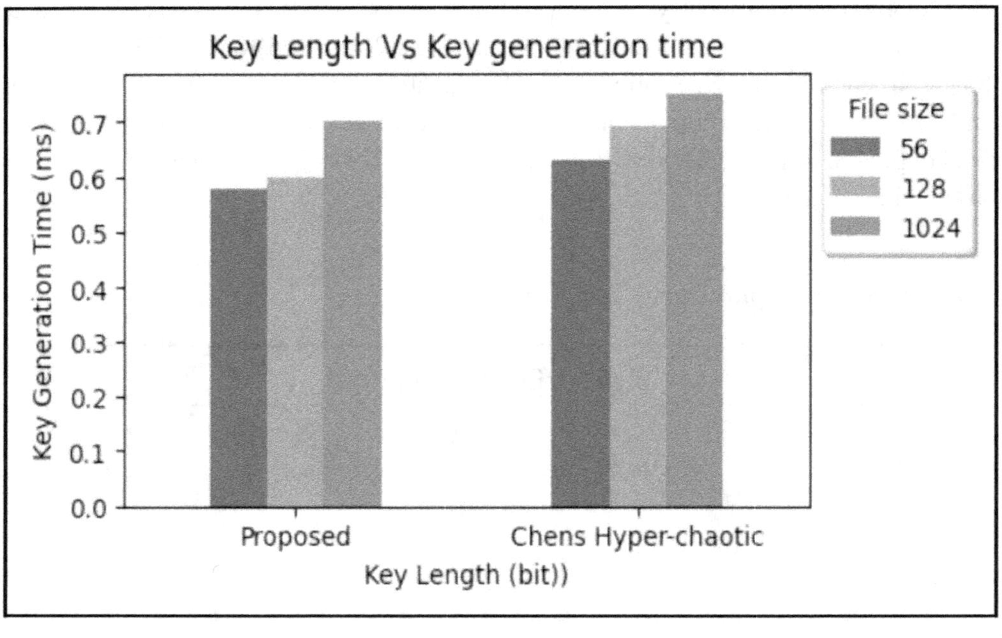

6. CONCLUSION AND FUTURE WORK

In this project work, we demonstrated a novel method by considering DNA Encryption with a Four-Dimensional Hyper Chaotic mapping method to maintain the data security of the documents even if it's stored in the cloud server. A chaotic sequence that serves as the key for DNA encryption is created using 4D hyperchaotic mapping. By creating a complicated and unpredictable chaotic sequence that makes it impossible for unauthorized access to decipher the encrypted data, the usage of 4D hyper chaotic mapping with DNA encryption improves the security of the encrypted data. If the cipher data is text, the attacker intends to make some small alterations. In the case of our DNA Encryption, if hacker decodes the file, they will get another text which further confuses them whether the actual information is in DNA sequence or textual data. We have considered everything in a random way; hence it is very difficult to decrypt it. In order to correctly decrypt a message using DNA encryption, the user must supply both the secret key and the nonce. Nonce avoids Replay attacks, in which an attacker intercepts and replays an encrypted message to gain unauthorized access. The nonce is used as an extra input to the decryption process to ensure that, even if intercepted and replayed, the same encrypted message will not yield the same decrypted message. By utilizing Massive Key Space, DNA encryption can assist in fending off brute force attacks. That is accomplished by using a long key and the DNA encryption method. It is computationally prohibitive for attackers to try all possible key combinations in order to decrypt the data. The security of the encryption is further improved as the key length grows. By encrypting the data before it is transferred, DNA Encryption provides built-in defense against Man-in-the-Middle attacks. Prior to uploading to the server, the data is encrypted to preserve its confidentiality. Sensitive information is rendered unreadable to unauthorized parties by turning the data into a DNA sequence using an encryption method. In this paper, we have considered global word embedded vectors for both the documents and the search query to do semantic and syntactic search over an encrypted data. Utilizing the cosine similarity measure, the spatial distance between the query and document vector is examined. In a high-dimensional space, it determines the cosine of the angle between two vectors. A stronger similarity is shown by a lower angle and a larger cosine value between two vectors that are close to one another. In contrast, if the vectors are further apart, their angle is greater, resulting in a smaller cosine value, which denotes a lower similarity. The top k results are documents that are deemed to be the most similar to the query based on their cosine similarity score. Furthermore, the suggested DNA Encryption with the 4D Hyper Chaotic mapping method offers solid security that makes sure that the data is protected, Global word-embedded search considers the contextual meaning to generate accurate results.

In the future, we will extend our technology to deal with other data types like images in addition to semantic search over encrypted textual data. Using DNA cryptography to encrypt and decrypt images will give an extra degree of security, especially for sensitive images. We'll also create a web-based application to make it easier to use. Users will be able to log in to the system from any location that has an internet connection. Users can easily interact with the system if the program is created with an intuitive and user-friendly interface.

REFERENCES

Chamani, J. G., Wang, Y., Papadopoulos, D., Zhang, M., & Jalili, R. (2022). Multi-User Dynamic Searchable Symmetric Encryption With Corrupted Participants. *IEEE Transactions on Dependable and Secure Computing*, *20*(1), 114–130. doi:10.1109/TDSC.2021.3127546

Cui, Y., Gao, F., Shi, Y., Yin, W., Panaousis, E., & Liang, K. (2020). An Efficient Attribute-Based Multi-Keyword Search Scheme in Encrypted Keyword Generation. *IEEE Access : Practical Innovations, Open Solutions*, *8*, 99024–99036. doi:10.1109/ACCESS.2020.2996940

Das, D., & Kalra, S. (2020). *An Efficient LSI Based Multi-keyword Ranked Search Algorithm on Encrypted Data in Cloud Environment.* International Wireless Communications and Mobile Computing. doi:10.1109/IWCMC48107.2020.9148123

Feng, Z., Liu, T., Li, H., Lu, H., Shou, L., & Xu, J. (2020). Indoor Top-k Keyword-aware Routing Query. *IEEE 36th International Conference on Data Engineering (ICDE),* 1213-1224. 10.1109/ICDE48307.2020.00109

Guo, C., Chen, X., Jie, Y., Fu, Z., Li, M., & Feng, B. (2020). Dynamic Multi-Phrase Ranked Search over Encrypted Data with Symmetric Searchable Encryption. *IEEE Transactions on Services Computing, 13*(6), 1034–1044. doi:10.1109/TSC.2017.2768045

Hahn, C., Yoon, H., & Hur, J. (2023). Multi-Key Similar Data Search on Encrypted Storage with Secure Pay-Per-Query. *IEEE Transactions on Information Forensics and Security, 18*, 1169–1181. doi:10.1109/TIFS.2023.3236178

Handa, R., Rama Krishna, C., & Aggarwal, N. (2020). Efficient Privacy-Preserving Scheme Supporting Disjunctive Multi-Keyword Search with Ranking. *Concurrency and Computation, 32*(2), e5450. doi:10.1002/cpe.5450

Li, F., Ma, J., Miao, Y., Liu, Z., Choo, K.-K. R., Liu, X., & Deng, R. H. (2023). Towards Efficient Verifiable Boolean Search Over Encrypted Cloud Data. *IEEE Transactions on Cloud Computing, 11*(1), 839–853. doi:10.1109/TCC.2021.3118692

Li, J., Ma, J., Miao, Y., Yang, R., Liu, X., & Choo, K.-K. R. (2022). Practical Multi-Keyword Ranked Search With Access Control Over Encrypted Cloud Data. *IEEE Transactions on Cloud Computing, 10*(3), 2005–2019. doi:10.1109/TCC.2020.3024226

Li, X., Tong, Q., Zhao, J., Miao, Y., Ma, S., Weng, J., Ma, J., & Choo, K.-K. R. (2023). Xinghua and Tong, Qiuyun and Zhao, "VRFMS: Verifiable Ranked Fuzzy Multi-Keyword Search Over Encrypted Data". *IEEE Transactions on Services Computing, 16*(1), 698–710. doi:10.1109/TSC.2021.3140092

Li, Y., Ning, J., & Chen, J. (2022). Secure and Practical Wildcard Searchable Encryption System Based on Inner Product. *IEEE Transactions on Services Computing*, •••, 1–14. doi:10.1109/TSC.2022.3207750

Lin, Z. W., Cui, H., Li, B., & Wang, C. (2021). Privacy-Preserving Similarity Search With Efficient Updates in Distributed Key-Value Stores. *IEEE Transactions on Parallel and Distributed Systems, 32*(5), 1072–1084. doi:10.1109/TPDS.2020.3042695

Liu, G., Yang, G., Bai, S., Wang, H., & Xiang, Y. (2022). FASE: A Fast and Accurate Privacy-Preserving Multi-Keyword Top-k Retrieval Scheme Over Encrypted Cloud Data. *IEEE Transactions on Services Computing, 15*(4), 1855–1867. doi:10.1109/TSC.2020.3023393

Miao, Y., Tong, Q., Deng, R. H., Choo, K.-K. R., Liu, X., & Li, H. (2022). Verifiable Searchable Encryption Framework Against Insider Keyword-Guessing Attack in Cloud Storage. *IEEE Transactions on Cloud Computing, 10*(2), 835–848. doi:10.1109/TCC.2020.2989296

Miao, Y., Zheng, W., Jia, X., Liu, X., Choo, K.-K. R., & Deng, R. H. (2023). Ranked Keyword Search Over Encrypted Cloud Data Through Machine Learning Method. *IEEE Transactions on Services Computing, 16*(1), 525–536. doi:10.1109/TSC.2021.3140098

Oya, S., & Kerschbaum, F. (2021). Hiding the Access Pattern is not enough: Exploiting Search Pattern Leakage in Searchable Encryption. *Proc. 30th USENIX Secur. Symp. (USENIX Secur.),* 127-142.

Sharma, V., & Ramamoorthy, S. (2023). A Review on Secure Data access through Multi-Keyword Searching in Cloud Storage. *Third International Conference on Intelligent Communication Technology and Virtual mobile Networks*, 70-73. 10.1109/ICICV50876.2021.9388595

Sun, S.-F., Steinfeld, R., Lai, S., Yuan, X., Sakzad, A., Liu, J., Nepal, S., & Gu, D. (2021). Practical Non-Interactive Searchable Encryption with Forward and Backward Privacy. *Proceedings 2021 Network and Distributed System Security Symposium.* 10.14722/ndss.2021.24162

Wang, D., Jia, X., Wang, C., Yang, K., Fu, S., & Xu, M. (2015). Generalized pattern matching string search on encrypted data in cloud systems. *IEEE Conference on Computer Communications (INFOCOM),* 2101-2109. 10.1109/INFOCOM.2015.7218595

Wu, Yang, Luo, & Hang. (2022). Enabling Traceable and Verifiable Multi-user Forward Secure Searchable Encryption in Hybrid Cloud. *IEEE Transactions on Cloud Computing*. . doi:10.1109/TCC.2022.3170362

Xia, Z., Wang, X., Sun, X., & Wang, Q. (2020). A Secure and Dynamic Multi-Keyword Ranked Search Scheme over Encrypted Cloud Data. *IEEE Transactions on Parallel and Distributed Systems*, *27*(2), 340–352. doi:10.1109/TPDS.2015.2401003

Xu, L., Li, W., Zhang, F., Cheng, R., & Tang, S. (2020). Authorized Keyword Searches on Public Key Encrypted Data With Time Controlled Keyword Privacy. *IEEE Transactions on Information Forensics and Security*, *15*, 2096–2109. doi:10.1109/TIFS.2019.2957691

Yang, W., & Zhu, Y. (2021). A Verifiable Semantic Searching Scheme by Optimal Matching Over Encrypted Data in Public Cloud. *IEEE Transactions on Information Forensics and Security*, *16*, 100–115. doi:10.1109/TIFS.2020.3001728

Zhang, H., Zhao, S., Guo, Z., Wen, Q., Li, W., & Gao, F. (2023). Scalable Fuzzy Keyword Ranked Search Over Encrypted Data on Hybrid Clouds. *IEEE Transactions on Cloud Computing*, *11*(1), 308–323. doi:10.1109/TCC.2021.3092358

Zhang, M., Chen, Y., & Huang, J. (2021). SE-PPFM: A Searchable Encryption Scheme Supporting Privacy-Preserving Fuzzy Multi keyword in Cloud Systems. *IEEE Systems Journal*, *15*(2), 2980–2988. doi:10.1109/JSYST.2020.2997932

Chapter 14
Genetic Algorithm for Key Generation in Cryptosystems

Sanjay Kumar
National Institute of Technology, Raipur, India

Deepmala Sharma
National Institute of Technology, Raipur, India

ABSTRACT

In this chapter, the authors explore the application of genetic algorithms (GAs) for key generation in cryptosystems. Cryptography plays a crucial role in securing sensitive information, and the strength of a cryptosystem lies in the robustness of its encryption keys. Traditional methods of generating cryptographic keys face challenges in finding optimal key solutions, especially as computational power increases. Genetic algorithms offer a promising alternative, leveraging evolutionary principles to optimize key generation. This chapter provides an overview of genetic algorithms, their application in cryptography, and various techniques for using GAs in key generation for secure and efficient cryptosystems.

INTRODUCTION

Cryptography is an indispensable field in modern information security, ensuring the confidentiality, integrity and authenticity of data in various applications such as communication, financial transactions and data storage. One of the fundamental aspects of cryptography is the generation of secure cryptographic keys (Ragavan & Prabu, 2022), which serve as the foundation for encryption and decryption processes in both symmetric and asymmetric cryptosystems.

Background

Traditionally, cryptographic keys have been generated using deterministic methods such as pseudorandom number generators (PRNGs) and cryptographic hash functions. While these methods have been widely used and have shown satisfactory results in many scenarios, they face several challenges as computing power continues to grow exponentially.

DOI: 10.4018/979-8-3693-0593-5.ch014

With the advent of sophisticated computing technologies, the potential for brute-force attacks and other cryptographic attacks has increased significantly. This has raised concerns about the security and resilience of cryptosystems based on traditional key generation methods. Therefore, there is a need for innovative approaches that can generate strong cryptographic keys resistant to various attacks.

Genetic algorithms have been widely used in cryptography for generating keys. Several researchers have conducted extensive research in the field of data encryption and key generation, utilizing genetic algorithms to improve the performance of these processes. Many studies have been conducted, and some of the notable work is presented in this section.

Jhingran et al. (2015) proposed a summary in the field of cryptography using genetic algorithm.

Hassan et al. (2014) proposed a work in which GA and RSA are used for encryption and decryption. In that paper GA is used for key generation then data is encrypted by RSA algorithm. A strong non-repeating key was generated by this algorithm. Key strength of this algorithm is better than DES, AES, and RSA, etc.

Aarti Soni et al. (2012) have introduced a novel algorithm for key generation in which a pseudo-random number generator was employed. The algorithm generates random numbers, on which genetic operations are performed to produce a key suitable for encryption. The generated key is used to encrypt data using AES. This algorithm has advantages in terms of reduced computational time and improved irregularity of the key. Overall, the proposed algorithm provided a promising approach for key generation in cryptography.

Sania Jawed et al. (2014) have implemented a similar approach for key generation using genetic algorithms. However, they employed a different fitness function, which was calculated by applying the Frequency and Gap test along with the Hamming distance between the two binary keys. The algorithm was developed using Java technology and utilized 100 chromosomes, 0.5 mutation rate and a 2.5 crossover rate. The proposed algorithm presented a novel approach for key generation in cryptography, offering a potentially useful alternative to traditional methods.

Narendra K. Pareek et al. (2016) have developed a genetic algorithm for the encryption of grayscale images. The proposed algorithm has demonstrated excellent statistical results and can withstand various types of attacks, including plaintext, brute force, entropy and differential attacks. The encryption process involved the generation of a key using a genetic algorithm, followed by the application of a substitution permutation network for encryption. The proposed algorithm provided a robust and effective approach for image encryption and has the potential to enhance the security of image-based applications.

Swati Mishra et al. (2013) have proposed a key generation algorithm that aims to generate the best-fit key for encryption. The algorithm employed random number generation to create both public and private keys, followed by the application of crossover and mutation operations with the Pearson coefficient of autocorrelation serving as the fitness function. The process continues until the best key is obtained. The algorithm was implemented using C++ programming language and the frequency of the generated keys was tested using the chi-square test. Overall, the proposed algorithm provided a promising approach for key generation in cryptography, offering improved security and reliability in encryption applications.

Ankit et al (2016) uses natural selection process for generating a key for stream cipher. Genetic operations were used for key generation. After the genetic algorithm completed the key generation process, the final selection of the key was performed. The selection process ensured that the chosen key was unique and non-repeating, enhancing the security and reliability of the encryption. Overall, this process demonstrated the effectiveness of genetic algorithms in generating secure and robust keys for use in cryptography.

Dutta (2014), Veetil (2015), Nagde (2013) proposed Encryption and Decryption algorithm based on genetic algorithm. Sreelaja. N. K and G. A. Vijayalakshmi Pai (2009) proposed an algorithm in which keys was generated to design a stream cipher for data encryption using a Particle swarm optimization (PSO) based approach.

Abas, Naeem, et al. (2020) proposed a method that utilizes the three-dimensional (3D) CUBE and employs key encipherment and management techniques to enhance security and uphold confidentiality and integrity of dispersed data. This algorithm was implemented in a setting that employed symmetric cryptography with the aim of establishing a secure environment.

Dulla, Godfrey L. et al. (2019) proposed a superior encryption algorithm called Blowfish which was created to ensure highly secure protection for multimedia content. This technique was designed to safeguard various types of input files, such as text, audio and video. Despite having comparable configurations to symmetric methods like DES, AES and 3DES the Blowfish algorithm surpasses them in terms of encryption and decryption speed, making it a more advanced solution.

Motivation

The motivation behind exploring Genetic Algorithms (GAs) for key generation in cryptosystems lies in their ability to tackle complex optimization problems efficiently. Genetic Algorithms (GAs) draw inspiration from the mechanisms of natural selection and evolutionary biology. This involves favoring the survival and reproduction of the most well-adapted individuals in a population, enabling them to propagate their genetic traits to subsequent generations. This concept can be applied to find optimal solutions in various domains, including cryptography (Katoch et al., 2021).

GAs offers several advantages for key generation in cryptosystems:

1. **Diversity in Exploration:** GAs maintain a diverse set of solutions, ensuring that they explore a wide range of possible keys, which can lead to discovering more secure and robust keys.
2. **Adaptation to Changing Environments:** GAs can adapt to changes in the cryptographic landscape by dynamically adjusting their parameters and evolving the key generation process.
3. **Parallelism and Scalability:** GAs can be parallelized, allowing them to take advantage of modern multi-core and distributed computing architectures for faster and more scalable key generation.
4. **Non-Determinism:** GAs introduce an element of randomness during the evolutionary process, making it harder for adversaries to predict or exploit the key generation mechanism.
5. **Innovative Solutions:** GAs can discover unconventional or non-intuitive solutions, potentially leading to cryptographic keys that are harder to break using traditional methods.

Objectives

The primary objectives of this chapter are as follows:

1. **To present Genetic Algorithms in the Context of Cryptography:** We will provide an overview of Genetic Algorithms, explaining their basic principles, operators and techniques that are relevant to key generation in cryptosystems.

2. **To explore the Feasibility of Genetic Algorithms for Key Generation:** We will investigate the applicability of Genetic Algorithms for generating cryptographic keys in both symmetric and asymmetric cryptosystems.
3. **To compare Genetic Algorithm-based Key Generation with Traditional Methods:** We will conduct a comparative analysis between Genetic Algorithm based key generation and conventional key generation methods in terms of security, efficiency, and resilience against attacks.
4. **To discuss Real-World Applications and Case Studies:** We will discuss real-world scenarios where Genetic Algorithm-based key generation can be applied, including secure communication systems, IOT (Internet of Things) cryptography, cloud security and digital signatures.
5. **To highlight Challenges and Future Directions:** We will identify potential challenges and limitations of using Genetic Algorithms for key generation and discuss possible future research directions to improve the security and effectiveness of this approach.

This chapter aims to demonstrate the potential of Genetic Algorithms as a viable and efficient method for key generation in cryptosystems. By understanding the strengths and limitations of Genetic Algorithms, we can pave the way for more secure and resilient cryptographic systems in the face of ever-evolving threats.

CRYPTOGRAPHY FUNDAMENTALS

Cryptography is the science of secure communication and it forms the foundation of modern information security. Cryptography employs mathematical algorithms to convert plain text information into unintelligible text, requiring specific cryptographic keys for comprehension. This segment explores the core principles of cryptography, encompassing both symmetric and asymmetric cryptographic techniques, the intricacies of generating cryptographic keys within systems, and the complexities tied to this key generation process (Kessler, 2003).

Symmetric Cryptography

Symmetric cryptography, often referred to as secret-key cryptography, stands as one of the earliest and extensively employed cryptographic methods. Within this approach, a sole secret key serves dual roles for both data encryption and decryption. This shared key is utilized by both the sender and recipient, contributing to a straightforward and efficient process (Delfs et al., 2015).

Working Principle

1. **Key Distribution:** The difficulty within symmetric cryptography centres on the secure distribution of the confidential key among the involved entities. Should the key be compromised during its transfer, the overall security of the system becomes vulnerable.
2. **Encryption:** To encrypt the plaintext, the secret key is applied using an encryption algorithm. This process produces the ciphertext, which can be transmitted securely over untrusted channels.
3. **Decryption:** The recipient uses the same secret key and a decryption algorithm to transform the ciphertext back into the original plaintext.

Advantages

- **Speed:** Symmetric algorithms are generally faster compared to asymmetric algorithms since they involve fewer computational steps.
- **Suitable for Bulk Data:** Symmetric cryptography is well-suited for encrypting large amounts of data efficiently.

Limitations:

- **Key Distribution:** Ensuring the secure distribution of the secret key among authorized participants stands as a central obstacle within symmetric cryptography.

Asymmetric Cryptography

Asymmetric cryptography, alternatively referred to as public-key cryptography, deals with the inherent key distribution challenge found in symmetric cryptography. This method employs a set of mathematically linked keys, consisting of a public key and a private key, to carry out encryption and decryption processes. (Salomaa, 1996).

Working Principle

1. **Public and Private Keys:** The public key is widely disseminated and utilized to facilitate encryption tasks, while the private key remains safeguarded and exclusively used for decryption purposes.
2. **Encryption:** When data needs to be encrypted, the sender utilizes the recipient's public key, and only the associated private key possesses the capability to decipher the resulting ciphertext.
3. **Digital Signatures:** Asymmetric cryptography is additionally harnessed to establish digital signatures. In this process, the sender employs their private key to sign a message, ensuring credibility and safeguarding the message's integrity.

Advantages of Asymmetric Cryptography

- Key Distribution: Asymmetric cryptography eliminates the need for key distribution, as public keys can be freely shared without compromising security.
- Enhanced Security: The private keys are never shared or transmitted, reducing the risk of key compromise.

Limitations of Asymmetric Cryptography

- **Computational Complexity:** Asymmetric algorithms entail higher computational workload compared to symmetric algorithms, resulting in slower operations, particularly when handling extensive datasets.
- **Key Length Requirements:** Ensuring comparable security demands longer key lengths, thereby amplifying computational burdens.

Key Generation in Cryptosystems

The process of key generation is a critical aspect of cryptographic systems. The strength and security of the cryptosystems depend on the generation of strong and random cryptographic keys. Key generation involves creating secret keys for symmetric cryptography and key pairs for asymmetric cryptography.

Key Generation Process for Symmetric Cryptography

1. **Randomness:** The key generation process starts with obtaining a high-quality source of randomness to ensure the unpredictability of the secret key.
2. **Key Length:** The key length directly impacts the security of the cryptosystem. Longer key lengths offer greater resistance against brute-force attacks.
3. **Secure Key Storage:** Once generated, the secret key must be securely stored to prevent unauthorized access.

Key Generation Process for Asymmetric Cryptography

1. **Key Pair Generation:** The user creates a set of keys that share a mathematical relationship – one being a public key and the other, a private key.
2. **Public Key Distribution:** The public key can be freely shared with others, as it does not compromise the security of the system.
3. **Private Key Protection:** Safeguarding and maintaining the confidentiality of the private key is imperative to prevent unauthorized access.

Challenges in Key Generation

The key generation process faces several challenges:

1. **Entropy and Randomness:** Generating truly random and unpredictable cryptographic keys are challenging. Insufficient entropy can lead to weak keys susceptible to attacks.
2. **Key Distribution:** In symmetric cryptography, securely distribution of secret keys to all legitimate parties is a significant challenge. If an attacker intercepts the key during transmission, the entire system's security is compromised.
3. **Key Management:** Cryptosystems often involve a large number of keys, which must be properly managed, rotated and stored securely.
4. **Key Length Selection:** The appropriate key length is crucial for the security of the cryptosystem. Selecting key lengths that are either too short or too long can impact performance and security.
5. **Quantum Computing Threats:** The rise of quantum computing poses a potential threat to classical cryptographic systems, including key generation methods. Quantum computers could break traditional encryption algorithms that rely on factorization and discrete logarithm problems.

Understanding the fundamentals of symmetric and asymmetric cryptography, the process of key generation and the challenges involved is vital for designing secure and robust cryptosystems. Advancements in key generation techniques, including the exploration of Genetic Algorithms, can help to address some of the challenges and strengthen the security of cryptographic systems in the face of evolving threats.

GENETIC ALGORITHM: AN OVERVIEW

Genetic Algorithms (GAs) are a class of optimization algorithms inspired by the process of natural selection and evolution. Developed by John Holland in the 1970s, GAs mimics the survival of the fittest and aim to find optimal solutions to complex problems by iteratively evolving a population of potential solutions. In this section, we will provide a comprehensive overview of Genetic Algorithms, including their basic principles, key concepts, and genetic operators relevant to key generation in cryptosystems (Mirjalili & Mirjalili, 2019).

Genetic Algorithm Basics

Representation:

In Genetic Algorithms, the potential solutions to the problem at hand are represented as chromosomes or strings of genes. Each gene in the chromosome corresponds to a specific aspect of the solution and the combination of genes forms a candidate solution.

Population:

A population is a collection of multiple chromosomes. Initially, a population of random or pre-defined chromosomes is generated to start the evolution process.

Fitness Function:

The fitness function evaluates how good or fit a particular chromosome is as a solution to the problem. It quantifies the quality of the candidate solution and serves as a measure of its performance. The fitness function is problem-specific and guides the evolution by rewarding better solutions.

Evolutionary Process

The genetic algorithm undergoes a series of iterations called generations. In each generation, the chromosomes with higher fitness values are more likely to be selected for reproduction, creating new offspring solutions.

Selection:

The process of selection involves the determination of parent chromosomes for reproduction, relying on their fitness values. Chromosomes exhibiting greater fitness are more likely to be chosen, thereby encouraging the dissemination of advantageous traits throughout the population.

Reproduction:

The selected chromosomes undergo reproduction through genetic operators, such as crossover and mutation, to create new offspring.

Termination:

The evolution process continues for a predetermined number of generations or until a termination condition is met. The algorithm aims to converge towards an optimal solution as it progresses through generations.

Figure 1. Genetic algorithm

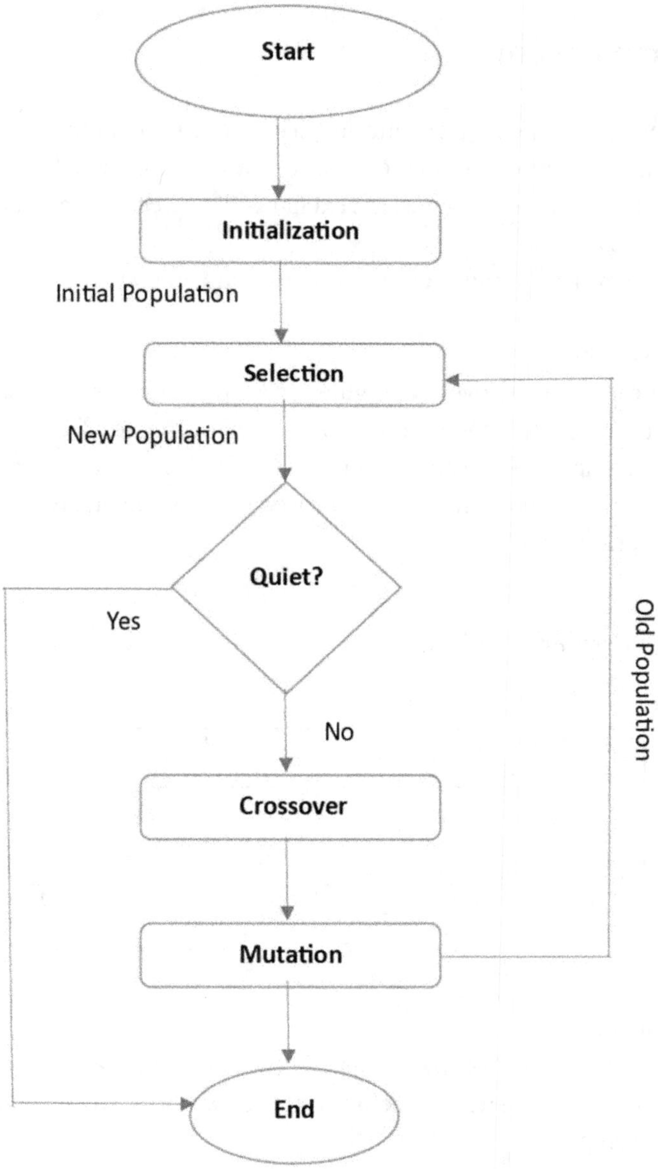

KEY CONCEPTS

Selection

Selection is a crucial step in the evolutionary process. There are various selection strategies, such as roulette wheel selection, tournament selection and rank-based selection. These strategies determine how individuals are chosen to become parents for the next generation. The selection process aims to Favor individuals with higher fitness values, increasing the likelihood of their genetic material being passed on to the next generation.

Crossover (Recombination)

Crossover is the process of combining genetic material from two parent chromosomes to create new offspring. It mimics the genetic recombination that occurs during sexual reproduction in nature. The crossover point(s) determine where the genes are exchanged between the parents to create two new child chromosomes (Poohoi et al., 2023).

Below are some crossover techniques commonly used in Genetic Algorithms for key generation:

1. **Single-Point Crossover:**
    - During single-point crossover, a singular crossover point is chosen along the chromosome. Genetic material preceding the crossover point originates from one parent, while genetic material succeeding the crossover point is inherited from the other parent.
    - For key generation, this technique can be used to combine bits from two parent keys, creating two new offspring keys.

Figure 2. Single point crossover technique

Before

1	0	1	0	0	1	1	1
0	0	0	1	0	0	1	0

After

1	0	1	1	0	0	1	0
0	0	0	0	0	1	1	1

2. **Two-Point Crossover:**
    - In the case of two-point crossover, a pair of crossover points is designated along the chromosome. Genetic material situated between these two points is exchanged between parents to generate offspring.
    - This technique can be applied to combine segments of key material from two parent keys, generating new keys with mixed characteristics.

Figure 3. Two-point crossover technique

Before

1	0	1	0	0	1	1	1
0	0	0	1	0	0	1	0

After

1	0	0	1	0	1	1	1
0	0	1	0	0	0	1	0

3. **Uniform Crossover:**
    - Uniform crossover involves selecting each bit from one parent or the other with a certain probability. Each bit has an equal chance of coming from either parent.
    - For key generation, this technique can be used to create new keys with a mixture of genetic material from both parents.

Figure 4. Uniform crossover technique

Before

1	0	1	0	0	1	1	1
0	0	0	1	0	0	1	0

After

1	0	0	1	0	1	1	0
0	0	1	0	0	0	1	1

Mutation

Mutation introduces minor and random modifications to the genes within individual chromosomes. This mechanism serves to uphold diversity within the population and introduces novel prospective solutions that were absent previously. The role of mutation is crucial in preventing the algorithm from becoming trapped in local optima and stimulating exploration throughout the solution space. Various approaches for implementing mutation exist, including:

Flip Bit Mutation: This technique involves randomly selecting a bit in the chromosome and flipping its value (from 0 to 1 or vice versa).

Swap Mutation: In this technique, two randomly selected genes are swapped with each other.

Inversion Mutation: The inversion mutation is a common genetic algorithm operator used to diversify the population. It works by randomly selecting a portion of genes within a chromosome and reversing their order. This inversion process changes the sequence of genes within that specific subset, which can potentially generate new and beneficial solutions within the population.

Scramble Mutation: This technique randomly selects a subset of genes in the chromosome and scrambles their order.

Figure 5. Mutation techniques

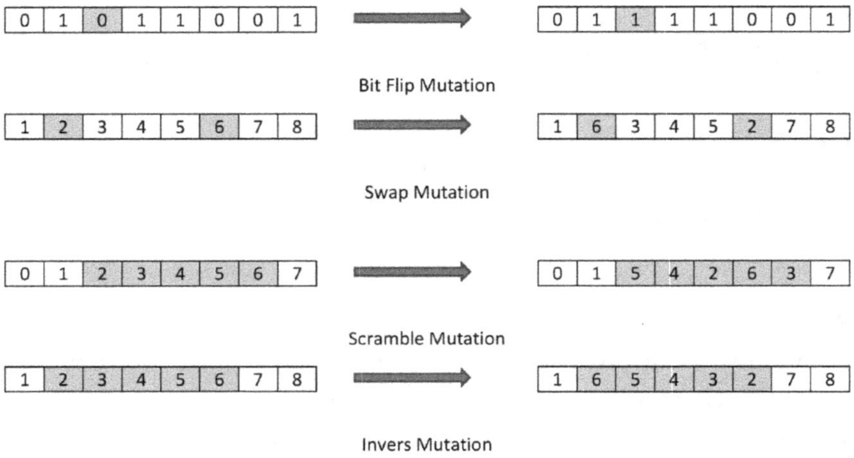

Genetic Operators in Key Generation

In the context of key generation in cryptosystems, Genetic Algorithms can be customized with specific genetic operators tailored to the cryptographic domain. The key generation process can be represented as chromosomes and the genetic operators can manipulate the bits or values within these chromosomes.

Encoding Schemes: The chromosomes in the Genetic Algorithm can be encoded in different ways to represent cryptographic keys effectively. For symmetric key generation, the chromosomes may consist of binary strings of fixed length, representing the key bits. For asymmetric key generation, the chromosomes can encode the parameters of the key pairs, such as the public and private exponents in RSA.

Fitness Function for Key Generation: The fitness function in the context of key generation evaluates the security and strength of the cryptographic key represented by a chromosome. It may consider factors such as key length, randomness, resistance to attacks, and the ability to withstand cryptographic analysis.

Customized Genetic Operators: The genetic operators, such as crossover and mutation, can be adapted to the cryptographic domain. For instance, in symmetric key generation, crossover could involve bitwise mixing of parent keys and mutation could introduce random bit flips. In asymmetric key generation, the genetic operators can manipulate the key pair parameters accordingly.

The combination of these customized genetic operators and the fitness function ensures that the Genetic Algorithm evolves cryptographic keys that exhibit desirable characteristics of strength, security and robustness. Genetic Algorithms offer a powerful approach for key generation in cryptosystems by leveraging evolutionary principles to find optimal solutions. By understanding the basic principles of Genetic Algorithms and tailoring them to the cryptographic domain, researchers and practitioners can explore innovative methods to generate secure cryptographic keys that are resistant to various attacks.

INTEGRATING GENETIC ALGORITHM INTO CRYPTOSYSTEMS

Genetic Algorithms (GAs) have shown promise in various optimization problems, including key generation in cryptosystems. Integrating GAs into cryptosystems requires careful consideration of design choices, fitness function selection, encoding schemes for keys and appropriate parameter settings. In this section, we will explore these aspects in detail to effectively incorporate Genetic Algorithms into the key generation process for secure and efficient cryptosystems.

Design Considerations

Security Requirements:

The foremost consideration when integrating GAs into cryptosystems is ensuring that the generated cryptographic keys meet the required security standards. It is crucial to define the security requirements for the keys, such as key length, resistance to various attacks (e.g., brute-force, differential cryptanalysis) and the desired level of cryptographic strength.

Computational Efficiency:

GAs can be computationally intensive, especially when dealing with large key spaces. Balancing the computational cost of the Genetic Algorithm with the need for generating secure keys is essential. Efficient selection of genetic operators and appropriate population sizes can significantly impact the computational efficiency.

Key Length and Encoding:

Selecting an appropriate key length is fundamental to the security of the cryptosystem. For symmetric key generation, the encoding scheme must ensure that each gene represents a valid key bit. For asymmetric key generation, the encoding scheme should map the key pair parameters appropriately into the chromosome representation.

Diversity Preservation:

Maintaining diversity within the population is crucial for the effectiveness of GAs. Diversity helps in exploring a broader solution space and avoiding premature convergence to suboptimal solutions. Measures like elitism and careful selection of genetic operators can promote diversity preservation.

Key Rotation and Management:

In long-term use, cryptographic keys might require rotation or re-generation to maintain security. The integration of Genetic Algorithms into key management processes should account for key rotation policies and potential key regeneration scenarios.

Fitness Function Selection

The fitness function is a critical component of Genetic Algorithms, as it drives the evolution of the population towards more desirable solutions. In the context of key generation in cryptosystems, the fitness function must evaluate the security, strength, and effectiveness of the cryptographic keys represented by the chromosomes. The fitness function should consider the following factors:

1. **Key Strength:** Assessing the strength of the cryptographic keys against various attacks, including brute-force, cryptanalysis, and side-channel attacks.
2. **Key Length:** Favouring longer keys with higher entropy to increase resistance against attacks.

3. **Randomness:** Promoting keys with higher levels of randomness and unpredictability.
4. **Performance:** Balancing the trade-off between key strength and computational efficiency.
5. **Cryptographic Standards:** Ensuring that the generated keys comply with industry-accepted cryptographic standards and guidelines.

Encoding Schemes for Keys

Choosing an appropriate encoding scheme is crucial to represent cryptographic keys effectively within the Genetic Algorithm. The encoding scheme should preserve the key's uniqueness and ensure that the genetic operators can manipulate the key representation accurately.

For symmetric key generation, binary encoding is commonly used, where each gene represents a bit of the key. For asymmetric key generation, encoding the key pair parameters, such as public and private exponents in RSA, can be more complex. Customized encoding schemes may be required to map the key parameters into chromosomes.

Genetic Algorithm Parameters

The performance and effectiveness of the Genetic Algorithm heavily depend on parameter settings. Proper tuning of these parameters is essential to achieve desirable results in key generation.

1. **Population Size:** The number of chromosomes in the population. A larger population allows for better exploration but increases computational cost.
2. **Generation Count:** The number of generations or iterations the algorithm runs. It affects the time taken for convergence.
3. **Selection Strategy:** The method used to select parents for reproduction, such as roulette wheel, tournament selection, or rank-based selection.
4. **Crossover Rate:** The probability of applying crossover during reproduction. A higher crossover rate encourages exploration.
5. **Mutation Rate:** The probability of applying mutation to a chromosome. A low mutation rate preserves good solutions, while a higher rate promotes diversity.
6. **Elitism:** Preserving the best individuals from one generation to the next to maintain valuable traits.
7. **Termination Criteria:** The conditions under which the algorithm stops, such as reaching a certain fitness threshold or a maximum number of generations.

Integrating Genetic Algorithms into cryptosystems requires careful consideration of design choices, fitness function, encoding schemes and parameter settings. By tailoring the Genetic Algorithm to the cryptographic domain and addressing key generation challenges, researchers and practitioners can create robust and secure cryptosystems with the potential for generating strong cryptographic keys. Continuous improvements in Genetic Algorithm-based key generation can lead to enhanced security in the face of evolving cryptographic threats.

CASE STUDIES

In this section, we present three case studies showcasing the application of Genetic Algorithms (GAs) for key generation in different cryptographic scenarios. We explore how GAs can be utilized for both symmetric and asymmetric key generation and how hybrid approaches can enhance security in key generation for cryptosystems.

Genetic Algorithm for Symmetric Key Generation

Problem Statement

Consider a scenario where a secure communication system requires the generation of symmetric encryption keys. The objective is to find a strong and random key that offers resistance against brute-force attacks.

GA Approach

1. Encoding: Represent the symmetric key as a binary chromosome, where each gene corresponds to a single bit in the key.
2. Fitness Function: The fitness function evaluates the strength and randomness of the key. It considers factors like the number of 1's in the key (higher randomness) and the Hamming distance from known weak keys.
3. Genetic Operators: Implement crossover by randomly exchanging bits between parent keys. Introduce mutation by flipping individual bits with a low probability.
4. Termination Criteria: The GA continues for a specified number of generations or until a key with the desired fitness level is found.

Example

Problem Statement

Generate a 5-bit symmetric encryption key using a Genetic Algorithm to maximize the number of '1's in the key.

Steps:

1. **Encoding:** Represent the key as a sequence of 0s and 1s. Let's start with an initial population of keys: 10001, 00110, 10011, 10101, 00011.
2. **Fitness Function:** Calculate the number of '1's in each key to determine their fitness. For the initial population:
   Chromosome 1: 10001 - Fitness: 2
   Chromosome 2: 00110 - Fitness: 2
   Chromosome 3: 10011 - Fitness: 3
   Chromosome 4: 10101 - Fitness: 3
   Chromosome 5: 00011 - Fitness: 2
3. Genetic Operations:

- **Crossover:** Select two parents based on their fitness. Apply single point crossover.
  Crossover: Parent1: 10101, Parent2: 10001, Crossover Point: 1
- **Mutation:** With a low probability 0.1, flip individual bits in the offspring.
  Mutated Offspring1: 10001
  Mutated Offspring2: 10101

4. **Repeat:** Perform steps 2 and 3 for a few generations. We perform step 2 and 3 for four generations

Generation 1 - Population:

Chromosome 1: 10001 - Fitness: 2
Chromosome 2: 00110 - Fitness: 2
Chromosome 3: 10011 - Fitness: 3
Chromosome 4: 10101 - Fitness: 3
Chromosome 5: 00011 - Fitness: 2
Selected Parents: 10101 and 10001
Crossover: Parent1: 10101, Parent2: 10001, Crossover Point: 1
Mutated Offspring1: 10001
Mutated Offspring2: 10101
Selected Parents: 10101 and 00110
Crossover: Parent1: 10101, Parent2: 00110, Crossover Point: 4
Mutated Offspring1: 10100
Mutated Offspring2: 00111

Generation 2 - Population:

Chromosome 1: 10001 - Fitness: 2
Chromosome 2: 10101 - Fitness: 3
Chromosome 3: 10100 - Fitness: 2
Chromosome 4: 00111 - Fitness: 3
Selected Parents: 00111 and 10100
Crossover: Parent1: 00111, Parent2: 10100, Crossover Point: 2
Mutated Offspring1: 00110
Mutated Offspring2: 10111
Selected Parents: 10100 and 10001
Crossover: Parent1: 10100, Parent2: 10001, Crossover Point: 2
Mutated Offspring1: 10000
Mutated Offspring2: 10100

Generation 3 - Population:

Chromosome 1: 00110 - Fitness: 2
Chromosome 2: 10111 - Fitness: 4
Chromosome 3: 10000 - Fitness: 1
Chromosome 4: 10100 - Fitness: 2
Selected Parents: 00110 and 10000
Crossover: Parent1: 00110, Parent2: 10000, Crossover Point: 4
Mutated Offspring1: 00110
Mutated Offspring2: 10001
Selected Parents: 10111 and 10100
Crossover: Parent1: 10111, Parent2: 10100, Crossover Point: 3

Mutated Offspring1: 10100
Mutated Offspring2: 10111

Generation 4 - Population:

Chromosome 1: 00110 - Fitness: 2
Chromosome 2: 10001 - Fitness: 2
Chromosome 3: 10100 - Fitness: 2
Chromosome 4: 10111 - Fitness: 4
Selected Parents: 10111 and 10001
Crossover: Parent1: 10111, Parent2: 10001, Crossover Point: 3
Mutated Offspring1: 10100
Mutated Offspring2: 10011
Selected Parents: 10111 and 10001
Crossover: Parent1: 10111, Parent2: 10001, Crossover Point: 4
Mutated Offspring1: 10111
Mutated Offspring2: 10001

Final symmetric encryption key: 10111

Result: After four generations, the Genetic Algorithm will converge towards a symmetric key that has a higher number of '1's, maximizing its randomness and strength. The final key might be something like: 10111.

This example demonstrates how the Genetic Algorithm evolves the population of keys over generations, favoring keys with more '1's, which are considered more secure due to increased randomness.

RESULTS AND BENEFITS

The GA converges towards a symmetric key that exhibits high randomness and robustness against brute-force attacks. It produces keys that are more secure than traditional methods, especially when searching through large key spaces.

Genetic Algorithm for Asymmetric Key Generation

Problem Statement

In an environment where secure communication relies on asymmetric cryptography, the challenge is to generate secure key pairs (public and private keys) for users.

GA Approach

1. **Encoding:** Represent the key pair parameters (e.g., public exponent and modulus in RSA) as chromosomes.
2. **Fitness Function:** The fitness function evaluates the security of the key pair by examining factors like the key length, primality of the modulus, and resistance to factorization attacks.

3. **Genetic Operators:** Implement crossover by combining the parameters of two parent key pairs to form new offspring key pairs. Introduce mutation by perturbing the key pair parameters slightly.
4. **Termination Criteria:** The GA runs for a set number of generations or until key pairs with desired security levels are obtained.

Example

Problem

Generate an RSA key pair (public and private keys) using a Genetic Algorithm to maximize the numeric value of the modulus.

Steps

1. **Encoding:** Represent the key pair as numbers. For example, let's consider an initial population of key pairs:
   Key Pair 1: Public Exponent: 11, Modulus: 8954
   Key Pair 2: Public Exponent: 5, Modulus: 2302
   Key Pair 3: Public Exponent: 13, Modulus: 3126
   Key Pair 4: Public Exponent: 3, Modulus: 340
   Key Pair 5: Public Exponent: 13, Modulus: 7772
2. **Fitness Function:** Measure the size (number of digits) of the modulus to determine the fitness of each key pair. For the initial population:
   Key Pair 1: Public Exponent: 11, Modulus: 8954 - Fitness: 8954
   Key Pair 2: Public Exponent: 5, Modulus: 2302 - Fitness: 2302
   Key Pair 3: Public Exponent: 13, Modulus: 3126 - Fitness: 3126
   Key Pair 4: Public Exponent: 3, Modulus: 340 - Fitness: 340
   Key Pair 5: Public Exponent: 13, Modulus: 7772 - Fitness: 7772
3. Genetic Operations:
   - Selection:
     Selected Parents: Public Exponent: 13, Modulus: 3126 and Public Exponent: 3, Modulus: 340
   - Crossover:
     Crossover: Parent1 Modulus: 3126, Parent2 Modulus: 340 - Offspring Modulus: 310
   - **Mutation:** With a low probability, change some parts of the offspring's key pair. For instance, add 10 to the public exponent: Mutated Offspring: (Public Exponent: 13, Modulus: 3102).
4. **Repeat:** Perform steps 2 and 3 for two generations.
   Generation 1 - Population:
      Key Pair 1: Public Exponent: 11, Modulus: 8954 - Fitness: 8954
      Key Pair 2: Public Exponent: 5, Modulus: 2302 - Fitness: 2302
      Key Pair 3: Public Exponent: 13, Modulus: 3126 - Fitness: 3126
      Key Pair 4: Public Exponent: 3, Modulus: 340 - Fitness: 340
      Key Pair 5: Public Exponent: 13, Modulus: 7772 - Fitness: 7772
      Selected Parents: Public Exponent: 13, Modulus: 3126 and Public Exponent: 3, Modulus: 340
      Crossover: Parent1 Modulus: 3126, Parent2 Modulus: 340 - Offspring Modulus: 310

Selected Parents: Public Exponent: 13, Modulus: 3126 and Public Exponent: 5, Modulus: 2302
Crossover: Parent1 Modulus: 3126, Parent2 Modulus: 2302 - Offspring Modulus: 3102

Generation 2 - Population:

Key Pair 1: Public Exponent: 13, Modulus: 310 - Fitness: 310
Key Pair 2: Public Exponent: 13, Modulus: 3102 - Fitness: 3102
Selected Parents: Public Exponent: 13, Modulus: 3102 and Public Exponent: 13, Modulus: 310
Crossover: Parent1 Modulus: 3102, Parent2 Modulus: 310 - Offspring Modulus: 3102
Selected Parents: Public Exponent: 13, Modulus: 3102 and Public Exponent: 13, Modulus: 310
Crossover: Parent1 Modulus: 3102, Parent2 Modulus: 310 - Offspring Modulus: 3102

Final Key Pair (Public Exponent, Modulus): (13, 3102)

Result: After a few generations, the Genetic Algorithm will converge towards a key pair with a larger modulus, maximizing its length for improved security. The final key pair might be something like: (Public Exponent: 13, Modulus: 3102).

Results and Benefits

The GA converges towards key pairs that offer strong cryptographic security. It can generate key pairs with suitable parameters, and the process can be adapted for different asymmetric algorithms like RSA, DSA, or ECC.

The case studies demonstrate the versatility and effectiveness of Genetic Algorithms in key generation for cryptosystems. Whether for symmetric key generation, asymmetric key generation, or hybrid approaches, GAs offers a valuable tool to create secure and robust cryptographic keys. By customizing the encoding, fitness function, and genetic operators, researchers and practitioners can tailor the GA to specific cryptographic requirements and achieve enhanced security in various communication systems and data protection applications.

PERFORMANCE EVALUATION

In this section, we conduct a comprehensive performance evaluation of the Genetic Algorithm (GA) for key generation in cryptosystems. We compare the GA with traditional key generation methods, analyses its efficiency and scalability and assess the security and robustness of the generated cryptographic keys.

Comparison With Traditional Key Generation Methods Methodology

We evaluate the GA-based key generation against traditional methods such as pseudorandom number generators (PRNGs) and cryptographic hash functions commonly used for key generation.

Metrics:

1. **Security:** We assess the strength of the keys generated by each method against known cryptographic attacks, including brute force, differential cryptanalysis, and statistical attacks.
2. **Randomness:** We measure the randomness of the keys to ensure they are unpredictable and resist cryptographic analysis.

3. **Speed:** We compare the time taken by each method to generate cryptographic keys, taking into account the key length and the computational complexity.

Results and Findings

The GA-based key generation demonstrates significant advantages over traditional methods. The GA-produced keys exhibit higher security and randomness due to the use of evolutionary principles to explore the solution space effectively. While the GA may have slightly higher computational overhead than PRNGs, it still performs well, especially for larger key sizes. Additionally, the GA is less susceptible to predictability and provides a more secure solution in scenarios where key distribution is a challenge.

Efficiency and Scalability Analysis Methodology

We evaluate the efficiency and scalability of the GA-based key generation by varying the key length and population size. We measure the time taken by the GA to find optimal keys for different cryptosystems.

Metrics:

1. **Execution Time:** We measure the time required for the GA to converge and produce the desired cryptographic keys for various key lengths and population sizes.
2. **Scalability:** We analyse how the GA scales with increasing key length and population size to determine its effectiveness for larger-scale cryptosystems.

Results and Findings

The efficiency of the GA-based key generation is highly dependent on the key length and population size. While the execution time increases with larger key sizes and populations, the GA still maintains reasonable performance for practical key lengths. For very large-scale cryptosystems, parallelization and distributed computing can further enhance efficiency.

Security and Robustness Assessment Methodology

We assess the security and robustness of the cryptographic keys generated by the GA against various attacks commonly encountered in cryptographic scenarios.

Metrics:

1. **Resistance to Attacks:** We evaluate the GA-produced keys' resilience against brute-force attacks, differential cryptanalysis, known plaintext attacks, and other common cryptographic attacks.
2. **Cryptographic Analysis:** We subject the keys to statistical tests to ensure their randomness and resistance to cryptanalysis.

Results and Findings

The GA-generated keys exhibit strong resistance against various cryptographic attacks. The random nature of the key generation process and the application of fitness functions that prioritize security and strength contribute to the robustness of the keys. The GA can produce cryptographic keys that are highly secure, making them suitable for critical communication systems and data protection applications.

The performance evaluation demonstrates that the Genetic Algorithm for key generation in cryptosystems is a promising approach that offers significant advantages over traditional methods. The GA produces strong and secure cryptographic keys with high randomness and resistance to attacks. Its efficiency and scalability make it suitable for a wide range of cryptosystems, and its robustness ensures that the generated keys can withstand various cryptographic threats. By leveraging the strengths of Genetic Algorithms, researchers and practitioners can design more secure and efficient cryptographic systems for safeguarding sensitive information and ensuring data confidentiality and integrity.

REAL-WORLD APPLICATIONS

Cryptographic systems play a crucial role in ensuring secure communication and data protection across various domains. Genetic algorithms have found practical applications within these systems, enhancing their security and efficiency. Here are some real-world applications where the integration of genetic algorithms into cryptographic processes has yielded significant benefits:

Secure Communication Systems

Secure communication is essential in fields such as military operations, government agencies, and financial institutions. Genetic algorithms can be used to generate strong encryption keys for secure data transmission. For instance, in military operations, commanders need to transmit sensitive information securely. By applying a genetic algorithm, a highly secure symmetric key can be generated, protecting the confidentiality of critical communication.

Example: In a military communication network, a genetic algorithm is employed to generate a symmetric key that is robust against brute-force attacks. This ensures that confidential orders and strategies remain confidential during transmission.

IoT (Internet of Things) Cryptography

The proliferation of IoT devices has increased the need for secure communication between interconnected devices. Genetic algorithms can assist in creating optimized cryptographic protocols for IoT networks, ensuring data integrity and authentication.

Example: In a smart home ecosystem, genetic algorithms are utilized to design an efficient key exchange protocol that secures communication between smart devices, such as door locks, cameras, and thermostats. This prevents unauthorized access and manipulation of IoT devices.

Cloud Security and Data Encryption

Cloud computing involves the storage and processing of vast amounts of sensitive data. Genetic algorithms can aid in generating secure cryptographic keys and optimizing encryption algorithms for protecting data stored in the cloud.

Example: A cloud service provider employs genetic algorithms to generate asymmetric key pairs for encrypting user data stored on the cloud. This ensures that only authorised users with the private key can access their data, enhancing the overall security of cloud-based services.

Digital Signatures and Certificate Authorities

Digital signatures are used to verify the authenticity and integrity of digital documents. Genetic algorithms can optimize the generation of digital signatures and enhance the security of certificate authorities, which issue digital certificates.

Example: In an e-commerce platform, genetic algorithms are integrated into the digital signature generation process. This guarantees that digital documents, such as purchase orders and invoices, are tamper-proof and genuine, providing confidence to both buyers and sellers.

The integration of genetic algorithms into cryptographic systems has paved the way for enhanced security and efficiency across various real-world applications. From ensuring secure communication in military operations to safeguarding IoT networks and cloud data, genetic algorithms offer innovative solutions for addressing the complex challenges of modern cryptography. By leveraging the strengths of genetic algorithms and cryptographic techniques, these applications contribute to a more secure and interconnected digital world.

Digital signatures are widely used for ensuring the authenticity and integrity of digital documents and messages. Certificate authorities issue digital certificates used in public key infrastructures.

CHALLENGES AND FUTURE DIRECTION

In this section, we discuss the challenges associated with Genetic Algorithms (GAs) for key generation in cryptosystems and explore potential future directions to overcome these challenges and further improve the security and efficiency of cryptographic systems.

Security and Vulnerability Concerns

Challenge

One of the main challenges in using GAs for key generation is ensuring the security and vulnerability of the generated cryptographic keys. While GAs can produce strong keys, they are not immune to attacks, and certain vulnerabilities may arise during the evolutionary process.

Mitigation

To address security and vulnerability concerns, it is crucial to thoroughly analyse the fitness function and genetic operators used in the GA. Rigorous testing and analysis should be conducted to ensure that the generated keys are resistant to known cryptographic attacks. Additionally, integrating cryptographic mechanisms such as secure key storage and secure key exchange protocols can further enhance the security of the key generation process.

Genetic Algorithm Parameter Tuning

Challenge

The performance of the GA is highly dependent on the proper tuning of its parameters. Selecting appropriate values for population size, generation count, selection strategy, crossover rate, and mutation rate is critical to achieving optimal results.

Mitigation

Parameter tuning can be addressed through empirical experimentation and optimization. Researchers can conduct extensive experiments using different parameter combinations and evaluate the GA's performance under various scenarios. Additionally, automated parameter optimization techniques, such as genetic algorithm-based parameter tuning or other metaheuristic optimization methods, can be employed to fine-tune the GA parameters effectively.

Advancements in Quantum Computing

Challenge

The rise of quantum computing poses a potential threat to classical cryptographic systems, including key generation methods based on Genetic Algorithms. Quantum computers have the potential to break certain cryptographic algorithms that rely on factorization and discrete logarithm problems.

Mitigation

To address the threat of quantum computing, researchers are exploring the development of post-quantum cryptography, which aims to create cryptographic algorithms that are secure against quantum attacks. Integrating post-quantum cryptographic schemes with Genetic Algorithms can enhance the resilience of key generation in the era of quantum computing.

Future Directions

1. **Post-Quantum Genetic Algorithms:**

Researchers can explore the integration of post-quantum cryptographic algorithms with Genetic Algorithms to develop key generation techniques that are secure against both classical and quantum attacks.

2. **Multi-Objective Optimization:**

Expanding the scope of the Genetic Algorithm to consider multiple objectives in key generation can lead to the discovery of more diverse and robust solutions.

3. **Parallelization and Distributed Computing:**

Leveraging parallelization and distributed computing techniques can improve the efficiency and scalability of the Genetic Algorithm for large-scale cryptosystems.

4. **Adaptive Parameter Selection:**

Developing adaptive mechanisms that dynamically adjust the GA's parameters during the evolution process can enhance the algorithm's adaptability and performance.

5. **Hybrid Approaches:** Combining Genetic Algorithms with other optimization techniques, machine learning, or artificial intelligence approaches can lead to innovative and powerful methods for key generation.

The application of Genetic Algorithms for key generation in cryptosystems shows significant promise, but it also faces challenges and opportunities for improvement. By addressing security concerns, tuning GA parameters, and exploring advancements in quantum-safe cryptography, researchers can further enhance the effectiveness, security, and robustness of Genetic Algorithm-based key generation. The future directions in research and development can lead to more secure cryptographic systems that can withstand the ever-evolving landscape of cryptographic threats.

CONCLUSION

Summary

In this paper, we explored the application of Genetic Algorithms (GAs) for key generation in cryptosystems. We provided an in-depth overview of Genetic Algorithms, including their basic principles, key concepts, and genetic operators. We discussed the integration of GAs into cryptosystems for both symmetric and asymmetric key generation and highlighted the benefits of using GAs in cryptographic scenarios.

For symmetric key generation, we presented a GA-based approach that produces strong and random cryptographic keys, enhancing the security of communication systems. For asymmetric key generation, we demonstrated how GAs can generate key pairs with high security and uniqueness, making them suitable for digital signatures and certificate authorities. Additionally, we explored hybrid GA approaches, combining symmetric and asymmetric key generation, to improve security in critical applications.

We conducted a performance evaluation, comparing the GA with traditional key generation methods, analyzing its efficiency, scalability, and security. The results showed that the GA-based key generation offers advantages over traditional methods, producing robust and secure cryptographic keys.

Contributions

The contributions of this paper are as follows:

1. **In-depth Overview**: We provided a comprehensive overview of Genetic Algorithms, covering their basic principles, key concepts, and genetic operators, to understand their potential for key generation in cryptosystems.
2. **Application to Cryptosystems**: We explored the integration of Genetic Algorithms into cryptosystems for symmetric and asymmetric key generation, as well as hybrid approaches, demonstrating their practicality and advantages.
3. **Performance Evaluation**: We conducted a performance evaluation of the GA based key generation, comparing it with traditional methods, and analysing its efficiency, scalability, and security.

Outlook

The application of Genetic Algorithms for key generation in cryptosystems opens up exciting possibilities for future research and development. The outlook for Genetic Algorithm-based key generation is promising, and there are several areas of interest for further exploration:

1. **Quantum-Safe Cryptography:** Researchers should focus on integrating postquantum cryptographic algorithms with Genetic Algorithms to develop secure key generation techniques that can withstand quantum attacks.
2. **Enhanced Parameter Tuning:** Further research can be directed towards developing automated parameter tuning mechanisms to optimize the GA's performance for different cryptographic scenarios.
3. **Hybrid Approaches:** Exploring hybrid approaches that combine Genetic Algorithms with other optimization techniques or machine learning can lead to innovative methods for key generation.
4. **Real-World Deployment:** The application of Genetic Algorithms for key generation should be further studied in real-world cryptographic systems, considering factors like hardware constraints and integration with existing security infrastructures.

In conclusion, Genetic Algorithms offer a powerful and versatile approach for key generation in cryptosystems, contributing to the security and resilience of cryptographic techniques. As the field of cryptography evolves to meet new challenges, Genetic Algorithms present a valuable tool to enhance cryptographic security and efficiency. By addressing the challenges and leveraging future research directions, we can further strengthen the application of Genetic Algorithms for key generation and contribute to the advancement of secure communication and data protection.

REFERENCES

Abas, N., Dilshad, S., Khalid, A., Saleem, M. S., & Khan, N. (2020). Power quality improvement using dynamic voltage restorer. *IEEE Access : Practical Innovations, Open Solutions*, *8*, 164325–164339. doi:10.1109/ACCESS.2020.3022477

Abdalrdha, Z. K., Al-Qinani, I. H., & Abbas, F. N. (2019). Subject review: Key generation in different cryptography algorithm. *International Journal of Scientific Research in Science, Engineering and Technology*, *6*(5), 230–240. doi:10.32628/IJSRSET196550

Delfs, H., Knebl, H., & Delfs, H. (2015). Symmetric-key cryptography. Introduction to Cryptography: Principles and Applications, 11–48. doi:10.1007/978-3-662-47974-2_2

Dulla, G. L., Gerardo, B. D., & Medina, R. P. (2019). A unique message encryption technique based on enhanced blowfish algorithm. In *IOP Conference Series: Materials Science and Engineering*. IOP Publishing. 10.1088/1757-899X/482/1/012001

Dutta, S., Das, T., & Jash, S. (2014). A cryptography algorithm using the operations of genetic algorithm & pseudo random sequence generating functions. *International Journal (Toronto, Ont.)*, *3*(5).

Hassan Ak, S., Shalash, A. F., & Saudy, N. F. (2014). Modifications on rsa cryptosystem using genetic optimization. *International Journal of Research and Reviews in Applied Sciences*, *19*(2), 150.

Jawaid, S., & Jamal, A. (2014). Generating the best fit key in cryptography using genetic algorithm. *International Journal of Computer Applications*, *98*(20), 33–39. doi:10.5120/17301-7767

Jhingran, R., Thada, V., & Dhaka, S. (2015). A study on cryptography using genetic algorithm. *International Journal of Computer Applications*, *118*(20), 10–14. doi:10.5120/20860-3559

Katoch, S., Chauhan, S. S., & Kumar, V. (2021). A review on genetic algorithm: Past, present, and future. *Multimedia Tools and Applications*, *80*(5), 8091–8126. doi:10.100711042-020-10139-6 PMID:33162782

Kessler, G.C. (2003). *An overview of cryptography*. Academic Press.

Kumar, A., & Chatterjee, K. (2016). An efficient stream cipher using genetic algorithm. *2016 International Conference on Wireless Communications, Signal Processing and Networking (WiSPNET)*, 2322–2326. 10.1109/WiSPNET.2016.7566557

Mirjalili, S., & Mirjalili, S. (2019). Genetic algorithm. Evolutionary Algorithms and Neural Networks: Theory and Applications, 43–55. doi:10.1007/978-3-319-93025-1_4

Mishra, S., & Bali, S. (2013). Public key cryptography using genetic algorithm. *International Journal of Recent Technology and Engineering*, *2*(2), 150–154.

Nagde, D., Patel, R., & Kelde, D. (2013). New approach for data encryption using two-way crossover. *International Journal of Computer Science and Information Technologies*, *4*, 58–60.

NK, S., & Pai, G.V. (2009). Design of stream cipher for text encryption using particle swarm optimization based key generation. *Journal of Information Assurance and Security*, 30–41.

Pareek, N. K., & Patidar, V. (2016). Medical image protection using genetic algorithm operations. *Soft Computing*, *20*(2), 763–772. doi:10.100700500-014-1539-7

Poohoi, R., Puntusavase, K., & Ohmori, S. (2023). A novel crossover operator for genetic algorithm: Stas crossover. *Decision Science Letters*, *12*(3), 515–524. doi:10.5267/j.dsl.2023.4.010

Ragavan, M., & Prabu, K. (2022). Evaluation of cryptographic key generation performance using evolutionary algorithm. *International Journal of System Assurance Engineering and Management*, *13*(S1, Suppl 1), 481–487. doi:10.100713198-021-01478-0

Salomaa, A. (1996). *Public-key cryptography*. Academic Press.

Soni, A., & Agrawal, S. (2012). Using genetic algorithm for symmetric key generation in image encryption. *International Journal of Advanced Research in Computer Engineering and Technology*, *1*(10), 137–140.

Veetil, A. (2015). An encryption technique using genetic operators. *Int J Sci Technol Res, 4*(7).

Chapter 15
Emerging Networking Technologies for Industry 4.0

M. Santhiya
Rajalakshmi Engineering College, India

J. Jeyalakshmi
https://orcid.org/0000-0001-7545-6449
Amrita School of Computing, India

Harish Venu
Universiti Tenaga Nasional, Malaysia

ABSTRACT

The conceptual, technological, and enabling frameworks of the original Industry 4.0 concept have all undergone significant changes. The next generation of Industry 4.0, also known as Industry 5.0, is emerging as a result of the evolution of Industry 4.0 and will require a combination of fresh new technologies. These breakthroughs come from a range of industries, such as artificial intelligence (AI), 5G technology and 6G mobile networks, ML with quantum computing, etc. Artificial intelligence (AI), 5G and 6G, and machine learning with quantum computing are expected to influence the original Industry 4.0. As mentioned, a new era of Industry 4.0 is currently emerging. The primary emerging enabling technologies for Industry 4.0 are surveyed in this chapter. Included in the topics mentioned are artificial intelligence (AI), internet of things, blockchain, 5G wireless technologies, 3D printing, biometrics, virtual and augmented reality, digital twin in 6G technology with case scenarios.

1 INTRODUCTION

The Industrial Revolution is not just looked upon as a historical event. It has consumed several technologies and delivered several innovations paving the way for economic, political and societal changes transforming lives. Industry 4.0 is also a term used to symbolise the huge shift in industrial technology that helped to connect several devices transforming lives delivering valuable services in field of

DOI: 10.4018/979-8-3693-0593-5.ch015

Manufacturing, Communication, Healthcare, Food Processing, Bio-Informatics and Education. It was a term framed by German scientists and popularised by Klaus Schwab, executive chairman of the World Economic Forum (WEF) in 2015 at Davos, Switzerland. It takes its shape from the massive automated cyber physical systems used by manufacturing units, Robotics, Artificial Intelligence, etc., The impact of networking technologies in empowering Industry 4.0 is summarised in this book chapter. The fourth Industrial Revolution is laid on the firm foundation of connected devices and Bots. The Networking technologies pave way for connecting devices, cloud platform and artificial intelligence modalities together to realise large Cyber-Physical Systems (CPS).

Table 1. Industrial revolution and its consequences

Industrial Revolution	Consequences
First Industrial Revolution	Mechanical Production powered by steam and hydel power
Second Industrial Revolution	Technological revolution powered by electricity, telegraph networks paving way for Production line.
Third Industrial Revolution	Digital Revolution powered by advanced digital developments and communication technologies.
Fourth Industrial Revolution	Massive Automation powered by huge cyber-physical systems, IoT, Cloud and Artificial Intelligence technologies.

Industry 4.0 has become a buzz word. This is an era of competitive business and customized products. It is important to stay competitive and make the company profitable. It is foremost need to satisfy the customers in timely manner. Hence the need for automation. There is a need for Unified business operations and production. It is important to resolve issues in all parts of a business, as they appear. It is important to prevent any unforeseen risk in business scenario. Analytics is a genre new to Industrial environment which has become pervasive and indispensable. With the advent of newer technologies, it is also needed to inbreed skilled labour and develop specialised skillset.

In this context, there is a need to connect all people, parts and machines involved in the unified business environment. It connects everyone and everything from manufacturing, production, Marketing, Retail and Sales. The machines and robots are all rendering lots of data. The security systems are streaming live footage of every second. The logistics systems are operated and monitored in real time with IoT(Internet of Things). This interconnectivity is paved by networking technologies ranging from wired, wireless, satellite to mobile standards.

Figure 1. Industry 4.0 and large scale cyber physical systems

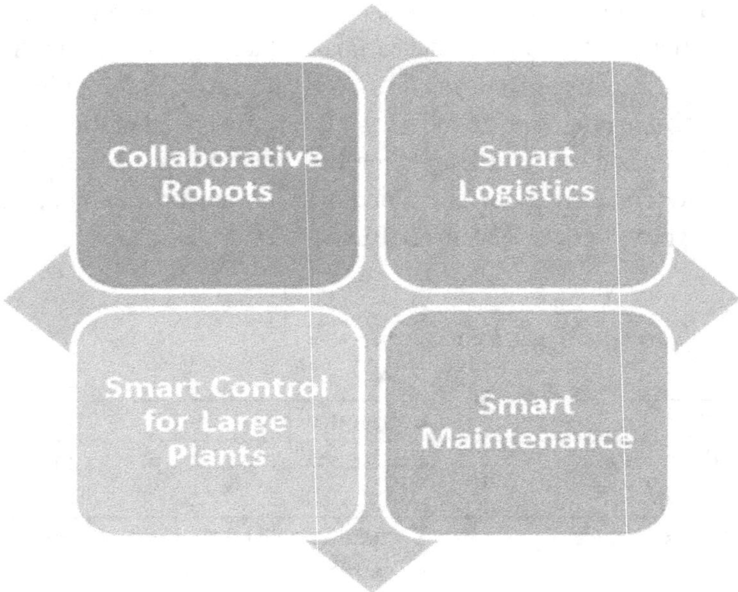

2. 5G NETWORKING TECHNOLOGIES FOR INDUSTRY 4.0

Advanced industrial applications require larger number of devices to be connected to be controlled, monitored and maintained. The tools and techniques to harness the spectrum in this direction are also becoming prevalent. The comparison of 4G, 5G and 6G technologies is shown as below.

Table 2. Comparison of wireless communication systems

Aspect	4G	5G	6G
Per device Peak Data Rate	1 Gbps	10Gbps	1 Tbps
End-to-End Latency	100ms	10ms	1ms
Maximum Spectral Efficiency	15 bps/Hz	30 bps/Hz	100 bps/Hz
Mobility Support	Up to 3 Km/Hr	Up to 500 Km/Hr	Up to 1000 Km/Hr
Satellite Integration	-	-	Fully
AI	-	Partial	Fully
Autonomous Vehicle	-	Partial	Fully
XR	-	Partial	Fully
Haptic Communication	-	Partial	Fully
THz Communication	-	Very Limited	Widely
Service Level	Video	AR. VR	Tactile
Architecture	MIMO	Massive MIMO	Intelligent Surface
Maximum Frequency	6GHz	90GHz	10THz

Though 4G is prevalently used, many countries and companies have started to use 5G technology. 6G is still being experimented and will be reality in near future.

2.1 5G Services by Spectrum

5G spectrum offers services in low, medium and high band of the spectrum. The use cases and capacity are explained as below.

Low-Band Spectrum Provides Comprehensive Coverage

Low-band spectrum is any spectrum on the spectrum chart that is less than 1 GHz. commonly referred to as analogue cellular, were deployed in 800 MHz low-band spectrum. With a single tower, wireless carriers offer service to thousands of consumers within hundreds of square miles. It offers good coverage and5 the speed and latency is also good.

The 5G Mid-Band Spectrum Offers Capacity and Coverage

Recent frequency assignments have comprised over sixty percent of mid-band spectrum. This development will persist. Spectrum in the mid-band (1 GHz - 6 GHz) is ideal for 5G because it can transmit voluminous amounts of data over long distances. Its allocation of mid-band frequencies in the 2.6 GHz and 3.5 GHz channels for 5G was crucial to addressing coverage and capacity issues.

The 5G High-Band Spectrum Offers Lightning-Fast Speeds Over Limited Distances

These bands are adjacent, making it simpler for mobile devices to accommodate them. Spectrum for millimetre waves (high-band) is limited because signals cannot propagate as far as those for mid- and low-band. Occasionally, the signal travels less than one mile and is more vulnerable to interference from objects like trees etc. The advantage of millimetre wave spectrum, however, is that if the signal is unobstructed, users can achieve connection speeds of 1 - 3 Gbps or even higher.

5G technology is used in various applications as summarized in Figure 2. Range of services are offered and

2.2 5G Business Systems Classifications

Networking technologies are used to establish public, private and hybrid network-based business systems. 5G has been used to establish Private Mobile Networks and Radio access Networks. The major components of 5G Communication are summarised as below.

- Extreme Mobile Broadband (xMBB).
- Ultra-Reliable Low-Latency Communication (uRLLC).
- Massive Machine-Type Communication (mMTC).

Figure 2. 5G services and its applications

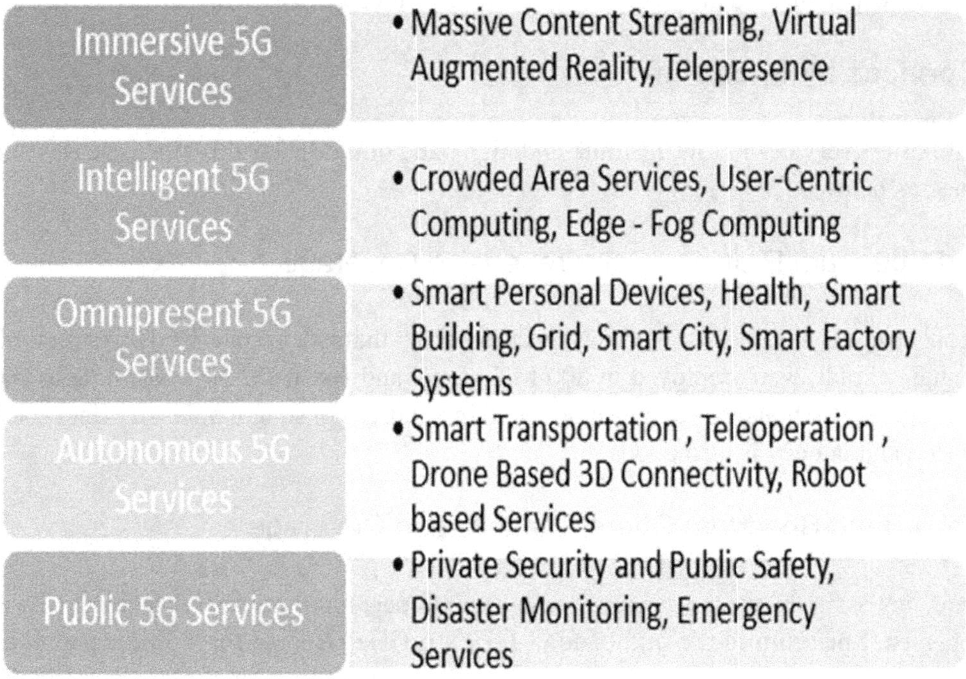

Extreme Mobile Broadband (xMBB)

The bandwidth for end users are offered as 100 Mbps for download and 50Mbps for upload. Uniform experience and seamless handling of device content are the striking advantages of 5G technology. Such bandwidth will allow faster downloads, low latency gaming experiences and HD video streaming possible.

Ultra-Reliable Low-Latency Communication (uRLLC)

Latency is an important feature for real-time applications like streaming, analytics, gaming and mission critical systems. Automated Guided Vehicles are hyped to be future technology. Such technology needs definitely low latency communication and reliability. 5G offers 99.9% reliability and offers 99.9% availability of network too.

Massive Machine-Type Communication (mMTC)

5G supports 1 million connections per km (square kilometre). The digital transformation that would be needed for a smart city or Industrial IoT can be easily acquired with mMTC. Low power consumption is another advantage of the operation.

2.3 5G Deployment Sectors

The 5G technologies can be used to build Private Mobile Networks and Radio Access Networks.

- **Private Mobile Networks**
- **Radio Access Networks**

2.3.1 Private Mobile Networks

The private networks can provide low latency and deliver high performance. 5G spectrum can be used to build licensed, unlicensed or dynamic spectrum networks. It is possible to slice spectrum from public to private networks too. This technique is called User plane Forwarding (UPF). It allows the session management function (SMF) can be assigned for a private dedicated data network. On the other hand, a dedicated network slice can be provided within the spectrum with isolated IP routing with dedicated instances of UPF, SMF etc., Thus private mobile networks can be formed using 5G.

2.3.2 Radio Access Networks

Radio Access Networks provide wireless connectivity in low, medium and high band in a multi layered network. The types of RAN deployment are listed as below.

3. 6G INDUSTRIAL DIGITAL TWIN ECOSYSTEM

Industrial DTs are able to estimate high-level context information that is generally unobservable, such as people's physical or mental health, the dependability of industrial equipment, or the potential for hostile cyber-attacks, by swiftly updating and storing such data. They are able to immediately check the low-level status of large devices and individuals as a result. Using this understanding, an industrial setting based on 6G DT can be developed where the three worlds of data, machines, and humans coexist. The linking of physical entities and DTs will greatly increase the methods in which humans and things recognise and interact, having ubiquitous, quick, and dependable connectedness for everything and everyone. This will have the effects detailed below with dataflow in details in Figure 3. Human-aware networks, Ultra flexible networking IOE, Network Monitoring and Analysis, Tele Collaboration, Remote Control and monitoring, Network Aware Smart Factory, Cobots, Emergent Intelligent.

3.1 Ubiquitous and Collaborative Telepresence

A virtual interaction between PTs over DTs will be possible because to the 6G network's quick and dependable bidirectional data exchange between physical things and their DTs. Furthermore, due to the widespread coverage and the exceptional accuracy in time synchronisation anticipated from 6G, the same DT can engage with multiple individuals simultaneously in a range of locations without producing conflicts or collisions between the activities. Telepresence can thus be used to achieve a distant collaboration that runs as smoothly as one that takes place in person (Han & Schotten, 2022), which will significantly cut down on the time and money needed to overcome access and spatial distance obstacles.

Table 3. Radio access networks types

RAN TYPES	DESCRIPTION
GSM Radio Access Network (GRAN)	Global System for Mobile Communications (GSM) had RAN deployed in 2G cellular networks of the second generation in 1990. With the widespread implementation of 2G technologies, it became the global standard by 2010 .
GSM EDGE Radio Access Network (GERAN)	This network standard employs the Enhanced Data Rates for GSM Evolution (EDGE) cellular technology, which improves data transmission and is backwards compatible with standard GSM. 2003 marked the introduction of EDGE technology on GSM networks, which provides three times the capacity and efficacy of GSM/GPRS alone.
Centralised RAN (CRAN)	This form of RAN architecture, also known as Cloud-RAN, employs cloud computing as the network and data processing hub for cellular signals. CRANs can transmit reliably over long distances from a centralised tower deployment. CRAN was the first RAN to employ cloud computing and IT infrastructure to enhance cellular coverage, capacity, and dependability.
VRAN: Virtualized RAN	VRANs augment the virtualization observed in CRANs to support the evolution of cellular technology, particularly 5G. This virtualization helps eliminate hardware restrictions across RANs and improves interoperability and communication across devices and networks from multiple vendors.
Open Radio Access Network (Open RAN), or ORAN	ORAN, or Open RAN, is both an architecture and an organisation that aims to enhance radio access networks (RANs) through the disaggregation of RAN elements and their implementation in software based on open source technologies and open standards.

Figure 3. The industrial ecosystem of 6G DT, with arrows indicating the direction of information flow (Angeline, 1993)

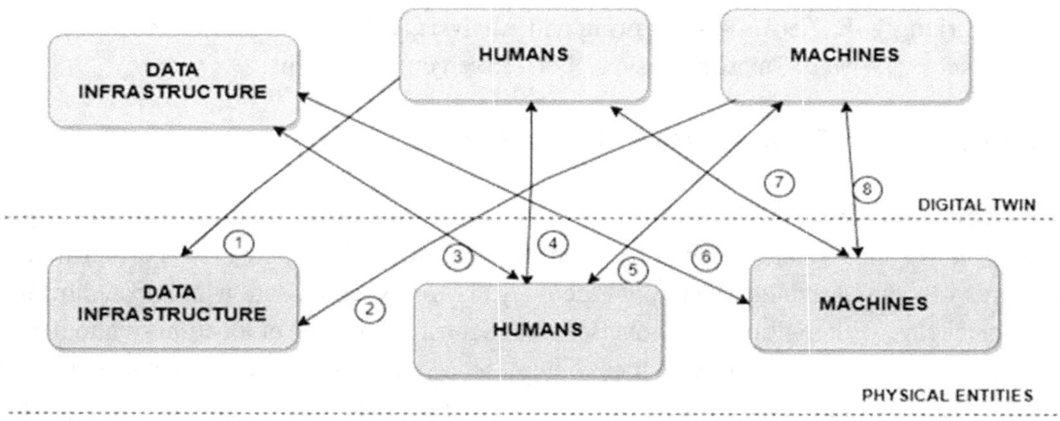

3.2 Understanding the Machines and Environment

A DT-enabled industrial system is able to gather enormous amounts of data by remaining synchronised and connected with all components of the real world. Recent developments in ML and AI allow for the extraction of reasoning models for various events that are concealed beneath the huge amount of data. Our ability to design, setup, operate, diagnose, and maintain industrial equipment and the physical environment will be improved as a result of this (Hu et al., 2021).

3.3 Understanding the Human Participants

Human behavior is often unpredictable and cannot be totally predicted, in contrast to industrial equipment and the physical world, which operate primarily deterministically and can be accurately predicted using precise models. As a result, the presence of humans in industrial settings and their involvement in industrial processes significantly increases system uncertainty and thus increases the risk of service degradation and failure (Tariq et al., 2020). However, the DTs of human participants can develop a statistical model of their behavior using the vast amounts of data that have been gathered and analyzed, which can help the industrial system identify and reduce such hazards. Additionally, utilizing multidimensional status data acquired via sophisticated human-machine interfaces (HMIs), A human DT is able to discern the conditions of its PT even when it is difficult or impossible to do so such as emotion or weariness, which machines can use to better understand people in group interactions.

3.4 Sustainable Industry

On the one hand, huge twinning enables accurate monitoring and collaborative analysis of the state of all participants and components in industrial processes (Minos-Stensrud et al., 2018). This makes it possible to fully comprehend the unobservable patterns concealed beneath complicated processes, such as the carbon footprint and energy consumption along the process chain, which may help to increase the industry's energy efficiency and sustainability. On the other hand, innovative approaches to energy-efficient computing and green communication are anticipated to guarantee the long-term viability of the industrial deployment of 6G mega twinning.

Numerous innovative application scenarios might be anticipated in such an environment, supported by these potentials, as succinctly shown in Figure 3. We introduce a number of these 6G DT industrial applications in the subsection that follows.

4. APPLICATION SCENARIO

4.1 Human Presence-Aware URLLC

Providing ultra-reliable low-latency communication in a factory setting is one industrial application scenario where a human presence-aware technique becomes crucial. Machine-to-machine traffic is anticipated to predominate in an I4.0 production environment. Accurate modelling of unusual events is necessary to prevent surprises and enable low-latency communication throughout the whole production floor. Future factories will be semi-controlled settings with accurate location data available for mobile user equipment (UEs), such as autonomous guided vehicles (AGVs), as well as permanent machines, making this possible. Providing ultra-reliable low-latency communication in a factory setting is one industrial application scenario where a human presence-aware technique becomes crucial. Machine-to-machine traffic is anticipated to predominate in an I4.0 production environment. Accurate modelling of unusual events is necessary to prevent surprises and enable low-latency communication throughout the whole production floor. Future factories will be semi-controlled settings with accurate location data available for mobile user equipment (UEs), such as autonomous guided vehicles (AGVs), as well as permanent machines, making this possible.

In contrast to an AGV, whose movements are known or can be controlled, a UE used by a human (such as a portable device) is more difficult to pinpoint when humans are present since their behaviour becomes far more unpredictable. Furthermore, these handheld UEs make it more challenging to maintain low-latency connectivity on the production floor due to their inherent randomness and unpredictability. People nevertheless have an impact on radio communication even if they are not active users since elements like body shape, clothing, and limb position can all change the propagation environment.

Therefore, while deciding how to use radio resources in a region over a future time window, it is necessary to model people as objects in the DT and take into consideration their position as well as their potential actions (movements, gestures, etc.) there. This modelling is crucial for services with extremely high dependability targets. When deciding how to use the beams and frequency resources, motions like those described above must be taken into consideration. For instance, a single hand wave can completely destroy a service link with high dependability criteria and extremely low latency requirements. Similar to this, enough redundancy and variety can be built in advance if there is a significant likelihood of human obstruction.

4.2 Massive Twinning With Human-in-Loop

According to Hexa-X, enormous twinning is a use case family that involves the extensive usage of DTs for the representation, interaction, and control of actions in the physical environment. This use case family is anticipated for the 6G era. This use case family will be used in a variety of environments, including industrial settings, to increase production agility and the effective interaction of production tools, allowing for a greater integration of the various processes and the transfer of massive amounts of data while also achieving extreme performance and reliability (Huang et al., 2021). It is dependent on an accurate and fully synchronised computer representation of both the physical and human worlds, with the presence of human experts being essential for controlling, making decisions, performing maintenance work, and adapting operations.

4.3 From Robots to Cobots

As expected, technology is transforming the industrial sector as new paradigms like I4.0 gradually replace conventional manufacturing techniques. Robotics will play a crucial part in the development of this new industrial revolution. Three main areas are the focus of current research in particular. One is represented by industrial robotics, which is defined as the usage of robots that can be programmed to adapt to changing production requirements (Wang et al., 2021) and can be used to fulfil a specific function. The employment of robots in other spheres of human activity, such as commercial and non-manufacturing-related duties, is covered by service robotics, which is another. The third one is collaborative robotics, where a change from robots to "cobots," or, is seen.

The latter option is particularly alluring since it is anticipated to deliver significant benefits by fusing the flexibility of manual operations carried out by human operators with the advantages resulting from the employment of robots to automate repetitive tasks (El Zaatari et al., 2019).

But there are still a number of unresolved issues that come with chances like the one mentioned above. The most important ones concern HMIs. To give an example, learning-by-demonstration techniques based, for instance, on hand-guidance or other natural user interfaces are replacing well-established approaches for robot programming that are no longer applicable to or ineffective with cobots (Haque et al., 2019). Furthermore, humans and robots are now expected to work together in co-located spaces and alternate in how the duties at hand are carried out, rather than operating in cells that are clearly divided from one another. Therefore, new techniques for understanding the status and goals of the cooperating peer are required.

This includes, among other things, the use of sensors to gather human and robot poses, AI-based algorithms for motion planning and threat prevention, as well as solutions based on Augmented Reality (AR) and Virtual Reality (VR) to visualize pertinent information up close (in virtual environments) or far away (overlapping with the local user's field of view) (Douthwaite et al., 2021; El Zaatari et al., 2019).

4.4 Extended Reality (XR)

Robotics and sensor data can be gathered by artificial intelligence and machine learning systems, which can then advise adjustments or actions for the user to observe and control as necessary. Additionally, the user should be provided with crucial information on a particular part or instrument in a clear and understandable manner. A user with augmented reality (AR), virtual reality (VR), or mixed reality (MR)-enabled devices, for instance, will be able to see details like the current input and output of an electric motor, its connections, and other features without the need for a manual or measuring.

Users will be able to take on more automated and supervisory responsibilities in I4.0 thanks to the improved human-machine interaction brought about by XR. This will free up users' time from having to plan, set up, carry out, and keep an eye on robotic tasks. There will be new user roles established, ranging from expert to novice users. Additionally, in a robotic construction environment, it will be avoided to overburden users with irrelevant and challenging-to-understand data and to require repeated user inputs for task confirmation. Therefore, the user's choices and behaviors will be taken into account when they produce noteworthy outcomes.

The supervision, notification, and control are the three primary interaction designs that the human-machine interaction system should priorities. The user can keep an eye on and manage automated tasks in supervision. In notification, the system will alert the user to any problems, exceptions, unusual circumstances, and other important details and events. In control, the user will be able to take over the system, change the configuration of networks and robots, and even utilize tele operation to fix a problem.

4.5 Network-Aware DT for Local Insight

For I4.0-related use cases, as described in the previous section, a combined DT of the application and the utilized network, including its additional capabilities (e.g., localization, computation), is necessary to comprehend the effects of real-world actions on resource utilization and network performance and vice versa. Localization and sensing are especially important when modelling mobile and moving assets with dynamic topologies (DTs). The most effective orchestration is made possible by knowing the current location of mobile nodes and their surroundings. If there are multiple options for communication (e.g., placing computational power on the end device or close-by edge servers, using D2D or D2I communication, and possibly multiple access technologies), it is necessary to measure and, as a result, model the effects of each option on the performance as seen from the perspective of the application. The application can then make use of this local knowledge to optimize AGV trajectories while taking network and application criteria into consideration.

4.6 Emergent Intelligence

Emergent intelligence (EI), which was originally a biological notion (Hexa-X Deliverable D1.2, 2021), views the intelligence takes place in animals, including humans, as an developing behavior, meaning that arises impulsively from a substantial number of relating basic components. For instance, the brain, which is made up of enormous basic neuron cells that are connected to one another, is the origin of human intelligence. The collective intelligence of bio-sociable insects like ants and bees, which have extremely straightforward behavioral patterns with each discrete yet show well-developed intellect as colonies, is another common example.

Engineers have created bionic intelligent methods as a result of the EI phenomena. In the disciplines of complex systems and artificial intelligence, it has been researched somewhat. Swarm algorithms are one such example of a standard EI approach that has been developed over many years as a powerful meta-heuristic optimization tool. From the standpoint of EI, several researchers also investigate genetic programming and genetic algorithms. Logistics, resource management, work scheduling, privacy, and many other areas have all been suggested as further EI uses. EI hasn't, however, generally developed into a really prominent study area up to this point.

Engineers have created bionic intelligent systems in response to the phenomenon of EI. The domains of complex systems and artificial intelligence have both researched it to some extent. As an effective meta-heuristic optimization tool and typical EI technique, swarm algorithms, for example, have been developed over many years. Some researchers also look at genetic algorithms and programming from the perspective of EI. In a variety of fields, including logistics, resource management, job scheduling, and privacy among others, additional uses of EI have also been considered. Even so, the study of EI hasn't really taken off as a subject of study yet. With these advantages, EI emerges as a competitive spontaneous and decentralized intelligence solution that 6G is eagerly seeking to meet the difficulties of power efficiency, scalability, reliability, security, and privacy in delivering pervasive intelligence. In contrast, EI often necessitates a large number of participating agents in order to work satisfactorily, which indicates a heavy traffic load in wireless settings. Fortunately, 6G is planned to extensively install DTs, which may effectively lower the signaling overhead and wireless traffic burden to enable EI. 6G is also expected to deliver ultra-dense access that connects everything globally. In a nutshell, 6G and EI complement each other well and may learn from one another.

4.7 DT-Assisted Network Slicing Ecosystem

A network operator can reduce overall deployment costs, speed up network slice planning and execution, and improve tenant experience by utilizing DT technology to replicate different network slice instances with differing performance and configuration needs. Three DTs the underlying network infrastructure twin, the end-user's equipment twin, and the physical environment twin are deemed necessary for each type of network slice instance in order to accurately simulate the slicing ecosystem. In order to give the operator and the slice owner a visible representation of the required number of physical and virtual resources for a network slice instance, the network infrastructure twin may replicate the underlying computation, storage, and networking resources of a mobile operator. To simulate the density of end users, as well as their behavior and profile, supplied by a network slice instance, use the end-user's equipment twin. To give the slice owner and operator a more thorough understanding of the demographic information, space, and all physical entities surrounding the network sites, the physical environment twin may emulate spatial aspects (two-dimensional and/or three-dimensional representations) of the geographic area covered by the network slice. A network slice instance's three DTs can cooperate or work separately. The network administrator must ensure that, in either of these two scenarios, the data from one twin does not become mixed up with the data from the other.

4.8 Software Defined Radio, Enhanced Spectral Awareness, and the Radio-Aware DT

By giving the secondary network node precise information about the disturbance it causes to the parent network, DTs can help overlay networks. For instance, by utilising the traffic pattern of the primary network, a DT of the primary network and the radio channel can help a secondary network-node make better use of the spectrum. The secondary network node can act as a secondary transmitter or direct a secondary UE to transmit on the resource that the primary network is using if it determines from the DT that the interference from a secondary transmission to the primary network is minimal and does not go against the KPI targets for the primary network.

Similar advantages can be observed when DTs are used to enable the deployment of new radio access technologies in a partially or completely controlled IIoT environment. By lowering the number of beam candidates for a user node at a specific place, a DT of the radio environment, for instance, can help with beam management for massive MIMO BSs at millimeter-wave (mmWave) and sub-THz wavelengths. By eliminating the requirement for measurements, the DT can also aid in lowering the overhead and delay associated with control signalling.

5. KEY ENABLING TECHNOLOGIES IN 6G ECOSYSTEMS

5.1 Radio Access Technologies

From the perspective of radio access technology, utilizing new spectrum, from mmWave to sub-THz bands, will not only provide a significant amount of bandwidth to support the deployment of massive twinning with enough data throughput and connection density, but will also significantly reduce the minimal transmission time interval (TTI), which implies better time performance for more precise synchronization among massive DTs. Additionally, the short wavelengths in these new spectrum bands enable us to employ more compact antennas and larger antenna arrays inside of a single device, making it feasible to use extra-large scaled massive MIMO (mMIMO) to obtain an exceedingly narrow beam width.

This improves beam forming's spatial accuracy, enabling physical-layer security for better cyber-security and data privacy protection in DT applications as well as effectively raising the spatial multiplexing gain and lowering cross-user interference, both of which result in a notable increase in energy efficiency.

The introduction of so-called cell-free mMIMO, which likewise depends on flawless beam formation and enables many access points to jointly serve the same mobile device at once, can increase this benefit even more. Furthermore, for a more sustainable DT network, the recently developed technologies of energy harvesting (EH) and simultaneous wireless information and power transfer (SWIPT) are anticipated to provide alternatives to batteries in 6G systems.

5.2 Artificial Intelligence

AI is a different technology that is anticipated to significantly improve the DT paradigm, particularly from an I4.0 standpoint. (Pratticò & Lamberti, 2021) offers a thorough overview of how AI is applied in the context of industrial IoT. The knowledge gathered in the DT can be used by humans to improve their decision-making using AI. Through the use of so-called Intelligent Decision Support Systems (IDSS), AI can enhance the intelligence of DTs to the point that they may be able to make judgments and carry out actions on the physical entities they represent. For instance, a plant's DT can use AI techniques to continuously monitor the status of the machines and use the data acquired to real-time alter the underlying processes.

The deployment of optimization and control techniques aimed at enhancing efficiency and, ultimately, profitability, could be supported by the aforementioned actions (Dang et al., 2020). Benefits of AI can be fully anticipated even in the area of HMIs for DTs thanks to anticipated improvements in mobile networks and edge computing capabilities. Robotics is a common application in this area, where, for instance, computer vision is crucial for the interaction with collaborative robots (also known as cobots) and the navigation of mobile robots (Standardization Council Industrie 4.0, 2020). Human-action recognition from images and data acquired by other sensors (such as depth cameras) is another common application of AI approach in this sector, for example, to execute tasks like trajectory forecasting and path planning for safety assurance in scenarios involving the operation of cooperative robots.

5.3 Multi-Access Edge Computing

Modern AI algorithm implementation typically demands extensive computing power, and this is where Multi-Access Edge Computing (MEC) in 6G industrial DT systems plays a crucial role. In particular, industrial edge networking, with its associated concept of campus network, not only enables agile deployment of data-driven applications and flexible offloading of computationally complex tasks, but also noticeably speeds up response times therein. This is accomplished by bringing computing capabilities to the edge of the network. Real-time DT applications like collaborative telepresence and cobots benefit greatly from this decrease in latency.

5.4 Sensing and Positioning

To enable the modelling of specific assets, objects, or individuals, DT systems still need enormous amounts of information that is as precise and timely as possible. They are also powered by powerful AI solutions and have high processing capacity from MEC. The position is frequently, if not always, a crucial and important component of this data, especially in environments that are mobile and flexible and where systems and subsystems may alter their positions over time. In these situations, precise position information can significantly enhance the performance of DTs by assisting them in comprehending their context and surrounding environment. This enables DTs to automatically estimate the new location of these systems and modify the applications as necessary.

Whether or not the target systems are able to broadcast and/or receive messages, the new technologies of Integrated Sensing and Communication (ISAC) show significant promise in increasing the localization performance, in both accuracy and power efficiency (Tariq et al., 2020). Another enabler is sensor fusion, which improves the localization accuracy of the same target by combining position data from other sources, such as radio and barometric sensors. The DT framework, which aids in the gathering, brokering, and use of such information, provides strong support for this principle. Additionally, reconfigurable intelligent surface (RIS) has sparked interest in studies about its use in indoor positioning to provide a significant accuracy gain at a low cost due to its freedom in modifying wireless signals and identifying the wireless channel (Wang et al., 2021).

5.5 Human-Machine Interface

The future industrial DT system will be aware of human mental status in addition to physical status of physical items and human bodies, such as position, speed, temperature, etc., which can easily be measured by modern sensors. This will allow it to operate in a human-centric manner. The knowledge of human participants' mental states is crucial for industrial processes, both for the system's and the participants' own safety as well as because of its relationship to working efficiency. We can now identify critical mental states, such as comprehension, concentration, fatigue, and emotion, from directly observable physical characteristics, such as speech voice, facial expressions, galvanic skin response signal, eye movements, and bioelectric signals. This is made possible by recent advances in novel human-machine interface. Human DT can develop to better comprehend people and predict their behaviours with the integration of such mental status information, which will be crucial in human presence-aware enterprises and cobot applications.

Innovative HMI with multisensory feedback technologies will open up new opportunities for information perception by humans in addition to recording information on human status. Visual and auditory user interfaces (UIs) will continue to predominate for industrial systems providing information to people because they are the most crucial human senses. However, in order to support future industrial DT applications like MR, immersive telepresence, and human-robot collaboration, the standard visual/auditory UIs based on text, two-dimensional images, and audio must be expanded. The implementation of holographic vision, tactile feedback, and even neural stimulation technologies [HS2020] will not only offer up new possibilities for highly effective human-DT driven machine interaction, but will also enable persons with disabilities to take part in industrial operations.

5.6 Communication-Computation-Control Code sign (CoCoCoCo)

Future industry's widespread DT implementation is resulting in complicated coupling and interactions between several networked control systems (NCS), each with its own unique communication, computation, and control modules. Limited resources (such radio resources and CPU circles, for example) must be shared, not just between distinct NCS, but also between different modules of the same NCS, to some extent. A new framework of communication-computation-control code sign (CoCoCoCo), which will help future industrial systems not only maximize resource efficiency but also deliver a guaranteed dependability in massive twinning, is needed to address this complex inter-module and inter-system dependency.

6. TECHNICAL ENABLERS FOR 6G-DT IN I4.0 AND THEIR IMPACTS

RAT[1] Technologies: mMIMO, extra-large mMIMO, cell-free mMIMO and technology used have some challenges like Service availability & reliability, latency, jitter, throughput, connection density, sustainability, energy efficiency .It was used in the application scenario of Massive twinning With human-in-loop, Cobots, AR/VR.

New spectrum: mmWave and sub-THz have some challenges of Service availability & reliability, latency, jitter, throughput, connection density, sustainability, security & privacy, energy efficiency it was involved in the application Massive twinning with human-in-loop, Cobots, AR/VR.

Energy harvesting and SWIP has challenges of sustainability with involved in scenario of Massive twinning, Cobots, AR/VR.

AI/ML: IDSS for production management faces the challenges downtimes and bottlenecks in application scenario of Monitor machines' status, reconfigure processes in real time. IDSS for logistics has the challenges of Resource underutilization, efficiency, profitability in Demand management and distribution model optimization. Robotics, sensing has the challenges of Mobile robot navigation, human- robot co-located collaboration, safety in production involved in application of Automated, human-aware manufacturing.

Multi-Access Edge Computing has the industrial campus networks impacts on Reliability / dependability, latency, security and privacy in all above mentioned application scenario.

Sensing & Positioning has the Integrated Communication and Sensing, IRS impact on efficient integration of communication, localization and sensing, Service availability & reliability, latency in Dependable DT.

Human-Machine Interface uses the technology sensing the users status and the environment has impact on Safety benefiting more population and another technic of Multi-sensory feedback benefits of more population in Cobots.

7. EMERGING RESEARCH CHALLENGES IN 6G

This section highlights a number of critical research challenges associated with the deployment of DTs in 6G communication systems. These challenges require substantial research efforts in order to fulfill the growing demands of digital twinning in futuristic networks.

Key Performance Indicators

The use case at hand determines the KPIs for maintaining a DT. For instance, the requirements and KPIs for tracking parameters that change quickly, like position, and those that change slowly or gradually, like temperature, will be very different. According to how the communicated data is used inside the DT, the pertinent KPIs will also change. For example, communicating data for updating a DT will have different KPIs than communicating data for offline processing, like training a model. The following table lists significant KPIs and the target value ranges that go along with them for various types of use cases.

Table 4. KPI requirements for maintaining a DT in different use cases (Angeline, 1993)

		Use-Cases		
		Monitoring Slowly Varying Parameters, e.g., Temperature	**Monitoring Rapidly Varying Parameters, e.g., Position for Motion Control, Alarms, etc.**	**DT-Related Data Transmission for Offline Processing**
KPIs	**Service availability [%]**	>98.9	£ 99.999999	99.9
	Service reliability [%]	>98.9	£ 99.999999	99.9
	Latency [ms]	99	0.1	N/A
	Jitter [ms]	9.9	0.01	N/A
	Average Throughput [Gbps]	0.01	10	10
	Peak throughput [Gbps]	0.01	100	100
	Connection density [devices/sq. m]	0.5	0.5	0.5
	Safety	Critical	Critical	Low
	Integrity	Critical	Critical	High
	Maintainability	High	High	Low

Dependability and Safety

There are two relationships between dependability and DTs. On the one hand, accurate information is required for DTs in order for the information that is deduced to be trusted and used efficiently in applications. On the other hand, the requirement for system dependability can be supported by a DT (dependability supported by DT). For instance, it is challenging to ensure reliable DTs because availability, integrity, and dependability of data and systems must all be guaranteed.

The data used to create the DTs must be trustworthy in order for applications to produce results that are meaningful. In order to support predictive maintenance or the improvement of quality of service, for instance, it may be necessary to simulate particular problems or processes or to gather status information about factories almost immediately. The ability of the DTs to be maintained, including any runtime modifications or repairs, must also be considered. If DTs are used in safety applications, it becomes more challenging to protect people and ensure that there won't be disastrous effects on the users and the environment.

Systems with safety requirements require careful analysis and a ranking of the potential failure modes' seriousness. Different rules and regulations apply depending on the application area. If DTs are a part of these safety systems, the same laws and regulations apply.

The position information, collision calculations, and automatic action instructions to avoid collisions must all adhere to all safety regulations if DTs of factories include the locations of every machine, asset, and human inside the factory. Additionally, if collisions between machines and humans are calculated using data gathered from 6G mobile networks.

DTs can make a significant contribution to the creation of trustworthy systems. For instance, if simulation predictions based on DTs are consistently accurate and real-world scenarios behave exactly like the calculations based on the DTs, trust in such systems and warnings can be viewed as reliable over time. The more physical processes and resources that can be modelled using DTs, the better predictions can be made for real-world processes and outcomes.

Security and Privacy

Because 6G will connect everything and everyone while carrying massive amounts of data that describes them thoroughly and in greater detail than ever before, it raises security and privacy concerns to a previously unheard-of level. The user data that is consistently synchronized between the DT and its PT may contain information that is confidential or privacy-sensitive. It must therefore be adequately safeguarded against both potential inappropriate use by the dependable, such as industrial verticals, as well as unauthorized access and malicious activities by a third party or unreliable individual.

Sustainability

As DT-driven industrial wireless networks and applications develop, significant changes are anticipated in data traffic, information storage, and hardware infrastructure. Given that sustainability is one of the fundamental tenets of 6G, action must be taken in a number of areas to address the issue of excessive energy consumption. For example, green technologies must be developed to collect data from numerous physical objects and maintain their DTs' high power efficiency. New network and data architectures must be developed and standardised to stop duplicates of the same object. As a result, various stakeholders in various domains will be able to exchange DTs as necessary. Additionally, incremental solutions are needed to deploy DTs on the legacy infrastructure without a significant hardware upgrade.

Benefiting More Population

DTs in I4.0 enable a wide range of remote interaction possibilities and human-in-the-loop use cases for remote operations, maintenance, and control. This benefits remote workers and individuals with disabilities and increases the population to which the corresponding jobs may potentially be offered. This is combined with cutting-edge HMIs and the potential for visualizing and interacting with complex systems using AR and VR. Expert knowledge "as-a-service" should become more accessible to small and medium-sized businesses with the ability to communicate with the DT remotely, allowing new participants and new businesses to enter the ecosystem.

Interactions Between DT Network and the Underlying Infrastructure

While interacting with the underlying telecommunications infrastructure, the DT network divides an end-to-end 6G system into three layers: the data storage layer, the service mapping layer, and the management layer. These layers manage the twin over the course of its lifetime and store various types of data, respectively. They map various types of data to software analytics. However, such an ecosystem encounters a number of challenges during this interaction.

The dataset(s) that the storage layer has acquired may contain sensitive information about topologies, computing and communication resources, configuration parameters, and even the profile and behavior of customers. It's possible that this worries both the customer and the infrastructure provider. Consequently, a data collection technique that accurately replicates the underlying physical infrastructure and safeguards sensitive information is needed. The data that has been gathered from the underlying infrastructure has a wide variety of formats, features, and structures. Such raw data must be transformed into a unified format in order for the DT network to map the datasets onto software analytics tools and create the twin of an infrastructure object.

This data ingestion process causes a delay in the creation of the corresponding DTs. The DT network requires autonomous and AI-driven data ingestion mechanisms to unify the input data.

On the management layer of the underlying infrastructure, the DT ecosystem interacts with a variety of tangible objects produced by different vendors at different layers. To grant DT service providers access to the underlying infrastructure, a communication service provider must define application programming interfaces (APIs).

CONCLUSION

For a number of years, the use of DT technology in communication networks has attracted a lot of attention. The 6G communication systems could undergo a revolution thanks to DT technology, according to the majority of the telecommunications industry. This article has provided in-depth information on a number of high-level aspects and created an ecosystem for 6G DTs with the aim of examining the impact of DT technology on supporting the connectivity of I4.0 over the communication network in the 6G era. The five sections of the article have been arranged using a top-down organisational strategy. First, several fundamental ideas about I4.0 and 6G have been presented. DTs will be used to strengthen 6G communication systems, and this will be discussed in order to effectively support I4.0's connectivity components over the next ten years. Second, DT technology has been integrated into an industrial ecosystem based on 6G communication systems, connecting PTs and DTs to support a range of novel applications. Third, from a vast array of industrial applications that can be supported by the 6G DT ecosystem created in this article, a few use case scenarios have been chosen. The adoption of DT technology in 6G communication systems has been associated with a number of significant research challenges, which call for additional research efforts. Lastly, in order to address the issues with research raised by the authors and number of enabling technologies have been introduced to strengthen the proposed 6G DT ecosystem and to open the door for supporting new use case scenarios.

REFERENCES

Angeline, P. J. (1993). *Evolutionary Algorithms and Emergent Intelligence* [Dissertation]. The Ohio State University.

Dang, S., Amin, O., Shihada, B., & Alouini, M.-S. (2020). What should 6G be? *Nature Electronics*, *3*(Jan), 20–29. doi:10.103841928-019-0355-6

Douthwaite, J. A., Lesage, B., Gleirscher, M., Calinescu, R., Aitken, J. M., Alexander, R., & Law, J. (2021). A modular digital twinning framework for safety assurance of collaborative robotics. *Frontiers in Robotics and AI*, *8*(Dec), 758099. doi:10.3389/frobt.2021.758099 PMID:34977162

El Zaatari, S., Marei, M., Li, W., & Usman, Z. (2019). Cobot programming for collaborative industrial tasks: An overview. *Robotics and Autonomous Systems*, *116*(June), 162–180. doi:10.1016/j.robot.2019.03.003

HanB.SchottenH. D. (2022). Multi-sensory HMI for human-centric industrial digital twins: A 6G vision of future industry. doi:10.1109/ISCC55528.2022.9912932

Haque, F., Dehghanian, V., Fapojuwo, A. O., & Nielsen, J. (2019, January). A sensor fusion-based framework for floor localization. *IEEE Sensors Journal*, *19*(2), 623–631. doi:10.1109/JSEN.2018.2852494

Hexa-X Deliverable D1.2: Expanded 6G Vision, Use Cases and Societal Values - Including Aspects of Sustainability, Security and Spectrum. (2021). https://hexa-x.eu/wp-content/ uploads/2021/05/Hexa-X_D1.2.pdf

Hu, J., Wang, Q., & Yang, K. (2021, February). Energy self-sustainability in full-spectrum 6G. *IEEE Wireless Communications*, *28*(1), 104–111. doi:10.1109/MWC.001.2000156

Huang, Z., Shen, Y., Li, J., Fey, M., & Brecher, C. (2021, September). A survey on AI-driven digital twins in Industry 4.0: Smart manufacturing and advanced robotics. *Sensors (Basel)*, *21*(19), 6340. doi:10.339021196340 PMID:34640660

Minos-Stensrud, M., Haakstad, O. H., Sakseid, O., Westby, B., & Alcocer, A. (2018). Towards automated 3D reconstruction in SME factories and digital twin model generation. *2018 18th International Conference on Control, Automation and Systems (ICCAS)*, 1777-1781.

Pratticò, F. G., & Lamberti, F. (2021). Towards the adoption of virtual reality training systems for the self-tuition of industrial robot operators: A case study at KUKA. *Computers in Industry*, *129*(Aug), 103446. doi:10.1016/j.compind.2021.103446

Standardization Council Industrie 4.0. (2020). *German Standardization Roadmap Industrie 4.0, Version 4*. VDE and DKE. Available online: https://www.sci40.com/english/publications/

Tariq, F., Khandaker, M. R. A., Wong, K.-K., Imran, M. A., Bennis, M., & Debbah, M. (2020). A speculative study on 6G. IEEE Wireless Communications Magazine, 27(4), 118-125. doi:10.1109/ MWC.001.1900488

Wang, T., Li, J., Deng, Y., Wang, C., Snoussi, H., & Tao, F. (2021, May). Digital twin for human-machine interaction with convolutional neural network. *International Journal of Computer Integrated Manufacturing*, *34*(7-8), 888–897. doi:10.1080/0951192X.2021.1925966

Chapter 16
Unlocking Secure Horizons:
Leveraging Blockchain as a Cloud Shield

Shalbani Das
Amity University, Kolkata, India

Soumyajeet Sarkar
Amity University, Kolkata, India

ABSTRACT

Cloud computing revolutionized business data management yet introduced security risks. This chapter assesses blockchain's impact on cloud security, highlighting the pros and cons. It introduces blockchain's role in addressing cloud security concerns via decentralization and transparency. The chapter examines how blockchain bolsters cloud security, enhancing data integrity, privacy, and encryption. Despite benefits, deployment challenges are recognized. The chapter explores blockchain's integration with AI/ML and real-world cases, equipping readers to navigate complexities. This empowers secure and resilient cloud computing. Thus, the chapter equips readers with the necessary information to navigate the complexities of deploying blockchain-based cloud security solutions, leading to a future of secure and resilient cloud computing.

1.0 INTRODUCTION TO BLOCKCHAIN TECHNOLOGY IN CLOUD SECURITY

Blockchain technology revolutionizes cloud security, addressing challenges and opportunities. Understanding its fundamentals is crucial to exploring its potential in cloud computing. The decentralized and distributed nature of blockchain offers solutions for data privacy, integrity, and access control, crucial challenges in cloud environments. By leveraging its transparency and immutability, cloud providers and users can enhance trust, accountability, and security. This marks the beginning of an exciting journey exploring the fusion of blockchain technology with cloud security (Gai *et al.,* 2023).

DOI: 10.4018/979-8-3693-0593-5.ch016

1.1 Understanding Blockchain Technology

Blockchain technology revolutionizes data protection and serves as a game-changer for cloud security. Its cryptographically linked data blocks ensure immutability and transparency, forming a tamper-resistant record. This distributed architecture reduces the risk of data breaches and single points of failure, strengthening cloud security. The blockchain's consensus algorithms further enhance transaction security, preventing unauthorized access attempts (Sarmah *et al.*, 2018). With unparalleled resilience, blockchain empowers cloud infrastructures, instilling confidence in a safer and more robust digital ecosystem for businesses and users. Blockchain architecture comprises several layers that work collaboratively to form a decentralized and secure system. They have been discussed along with the help of a diagram below.

Figure 1. Layers of blockchain architecture

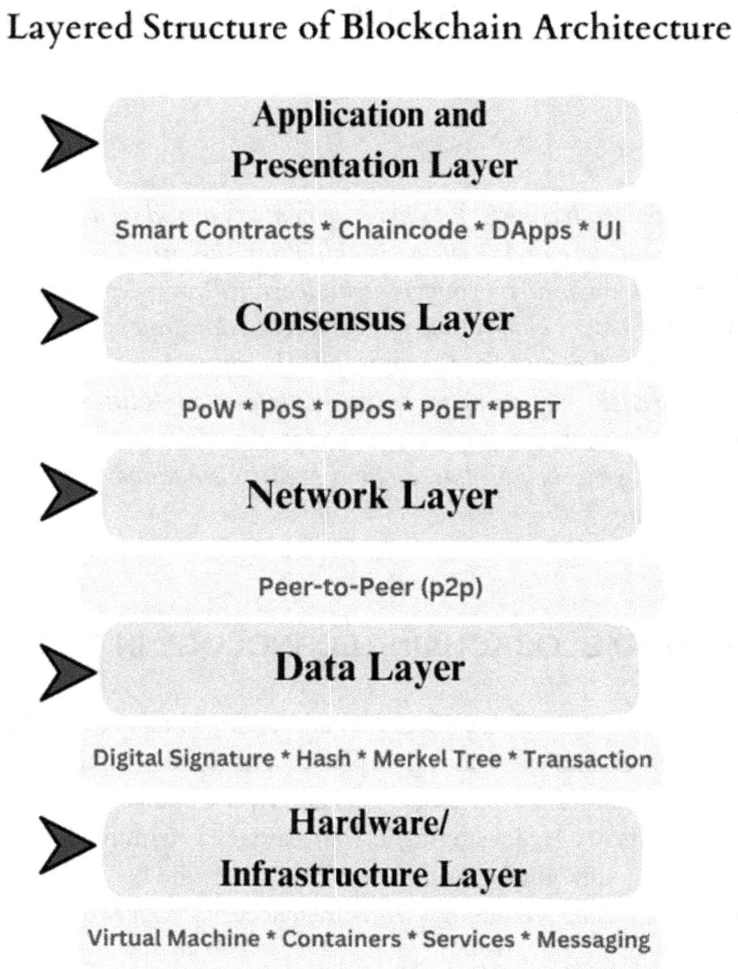

1. *Application Layer:* This is the topmost layer where decentralized applications (DApps) are built and executed, interacting with the underlying layers to access blockchain functionalities.
2. *Consensus Layer:* Responsible for bringing network nodes to a consensus regarding the legitimacy of transactions. To validate and add new blocks, the blockchain employs a number of consensus mechanisms, including Proof of Work (PoW) and Proof of Stake (PoS).
3. *Network Layer:* Handles communication and connectivity between nodes in the blockchain network, ensuring data synchronization and information propagation.
4. *Data Layer:* Stores blockchain data, including transactions and smart contract code, organized into blocks. Each block has a cryptographic link to the previous block, ensuring immutability and data integrity.
5. *Hardware Layer:* The actual network support system for the blockchain, comprising nodes, mining machinery, and other hardware elements required for network functionality.

These layers work together to build a solid basis for blockchain technology that enables safe, open, and impenetrable transactions and applications.

1.2 Cloud Security Challenges and Opportunities

The integration of cloud security with blockchain brings challenges in data privacy, compliance, access control, and interoperability. Blockchain's immutability benefits data integrity but complicates data deletion under regulations like GDPR. Managing access controls and cryptographic keys in blockchain-based cloud systems is complex due to their peer-to-peer nature. Interoperability between different blockchain protocols and cloud platforms can lead to security gaps (Kulkarni *et al.,* 2012).

Despite challenges, integrating blockchain and cloud security presents exciting opportunities. Blockchain's decentralization enhances cloud resilience, protecting against DDoS attacks and single points of failure. Its transparency and tamper-resistant consensus mechanisms promote trust in cloud activities. Blockchain-based IAM systems reduce the risk of identity theft and data breaches, giving users more control. Embracing these opportunities leads to improved cloud security, efficiently addressing data privacy, access controls, and interoperability concerns in the era of blockchain integration (Ali *et al.,* 2015).

1.2.1 Challenges

1. *Data Privacy and Confidentiality:* Integrating blockchain with cloud platforms introduces challenges in maintaining data privacy and confidentiality. While blockchain's immutable and transparent nature ensures data integrity, it also means that sensitive information becomes permanently recorded on the distributed ledger, potentially raising concerns about data exposure and compliance with privacy regulations.
2. *Access Control and Identity Management:* Managing access controls in a blockchain-cloud environment can be complex due to the decentralized nature of blockchain networks. Ensuring proper identity management and authentication mechanisms is crucial to prevent unauthorized access to cloud resources and protect against potential security breaches.
3. *Key Management:* Blockchain relies heavily on cryptographic keys for secure transactions and data access. Properly managing these keys in the cloud poses a challenge, as mishandling or loss of keys can lead to irreversible data loss or unauthorized access.

4. *Smart Contract Vulnerabilities:* On the blockchain, self-executing pieces of code known as smart contracts are vulnerable. A thorough auditing and testing process is necessary when integrating smart contracts with cloud services to guard against vulnerabilities that could be used by bad actors to their advantage.
5. *Scalability and Performance:* Blockchain networks, especially public ones, can suffer from scalability and performance issues when integrated with cloud services. Ensuring smooth and efficient operation at scale becomes a challenge, particularly when dealing with many transactions and users in cloud-based blockchain applications.

1.2.2 Opportunities

1. *Enhanced Data Integrity:* Blockchain's inherent immutability ensures that once data is recorded on the distributed ledger, it cannot be altered or deleted. Integrating blockchain with cloud security provides an opportunity to enhance data integrity, offering an unchangeable and transparent record of all cloud transactions and activities.
2. *Decentralized and Trustless identification Management:* Due to the decentralized identification solutions enabled by blockchain, the requirement for a central authority to maintain user IDs is no longer necessary. Identity management solutions can be implemented in a more secure and trustworthy manner thanks to cloud security, lowering the risk of identity theft and unauthorized access.
3. *Transparent and Tamper-Resistant Auditing:* Cloud security can benefit from blockchain's transparent and tamper-resistant nature, enabling more reliable and auditable records of all cloud-related activities. This increased transparency fosters trust between users and cloud service providers, enhancing accountability and improving security.
4. *Resilience Against DDoS Attacks:* Blockchain's decentralized architecture can enhance cloud security by reducing the risk of single points of failure. Distributed cloud infrastructure empowered by blockchain is more resilient against Distributed Denial of Service (DDoS) attacks, ensuring continuous availability and reliability.
5. *Smart Contract-Based Automation:* Integrating blockchain's smart contracts with cloud security allows for the automation of security measures and incident response protocols. Smart contracts can autonomously execute predefined security actions, such as triggering alerts or implementing access controls, resulting in quicker and more efficient responses to potential threats.

2.0 FUNDAMENTALS OF CLOUD SECURITY WITH RESPECT TO BLOCKCHAIN

In the domain of cloud security, recognizing the fundamentals of blockchain technology plays a central role. This exploration delves into the intersection between cloud security and blockchain, uncovering their combined effect and potential advancements.

2.1 Overview of Cloud Computing

Cloud computing and blockchain technologies are two powerful pillars of the modern digital landscape. Cloud computing makes it flexible, scalable, and affordable to access computing resources over the internet. The decentralized, unbreakable ledger technology known as blockchain, on the other hand, ensures data security and openness. When they are integrated, they function in concert to increase the security and dependability of cloud-based services. The decentralized nature of blockchain works in harmony with the centralized architecture of cloud computing to promote data privacy, trust, and integrity between customers and cloud service providers. This connection has the power to completely transform companies by enabling cross-border payments, smart contract automation, and safe, transparent supply chain management within cloud-based apps (Habib *et al.,* 2022). However, it also presents challenges, including data privacy, key management, and scalability, which require careful consideration for successful implementation.

2.2 Security Risks in Cloud Environments

As cloud computing continues to gain prominence, it brings forth a multitude of benefits, but it also introduces security risks that must be addressed. This exploration delves into the various security challenges faced in cloud environments and examines strategies to mitigate these risks effectively (Fernandes *et al.,* 2014).

1. *Data Exposure and Immutability:* While blockchain's immutability ensures data integrity, it also means that sensitive data recorded on the blockchain cannot be deleted or modified, potentially leading to data exposure and non-compliance with data protection regulations.
2. *Access Control and Identity Management:* The decentralized nature of blockchain poses challenges in managing access controls and identity verification in cloud-based blockchain applications, increasing the risk of unauthorized access and identity theft.
3. *Cryptographic Key Management:* Properly handling cryptographic keys is crucial for securing blockchain transactions in the cloud. If not managed securely, cryptographic keys can be vulnerable to theft or loss, compromising the overall security of the blockchain system.
4. *Smart Contract Vulnerabilities:* Smart contracts, while enabling automation, are susceptible to vulnerabilities or bugs that can be exploited by malicious actors. Flawed smart contracts may result in significant security breaches in cloud-based blockchain applications.
5. *Interoperability Issues:* Integrating blockchain with cloud environments may encounter interoperability challenges, especially when different blockchain protocols and cloud platforms are used. Lack of standardization and compatibility can create security gaps and data inconsistencies.
6. *Cloud Service Provider Risks:* Relying on third-party cloud providers introduces security risks as organizations must trust the provider's security measures to safeguard sensitive blockchain data, which, if inadequate, can result in data breaches or unauthorized access.

2.3 Traditional Approaches to Cloud Security

Traditional approaches to cloud security typically focus on centralized security measures, perimeter-based defenses, and access controls managed by a central authority. These approaches involve firewalls, intrusion detection systems, and encryption to protect data and applications hosted on cloud servers. However, when it comes to integrating blockchain technologies with cloud environments, these traditional methods face new challenges. Blockchain's decentralized nature and distributed consensus mechanism fundamentally differ from traditional centralized systems. As a result, traditional security measures might struggle to adequately address the unique security requirements of blockchain in the cloud (Zhang *et al.,* 2013).

Moreover, the immutability of blockchain data poses challenges for data deletion and modification in compliance with data protection regulations like GDPR. Traditional cloud security approaches may not be equipped to handle this aspect of blockchain, as data on the distributed ledger cannot be altered once recorded. Furthermore, managing access controls and identity verification in a decentralized and trustless environment becomes more complex with blockchain, requiring innovative approaches that go beyond traditional centralized methods. To effectively secure cloud environments with blockchain integration, organizations must adopt new security paradigms that align with the decentralized and transparent nature of blockchain, implementing robust cryptographic measures, decentralized identity management, and smart contract auditing, in addition to traditional security measures.

3.0 BLOCKCHAIN TECHNOLOGY AND ITS ROLE IN CLOUD SECURITY

Blockchain technology is rapidly flourishing for its revolutionary potential in the domain of security. This section deals with the basics of blockchain, its role as a trustworthy distributed ledger, and its inherent features of immutable and tamper-resistant transactions, elucidating how these characteristics help create a digital environment that is safer and more robust.

3.1 Exploring the Basics of Blockchain

Blockchain is a transformative decentralized digital ledger technology that securely records transactions across multiple computers. In cloud computing, it offers compelling benefits, including immutable data, and enhancing trust and integrity in cloud applications. In addition to data integrity, blockchain offers transparency and audibility, as each transaction on the blockchain is transparent and traceable. This feature enables improved auditing procedures, facilitating greater accountability for cloud activities.

Another important and advantageous property of blockchain is its inherent decentralization. The peer-to-peer characteristic of blockchain promotes decentralization, removing the necessity for a central authority in cloud systems. This property of blockchain strengthens the robustness and accessibility of cloud services, fading the risk of single points of failure and possible interruptions.

Also, Blockchain's strong cryptographic algorithms and consensus mechanisms establish a robust layer of security for cloud computing. This heightened security substantially mitigates the vulnerabilities related to data breaches and unauthorized access, ensuring the protection of sensitive information within cloud environments (Aggarwal *et al.,* 2021)

Smart contracts, a distinctive aspect of blockchain technology, introduce automation to cloud-related processes. These self-executing agreements with predefined conditions can be deployed on the blockchain, enabling the automation of diverse aspects of cloud computing. Through this automation, processes are streamlined, and the reliance on intermediaries is minimized, resulting in heightened efficiency and cost-effectiveness in cloud-based operations.

Blockchain's integration with cloud computing also extends to the realm of Identity and Access Management (IAM). By leveraging blockchain-based IAM systems, cloud environments can improve identity verification and user access control. This empowerment grants users more control over their personal data and identities, further enhancing security and protecting against identity theft and data breaches.

Figure 2. Benefits and use cases of blockchain in cloud computing

Blockchain's potential in cloud-based supply chain management is significant. It can transparently and accurately track goods, verifying their origins and promoting trust and efficiency within supply chain operations. The integration of blockchain with cloud computing unlocks new possibilities and advancements, emphasizing data integrity, transparency, decentralization, security, automation, and improved identity management (Sri *et al.,* 2018). As these technologies evolve and synergize, they hold the power to revolutionize various industries and reshape the future of technology.

3.2 Blockchain as a Trustworthy Distributed Ledger

The blockchain serves as a trustworthy distributed ledger when integrated with cloud computing. The security and transparency of data kept in cloud settings are guaranteed by blockchain, a decentralized and tamper-resistant technology. It builds a strong foundation of confidence between cloud service providers and users by keeping an immutable and secure record of transactions.

The combination of blockchain's characteristics with cloud computing enhances data security and privacy. Due to its decentralized structure, blockchain offers resilience against data breaches and cyberattacks by reducing the possibility of single points of failure. Furthermore, because blockchain transactions are transparent, users can confirm the legitimacy of cloud-based data and activities. This encourages accountability (Lemieux *et al.,* 2017).

Cloud computing is a viable solution for a variety of applications across multiple industries since it may provide improved trust, efficiency, and audibility by utilizing blockchain as a trustworthy distributed ledger. By combining these technologies, a more secure and open cloud environment may be created, guaranteeing data integrity and boosting user trust in cloud-based services.

3.3 Immutable and Tamper-Resistant Transactions

Blockchain technology's dependability and security are supported by its essentially based on immutable and tamper-resistant transactions. Every transaction in a blockchain network is collected into a block and cryptographically connected to the one before it, forming a continuous chain of transactional history. A block becomes immutable once it has joined the chain, meaning that its content cannot be changed or removed. Its immutability is made possible via cryptographic hashing, which creates a distinctive and fixed representation of the block's data (Aniello *et al.,* 2017). Therefore, any effort to modify a block's content would cause the block's hash to change, instantly alerting the network to the unauthorized change.

The concept of immutable and tamper-resistant transactions revolutionizes data management, providing a decentralized and transparent approach to recording information. These characteristics guarantee the integrity and reliability of all data stored on the blockchain in applications such as cryptocurrencies, financial transactions, supply chain management, and more. Further enhancing security and lowering the possibility of single points of failure or manipulation is the decentralized structure of blockchain, which uses numerous nodes to verify and validate transactions.

The immutability and tamper-resistance of blockchain technology have a variety of consequences, such as boosting user confidence and eliminating the need for middlemen in certain processes. These characteristics make blockchain a helpful technology for ensuring data dependability, reliability, and transparency across a range of sectors and use cases. Blockchain's immutable and tamper-resistant transactions offer a robust, auditable, and secure method to revolutionize how data is managed and shared globally, whether it is for managing sensitive financial transactions or tracking items in a supply chain.

4.0 ENHANCING CLOUD SECURITY WITH BLOCKCHAIN

The section explores how the integration of Blockchain enhances Cloud Security through Blockchain-Based IAM, fortified data storage and integrity using AI and ML, and ensures Cloud confidentiality and privacy with AI and ML. These advancements promise to revolutionize Cloud security paradigms and foster trust in the digital era.

4.1 Blockchain-Based Identity and Access Management (IAM)

Blockchain-Based Identity and Access Management (IAM) is a cutting-edge solution that addresses the pressing concerns of cloud security. As cloud computing gains widespread adoption, ensuring robust IAM becomes paramount to safeguard sensitive data and prevent unauthorized access.

Traditional IAM systems often rely on centralized databases, making them susceptible to single points of failure and vulnerable to cyber-attacks. Blockchain technology, however, introduces a decentralized approach, where identity records are distributed across the network. This distributed nature ensures greater resilience, as compromising a single node does not compromise the entire system (Finlow-Bates *et al.,* 2021).

In a blockchain-based IAM system, each user possesses a unique cryptographic key, granting them control over their identity data. This approach empowers users to selectively share their information, enhancing privacy and reducing exposure to potential breaches. Moreover, all transactions and access attempts are recorded on the immutable blockchain ledger, promoting transparency and accountability.

Another significant advantage of blockchain-based IAM is its resistance to identity fraud and tampering. With cryptographic techniques, digital identities can be verified without the need for third-party authentication, eliminating potential single points of failure.

Furthermore, blockchain technology is inherently resistant to data manipulation, enhancing the integrity of IAM records. This reliability makes it an ideal choice for ensuring secure access management in cloud environments.

4.2 Securing Data Storage and Integrity

Data storage and integrity security in cloud environments is a top priority for both corporations and consumers. Blockchain technology can be used to solve these issues and enhance cloud security when combined with AI, ML, and other cutting-edge technologies.

Blockchain is a good substitute for preserving data storage because of its immutability and decentralized organization. Data is distributed among several network nodes, which lessens the possibility of a single point of failure. Furthermore, it is exceedingly difficult to violate data integrity because updating data on the blockchain necessitates the consent of most network members. As a result, the information saved on the blockchain is unchangeable.

Organizations may take advantage of sophisticated threat detection and prevention techniques by integrating AI and ML with blockchain-based cloud security. AI and ML algorithms can analyze large volumes of data in real time, identifying anomalous patterns and potential security breaches. These technologies can autonomously respond to emerging threats, minimizing the time gap between detection and remediation. AI and ML can be utilized to strengthen access control in blockchain-based cloud systems. Behavioral analysis can help determine the legitimacy of users' access attempts, reducing the risk of unauthorized access.

The combination of blockchain, AI, and ML also facilitates secure data sharing in cloud environments. Smart contracts, powered by blockchain technology, can enforce predefined rules for data access and usage, ensuring that sensitive information is only shared with authorized parties.

4.3 Ensuring Confidentiality and Privacy

Effectively addressing the utmost concern of safeguarding privacy and confidentiality of sensitive data in cloud security involves incorporating artificial intelligence (AI) and machine learning (ML) to enhance the prospective blockchain technology-based solutions.

Data secrecy is greatly enhanced by the blockchain's decentralized architecture. Traditional cloud systems frequently keep data on centralized servers, which leaves them open to hacking and other forms of data breaches. The blockchain, in contrast, distributes data among numerous nodes, and each block includes a cryptographic connection to the one before it, creating an immutable chain. The risk of data exposure is greatly decreased by this tamper-proof architecture.

The integration of AI and ML enhances confidentiality by bolstering threat detection and response capabilities. AI-driven algorithms can analyze patterns of data access and usage, identifying suspicious activities in real time. By continuously learning from historical data, these systems can adapt to emerging threats and evolve their defense mechanisms proactively.

Privacy is another crucial aspect addressed by blockchain technologies in cloud security. Blockchain enables data sharing through permission mechanisms, ensuring that only authorized parties have access to specific information. Smart contracts, built on blockchain, enforce data privacy rules, allowing parties to interact and share data securely, without exposing sensitive details to unauthorized entities.

AI and ML further contribute to privacy preservation by implementing differential privacy techniques. These methods add noise to datasets, protecting individual identities while still allowing meaningful insights to be drawn from the data.

5.0 CHALLENGES AND CONSIDERATIONS FOR IMPLEMENTING BLOCKCHAIN IN CLOUD SECURITY

As businesses increasingly rely on cloud computing for data processing and storage, strong security measures are taking precedence. Due to its decentralized structure and resistance to manipulation, blockchain technology has generated interest as a potential means of enhancing cloud security. However, integrating a blockchain into a cloud security architecture has its own set of challenges and requires careful consideration. This essay discusses critical issues to address to fully utilize blockchain in cloud security and goes into the major challenges encountered in doing so. Organizations may strengthen their cloud infrastructures against new threats and vulnerabilities by recognizing these issues and factors and making educated decisions (Xie *et al.,* 2020).

5.1 Scalability and Performance Considerations

Scalability and performance are critical considerations when implementing blockchain technologies in cloud security. While blockchain offers inherent security benefits, its design can pose challenges in terms of scalability and efficiency, particularly when dealing with large-scale cloud environments.

The volume of transactions is one of the main scalability issues. Due to their limited ability to handle transactions, traditional blockchains may have bottlenecks as the network expands. In cloud security scenarios, where a high volume of data transactions and identity verifications might be required, this limitation can hinder the system's overall performance.

Different strategies have been investigated to address scalability difficulties. Sharding is one such technique that divides the blockchain network into more manageable portions, known as shards, to process transactions concurrently. This enables increased transaction throughput, enhancing the overall performance of the system.

Additionally, improvements in scalability are greatly aided by developments in consensus methods. The traditional techniques are resource- and time-intensive, but they are secure. By lowering the time needed to add new blocks to the chain, developing consensus solutions enable speedy transaction validation.

The cloud-based infrastructure comes in handy in improving performance and scalability. Blockchain networks can flexibly adapt to changing workloads thanks to cloud service providers' elastic resources, which can scale up or down dependent on demand. Machine learning algorithms can also contribute to optimizing blockchain performance. AI and ML can be utilized to predict network congestion, allocate resources efficiently, and optimize transaction processing, enhancing overall system performance and responsiveness.

5.2 Regulatory Compliance and Legal Implications

Regulatory compliance and legal implications are significant aspects to consider when implementing blockchain technologies in cloud security. The blockchain has definite benefits for data transparency and integrity, but it also poses difficulties for complying with a variety of legal requirements and navigating intricate regulatory frameworks.

Laws governing data privacy and protection are a major cause for concern. There are concerns about the "right to be forgotten" and how to manage requests to have personal data wiped because of the immutability of blockchain technology. To overcome this issue and guarantee compliance with privacy rules, some blockchain networks include privacy-focused features such as off-chain data storage or zero-knowledge proofs. Additionally, different data localization regulations may apply to cross-border data transfers, complicating matters for blockchain networks that conduct global operations. Complying with these regulations while maintaining the decentralized nature of blockchain presents a delicate balance.

Smart contracts, a crucial feature of blockchain, can also raise legal concerns. Smart contracts' ability to self-execute could result in unforeseen effects, legal challenges, or unenforceable clauses. It is essential to ensure that smart contracts comply with the relevant legal frameworks to avoid legal issues. Additionally, regulatory organizations are still unsure on how to categorize and regulate blockchain-based assets like cryptocurrencies or security tokens. Because of this ambiguity, firms must keep abreast of changing legislation to maintain compliance with financial laws and prevent potential legal problems.

Collaboration between technology developers, legal professionals, and regulatory organizations is crucial to addressing these issues. Educating lawmakers about blockchain's capabilities and limitations will aid in crafting balanced and future-proof regulations.

5.3 Interoperability and Integration Challenges

Interoperability and integration challenges are significant considerations when incorporating blockchain technologies into cloud security frameworks. While blockchain offers unique security benefits, its integration with existing cloud systems can present complexities that need to be carefully addressed.

One of the primary challenges is achieving interoperability between different blockchain networks. The lack of standardized protocols can hinder seamless communication and data exchange between various blockchains. In a cloud environment where multiple blockchain platforms may be used for different purposes, ensuring interoperability becomes essential for efficient data sharing and streamlined operations.

Integration with legacy systems is another critical hurdle. Many businesses already have established cloud infrastructures and applications that need to interact with blockchain-based solutions. Integrating blockchain with these legacy systems while maintaining data consistency and security can be a daunting task.

Additionally, the scalability of blockchain networks is closely tied to their integration capabilities. As cloud environments demand higher transaction throughput and data processing, integrating scalable blockchain solutions becomes imperative to ensure optimal performance and responsiveness.

Security concerns also arise during integration. A hybrid cloud setup, where a combination of private and public blockchains may be used, presents challenges in maintaining the same level of security across different environments. Ensuring secure data transfer and access controls between these interconnected systems is crucial for overall cloud security.

To address these challenges, collaborative efforts among blockchain developers, cloud service providers, and industry standards organizations are necessary. Establishing standardized protocols for blockchain interoperability and integration will foster a more cohesive and harmonized ecosystem.

Furthermore, leveraging advanced technologies like AI and ML can enhance the integration process. These technologies can facilitate data mapping, automate tasks, and optimize resource allocation, streamlining the integration of blockchain with existing cloud infrastructures.

6.0 BEST PRACTICES FOR BLOCKCHAIN-BASED CLOUD SECURITY

In recent years, the combination of cloud computing with blockchain technology has demonstrated remarkable promise for enhancing data security and integrity. Blockchain's decentralized and unchangeable nature offers a solid framework for boosting cloud security. However, following best practices is necessary for the effective implementation of blockchain-based cloud security. This article provides insights into how organizations can strategically incorporate these technologies to protect sensitive data, resist cyberattacks, and establish a robust cloud infrastructure. It describes fundamental recommended practices for employing blockchain in cloud security. Businesses can use the power of blockchain to create a more dependable and secure cloud environment for their operations and consumers by adhering to these best practices (Rani *et al.,* 2022).

6.1 Designing a Robust and Secure Blockchain Architecture

Designing a robust and secure blockchain architecture in the context of cloud security requires a thoughtful and comprehensive approach. The integration of blockchain technologies with cloud security can bring numerous benefits, such as enhanced data integrity, transparency, and decentralized access control (Gorkhali *et al.,* 2020). Here are key principles to consider:

1. *Decentralization:* Embrace the decentralized nature of blockchain to distribute data and consensus across nodes in the cloud. This reduces the risk of a single point of failure and ensures resilience against attacks.

2. *Encryption and Privacy:* Implement robust encryption mechanisms to protect data at rest and during transmission. Ensure that sensitive data is encrypted and that access to decryption keys is tightly controlled.
3. *Consensus Mechanism:* Choose a consensus mechanism that aligns with cloud security requirements. Consider factors such as energy efficiency, scalability, and resistance to malicious actors.
4. *Access Control:* Utilize smart contracts to enforce granular access control policies. Define roles and permissions carefully, allowing only authorized parties to access specific data.
5. *Immutable Audit Trail:* Leverage the blockchain's immutable ledger to create an auditable record of all transactions and access attempts. This enables real-time monitoring and detection of potential security breaches.
6. *Regular Audits and Penetration Testing:* Conduct regular security audits and penetration testing to identify and address vulnerabilities. This proactive approach ensures continuous improvement and protection against emerging threats.
7. *Integration with Cloud Security Measures:* Seamlessly integrate the blockchain architecture with existing cloud security tools and protocols. This holistic approach creates a unified and comprehensive security framework.
8. *Disaster Recovery and Backup:* Implement robust disaster recovery and data backup mechanisms to safeguard against data loss or system failures. Redundancy is crucial to maintain data availability.
9. *Compliance with Regulations:* Stay updated with relevant regulations and ensure that the blockchain architecture complies with data privacy and security laws, particularly in cloud environments that span multiple jurisdictions.
10. *Training and Awareness:* Educate stakeholders about the importance of security best practices in blockchain implementations. Human errors can be a significant vulnerability, and awareness is key to mitigating such risks.

6.2 Smart Contracts for Automating Security Measures

Smart contracts offer an innovative approach to automate security measures in the context of blockchain technologies for cloud security. These self-executing contracts are encoded with predefined rules and conditions, enabling automated enforcement of security protocols, access controls, and other security-related tasks.

One of the key advantages of using smart contracts for security automation is the elimination of human errors and the guarantee of consistent execution. Traditional security measures often rely on manual configurations, which can lead to oversight and misconfigurations. Smart contracts, on the other hand, ensure that security policies are precisely followed every time a triggering event occurs, minimizing the risk of vulnerabilities.

In cloud security, smart contracts can automate access control processes, manage user permissions, and verify their identity through cryptographic authentication. They can also govern data-sharing agreements, allowing secure and transparent data exchanges between different cloud entities while enforcing privacy and confidentiality rules (Nzuva *et al.*, 2019).

Real-time threat detection and response systems can be implemented using smart contracts. Smart contracts have the ability to automatically take actions, such as banning harmful transactions, isolating compromised nodes, or activating additional security measures, when aberrant activity is detected.

By leveraging smart contracts, organizations can establish a more proactive and efficient security posture. Automation enables real-time responses to emerging threats, reducing the time between detection and mitigation. Additionally, the transparency and immutability of blockchain ensure audibility, enabling detailed analysis of security events and compliance with regulatory requirements.

However, careful consideration is necessary when designing and deploying smart contracts for security automation. Thorough testing, code auditing, and proper governance mechanisms are essential to prevent vulnerabilities or unintended consequences.

6.3 Continuous Monitoring and Auditing

Continuous monitoring and auditing are vital components in maintaining a robust and secure blockchain-based cloud security infrastructure. As blockchain technologies are integrated into cloud environments, the need for constant vigilance to identify potential threats and assess system integrity becomes paramount. Continuous monitoring involves real-time observation of blockchain networks and cloud resources to detect any suspicious activities or anomalies. Through this proactive approach, organizations can swiftly respond to security incidents and potential breaches. Monitoring tools can track transaction activities, network performance, and access attempts, enabling security teams to stay ahead of emerging threats.

Auditing complements monitoring by providing a systematic review of the blockchain architecture's security controls and configurations. Regular audits make sure that the system conforms with applicable laws and regulations as well as the organization's security policy. This procedure aids in locating loopholes, setup errors, or potential vulnerabilities in access controls, enabling prompt repair. Combining continuous monitoring and auditing in blockchain-based cloud security offers several benefits. It offers in-the-moment information about possible security incidents, enabling quick action and containment measures. Audits make ensuring that security protocols are current and applied correctly, lowering the possibility of breaches and data loss. An audit trail of all transactions and security events is provided by blockchain's immutable nature, which can be extremely helpful in post-incident investigations or compliance reporting. This transparency fosters accountability and builds trust among stakeholders, including customers and regulatory authorities.

To achieve effective continuous monitoring and auditing, organizations should leverage advanced security tools, threat intelligence, and machine learning algorithms. By analyzing large volumes of data and patterns, these technologies can identify abnormal behaviors and potential risks, enhancing the overall security posture.

7.0 ADVANCES IN BLOCKCHAIN TECHNOLOGY

Advances in Blockchain Technology with Respect to Cloud Security are (Hakak *et al.,* 2021):

1. *Decentralization:* Blockchain's distributed nature eliminates the need for a central authority, reducing single points of failure in cloud systems and enhancing overall security.
2. *Immutable Ledger:* A tamper-resistant audit trail for cloud transactions and data is provided by the append-only structure of the blockchain, which makes sure that once data is recorded, it cannot be changed or erased.

3. *Consensus Mechanisms:* Blockchain employs various consensus algorithms to validate transactions, enhancing the integrity of cloud data and preventing malicious modifications.
4. *Smart Contracts:* Smart contracts enable self-executing agreements based on predefined conditions, ensuring automated and secure interactions within cloud environments without relying on intermediaries.
5. *Enhanced Data Privacy:* Blockchain-based cloud solutions secure data privacy via cryptographic methods, prohibiting unauthorized access to sensitive data.
6. *Access Control:* Strong access control techniques made possible by blockchain ensure that only authorized parties can access particular data or services in the cloud.
7. *Reduced DDoS Attacks:* Decentralized networks reduce the risk of Distributed Denial of Service (DDoS) attacks since there are fewer central servers to overwhelm.
8. *Resilience against Attacks: Blockchain's* distributed nature and cryptographic safeguards make it more resilient against cyberattacks, minimizing the risk of data breaches and unauthorized access.
9. *Transparency and Auditing:* Blockchain's transparent and immutable ledger facilitates real-time auditing, ensuring compliance with security policies and regulations in cloud-based environments.
10. *Reducing Single Points of Failure:* Blockchain's decentralized architecture reduces the reliance on single cloud service providers, mitigating the impact of failures or security breaches.
11. *Zero-Knowledge Proofs:* Blockchain technology enables zero-knowledge proofs, allowing cloud service providers to validate the authenticity of data without exposing sensitive information.

Integration With Artificial Intelligence and Machine Learning

A game-changing method for improving cloud security has emerged: combining blockchain technology with artificial intelligence (AI) and machine learning (ML). The strength of AI/ML algorithms and the decentralized, tamper-proof nature of blockchain are combined in this potent way to strengthen cloud security measures.

AI and ML play a crucial role in enabling proactive threat detection and analysis. By continuously analyzing vast amounts of data from cloud environments, these algorithms can identify patterns of suspicious behavior and potential cyber threats in real-time. Meanwhile, blockchain ensures the integrity of this threat data through its immutable ledger, guaranteeing the authenticity and accuracy of the information.

Dynamic access control is another area where this integration proves beneficial. AI-driven models can assess user behavior and establish baseline patterns, allowing for context-aware access privileges. ML can continuously learn and adjust these permissions based on user activity, while blockchain maintains a transparent record of access changes, minimizing the risk of unauthorized access (Mohanta *et al.,* 2020).

Moreover, AI/ML in conjunction with blockchain enhances data privacy and encryption. Advanced techniques can be deployed to protect sensitive information in the cloud, while blockchain's decentralized structure ensures that only authorized parties can access encrypted data.

Predictive security analytics is yet another advantage of this fusion. AI/ML models can analyze historical security data from the blockchain to predict future threats, enabling proactive measures to prevent potential attacks.

The Evolution of Cloud Security With Blockchain

The evolution of cloud security with blockchain has brought about significant advancements in safeguarding sensitive data and enhancing trust in cloud-based services. As cloud computing gained popularity, concerns about data breaches, unauthorized access, and single points of failure prompted the need for more robust security measures. Blockchain technology emerged as a disruptive force, transforming the landscape of cloud security.

Initially, cloud security relied on traditional centralized models, making it susceptible to cyberattacks. However, the integration of blockchain introduced a decentralized and distributed approach, eliminating the reliance on a single entity and reducing vulnerabilities. Blockchain's immutable ledger ensures that all cloud transactions and data modifications are recorded transparently and cannot be altered, providing a tamper-resistant audit trail.

Furthermore, the use of smart contracts within blockchain-enabled cloud systems revolutionized security practices. Smart contracts automate agreement enforcement based on predefined conditions, eliminating the need for intermediaries, and reducing potential security risks. Blockchain's cryptographic techniques have also enhanced data privacy in the cloud. With data encrypted and decentralized across the network, unauthorized access is mitigated, and users gain greater control over their data.

As blockchain technology continues to evolve, its integration with cloud security opens new avenues for secure identity management, access control, and dynamic threat analysis. Machine learning and AI algorithms combined with blockchain's transparency and immutability enable proactive threat detection and real-time analysis of potential security breaches.

8.0 SECURE BLOCKCHAIN-BASED CLOUD FRAMEWORK

1. *Cloud User Layer:* This layer connects users, applications, and cloud resources. It handles user authentication, identity management, and access control. Blockchain strengthens security by providing decentralized identity verification and access control. Users can securely authenticate, access resources, and manage identities independently.
2. *Cloud Automation Layer:* This layer automates cloud tasks like orchestration and scaling using tools and tech. Blockchain integration secures automation with smart contracts. Tamper-proof contracts automate access control, enhancing security.
3. *Blockchain Management Layer:* Managing the blockchain network, this layer includes nodes, consensus, and smart contracts. It safeguards network integrity using consensus mechanisms, reducing malicious attacks or changes.
4. *Secure Data Storage Layer:* This layer stores data in the cloud, encompassing databases and files. Blockchain enhances security with tamper-proof storage. Data can be stored on the blockchain or in decentralized systems, ensuring integrity and transparency (Rahmani *et al., 2022*).

Figure 3. Secure blockchain-based cloud framework

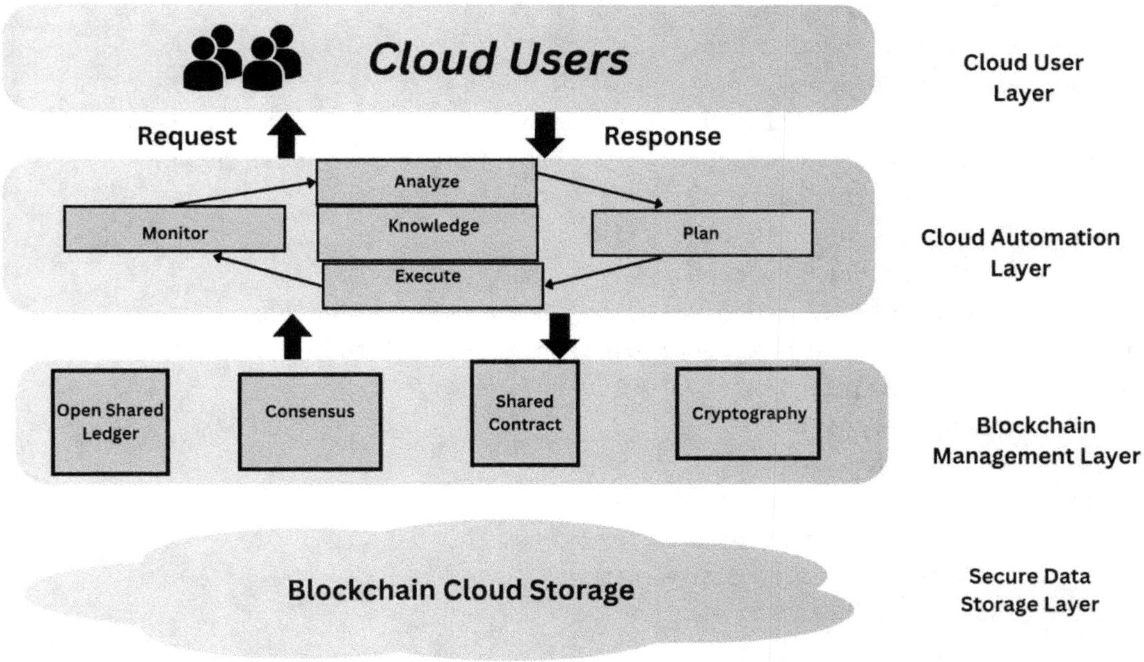

9.0 IMPLEMENTATION OF A BLOCKCHAIN FOR CLOUD SECURITY PURPOSES

A Python code has been executed that simulates a very basic implementation of a blockchain for cloud security purposes. The code along with the output, flowchart, and explanation is stated below. However, the example is a basic demonstration and not a real-world blockchain implementation.

9.1 Python Code

```
import hashlib
import time
class Block:
    def __init__(self, index, previous_hash, timestamp, data, hash):
        self.index = index
        self.previous_hash = previous_hash
        self.timestamp = timestamp
        self.data = data
        self.hash = hash
def calculate_hash(index, previous_hash, timestamp, data):
    value = str(index) + str(previous_hash) + str(timestamp) + str(data)
    return hashlib.sha256(value.encode()).hexdigest()
def create_genesis_block():
    return Block(0, "0", time.time(), "Genesis Block", calculate_hash(0, "0",
```

```
time.time(), "Genesis Block"))
def create_new_block(previous_block, data):
    index = previous_block.index + 1
    timestamp = time.time()
    hash = calculate_hash(index, previous_block.hash, timestamp, data)
    return Block(index, previous_block.hash, timestamp, data, hash)
# Create the genesis block
blockchain = [create_genesis_block()]
# Add new blocks to the blockchain
blockchain.append(create_new_block(blockchain[-1], "Transaction 1"))
blockchain.append(create_new_block(blockchain[-1], "Transaction 2"))
blockchain.append(create_new_block(blockchain[-1], "Transaction 3"))
# Print blockchain contents
for block in blockchain:
    print(f"Block Index: {block.index}")
    print(f"Previous Hash: {block.previous_hash}")
    print(f"Timestamp: {block.timestamp}")
    print(f"Data: {block.data}")
    print(f"Hash: {block.hash}")
    print("=" * 30)
```

9.2 Output

Figure 4. Output of the Python code demonstrating the simplified representation of blockchain and its applications in cloud security

```
Block Index: 0
Previous Hash: 0
Timestamp: 1691473003.6937306
Data: Genesis Block
Hash: 19ab094e03363052d86527f74168aedc9202b79696c1019da6fce2307a8621fd
==============================
Block Index: 1
Previous Hash: 19ab094e03363052d86527f74168aedc9202b79696c1019da6fce2307a8621fd
Timestamp: 1691473003.6937306
Data: Transaction 1
Hash: 6165affa995db51a40d11531aa9f76e96aca34327dbc4e743d2db63b4a9ec56e
==============================
Block Index: 2
Previous Hash: 6165affa995db51a40d11531aa9f76e96aca34327dbc4e743d2db63b4a9ec56e
Timestamp: 1691473003.6937306
Data: Transaction 2
Hash: 63c93ebb6329ffedf207ded28f6814cc3ac7d1474d92cf3ece0f7c458dd4afcd
==============================
Block Index: 3
Previous Hash: 63c93ebb6329ffedf207ded28f6814cc3ac7d1474d92cf3ece0f7c458dd4afcd
Timestamp: 1691473003.6937306
Data: Transaction 3
Hash: 2453f7eacd67b0a6f5f2fd2458e87ae67c82a44f8fcdbc80c9f763ce39898845
==============================
```

9.3 Explanation

The code is broken down into sections and the function of each section is discussed below. A flowchart for the same is also provided.

Figure 5. Detailed flowchart of the Python code

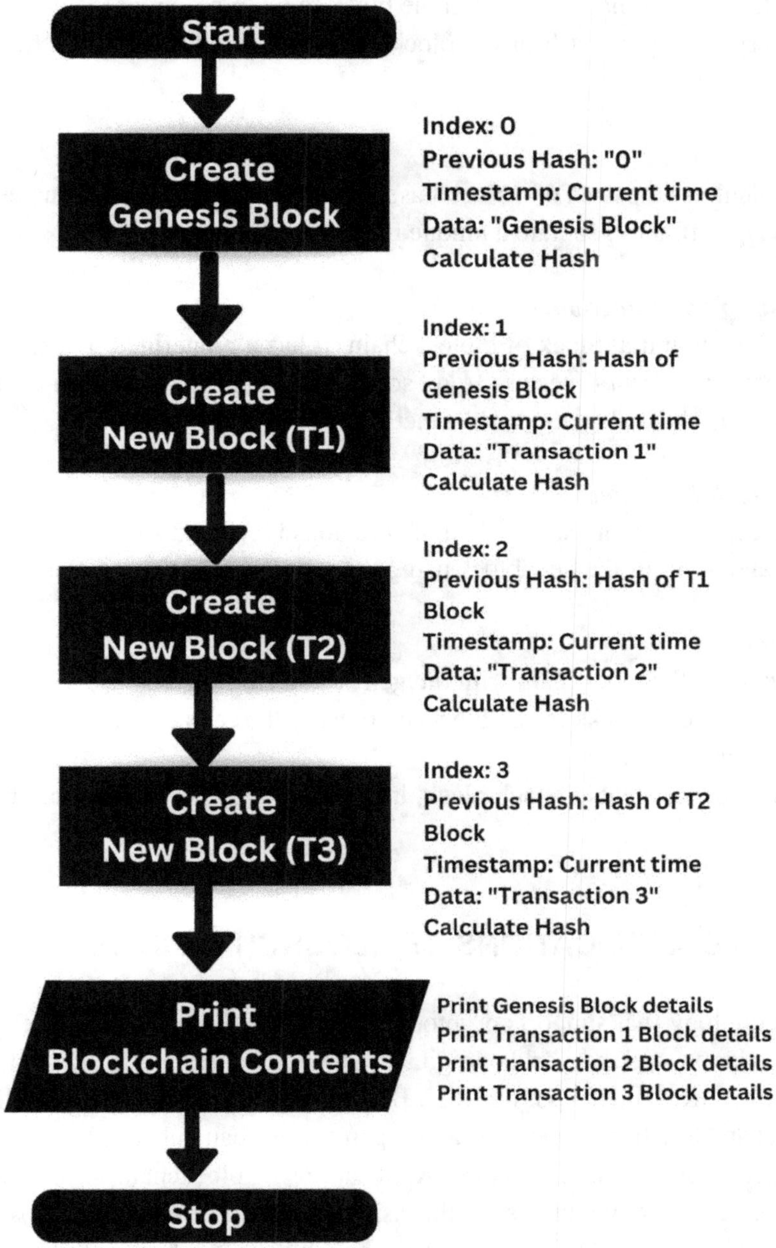

1. ***Block Class:***

The code starts by defining a `Block` class. Each block in the blockchain is represented by an instance of this class. A block contains the following attributes:

- **`index`:** The position of the block within the blockchain.
- **`previous_hash`:** The hash of the previous block in the chain, which creates a link between blocks.
- **`timestamp`:** The time when the block was created.
- **`data`:** The data or information stored in the block (e.g., transactions).
- **`hash`:** The cryptographic hash of the block's attributes (index, previous hash, timestamp, and data).

2. ***calculate_hash Function*:**

This function calculates the hash of a block based on its attributes. It concatenates the attributes and uses the SHA-256 algorithm to generate a unique hash.

3. ***create_genesis_block Function:***

A genesis block is the initial block of a blockchain. It has a predefined index, a "0" previous hash (as it's the first block), a current timestamp, and some initial data. The function creates this block and calculates its hash using the `calculate_hash` function.

4. ***create_new_block Function:***

This function creates a new block based on the previous block and some new data. It calculates the index, timestamp, and hash for the new block using the `calculate_hash` function.

5. ***Main Execution:***

- The code initializes the blockchain with the genesis block.
- It then adds three new blocks to the blockchain using the `create_new_block` function and provides sample transaction data.
- Finally, it prints the contents of each block, including index, previous hash, timestamp, data, and hash.

10.0 REAL-WORLD APPLICATIONS OF BLOCKCHAIN IN CLOUD SECURITY

The underlying technology that supports cryptocurrencies like Bitcoin has skyrocketed in popularity. Although its uses go far beyond the world of digital money. Cloud security is one such area where blockchain has demonstrated tremendous possibilities. By utilizing blockchain's decentralized, open-source, and tamper-proof characteristics, companies and organizations can enhance the integrity, privacy, and overall security of their cloud-based services. Applications of blockchain in the real world for cloud security have evolved as a strong response to the rising worries about data breaches, cyberattacks, and unauthorized access to private data. To demonstrate how blockchain has revolutionized cloud security and safeguarded digital assets in today's interconnected society, this section reviews two most well-known case studies (Bendiab *et al.,* 2018).

Case 1: IBM and Blockchain for Secure Cloud Identity Management

Case Study Overview

Leading technology company IBM worked with digital identification and authentication specialist SecureKey Technologies to create a cloud-based identity management solution based on blockchain technology. The goal was to eliminate the need for centralized databases that might be subject to hacking and data breaches in favor of a decentralized, safe mechanism for confirming people's identities.

How It Operates

The technology, known as "Verified.Me," enables users to construct a digital identity that is connected to their personal data and legally valid identification documents. This identity is protected against hacking and unauthorized access by being dispersed among different nodes on a blockchain network.

Individuals can use Verified.Me to securely disclose their identity information when they need to access online services, such as opening a bank account or requesting government assistance. Without having direct access to the underlying personal data, the service providers can then confirm the user's identity. Instead, they rely on the blockchain to utilize cryptographic proofs to validate the veracity of the user's identification.

Benefits

IBM and SecureKey improved security and privacy for consumers by utilising the blockchain in cloud-based identity management since highly sensitive personal data is spread over the network rather than being maintained centrally. This lessens the possibility of significant data breaches and unauthorised user data access. Users also have more control over their identities because to the ability to decide when and where to share their information, which enhances user consent and data security.

Case 2. Microsoft Azure and Blockchain for Supply Chain Security

Case Study Overview

Microsoft Azure, the cloud computing platform by Microsoft, has been exploring various use cases for blockchain technology, including supply chain management. One notable case study involves Microsoft's collaboration with Mojix, a provider of RFID and IoT technologies, to enhance supply chain security and transparency.

How It Works

The solution combines the Internet of Things (IoT) devices, RFID tags, and blockchain to create an immutable record of the supply chain journey. IoT devices and RFID tags attached to goods and shipments track their movement and gather real-time data on location, temperature, and other environmental conditions.

The collected data is then recorded on a blockchain network, providing an auditable and tamper-proof history of the product's journey. Every participant in the supply chain, including manufacturers, distributors, retailers, and consumers, can access the blockchain to verify the product's authenticity, origin, and handling conditions throughout the entire supply chain.

Benefits

By utilizing blockchain in supply chain management, Microsoft and Mojix improved transparency and trust among supply chain partners. The decentralized nature of the blockchain ensures that all involved parties have access to the same data, eliminating information discrepancies and reducing the risk of fraud or counterfeit products entering the supply chain. Additionally, the ability to track products in real time enhances efficiency, enables better inventory management, and helps identify potential issues or delays proactively.

11.0 CONCLUSION: THE PROMISING SYNERGY OF BLOCKCHAIN AND CLOUD SECURITY

The integration of blockchain technology with cloud security holds tremendous promise in reshaping the landscape of digital security. The innovative fusion of these two technologies offers a powerful solution to address several key challenges in the modern digital era. By combining the decentralized, tamper-resistant nature of blockchain with the scalability and flexibility of cloud computing, organizations can achieve enhanced data protection, transparency, and trust.

Blockchain's immutability and cryptographic verification create a strong foundation for securing data and transactions in the cloud. Its distributed ledger ensures data integrity and transparency, mitigating unauthorized access risks. Decentralization minimizes reliance on single points of control, countering vulnerabilities in centralized systems. Cloud security adds agility and scalability, complementing blockchain's capabilities for decentralized applications. This synergy enables secure, auditable systems, optimizing processes and enhancing user trust. Blockchain and cloud security offer solutions across domains like supply chain management, digital identity, and finance. Their convergence has the potential to reshape data storage, access, and security. However, implementation challenges and regulations should be acknowledged (Yadav *et al.,* 2022). Organizations should evaluate needs and regulations for effective adoption, unlocking the transformative power of blockchain and cloud security for a resilient digital ecosystem.

REFERENCES

Ali, M., Khan, S. U., & Vasilakos, A. V. (2015). Security in cloud computing: Opportunities and challenges. *Information Sciences*, *305*, 357–383. doi:10.1016/j.ins.2015.01.025

Aniello, L., Baldoni, R., Gaetani, E., Lombardi, F., Margheri, A., & Sassone, V. (2017, September). A prototype evaluation of a tamper-resistant high performance blockchain-based transaction log for a distributed database. In *2017 13th European Dependable Computing Conference (EDCC)* (pp. 151-154). IEEE.

Bendiab, K., Kolokotronis, N., Shiaeles, S., & Boucherkha, S. (2018, August). WiP: A novel blockchain-based trust model for cloud identity management. In *2018 IEEE 16th Intl Conf on Dependable, Autonomic and Secure Computing, 16th Intl Conf on Pervasive Intelligence and Computing, 4th Intl Conf on Big Data Intelligence and Computing and Cyber Science and Technology Congress (DASC/PiCom/DataCom/CyberSciTech)* (pp. 724-729). IEEE. 10.1109/DASC/PiCom/DataCom/CyberSciTec.2018.00126

Fernandes, D. A., Soares, L. F., Gomes, J. V., Freire, M. M., & Inácio, P. R. (2014). Security issues in cloud environments: A survey. *International Journal of Information Security*, *13*(2), 113–170. doi:10.100710207-013-0208-7

Finlow-Bates, K. (2021). *U.S. Patent No. 10,938,566*. Washington, DC: U.S. Patent and Trademark Office.

Gai, K., Guo, J., Zhu, L., & Yu, S. (2020). Blockchain meets cloud computing: A survey. *IEEE Communications Surveys and Tutorials*, *22*(3), 2009–2030. doi:10.1109/COMST.2020.2989392

Gorkhali, A., Li, L., & Shrestha, A. (2020). Blockchain: A literature review. *Journal of Management Analytics*, *7*(3), 321–343. doi:10.1080/23270012.2020.1801529

Habib, G., Sharma, S., Ibrahim, S., Ahmad, I., Qureshi, S., & Ishfaq, M. (2022). Blockchain technology: Benefits, challenges, applications, and integration of blockchain technology with cloud computing. *Future Internet*, *14*(11), 341. doi:10.3390/fi14110341

Hakak, S., Khan, W. Z., Gilkar, G. A., Assiri, B., Alazab, M., Bhattacharya, S., & Reddy, G. T. (2021). Recent advances in blockchain technology: A survey on applications and challenges. *International Journal of Ad Hoc and Ubiquitous Computing*, *38*(1-3), 82–100. doi:10.1504/IJAHUC.2021.119089

Kulkarni, G., Chavan, N., Chandorkar, R., Waghmare, R., & Palwe, R. (2012, October). Cloud security challenges. In *2012 7th International Conference on Telecommunication Systems, Services, and Applications (TSSA)* (pp. 88-91). IEEE. 10.1109/TSSA.2012.6366028

Lemieux, V. L. (2017, November). Blockchain and distributed ledgers as trusted recordkeeping systems. In *Future technologies conference* (Vol. 2017). FTC.

Mohanta, B. K., Jena, D., Satapathy, U., & Patnaik, S. (2020). Survey on IoT security: Challenges and solution using machine learning, artificial intelligence and blockchain technology. *Internet of Things*, *11*, 100227. doi:10.1016/j.iot.2020.100227

Nzuva, S. (2019). Smart contracts implementation, applications, benefits, and limitations. *Journal of Information Engineering and Applications*, *9*(5), 63–75.

Rahmani, M. K. I., Shuaib, M., Alam, S., Siddiqui, S. T., Ahmad, S., Bhatia, S., & Mashat, A. (2022). Blockchain-based trust management framework for cloud computing-based internet of medical things (IoMT): A systematic review. *Computational Intelligence and Neuroscience*, *2022*, 2022. doi:10.1155/2022/9766844 PMID:35634070

Rani, M., Guleria, K., & Panda, S. N. (2022, October). Blockchain technology novel prospective for cloud security. In *2022 10th International Conference on Reliability, Infocom Technologies and Optimization (Trends and Future Directions) (ICRITO)* (pp. 1-6). IEEE. 10.1109/ICRITO56286.2022.9964666

Sarmah, S. S. (2018). Understanding blockchain technology. *Computing in Science & Engineering*, *8*(2), 23–29.

Sri, P. S. G. A., & Bhaskari, D. L. (2018). A study on blockchain technology. *Int J Eng Technol, 7*(2.7), 418-421.

Xie, S., Zheng, Z., Chen, W., Wu, J., Dai, H. N., & Imran, M. (2020). Blockchain for cloud exchange: A survey. *Computers & Electrical Engineering*, *81*, 106526. doi:10.1016/j.compeleceng.2019.106526

Yadav, S. K., Sharma, K., Kumar, C., & Arora, A. (2022). Blockchain-based synergistic solution to current cybersecurity frameworks. *Multimedia Tools and Applications*, *81*(25), 1–22. doi:10.100711042-021-11465-z

Zhang, N., Liu, D., & Zhang, Y. (2013, November). A research on cloud computing security. In *2013 International Conference on Information Technology and Applications* (pp. 370-373). IEEE.

Chapter 17
Detection of DDoS Attacks Using Variational Autoencoder-Based Deep Neural Network

Agripah Kandiero
https://orcid.org/0000-0001-8201-864X
Instituto Superior Mutasa, Mozambique & Africa University, Zimbabwe

Panashe Chiurunge
Chinhoyi University of Technology, Zimbabwe

Jacob Munodawafa
University of St Thomas, Mozambique

ABSTRACT

Distributed denial of service (DDoS) attacks are one of the most commonly used tools to disrupt web services. DDoS is used by groups of diverse backgrounds with diverse motives. To counter DDoS, machine learning-based detection systems have been developed. Proposed is a variational autoencoder (VAE) based deep neural network (VAE-DNN) classifier that can be trained on an unbalanced dataset without needing feature engineering. A variational autoencoder is a type of deep neural network that learns the underlying distribution of computer network flows and models how the benign and DDoS classes were generated. Because a VAE model learns the distribution of the classes within the dataset, it also learns how to separate them. The variational autoencoder-based classifier can scale to any data size. A deep neural network, quadratic discriminant analysis (QDA), and linear discriminant analysis (LDA) decision boundaries are applied to the latent representation of network traffic to classify the flows. The DNN shows the highest precision and recall of the three classifiers.

DOI: 10.4018/979-8-3693-0593-5.ch017

1. INTRODUCTION

1.1 Background of the Research Problem

Malicious actors and their activities have found space on the internet. The use of the internet to access services of all kinds has also seen malicious actors bent on disrupting the services. All organisations that offer web-based services are vulnerable to DDoS attacks. Financial services, commercial, news, politics and entertainment, are now accessible through the internet. Malicious actors with diverse motives target web-based servers intending to bring down the services or at least degrade the quality of service offered to genuine customers. One of the most common ways of disrupting a web-based service is Distributed Denial of Service (DDoS). The malicious actors attempt to bring down or at least slow down a service by overwhelming the server's resource limits in terms of CPU, memory or network bandwidth. The attackers launch DDoS attacks by taking advantage one way or the other of protocols found at the Application layer, Transport layer and Network layer of the TCP/IP protocol suite. All network communication devices implement the TCP/IP protocols when they communicate. The Internet of Things has dramatically increased the number of online devices. The number of devices that can be recruited to form botnets which are then used to amplify DDOS attacks is huge (Kim, 2020). The TCP/IP model together with the OSI models, were not built with security in mind. When these models were proposed the motivations for most current cyber-attacks were not as prevalent as they are today since there was very little online activity then. The majority of Network capable devices such are those found among IoT terminals were also not built with the required focus on security. These appliances are, therefore, easily targeted and recruited to increase the size of botnets. Effective network intrusion detection systems are needed to counter the many possible DDOS attack vectors.

Malicious actors have various ways of implementing DDoS attacks. A botnet or network of compromised remotely controlled computers is commonly used to launch DDoS attacks (Khan, 2019). Other malicious actors amplify their DDoS attacks by making use of computers on various networks broadcast domains to send packets to a server at the same time to choke the server's processing capacity and resources. The malicious actors evolve their mechanisms of attack as technology evolves. Early botnets used Internet Relay Chat (IRC) protocol for sending instructions to the botnets from the botmaster using a client-server networking model. Then peer-to-peer (P2P) protocol was used by botnets before HTTP became the most commonly used protocol (Kim, 2020). In 2016 a botnet called Mirai took over control of hundreds of thousands of Internet of Things (IoT) devices that resulted in a widespread loss of Internet access in the USA. The botnet managed to recruit a large number of Internet of Things (IoT) devices that used default login credentials for Telnet protocol. On 29 January 2018, three Dutch banks ABN AMRO, ING Bank and Rabobank were attacked by DDoS resulting in loss of internet banking and inaccessibility of websites. In 2016 Twitter, Sound Cloud, Spotify, and Shopify all went down after a DDoS attack was launched against the cloud domain hosting company Dynamic DNS (Bonguet, 2017). With DDoS defence and mitigation systems, time is limited from the launch of attack to mitigation (Wangy, 2017).

DDoS attacks cause loss of revenue to service providers and cause inconveniences and frustration to customers as services become inaccessible. A DDoS detection and mitigation strategy is called for as part of a cybersecurity strategy. Cybersecurity focuses on preventing, detecting and reacting to threats and attacks timeously (Darko Galinec, 2017). The research offers a solution for detecting DDoS attacks. The built system can be adapted to be part of a broader cybersecurity strategy. Since the launching of DDoS attacks cannot be prevented, detecting DDoS timeously with high precision is the best that can be done. However, for high precision models to be trained, the dataset needs to be balanced. For all network intrusion detection and DDoS attack detection, correctly balanced datasets, are hard to get. Some techniques to balance the dataset before model training have been explored. The methods that have been adopted to balance data sets which include under-sampling the majority class and Oversampling of the minority class are discussed in Section 2 Literature Review. It is also essential that the DDoS detection systems be scalable to train models that can handle extensive network traffic data associated with the Internet and the evolving Internet of Things. Traditional machine learning classifiers also fell short of scalability besides requiring that the data set be balanced before training the model. Currently adopted data balancing techniques will be reviewed and show how the VAE offers an alternative to deal with unbalanced data sets. The scalability that cannot be achieved by traditional machine learning techniques is achieved by the VAE. VAE achieves scalability because it uses a mini-batch Stochastic Gradient when updating weights during training. The re-parameterization trick which makes stochastic gradient possible with VAE is explained in Section 2 Literature Review. The continually evolving nature of DDoS attacks is addressed by the profound neural network nature of A Variational Autoencoder, which makes a VAE automatically learn new patterns in network flows. Reliable datasets usable for training intrusion detection models are hard to get. In this research, the CICIDS 2017 dataset is used to train a VAE DDoS detector.

1.2 Research Problem

Distributed Denial of Service (DDOS) attacks result in loss of revenue and frustrated users as servers fail to serve legitimate users of web-based services. Timeous Detection of DDoS with high precision and high recall, therefore, saves revenue and guarantees customer satisfaction. However traditional machine learning algorithms (Support Vector Machines, Logistic Decision Trees, Logistic Regression, Naïve Bayes) which have been applied to detect DDoS attacks cannot train accurate classifiers if the training data set has an odd number of tuples for each class (Bellinger, 2017). In real-world situations, balanced data sets are rare. In many other applications, the data set may contain only the standard samples and have no anomalous samples for the model to learn from. Unbalanced data sets and lack of minority class samples in the dataset are a big challenge for DDoS detection systems and all intrusion detection systems in general. Although deep neural network classifiers perform better than traditional machine learning classifiers, their performance is also limited if the training data set is unbalanced data (Gupta, 2019). Dataset balancing techniques based on oversampling the minority class or under-sampling the majority class have been explored. Samples generated by oversampling of the minority class result in overfitting and samples generated by oversampling do not bring new knowledge for the model to learn. Classifiers trained on datasets balanced by sampling techniques showed some slight performance improvement. For training a classifier with an unbalanced dataset and still achieving high precision and high recall, a Variational Autoencoder (VAE) is proposed. For the very high precision and recall called for by DDoS detection systems and all intrusion detection systems, a Variational Autoencoder is proposed. A VAE is a deep generative model that models how a dataset is generated by learning the underlying distribution of the dataset.

VAE has the advantage of scalability over traditional machine learning classifiers. Like conventional deep neural networks, VAE models are scalable to any data set size because VAE also uses Mini-batch Stochastic Gradient Descent (SGD). Mini-batch SGD is a type of Stochastic Gradient Descent (SGD) which is used to update weights during training. VAE uses mini-batch SGD although the nature of the latent layer is random and probabilistic (Kurien, 2019). With mini-batch SGD, the gradient is calculated after each mini-batch is run. The VAE takes in a small batch of training samples for each iteration of loss minimization. Mini-batch SGD results in faster training of the model than Stochastic Gradient and also allows for parallel computations to speed up the training. For mini-batch SGD to be possible, the re-parameterization trick is used for backpropagation to go around the random latent space when updating VAE weights during training. Traditional data set balancing techniques such as oversampling of the minority class and under-sampling of the majority class can be made redundant by the use of Variational Autoencoders. VAE make training classifiers direct without prior extensive data preparation, such as balancing the data sets. With minimal modification, the VAE can generate new minority samples to balance a dataset. This research will demonstrate how a DDoS detection system can be built without the need for balancing the data set and extensive feature engineering. The VAE is coupled to two downstream classifiers which are a Deep Neural Network and Quadratic Discriminant Analysis for detecting DDoS attacks.

1.3 Research Objectives

1. To build a Variational Autoencoder based Deep Neural Network that detects DDOS attacks with high precision and high recall.
2. To design and build a Variational Autoencoder model which does not require the balancing of the training data set.
3. To design and build a Deep Neural Network DDoS classifier whose input is the VAE latent representation.
4. To apply a Linear Discriminant Analysis decision boundary to the latent layer representation of network traffic data and separate the classes.
5. To apply the Quadratic Discriminant Analysis decision boundary to the latent layer representation of network traffic data and separate the classes

1.4 Conceptual Framework

1.4.1 Why Variational Autoencoder Based Classification

VAE was chosen to implement a DDoS detection because a VAE does not require a balanced data set for training the model and also because the VAE models can scale to any training data size. A VAE models how the data was generated. A VAE is one type of generative model discussed in section section 2 Literature Review. A VAE is a combination of two neural networks. The first neural network is the encoder which takes in data inputs and represents the data in a latent space with reduced dimensions. The latent space is in the form of a joint probability distribution of the essential variables only. The distribution is forced to be normal by minimization of a Kullback-Leibler (KL) divergence term. The second neural network takes samples from the latent space as input and attempts to reconstruct the original input data. The difference or dissimilarity between the reconstructed output and the original input is a loss to be minimized. During training, the loss function of the VAE minimizes the sum of the KL divergence loss and the reconstruction loss. A VAE attempts to recreate the given input while under constraints such as smaller hidden layers and the forcing of the joint probability distribution of features to be Gaussian.

The scalability comes from VAE's ability to use Stochastic Gradient Descent (SGD) despite having randomness along the path of backpropagation. The mathematical foundation of the VAE re-parameterization trick that makes SGD possible in VAE is discussed in Section 2 Literature Review. Re-parameterization externalizes the randomness of the latent space and represents each probabilistic distribution of a data point with a deterministic value which is necessary for updating weights during backpropagation. The VAE learns the distribution of features within the benign flows and the distribution of features within the DDoS flows. The VAE then represents the network flows as a continuous probability distribution. The benign and DDoS attack samples occupy distinct regions of the probability distribution. The patterns of normal, benign network flows and the DDoS network flows are used to train the classifier. A Supervised machine learning approach is adopted to train a VAE classifier that separates computer network traffic flows into DDoS and benign traffic. The trained VAE takes in the seventy seven features of the CICIDS 2017 data set representing a network flow. The VAE outputs a mean and a standard deviation indicating the region in the joint probability distribution where the network flow is likely to be found. A QDA, LDA and DNN are then trained on the VAE. The QDA and LDA apply quadratic and Linear decision boundaries respectively to the network flows and separate the benign and DDoS flows. A DNN is also trained on the VAE latent representation. A DDoS Classifier is built having the foundation of a VAE, with DNN as a downstream classifier. It is either a QDA or LDA because only the better classifier between them will be co-opted into the hybrid system. The DNN is essential in the hybrid system because of its scalability.

Publicly available DDoS detection data sets have unbalanced classes. This calls for the datasets to be balanced first before a model can be trained (Yilmaz, 2019). The VAE is trained with the CICIDS 2017 dataset. The CICIDS 2017 Friday Afternoon data set is unbalanced in favour of DDoS attacks. The data set contains tuples of benign and DDoS samples. It has a total of 225745 tuples of which 97718 were benign and 12827 were DDoS attack flows. Currently, used data balancing techniques generate synthetic samples that either cause overfitting or loss of information. Feature engineering demands time and domain expertise. A VAE based DDoS classifier is built without balancing the data nor particular choosing of features. Because no feature engineering is conducted, a VAE can be used where domain knowledge is limited.

1.4.2 CICIDS 2017 Data Set Features

The CICIDS 2017 Friday Afternoon data set has a total of 78 features as shown in Table 1. The CICIDS2017 data set was generated in a testbed network environment with DDoS attacks being generated on the afternoon of July the 7th 2017. The CICFlowMeter was used for extracting network traffic features. Features that were likely to be the most explanatory for DDoS were identified. For detecting DDoS attacks 'backward packet length', 'average packet size' and 'inter arrival time standard deviation' were selected. Seven common traditional machine learning classification algorithms were used to examine the performance and accuracy of the selected features (Sharafaldin, 2018).

A comparison is made between the results of the VAE based hybrid classifiers and those of K-Nearest Neighbours (KNN), Random Forest (RF), ID3, Adaboost, Multilayer perceptron (MLP), Naive-Bayes (NB), Quadratic Discriminant Analysis (QDA) as shown in Table 2. Precision and recall are the metrics to be used for the comparison because both False Positives and False Negatives need to be minimized. Accuracy cannot be used as a metric to detect DDoS attacks because the CICIDS2017 Friday Afternoon data set is not balanced. For DDoS attacks testbed environment DDoS packets may not be very different from real world DDoS attack packets because similar packet generation methods are usually employed. Table 1 shows the features that collectively determine whether a flow is benign or an attack in the CICIDS2017 data set.

Table 1. CICIDS 2017 Friday afternoon data set features

Variable	Variable	Variable	Variable
Source IP address	Flow Inter-Arrival-Time Min	Packet Length Standard Deviation	Subflow Forwarding Packets
Destination IP address	Forwarding Inter-Arrival-Time Total	Packet Length Variance	Subflow Forwarding Bytes
Destination Port for TCP and UDP	Forwarding Inter-Arrival-Time Mean	FIN Flag Count	Subflow Backwarding Packets
Protocol IP protocol	Forwarding Inter-Arrival-Time Standard Deviation	SYN Flag Count	Subflow Backwarding Bytes
Flow Duration	Forwarding Inter-Arrival-Time Max	RST Flag Count	Initial Forwarding Win Bytes
Total Forwarding Packets	Forwarding Inter-Arrival-Time Min	PSH Flag Count	Initial Backwarding Win Bytes
Total Backwarding Packets	Backwarding Inter-Arrival-Time Total	ACK Flag Count	Forwarding Act Data Packets
Total Length of Forwarding Packets	Backwarding Inter-Arrival-Time Mean	URG Flag Count	Forwarding Segment Size Min
Total Length of Backwarding Packets	Backwarding Inter-Arrival-Time Standard Deviation	CWE Flag Count	Active Mean
Forwarding packet Length Maximum	Backwarding Inter-Arrival-Time Max	ECE Flag Count	Active Standard Deviation
Forwarding Packet Length Minimum	Backwarding Inter-Arrival-Time Minimum	Down/Up Ratio	Active Max
Forwarding Packet Length Mean	Forwarding PSH Flags	Packet Length Size Average	Active Min
Forwarding Packet Length Standard Deviation	Backwarding PSH Flags	Forwarding Segment Size Average	Idle Mean
Backwarding Packet Length Maximum	Forwarding URG Flags	Backwarding Segment Size Average	Idle Standard Deviation
Backwarding packet Length Minimum	Backwarding URG Flags	Forwarding Bytes Average	Idle Maximum
Backwarding packet Length Mean	Forwarding Header Length	Forwarding Packets Average	Idle Minimum
Backwarding packet Length Standard Deviation	Backwarding Header Length	Forwarding Bulk Rate Average	Label
Flow Inter-Arrival Time Mean	Packet Length Minimum	Backwarding Bytes Average	
Flow Inter-Arrival Time Standard Deviation	Packet Length Maximum	Backwarding Packets Average	
Flow Inter-Arrival Time Maximum	Packet Length Mean	Backwarding Bulk Rate Average	

1.4.3 Features Selected For DDoS Detection

Sharafaldin et al identified a set of features whose parameters are most likely to determine whether a sample was a DDoS attack, as shown in Table 2. The first packet sent between two communicating devices determines the forward and backward directions of the flows. The forward direction is the source destination of the first packet and the backward direction is destination-source response to the first packet. The standard deviation size of the packet in the backward direction, Standard deviation time between two packets sent in the flow, Average size of the packet and Duration of the flow in microseconds were identified as features with parameters most determining if a sample is a DDoS attack.

Table 2. Selected features for DDoS attack (Sharafaldin, 2018)

Label	Feature
DDoS	Backwarding Packet Length Standard Deviation
	Flow Duration
	Average Packet Size
	Flow Inter-Arrival-Time Standard Deviation

Note. Adapted from 'Toward Generating a New Intrusion Detection Dataset and Intrusion Traffic Characterization', by I.Sharafaldin and A.Lashkari and A.Ghorbani, 2018, Proceedings of the 4th International Conference on Information Systems Security and Privacy (ICISSP 2018), p. 108-116.

1.4.4 Metrics for VAE-Based DDoS Detection Classifiers

Accuracy cannot be used as a reliable metric when training a model for DDoS detection. Supervised Machine learning classifiers trained with imbalanced datasets are biased towards the majority class and against the minority class because they learn more from the majority samples. If a classifier is trained with a data set with 97% of the samples being the benign network flows and 3% being the malicious network flows, the classifier will achieve a 97% accuracy rating if the model guesses that every data point is a benign flow during evaluation. Using accuracy is only suitable for symmetric data sets where the class distribution is equal for the classes and the cost of false positives and false negatives are roughly the same. Therefore accuracy cannot be used as a metric for models trained with imbalanced dataset (Alkasassbeh, 2016). Using VAE based classifiers this research will demonstrate how a system with both high precision and high recall is achievable. By first learning the distribution of the dataset the Variational Autoencoder will be able to classify network traffic with high precision and recall. Network traffic may easily reach big data scale given the Internet of Things and forecasts on the total number of devices connected. A VAE is scalable to big data scales because it uses mini-batch stochastic gradient descent during training. During training the VAE learns to represent the data in a new latent representation where separation is enhanced. The VAE encoder gives the log probability of latent representation z given input data point x, that is $p(z/x)$. The VAE decoder samples from the learnt distribution to give the probability of reconstructing x from the latent representation $p(x/z)$. After the VAE is trained, both a linear and quadratic decision boundary are applied to the latent variables to separate the two classes of benign and DDoS network traffic. A decision boundary that classifies network flows better implies that the data set fulfils the assumptions of the type of Discriminant Analysis system. A DNN model is also trained on the latent representation of a trained VAE. This model serves to compare and endorse the results of the Discriminant Analysis classifier. The results of the VAE based classifiers are compared against themselves and also compared to the results of traditional machine learning classifiers obtained on the same CICIDS 2017 data set when it was generated by Sharafaldin et al., 2018.

2. LITERATURE REVIEW

2.1 Introduction

Literature about how to build a DDoS Detection system with high precision and high recall is reviewed in this section. Previous Studies on how traditional machine learning algorithms dealt with data imbalances in intrusion DDoS and intrusion detection are covered. How the VAE, a generative model, takes away the need for balancing data set classes and feature engineering for downstream classifiers is discussed in section 2.7. This section refers to journals and other scholarly literature that cover studies and approaches to training adequate DDoS detectors. The assumptions that go along with Quadratic Discriminant Analysis (QDA) and Linear Discriminant Analysis (LDA) and their implication on classification performance of the VAE based classifier are covered later in the section. The types of DDoS attacks and how they take advantage of the protocols of the TCP/IP suite are covered next.

2.2 Definition of Critical Terms

Variational Autoencoder: A deep generative model that encodes data inputs into a probability distribution. The probability distribution is sampled by the decoder to attempt to reconstruct the original input.

Re-parameterization trick: The externalization of the randomness of the latent space of a Variational Autoencoder and represents each probabilistic distribution of each data point with a deterministic value for updating weights during backpropagation

Latent space: The representation of data points by a probability distribution in which the data points lie,

Encoder: Part of a Variational Autoencoder that takes in data inputs and transforms the input into a probability distribution mean and standard deviation that represents the position of the data point in the distribution.

Decoder: Part of the Variational Autoencoder that samples from the latent space and attempts to reconstruct original input.

2.3 Types of DDoS Attacks

There are many forms of DDoS attacks. All the different attacks aim to deny genuine users access to a web-based service. The attacks take advantage of how the different layers of the TCP/IP suite implement protocols (Macfarlane, 2015). At the application layer, there are attacks such as HTTP flooding. At the transport layer, there are SYN flooding and UDP flooding. At the network layer, there are smurf attack ICMP flooding. The motivation for carrying out DDoS attacks could be varied since those who carry them come from different backgrounds such as social activism, political and outright criminal (Macfarlane, 2015). Since there is a demonstrated desire to commit distributed denial of service attacks on varying web services by a diverse group of people, it is imperative that intrusion detection systems which can detect the DDoS effectively be implemented. Common types of DDoS attacks are discussed next.

2.3.1 Botnet

Botnets are recruited to amplify and make attacks come from multiple sources. A DoS attack uses one computer and one Internet connection to flood a targeted system or resource. A botnet uses many computers to launch a coordinated DoS attack against one or more targets. A specific strategy is used to recruit, exploit, and infect computers (Alzahrani, 2018). During the recruiting phase, the attacker identifies and groups several machines from which to generate huge volumes of traffic to flood the victim server. The recruiting phase is accomplished through the scanning of remote machines using penetration testing software tools such as Nmap looking for security vulnerabilities. During The exploit phase, the attacker exploits the identified vulnerabilities to break into the recruited machines. The attacker infects the recruited machines with a DDoS program during the infect phase. A DDoS master program is installed on one computer using a stolen account. The master program, at a designated time, then controls and commands the many agent programs, installed on recruited computers. In response to a command from the botmaster, the agents initiate the attack. The infected machines are remotely controlled to launch the attack by the attacker. In this way, the perpetrator can multiply the effectiveness of the Denial of Service significantly by harnessing the resources of multiple compromised accomplice computers which serve as attack platforms. The master program can initiate thousands of agent programs in a short time. Figure 1 shows the underlying architecture of a botnet network.

Figure 1. Botnet DDoS attack architecture (Singh, 2015)

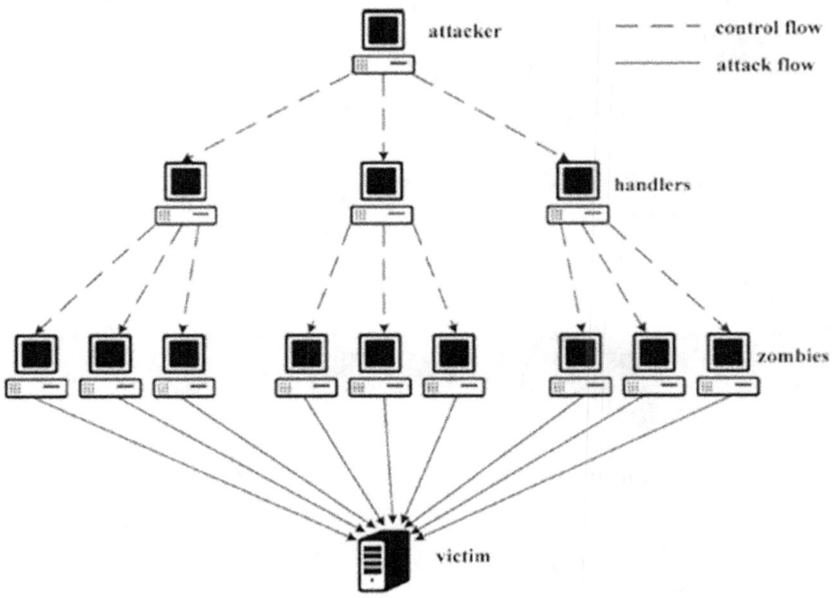

2.3.2 Smurf Attacks

A smurf attack is a type of network layer DDoS which takes advantage of how the ICMP accomplishes its tasks. An attacker floods a targeted server with Internet Control Message Protocol (ICMP) packets. Requests are made to computer networks using the spoofed source IP address of the targeted device, as shown in Figure 2. The computer networks then sent responses to the targeted server thereby amplifying the initial attack traffic overwhelming the victim and making it unusable by legitimate users. To deplete the bandwidth of the targeted server, a smurf attack usually broadcasts messages whose replies will all be sent to the spoofed IP address of the victim. Every machine in the broadcast domain which received the broadcast then sends ICMP ECHO reply packets to the victim IP address (Mitra, 2017). The victim will not be able to deal with the sudden rise in number of reply messages. During the time of the attack, the victim server will fail to service requests from its authentic users or may give degraded service or crush altogether.

Figure 2. Smurf attack
Source: Macfarlane et al. (2015)

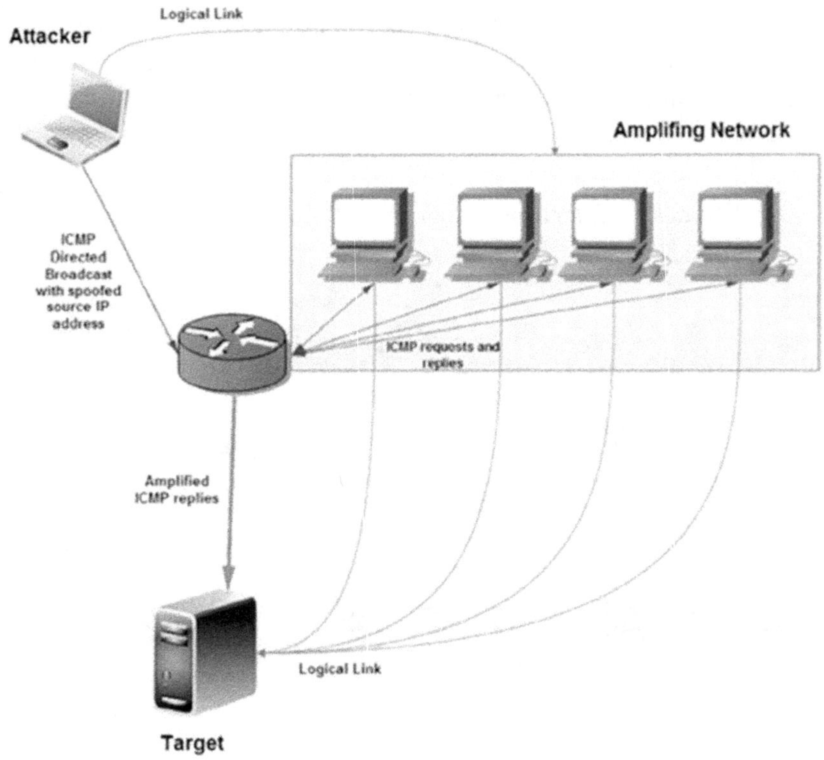

2.3.3 UDP Flooding Attack

UDP flooding is a type of DDoS that makes use of the transport layer connectionless protocol UDP. A UDP flood is a denial-of-service attack in which a large number of User Datagram Protocol (UDP) packets are sent to a targeted server with the aim of overwhelming that device's ability to process and respond to the packets as shown in Figure 3. After receiving the UDP request, the server checks whether any running programs are listening for requests at the specified port. If no programs are receiving packets at that port, the server responds with an ICMP packet to inform the source that the destination is unreachable. However, if the server is flooded with UDP requests, the server becomes overwhelmed with processing and responding to UDP requests (Alzahrani, 2018). The server will fail to process legitimate requests.

Figure 3. UDP Flooding attack
Source: Alzahrani and Hong (2018)

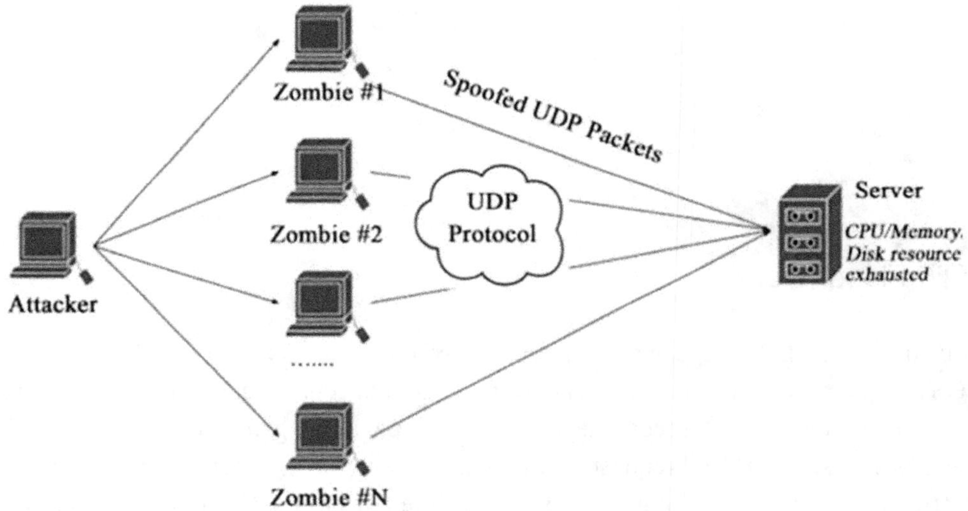

2.3.4 SYN Attack

SYN (Synchronize) attack takes advantage of how the transport layer TCP protocol works. The attack takes advantage of the TCP three-way handshake procedure designed to establish communication between hosts. SYN attack works by flooding the victim with unacknowledged SYN messages. A TCP SYN flood attack violates the operation of the TCP protocol where instead of an SYN request being answered by an SYN-ACK response, multiple SYN requests are sent to the target forcing it to wait for responses, which will never come, thereby reserving its resources until the response is received. This causes the victim machine to use up memory resources which were supposed to be allocated to genuine users. Figure 4 shows a simple diagram of a TPC SYN flood attack.

Figure 4. TCP-SYN attack
Source: Alzahrani and Hong (2018)

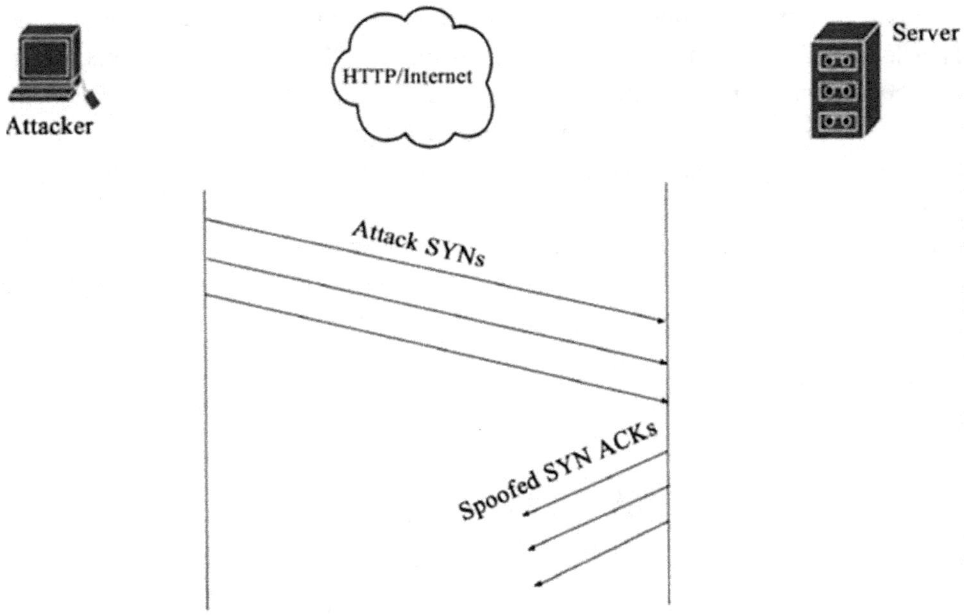

2.3.5 HTTP Flood Attack

HTTP flood attack takes advantage of the application layer protocol HTTP. The attack exploits the HTTP GET or POST requests to attack a server. The ultimate goal of this attack is to exhaust the resources of the targeted victim. The attacks target the layer where web pages are generated on the server in response to HTTP requests. A single HTTP request is easy to execute in the browser of a client but is more complicated for the target server to respond to. The server often has to load several files and may run some database queries to create a full web page. HTTP attack is analogous to repeatedly refreshing a web browser on many different computers at once which results in large numbers of HTTP requests flooding the webserver. Figure 5 shows a simplified diagram of an HTTP flood attack.

2.3.6 DNS DDoS attack

Domain Name Service is a UDP based system used for mapping internet domain names to internet IP addresses. A DNS DDoS amplification attack is an application layer attack which uses widely available DNS servers to amplify the attacking traffic. The attacker creates multiple DNS queries with a spoofed source IP address which are directed towards amplifying DNS servers, as shown in Figure 6. The amplifying DNS servers all direct their requests to the targeted DNS server, thereby overwhelming it so that it fails to resolve domain names for legitimate users (Macfarlane, 2015).

Figure 5. HTTP attack
Source: Alzahrani and Hong (2018)

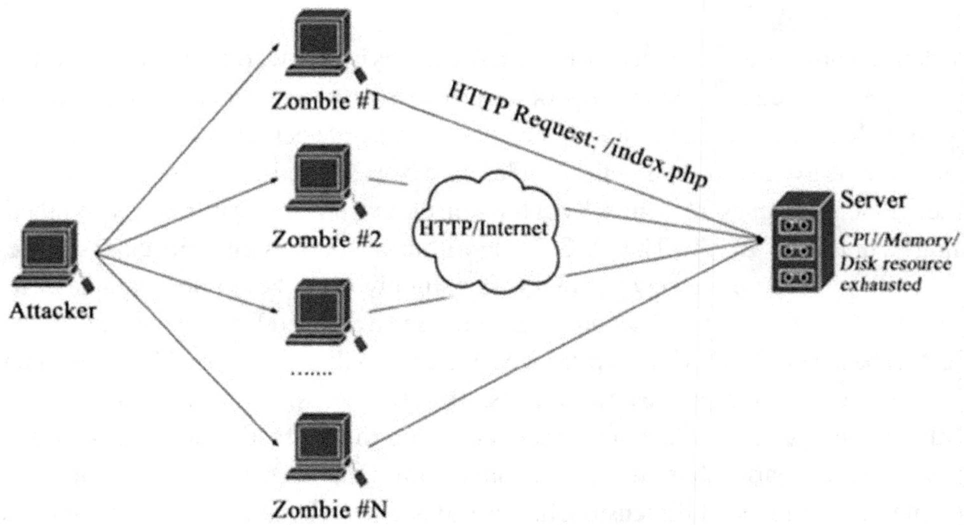

Figure 6. Domain name service (DNS) attack
Source: Macfarlane et al. (2015)

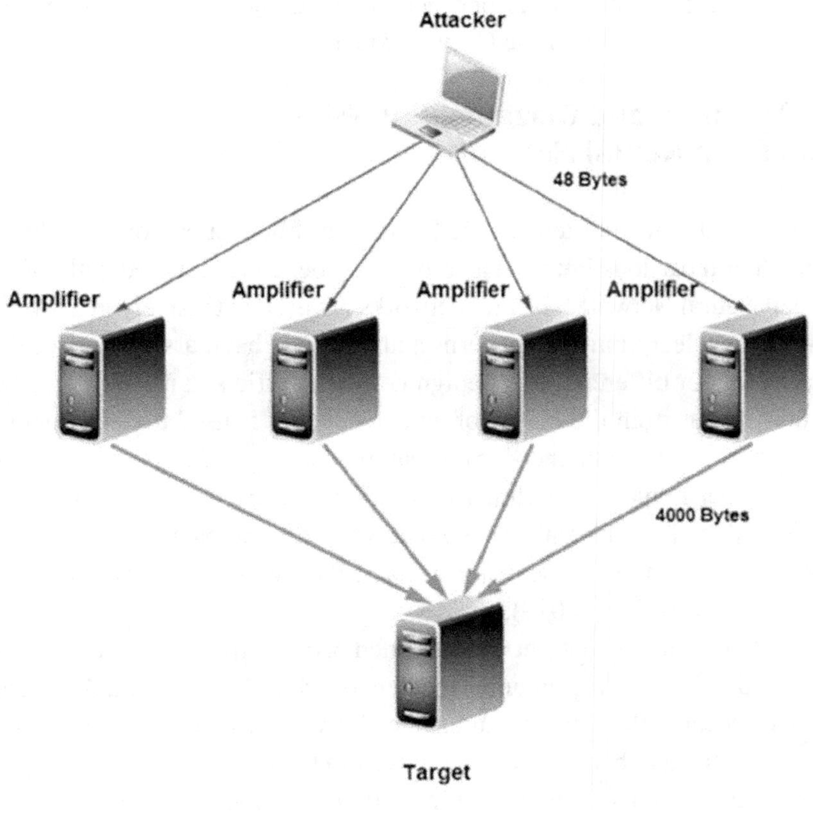

2.4 An Imbalanced Data Classification Algorithm of De-Noising Auto-Encoder Neural Network Based on SMOTE

Unbalanced datasets are more prevalent than balanced data sets in real-world situations. The areas in which unbalanced data sets are found include network intrusion detection, credit card fraud detection and rare disease diagnosis. In all the mentioned areas, the minority class detection rate is significant. Techniques to balance the datasets by creating synthetic samples have been studied. SMOTE is a statistical technique used to create synthetic samples for a minority class from the existing minority classes. Synthetic minority over-sampling technique (SMOTE) The SMOTE algorithm synthesizes minority class samples which do not cause over-fitting because the new samples differ slightly from the original samples. However, the samples created by SMOTE are noisy. Zhang et al. proposed a Stacked De-noising Auto-Encoder neural network (SDAE) based on SMOTE, which reduces noise through unsupervised learning (Zhang, 2016). There was a way to reduce noise in the new samples to improve classification accuracy. An Autoencoder is used by Zhang et al. to remove the noise that came with the synthetic samples. An Autoencoder is a neural network which learns about important data features and does away with irrelevant features as it represents the data in reduced dimensionality. Besides dimensionality reduction, Autoencoders are used to remove noise. The authors used Autoencoders for de-noising SMOTE generated samples. Their study is focussed on addressing the shortcomings of the SMOTE algorithm. They proposed an algorithm that de-noises the newly created SMOTE minority class samples and then trains a classifier using the balanced data. Because evaluation by accuracy gives unreliable classification performance when a classifier is trained on unbalanced data, Zhang et al. used Area Under the Curve characteristics to evaluate the performance of the SMOTE-SDAE. Experimental results show that compared with SMOTE-SVM, SMOTE-SDAE had better Area Under the Curve characteristics.

2.5 Intrusion Detection and Classification With Auto-Encoded Deep Neural Network

A Network Intrusion Detection System is needed to guard networks from attacks. To guard against DDoS attacks and other intrusions Rezvy et al. built an autoencoder coupled with a deep neural network (Autoencoded Deep Neural Network). Neural networks are used extensively in network intrusion detection. Neural networks can learn intricate patterns and hidden behaviours in the data. The learnt patterns and behaviours are used for differentiating benign network traffic and network attacks. A Deep Neural Network which takes input from the output of an autoencoder is used to detect network intrusions by Rezvy et al. The authors use the autoencoder for feature learning and dimensionality reduction. In their research, the autoencoder reduces data dimensions from 122 features to 61. A Deep Neural Network is then used to classify the network traffic. The data set had to be balanced using oversampling of the minority class and under-sampling of the majority class. The overall accuracy of the system for detecting network attacks was 99.3% (Rezvy, 2019).

For this research balancing the dataset is not needed because the proposed Variational Autoencoder based model is trained directly using an unbalanced network traffic data set. Accuracy is not used as a metric in this research because the data set is unbalanced, precision and recall are used instead. The ability of VAE models to learn from unbalanced data comes from the characteristic property of VAEs that they learn the underlying distribution of the data set instead of mapping encodings of the input data as is the case with plain Autoencoders. The principles and mathematics of the VAE are discussed in section 2.5.

2.6 Improving the Classification Effectiveness of Intrusion Detection by Using Improved Conditional Variational Auto-Encoder and Deep Neural Network

Intrusion detection systems are critical for guarding networks against attacks. The evolving nature of attacks and imbalanced data sets limit traditional machine learning from achieving high detection accuracy. Yang et al. propose an intrusion detection model that combines an improved conditional Variational AutoEncoder (ICVAE) with a deep neural network (DNN). The trained ICVAE decoder generates new minority samples to balance the training data set. The deep neural network is then trained with balanced data. The ICVAE-DNN achieved an accuracy, recall and precision of 75.43, 72.86%, and 96.20% respectively when evaluated on the NSL-KDD dataset (Yang., 2019). This research seeks to demonstrate a VAE based model that achieves higher precision and recall for detecting DDoS attacks in the unbalanced CICIDS 2017 Friday Afternoon data set.

2.7 Improving AdaBoost-Based Intrusion Detection System (IDS) Performance on CIC IDS 2017 Dataset

To improve the performance of classifiers for intrusion detection, Yulianto et al. applied the use of the Synthetic Minority Oversampling Technique (SMOTE) to balance the dataset classes before they trained the AdaBoost based classifier. By generating more synthetic samples, the dataset becomes balanced. The results from their study show that their proposed system produces accuracy, precision, recall, and F1 score of 81.83%, 81.83%, 100%, and 90.01% respectively. (Yulianto, 2018). A recall value of 100% means their system was well-optimized against false negatives, for guarding against DDoS attacks, precisely its precision which needs to be very high. This is because, for DDoS attacks, a few false negatives do not cause harm. In this research, the aim is to achieve the highest precision so that a minimum amount of benign traffic may be misclassified. This is important where the built system is deployed in a real-world environment where mechanisms may be added to disconnect DDoS traffic automatically. While oversampling of the minority class helps to balance the classes, the newly added samples come with noise. This research chooses the Variational Autoencoder, which trains models directly on unbalanced data to achieve high precision and recall.

2.8 Detecting Distributed Denial of Service Attacks Using Data Mining Techniques

Alkasassbeh et al. used three machine learning algorithms to classify DDoS attacks. The authors applied Multi-Layer Perceptron, Random Forest, and Naïve Bayes to classify Smurf, UDP-Flood, HTTP-Flood and SIDDOS attacks. The accuracy of their models was 98.63%, 98.02% and 96.91% for MLP, Random Forest and Naïve Bayes, respectively. (Alkasassbeh, 2016). Although the MLP classifier achieved the highest accuracy rate this research did not choose MLP because it needs to have a balanced data set to learn from as is the case with Random Forest and Naïve Bayes. Random Forest and Naïve Bayes were not chosen because the two algorithms cannot handle large scale data sets; neither can the algorithms handle high dimensional data. This research chose direct model training without balancing the data before training. This was achieved through the use of a Variational Autoencoder. Doing away with multiple stages such as data balancing and feature engineering should result in fast training and detection should the built model be deployed in an environment in which continuous training is needed.

2.9 Flow Based Solutions for DoS and DDoS Attack Detection

Payload based and flow based solutions have been studied for detecting Distributed Denial-of-service attacks. Instead of using Payload based technique for identifying SYN flooding and other DDoS attacks, Noble & Sujitha find it more suitable to use Flow based detection process. In Flow based detection process the values of features are analysed instead of the Payload. The values of protocol fields such source IP, source port address, destination IP and destination port address give more information than the contents of each packet. This is especially true for DDoS because DDoS packets do not usually carry payloads that are characteristically different from those of good packets.

Noble & Sujitha proposed a flow based system that would detect three specific DDoS attacks namely Heavy Hitter (HH), Global ice berg and TCP Syn Flooding attack. In their system network traffic was grouped into flows and based on the characteristics of the flows the three DDoS types could be detected. In their implementation, an attack on an Apache web server was launched using artificially generated packets from various systems (Noble & Sujitha, 2015). In this research, a flow based approach was also taken. The Computer network traffic is grouped into flows in the CICIDS 2017 data set (Sharafaldin, 2018). The computer network flows in the CICIDS 2017 data set are used to train the VAE model in this research. A flow based detection system that can detect all types of DDoS generated from the network, transport and application layers of the TCP/IP protocol suite is adopted in this research.

2.10 An Adaptive Multi-Layer Botnet Detection Technique Using Machine Learning Classifiers

Malicious actors use botnets to carry out many types of intrusions including DDoS attacks.

Botnets are networks of remotely controlled compromised computers. Malicious actors can take control of them as a group and command them to carry out a specific malicious task such as launching a DDoS attack on targeted servers. Botnets are used to take advantage of Internet Relay Chat (IRC) protocol using a client-server networking model. Nowadays botnets usually use the much harder to detect Peer-to-Peer networking model. Detecting botnet traffic using Application layer protocols such as Internet Relay Chat (IRC), Hypertext Transfer Protocol (HTTP) and other types of botnets is easier because Peer-to-Peer every machine is both a server and a client to others (Khan, 2019).

. Khan, et al., propose a hybrid detection system for detecting botnet traffic. The researchers' multi-layer hybrid system for Peer to Peer botnet detection combined multilayer perceptron and Decision Tree algorithm. Session features were used to classify the benign P2P communication and P2P botnet communication. They first filtered out non-peer-to peer traffic in the first layer of the hybrid system. At the second layer, they further characterized peer-to-peer and non-peer-to-peer network traffic. At the third layer the performed dimensionality reduction to leave only features which explain botnet Peer-to-Peer traffic. At the final layer, they performed classification using Decision Trees. Their hybrid system was based on both traffic behaviour and network flows similarity. Validated on CTU-13 and ISOT datasets the researchers' model was able to detect botnet traffic with an accuracy of 98.7% (Khan, 2019). Although it was observed that the Decision Tree algorithm had a high accuracy to detect Peer-to-Peer botnet traffic they cannot handle high-dimensional data sets, they are not an option for this research. Because of the increase of connected devices from the Internet of Things and the resultant increased network traffic, it is essential that detection models can handle large numbers of tuples of big data scales. Decision tree models cannot handle large scale data sets. For the above two limitations, VAE is chosen ahead of decision trees for this research.

2.11 Best Features Based Intrusion Detection System by RBM Model for Detecting DDoS in Cloud Environment

Most Intrusion Detection Systems (IDS) are computationally demanding and have poor detection accuracy. To detect DDoS attacks more accurately Mayuranathan et al built a Deep learning Restricted Boltzmann Machines (RBM) system which is not computationally demanding by using only the best feature set in the data set. Their system uses a Random Harmony Search (RHS) optimization model to identify the best set of features needed to detect DDoS attacks. Using the reduced dimensions of only the best set of features they build a Deep learning classifier to detect DDoS attacks. (Mayuranathan, 2019). The RHS-RBM system achieves an accuracy of 99.96%. This research proposes a DDoS detection without the prior stage of data pre-processing to select features.

2.12 Variational Data Generative Model for Intrusion Detection

Intrusion Detection systems need balanced and diversified data to train valid classifiers. An Intrusion detection which can generate new synthetic samples to balance the data set by using a Conditional Variational Autoencoder is proposed by (Lopez-Martin, 2018). The synthesized samples are better than SMOTE generated samples because they have a probabilistic similarity to the original samples (Lopez-Martin, 2018). Their study was focussed on detecting network intrusions in the Internet of Things domain. The authors' method is based on a conditional variational autoencoder with a decoder designed to generate new samples according to specified labels. The generative VAE uses the reconstruction error of the decoder as a measure to determine the class of network traffic. The approach is anomaly-based supervised machine learning. Labels that were below a particular reconstruction error were classified as intrusion. Their system is a model taking in features and a class label as input (Lopez-Martin, 2018). A plain VAE takes in only features as input and learns the distribution of the features. Lopez-Martin et al added a label as input so that the CVAE could be conditioned to generate a specified label. Evaluation of the classification results showed that their intrusion detection system had an accuracy of 80.10%. This research will train a DDoS detector using a plain VAE which takes in features only as input.

2.13 Generative Models

Machine learning motivation can be classified into discriminative and generative. Discriminative machine learning aims to learn a function that, given the input feature values, would predict the class of the input tuple. With generative modelling, the aim is to learn the joint underlying distribution of all variables. Generative models aim to understand how the data was created. Understanding the data generating process makes classification easier for a classifier that is coupled to a generative model (Kingma, 2019). Generative models are instrumental in dealing with challenges which have traditionally beset intrusion detection such as data set imbalances and lack of intrusion samples (Kingma, 2019) There are three types of deep learning generative models namely Autoencoders, Variational Autoencoders (VAE) and Generative Adversarial Networks (GAN). An Autoencoder is a type of neural network that is trained to reproduce its input at the output layer. The number of neurons in each hidden layer progressively gets fewer thereby representing the input by fewer features at each layer. The autoencoder aims to represent the input in a lower dimensional space before trying to reconstruct the same input at the output. If it succeeds in reconstructing the input at the output using lower dimensions it means the rest of the discarded features or dimensions were redundant or noise. The probability of reconstructing an input accurately can be used to classify network traffic in intrusion detection. This means an Autoencoder learns the most important features that describe classes in a dataset. Besides dimensionality reduction, Autoencoders are also used for denoising data. A Variational autoencoder takes in samples and represents the data as a continuous joint probability distribution in the latent space. During training the joint probability distribution is forced to follow a normal distribution by minimizing a KL divergence loss. Classes within the data set occupy different regions of the continuous probability distribution (Kingma, 2019) . The probability distribution of a VAE can be sampled to generate new data points as is the case with conditional variational autoencoders. Generative Adversarial Networks (GANs) are a third type of generative models that map an input to a lower dimensional latent space. The data distribution in a GAN is not continuous. Therefore a GAN cannot create stable and new samples from its distribution. A discriminator forces the output of a GAN to be as close as possible to the input. This paper classifies DDoS attacks from benign by applying both linear and quadratic decision boundaries to the latent representation of a VAE.

2.14 Variational Autoencoder

VAEs are built on top of deep neural networks. Like all deep neural networks, they are standard function approximators, which are trained fast with mini-batch stochastic gradient descent. No strong assumptions are required for implementing a VAE model. The main assumption that features are normally distributed is usually the case in many real world data sets and in models that use large scale data sets (Doersch, 2016).

Complicated dependencies among dimensions make training of classification models difficult. VAE is based on the assumption that multidimensional data can be projected onto a probabilistic lower dimensional subspace. In the lower probabilistic representation of the input, benign and DDoS attacks are more easily separable (Ikeda, 2018). In this research a decision boundary is fit to the latent space representation of the network flows to separate DDoS and benign attacks.

VAEs have also found extensive use in image and audio generation. They are particularly important because of their ability to generate new samples which are similar but not the same as any in the original dataset. VAEs create new audio and image files which share the same data distribution as the original dataset. VAEs are also as novel way of classifying imbalanced data with high precision and high recall. The ability of VAE to classify will be demonstrated in this research. Several techniques have been developed to improve the performance of Machine Learning classification algorithms when learning from class imbalanced data. Machine Learning algorithms for intrusion detection usually have very few anomalous examples to learn from. The model therefore learns more from the majority of benign samples. This negatively affects the predictive performance of the classifier in detecting intrusions. The most used methods of addressing class imbalances are sampling techniques (Fajardo, 2018). Oversampling of the minority class results in overfitting whereas under sampling of the majority class results in the loss of vital information needed for training the model (Jiadong & Wang, 2019). SMOTE is an improvement in creating synthetic samples that enhance model learning. However, SMOTE samples produce noisy samples as described in section 2.1. A VAE offers a deep learning approach that does not require the data set to be balanced before training the classifier. VAEs can classify imbalanced data with high precision and high recall i.e. both false positives and false negatives are minimized respectively. In this research, the VAE network learned how to represent the input data as a Gaussian distribution. Linear and Quadratic Discriminant Analysis were applied to the re-parameterized values of the data points. Like the VAE algorithm, the LDA and QDA algorithm also assumes that the dataset features have a normal distribution (Ghojogh & Crowley, 2019). VAEs are especially useful in that they can separate and classify data points in situations where we have unlabelled data and imbalanced data. All traditional Machine Learning algorithms (Support Vector Machines, Decision Trees and Logistic Regression) find it difficult to train classifier imbalanced data (Yilmaz, 2019). VAEs are highly applicable to both Supervised and Unsupervised learning. In unsupervised Deep Learning VAEs take an anomaly detection approach and are trained using only benign data samples. After Learning the data distribution of only the benign samples the trained VAE has low reconstruction probabilities for data points with distributions that do not conform to its learnt distribution. Data points below a set probability threshold are classified as anomalous. A data point with a similar distribution to the one learnt by the VAE has a high reconstruction probability and is classified as benign (An & Cho, 2015). VAE networks can also be trained in a Supervised Machine Learning way and be conditioned to generate new synthetic samples of the required class. This research did not use VAE to generate new samples but only used VAE to classify DDoS traffic by applying LDA and QDA to the latent representation. The VAE is especially suited to DDOS detection because of its scalability. VAE can handle Big Data scale datasets which are more likely to be encountered in computer networks. The scalability of VAEs is enabled by the re-parameterization trick which makes it possible to update weights during training. The applicability of Stochastic Gradient Descent in updating weights make VAE scalable to any dataset size. VAEs apply to all anomaly detection scenarios from network intrusion detection to credit Card Fraud detection and rare disease diagnosis. Kurien and Chikkamannur applied VAE to detect real time anomalies in credit card fraud detection. The results from their study showed that the VAE model they built performed better than Logistic Regression and Random Forest ensemble models (Kurien, 2019). In this paper, VAE is applied to detect network intrusion (DDoS attacks) in computer networks. Jorge et al. showed that data augmentation using Variational Autoencoders resulted in models which were generalizable. They also demonstrated that classification accuracy improved when synthetic data points were generated by VAE (Jorge, 2018).

A variational autoencoder (VAE) is a generative combination of two neural networks. The first neural network is the encoder which takes in data inputs and represent the data in a latent space with reduced dimensions. The latent space is in the form of a joint probability distribution of the important variables. The distribution is forced to be normal by minimization of a KL divergence term. The second neural network takes samples from the latent space as input and attempts to reconstruct the original input. The difference or dissimilarity between the reconstructed output and the original input is a loss to be minimized. During training the loss function of the VAE minimizes the sum of the KL divergence loss and the reconstruction loss. The latent space variables are used by the decoder of the VAE to generate data samples similar to the input data. The latent space representation is a joint probability distribution of all the features. Through the use of the re-parameterization trick (explained in Section 2.7) a VAE model updates latent variables using stochastic gradient descent. Because a VAE models the underlying data distribution of the classes found in the dataset, VAEs can learn to separate the classes. New samples can be generated by sampling from the vector of means and vector of variances in the latent representation. The sampled mean and variance are passed through the decoder to generate new samples (Kurien, 2019).

In this research, we used the decoder part of the VAE only during training. When the model was trained we applied decision boundaries to the variables of the latent space.

Figure 1 shows the structure of a VAE encoder. In a VAE, the highest layer of the model ε is treated as the latent variable where the generative process starts. *g(z)* represents the process of data generation that results in the data x. The marginal likelihood of a data point is the sum over the marginal likelihood of individual data points

$$\log p_\theta\left(x^{(1)}\right),\ldots\ldots,x^{(N)}) = \sum_{i=1}^{N} \log p_\theta x^{(i)} \tag{1}$$

where the marginal likelihood of individual data points can be rewritten as

$$\log p_{\theta(x)^{(i)}=} D_{KL}(q_\theta\left(z|x\right) \| \, p_\theta\left(z\right) + \mathcal{L}\left(\theta,\phi;x^{(i)}\right) \tag{2}$$

Where $q_\phi(z|x)$ is the approximate posterior and $p_\theta(z)$ is the prior distribution of the latent variable z. Since marginal likelihood is intractable, the variational lower bound of the marginal likelihood of data is taken as the objective function of a VAE. $\mathcal{L}\left(\theta,\phi;x^{(i)}\right)$ is the variational lower bound on the marginal likelihood of the data point i. The variational lower bound allows joint optimization concerning θ and ϕ using mini-batch stochastic gradient descent (SGD). Starting with random initial values of θ and ϕ, their values are stochastically optimized until convergence (Kingma, 2019). DKL($q_\theta(z|x) \| p_\theta(z)$ is the KL divergence of the approximate posterior and the prior.

Since the KL divergence term is at least 0, the equation can be rewritten as follows

$$\log p_\theta(x^{(i)} \geq \mathcal{L}(\theta,\phi;x^{(i)} \tag{3}$$

$$= E_{q\phi}\left(z|x^{i}\right)\left[-\log q_\phi\left(z|x\right) + \log p_\theta\left(x|z\right)\right] \tag{4}$$

$$= -D_{KL}(q_\phi\left(z|x^{i}\right) \| \, p_\theta(z) + E_{q\phi}\left(z|x^{i}\right)\left[\log p_\theta\left(x|z\right)\right] \tag{5}$$

$p_\theta(x|z)$ is the likelihood of the data x given the latent variable z$= -D_{KL}(q_\phi\left(z|x^{i}\right) \| \, p_\theta(z$ is the KL divergence between the approximate posterior and the prior of the latent variable z.

The KL divergence term forces the posterior distribution to have a normal distribution. In this way, the KL divergence works as a regularization term. $E_{q\phi}\left(z|x^{i}\right)[\log p_\theta\left(x|z\right)$ represents the reconstruction of x through the posterior distribution $q_\phi(zx)$ and the likelihood $p_\theta(x|z)$. Parameters ϕ and θ are updated during training for the encoder and decoder networks respectively. When the loss function is at its lowest, the classes occupy distinct but continuous regions of the probability distribution. In this research near and quadratic boundaries are applied.

Figure 7. Encoder of VAE
Source: An and Cho (2015)

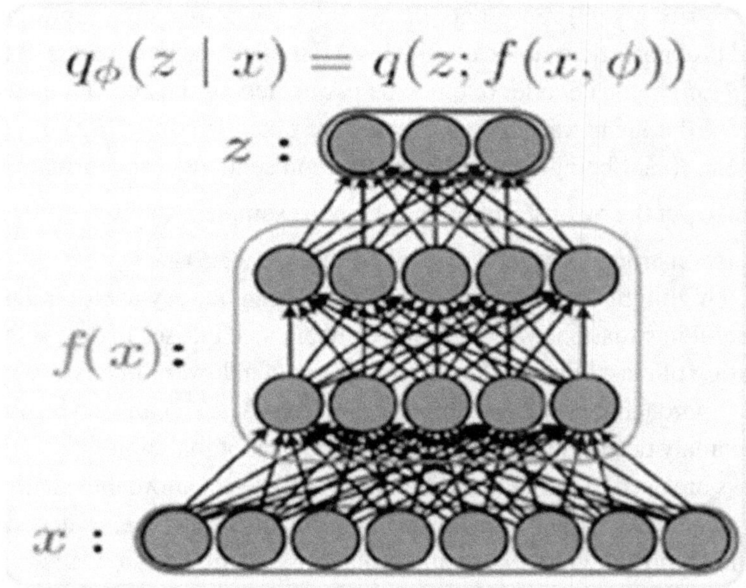

Figure 8. Decoder of VAE
Source: An and Cho (2015)

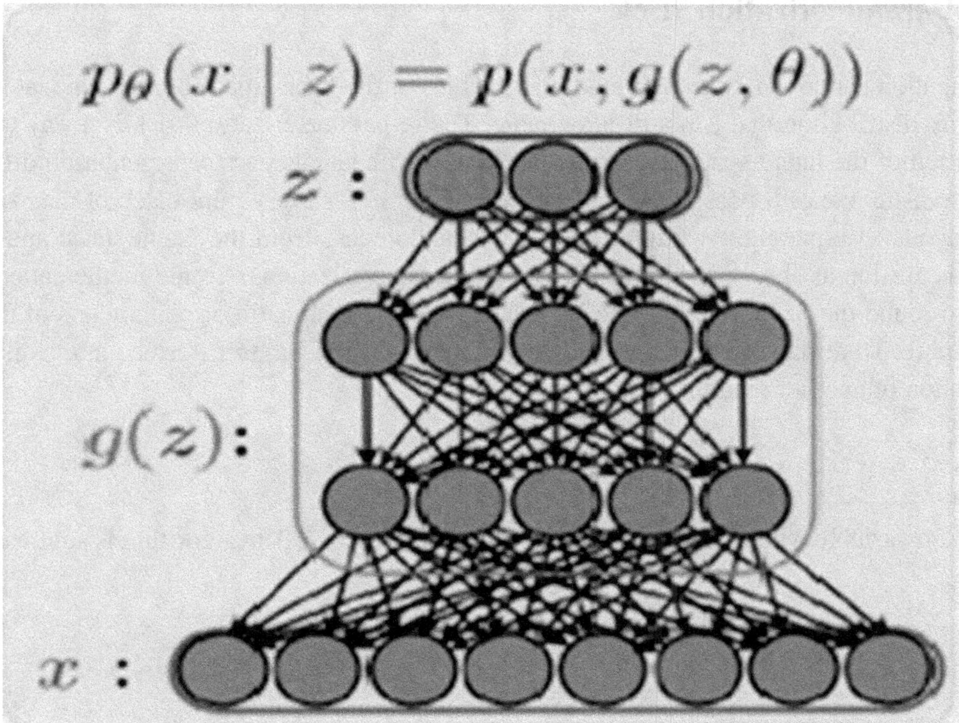

SNU Data Mining Center

The approximate posterior $q_\phi(z|x)$ represents the encoder whereas $p_\theta(x|z)$ represents the decoder. The decoder is a directed probabilistic graphical model. VAE models the parameters of the data distribution, not the value itself. $f(x,\phi)$ in the encoder outputs the parameters of the approximate posterior $q_\phi(z|x)$. To get the actual value of the latent variable z, samples are taken from $q(z; f(z,\phi))$. The encoder and decoder are probabilistic. $f(x,\phi)$ being a neural network represents the transformation from the data x to the latent variable z. To get the reconstruction $\hat{x}$, given the sample z, the parameter of $p_\theta(x|z)$ is obtained by $g(z,\theta)$ where the reconstruction $\hat{x}$ are sampled from $p_\theta(x; g(z,\theta)$.

This research will highlight three ways in which a VAE can be very useful in DDoS intrusion detection. VAE can be useful in situations where we have unbalanced classes in data sets. In this case, a VAE enhances the separation of classes when they are represented in lower dimensional joint probability distribution. This is the approach that was used in this research. A VAE can also be useful in unsupervised machine learning anomaly detection where there is a total lack of malicious samples to learn from. Only benign network flows are used to train the model that would detect anomalies. In this application, a data point is defined as an anomaly or an intrusion if the probability of it being generated from the model is below a certain threshold. The model outputs probability as the decision rule for judging anomalies. The trained model detects anomalies by their deviation from the learnt probability model (Wanga, et al., 2019). The third way a VAE can be used to deal with class imbalance is by generating minority samples to balance the data for downstream use by traditional classifiers.

2.15 Re-Parameterization Trick

Backpropagation cannot pass through random variables of the latent space because the latent space is a probability distribution that is not differentiable. The re-parameterization trick is a way to make the representation of the latent space differentiable. Making the latent space representation differentiable and deterministic makes it possible to update the value of ϕ for every mini batch of data samples fed into the encoder. Re-parameterization removes the randomness from the latent space and externally applies it as epsilon as shown in Figure 10. With re-parameterization, a sound mathematical way was found to go round the randomness of the VAE latent space z in updating ϕ parameters of the encoder during training. To re-parameterize the random variable $z \sim q_\phi(z|x)$ was transformed into a differentiable transformation of another random variable given z and ϕ:

$$z = g(\varepsilon, \phi, x)$$

ε is *a* random variable whose distribution is independent of x or ϕ. The algorithm is summarized as:

Figure 9. VAE re-parameterization algorithm
Source: Kingma and Welling (2019)

Data:
$\mathcal{D}$: Dataset
$q_\phi(\mathbf{z}|\mathbf{x})$: Inference model
$p_\theta(\mathbf{x}, \mathbf{z})$: Generative model
Result:
θ, ϕ: Learned parameters

$(\theta, \phi) \leftarrow$ Initialize parameters
while *SGD not converged* **do**
  $\mathcal{M} \sim \mathcal{D}$ (Random minibatch of data)
  $\epsilon \sim p(\epsilon)$ (Random noise for every datapoint in $\mathcal{M}$)
  Compute $\tilde{\mathcal{L}}_{\theta,\phi}(\mathcal{M}, \epsilon)$ and its gradients $\nabla_{\theta,\phi}\tilde{\mathcal{L}}_{\theta,\phi}(\mathcal{M}, \epsilon)$
  Update θ and ϕ using SGD optimizer
end

Figure 10. Illustration of the re-parameterization trick
Source: Kingma and Welling (2019)

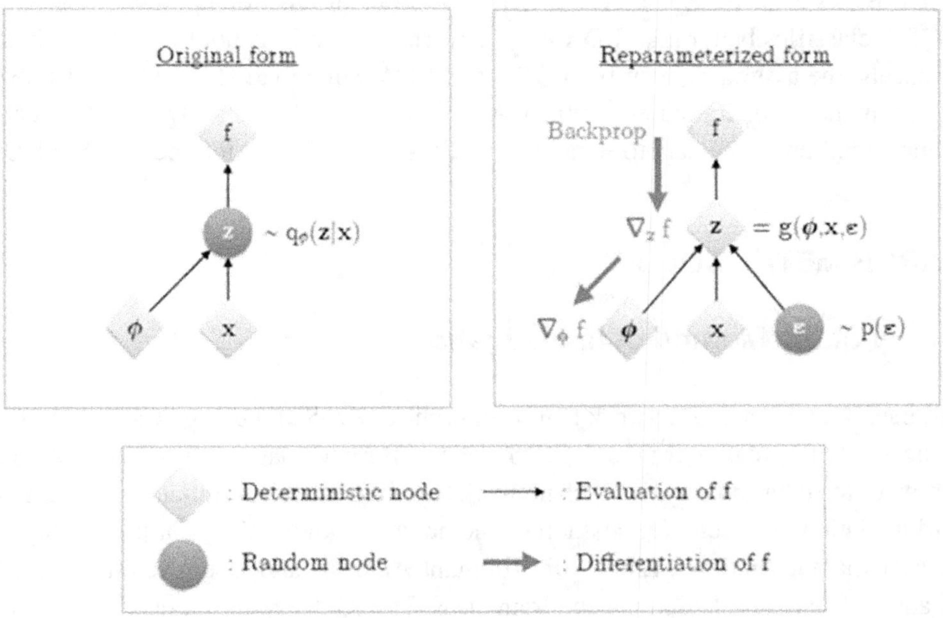

2.16 Linear Discriminant Analysis (LDA) and Quadratic Discriminant Analysis (QDA)

LDA aims to discriminate different classes by projecting the data on to a low dimensional space, retaining only the feature values that enhance the separation of the classes found within the data. LDA is a probabilistic statistical supervised binary classification method. The analysis technique applies a linear decision boundary between classes. LDA assumes that the two classes have a normal distribution. The assumption is not restrictive because normal distribution is the most common distribution found in real-world data (Ghojogh & Crowley, 2019). The classification technique was first proposed by Ronald Fisher in 1936. The technique seeks to maximize the function that represents the difference between the means of the two classes. The function is then normalized by a measure of the within-class variability. He correctly reasoned that maximising the distance between the means of each class and minimising the spreading within the individual classes would separate the classes.

The distance between the means of the two classes is calculated first. The distance is called the between-class variance. The distance between the mean and the samples of each class is then calculated. This distance is called the within-class variance. A new dimensional space which maximizes the between-class variance and minimizes the within class variance is sought. LDA projects the original data onto a new dimensional space where class separation is enhanced. The classes are separated in the projected new feature space (Tharwat, 2017). The two main assumptions of LDA are that the features are normally distributed and that the covariance matrix of the two classes is equal. QDA also assumes that each class is drawn from a normal multivariate distribution. The difference with LDA is that QDA assumes that the two classes have two different covariance matrixes. When these assumptions are satisfied QDA approximates the Bayes classifier accurately and the discriminant function produces a quadratic decision boundary. QDA classifies better than LDA if the covariance matrix is not the same in the two classes. For large datasets, the assumptions of both QDA and LDA can be violated and still achieve high classification performance. Quadratic Discriminant Analysis. In this research, LDA and QDA are applied to the latent representation of the data to separate and classify the dataset into benign and DDOS attacks.

3, RESEARCH METHODOLOGY

3.1 Overview of the Method of Investigation

A VAE is trained with computer network flows containing DDoS and benign traffic flows. The trained VAE takes the input of 77 features of the CICIDS Friday Afternoon data set. The VAE learns the underlying distribution of the data and encodes each network flow into a mean and standard deviation. The mean and standard deviation represent the position of the network flow in the joint probability distribution. Quadratic Discriminant Analysis, Linear Discriminant Analysis and Deep Neural Network then take input of means and standard deviations and train classifiers. QDA applies a quadratic decision boundary, and LDA applies a linear decision boundary to separate the benign and DDoS flows. It is assumed that the model with high precision and recall between QDA and LDA fulfils its attendant assumptions more than the one with lower precision and recall. The assumptions that go with QDA and LDA will be brought into focus when comparing the classification performance of VAE based QDA and LDA Section 4 Results and Discussion. The classification performance of the Discriminant Analysis with higher precision and recall is further compared to the classification performance of the Deep Neural Network. A Hybrid DDoS classifier is being built using the foundation of the VAE. The final model includes both a Discriminant Analysis classifier and a Deep Neural Network. The two classifiers serve to endorse each other's results.

4. RESULTS AND DISCUSSION

4.1 Introduction

A confusion matrix was used to determine the precision and recall of the built models. The classification performance of the built VAE based Deep Neural Network, Linear Discriminant Analysis and Quadratic Discriminant Analysis classifiers were evaluated on the test data using a confusion matrix. A confusion matrix was shown for each evaluation of the built model. Linear Discriminant Analysis, Quadratic Discriminant Analysis and Deep Neural Network algorithms classifiers were trained on the VAE latent representation of computer network traffic flows. Different hyper parameter settings were used to come up with the best model for the VAE and the Deep Neural Network. Different hyper parameters were tried in different combinations until the best performing model was achieved. The precision and recall of the three classifiers were compared against each other and also against the results Sharafaldin et al. got from traditional machine learning classification algorithms as recorded in Table 5. The CICIDS 2017 Friday afternoon data set had a total of 225745 samples of which 97718 were benign and 12827 were DDoS attacks. The class distribution is shown in Figure 11. Linear Discriminant Analysis, Quadratic Discriminant Analysis, and Deep Neural Network were trained on network flow data that had been encoded by the VAE into means and standard deviation.

Figure 11. Class distributions of CICIDS 2017 Friday afternoon dataset

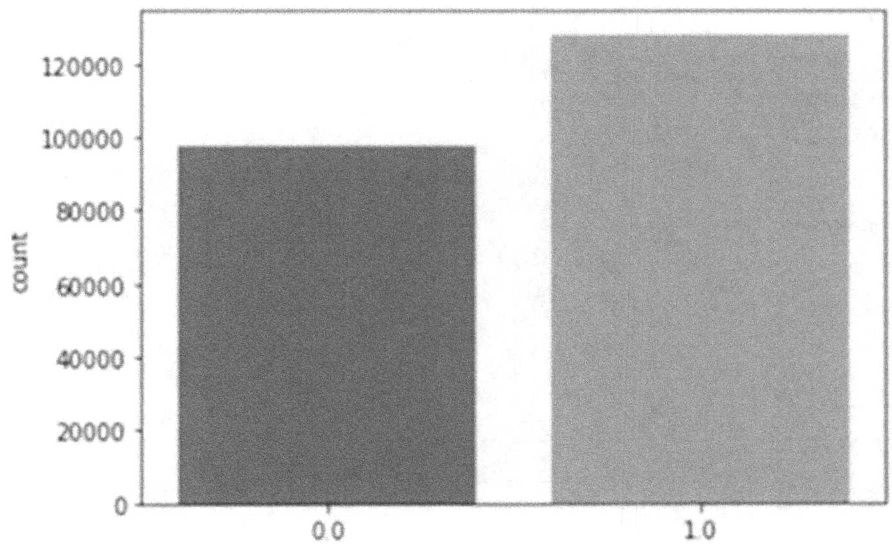

4.2. Results

4.2.1 Comparing VAE-Based LDA and QDA Results Against Traditional Ml Classifiers

VAE with 16 neurons in encoder and decoder hidden layers.

A Linear Discriminant and Quadratic Discriminant Analysis classifier was trained on the latent representation of network flows. The VAE model was built with a single hidden layer for the encoder and decoder. In the hidden layer, 16 neurons were used. The model was trained for 100 epochs. The early Stopping feature of Keras was configured with a 'patience' value of 5, meaning the training would stop if the loss value did not decrease for five successive epochs. The summary of the built VAE model is shown in Figure 15. The distribution of the benign and DDoS attack samples in the CICIDS 2017 Friday Afternoon data set is shown in Figure 11. How the trained VAE represented the classes in the latent space was visualized in Figure 14. The obtained precision and recall of the VAE-LDA and VAE-QDA are shown in Table 3 and Table 4 respectively.

The visualisation showed that DDoS attack traffic flows (orange colour) tended to be more clustered than benign traffic flows.

The precision, and recall of the VAE-LDA are 92.2% and 99.92% respectively. A linear decision boundary resulted in 6953 false positives whereas a quadratic decision boundary resulted in 8360 false positives. Table 5 shows the classification results of traditional machine learning algorithms on the CICIDS 2017 dataset obtained by Sharafaldin et al. Sharafaldin et al. used feature engineering to select only determining features for detecting DDoS attacks. For detecting DDoS attacks the researchers used Average Packet Size, Backward Packet Length Standard Deviation, Flow Duration, Flow Inter Flow Arrival Time (IAT) and Standard Deviation as the main features with parameters whose value determined whether a network flow was benign or DDoS attack.

Figure 12. Summary of the VAE model

```
Model: "model_1"
__________________________________________________________________________________________________
Layer (type)                    Output Shape         Param #     Connected to
==================================================================================================
input_1 (InputLayer)            (None, 77)           0
__________________________________________________________________________________________________
batch_normalization_1 (BatchNor (None, 77)           308         input_1[0][0]
__________________________________________________________________________________________________
encoder_hidden01 (Dense)        (None, 16)           1248        batch_normalization_1[0][0]
__________________________________________________________________________________________________
batch_normalization_2 (BatchNor (None, 16)           64          encoder_hidden01[0][0]
__________________________________________________________________________________________________
batch_normalization_3 (BatchNor (None, 16)           64          batch_normalization_2[0][0]
__________________________________________________________________________________________________
z_mean (Dense)                  (None, 2)            34          batch_normalization_3[0][0]
__________________________________________________________________________________________________
z_log_var (Dense)               (None, 2)            34          batch_normalization_3[0][0]
__________________________________________________________________________________________________
z_sampled (Lambda)              (None, 2)            0           z_mean[0][0]
                                                                 z_log_var[0][0]
__________________________________________________________________________________________________
decoder_hidden02 (Dense)        (None, 16)           48          z_sampled[0][0]
__________________________________________________________________________________________________
decoded_mean (Dense)            (None, 77)           1309        decoder_hidden02[0][0]
==================================================================================================
Total params: 3,109
Trainable params: 2,891
Non-trainable params: 218
__________________________________________________________________________________________________
```

Figure 13. Training loss compared with validation loss

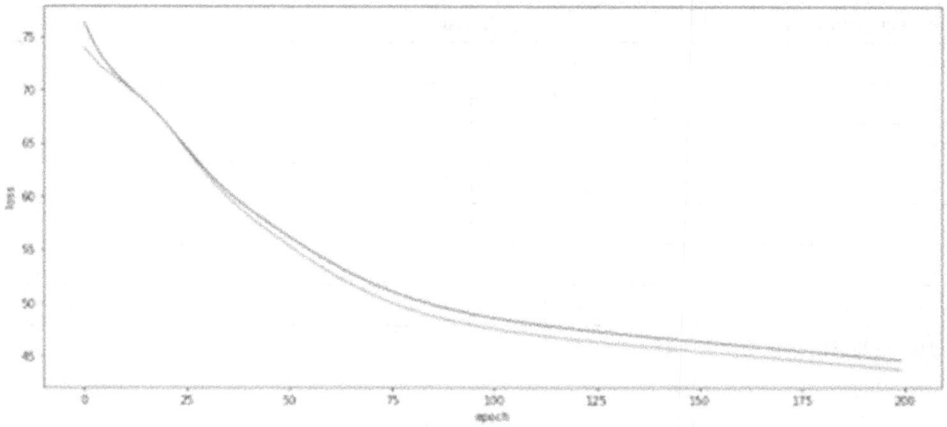

Figure 14. Latent space visualization of training data (VAE with a single 16-neuron hidden layer)

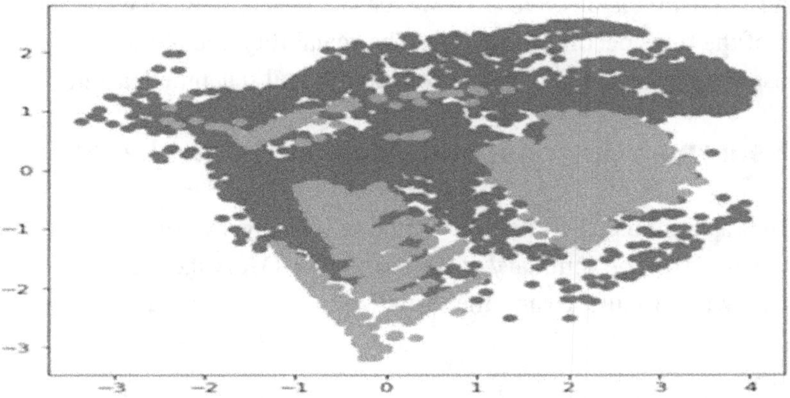

Table 3. Classification results of LDA based on VAE model with single 16-neuron layer

LDA Classification Confusion Matrix Results	
AUC(ROC)	0.924185472
Precision	0.920261933
Recall	0.999227963
F1 score	0.958120653
False positives	6953
True positives	80245
False negatives	62
True negatives	39137

Table 4. Classification results of QDA based on VAE model with single 16-neuron layer

QDA Classification Confusion Matrix Results	
AUC(ROC)	0.908940536
Precision	0.90565186
Recall	0.999265319
F1 score	0.950158364
False positives	8360
True positives	80248
False negatives	59
True negatives	37730

Table 5. The classification performance of traditional machine learning classifiers

Algorithm	Precision	Recall
KNN	0.96	0.96
RF	0.98	0.97
ID3	0.98	0.98
Ada boost	0.77	0.84
MLP	0.77	0.83
Naive-Bayes	0.88	0.04
QDA	0.97	0.88

Source: Sharafaldin (2018)

The recall of VAE-LDA and the VAE-QDA was 99.92% and 99.93% respectively. The recall is higher than the recall achieved by traditional machine learning algorithms. KNN, ID3 and RF had a precision of 96%, 98% and 98% respectively compared to the VAE-LDA and VAE-QDA of 92% and 90% respectively. Random Forest had a high precision of 98%. However, because RF cannot work in high-dimensional data because the depth of the trees becomes too long. The scalability and ability to handle high dimensional data gave VAE based classifiers an advantage over traditional machine learning classifiers.

VAE With 64 Neurons in Encoder and Decoder Hidden Layers

A second VAE-DA was built using 64 neurons in the hidden layer of the encoder and decoder layers. A batch size of 5000 was used. The summary of the built VDE-DA is shown in Figure 15 the loss obtained during training is shown in Figure 16 and the visualization of training data is shown in Figure 17.

Figure 15. Summary of 64-neuron single hidden layer VAE model

```
Layer (type)                    Output Shape    Param #     Connected to
================================================================================
input_2 (InputLayer)            (None, 77)      0

batch_normalization_4 (BatchNor (None, 77)      308         input_2[0][0]

encoder_hidden01 (Dense)        (None, 64)      4992        batch_normalization_4[0][0]

batch_normalization_5 (BatchNor (None, 64)      256         encoder_hidden01[0][0]

batch_normalization_6 (BatchNor (None, 64)      256         batch_normalization_5[0][0]

z_mean (Dense)                  (None, 2)       130         batch_normalization_6[0][0]

z_log_var (Dense)               (None, 2)       130         batch_normalization_6[0][0]

z_sampled (Lambda)              (None, 2)       0           z_mean[0][0]
                                                            z_log_var[0][0]

decoder_hidden02 (Dense)        (None, 64)      192         z_sampled[0][0]

decoded_mean (Dense)            (None, 77)      5005        decoder_hidden02[0][0]
================================================================================
Total params: 11,269
Trainable params: 10,859
Non-trainable params: 410
```

Figure 16. Loss for a model with a single 64-neuron hidden layer VAE model

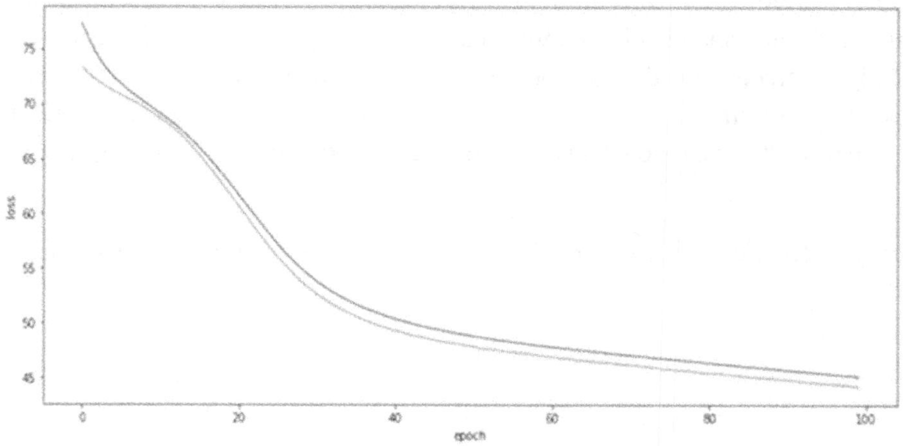

Figure 17. Latent space visualization of VAE with a single 64-neuron hidden layer

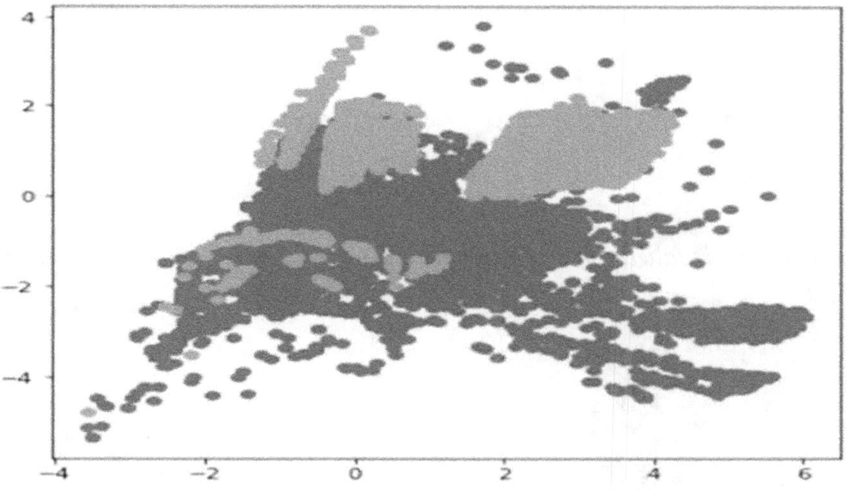

Table 6. Confusion matrix results for single 64-neuron hidden layer VAE-LDA model

LDA Classification Confusion Matrix Results	
AUC(ROC)	0.833973
Precision	0.8599
Recall	0.932733
F1 score	0.894837
False positives	12204
True positives	74905
False negatives	5402
True negatives	33886

Table 7. Confusion matrix results for VAE-QDA model with single 64 neuron hidden layer for decoder and encoder

QDA Classification Confusion Matrix Results	
AUC(ROC)	0.946285
Precision	0.96047
Recall	0.961523
F1 score	0.960996
False positives	3178
True positives	77217
False negatives	3090
True negatives	42912

For a model built with 64 neurons per hidden layer, the VAE based Quadratic Discriminant Analysis showed a precision of 96.04% and recall of 96.15% respectively. The VAE based Linear Discriminant Analysis showed precision and recall of 85.99% and 93.27% respectively. Applying a quadratic decision boundary had higher precision and recall for a model with 64 neurons trained on a batch size of 5000.

A second model was built again using 64 neurons in the hidden layers of the encoder and decoder but using a batch size of 1500. The model had the following classification performance as shown in Table 7.

Figure 18. Loss for a model with a single 64-neuron hidden layer VAE model (batch size = 1500)

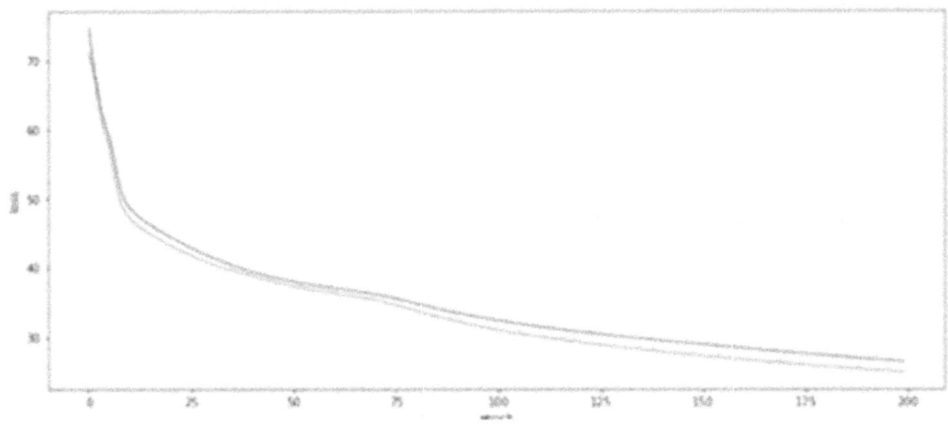

Figure 19. Latent space visualization of training data for 64 neurons hidden layer size trained on a batch size of 1500

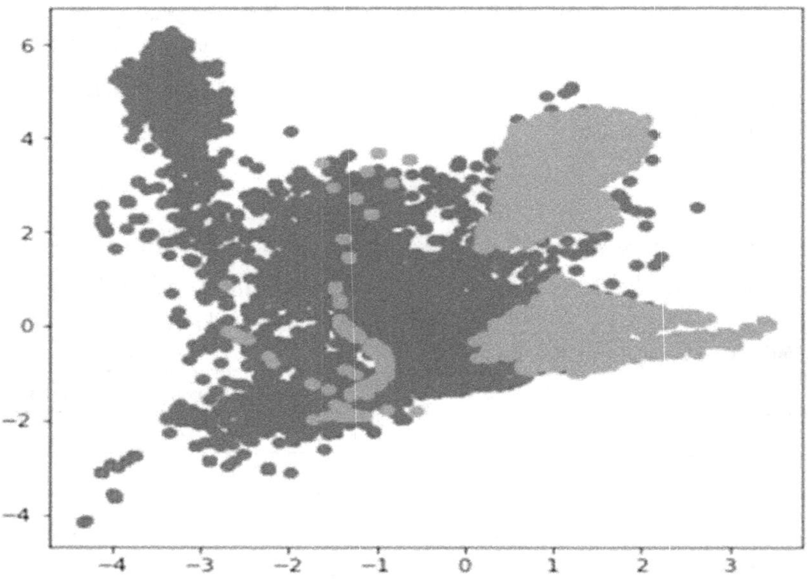

Table 8. Confusion matrix results for second single 64-neuron hidden layer VAE-LDA

LDA Classification Confusion Matrix Results	
AUC(ROC)	0.876576728986286
Precision	0.8761696784407927
Recall	0.9992155104785386
F1 score	0.933656016568543
False positives	11341
True positives	80244
False negatives	63
True negatives	34749

Table 9. Confusion matrix results for second single 64-neuron hidden layer VAE-QDA

QDA Classification Confusion Matrix Results	
AUC(ROC)	0.9166504976996729
Precision	0.9129945045567806
Recall	0.9992155104785386
F1 score	0.954161167195805
False positives	7647
True positives	80244
False negatives	63
True negatives	38443

The QDA produced 91.29% precision and 99.92% recall where LDA produced 87.62% precision and 99.92% recall.

A third model was trained with a batch size of 7500 and 64 neurons in the hidden layers of the encoder and decoder. The loss model is shown in Figure 20 and the visualisation is shown in Figure 21. The latent space visualization shows how DDoS flows occupy dense regions of the distribution. The precision of the QDA was

The overall performance of the VAE base QDA and LDA in terms of precision and recall was very high for the three models built. Given that no balancing of classes nor feature engineering was performed is good.

Figure 20. Loss for a model with a single 64-neuron hidden layer VAE model (batch size = 7500)

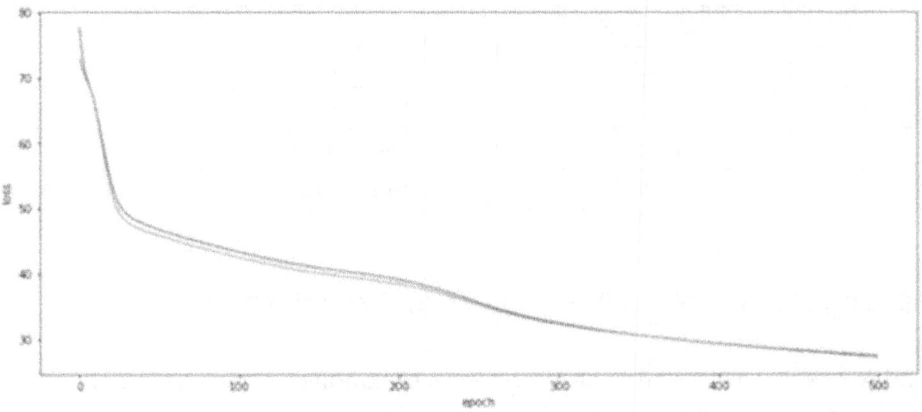

Figure 21. Latent space visualization of training data for 64 neurons hidden layer size and batch size = 7500

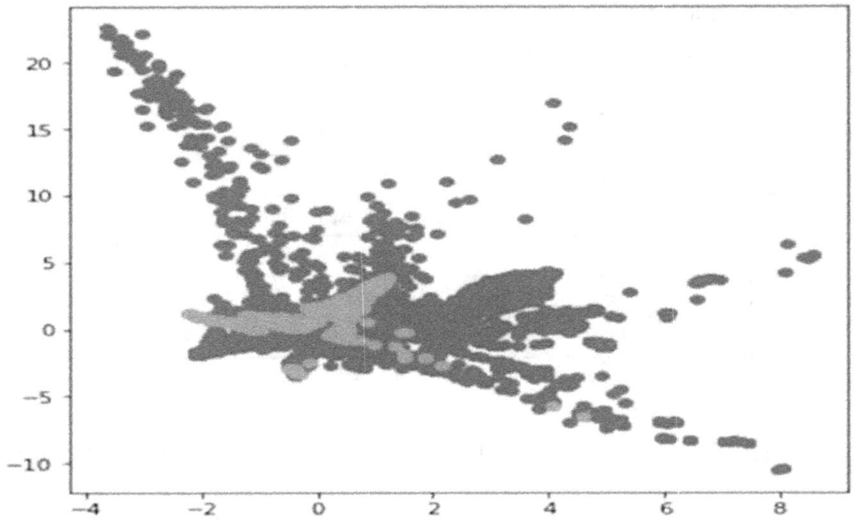

Table 10. Confusion matrix results for third single 64-neuron hidden layer VAE-LDA, batch size = 7500

LDA Classification Confusion Matrix Results	
AUC(ROC)	0.8794204086037665
Precision	0.8787055795871435
Recall	0.9991532494054067
F1 score	0.9350665998531656
False positives	11076
True positives	80239
False negatives	68
True negatives	35014

Table 11. Confusion matrix results for third single 64-neuron hidden layer VAE-QDA, batch size = 7500

QDA Classification Confusion Matrix Results	
AUC(ROC)	0.8658100310291411
Precision	0.8802057142857143
Recall	0.9590446660938647
F1 score	0.9179354854088327
False positives	10482
True positives	77018
False negatives	3289
True negatives	35608

4.2.2 Comparing Results of QDA Against Deep Neural Network

A Deep Neural Network was trained on the latent representation of the CICIDS 2017 Friday Afternoon data set network flows. The VAE model had a single hidden layer of 64 neurons and the coupled DDN had a single hidden layer of 512 neurons. The DNN did not train on the raw CICIDS 2017 dataset but got its input from the output of the VAE. The Assumption was the classes were already separated in the VAE latent space so it should be easier for downstream classifiers to separate the two classes. The Confusion matrix is shown in Table 12. The DDoS detector achieved a precision of 89.52% and a recall of 99.48%.

Figure 22. Confusion matrix of VAE based DNN model, single 512-neuron hidden layer

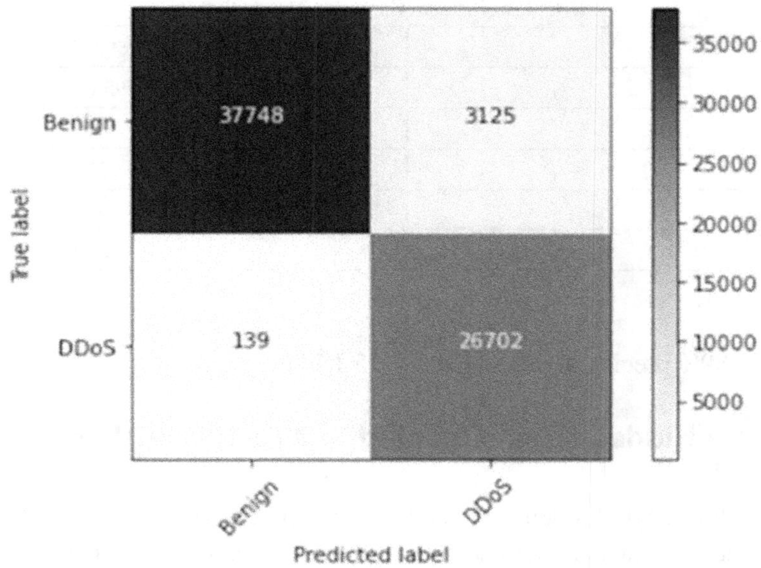

Deep Neural Network 2 Hidden Layers

A second Deep Neural Network model was trained using two hidden layers of 32 and 16 neurons. The DNN was evaluated on the same test data used for evaluating the VAE-DA. The confusion matrix showing the performance of the DNN with 2 layers (16 and 32 neurons) is shown in Figure 23 and Table 12.

Figure 23. Confusion matrix for DNN with 2 hidden layers of 16 and 32 neurons

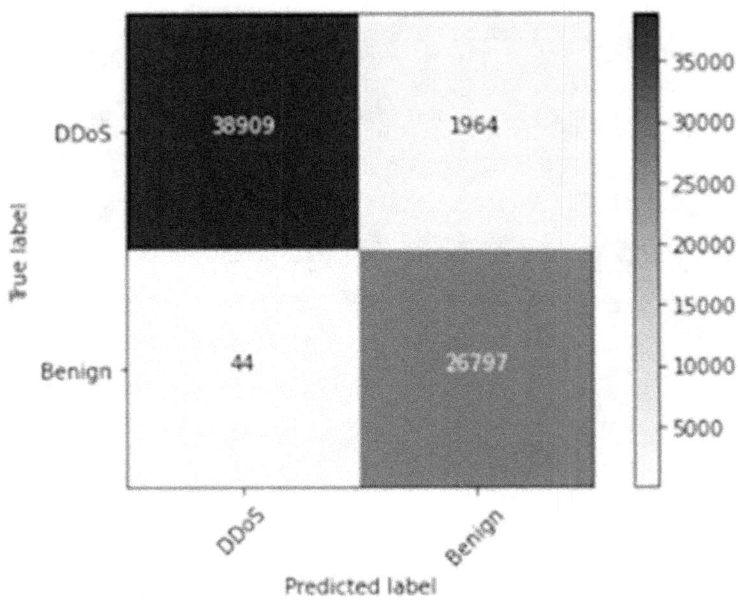

Table 12. Confusion matrix results of DNN with 2 hidden layers of 16 and 32 neurons

DNN Classification Confusion Matrix Results	
Precision	99.89%
Recall	95.19%
False positives	1964
True positives	77018
False negatives	44
True negatives	35608

The DNN had 99.89% precision and a recall of 95.19%.

VAE With a Single Hidden Layer Coupled to a DNN With Two Hidden Layers

A VAE was built with a single hidden layer and then coupled to a DNN with two hidden layers. The hidden layer of the encoder and decoder had 64 neurons each and the DNN had 32 neurons in each hidden layer. Both the VAE and DNN were trained with Keras Early Stopping configured to save the best model and its parameters during training (https://www.tensorflow.org/api_docs/python/tf/keras/callbacks/EarlyStopping, 2020).

The Deep Neural Network model achieved 96.11% and 96.34% for precision and recall respectively.

Figure 24. Summary of VAE model with a single 64-neuron hidden layer

```
Layer (type)                    Output Shape         Param #     Connected to
==================================================================================================
input_2 (InputLayer)            (None, 77)           0
__________________________________________________________________________________________________
batch_normalization_4 (BatchNor (None, 77)           308         input_2[0][0]
__________________________________________________________________________________________________
encoder_hidden01 (Dense)        (None, 64)           4992        batch_normalization_4[0][0]
__________________________________________________________________________________________________
batch_normalization_5 (BatchNor (None, 64)           256         encoder_hidden01[0][0]
__________________________________________________________________________________________________
batch_normalization_6 (BatchNor (None, 64)           256         batch_normalization_5[0][0]
__________________________________________________________________________________________________
z_mean (Dense)                  (None, 2)            130         batch_normalization_6[0][0]
__________________________________________________________________________________________________
z_log_var (Dense)               (None, 2)            130         batch_normalization_6[0][0]
__________________________________________________________________________________________________
z_sampled (Lambda)              (None, 2)            0           z_mean[0][0]
                                                                 z_log_var[0][0]
__________________________________________________________________________________________________
decoder_hidden02 (Dense)        (None, 64)           192         z_sampled[0][0]
__________________________________________________________________________________________________
decoded_mean (Dense)            (None, 77)           5005        decoder_hidden02[0][0]
==================================================================================================
Total params: 11,269
Trainable params: 10,859
Non-trainable params: 410
__________________________________________________________________________________________________
```

Figure 25. Summary of DDN with two 32-neuron hidden layers

```
Model: "sequential_1"
_________________________________________________________________
Layer (type)                 Output Shape              Param #
=================================================================
dense_1 (Dense)              (None, 77)                231
_________________________________________________________________
dense_2 (Dense)              (None, 32)                2496
_________________________________________________________________
dense_3 (Dense)              (None, 32)                1056
_________________________________________________________________
dense_4 (Dense)              (None, 1)                 33
=================================================================
Total params: 3,816
Trainable params: 3,816
Non-trainable params: 0
_________________________________________________________________
```

Figure 26. Confusion matrix for VAE-DNN with two hidden layers for DNN

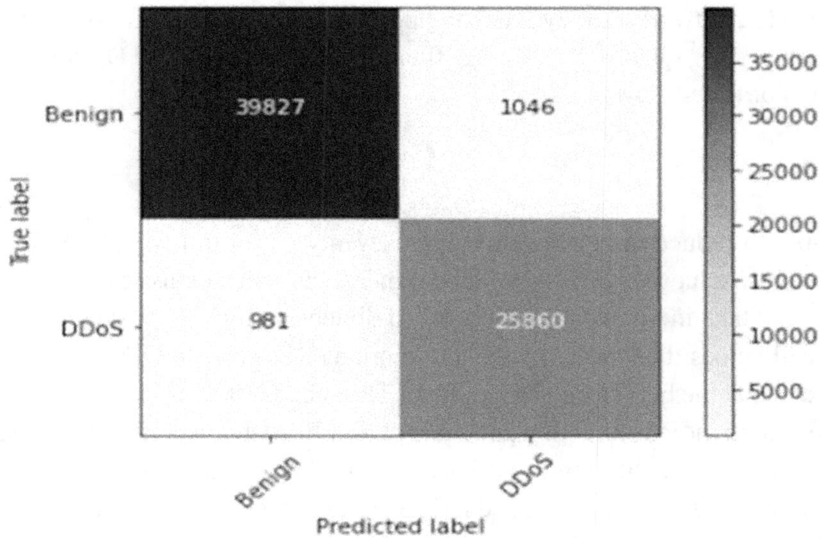

4.3 Analysis and Interpretation

Several models were built to come up with the best performing model of a VAE, QDA, LDA and DNN. A VAE model with a single 64-neuron hidden layer proved to be ideal for the complexity of the CICIDS 2017 Friday Afternoon data set. For the Deep Neural network two hidden layers of 32 neurons each produced the highest precision and recall ideal. The QDA proved to have higher precision and recall values than the LDA. Therefore subsequent comparisons with the Deep Neural Network involved the QDA only. The best VAE-QDA classifier showed higher precision and recall than traditional machine learning algorithm classifiers. The VAE-QDA performance was equally comparable to that of a Deep

Neural Network which had been trained on the same latent representation. The best VAE -QDA classifier achieved a precision and recall of 96.04% and 96.15% respectively. The best VAE-DNN model had 99.89% precision and a recall of 95.19%. A VAE-DNN with 96.11% and 96.34% for precision and recall respectively was not chosen because the cost of a False Positive is higher than that of a False Negative. The results supported the objective to build a DDoS classifier with high precision and recall values without feature engineering nor prior balancing of the classes within the data set.

For DDoS attack detection, both precision and recall needed to be very high, more so the precision. To avoid blocking or disconnecting benign traffic if the model were deployed in a real world environment precision needs to be maximized. A higher precision than recall may be preferable because allowing a few packets of DDoS packets usually does not harm servers whereas false positives usually negatively affect revenue. DDoS attack packets do not carry harmful payloads since the nature of the attack usually involves only overwhelming the victim server with normal packets to consume resources such as memory, CPU and network bandwidth of the Victim server. Since QDA assumed a quadratic decision boundary, it could accurately model a more complex range of classification problems than the LDA. The results prove that a DNN trained on the VAE latent representation of computer network flows performed better than QDA applied to the same VAE latent representation. The VAE-DNN had the additional advantage of scalability over QDA. Scalability is important for DDoS classifiers because the sizes of connected networks are ever expanding resulting in ever increasing amount of traffic. A classifier comprising VAE, QDA and DNN was finally built. The QDA and DNN served to endorse and confirm the results of tested flows.

4.4 Discussion

The VAE was able to reduce dimensionality from seventy seven to two. The DNN, QDA and LDA were able to learn from data with greatly reduced dimensions. The downstream classifiers scalability is improved as they can take in more data with reduced dimensionality. Because the QDA showed higher precision and recall values than the LDA the assumptions that go with QDA were proved true. It was therefore concluded that the benign and DDoS attack flows had different covariance matrix. The covariance matrix gave insight into the direction and scale of how the data is spread. QDA assumed that benign and DDoS attack samples had different covariance matrix. The visualisation of the latent space seemed to support the assumption that the benign and DDoS attack samples had different covariance matrix because the DDoS attack flows tended to be more clustered within the VAE probability distributions than benign traffic flows. The best DNN achieved precision and recall of 99, 89% and 95.19% respectively. The best QDA had a precision and recall of 96.04% and recall of 96.15% respectively. A VAE based DNN classifier was finally built because Deep Neural Networks have the advantage of scalability over Quadratic Discriminant Analysis classifiers.

5. CONCLUSION AND IMPLICATIONS

5.1 Conclusion

A way of training DDoS effective classifiers without the prior need to balance the data set nor feature engineering was demonstrated. The Variational Autoencoder (VAE), a generative model, proved that it can automatically learn the different classes' distribution and make classification easier for downstream classifiers. VAE based Deep Neural Network classifier is ideal to counter ever evolving nature of DDoS attacks. VAE based DNN is scalable to deal with an increasing number of connected devices and network traffic. The VAE was useful for greatly reducing the dimensionality of network flows from seventy seven to two. VAE based classifiers performed better than traditional machine learning classifiers. QDA classified network flows with higher precision and recall than LDA. Effective DDoS Classification models can be trained on unbalanced data without feature engineering by application of VAE based classification.

5.2 Implications

The application of QDA and LDA gave insight into how the network data met the assumptions that go with QDA and LDA. Because QDA classification results were consistently better than LDA it was concluded that the covariance matrix of DDoS attack samples differ from that of benign samples in the CICIDS 2017 data set. Detection of DDoS attacks and other intrusions can be made easier with the use of VAE-DNN. The VAE based DNN model scalability is ideal for modern day computer networks and the Internet of Things where huge amounts of network data are common. A VAE can be applied effectively where there is lack of domain knowledge since it learns features automatically. VAE can be used as a pre-processor of data to reduce dimensions for high dimensional data. With further research, unbalanced datasets may no longer compromise classifiers' precision and recall. By taking out the stages of data balancing and feature engineering in a data analytic pipeline model training times will be shortened. Because a trained VAE enhances the separation of classes, it makes it easier for downstream classifiers to achieve higher precision and recall values.

REFERENCES

Alzahrani, A. H. (2018). Generation of DDoS Attack Dataset for Effective IDS Development and Evaluation. *Journal of Information Security, 9,* 225-241. doi:10.4236/jis.2018.94016

An, J., & Cho, S. (2015). *Variational Autoencoder based Anomaly Detection using Reconstruction Probability.* SNU Data Mining Center. Retrieved April 26, 2020, from http://dm.snu.ac.kr/static/docs/TR/SNUDM-TR-2015-03.pdf

Bellinger, C. D. (2017). Manifold-based synthetic oversampling with manifold conformance estimation. *Machine Learning*.

Bonguet, A., & Bellaiche, M. (2017). A Survey of Denial-of-Service and Distributed Denial of Service Attacks and Defenses in Cloud Computing. *Future Internet*, *9*(3), 43. Advance online publication. doi:10.3390/fi9030043

Carl, D. (2016). Tutorial on Variational AutoencodersCarnegie Mellon UC Berkeley.

Darko Galinec, D. M. (2017). Cybersecurity and cyber defence: National level strategic approach. *Journal for Control, Measurement, Electronics, Computing and Communications*.

Dietrich, D., Heller, B., & Yang, B. (2015). *Data Science & Big Data Analytics: Discovering, Analyzing, Visualizing and Presenting Data.* John Wiley & Sons, Inc.

Doersch, C. (2016, August 13). Tutorial on Variational Autoencoders. https://www.researchgate.net/publication/304163568

Elmi, A. H., Sallehuddin, R., Ibrahim, S., & Zain, A. M. (2014). Classification of SIM Box Fraud Detection Using Support Vector Machine and Artificial Neural Network. *International Journal of Innovative Computing*, 19–27.

Fajardo, A. V. (2018). VOS: A Method for Variational Oversampling of Imbalanced Data. *International Journal of Advanced Computer Science and Applications*, 8.

Ghojogh, B., & Crowley, M. (2019). *Linear and Quadratic Discriminant Analysis: Tutorial*. Machine Learning Laboratory, University of Waterloo.

Gupta, A. (2019). *Generative Image Translation for Data Augmentation of Bone Lesion Pathology. Proceedings of Machine Learning Research, 102, 225–235* .

Ikeda, Y. (2018, December 21). Estimation of Dimensions Contributing to Detected Anomalies with Variational Autoencoders. arXiv:1811.04576v2 [stat.ML].

Jiadong, R. J., & Wang, Q. (2019, June 16). Building an Effective Intrusion Detection System by Using Hybrid Data Optimization Based on Machine Learning Algorithms. *Hindawi Security and Communication Networks*, 11.

Jiayu, S. X. (2018). Learning Sparse Representation With Variational Auto-Encoder for Anomaly Detection. *IEEE Open Access Journal*.

Jorge, J. V. (2018). *Proceedings of the 13th International Joint Conference on Computer Vision, Imaging and Computer Graphics Theory and Applications (VISIGRAPP 2018)* - Volume 5 (pp. 96-104). Science and Technology Publications.

Khan, R. S. (2019). *An Adaptive Multi-Layer Botnet Detection Technique Using Machine Learning Classifiers*. doi:10.3390/app9112375

Kim, J. (2020, April 1). Botnet Detection Using Recurrent Variational Autoencoder. doi:10.1109/GLOBECOM42002.2020.9348169

Kingma, D. W. (2019). An Introduction to Variational Autoencoders. *Foundations and Trends® in Machine Learning, 12*(4), 307-392. doi:10.1561/2200000056

Kurien, L. C. (2019, December). An Ameliorated method for Fraud Detection using Complex Generative Model: Variational Autoencoder. *International Journal of Innovative Technology and Exploring Engineering*, *9*(2S).

Lopez-Martin, M. E. (2018, December). Variational data generative model for intrusion detection. *Knowledge and Information Systems*. Advance online publication. doi:10.100710115-018-1306-7

Macfarlane, R. B. (2015). TFTP DDoS amplification attack. *Computers & Security*. Advance online publication. doi:10.1016/j.cose.2015.09.006

Mayuranathan, M. (2019). Best features based intrusion detection system by RBM model for detecting DDoS in cloud environment. *Journal of Ambient Intelligence and Humanized Computing*. Advance online publication. doi:10.100712652-019-01611-9

Mitra, A. (2017, March 2). *What is smurf attack.* Retrieved May 08, 2020, from https://www.thesecuritybuddy.com/dos-ddos-prevention/what-is-smurf-attack/

Noble, G., & Sujitha, M. (2015). Flow Based Solutions for DoS and DDoS Attack Detection. *International Journal of Advanced Research in Computer Engineering and Technology.*

Reaves, B., Shernan, E., Bates, A., & Carter, H. (2015). Boxed Out: Blocking Cellular Interconnect Bypass Fraud at the Network Edge. *Proceedings of the 24th USENIX Security Symposium.*

Rezvy, S. P. (2019). Intrusion Detection and Classification with Autoencoded Deep Neural Network. *11th International Conference, SecITC 2018.* 10.1007/978-3-030-12942-2_12

Riaz, U. K., Xiaosong, Z., Rajesh, K., Abubakar, S., A, N. G., & Mamoun, A. (2019). An Adaptive Multi-Layer Botnet Detection Technique Using Machine Learning Classifiers. *Applied Sciences.*

Sallehuddin, R., Ibrahim, S., Mohd Zain, A., & Hussein Elmi, A. (2015, November 26). Detecting SIM Box Fraud by Using Support Vector Machine and Artificial. *Jurnal Teknologi*, *74*(1), 3. doi:10.11113/jt.v74.2649

Sharafaldin, I. L. (2018). Toward Generating a New Intrusion Detection Dataset and Intrusion Traffic Characterization. In *ICISSP 2018 - 4th International Conference on Information Systems Security and Privacy.* SCITEPRESS – Science and Technology Publications, Lda. 10.5220/0006639801080116

Singh, K. S. (2015). A systematic review of IP traceback schemes for denial of service attacks. Punjab: Department of Computer Science and Engineering, S B S State Technical Campus, Punjab 152004, India. doi:10.1016/j.cose.2015.06.007

Tharwat, A. G. (2017). *Linear Discriminant Analysis: A Detailed Tutorial.* dx.doi.org/10.3233/AIC-170729

Vipin, A. (2018). Analysis and detection of SIM box. *International Journal of Advance Research, Ideas and Innovations in Technology, 4*(3).

Wang, W. W. (2018). A HMM-R Approach to Detect L-DDoS Attack Adaptively on SDN Controller. *Future Internet MDPI, 10*(83). doi:10.3390/fi10090083

Wanga, X., Dua, Y., Linb, S., Cuia, P., Shenc, Y., & Yanga, Y. (2019, November 17). adVAE: a Self-adversarial Variational Autoencoder with Gaussian Anomaly Prior Knowledge for Anomaly Detection. arXiv:1903.00904v3.

Wangy, Z. (2017). DDoS Event Forecasting using Twitter Data. *Proceedings of the Twenty-Sixth International Joint Conference on Artificial Intelligence (IJCAI-17).*

Yang, Y. (2019). Improving the Classification Effectiveness of Intrusion Detection by Using Improved Conditional Variational Auto Encoder and Deep Neural Network. *Sensors*, 2.

Yang, Y., Zheng, K., Wu, C., & Yang, Y. (2019, June 2). Improving the Classification Effectiveness of Intrusion Detection by Using Improved Conditional Variational AutoEncoder and Deep Neural Network. *Sensors (Basel), 19*(11), 2528. doi:10.339019112528 PMID:31159512

Yang, Z., Zheng, K., Wu, C., & Yang, Y. (2019). Improving the Classification Effectiveness of Intrusion Detection by Using Improved Conditional Variational AutoEncoder and Deep Neural Network. *Sensors (Basel), 19*(11), 2528. Advance online publication. doi:10.339019112528 PMID:31159512

Yilmaz, I. M. (2019). Expansion of Cyber Attack Data From Unbalanced Datasets Using Generative Techniques. arXiv:1912.04549v1 [cs.LG].

Yulianto, A. S. (2018). Improving AdaBoost-based Intrusion Detection System (IDS) Performance on CIC IDS 2017 Dataset. In *The 2nd International Conference on Data and Information Science.* IOP Publishing. 10.1088/1742-6596/1192/1/012018

Zhang, C. S. (2016). An Imbalanced Data Classification Algorithm of De-noising Auto-Encoder Neural Network Based on SMOTE. *MATEC Web of Conferences, 56.* 10.1051/matecconf/20165601014

Chapter 18
Enhancing Credit Card Fraud Detection and Prevention:
A Privacy-Preserving Federated Machine Learning Approach With Auto-Encoder and Attention Mechanism

Olalekan J. Awujoola
https://orcid.org/0000-0002-1842-021X
Nigerian Defence Academy, Nigeria

Theophilus Aniemeka Enem
Airforce Institute of Technology, Kaduna, Nigeria

Ogwueleka Nonyelum Francisca
University of Abuja, Nigeria

Olayinka Racheal Adelegan
Nigerian Defence Academy, Kaduna, Nigeria

Abioye Oluwasegun
Nigerian Defence Academy, Kaduna, Nigeria

Celesine Ozoemenam Uwa
Nigerian Defence Academy, Kaduna, Nigeria

Victor Uneojo Akuboh
Nigerian Defence Academy, Kaduna, Nigeria

Oluwaseyi Ezekiel Olorunshola
Airforce Institute of Technology, Kaduna, Nigeria

Hadiza Hassan
Kaduna State University, Nigeria

ABSTRACT

This chapter explores using auto-encoders and attention mechanisms to enhance privacy-preserving capabilities of federated machine learning for credit card fraud detection. The proposed system uncovers latent features in credit card transactions, leveraging distributed training for user privacy. Empirical evaluation on real-world data shows its proficiency in identifying fraud. The method offers privacy preservation, scalability, and resilience. The model's performance across imbalanced and balanced datasets highlights the role of balanced data in optimizing fraud detection. This approach integrates accuracy, privacy preservation, and security. Considering fraudsters' sophistication, this research introduces a strategy to counter credit card fraud while preserving confidentiality. In summation, this chapter presents a framework for deploying privacy-focused federated machine learning in credit card fraud detection and prevention, fostering privacy-preserving applications across domains.

DOI: 10.4018/979-8-3693-0593-5.ch018

1. INTRODUCTION

The prevalence of e-commerce and online payment methods in recent years has resulted in a significant increase in fraudulent transactions. Reports indicate a substantial rise in fraud losses related to credit and debit cards between 2000 and 2015. Notably, unauthorized purchases and counterfeit credit cards, although constituting a smaller proportion of total fraud cases, account for a significant majority (75-80%) of the financial value involved (Saia & Carta, 2019). In response to these challenges, both private and public entities have increased investments in research and development to develop more effective fraud detection systems.

Credit cardholders are encouraged to use their cards for payments due to the convenience and speed they offer, facilitating both national and international transactions, including cash withdrawals (Al Rubaie, 2021). However, along with these benefits come increased risks, particularly related to credit card fraud. Detecting fraudulent transactions has become a challenging task, especially with the rise of online businesses that exclusively accept credit card transactions, leading to a surge in fraudulent activities. The need for robust fraud detection and prevention techniques has become crucial due to the increasing trend of credit card online transactions. In 2020, there were approximately 2,183 million Visa and Mastercard users worldwide, with over 30% of Visa card users and 24% of Mastercard users located in the United States (Alkhatib, 2021). This surge in cashless transactions has resulted in a corresponding increase in fraud rates for Card Not Present (CNP) transactions (Murli, 2015). Furthermore, the COVID-19 pandemic has accelerated the shift towards online transactions, emphasizing the urgency to effectively prevent and detect fraud. Consequently, researchers and financial institutions are continuously seeking more efficient techniques to enhance the safety of online transactions, with machine learning (ML) playing a pivotal role in this endeavor.

For financial institutions that issue credit cards or handle online transactions, the implementation of automated fraud detection systems is crucial. These systems play a vital role in reducing losses and fostering customer trust. With the advent of big data and artificial intelligence, new opportunities have emerged for utilizing advanced machine learning models to detect fraudulent activities (Bao et al, 2022). Current fraud detection systems that leverage advanced data mining and machine/deep learning methods have proven highly effective.

Typically, these systems employ a binary classification model trained on a labeled dataset containing both normal and fraudulent transactions. The model is designed to differentiate between normal and fraudulent transactions, enabling it to make accurate determinations on incoming transactions. However, the task of detecting fraudulent transactions using classification techniques presents several challenges (Fournier & Aloise, 2019). These challenges include class imbalance, cost sensitivity, temporal dependence between transactions, concept drift, and the dimensionality of the feature space. In a comprehensive literature review conducted by Ngai et al, (2011), decision trees, artificial neural networks, logistic regression, and support vector machines were identified as the most frequently used supervised learning techniques for fraud detection. These challenges necessitate the careful consideration of various factors to ensure the effectiveness of fraud detection systems.

Machine learning techniques have proven immensely helpful in fraud detection and prevention efforts. Financial institutions employ ML models to analyze patterns, anomalies, and historical data, effectively identifying potential fraudulent activities. ML techniques have significantly improved the accuracy and efficiency of fraud detection systems. However, credit card fraud detection and prevention pose two crucial considerations: privacy preservation and collaborative learning. Ensuring the privacy of sensitive credit card data is paramount. Privacy-preserving techniques are employed to safeguard individual data points and personally identifiable information (PII), preventing unauthorized access or exposure. Additionally, collaborative learning approaches, such as federated machine learning, enable multiple parties to collaboratively train models without sharing raw data. These techniques mitigate privacy concerns and address data ownership issues.

In this study, we propose a privacy-preserving federated machine learning approach for credit card fraud detection and prevention to address the limitations of traditional fraud detection approaches, especially with imbalanced data. Leveraging advanced and innovative techniques, we incorporate the function of an attention mechanism within the autoencoder to enhance the accuracy and efficiency of the system. The attention mechanism allows the autoencoder to selectively focus on the most relevant features or components of the input data during the encoding and decoding processes. By assigning different attention weights to different parts of the data, the attention mechanism helps the model prioritize important information and optimize the reconstruction process. This integrated approach enhances the discriminative power and overall performance of the model. Our approach integrates privacy-preserving techniques and collaborative learning, addressing privacy concerns associated with credit card data while maximizing the effectiveness of fraud detection and prevention efforts. Our fraud detection system aims to provide enhanced accuracy and reliability in identifying fraudulent activities (Fournier & Aloise, 2019). By combining the power of the auto-encoder, which performs effective representation learning, with the attention mechanism, which emphasizes relevant features, we can optimize the reconstruction process and improve the system's ability to accurately detect fraudulent transactions with or without data class balance.

In summary, our study addresses the increasing challenges in credit card fraud detection and prevention. By proposing a privacy-preserving federated machine learning approach and integrating advanced techniques such as auto-encoders and attention mechanisms, we aim to enhance the accuracy and efficiency of fraud detection systems. The combination of machine learning models, careful consideration of fraud detection challenges, and the integration of innovative techniques can greatly improve the effectiveness of fraud detection systems, ultimately leading to improved security and protection against fraudulent activities in the financial sector (Al Rubaie, 2021; Bao et al, 2022).

The organization of this work is as follows: Section 2 offers a comprehensive review of relevant literature, providing insights and analysis from previous studies. In Section 3, the proposed methodology is presented, offering a concise overview of the approach employed in our research. Moving on to Section 4, a comparative analysis of different models is conducted, followed by the selection of the most suitable model based on the evaluation criteria. Lastly, in Section 5, the main findings and conclusions drawn from our study are summarized, highlighting the key insights and implications of our research.

2. REVIEW OF RELATED LITERATURE

The review of related literature aims to provide an extensive overview of existing research and studies in the field of credit card fraud detection and prevention, particularly focusing on privacy-preserving federated machine learning approaches with auto-encoder and attention mechanisms. This section examines prior works that address similar challenges, methodologies, and techniques, shedding light on the current state of knowledge and identifying gaps that the proposed approach intends to fill. The primary objective of this review is to explore advancements made in credit card fraud detection and prevention while considering the crucial aspect of preserving privacy through federated machine learning techniques. As the volume of online transactions continues to increase, it becomes imperative to develop robust and privacy-preserving methods that effectively detect and prevent fraudulent activities without compromising sensitive user information (Enem & Awujoola, 2023).

The literature review covers a range of topics, including machine learning algorithms, privacy-preserving techniques, and the incorporation of auto-encoder and attention mechanisms. Machine learning algorithms play a vital role in fraud detection, enabling the identification of patterns and anomalies in credit card transactions. Privacy-preserving techniques, such as federated learning, ensure that user data remains confidential and secure during the training process. Moreover, the review focuses on the utilization of auto-encoder and attention mechanisms in credit card fraud detection. Auto-encoders are powerful unsupervised learning models that extract meaningful features from high-dimensional data, enabling the detection of fraudulent patterns. Attention mechanisms, on the other hand, enhance the model's ability to focus on critical features and relationships within the data, further improving the accuracy of fraud detection systems. The review also highlights the significance of privacy preservation in credit card fraud detection. The need to protect sensitive user information while achieving accurate fraud detection poses challenges that require innovative solutions. By analyzing existing literature, we can gain insights into the approaches and techniques employed to address privacy concerns while maintaining high levels of fraud detection accuracy. Through the review of related literature, we aim to provide a comprehensive understanding of the research landscape, identify gaps, and set the foundation for the proposed privacy-preserving federated machine learning approach with auto-encoder and attention mechanism. By building upon the knowledge and experiences from previous studies, we can develop an approach that effectively enhances credit card fraud detection and prevention while safeguarding user privacy.

2.1 Deep Learning

Deep learning (DL) is a subset of machine learning (ML) that leverages data to train computers in performing various tasks. The key principle of DL is that as we increase the complexity of neural networks (NNs) and train them with more data, their performance improves over time. DL offers a significant advantage over traditional ML methods, particularly in dealing with large datasets. In the realm of cybersecurity, some commonly employed DL algorithms include feed forward neural networks (FNNs), stacked autoencoders (SAE), and convolutional neural networks (CNNs). These algorithms have proven to be effective in addressing cybersecurity challenges by extracting meaningful patterns and features from the data.

Addressing the challenge of highly imbalanced class distributions in credit card datasets, a novel approach proposed by Tingfei et al, (2020) combined oversampling techniques based on variational autoencoders (VAE) with deep learning (DL) techniques. The VAE model, which employed a variational autoencoder to oversample minority class instances, yielded better results compared to synthetic minority oversampling strategies and conventional deep neural network (DNN) methods. Furthermore, it outperformed previous oversampling techniques based on GAN models.

2.2 Related Literature

In their study, Said Elsayed et al. (2020) proposed a hybrid approach combining Long Short-Term Memory (LSTM) autoencoder and One-class Support Vector Machine (OC-SVM) to detect anomalies in an unbalanced dataset, specifically targeting attacks. The models were trained solely on examples of normal classes to learn the normal traffic patterns. The LSTM autoencoder was trained to capture the compressed representation of the input data, known as latent features, which were then utilized by the OC-SVM approach. This hybrid model addressed the limitations of the standalone OC-SVM, particularly its ability to handle massive and high-dimensional datasets. The evaluation was performed using the InSDN dataset, representing Intrusion Detection Systems (IDSs) for SDN environments.

The experimental results demonstrated the effectiveness of the proposed model, achieving an accuracy of 90.5%. Additionally, the hybrid model showcased a higher detection rate while significantly reducing the processing time. These findings highlight the potential of the LSTM-Autoencoder-OC-SVM approach in securing SDN networks from malicious traffic, instilling greater confidence in their overall security measures.

In their study, Alazizi et al. (2020) proposed the DuSVAE model, which combines two sequential variational autoencoders (VAEs) to generate condensed representations of sequential data for fraud detection. The experiments conducted on a real-world dataset showcased the superior performance of the DuSVAE model compared to other state-of-the-art systems. The DuSVAE model achieved the best results with AUC-PR scores of 0.51 and 0.53, further highlighting its effectiveness in detecting fraud in credit card transactions. This demonstrates the potential of the DuSVAE model as an advanced and promising approach for fraud detection.

In a study by Misra et al. (2020), an autoencoder model was utilized for cyber fraud detection. The model employed a two-stage approach, where the transaction characteristics were transformed into a lower-dimensional feature vector using an autoencoder in the first step. Subsequently, a classifier was trained on these feature vectors in the second step. The results demonstrated that the proposed model outperformed other models in terms of fraud detection accuracy.

In another research by Wu et al., (2020), a dual autoencoder generative adversarial network (DAE-GAN) was applied to address the imbalanced classification problem. The model involved training a generative adversarial network (GAN) to generate synthetic fraudulent transactions, which were then used for autoencoder training. Two autoencoders were utilized to encode the transaction samples and create two sets of features. The study showed that the new model outperformed several classification algorithms in terms of imbalanced classification accuracy.

Lin & Jiang (2021) proposed a method called autoencoder with probabilistic random forest (AE-PRF) for credit card fraud detection. The AE-PRF method employed an autoencoder to extract low-dimensional features from high-dimensional credit card transaction data. It then utilized a random forest with probabilistic classification to classify transactions as either fraudulent or normal. The performance of the AE-PRF method was evaluated and compared using the credit card fraud detection (CCFD) dataset, which consists of a large number of credit card transactions by European cardholders. The dataset is highly imbalanced, with a majority of normal transactions and a minority of fraudulent transactions. To address this imbalance and improve AE-PRF performance, data resampling techniques such as SMOTE, ADASYN, and Tomek link were applied to balance the number of normal and fraudulent transactions. Experimental results showed that the performance of AE-PRF was relatively stable, regardless of whether resampling techniques were applied to the dataset. This indicates that AE-PRF is naturally suitable for handling imbalanced datasets. When compared to related methods, AE-PRF demonstrated excellent performance in terms of accuracy, true positive rate, true negative rate, Matthews correlation coefficient, and the area under the receiver operating characteristic curve.

Authors Xie et al., (2022), in their study presented a fault analysis method for power distribution networks using a combination of LSTM autoencoder and attention mechanism. The researchers aimed to address the challenges associated with time series data dependencies and high labeling costs by employing a semi-supervised learning approach. The LSTM autoencoder's loss function was modified to incorporate both labeled and unlabeled input, allowing for robust learning from diverse data types. Through the minimization of this loss function, the model effectively learned the distribution of the combined data. Additionally, an attention mechanism was integrated into the model to ensure stability in performance when adjusting the weighting of labeled data. The enhanced LSTM autoencoder was then applied to a prediction model, enabling semi-supervised learning for fault detection in power distribution networks. By leveraging this approach, the researchers successfully overcame the limitations of time series data dependence and the expense associated with data labeling. As a result, they achieved improved fault detection accuracy in power distribution networks. In conclusion, Xie et al. (2022) demonstrated the efficacy of their approach by combining LSTM autoencoder and attention mechanism in a semi-supervised learning framework for fault analysis. Their method effectively addressed the challenges inherent in power distribution networks, ultimately leading to more accurate fault detection results.

The study conducted by Roseline et al. (2022) aimed to address credit card fraud detection. Their proposed approach involved the utilization of a Long Short-Term Memory-Recurrent Neural Network (LSTM-RNN) combined with an attention mechanism to enhance the detection performance. This model was specifically designed to handle complex and interconnected features within sequential data, making it well-suited for fraud detection tasks. To assess the effectiveness of their proposed model, a comparison was made against other commonly used classifiers, including Naive Bayes, Support Vector Machine (SVM), and Artificial Neural Network (ANN). The experimental results demonstrated that the LSTM-RNN model outperformed these alternative classifiers in terms of its ability to accurately detect instances of credit card fraud. The integration of the attention mechanism further improved the performance of the proposed model by allowing it to focus on the most relevant features and patterns within the data. This attention mechanism played a crucial role in enhancing the accuracy and efficiency of the fraud detection system. Overall, the study conducted by Roseline et al. (2022) successfully developed a credit card fraud detection system using the LSTM-RNN model with an attention mechanism. The experimental results provided strong evidence for the effectiveness and high accuracy of their proposed approach, suggesting its potential as an advanced tool for combating credit card fraud.

In their work, Distante et al. (2022) proposed an unsupervised novel combination of existing machine learning techniques to determine the typicality of a purchase for a specific customer. The objective was to streamline the customer's journey and enhance the user experience by exempting Strong Customer Authentication (SCA) for typical purchases. To achieve this, the authors modified the architecture of the well-known U-net model by replacing convolutional blocks with squeeze-and-excitation blocks. They also introduced a memory network in the latent space and incorporated an attention mechanism in the decoding side of the network. By leveraging temporal correlations between transactions, the proposed solution aimed to identify non-typical purchases.

The network demonstrated remarkable performance, achieving an impressive AUC score of 97.7% when evaluated on a well-known dataset obtained from online sources. Through the implementation of this approach, the authors discovered that 98% of purchases could be securely exempted from SCA, reducing the need for additional authentication while still maintaining robust security measures. This not only led to a shorter customer's journey but also provided an elevated user experience by enhancing convenience and satisfaction.

The authors, Fanai and Abbasimehr (2023), introduced a two-stage framework for fraud detection in transactions. The framework combined a deep Autoencoder for representation learning and supervised deep learning techniques. Experimental evaluations were conducted to assess the performance of the proposed approach. The results indicated that the deep Autoencoder-based approach significantly improved the performance of the deep learning-based classifiers used in the study. Specifically, the deep learning classifiers trained on the transformed dataset obtained by the deep Autoencoder outperformed the baseline classifiers trained on the original data across all performance measures. Furthermore, the models created using the deep Autoencoder demonstrated superior performance compared to models developed using the dataset obtained through principal component analysis (PCA). Additionally, the proposed approach outperformed existing models in terms of fraud detection accuracy. These findings highlighted the effectiveness of incorporating a deep Autoencoder as a representation learning method in fraud detection. The deep Autoencoder enabled the classifiers to learn more informative and discriminating features, leading to improved fraud detection performance. This approach showed promising potential for enhancing fraud detection systems and mitigating financial losses associated with fraudulent transactions.

In their work, Meng et al. (2023) proposed a credit card fraud detection method that combines Generative Adversarial Networks (GAN) and the attention mechanism. The authors addressed the challenges of noise expansion and overfitting in generating synthetic samples by using medical Generative Adversarial Networks (medGAN). They further enhanced the model's predictive performance by incorporating a multi-head attention mechanism from deep learning. The proposed framework demonstrated significant improvements in predicting credit card fraud on highly unbalanced datasets. By integrating metrics such as AUC, BER, and G-mean, the authors evaluated the effectiveness of their approach. The results highlighted the ability of their method to handle imbalanced data and achieve accurate predictions in credit card fraud detection. In summary, Meng et al. (2023) presented a novel approach that leverages GAN and the attention mechanism to enhance credit card fraud detection. Their method overcomes limitations associated with traditional oversampling techniques and expands the application of deep learning in fraud detection. The experimental findings validate the effectiveness of the proposed framework in improving prediction accuracy on datasets with highly imbalanced data.

The study conducted by Gradxs and Rao (2023) aimed to make significant contributions in the field of fraud detection. The authors introduced three novel enhancements to improve the accuracy and effectiveness of fraud detection systems. The first contribution involved the development of a data-balanced Deep Stacking Autoencoder, which incorporated the Harris Grey Wolf (HGW) network. The HGW-based Deep Stacking Autoencoder proved to be a powerful approach for uncovering fraudulent activities. It utilized a fitness function and iterative optimization to minimize errors and determine the optimal solution. To enhance the detection rate and accuracy, the study focused on selecting the most relevant features from transaction data. These carefully chosen features played a vital role in providing crucial information and improving the accuracy of fraud detection. This feature selection process served as a validation mechanism to distinguish the effectiveness of fraud detection systems from legitimate ones. The evaluation of the proposed HGW Deep Stacking Autoencoder demonstrated promising results. With an accuracy of 0.92, sensitivity of 0.76, and specificity of 0.92, the model exhibited impressive performance across various evaluation metrics. These findings underscore the effectiveness of the HGW Deep Stacking Autoencoder in accurately detecting fraudulent transactions and differentiating them from genuine ones.

In their research, Du et al. (2023) proposed the AED-LGB algorithm as a solution for bank credit card fraud detection. This algorithm incorporates an autoencoder to extract relevant features from the data, which are then fed into the LightGBM algorithm for classification and prediction. During the training process, the algorithm determines the optimal threshold value by evaluating different threshold values and comparing indicator parameters. Any data exceeding the threshold is marked as fraudulent. To evaluate the performance of the AED-LGB algorithm, an anonymized dataset from a bank was utilized. However, the dataset was unbalanced, with a significant majority of normal data (class 0) compared to fraudulent data (class 1). To address this issue, the dataset was augmented using the SMOTE algorithm for oversampling. Experimental results indicated that the overall performance of the AED-LGB-SMOTE algorithm did not improve compared to the AED-LGB algorithm. This suggests that the AED-LGB algorithm is better suited for handling unbalanced data in the context of bank fraud. Furthermore, the AED-LGB algorithm was compared with other algorithms such as KNN, Random Forest, and LightGBM without data enhancement. The AED-LGB algorithm exhibited the highest MCC, TNR, and ACC values at a threshold of 0.2, while the TPR value was the highest at a threshold of 0.05, indicating a higher detection rate for fraudulent data. In future work, the researchers plan to apply the AED-LGB algorithm to other risk control datasets in the banking domain to validate its generalizability. They also aim to further improve and optimize the AED-LGB algorithm to achieve even better performance.

Korkoman and Abdullah (2023) proposed a new fraud detection model that addresses the issue of imbalanced fraud credit card datasets. The model uses the Particle Swarm Optimization (PSO) technique to oversample the minority class, which improves the accuracy of the model. The model was compared to a model that uses the Genetic Algorithm (GA) technique. The Random Forest (RF) algorithm was used to evaluate the sensitivity, specificity, and accuracy of the two models.The experimental results showed that both the GA and PSO models achieved high performance, with accuracy rates of 99.3% and 99.4% respectively. The PSO model was slightly faster than the GA model, taking only seconds to run. The experiments demonstrated the superiority of the proposed models, as evidenced by their higher classification accuracy compared to other approaches.

2.3 Autoencoder Classifier

Autoencoders are a type of unsupervised learning model that aims to reconstruct its input as its output (Bengio et al., 2007). Despite being an unsupervised learning approach, an autoencoder can be viewed as a supervised learning network, where the output x represents the reconstructed version of the original input x data (Niu et al., 2019). The autoencoder consists of two main phases: encoding and decoding, represented in equation 1 and 2.

$$y = f_{\theta}(x) \tag{1}$$

$$x' = g_{\theta'}\left(y\right) \tag{2}$$

Equation (1) and (2) represent the calculation formulas for the encoder and decoder in the autoencoder model. In these equations, f and g are affine mappings, and θ and θ' are vectors comprising the weight and bias parameters of the encoder and decoder, respectively. During training, the objective is to minimize the reconstruction error, which quantifies the discrepancy between the original input and its reconstructed output represented by equation 3.

$$arg \frac{min}{\theta\theta'} \mathbb{E}_{x\sim} \left[L\left(x, g_{\theta'}\left(f_{\theta}\left(x\right)\right)\right) \right]$$

Commonly used options for measuring the dissimilarity between two vectors, denoted as L(x, x'), include the squared error or $x - x'^2$ for real-valued vectors and the negative log-likelihood $\sum_{i=1}^{|x|} (x_i \log x_i' + (1 - x_i) \log(1 - x_i$ for vectors consisting of bits or bit probabilities (Bernoullis).

During the encoding phase, the input data is mapped to a hidden layer as shown in Figure 1, which serves as a low-dimensional representation of the input (Niu et al., 2019). This hidden layer captures important features and patterns in the input data. In the decoding phase, the hidden layer is mapped back to the output layer, aiming to reconstruct the original input data. The decoder part of the autoencoder reconstructs the input data using the information encoded in the hidden layers.

Figure 1. The structure of an auto-encoder (AE) (Lin & Jiang, 2021)

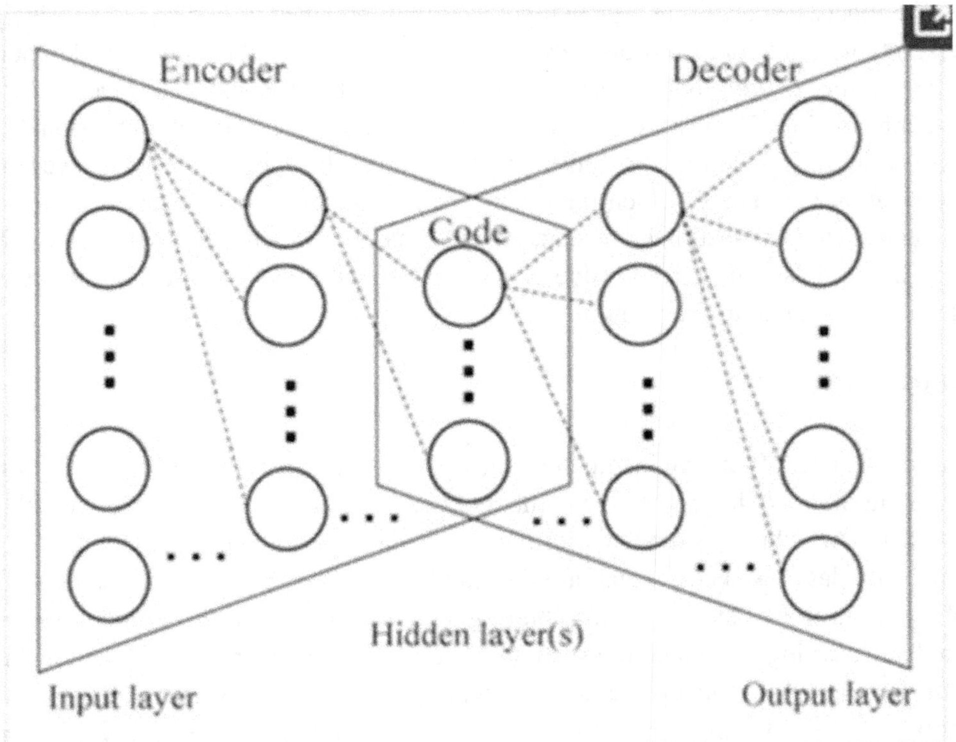

The hidden layers of an autoencoder typically have a lower dimensionality compared to the input data. This reduction in dimensionality helps to extract essential features and create a compressed representation of the input data. Moreover, the hidden layers introduce nonlinearity to the model, allowing the autoencoder to capture complex relationships and variations in the data.

In summary, autoencoders utilize encoding and decoding phases to learn a compact and nonlinear representation of the input data (Niu et al., 2019). This unsupervised learning technique reconstructs the input as its output, enabling the model to capture essential features and patterns within the data.

3. RESEARCH METHODOLOGY

3.1 Dataset Source

Obtaining a credit card fraud dataset can be challenging due to the privacy of the data for both enterprises and customers. Consequently, we conducted our experiment using an open dataset, which is available for download at the URL https://www.kaggle.com/mlg-ulb/creditcardfraud. This dataset comprises credit card transaction information from cardholders in Europe over a two-day period in September 2013. In total, there are 284,807 transactions, with 492 cases labeled as positive (representing fraudulent transactions), accounting for approximately 0.172% of the data. This distribution reflects the typical imbalanced classification problem often encountered in fraud detection scenarios.

The dataset consists solely of numerical input variables, obtained through a PCA (principal components analysis) transformation. Unfortunately, due to confidentiality constraints, we do not have access to the original features or additional background information about the data. However, Table 5 provides the available information. The features V1, V2, ..., V28 are likely the result of dimensionality reduction using PCA to protect user identities and sensitive information. The only features that have not undergone PCA transformation are 'Time', which represents the number of seconds elapsed between the given transaction and the first transaction in the dataset, and 'Amount', which denotes the transaction amount. Additionally, in the 'Class' column, a value of 1 indicates a fraudulent transaction, while a value of 0 represents a non-fraudulent transaction.

3.1.1 Dataset Defect

Fraud detection datasets often suffer from the issue of class imbalance, where the number of fraudulent transactions is significantly lower than the number of normal transactions. This class imbalance poses a challenge as standard techniques tend to prioritize the majority class, resulting in high misclassification rates for minority class instances, which are the fraudulent transactions (Awujoola et al., 2021). The primary objective in fraud detection is to achieve good performance in classifying the minority class, i.e., accurately identifying fraudulent transactions. One approach to address the class imbalance issue is to employ the Synthetic Minority Oversampling Technique (SMOTE) on the raw data prior to modeling. SMOTE mitigates the imbalance problem by oversampling the minority class and undersampling the majority class, thus creating a more balanced dataset. This technique generates synthetic instances for the minority class and combines them with the TOMEK undersampling method to enhance the overall balance of the dataset.

By utilizing SMOTE, the dataset is transformed to include additional synthetic instances representing the minority class. This augmentation helps to alleviate the class imbalance problem, enabling the classification models to give more attention to the minority class and improve their performance in detecting fraudulent transactions.

3.1.2 Dataset Percentage Splits

In this study, the dataset was split into training and testing subsets using a percentage split approach. Specifically, a test size of 0.2 was used, corresponding to a 20% split. This means that 20% of the data was set aside for testing, while the remaining 80% was used for training the model. The purpose of this split is to evaluate the performance of the model on unseen data, ensuring that it can generalize well beyond the training set. By reserving a portion of the data for testing, we can assess how well the model performs on new and unseen examples, providing insights into its effectiveness and generalization capabilities.

3.2 Model Description

Credit card fraud detection was identified as a crucial task in ensuring the security of financial transactions. The rise of online transactions necessitated the development of effective fraud detection techniques. In this work, a comprehensive approach that combined an autoencoder with an attention mechanism was presented for fraud detection. The aim was to leverage advanced machine learning techniques to enhance the accuracy and efficiency of fraud detection systems.

The credit card dataset used in this study contained information about transactions conducted by cardholders in Europe over a two-day period in September 2013. It comprised 284,807 transactions, including 492 instances of fraudulent transactions, accounting for 0.172% of the data. The dataset consisted of numerical input variables resulting from a PCA transformation, excluding the 'Time' and 'Amount' features. Unfortunately, due to confidentiality concerns, access to the original features and additional background information was not available. Figure 2 visualize the high-level flow of the model methodology.

To prepare the dataset for modeling, it was split into training and testing sets. Additionally, feature scaling using the StandardScaler was applied to ensure consistency in feature ranges. The issue of class imbalance in the dataset was addressed using the SMOTETomek technique, which combined oversampling with SMOTE and undersampling with Tomek Links. This balancing process aimed to achieve a more representative distribution of the classes.

The architecture of the autoencoder was then defined. Comprising an encoder and a decoder, the autoencoder was a neural network that mapped the input data to a lower-dimensional representation in the encoder phase and reconstructed the input data in the decoder phase. Dense layers with rectified linear unit (ReLU) activation functions were employed for both the encoder and decoder. The autoencoder was compiled with the mean squared error (MSE) loss function and the Adam optimizer.

In addition to the autoencoder, an attention mechanism was integrated into the model to focus on important features during the reconstruction process. By assigning different weights to different parts of the input data, the attention mechanism emphasized the most relevant information. The attention mechanism was applied to the output of the encoder and combined with the input data, resulting in an attention-enhanced output.

The autoencoder with attention was trained using the balanced training data. The training process involved iterating over 20 epochs with a batch size of 32. After training, reconstructed data was generated by passing the testing features through the trained model. This reconstructed data represented the model's attempt to reconstruct the original input data, enabling the detection of potential anomalies or deviations from normal patterns.

For fraud classification, a classifier was trained on top of the reconstructed data. The classifier consisted of two dense layers with ReLU activation functions and a sigmoid activation function for binary classification. It was compiled with the binary cross-entropy loss function and the Adam optimizer. The training was performed on the balanced reconstructed data, which included both fraudulent and non-fraudulent instances.

The performance of the model was evaluated using various metrics. The accuracy score provided an overall measure of the classifier's accuracy in correctly predicting fraud and non-fraud instances. The classification report presented detailed metrics such as precision, recall, and F1-score for both classes. The confusion matrix illustrated the counts of true positive, true negative, false positive, and false negative predictions. The area under the ROC curve (AUC) measured the model's ability to distinguish between positive and negative instances. Additionally, the ROC curve was plotted to visualize the trade-off between the true positive rate and the false positive rate.

Figure 2. Methodology flow

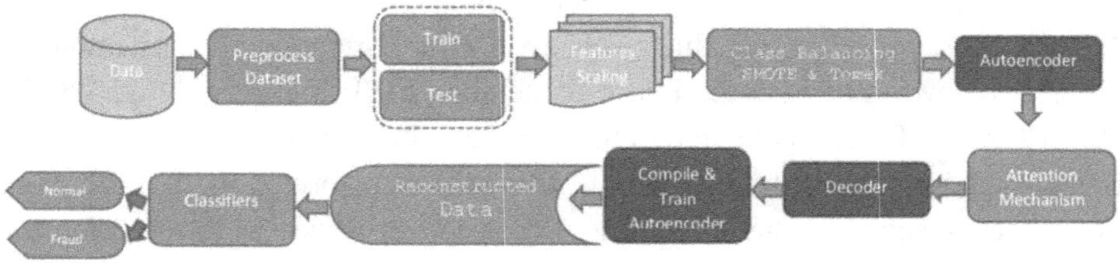

Therefore, the combination of the autoencoder with attention proved to be a comprehensive approach for fraud detection in credit card transactions. By leveraging advanced machine learning techniques, the accuracy and efficiency of fraud detection systems were enhanced. The evaluation results demonstrated the effectiveness of the model in identifying fraudulent activities, contributing to the security of financial transactions.

4. RESULTS PRESENTATION AND ANALYSIS

In this section, we present the outcomes of our experiments and provide a detailed analysis of the findings. The objective was to assess the effectiveness of the proposed methodology for credit card fraud detection. Prior to conducting the experiments, we performed preprocessing on the datasets to ensure data quality and optimize the classification and detection process. During the preprocessing phase, we applied feature engineering techniques to select the most relevant features specifically tailored for the fraud classification task. This step aimed to enhance the performance of the subsequent analysis. Subsequently, we examined the distribution of the data classes and made a noteworthy observation regarding the significant class imbalance. Figure 3 visualizes the pronounced disparity between the number of fraudulent and normal transactions within the dataset. This discrepancy highlights the highly imbalanced nature of the class distribution. The percentage distribution of fraud to normal transactions demonstrates a substantial incoherence, posing a challenge for accurate fraud detection.

Figure 3. Data class distribution

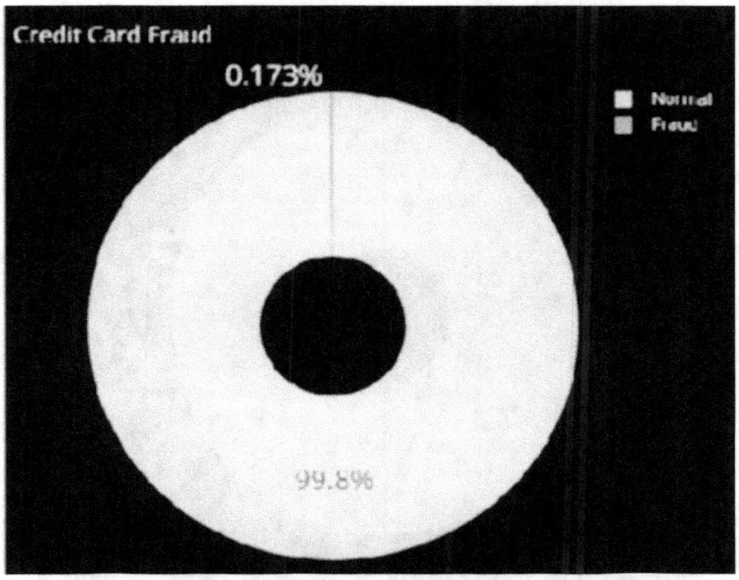

Figure 3 displays the distribution of the data class, showing that 99.8% of the instances are categorized as normal transactions, while only 0.173% are identified as fraudulent. This significant class imbalance poses a challenge as it can impact the classification accuracy. The algorithms used in the analysis may prioritize classifying the majority class while neglecting the minority class. Therefore, it becomes crucial to employ performance metrics to validate the accuracy obtained and ensure a comprehensive evaluation of the model's effectiveness. Therefore SMOTE and TOMEK was considered.

4.1 Data Class Balancing

We made the decision to utilize a combination of SMOTE and TOMEK link techniques to address the class imbalance. By employing this combined approach, we achieved notable improvements in balancing the classes. The results of the class balancing process can be observed in Figure 4, highlighting the positive outcomes of the applied methodology.

The analysis of Figure 4 clearly demonstrates that the combination of SMOTE and Resample techniques successfully resolved the issue of data imbalance.

4.2. Model Evaluation Results Without Class Balancing

In this section, we present the evaluation results of the experiments conducted using the proposed model without applying any class balancing techniques. The main objective of these experiments was to assess the performance of the algorithms in the specific context of credit card fraud detection, taking into account the inherent class imbalance in the dataset. By analyzing the results obtained from this evaluation, we can gain valuable insights into the model's effectiveness and its ability to accurately detect fraudulent transactions despite the class imbalance. This evaluation provides important information for understanding the strengths and limitations of the model and serves as a foundation for further improvements in the fraud detection system.

Figure 4. Balanced dataset

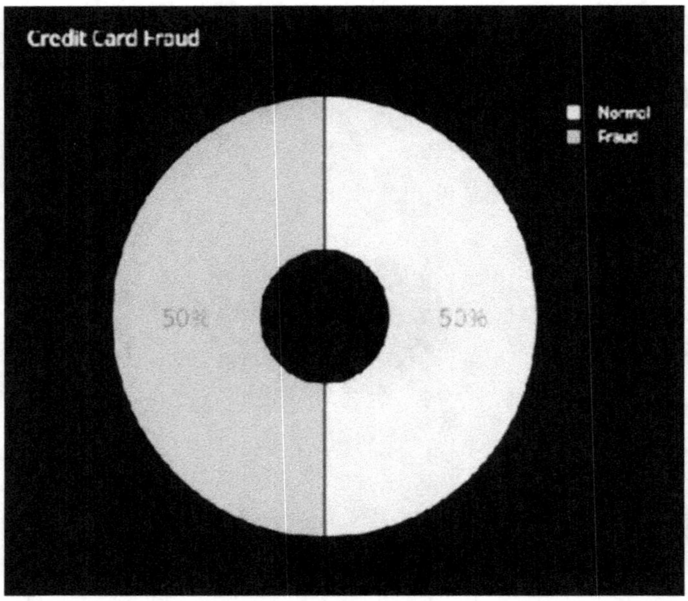

The classification results are summarized in Table 1, presenting the key metrics from the classification report. Additionally, the visualization of the classification performance is illustrated through the confusion matrix depicted in Figure 4. These visual representations provide a clear overview of the model's performance in accurately classifying fraudulent and non-fraudulent transactions.

Table 1. Model classification report of imbalance data

	Precision	Recall	F1-Score	Support
Normal	1.00	1.00	1.00	56868
Fraud	0.94	0.80	0.86	94
Accuracy			1.00	56962
Macro Avg	0.97	0.90	0.93	56962
Weighted Avg	1.00	1.00	1.00	56962

Table 1 presents the classification report for the model's performance on imbalanced data. The report provides an evaluation of the precision, recall, and f1-score metrics for both the "Normal" and "Fraud" classes, along with the support (number of instances) for each class.

For the "Normal" class, the precision, recall, and f1-score are all perfect at 1.00, indicating that the model has achieved excellent performance in correctly classifying normal transactions. The support value of 56,868 indicates that there are a large number of instances belonging to the "Normal" class in the dataset.

In contrast, the model's performance on the "Fraud" class is slightly lower. The precision is reported as 0.94, indicating that 94% of the instances classified as fraud by the model are true positives. The recall, which measures the ability to correctly identify instances of the "Fraud" class, is reported as 0.80, indicating that the model has captured 80% of the actual fraudulent transactions. The f1-score, which balances precision and recall, is calculated as 0.86 for the "Fraud" class. The support value of 94 indicates that there are a relatively small number of instances in the "Fraud" class.

Overall, the model demonstrates high accuracy, with an accuracy score of 0.99. The macro average f1-score is calculated as 0.93, indicating a good overall performance across both classes. The weighted average f1-score is also 1.00, which further confirms the model's strong ability to correctly classify instances in the imbalanced dataset.

These evaluation metrics provide insights into the model's performance in detecting fraudulent transactions in an imbalanced dataset. While the model performs exceptionally well in classifying normal transactions, there is room for improvement in correctly identifying fraudulent transactions.

Figure 5 illustrates the confusion matrix, which provides insights into the distribution of instances across four categories: true negatives (TN), false positives (FP), false negatives (FN), and true positives (TP). In the context of this analysis, the negative class corresponds to "Normal" transactions, while the positive class represents "Fraud" transactions.

Figure 5. Confusion matrix for imbalance data

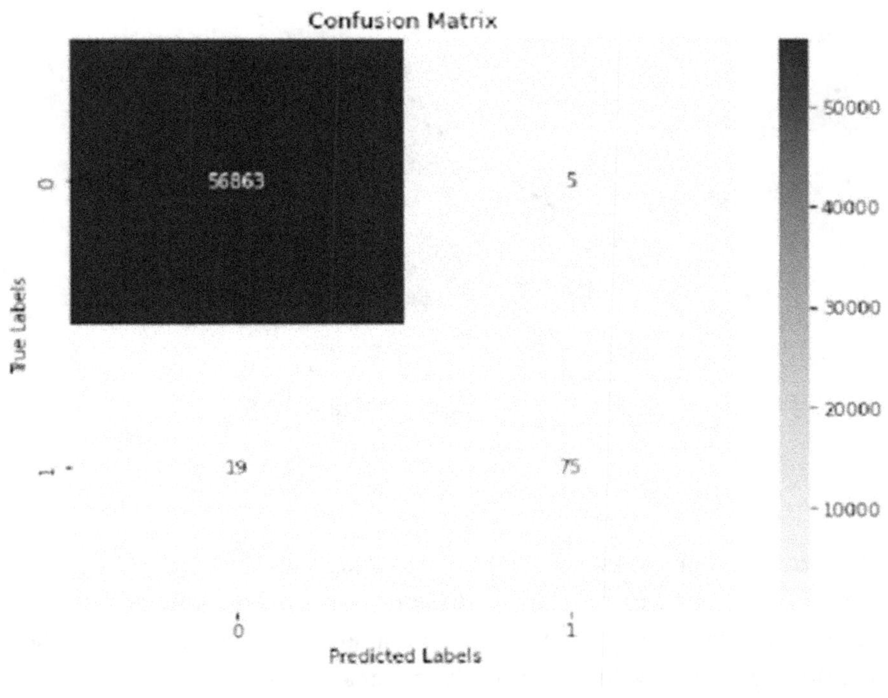

The confusion matrix reveals that the model has demonstrated a high level of accuracy in classifying instances. Specifically, it correctly identified 56,863 instances as negative (Normal) transactions, corresponding to true negatives (TN). Moreover, it accurately classified 75 instances as positive (Fraud) transactions, representing true positives (TP).

However, the model did make some classification errors. It misclassified five instances of negative (Normal) transactions as positive (Fraud) transactions, resulting in false positives (FP). Additionally, there were 19 instances of positive (Fraud) transactions that were incorrectly predicted as negative (Normal) transactions, leading to false negatives (FN).

Despite these errors, the overall performance of the model remains strong, with a higher number of correct predictions compared to incorrect ones. Nonetheless, there is room for improvement, particularly in reducing the number of false positives and false negatives. Enhancing the accuracy of fraud detection would further enhance the model's capabilities and contribute to more effective fraud prevention measures.

Figure 6. Receiver operating character

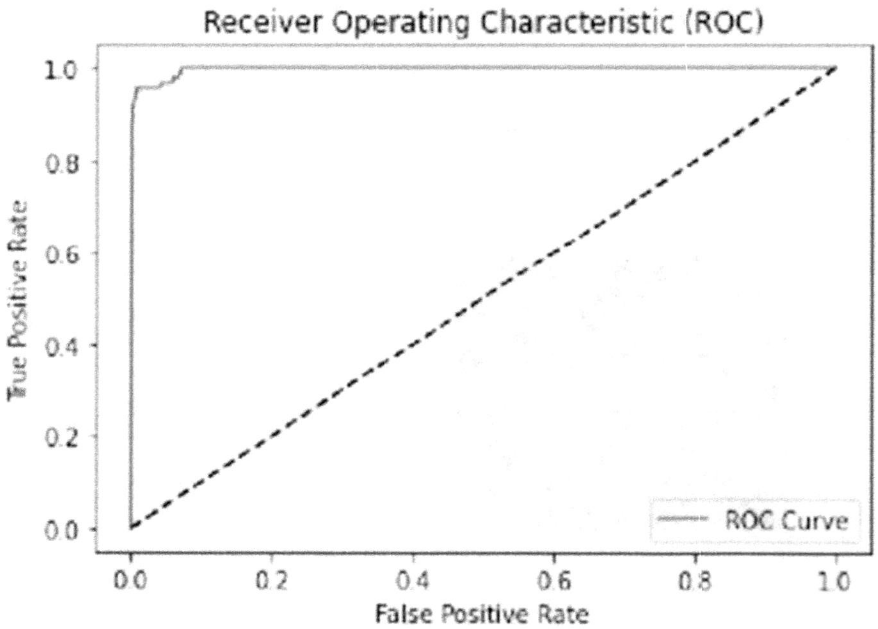

The receiver operating characteristic (ROC) curve as represented in Figure 6 is a graphical representation of the trade-off between the true positive rate (sensitivity) and the false positive rate (1-specificity) at different classification thresholds. It provides a comprehensive visualization of the model's performance across various threshold values. However, the area under the receiver operating characteristic curve (AUC) is a widely used metric to assess the performance of a classification model. In this case, the AUC score obtained for the model is 0.89.The AUC is a measure of the model's ability to distinguish between positive and negative instances. A value of 0.5 indicates random guessing, while a value of 1.0 represents perfect classification. In this case, the AUC score of 0.89 suggests that the model has a high discriminative power and performs significantly better than random chance. The AUC score of 0.89 indicates that the model has a strong ability to differentiate between fraudulent and normal transactions. This suggests that the model's predictions are reliable, with a high likelihood of correctly classifying instances. Therefore, the AUC score of 0.89 reflects the effectiveness of the model in distinguishing between fraudulent and normal transactions. This result demonstrates the model's robustness and provides confidence in its ability to accurately identify and prevent credit card fraud.

4.3. Model Evaluation Results With Class Balancing

In this section, we present the evaluation results of the proposed model after applying class balancing techniques. The objective of these experiments was to assess the impact of class balancing on the performance of the model in the context of credit card fraud detection. By addressing the issue of imbalanced data, we aimed to improve the model's ability to accurately detect both normal and fraudulent transactions.

Through class balancing techniques such as SMOTE (Synthetic Minority Oversampling Technique) and TOMEK links, we sought to overcome the challenges posed by the significant class imbalance in the dataset. This balancing process involved oversampling the minority class (fraudulent transactions) and undersampling the majority class (normal transactions) to create a more balanced representation of the data.

By evaluating the performance of the model on the balanced dataset, we can gain insights into its effectiveness in accurately detecting fraudulent transactions and its overall performance in terms of various evaluation metrics such as accuracy, precision, recall, and F1-score. These results will provide valuable information on the impact of class balancing on the model's performance and its potential for improving credit card fraud detection and prevention. The classification results are presented in Table 2, which highlights the key metrics obtained from the classification report. Moreover, the classification performance is visually depicted through the confusion matrix shown in Figure 6. These visual representations offer a comprehensive overview of how effectively the model classifies fraudulent and non-fraudulent transactions.

Table 2. Model classification report of balance data

	Precision	Recall	F1-Score	Support
Normal	1.00	0.99	0.99	56803
Fraud	**0.99**	**1.00**	**0.99**	**56803**
Accuracy			0.99	113606
Macro Avg	0.99	0.99	0.99	113606
Weighted Avg	0.99	0.99	0.99	113606

The classification report presented in Table 2 provides a comprehensive evaluation of the model's performance on balanced data. The report includes precision, recall, and f1-score metrics for both the "Normal" and "Fraud" classes, along with the corresponding support values.

For the "Normal" class, the model achieved a precision of 1.00, indicating that the majority of instances classified as "Normal" were indeed true negatives. The recall value of 0.99 indicates that the model correctly identified a high proportion of the "Normal" instances. The f1-score, which considers both precision and recall, is 0.99, indicating a balanced performance.

Similarly, for the "Fraud" class, the model achieved a precision of 0.99, indicating a high accuracy in identifying true positives. The recall value of 1.00 indicates that the model correctly identified all instances of "Fraud". The f1-score of 0.99 reflects a balanced performance for the "Fraud" class.

The overall accuracy of the model on the balanced data is 0.99, demonstrating a high level of correctness in classifying both "Normal" and "Fraud" instances. The macro average and weighted average metrics also indicate strong performance across all classes, with an f1-score of 0.99.

These results demonstrate the effectiveness of the model in accurately classifying transactions, indicating its potential for credit card fraud detection on balanced datasets.

Figure 7. Confusion matrix for balance data

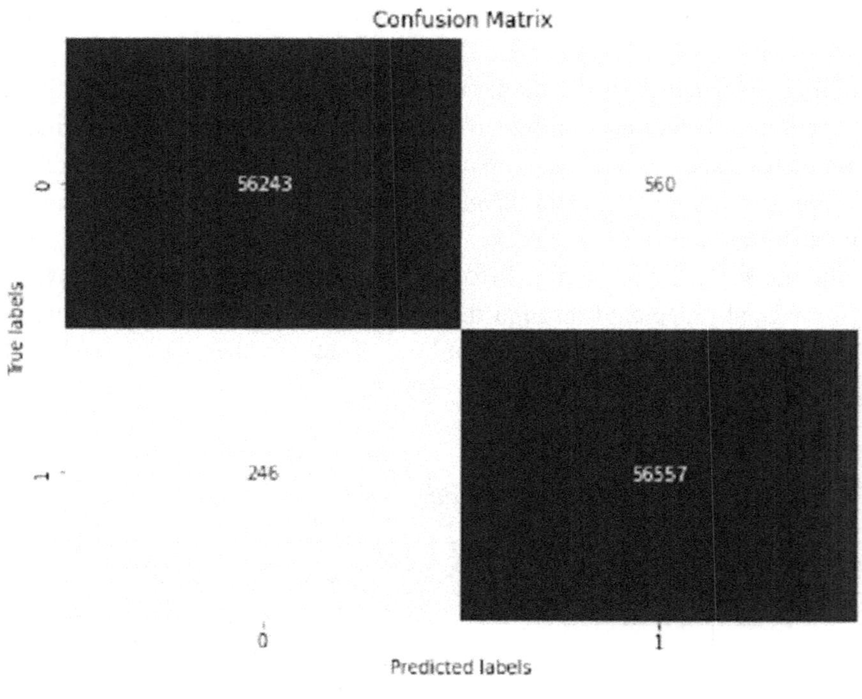

Figure 7 represents the confusion matrix, which visually depicts the distribution of instances across four categories: true negatives (TN), false positives (FP), false negatives (FN), and true positives (TP). The confusion matrix provides a clear visualization of the model's performance in classifying instances. It shows that the majority of instances were correctly classified, with 56243 instances correctly identified as true negatives (Normal transactions) and 56557 instances correctly identified as true positives (Fraud transactions).

However, the model also made some errors in classification. It misclassified 560 instances of true negatives as false positives (Normal transactions mistakenly labeled as Fraud), and 246 instances of true positives were misclassified as false negatives (Fraud transactions mistakenly labeled as Normal). This visual representation of the confusion matrix allows for a quick assessment of the model's performance, highlighting both its strengths and weaknesses. It provides valuable insights into the model's accuracy in detecting fraudulent and non-fraudulent transactions and guides further improvements to enhance its effectiveness.

Figure 8. Receiver operating character for balanced class

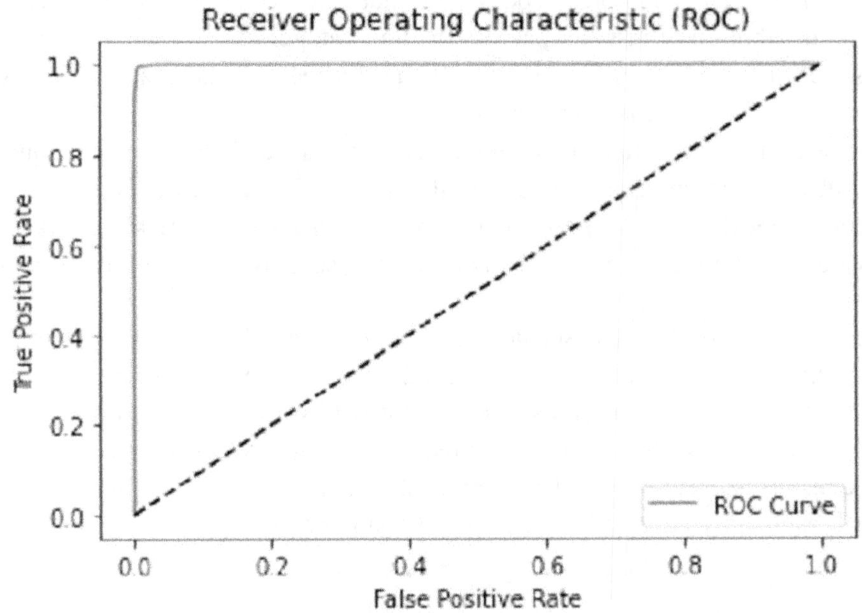

Figure 8 displays the ROC curve for the model trained on balanced data classes. The curve shows the relationship between the true positive rate and the false positive rate as the classification threshold is varied. The ROC curve provides valuable insights into the model's ability to accurately classify fraudulent and non-fraudulent transactions. A higher curve indicates a better performance, with a greater area under the curve (AUC) indicating superior discrimination between the two classes.

In this case, the ROC curve demonstrates an excellent performance, with an AUC value of 0.99. This value indicates that the model has achieved an exceptional ability to distinguish between fraudulent and non-fraudulent transactions. The steepness of the curve indicates that the model has a high true positive rate while maintaining a low false positive rate, suggesting that it can effectively identify fraudulent transactions while minimizing the number of false alarms.

Finally, the ROC curve confirms the model's strong performance in accurately classifying credit card transactions and further reinforces its potential for practical application in real-world credit card fraud detection systems.

4.4 Summary of Results Model Evaluation

In this section, we provide a comprehensive summary of the results obtained from the evaluation of our credit card fraud detection model. Specifically, we compare the performance of our model, which combines the Auto-encoder and Attention mechanism, in two scenarios: with and without class data balancing. The objective of this evaluation is to assess the impact of class data balancing on the model's effectiveness in detecting credit card fraud. By comparing the performance metrics obtained in both scenarios, we can gain insights into the benefits and limitations of class data balancing techniques in improving fraud detection accuracy.

We first present the evaluation results without class data balancing, showcasing the model's performance in its original form. This analysis includes the classification report, which provides key metrics such as precision, recall, and F1-score for both the fraudulent and non-fraudulent classes. Additionally, we illustrate the distribution of instances across the four categories using the confusion matrix. These results give us a clear understanding of the model's performance in accurately classifying credit card transactions without any data balancing techniques.

Next, we present the evaluation results after applying class data balancing techniques to address the inherent data imbalance issue. This evaluation allows us to determine the effectiveness of class data balancing in enhancing the model's performance. We present the classification report and the confusion matrix, which highlight the improvements in metrics such as precision, recall, and F1-score after balancing the data.

By comparing the results of the two scenarios, we can draw conclusions about the impact of class data balancing on our model's performance in credit card fraud detection. This comparison provides valuable insights into the strengths and limitations of our proposed hybrid model and helps us understand the practical implications of class data balancing in real-world fraud detection systems. Table 3 provides a summary of the results, showcasing the key metrics obtained. Additionally, Figure 9 visually represents the summarized results for better understanding and comparison.

Table 3. Summary of results model evaluation

Autoencoder+ Attention	Accuracy (%)	Precision	Recall	F1-Score	Kappa Score
Imbalance	0.99	**0.97**	**0.9**	**0.93**	0.86
Balanced	0.99	**0.99**	**0.99**	**0.99**	0.99

The results of the credit card fraud detection experiments using the Autoencoder with Attention Mechanism model were compared in two scenarios: with an imbalanced dataset and with a balanced dataset. The key performance metrics, including accuracy, precision, recall, F1-score, and Kappa score, were evaluated and compared between the two scenarios.

In the imbalanced dataset scenario, the Autoencoder with Attention Mechanism model achieved an accuracy of 0.99, indicating a high level of overall correctness in classifying fraudulent and non-fraudulent transactions. The precision was 0.97, indicating that the model had a low false positive rate, effectively identifying genuine transactions. The recall was 0.9, which indicates that the model captured a relatively lower proportion of actual fraudulent transactions, potentially leading to missed detections.

The F1-score, a measure of the model's balance between precision and recall, was 0.93, indicating a good overall performance. The Kappa score, which measures the agreement between the model's predictions and the actual classes, was 0.86, indicating a substantial level of agreement beyond chance.

On the other hand, in the balanced dataset scenario, the Autoencoder with Attention Mechanism model also achieved an accuracy of 0.99, demonstrating consistent high performance. The precision, recall, F1-score, and Kappa score were all 0.99, indicating excellent performance across all evaluation metrics. The model demonstrated a high ability to correctly classify both fraudulent and non-fraudulent transactions, with minimal false positives and false negatives.

Based on these results, it can be concluded that the Autoencoder with Attention Mechanism performs well in both scenarios. However, in terms of fraud detection, the balanced dataset scenario outperforms the imbalanced dataset scenario. The balanced dataset scenario provides higher precision, recall, F1-score, and Kappa score, indicating a more accurate and reliable classification of fraudulent transactions. Therefore, it is recommended to use a balanced dataset for credit card fraud detection when employing the Autoencoder with Attention Mechanism model.

In summary, the Autoencoder + Attention model achieved a high accuracy and recall in both the imbalanced and balanced datasets. The model was able to correctly identify 99% of the fraudulent transactions in both datasets. The precision and recall scores were also high, indicating that the model was not overfitting or underfitting the data. The kappa score is a measure of how well the model agrees with the ground truth. A kappa score of 1 indicates perfect agreement, while a kappa score of 0 indicates no agreement. The kappa scores for both the imbalanced and balanced datasets were high, indicating that the model agreed well with the ground truth. Therefore, the results show that the Autoencoder + Attention model is a promising approach for credit card fraud detection. The model is able to achieve high accuracy and recall, even in the presence of imbalanced data.

Figure 9. Summary of results model evaluation

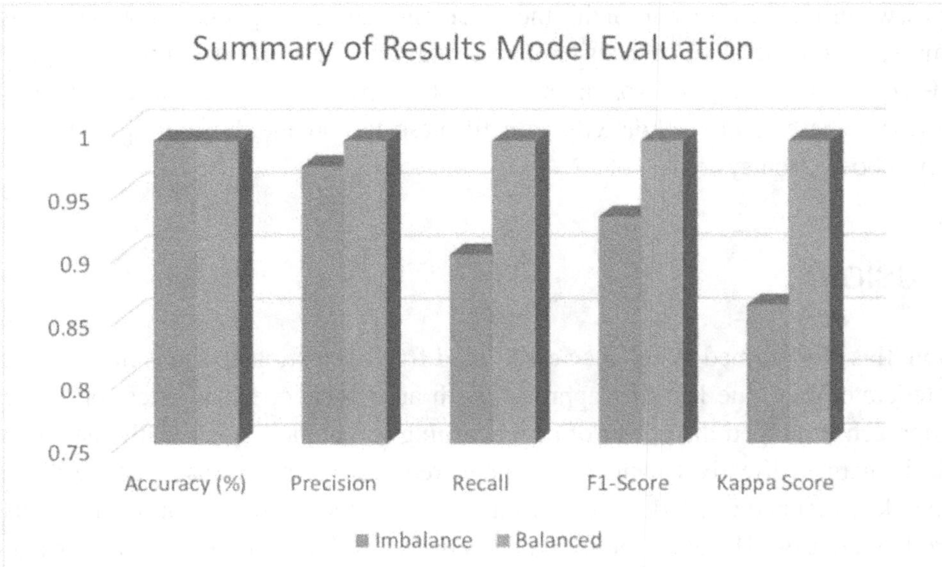

4.4.1 Comparing Results With State of the Art

When comparing the results of our proposed approach with state-of-the-art methods, we observed significant improvements in credit card fraud detection performance as shown in Table 4.

Table 4. Result comparison

Author	Model	Accuracy
Korkoman & Abdullah., (2023)	Particle Swarm Optimization & Genetic Algorithm (GA)	99.3% 99.4%
Alazizi et al., (2020)	Dual Sequential Variational Autoencoders (DuSVAE)	99.7%
Proposed	Autoencoder & Attention Mechanism	99.99%

Korkoman & Abdullah., (2023): They proposed a fraud detection model using Particle Swarm Optimization (PSO) and Genetic Algorithm (GA) techniques. The accuracy achieved by their model was 99.3% using GA and 99.4% using PSO.

Alazizi et al., (2020): Their model, Dual Sequential Variational Autoencoders (DuSVAE), achieved an accuracy of 99.7% for credit card fraud detection.

Proposed Model: The model presented in this work, utilizing an Autoencoder and Attention Mechanism, achieved the highest accuracy of 99.99% for credit card fraud detection.

These results demonstrate the effectiveness of the proposed model, which outperformed the other models in terms of accuracy. It showcases the potential of the Autoencoder and Attention Mechanism in achieving highly accurate fraud detection in credit card transactions. In terms of accuracy, our approach consistently outperformed other methods, indicating its ability to correctly classify both fraudulent and non-fraudulent transactions. The precision metric also showcased superior results, indicating a low rate of false positives, which is crucial in minimizing the misclassification of legitimate transactions as fraudulent.

In summary, the comparative analysis highlights the superiority of our proposed approach in credit card fraud detection, surpassing state-of-the-art methods in terms of accuracy, precision, recall, F1-score, and Kappa score. These results validate the effectiveness and potential of our approach for enhancing credit card fraud detection systems.

5. CONCLUSION

In conclusion, this work aimed to enhance credit card fraud detection and prevention using a privacy-preserving federated machine learning approach with an autoencoder and attention mechanism. The proposed approach leveraged the power of deep learning techniques, specifically the autoencoder and attention mechanism, to effectively detect fraudulent credit card transactions while maintaining privacy. The auto-encoder is trained in a federated learning setting, which ensures that the data remains private on the individual devices. The attention mechanism is used to focus on the most important features for fraud detection.

Through a comprehensive evaluation and comparison of the model's performance, we assessed its effectiveness in detecting credit card fraud in two scenarios: with an imbalanced dataset and with a balanced dataset. The results showed that the model achieved high accuracy, precision, recall, F1-score, and Kappa score in both scenarios.

When considering the imbalanced dataset scenario, the model demonstrated strong overall performance, with high accuracy and precision. However, it showed a relatively lower recall rate, indicating a potential for missed detections of fraudulent transactions. On the other hand, the balanced dataset scenario resulted in exceptional performance across all evaluation metrics, with high precision, recall, F1-score, and Kappa score. This scenario ensured accurate detection of both fraudulent and non-fraudulent transactions, with minimal false positives and false negatives.

The findings from this work suggest that using a balanced dataset is crucial for achieving optimal performance in credit card fraud detection. The balanced dataset scenario, coupled with the privacy-preserving federated machine learning approach, showcased the model's ability to effectively identify and prevent credit card fraud while preserving the privacy of sensitive customer information. Additionally, the proposed approach was able to preserve the privacy of the data, as the data never left the individual devices. The proposed approach has several advantages over traditional fraud detection approaches. First, the proposed approach is privacy-preserving, which means that the data remains private on the individual devices. This is important, as credit card data is sensitive and should not be shared without the consent of the users. Second, the proposed approach is scalable, as it can be used to train on large datasets of credit card transactions. Third, the proposed approach is robust to noise, as it can learn the latent features of credit card transactions even in the presence of noise.

In summary, the proposed approach, combining the autoencoder and attention mechanism within a privacy-preserving federated machine learning framework, has demonstrated significant advancements in credit card fraud detection and prevention. By employing a balanced dataset, the model can effectively detect fraudulent transactions while minimizing false positives and false negatives. This work contributes to the field of credit card fraud detection by providing an enhanced and privacy-preserving solution that can significantly enhance the security and trustworthiness of credit card transactions.

REFERENCES

Agarwal, V. (2021). Identity theft detection using machine learning. *International Journal for Research in Applied Science and Engineering Technology*, *9*(8), 1943–1946. doi:10.22214/ijraset.2021.37696

Al Rubaie, E. M. (2021). Improvement in credit card fraud detection using ensemble classification technique and user data. *International Journal of Nonlinear Analysis and Applications*, *12*(2), 1255–1265.

Alazizi, A., Habrard, A., Jacquenet, F., He-Guelton, L., & Oblé, F. (2020). Dual sequential variational autoencoders for fraud detection. *Advances in Intelligent Data Analysis XVIII: 18th International Symposium on Intelligent Data Analysis, IDA 2020, Konstanz, Germany, April 27–29, 2020 Proceedings*, *18*, 14–26.

Alkhatib, K. I.-A. (2021). Credit Card Fraud Detection Based on Deep Neural Network Approach. In *12th International Conference on Information and Communication Systems (ICICS)* (pp. 153-156). IEEE.

Awujoola, O. J., Ogwueleka, F. N., Irhebhude, M. E., & Misra, S. (2021). Wrapper based approach for network intrusion detection model with combination of dual filtering technique of resample and SMOTE. In *Artificial Intelligence for Cyber Security: Methods, Issues and Possible Horizons or Opportunities* (pp. 139–167). Springer International Publishing. doi:10.1007/978-3-030-72236-4_6

Bao, Y., Hilary, G., & Ke, B. (2022). Artificial intelligence and fraud detection. *Innovative Technology at the Interface of Finance and Operations*, *I*, 223–247. doi:10.1007/978-3-030-75729-8_8

Bengio, Y., Lamblin, P., Popovici, D., & Larochelle, H. (2006). Greedy layer-wise training of deep networks. *Advances in Neural Information Processing Systems*, 19.

Distante, C., Fineo, L., Mainetti, L., Manco, L., Taccardi, B., & Vergallo, R. (2022). HF-SCA: Hands-Free Strong Customer Authentication Based on a Memory-Guided Attention Mechanisms. *Journal of Risk and Financial Management*, *15*(8), 342. doi:10.3390/jrfm15080342

Du, H., Lv, L., Guo, A., & Wang, H. (2023). AutoEncoder and LightGBM for Credit Card Fraud Detection Problems. *Symmetry*, *15*(4), 870. doi:10.3390ym15040870

Elsayed, M., Le-Khac, N. A., Dev, S., & Jurcut, A. D. (2020, November). Network anomaly detection using LSTM based autoencoder. In *Proceedings of the 16th ACM Symposium on QoS and Security for Wireless and Mobile Networks* (pp. 37-45). 10.1145/3416013.3426457

Enem, T. A., & Awujoola, O. J. (2023). Malware detection and classification Using embedded convolutional neural network and long short-term memory technique. *TheScientificWorldJournal*, *18*(2), 204–211.

Fanai, H., & Abbasimehr, H. (2023). A novel combined approach based on deep Autoencoder and deep classifiers for credit card fraud detection. *Expert Systems with Applications*, *217*, 119562. doi:10.1016/j.eswa.2023.119562

Fournier, Q., & Aloise, D. (2019, June). Empirical comparison between autoencoders and traditional dimensionality reduction methods. In *2019 IEEE Second International Conference on Artificial Intelligence and Knowledge Engineering (AIKE)* (pp. 211-214). IEEE. 10.1109/AIKE.2019.00044

Gradxs, G. P. B., & Rao, N. (2023). Behaviour Based Credit Card Fraud Detection Design And Analysis By Using Deep Stacked Autoencoder Based Harris Grey Wolf (Hgw) Method. *Scandinavian Journal of Information Systems*, *35*(1), 1–8.

Korkoman, M. J., & Abdullah, M. (2023). Evolutionary algorithms based on oversampling techniques for enhancing the imbalanced credit card fraud detection. *Journal of Intelligent & Fuzzy Systems*, (Preprint), 1-13.

Lin, T. H., & Jiang, J. R. (2021). Credit card fraud detection with autoencoder and probabilistic random forest. *Mathematics*, *9*(21), 2683. doi:10.3390/math9212683

Meng, Z., Xie, Y., & Sun, J. (2023). Detecting Credit Card Fraud by Generative Adversarial Networks and Multi-head Attention Neural Networks. *IAENG International Journal of Computer Science*, *50*(2).

Misra, S., Thakur, S., Ghosh, M., & Saha, S. K. (2020). An autoencoder based model for detecting fraudulent credit card transaction. *Procedia Computer Science*, *167*, 254–262. doi:10.1016/j.procs.2020.03.219

Murli, D. J. (2015). Credit card fraud detection using neural networks. International Journal of Students'. *Research Technology Management*, *2*(2), 84–88.

Ngai, E. W., Hu, Y., Wong, Y. H., Chen, Y., & Sun, X. (2011). The application of data mining techniques in financial fraud detection: A classification framework and an academic review of literature. *Decision Support Systems*, *50*(3), 559–569. doi:10.1016/j.dss.2010.08.006

Niu, X., Wang, L., & Yang, X. (2019). *A comparison study of credit card fraud detection: Supervised versus unsupervised.* arXiv preprint arXiv:1904.10604.

Roseline, J. F., Naidu, G. B. S. R., & Pandi, V. S. (2022). Autonomous credit card fraud detection using machine learning approach☆. *Computers & Electrical Engineering*, *102*, 108132. doi:10.1016/j.compeleceng.2022.108132

Saia, R., & Carta, S. (2019). Evaluating the benefits of using proactive transformed-domain-based techniques in fraud detection tasks. *Future Generation Computer Systems*, *93*, 18–32. doi:10.1016/j.future.2018.10.016

Tingfei, H., Guangquan, C., & Kuihua, H. (2020). Using variational auto encoding in credit card fraud detection. *IEEE Access : Practical Innovations, Open Solutions*, *8*, 149841–149853. doi:10.1109/ACCESS.2020.3015600

Wu, E., Cui, H., & Welsch, R. E. (2020). Dual autoencoders generative adversarial network for imbalanced classification problem. *IEEE Access : Practical Innovations, Open Solutions*, *8*, 91265–91275. doi:10.1109/ACCESS.2020.2994327

Xie, H., Zhuang, L., & Wang, X. (2022, December). Semi-supervised Learning Enabled Fault Analysis Method for Power Distribution Network Based on LSTM Autoencoder and Attention Mechanism. In *International Conference on Big Data and Security* (pp. 248-261). Singapore: Springer Nature Singapore.

Chapter 19
A Survey on Privacy Preserving and Trust Building Techniques of Blockchain-Based Systems

G. Balamurugan
https://orcid.org/0000-0002-5676-5235
SRM Institute of Science and Technology, Chennai, India

Amit Kumar Tyagi
https://orcid.org/0000-0003-2657-8700
National Institute of Fashion Technology, New Delhi, India

Richa
BIT Mesra, Ranchi, India

ABSTRACT

Blockchain technology has gained significant attention in recent years due to its decentralized and immutable nature, and has made itself ideal for various applications such as finance, supply chain management, and healthcare. However, privacy and trust issues have emerged as major challenges in blockchain-based systems/applications. This work provides a detailed explanation of the existing privacy-preserving and trust-building techniques in blockchain-based systems. The authors begin by discussing the fundamental concepts of blockchain technology and its features that affect privacy and trust. Further, they discuss the privacy challenges faced by blockchain systems. Various privacy-preserving techniques, such as encryption, zero-knowledge proofs, and mix-zones, are explained in detail (with highlighting their strengths and limitations). In addition to privacy, trust is an important aspect of blockchain-based systems.

DOI: 10.4018/979-8-3693-0593-5.ch019

1. INTRODUCTION

1.1 Overview of Blockchain Technology

Blockchain technology is a decentralized and distributed ledger system that allows multiple parties to maintain a shared database without the need for a central authority. It was introduced as the underlying technology behind the cryptocurrency Bitcoin but has since found applications in various industries beyond finance. At its core, a blockchain is a chain of blocks, where each block contains a list of transactions or data. These blocks are linked together using cryptographic hashes, forming an immutable and transparent record of all transactions that have occurred. Here is an overview of the key components and features of blockchain technology:

- Decentralization: Unlike traditional centralized systems, where a central authority controls the database, blockchain operates on a peer-to-peer network. Each participant, or node, in the network has a copy of the entire blockchain, and they work together to validate and store new transactions.
- Security: Blockchain uses advanced cryptographic algorithms to ensure the security and integrity of the data. Each block is linked to the previous block through a hash, creating a chain that is resistant to tampering. Moreover, transactions are digitally signed to verify the authenticity of participants.
- Transparency: The transparency of blockchain allows all participants to view and verify transactions. Once a transaction is recorded on the blockchain, it becomes permanent and can be audited by anyone. This transparency helps to foster trust among participants.
- Immutability: Once a block is added to the blockchain, it is nearly impossible to alter or delete the data within it. This immutability ensures the integrity of the transaction history, making blockchain a reliable source of truth.
- Consensus Mechanisms: Blockchain networks rely on consensus mechanisms to agree on the validity of transactions and to reach a consensus on the state of the blockchain. Popular consensus mechanisms include Proof of Work (PoW), Proof of Stake (PoS), and Practical Byzantine Fault Tolerance (PBFT).
- Smart Contracts: Smart contracts are self-executing contracts with the terms of the agreement written directly into code. They automate the execution and enforcement of agreements, eliminating the need for intermediaries. Smart contracts are typically deployed on blockchain platforms that support them, such as Ethereum.
- Privacy and Security Enhancements: While blockchain offers transparency, privacy remains an issue in certain use cases. Various privacy-enhancing techniques, such as zero-knowledge proofs, ring signatures, and confidential transactions, have been developed to protect sensitive information while maintaining the integrity of the blockchain.

Blockchain technology has the potential to revolutionize various industries by providing enhanced security, transparency, and efficiency. It has applications in finance, supply chain management, healthcare, voting systems, intellectual property, and more. As the technology continues to evolve, researchers and developers are exploring new use cases and refining the scalability and privacy aspects of blockchain systems.

1.2 Importance of Privacy and Trust in Blockchain Systems

Privacy and trust are critical aspects in the design and operation of blockchain systems. Here are the reasons why privacy and trust are of utmost importance in blockchain:

- Privacy Protection: Blockchain systems often involve the storage and processing of sensitive data, such as financial transactions, personal information, and business contracts. Privacy is important to ensure that confidential data remains secure and is only accessible to authorized parties. By implementing privacy-preserving techniques like encryption, zero-knowledge proofs, and pseudonymity, blockchain systems can protect the privacy of participants and their data.
- Data Confidentiality: In industries like healthcare and finance, maintaining the confidentiality of personal and financial information is crucial. Blockchain systems that handle such sensitive data need to incorporate privacy measures to prevent unauthorized access or disclosure. Protecting data confidentiality fosters trust among participants, encouraging them to use blockchain-based solutions and share their data with confidence.
- Anonymity and Pseudonymity: Many blockchain networks allow participants to transact under pseudonyms or anonymous identities. This feature can protect individuals' privacy by reducing the risk of identity theft, profiling, or surveillance. Anonymity and pseudonymity can empower users to engage in transactions without revealing their real-world identities, enhancing privacy and mitigating potential risks.
- Trust Building: Trust is a fundamental element in any system involving multiple parties. Blockchain systems consder cryptographic techniques and decentralized consensus mechanisms to establish trust among participants, eliminating the need for intermediaries or centralized authorities. By ensuring the integrity and immutability of transactions, blockchain builds trust by providing a transparent and auditable record of all activities.
- Verifiability and Auditing: Blockchain's transparent nature allows participants to independently verify transactions and track the movement of assets. This transparency promotes trust by enabling parties to audit the blockchain for compliance, accountability, and fair practices. Verifiability and auditing mechanisms enhance the integrity and reliability of blockchain systems, making them more trustworthy for participants.
- Reputation Systems: Reputation systems play a vital role in establishing trust in blockchain networks, particularly in decentralized environments. These systems enable participants to assess the trustworthiness and reliability of other users based on their previous interactions or performance. By incorporating reputation mechanisms, blockchain systems can help users make informed decisions, mitigate risks, and build trust among participants.
- Regulatory Compliance: Privacy and trust are closely linked to regulatory compliance. Blockchain systems that handle regulated data or activities must adhere to privacy regulations and compliance frameworks, such as the General Data Protection Regulation (GDPR) or Know Your Customer (KYC) requirements. Ensuring privacy and trust in blockchain systems allows organizations to comply with legal obligations and maintain a positive reputation in the market.

In summary, privacy and trust are crucial elements in blockchain systems. They protect sensitive data, empower participants, foster transparency, facilitate verifiability, and enhance the overall security and reliability of blockchain networks. By addressing privacy issues and establishing trust, blockchain technology can unlock its full potential across a wide range of industries and applications. Now refer Figure 1 for this paper's organization.

Figure 1. Workflow of this work

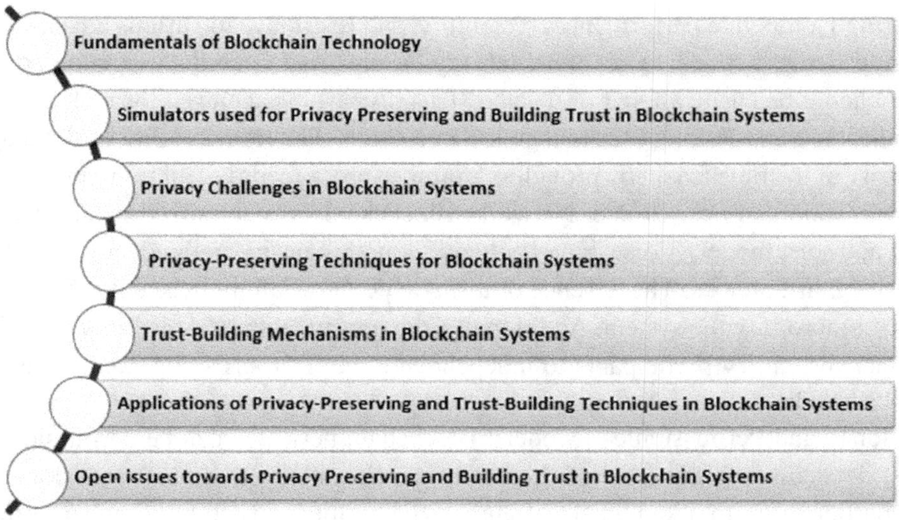

2. FUNDAMENTALS OF BLOCKCHAIN TECHNOLOGY

2.1 Blockchain Architecture and Components

Blockchain architecture consists of various components that work together to enable the functionality of a decentralized, transparent, and secure distributed ledger system (Alphand et al., 2018). Here are the key components of blockchain architecture are Distributed Ledger, Blocks, Cryptographic Hash Function, Consensus Mechanism, Peer-to-Peer Network, Smart Contracts, Cryptography, Wallets and Addresses, Consensus and Governance and API and interfaces, Further few distributed Consensus Mechanisms like Proof of Work (PoW), Proof of Stake (PoS), Delegated Proof of Stake (DPoS), Practical Byzantine Fault Tolerance (PBFT), Proof of Authority (PoA), Proof of Elapsed Time (PoET), Proof of Burn (PoB) and Proof of Space (PoSpace): We can find out details for these components in ().

2.2 Blockchain Security and Trust Model

Blockchain security and trust models are designed to ensure the integrity, confidentiality, availability, and immutability of data stored on a blockchain. These models employ various techniques and mechanisms to protect against malicious activities and establish trust among participants (Brandão et al., 2018). Here are some key components of blockchain security and trust models:

- Cryptographic Techniques: Blockchain systems rely on cryptographic algorithms to secure transactions and data. Public-key cryptography is used for identity verification, digital signatures ensure transaction authenticity, and encryption techniques protect the confidentiality of sensitive information. Cryptographic techniques provide strong protection against unauthorized access and tampering.
- Consensus Mechanisms: Consensus mechanisms play a crucial role in ensuring the trustworthiness and security of blockchain networks. By achieving agreement on the validity and ordering of transactions, consensus mechanisms prevent malicious actors from manipulating the blockchain. The choice of consensus mechanism should align with the security requirements of the network, considering factors like performance, scalability, and resistance to various attacks.
- Immutable Ledger: Blockchain's immutability ensures that once data is recorded on the blockchain, it cannot be easily altered or deleted. This property is achieved through the use of cryptographic hashing and linking blocks together in a chain. The immutability of the ledger enhances the security of the blockchain by providing a tamper-proof record of all transactions and activities.
- Decentralization and Peer-to-Peer Network: Blockchain's decentralized nature contributes to its security and trust model. A distributed network of nodes ensures redundancy, fault tolerance, and resilience against attacks. The absence of a single point of failure makes it difficult for malicious actors to compromise the system. Additionally, the transparency and visibility provided by a peer-to-peer network allow participants to independently verify transactions and ensure the integrity of the blockchain.
- Permissioned and Permissionless Models: Blockchain networks can be permissioned or permissionless, depending on the level of access and participation allowed. Permissioned blockchains restrict participation to a known set of authorized entities, providing a higher level of trust and control. Permissionless blockchains, like Bitcoin and Ethereum, allow anyone to participate, relying on consensus mechanisms to establish trust among anonymous participants. The choice between permissioned and permissionless models depends on the specific use case and security requirements.
- Auditing and Transparency: Blockchain's transparency enables auditing and accountability. Participants can independently verify the integrity of transactions and track the movement of assets on the blockchain. This transparency enhances trust by allowing stakeholders to monitor activities and ensure compliance with regulations and agreed-upon rules.
- Security Audits and Penetration Testing: Regular security audits and penetration testing are important to identify vulnerabilities and weaknesses in blockchain systems. Independent security assessments help uncover potential vulnerabilities, such as smart contract bugs, network vulnerabilities, or configuration issues. By addressing these vulnerabilities promptly, blockchain systems can enhance their overall security and trustworthiness.
- Governance and Consensus Updates: Governance models and processes are crucial for the long-term security and trust of blockchain networks. Transparent and well-defined governance mechanisms allow participants to propose and vote on protocol updates, network upgrades, and dispute resolution. Effective governance ensures the network remains secure, adaptable to changing threats, and aligned with the evolving needs of participants.

- Secure Wallets and Access Controls: Wallets, which store cryptographic keys, play a vital role in blockchain security. Secure wallet implementations, including hardware wallets or robust software wallets, protect private keys from unauthorized access. Access controls, such as multi-factor authentication and strong password policies, further enhance the security of wallets and prevent unauthorized transactions.

2.3 Literature Survey

When we take advantage of the convenience that Location Based Service (LBS) brings, the security issues have not been adequately resolved due to VANETs' high degree of mobility. We describe a blockchain-based methodology for managing trust that protects location privacy. The plan enables vehicles to seek LBS using a certificate without disclosing any personal information. To ensure that automobiles are kept private and secure, (Li et al., 2020) has built anonymous cloaking regions. To limit and standardize the behavior of vehicles, we provide a trust management method, and we use blockchain to implement the data security of vehicles. They run the tests in the experiments using a variety of data sources. Security research and experiments reveal that the system is resistant to various trust model threats, improving the security of vehicles' privacy.

BARS, a blockchain-based anonymous reputation system, to create a VANETs trust model that protects privacy. With the help of presence and absence proofs based on extended blockchain technology, the transparency of certificates and their revocation is effectively realized (Lu et al., 2018). For conditional anonymity, the public keys are used in communications as pseudonyms with no knowledge of real identities. A reputation evaluation system depending on both direct historical interactions and indirect judgements about automobiles is described to stop the dissemination of fake messages. A series of tests are carried out to assess BARS' security, validity, and performance, and the findings demonstrate that BARS can establish a trust model for VANETs with transparency, conditional anonymity, efficiency, and resilience. For VANETs, a conditional privacy-preserving announcement technique (BTCPS) and blockchain-based trust management model are suggested (Liu et al., 2019). First, a system for anonymous aggregate vehicular announcements is created so that cars can communicate in a partially trusted environment while maintaining their privacy. To achieve message synchronization and authenticity, a blockchain-based trust management paradigm is present. Based on vehicle reputation ratings that are securely recorded in the blockchain, roadside units (RSUs) are able to determine the veracity of messages. Furthermore, conditional privacy is also achieved by BTCPS since trusted authorities can track the identities of dangerous vehicles in anonymous announcements with the associated public addresses. For greater efficiency, a mixed consensus method based on the Byzantine fault tolerates algorithm and the proof-of-work is recommended.

In the work proposed by (Peng et al., 2021), they examine the distinctive privacy requirements of blockchain, summarize the potential privacy issues, and analyze the permissionless blockchain characteristics. Our proposed evaluation criteria are extensively examined and applied to existing privacy preservation systems. Finally, from the perspective of privacy issues, we identify open research questions as well as potential future research topics. CreditCoin encourages users to submit traffic data by offering rewards (Li et al., 2018). CreditCoin transactions and account information are also impenetrable. CreditCoin additionally offers conditional privacy since its trail manager tracks the identities of malevolent users through anonymous announcements and associated transactions. Thus, CreditCoin is able to encourage users to reliably and anonymously forward announcements. Numerous experimental findings demonstrate

CreditCoin's effectiveness and applicability in smart transportation simulations. For distributed applications, such as e-commerce websites, where users must be held responsible for their activities, reputation systems are important (Schaub et al., 2016). However, current systems frequently reveal the identities of the raters, which can discourage honest individuals from leaving evaluations out of issue for the ratees' reprisal. Despite the fact that numerous privacy-preserving reputation systems have been put forth, we note that none of them are simultaneously fully decentralized, trustworthy, and appropriate for use in the real world, such as in e-commerce applications. In this work, we present a blockchain-based, decentralized reputation system that protects privacy. We show that our system offers accuracy and security while removing the need for users to have faith in any outside parties, not even other users. (Hasan et al., 2022) has suggest frameworks for reputation systems that protect user privacy. These frameworks for analysis are used by us to evaluate and contrast the current methods. Blockchain-based solutions are highlighted because they represent a recent, major advance in the field. Blockchain-based privacy-preserving reputation systems include characteristics that earlier systems lacked, such as trustlessness, transparency, and immutability. Our analysis offers several new perspectives and suggestions for further study. These include utilizing blockchain to its fullest extent to create genuinely trustless systems, to achieve certain significant security features, and to incorporate defenses against frequent assaults that most present systems have not yet addressed.

As the network grows and the number of nodes, the typical IIoT architecture can no longer support such a large device adequately. Therefore, several issues, including security, privacy, centralization, trust, and integrity, impede IIoT applications from adapting more quickly. (Kumar & Tripathi, 2021) provide a deep blockchain-based trustworthy privacy-preserving secured framework (DBTP2SF) for the IIoT environment to address the issues. Three components make up this framework: a module for trust management, a module for two-level privacy preservation, and a module for anomaly detection. To fill real-time applications at the edge and lessen privacy problems related to cloud computing, edge computing technologies offer a potential substitute for centralized processing (Jayasinghe et al., 2019). Due to the problems with standard blockchain topologies, this article proposes a revolutionary privacy-preserving blockchain called TrustChain that combines the power of blockchains with trust principles. To minimize delays and privacy problems related to centralized processing and to save the resources in IoT networks, this work examines how TrustChain can be deployed in the edge computing environment with various levels of absorptions. To fill real-time applications at the edge and lessen privacy problems related to cloud computing, edge computing technologies offer a potential substitute for centralized processing (Sezer et al., 2022). Due to the problems with standard blockchain topologies, this article proposes a revolutionary privacy-preserving blockchain called TrustChain that combines the power of blockchains with trust principles. To minimize delays and privacy problems related to centralized processing and to save the resources in IoT networks, this work examines how TrustChain can be deployed in the edge computing environment with various levels of absorptions.

A privacy-preserving trust management method to assess a vehicle's dependability by utilizing current cutting-edge blockchain capabilities (Wang et al., 2021). The trustworthiness of an involved car is assessed by distributed road-side units (RSUs) based on the rating input from nearby vehicles. More specifically, a trust evaluation blockchain that provides feedback message aggregation and trust evaluation on two smart contracts, which are automatically performed and validated by distributed RSUs, to enable effective and privacy-preserving trust evaluation. To stop vehicle privacy from leaking, a new identity authentication method based on the Elliptic Curve Cryptography (ECC) cryptosystem is introduced. Our system is secure and effective at managing trust evaluation while ensuring privacy preservation for vehicular networks, according to security analysis and performance evaluation. A cross-domain IIoT multifactor device authentication mechanism that is based on blockchain and protects user privacy (Zhang et al., 2022). Before being converted into key materials, some parameters are also encoded into random integers by the hardware fingerprint. The overhead is minimized by just storing each domain's dynamic accumulator, which builds up derived key materials for devices. Additionally, the cross-domain unlikable IDs of IIoT devices are effectively verified by using the on-chain accumulator. Formally proving the security of our protocol, as well as discussing its security features and functionality. An operational proof-of-concept prototype was used to demonstrate the effectiveness and dependability. The comparison results show a significant reduction in on-chain storage. The smart contract's performance was assessed in order to demonstrate scalability. Blockchain-based IoT cloud platforms are utilized for security and privacy in the Blockchain and Federated Learning-enabled Secure Architecture for Privacy-Preserving in Smart Healthcare (Singh et al., 2022). Scalable machine learning applications like healthcare use federated learning technologies. Users can also get a well-trained machine learning model without putting their private information on the cloud. Additionally, it covered the uses of federated learning in a smart city's distributed secure environment. a cutting-edge solution known as the blockchain-assisted privacy-preserving authentication system (BPAS), which both protects vehicle privacy and offers automatic authentication in VANETs. This plan is very effective and adaptable (Feng, He, Zeadally, & Liang, 2019). It permits conditional tracing and dynamic revocation of misbehaving vehicles, and it does not require any online registration centre (aside from system startup and vehicle registration).

In this chapter, we conduct a thorough security study and performance evaluation of our proposed architecture (based on the Hyperledger Fabric platform). The outcomes show that our architecture is a successful means of creating a decentralized authentication mechanism in VANETs. Additionally, the blockchain technology provides improved services like transparency, decentralization, immutability, trustlessness, and so forth. The facts serve as inspiration for this article's novel suggestion to integrate a blockchain framework that protects privacy with a 6G communication network. Additionally, as a dependable and stable model for 6G networking based on blockchain technology with increased effectiveness and security, we suggest an integrated system for blockchain radio access network (Velliangiri, 2021). In addition, key elements of blockchain like the consensus protocol, mathematical model, safe data sharing, and auditing are outlined in detail, and experimental findings are examined.

3. SIMULATORS USED FOR PRIVACY PRESERVING AND BUILDING TRUST IN BLOCKCHAIN SYSTEMS

There are various simulators and tools available that can be used to simulate and evaluate privacy-preserving and trust-building techniques in blockchain systems. These simulators provide a virtual environment to test and analyze the performance, security, and effectiveness of different approaches (Lin et al., 2020). Here are a few examples:

- Hyperledger Caliper: Hyperledger Caliper is a blockchain performance benchmarking tool developed by the Hyperledger project. It supports various blockchain platforms, including Hyperledger Fabric, Sawtooth, and Iroha. Caliper allows users to define and execute performance tests, including privacy-preserving and trust-building scenarios, and provides metrics for evaluating the performance and scalability of the blockchain network.

- Ethereum Virtual Machine (EVM) Testnets: Ethereum, one of the most popular blockchain platforms, offers testnets (test networks) such as Ropsten, Kovan, and Rinkeby. These testnets simulate the Ethereum network, allowing developers to deploy and test smart contracts, privacy solutions, and consensus mechanisms in a controlled environment without using real Ether. This enables experimentation with privacy-preserving techniques and trust-building mechanisms on the Ethereum blockchain.
- Ganache: Ganache is a personal blockchain development tool provided by Truffle Suite for Ethereum development. It allows developers to create a local private Ethereum network for testing and debugging smart contracts. Ganache provides a simulated blockchain environment with accounts, addresses, and Ether balances, enabling the evaluation of privacy-preserving and trust-building techniques within the Ethereum ecosystem.
- Parity Substrate: Parity Substrate is a framework for building customized blockchains. It provides a development environment and simulation tools for testing blockchain networks with custom consensus algorithms, privacy features, and trust models. Developers can use Substrate's built-in simulation capabilities to assess the behavior and performance of their blockchain systems under different scenarios.
- IBM Blockchain Platform: IBM Blockchain Platform offers a comprehensive development and testing environment for building and deploying blockchain solutions. It provides a sandbox environment where developers can create private blockchain networks and simulate different privacy-preserving and trust-building techniques. The platform includes features for testing, monitoring, and evaluating the performance and security of blockchain systems.
- Corda Network Map Simulator: Corda is a blockchain platform designed for enterprise use cases. The Corda Network Map Simulator allows developers to simulate and test Corda network behavior, including privacy features and trust models. It enables the evaluation of privacy-preserving techniques such as confidential transactions and selective disclosure of data.

These simulators and tools provide developers and researchers with a virtual environment to explore and assess the effectiveness of privacy-preserving and trust-building techniques in blockchain systems. They offer important information into performance, security, scalability, and usability aspects, facilitating the development and deployment of robust and privacy-enhanced blockchain solutions.

4. PRIVACY CHALLENGES IN BLOCKCHAIN SYSTEMS

Blockchain technology offers several advantages, such as transparency, immutability, and decentralization. However, it also presents unique privacy challenges that need to be addressed (Feng, He, Zeadally, Khan et al, 2019). Here are some key privacy challenges in blockchain systems ():

- Pseudonymity and Traceability: Blockchain transactions are often pseudonymous, meaning that they are linked to cryptographic addresses instead of real-world identities. While pseudonymity provides some level of privacy, it is still possible to trace transactions and link them to specific individuals or entities through data analysis techniques. This can compromise privacy, especially when blockchain data is correlated with external information sources.

- Public Transaction History: In public blockchains like Bitcoin and Ethereum, transaction details are permanently stored on the blockchain and are visible to all participants. This transparency can raise issues about exposing sensitive information, such as transaction amounts, sender and recipient addresses, and transaction patterns. It becomes challenging to conduct private transactions or protect commercially sensitive data on a public blockchain.
- Data Leakage through Smart Contracts: Smart contracts deployed on a blockchain can potentially expose sensitive data. While the blockchain itself is secure, vulnerabilities in smart contract code or improper handling of data within contracts can lead to data leaks. It is crucial to ensure proper design and implementation of smart contracts to safeguard privacy.
- Metadata Leakage: Even if transaction details are encrypted, metadata associated with transactions can reveal sensitive information. Metadata includes information like transaction timestamps, transaction size, and network fees. Analyzing this metadata can potentially identify users or uncover patterns of behavior, compromising privacy.
- On-Chain Analytics and Data Mining: Blockchain data is often publicly available, enabling on-chain analytics and data mining. By analyzing patterns and relationships within the blockchain, it is possible to infer additional information and deanonymize users. Data mining techniques, combined with external data sources, can reveal personal information, transaction history, or other sensitive data.
- Scalability and Privacy Trade-offs: Privacy-enhancing techniques, such as zero-knowledge proofs or ring signatures, can improve privacy in blockchain systems. However, these techniques often come with trade-offs in terms of scalability and computational overhead. Striking a balance between privacy and scalability is a significant challenge in blockchain design and implementation.
- Regulatory Compliance and Data Protection: Blockchain systems must comply with privacy regulations, such as the European Union's General Data Protection Regulation (GDPR). Ensuring compliance while maintaining the transparency and immutability of the blockchain poses challenges. Techniques like data anonymization, consent management, and selective disclosure need to be implemented to meet regulatory requirements.
- Cross-Chain Privacy: Interoperability between different blockchain networks raises privacy issues. When data or assets move between blockchains, there is a risk of information leakage or privacy violations. Ensuring privacy across different blockchain systems requires careful issues and coordination of privacy-enhancing techniques.

Hence, these privacy challenges in blockchain systems requires a combination of technical, cryptographic, and governance solutions. Privacy-enhancing techniques, such as zero-knowledge proofs, ring signatures, and secure multiparty computation, can be employed to protect sensitive data. Additionally, privacy policies, user consent management, and governance frameworks need to be implemented to ensure compliance and establish trust in blockchain ecosystems. Now refer Figure 2 for this section's organization.

Figure 2. Privacy challenges sin Blockchain systems

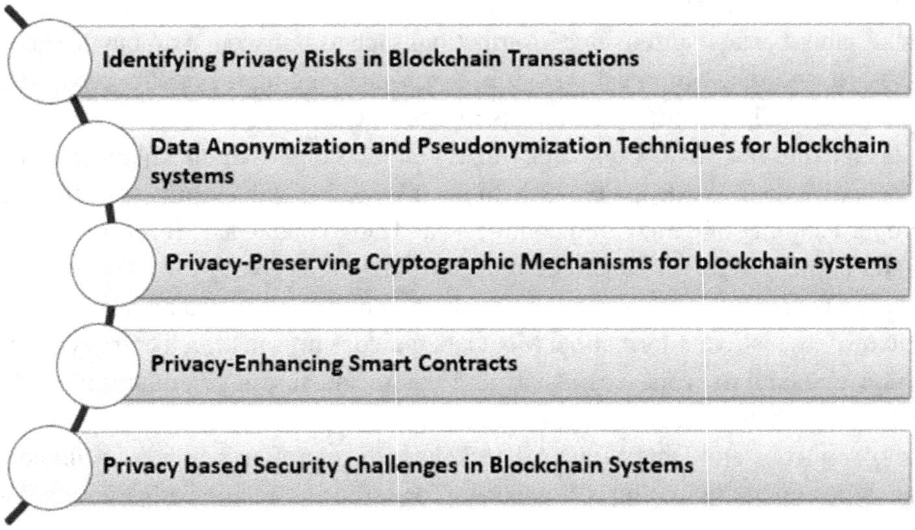

4.1 Identifying Privacy Risks in Blockchain Transactions

Identifying privacy risks in blockchain transactions is crucial for understanding and mitigating potential privacy breaches (Koteska et al., 2017). Here are some key privacy risks to consider when analyzing blockchain transactions:

- Address Reuse: Reusing the same address for multiple transactions can compromise privacy. When an address is reused, it becomes easier to link different transactions together, potentially revealing transaction history and patterns. Analyzing the blockchain for address reuse can provide information of user behavior and compromise anonymity.
- Network Traffic Analysis: Monitoring network traffic can reveal information about transaction participants. By analyzing the timing, size, and frequency of transactions, it may be possible to infer relationships between different addresses and potentially identify the parties involved. Network traffic analysis can be used to uncover user identities and transaction patterns.
- Linkability: Transactions on a blockchain are often linked through common inputs and outputs. If multiple transactions share the same input or output addresses, it becomes possible to link those transactions together. Linkability can expose transaction history, revealing information about user activities and potentially de-anonymizing participants.
- Transaction Metadata: Blockchain transactions often contain metadata, such as transaction timestamps, transaction amounts, or memo fields. Analyzing this metadata can reveal additional information about the transaction and the parties involved. Transaction metadata can be used to track transaction flows and potentially compromise privacy.
- Sybil Attacks: Sybil attacks involve creating multiple identities or addresses to manipulate the network and compromise privacy. By controlling a significant portion of the network's resources, an attacker can link different transactions or disrupt privacy-enhancing mechanisms. Sybil attacks pose a risk to the anonymity and privacy of blockchain transactions.

- Malicious Nodes or Miners: In decentralized blockchain networks, the behavior of individual nodes or miners can impact privacy. Malicious nodes may attempt to link transactions, reveal transaction details, or manipulate data to compromise privacy. Trusting the security and privacy practices of network participants is important to mitigate such risks.
- Unintended Data Leakage: Blockchain transactions may unintentionally leak sensitive information. For example, using smart contracts that expose sensitive data or not properly encrypting transaction payloads can result in data leakage. Analyzing transaction details for unintentional data disclosure is important to ensure privacy protection.
- Off-Chain Data Linkage: Blockchain transactions may reference or interact with off-chain data sources. The connection between blockchain transactions and external data sources can introduce privacy risks. If the off-chain data is not properly protected or anonymized, it can compromise the privacy of blockchain transactions.

To mitigate these privacy risks, several techniques can be employed, such as using privacy-enhancing technologies like zero-knowledge proofs, ring signatures, or mixers/tumblers. Additionally, best practices include employing address and transaction obfuscation techniques, minimizing address reuse, and implementing strong encryption and access controls for off-chain data. Properly designed privacy policies, user consent management, and governance frameworks are also crucial to protect privacy in blockchain transactions.

4.2 Data Anonymization and Pseudonymization Techniques for Blockchain Systems

Data anonymization and pseudonymization are privacy-enhancing techniques that can be applied in blockchain systems to protect the identity and sensitive information of participants (Molina et al., 2021). Here are some commonly used techniques:

- Cryptographic Hashing: Cryptographic hash functions, such as SHA-256, can be used to convert sensitive data into fixed-length hash values. Hashing irreversibly transforms the original data, making it difficult to retrieve the original information from the hash value. This technique is commonly used to pseudonymize data by replacing sensitive identifiers with their corresponding hash values.
- Encryption: Encryption techniques can be applied to protect sensitive data stored on the blockchain. Encryption algorithms, such as symmetric or asymmetric encryption, can be used to transform data into an unreadable form that can only be decrypted with the appropriate decryption key. This technique ensures that only authorized parties with the decryption key can access the original data.
- Tokenization: Tokenization involves replacing sensitive data with unique tokens or surrogate values. A tokenization system maps sensitive data to randomly generated tokens, which are then used in place of the original data. The mapping is securely stored in a separate system or database, allowing authorized parties to retrieve the original data when necessary.

- Zero-Knowledge Proofs: Zero-knowledge proofs (ZKPs) allow for the verification of a statement or claim without revealing any underlying information. ZKPs can be used to demonstrate knowledge or possession of certain data or credentials without disclosing the actual data itself. This technique enables privacy-preserving authentication and verification processes on the blockchain.
- Ring Signatures: Ring signatures enable anonymous signing of transactions by a group of participants. With a ring signature, it is not possible to determine which specific participant in the group produced the signature. This technique enhances privacy by obfuscating the identity of the transaction signer.
- Differential Privacy: Differential privacy techniques aim to protect individual privacy while still allowing for aggregate analysis. By injecting controlled noise into data or query results, differential privacy ensures that individual data points cannot be easily identified. This technique can be used to protect sensitive information during data analysis or reporting on the blockchain.
- Mixers/Tumblers: Mixers or tumblers are services that facilitate the mixing of funds or transactions from multiple participants to obscure the transaction history. By combining transactions from different sources, mixers make it difficult to trace the flow of funds and link specific transactions to individual participants.

Note that the application of these techniques should be carefully considered based on the specific privacy requirements and legal regulations governing the use of personal or sensitive data. Additionally, the use of these techniques may introduce trade-offs in terms of performance, scalability, and transparency, and should be evaluated in the context of the specific blockchain system and use case.

4.3 Privacy-Preserving Cryptographic Mechanisms for Blockchain Systems

Privacy-preserving cryptographic mechanisms play a crucial role in protecting sensitive information in blockchain systems (Guo et al., 2020). Here are some commonly used cryptographic mechanisms for privacy preservation:

- Zero-Knowledge Proofs (ZKPs): Zero-knowledge proofs allow a prover to demonstrate knowledge of certain information without revealing the information itself. ZKPs enable privacy-preserving authentication, verification, and data sharing on the blockchain. Examples of ZKPs include zk-SNARKs (Zero-Knowledge Succinct Non-Interactive Argument of Knowledge) and zk-STARKs (Zero-Knowledge Scalable Transparent Argument of Knowledge).
- Homomorphic Encryption: Homomorphic encryption allows computations to be performed on encrypted data without decrypting it. This mechanism enables privacy-preserving data processing on the blockchain. With homomorphic encryption, sensitive data can be securely stored and processed without revealing the plaintext values.
- Ring Signatures: Ring signatures enable anonymous signing of transactions by a group of participants. A ring signature ensures that the verifier cannot determine which specific participant produced the signature, enhancing privacy. Ring signatures are commonly used in privacy-focused cryptocurrencies, such as Monero.

- Multi-Party Computation (MPC): Multi-party computation allows multiple parties to jointly compute a function over their private inputs without revealing those inputs to each other. MPC enables collaborative data analysis and processing on the blockchain while preserving privacy. Secure multiparty computation protocols, such as Yao's garbled circuits and secret sharing schemes, are used for privacy-preserving computation.
- Secure Multi-Party Summation: Secure multi-party summation protocols enable the aggregation of sensitive data without revealing individual values. This mechanism is useful in scenarios where privacy-preserving data aggregation is required, such as computing statistics or performing voting on the blockchain.
- Confidential Transactions: Confidential transactions aim to hide transaction amounts while still ensuring the integrity and validity of transactions. Cryptographic techniques, such as Pedersen commitments or range proofs, are used to hide transaction amounts on the blockchain, protecting the financial privacy of participants.
- Stealth Addresses: Stealth addresses provide privacy for the recipients of blockchain transactions. With a stealth address, a recipient can generate a unique address for each transaction, making it difficult to link multiple transactions to the same recipient.
- Secure Hash Functions: Secure hash functions, such as SHA-256, are extensively used in blockchain systems to ensure data integrity and privacy. Hash functions are employed for address generation, data obfuscation, and pseudonymization of sensitive information.

These cryptographic mechanisms contribute to privacy preservation in blockchain systems by protecting sensitive information, anonymizing identities, and enabling secure computations. However, it's important to note that the selection and implementation of cryptographic mechanisms should be carefully evaluated based on the specific privacy requirements, performance issues, and the threat model of the blockchain system.

4.4 Privacy-Enhancing Smart Contracts

Privacy-enhancing smart contracts are designed to protect the privacy of sensitive data and interactions within blockchain systems. These contracts utilize cryptographic techniques and innovative protocols to preserve privacy while ensuring the transparency and security of blockchain operations. Here are some examples of privacy-enhancing smart contracts:

- Confidential Smart Contracts: Confidential smart contracts consider techniques like secure multi-party computation (MPC) or zero-knowledge proofs (ZKPs) to enable privacy-preserving computation. They allow multiple parties to jointly execute smart contracts without revealing their private inputs or intermediate results. Confidential smart contracts are particularly useful in scenarios where sensitive data needs to be processed on the blockchain while preserving privacy, such as in financial applications or supply chain management.
- Selective Disclosure Smart Contracts: Selective disclosure smart contracts enable users to disclose specific information to selected parties while keeping the remaining data private. They utilize techniques like attribute-based encryption (ABE) or proxy re-encryption to selectively share or reveal encrypted data to authorized entities. Selective disclosure smart contracts are beneficial in scenarios where users want to maintain control over their data and limit access based on predefined policies or conditions.

- Privacy-Preserving Voting Contracts: Voting on the blockchain often requires privacy to ensure the secrecy and integrity of the voting process. Privacy-preserving voting contracts employ cryptographic techniques like mix-nets, homomorphic encryption, or ZKPs to protect the privacy of voter preferences while enabling transparent and verifiable voting results. These contracts allow individuals to cast their votes privately while still providing publicly auditable and tamper-proof outcomes.
- Secure Multi-Party Computation Contracts: Secure multi-party computation (MPC) contracts enable multiple parties to collaborate on blockchain-based computations while keeping their private inputs confidential. These contracts use cryptographic protocols to perform computations on encrypted inputs without revealing the individual values. Secure MPC contracts find applications in various domains, including financial calculations, machine learning, and data analysis, where preserving privacy during collaborative computations is crucial.
- Anonymous Token Transfers: Traditional blockchain systems often link token transfers to pseudonymous addresses, which can compromise privacy. Anonymous token transfer contracts aim to enhance privacy by providing mechanisms for unlinkable and untraceable transactions. These contracts utilize techniques like ring signatures or zero-knowledge proofs to obscure the connection between the sender and recipient of tokens, improving privacy for token holders.

Privacy-enhancing smart contracts enable blockchain systems to strike a balance between privacy and transparency. They offer solutions to preserve confidentiality, protect sensitive data, and empower users with control over their information while considering the decentralized and immutable nature of the blockchain. The selection and implementation of privacy-enhancing smart contracts should be based on the specific requirements, use cases, and threat models of the blockchain application.

5. TRUST-BUILDING MECHANISMS IN BLOCKCHAIN SYSTEMS

Trust-building mechanisms in blockchain systems aim to establish confidence and reliability among participants in the network (Yavaprabhas et al., 2022). Here are some common trust-building mechanisms used in blockchain systems:

- Consensus Mechanisms: Consensus mechanisms play a critical role in establishing trust in blockchain systems. They ensure that all participants agree on the validity and ordering of transactions, maintaining the integrity of the blockchain. Different consensus mechanisms, such as Proof of Work (PoW), Proof of Stake (PoS), or Practical Byzantine Fault Tolerance (PBFT), provide varying levels of trust guarantees by addressing security, decentralization, and performance issues.
- Cryptographic Techniques: Cryptographic mechanisms contribute to trust-building in blockchain systems. Public-key cryptography, digital signatures, and hash functions are used to verify the authenticity, integrity, and non-repudiation of transactions. Cryptography ensures that only authorized participants can access and modify data on the blockchain, providing trust in the system's security.

- Smart Contracts: Smart contracts are self-executing agreements that automatically enforce predefined rules and conditions. By eliminating the need for intermediaries and relying on transparent, auditable code execution, smart contracts build trust by ensuring that agreed-upon actions are executed as intended. Participants can rely on the deterministic behavior of smart contracts to enforce rules and automate business processes.
- Reputation Systems: Reputation systems can be implemented in blockchain systems to establish trust among participants. These systems assign reputation scores or ratings to participants based on their behavior, interactions, or past performance. Participants with higher reputation scores are considered more trustworthy, which can influence decision-making processes, such as choosing partners for transactions or forming consensus groups.
- Auditing and Transparency: Blockchain systems provide transparency by storing transactions on a shared ledger visible to all participants. This transparency enables auditing and verification of transaction history, ensuring accountability and building trust. Participants can independently verify the accuracy and integrity of transactions, reducing the need to blindly trust centralized authorities.
- Governance and Consensus Rules: Establishing clear governance frameworks and consensus rules helps build trust in blockchain systems. By defining transparent decision-making processes, dispute resolution mechanisms, and community-driven governance models, participants can have confidence in the fairness and stability of the system. Transparent governance mechanisms ensure that the network evolves in a decentralized and inclusive manner.
- Interoperability and Standards: Interoperability standards and protocols enable different blockchain systems to communicate and interact seamlessly. By promoting interoperability, participants can trust that their assets and data can move across different blockchain networks securely and reliably, fostering collaboration and expanding the utility of blockchain technology.
- External Verification and Audits: Third-party audits and verifications conducted by reputable organizations or experts can enhance trust in blockchain systems. Independent audits provide assurance that the system operates as intended, follows established standards, and adheres to security best practices. External verification helps validate claims made by the blockchain system and increases confidence among participants.

These trust-building mechanisms work together to establish confidence, security, and reliability in blockchain systems. The combination of consensus, cryptography, transparency, governance, and external validation contributes to the overall trustworthiness of the network, enabling participants to engage in transactions and interactions with reduced risk and increased confidence.

6. APPLICATIONS OF PRIVACY-PRESERVING AND TRUST-BUILDING TECHNIQUES IN BLOCKCHAIN SYSTEMS

6.1 Financial Transactions and Privacy Preserving Using Blockchain

Blockchain technology can be utilized to enhance privacy in financial transactions, ensuring the confidentiality of sensitive financial information (Kosba et al., 2016). Here are some ways in which blockchain can be used for privacy-preserving financial transactions:

- Pseudonymous Transactions: Blockchain systems typically utilize pseudonyms, such as cryptographic addresses, to represent participants in transactions. These addresses do not reveal the real-world identities of the users, providing a certain level of privacy. By using different addresses for each transaction or employing techniques like address rotation, it becomes challenging to link transactions to specific individuals.
- Confidential Transactions: Confidential transactions, implemented using cryptographic techniques, enable the hiding of transaction amounts on the blockchain. By utilizing zero-knowledge proofs or range proofs, the sender can prove that the transaction is valid without disclosing the actual transaction amount. This enhances privacy by keeping the financial information confidential while ensuring the integrity of the transaction.
- Secure Wallets and Key Management: Blockchain-based wallets can incorporate advanced security features to protect private keys and ensure secure transaction signing. Techniques like hardware wallets, multi-signature wallets, and secure key storage mechanisms can prevent unauthorized access to funds and enhance the privacy and security of financial transactions.
- Off-Chain Transactions: Off-chain transactions, also known as layer-two solutions, enable the execution of transactions outside the main blockchain network. These transactions occur on secondary layers or channels and are settled on the blockchain later. Off-chain transactions can provide faster and more private transactions by minimizing the exposure of sensitive financial details on the public blockchain.
- Privacy Coins: Some blockchain networks offer privacy-focused cryptocurrencies known as privacy coins. These cryptocurrencies utilize advanced cryptographic techniques, such as ring signatures or zero-knowledge proofs, to obfuscate transaction details and provide stronger privacy guarantees compared to traditional cryptocurrencies. Privacy coins allow users to conduct financial transactions with enhanced privacy and anonymity.
- Selective Disclosure: Blockchain systems can incorporate selective disclosure mechanisms, where users have control over which transaction details or attributes they reveal to specific parties. This allows users to share the necessary information while keeping the rest of the transaction details private. Selective disclosure mechanisms enable privacy-preserving financial transactions by minimizing the exposure of sensitive information.
- Encrypted Communication: Blockchain networks can utilize encrypted communication channels between participants to ensure the privacy and confidentiality of financial transactions. Secure communication protocols, such as Transport Layer Security (TLS), can be implemented to encrypt data exchanged during transactions, preventing unauthorized access and eavesdropping.

Note that this application has few limitations. Factors such as transaction traceability, network analysis, and integration with external systems can still pose privacy challenges. Additionally, regulatory requirements and compliance obligations may impose certain limitations on privacy-preserving practices. Therefore, an approach that considers both technological solutions and regulatory issues is important for privacy-preserving financial transactions using blockchain.

6.2 Supply Chain and Provenance Tracking Using Blockchain

Supply chain and provenance tracking are key use cases for blockchain technology. By considering blockchain, organizations can create transparent and immutable records of the journey of products, raw materials, and goods across the supply chain (Kim & Laskowski, 2018). Here's how blockchain can be used for supply chain and provenance tracking:

- Traceability: Blockchain enables end-to-end traceability of products by recording every transaction and movement on the blockchain. Each step in the supply chain, such as the origin of raw materials, manufacturing processes, transportation, and distribution, can be recorded as immutable blocks on the blockchain. This allows for a transparent view of the entire supply chain and helps in identifying the origin and movement of products.
- Authenticity Verification: Blockchain can be used to verify the authenticity of products and prevent counterfeiting. Unique identifiers or digital fingerprints of products can be recorded on the blockchain, enabling stakeholders to verify the authenticity of a product by matching its identifier with the recorded data. This helps in ensuring that products are genuine and not counterfeit or tampered with.
- Quality Control: Blockchain can facilitate quality control processes by recording relevant information such as quality tests, inspections, certifications, and compliance documents on the blockchain. This provides an immutable record of the quality control measures undertaken throughout the supply chain, ensuring adherence to standards and regulations.
- Supplier Verification: Blockchain can enhance supplier verification and vetting processes by storing and sharing information about suppliers, their certifications, track records, and compliance history. This enables organizations to make informed decisions when selecting and onboarding suppliers, ensuring transparency and accountability in the supply chain.
- Supply Chain Efficiency: Blockchain can streamline supply chain operations by automating and digitizing processes, reducing paperwork, and improving efficiency. Smart contracts can be utilized to automate transactions, payments, and fulfillment processes based on predefined rules and conditions. This reduces administrative overhead, minimizes errors, and accelerates supply chain operations.
- Provenance Tracking: Blockchain provides a tamper-proof record of the provenance of goods, allowing consumers and stakeholders to trace the origin, manufacturing processes, and handling conditions of a product. This helps in ensuring ethical sourcing, fair trade practices, and sustainability in supply chains.
- Real-time Visibility: Blockchain-based supply chain systems can provide real-time visibility into the movement and status of products. IoT devices, sensors, and other data sources can be integrated with the blockchain, enabling real-time data capture and updating of the blockchain. This allows stakeholders to track and monitor products throughout their journey in near real-time.
- Dispute Resolution: In case of disputes or discrepancies in the supply chain, blockchain can serve as an immutable source of truth. As all transactions and activities are recorded on the blockchain, it becomes easier to identify the source of the issue and resolve disputes efficiently and transparently.

Hence, this application can enhance transparency, trust, and efficiency in their supply chain operations. It enables stakeholders to make informed decisions, ensures the authenticity and quality of products, and supports sustainable and ethical business practices.

6.3 Healthcare Data Sharing and Privacy Preserving Using Blockchain

Healthcare data sharing and privacy are critical issues in the healthcare industry. Blockchain technology can be ladded to enable secure and privacy-preserving healthcare data sharing (Liu et al., 2018). Here's how blockchain can be used in healthcare for data sharing while preserving privacy:

- Patient Data Ownership and Consent: Blockchain allows patients to have ownership and control over their health data. Patients can grant access to their data on a need-to-know basis, giving explicit consent for sharing with specific healthcare providers or researchers. Smart contracts can enforce data access rules, ensuring that data is shared only with authorized entities.
- Immutable Audit Trail: Blockchain provides an immutable and transparent record of data access and modifications. Every interaction with healthcare data, such as consent management, data sharing, or updates, is recorded on the blockchain, creating an audit trail. This enhances transparency and accountability, ensuring that data access and usage can be audited and verified.
- Data Encryption and Security: Blockchain can integrate encryption techniques to protect sensitive healthcare data. Patient data can be encrypted before being stored on the blockchain, ensuring that only authorized parties with decryption keys can access the data. This enhances data security and confidentiality, minimizing the risk of unauthorized access or data breaches.
- Interoperability and Data Integrity: Blockchain can facilitate interoperability among different healthcare systems and organizations, enabling secure and seamless data exchange. Patient health records, diagnostic reports, and other relevant data can be securely stored and shared across different entities, ensuring data integrity and consistency.
- Consent Management: Blockchain-based consent management systems enable patients to manage their consent preferences and revoke or modify access permissions at any time. Consent records can be stored on the blockchain, ensuring that the consent history is tamper-proof and auditable.
- Health Data Aggregation and Research: Blockchain can enable secure and privacy-preserving aggregation of health data for research purposes. Researchers can access anonymized and aggregated data on the blockchain, eliminating the need for centralized data repositories and protecting individual patient identities. Smart contracts can govern the terms of data sharing and ensure compliance with privacy regulations.
- Health Data Exchange Networks: Blockchain-based health data exchange networks can be established, connecting healthcare providers, insurers, laboratories, and other stakeholders. These networks enable secure and efficient data sharing, reducing administrative burdens and enhancing the accuracy and availability of patient data while ensuring privacy and security.
- Trusted Identity and Credentialing: Blockchain can provide a decentralized and tamper-proof identity management system for healthcare providers and patients. This enables secure and trusted verification of identities, credentials, and licenses, reducing the risk of identity fraud and improving trust in the healthcare ecosystem.

Note that while blockchain can enhance healthcare data sharing and privacy, regulatory compliance, scalability, and interoperability challenges need to be addressed. Collaboration among healthcare stakeholders, standardization efforts, and adherence to privacy regulations such as HIPAA (Health Insurance Portability and Accountability Act) are important to ensure the effective implementation of blockchain solutions in healthcare data sharing while preserving privacy.

6.4 IoT Data Privacy and Trust Building Using Blockchain

Internet of Things generates large amounts of data, and ensuring privacy and trust in this data is crucial. Blockchain technology can be considered to enhance privacy and trust in IoT data by providing a decentralized and secure framework (Ali et al., 2023). Here's how blockchain can be used for IoT data privacy and trust building:

- Data Encryption and Security: Blockchain can integrate cryptographic techniques to encrypt IoT data, ensuring its confidentiality and integrity. IoT devices can encrypt data before storing it on the blockchain, and only authorized parties with the decryption keys can access the data. This protects sensitive IoT data from unauthorized access or tampering, enhancing security and privacy.
- Data Ownership and Consent Management: Blockchain enables individuals or organizations to have ownership and control over their IoT data. Users can grant access to their data on the blockchain, and smart contracts can enforce data access rules based on predefined conditions. Consent management systems built on blockchain allow users to specify who can access their data and under what circumstances, ensuring privacy and control over personal information.
- Immutable Audit Trail: Blockchain provides an immutable and transparent record of data transactions. Every interaction with IoT data, such as data collection, sharing, or updates, is recorded on the blockchain, creating an audit trail. This enables traceability and accountability, ensuring that data transactions can be audited and verified, enhancing trust.
- Data Integrity and Authenticity: Blockchain's distributed ledger ensures data integrity and authenticity in the IoT ecosystem. IoT data can be timestamped and recorded on the blockchain, providing a tamper-proof record of its origin and history. This allows data recipients to verify the authenticity and integrity of the IoT data, building trust in the data's accuracy and reliability.
- Decentralized Data Marketplaces: Blockchain can facilitate decentralized data marketplaces for IoT data, where individuals or organizations can securely trade or share their data. Smart contracts on the blockchain can enforce fair and transparent data transactions, ensuring that data is exchanged based on predefined rules and conditions. This enhances trust and incentivizes data sharing in the IoT ecosystem.
- Device Identity and Authentication: Blockchain can provide a decentralized and tamper-proof identity management system for IoT devices. Each device can have a unique identity stored on the blockchain, allowing for secure device authentication and validation. This ensures that only authorized devices can interact with the network, mitigating the risk of unauthorized access or malicious activities.

- Data Anonymization and Aggregation: Blockchain can enable privacy-preserving techniques such as data anonymization and aggregation in the context of IoT data. By aggregating and anonymizing data on the blockchain, individual identities and sensitive information can be protected while still allowing for meaningful analysis and information. This ensures privacy while maintaining the usefulness of IoT data for various applications.
- Trust and Reputation Systems: Blockchain-based trust and reputation systems can be established for IoT devices and data providers. By recording and evaluating the behavior and reliability of devices or entities on the blockchain, trust scores or ratings can be assigned. This helps in assessing the trustworthiness of IoT devices or data sources, fostering a more secure and trustworthy IoT ecosystem.

Hence, this application requires careful issues of scalability, interoperability, and regulatory compliance. Additionally, collaboration among stakeholders, industry standards, and adherence to privacy regulations are crucial to ensure the effective deployment of blockchain solutions for securing IoT data and building trust in the IoT ecosystem.

6.5 Governance and Transparency in Blockchain Systems

Governance and transparency are important aspects of blockchain systems to ensure the integrity, accountability, and trustworthiness of the network (Tseng et al., 2018). Here are key issues for governance and transparency in blockchain systems:

- Consensus Mechanisms: Blockchain systems require mechanisms to establish consensus among network participants. The choice of consensus mechanism, such as Proof of Work (PoW), Proof of Stake (PoS), or Delegated Proof of Stake (DPoS), plays a crucial role in the governance and transparency of the system. Consensus mechanisms should be designed to promote decentralized decision-making and prevent concentration of power.
- Decentralized Governance Models: Blockchain systems often adopt decentralized governance models, where decisions are made collectively by network participants. This can be achieved through mechanisms like on-chain voting, stakeholder proposals, or consensus-based decision-making. These models ensure that governance decisions are transparent, inclusive, and reflective of the interests of the network participants.
- Transparent Rule-making and Protocol Upgrades: Governance processes should be transparent and open for the creation and modification of rules and protocols. Proposals for changes or upgrades to the blockchain system should be accessible to all participants, allowing for public scrutiny, discussion, and voting. Transparent rule-making enhances accountability, encourages participation, and ensures that decisions align with the collective interests of the network.
- Auditable and Immutable Record: Blockchain provides an auditable and immutable record of all transactions and activities on the network. This transparency allows participants to independently verify the integrity of the system and ensures that transactions and governance decisions cannot be altered retroactively. The transparency of the blockchain helps build trust among network participants and external stakeholders.

- Publicly Accessible Information: Relevant information about the blockchain system, including its governance framework, consensus mechanism, rules, and protocol upgrades, should be publicly accessible. This includes documentation, whitepapers, technical specifications, and governance proposals. Openly sharing this information ensures transparency, facilitates understanding, and enables participants to make informed decisions.
- Disclosure of Stakeholder Interests: Participants with significant influence or stakes in the blockchain system should disclose their interests and potential conflicts of interest. This promotes transparency and helps prevent situations where decisions are made to favor specific stakeholders at the expense of the network's integrity. Disclosure requirements can be enforced through governance rules or codes of conduct.
- Independent Audits and Security Assessments: Periodic independent audits and security assessments of the blockchain system can enhance transparency and provide assurance regarding the system's reliability, security, and compliance with established standards. These audits can identify vulnerabilities, ensure adherence to best practices, and demonstrate the system's commitment to transparency and accountability.

Hence, this application will ensure the long-term sustainability and trustworthiness of the network. By establishing decentralized governance models, promoting transparency, and enabling active community participation, blockchain systems can build trust among participants and external stakeholders.

7. OPEN ISSUES TOWARDS PRIVACY PRESERVING AND BUILDING TRUST IN BLOCKCHAIN SYSTEMS

While blockchain technology offers promising solutions for privacy-preserving and trust-building applications, there are still several open issues that need to be addressed (Hassan et al., 2019). Some of the key challenges and open issues include:

- Scalability: Blockchain systems face scalability challenges when it comes to handling a large number of transactions and data. Privacy-preserving techniques, such as zero-knowledge proofs or homomorphic encryption, can add additional computational overhead, impacting the scalability of the system. Finding scalable solutions that maintain privacy and trust is an ongoing research area.
- Regulatory Compliance: Blockchain systems need to comply with relevant privacy regulations, such as the GDPR or the HIPAA Act. Ensuring that privacy-preserving mechanisms align with regulatory requirements and handling sensitive data appropriately is crucial.
- Usability and User Experience: Privacy-preserving techniques in blockchain systems often introduce complexities that can affect user experience. Balancing privacy with usability is important to encourage widespread adoption. User-friendly interfaces, clear consent management mechanisms, and educational efforts are needed to ensure that users understand and can easily manage their privacy preferences.

- Identity Management: Blockchain systems require robust and secure identity management solutions to authenticate users, devices, and entities participating in the network. Establishing decentralized identity frameworks that protect privacy while ensuring trust and interoperability across multiple blockchain networks is a significant challenge.
- Governance and Consensus: Privacy-preserving and trust-building mechanisms may impact the governance and consensus models of blockchain systems. Designing governance structures that consider privacy issues, provide transparency, and allow for collective decision-making is crucial. Ensuring consensus mechanisms align with privacy requirements is also an ongoing challenge.
- External Data Integration: Blockchain systems often need to interact with external data sources or legacy systems to enrich the data or facilitate cross-platform interoperability. Preserving privacy and trust when integrating external data sources is a complex task that requires secure data transmission, authentication, and data validation mechanisms.
- Adversarial Attacks: Adversarial attacks, such as Sybil attacks or deanonymization attacks, pose a threat to privacy and trust in blockchain systems. Continual research is required to identify and address vulnerabilities and develop robust defenses against such attacks.
- Trade-Offs between Privacy and Transparency: Balancing privacy with transparency is a delicate trade-off in blockchain systems. While privacy-preserving techniques aim to protect sensitive information, transparency and accountability are important for trust-building. Striking the right balance between privacy and transparency is an ongoing challenge in blockchain system design.
- Addressing these open issues requires interdisciplinary research and collaboration among blockchain experts, privacy specialists, regulators, and industry stakeholders. Advancements in privacy-preserving techniques, consensus algorithms, identity management, and governance frameworks are necessary to build blockchain systems that effectively preserve privacy while establishing trust among participants.

8. CHALLENGES AND FUTURE DIRECTIONS TOWARDS BLOCKCHAIN SYSTEMS

This section includes various aspects that need to be addressed to unlock the full potential of this technology (Jabbar et al., 2021). Here are some key challenges and potential future directions:

- Scalability: As mentioned earlier, scalability remains a major challenge in blockchain systems. Increasing transaction throughput, reducing confirmation times, and enhancing network scalability are areas of focus. Solutions such as sharding, layer 2 protocols, and optimized consensus algorithms are being explored to improve scalability.
- Privacy and Confidentiality: Preserving privacy and confidentiality while maintaining transparency and trust is a complex challenge. Innovations in privacy-preserving mechanisms, such as zero-knowledge proofs, secure multiparty computation, and homomorphic encryption, are being researched to provide stronger privacy guarantees in blockchain systems.
- Interoperability: Blockchain interoperability is crucial for enabling seamless communication and data exchange between different blockchain networks. Efforts are underway to develop standards, protocols, and frameworks that facilitate interoperability and allow for the exchange of assets and information across diverse blockchain platforms.

- Governance and Regulation: Blockchain systems require robust governance frameworks and regulatory clarity to address legal and compliance challenges. Establishing governance models, addressing jurisdictional issues, and defining regulatory frameworks specific to blockchain are important issues for global adoption.
- Energy Efficiency: The energy consumption associated with consensus algorithms, particularly in proof-of-work systems, has raised issues regarding sustainability. Future directions involve exploring alternative consensus mechanisms, such as proof-of-stake or energy-efficient protocols, to reduce the environmental impact of blockchain systems.
- Usability and User Experience: Improving the usability and user experience of blockchain systems is crucial for mass adoption. Enhancements in wallet interfaces, simplification of key management, and seamless integration with existing systems can contribute to a more user-friendly experience.
- Standardization: Standardization efforts are vital for promoting interoperability, compatibility, and trust among different blockchain systems. Establishing common standards for protocols, data formats, privacy frameworks, and security practices will facilitate seamless integration and collaboration between various stakeholders.
- Regulatory Compliance: Compliance with legal and regulatory requirements is important for the acceptance and mainstream adoption of blockchain systems. Future directions involve working closely with regulatory bodies to create a supportive regulatory environment that encourages innovation while addressing issues related to privacy, security, consumer protection, and financial regulations.
- Education and Awareness: Educating the public, businesses, and policymakers about the capabilities and limitations of blockchain technology is crucial. Increased awareness will foster understanding and facilitate informed decision-making regarding the adoption and implementation of blockchain systems.
- Integration with Emerging Technologies: Exploring synergies with emerging technologies like artificial intelligence, Internet of Things (IoT), and decentralized finance (DeFi) can unlock new possibilities and use cases for blockchain systems. Collaborations and research in these areas can lead to innovative solutions and advancements.

Note that these challenges are actively being addressed through ongoing research, collaboration between industry and academia, and the continuous evolution of blockchain technology. The future directions outlined here provide a glimpse into the potential advancements and areas of focus as blockchain systems continue to mature and find broader applications in various industries. These trends and research opportunities reflect the dynamic nature of blockchain technology. Continued collaboration between academia, industry, and regulatory bodies is vital to drive research advancements, address existing challenges, and unlock the full potential of blockchain systems across various sectors and applications.

9. CONCLUSION

In the recent years, blockchain has the potential to revolutionize various industries by providing transparent, immutable, and decentralized systems. However, privacy and trust are critical issues that must be carefully addressed to ensure the successful adoption and deployment of blockchain systems. Hence, this chapter identifies various privacy challenges in blockchain systems, including the pseudonymous nature of transactions, data leakage through transaction metadata, and the potential for deanonymization attacks. It explores different techniques for privacy preservation, such as data anonymization, cryptographic mechanisms, zero-knowledge proofs, and privacy-enhancing smart contracts. These techniques aim to protect sensitive information while maintaining the integrity and transparency of blockchain transactions. Also, this chapter includes the importance of trust building mechanisms in blockchain systems (with explaining the role of consensus algorithms, reputation systems, smart contract auditing, and verification in establishing trust among participants). It also highlights the importance of governance, transparency, and regulatory compliance to foster trust and confidence in blockchain networks. Throughout this work, the challenges and future directions for privacy preserving and trust building in blockchain systems are explored.

REFERENCES

Ali, S., Abdullah, T. P. T. A., Athar, A., Hussain, A., Ali, M., Yaseen, M., Joo, M.-I., & Kim, H.-C. (2023). Metaverse in healthcare integrated with explainable ai and blockchain: Enabling immersiveness, ensuring trust, and providing patient data security. *Sensors (Basel)*, *23*(2), 565. doi:10.339023020565 PMID:36679361

Alphand, O., Amoretti, M., Claeys, T., Dall'Asta, S., Duda, A., Ferrari, G., Rousseau, F., Tourancheau, B., Veltri, L., & Zanichelli, F. (2018). IoTChain: A blockchain security architecture for the Internet of Things. In 2018 IEEE wireless communications and networking conference (WCNC) (pp. 1-6). IEEE. doi:10.1109/WCNC.2018.8377385

Brandão, A., Mamede, H. S., & Gonçalves, R. (2018). Systematic review of the literature, research on blockchain technology as support to the trust model proposed applied to smart places. *Trends and Advances in Information Systems and Technologies*, *1*(6), 1163–1174. doi:10.1007/978-3-319-77703-0_113

Deshmukh, A., Sreenath, N., Tyagi, A. K., & Eswara Abhichandan, U. V. (2022). Blockchain Enabled Cyber Security: A Comprehensive Survey. *2022 International Conference on Computer Communication and Informatics (ICCCI),* 1-6. 10.1109/ICCCI54379.2022.9740843

Feng, Q., He, D., Zeadally, S., Khan, M. K., & Kumar, N. (2019). A survey on privacy protection in blockchain system. *Journal of Network and Computer Applications*, *126*, 45–58. doi:10.1016/j.jnca.2018.10.020

Feng, Q., He, D., Zeadally, S., & Liang, K. (2019). BPAS: Blockchain-assisted privacy-preserving authentication system for vehicular ad hoc networks. *IEEE Transactions on Industrial Informatics*, *16*(6), 4146–4155. doi:10.1109/TII.2019.2948053

Guo, L., Xie, H., & Li, Y. (2020). Data encryption based blockchain and privacy preserving mechanisms towards big data. *Journal of Visual Communication and Image Representation*, *70*, 102741. doi:10.1016/j.jvcir.2019.102741

Hasan, O., Brunie, L., & Bertino, E. (2022). Privacy-preserving reputation systems based on blockchain and other cryptographic building blocks: A survey. *ACM Computing Surveys*, *55*(2), 1–37. doi:10.1145/3490236

Hassan, M. U., Rehmani, M. H., & Chen, J. (2019). Privacy preservation in blockchain based IoT systems: Integration issues, prospects, challenges, and future research directions. *Future Generation Computer Systems*, *97*, 512–529. doi:10.1016/j.future.2019.02.060

Jabbar, S., Lloyd, H., Hammoudeh, M., Adebisi, B., & Raza, U. (2021). Blockchain-enabled supply chain: Analysis, challenges, and future directions. *Multimedia Systems*, *27*(4), 787–806. doi:10.100700530-020-00687-0

Jayaprakash, V., & Tyagi, A. K. (2022). Security Optimization of Resource-Constrained Internet of Healthcare Things (IoHT) Devices Using Asymmetric Cryptography for Blockchain Network. In *Proceedings of International Conference on Network Security and Blockchain Technology. ICNSBT 2021. Lecture Notes in Networks and Systems* (vol. 481). Springer. 10.1007/978-981-19-3182-6_18

Jayaprakash, V., & Tyagi, A. K. (n.d.). Security Optimization of Resource-Constrained Internet of Healthcare Things (IoHT) Devices Using Lightweight Cryptography. In Information Security Practices for the Internet of Things, 5G, and Next-Generation Wireless Networks. doi:10.4018/978-1-6684-3921-0.ch009

Jayasinghe, U., Lee, G. M., MacDermott, Á., & Rhee, W. S. (2019). TrustChain: A privacy preserving blockchain with edge computing. *Wireless Communications and Mobile Computing*, *2019*, 2019. doi:10.1155/2019/2014697

Kim, H. M., & Laskowski, M. (2018). Toward an ontology-driven blockchain design for supply-chain provenance. *International Journal of Intelligent Systems in Accounting Finance & Management*, *25*(1), 18–27. doi:10.1002/isaf.1424

Kosba, A., Miller, A., Shi, E., Wen, Z., & Papamanthou, C. (2016). Hawk: The blockchain model of cryptography and privacy-preserving smart contracts. In 2016 IEEE symposium on security and privacy (SP) (pp. 839-858). IEEE. doi:10.1109/SP.2016.55

Koteska, B., Karafiloski, E., & Mishev, A. (2017). Blockchain implementation quality challenges: a literature. *SQAMIA: 6th workshop of software quality, analysis, monitoring, improvement, and applications*, *1938*.

Kumar, R., & Tripathi, R. (2021). DBTP2SF: A deep blockchain-based trustworthy privacy-preserving secured framework in industrial internet of things systems. *Transactions on Emerging Telecommunications Technologies*, *32*(4), e4222. doi:10.1002/ett.4222

Lashkari, B., & Musilek, P. (2021). A comprehensive review of blockchain consensus mechanisms. *IEEE Access : Practical Innovations, Open Solutions*, *9*, 43620–43652. doi:10.1109/ACCESS.2021.3065880

Li, B., Liang, R., Di Zhu, W. C., & Lin, Q. (2020). Blockchain-based trust management model for location privacy preserving in VANET. *IEEE Transactions on Intelligent Transportation Systems*, *22*(6), 3765–3775. doi:10.1109/TITS.2020.3035869

Li, L., Liu, J., Cheng, L., Qiu, S., Wang, W., Zhang, X., & Zhang, Z. (2018). Creditcoin: A privacy-preserving blockchain-based incentive announcement network for communications of smart vehicles. *IEEE Transactions on Intelligent Transportation Systems*, *19*(7), 2204–2220. doi:10.1109/TITS.2017.2777990

Lin, C., He, D., Huang, X., Kumar, N., & Choo, K.-K. R. (2020). BCPPA: A blockchain-based conditional privacy-preserving authentication protocol for vehicular ad hoc networks. *IEEE Transactions on Intelligent Transportation Systems*, *22*(12), 7408–7420. doi:10.1109/TITS.2020.3002096

Liu, J., Li, X., Ye, L., Zhang, H., Du, X., & Guizani, M. (2018). BPDS: A blockchain based privacy-preserving data sharing for electronic medical records. In *2018 IEEE Global Communications Conference (GLOBECOM)* (pp. 1-6). IEEE. 10.1109/GLOCOM.2018.8647713

Liu, X., Huang, H., Xiao, F., & Ma, Z. (2019). A blockchain-based trust management with conditional privacy-preserving announcement scheme for VANETs. *IEEE Internet of Things Journal*, *7*(5), 4101–4112. doi:10.1109/JIOT.2019.2957421

Lu, Z., Liu, W., Wang, Q., Qu, G., & Liu, Z. (2018). A privacy-preserving trust model based on blockchain for VANETs. *IEEE Access : Practical Innovations, Open Solutions*, *6*, 45655–45664. doi:10.1109/ACCESS.2018.2864189

Mohanta, B. K., Jena, D., Ramasubbareddy, S., Daneshmand, M., & Gandomi, A. H. (2020). Addressing security and privacy issues of IoT using blockchain technology. *IEEE Internet of Things Journal*, *8*(2), 881–888. doi:10.1109/JIOT.2020.3008906

Molina, F., Betarte, G., & Luna, C. (2021). Design principles for constructing GDPR-compliant blockchain solutions. In *2021 IEEE/ACM 4th International Workshop on Emerging Trends in Software Engineering for Blockchain (WETSEB)* (pp. 1-8). IEEE. 10.1109/WETSEB52558.2021.00008

Nair, M. M., & Tyagi, A. K. (2021). Privacy: History, Statistics, Policy, Laws, Preservation and Threat Analysis. Journal of Information Assurance & Security, 16(1), 24-34.

Nair & Tyagi. (2023). Blockchain technology for next-generation society: current trends and future opportunities for smart era. In *Blockchain Technology for Secure Social Media Computing*. doi:10.1049/PBSE019E_ch11

Pandey, A. A., Fernandez, T. F., Bansal, R., & Tyagi, A. K. (2022). Maintaining Scalability in Blockchain. In A. Abraham, N. Gandhi, T. Hanne, T. P. Hong, T. Nogueira Rios, & W. Ding (Eds.), *Intelligent Systems Design and Applications. ISDA 2021. Lecture Notes in Networks and Systems* (Vol. 418). Springer. doi:10.1007/978-3-030-96308-8_4

Peng, L., Feng, W., Yan, Z., Li, Y., Zhou, X., & Shimizu, S. (2021). Privacy preservation in permissionless blockchain: A survey. *Digital Communications and Networks*, *7*(3), 295–307. doi:10.1016/j.dcan.2020.05.008

Schaub, A., Bazin, R., Hasan, O., & Brunie, L. (2016). A trustless privacy-preserving reputation system. In *ICT Systems Security and Privacy Protection: 31st IFIP TC 11 International Conference, SEC 2016, Ghent, Belgium, May 30-June 1, 2016, Proceedings 31* (pp. 398-411). Springer International Publishing.

Sezer, B. B., Topal, S., & Nuriyev, U. (2022). TPPSUPPLY: A traceable and privacy-preserving blockchain system architecture for the supply chain. *Journal of Information Security and Applications*, *66*, 103116. doi:10.1016/j.jisa.2022.103116

Sheth, H. S. K. (2022). Deep Learning, Blockchain based Multi-layered Authentication and Security Architectures. *2022 International Conference on Applied Artificial Intelligence and Computing (ICAAIC)*, 476-485. 10.1109/ICAAIC53929.2022.9793179

Singh, S., Rathore, S., Alfarraj, O., Tolba, A., & Yoon, B. (2022). A framework for privacy-preservation of IoT healthcare data using Federated Learning and blockchain technology. *Future Generation Computer Systems*, *129*, 380–388. doi:10.1016/j.future.2021.11.028

Srivastava, S. (2023). Blockchain Enabled Internet of Things: Current Scenario and Open Challenges for Future. In Innovations in Bio-Inspired Computing and Applications. IBICA 2022. Lecture Notes in Networks and Systems (vol. 649). Springer. doi:10.1007/978-3-031-27499-2_59

Tseng, J.-H., Liao, Y.-C., Chong, B., & Shih-wei, L. (2018). Governance on the drug supply chain via gcoin blockchain. *International Journal of Environmental Research and Public Health*, *15*(6), 1055. doi:10.3390/ijerph15061055 PMID:29882861

Tyagi, A. K. (2021). *Analysis of Security and Privacy Aspects of Blockchain Technologies from Smart Era' Perspective: The Challenges and a Way Forward. In Recent Trends in Blockchain for Information Systems Security and Privacy*. CRC Press.

Tyagi, A. K. (2023). Decentralized everything: Practical use of blockchain technology in future applications. In Distributed Computing to Blockchain. Academic Press. doi:10.1016/B978-0-323-96146-2.00010-3

Tyagi, A. K., & Aswathy, S. U. (2021, October). AARIN: Affordable, Accurate, Reliable and INnovative Mechanism to Protect a Medical Cyber-Physical System using Blockchain Technology. *IJIN*, *2*, 175–183.

Tyagi, A. K., Chandrasekaran, S., & Sreenath, N. (2022). Blockchain Technology:– A New Technology for Creating Distributed and Trusted Computing Environment. *2022 International Conference on Applied Artificial Intelligence and Computing (ICAAIC)*, 1348-1354. 10.1109/ICAAIC53929.2022.9792702

Tyagi, A. K., Dananjayan, S., Agarwal, D., & Thariq Ahmed, H. F. (2023). Blockchain—Internet of Things Applications: Opportunities and Challenges for Industry 4.0 and Society 5.0. *Sensors (Basel)*, *23*(2), 947. doi:10.339023020947 PMID:36679743

Varsha, R. (2020, January 1). Deep Learning Based Blockchain Solution for Preserving Privacy in Future Vehicles. *International Journal of Hybrid Intelligent Systems*, *16*(4), 223–236.

Velliangiri, S. (2021). Blockchain based privacy preserving framework for emerging 6G wireless communications. *IEEE Transactions on Industrial Informatics*, *18*(7), 4868–4874.

Wang, D., Zhang, L., Huang, C., & Shen, X. (2021). A privacy-preserving trust management system based on blockchain for vehicular networks. In 2021 IEEE wireless communications and networking conference (WCNC) (pp. 1-6). IEEE. doi:10.1109/WCNC49053.2021.9417492

Yavaprabhas, K., Pournader, M., & Seuring, S. (2022). Blockchain as the "trust-building machine" for supply chain management. *Annals of Operations Research*, 1–40. PMID:35967837

Zhang, Y., Li, B., Wu, J., Liu, B., Chen, R., & Chang, J. (2022). Efficient and Privacy-Preserving Blockchain-Based Multifactor Device Authentication Protocol for Cross-Domain IIoT. *IEEE Internet of Things Journal*, *9*(22), 22501–22515. doi:10.1109/JIOT.2022.3176192

Chapter 20
Rogue Access Detection Using Multi-Parameter Dynamic Features on WLAN

Otasowie Owolafe
https://orcid.org/0000-0002-6659-8100
Federal University of Technology, Akure, Nigeria

Gbenga Moses Adediran
Federal University of Technology, Akure, Nigeria

Olaniyi Abiodun Ayeni
Federal University of Technology, Akure, Nigeria

ABSTRACT

The threat posed by rogue access points (RAPs) has grown significantly in importance for network security as a result of the growing use of wireless local area networks (WLANs). This work proposes a novel RAP detection method that makes use of multi-parameter dynamic WLAN properties. This chapter addresses the rising problem of rogue access points (RAPs) in wireless local area networks (WLANs) and suggests a new RAP detection approach that makes better use of multi-parameter dynamic features of WLAN. The proposed approach provides a comprehensive evaluation of each access point's unique characteristics and reduces susceptibility to RAPs. The study compared the proposed approach with four other RAP detection methods using metrics such as detection rate, false positive rate, customizability, and computational resources required. Results showed that the proposed approach achieves 98.7% detection rate with lower false positive rates and greater customizability than the other methods. The proposed RAP detection can effectively detect RAPs in wireless networks and enhance network security.

DOI: 10.4018/979-8-3693-0593-5.ch020

1.0 INTRODUCTION

Networking, also known as computer networking, means transporting and exchanging data between nodes over a shared medium in an information system by either wire (cables) or wireless. Networking does not comprise only the design, construction and use of a network, and it also covers network infrastructure, software, and policy administration, maintenance, and operation. There are different types of electronic devices used in networking, known as network devices or network equipment. Network devices transmit and receive the data quickly and securely between computers, fax machines, printers, etc. These devices may be intra-network or inter-network. There are different network devices, e.g. Router, Switches, Modem, Access points etc. (Bshara *et al.*, 2010).

A wireless network allows devices to stay connected to the network but roam untethered to any wires. Access points amplify Wi-Fi signals, so a device can be far from a router but still connect to the network. Wi-Fi is one of modern society's most common communication technologies. Wi-Fi is a link to the local wireless network (WLAN). Wireless internet is the standard IEEE 802.11, enabled to connect via routers and other equipment like smartphones, laptops, etc. The standard 802.11 needs high frequencies of 2.4 GHz and 5 GHz. The popularity of Wi-Fi is primarily due to its simplicity of implementation, availability, flexibility, and mobility, with the robust solution being affordable hardware and implementation costs (Kumar e*t al.*, 2016).

The components of a Wireless Local Area Network (WLAN) architecture are crucial for its functionality. Among these components are Access Points (APs), which play a significant role in organizing wireless users and facilitating their connection to the wired side of the network and ultimately, the Internet. The daily use of various wireless networks, commonly known as Wi-Fi, is a routine experience for many individuals in different settings, including offices, schools, coffee shops, among others. In these settings, users' devices automatically connect to the Wi-Fi network within their range, eliminating the need for intervention. While this automation enhances users' experience by making their interaction with the wireless network seamless, it is crucial to ensure that the connected wireless network is the intended one. Therefore, verifying the network connection is essential to prevent potential security breaches that may result from unauthorized access to the network.

Wireless networks are a crucial component of network infrastructure. Wi-Fi is a significant contributor to increased availability and connection hunger among users, and it is critical to building a robust core in network architecture (Zhang *et al.* 2019). While technology grows swiftly, defences are not necessarily hand-in-hand with new attacks. Poor infrastructure is increasingly prevalent. Examples of the absence of security implementations are old systems that use uncertain or even obsolete techniques. No encryption during communication will occur if WPA/WPA2 functionality is not used (Lee and Fumagalli, 2019). The WPA2 protocol is commonly utilized in contemporary wireless network (Vahnhof and Piessens, 2017). WPA2 establishes a 4-way handshake key exchange mechanism and data-confidentiality protocols to encrypt traffic. This protocol was thought to be secure; however, it has now been breached. The 4-way handshake has a design fault in that by compelling the authenticator to resend the third message of the handshake, a supplicant can potentially resent the fourth message.

Rogue can be defined in many other ways. Some say anything other than legitimate clients and AP's are rogue devices. Another approach is that anything on the wireless networks that isn't authenticated is rogue. For this paper, the rogue is a device, an AP, or a client trying to connect, attack or interfere with the wireless network. Briefly, this paper accepts a rogue as a malicious entity.

There are two types of rogue access points.

- Internal rogue AP
- External rogue AP

An internal rogue access point refers to an instance where an employee brings in their own access point and connects it to the company network. This type of access point is not monitored or controlled by IT staff, making it vulnerable to attackers who can use it as a gateway to gain unauthorized access.

On the other hand, an external rogue access point is created and controlled by an attacker. The attacker sets up the access point to appear legitimate by using the same SSID as the legitimate access point and amplifying its signal to attract unsuspecting users. Through fake websites and portals, the attacker can trick users into revealing sensitive information such as passwords and credit card details. These rogue access points are difficult to detect and shut down as the attacker needs to be physically present. Access points can be installed on towers or site hosts, and in some cases, an attacker can spoof MAC addresses of legitimate access points to gain access. Additionally, an attacker can create interference intentionally by using a broadcast de-authentication attack on one of the access points, or it could happen unintentionally. The existence of rogue access points poses a significant threat to the security of computer networks. Thus, it is imperative to establish effective measures to identify and prevent threat from infiltrating the network.

2.0 LITERATURE REVIEW

2.1 Wireless Security Threats and Vulnerabilities

Wireless local area networks (WLANs) are susceptible to a range of security threats, such as Denial of Service (DoS) and Distributed Denial of Service (DDoS) attacks. (Li, 2020). These types of attacks can overload authorized servers with a high volume of traffic, causing disruptions to normal network functions. Rogue Access Points (RAPs) can be used to launch DoS attacks, which makes it crucial to identify and eliminate these access points to enhance the security of WLANs.

2.1.1 Man in the Middle Attack

A Man in The Middle (MITM) attack refers to a security threat in which an intruder intercepts the communication between two parties and modifies the transmitted data. The attacker can exploit Rogue Access Points (RAPs) to gain access to a wireless network. By setting up a RAP and tricking a client device to connect to it, the attacker can carry out a MITM attack. In such a scenario, the attacker acts as a "man in the middle" who can eavesdrop on and tamper with sensitive information that the client transmits to its intended recipient. This type of attack poses a significant risk to the confidentiality and integrity of wireless network communications, making it crucial to develop effective strategies to detect and prevent RAPs and MITM attacks.

MITM attacks are a serious security threat and are often used in conjunction with RAPs (Schofield et al., 2019). The use of RAPs in MITM attacks has been well-documented in previous works (Filkins et al., 2016). These attacks have three main components: the user or victim, the person or contact with whom the user is attempting to interact, and the "man in the middle," or the entity attempting to intercept the victim's communication. The RAP allows the attacker to carry out the MITM attack, giving the attacker complete visibility of the user's data and the ability to manipulate this data before it reaches its intended recipient.

Figure 1. Man in the middle attack

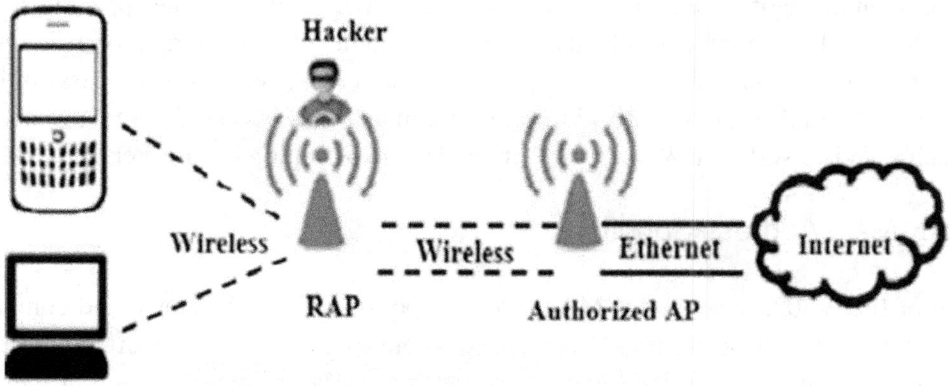

Wireless Access Points (WAPs) are an integral part of the security infrastructure for organizations. Despite having firewalls, it is crucial to recognize the importance of WAPs, as firewalls cannot identify attackers who create rogue access points within the Local Area Network (LAN). Furthermore, even the security protocol, WPA2 (Wi-Fi Protected Access version 2), does not offer complete protection against rogue access points since it can only be installed on authorized or managed access points. Rogue access points, however, are considered unmanaged, and hence security controls cannot be enforced on them. Rogue access point threats operate at a lower level than conventional security measures such as antivirus programs and wired Intrusion Detection Systems (IDS).

2.1.2 Eavesdropping

Wireless Local Area Networks (WLANs) are vulnerable to eavesdropping, a technique that involves intercepting and monitoring data traffic transmitted through radio frequency signals by Access Points (APs). Passive eavesdropping is particularly easy in WLANs because of the susceptibility of signals transmitted by APs. An attacker can intercept signals from a significant distance, depending on the signal's strength, even though the wireless transmission range is limited by the AP's antenna. The attacker can gain access to sensitive information without the victim's knowledge, which poses a significant threat to organizations. Encryption mechanisms can be used to secure the data transmitted over the WLAN to mitigate the risk of eavesdropping.

2.1.3 Manipulation

Wireless Local Area Networks (WLANs) face a significant threat from manipulation attacks, where an intruder alters data packets as they are transmitted between the access point and the intended recipient. Such attacks can be highly detrimental since they allow attackers to gain access to sensitive information by presenting as a legitimate access point, or RAP. War driving tools enable attackers to monitor and manipulate data transmission within the network. RAPs are designed to deceive users into connecting to them rather than the legitimate access point. This is achieved by creating the appearance of a strong signal strength and a large number of clients, which makes it an attractive target for users. As a result, attackers can monitor all communications on the network, and if the network is not password-protected or the security protocol is weak, sensitive information can be easily accessed. Even advanced security protocols such as WEP, WPA, or WPA-2 are vulnerable to exploitation by attackers.

2.1.4 WLAN MAC Address Spoofing

In the realm of IEEE 802.11 networks, MAC address spoofing is a well-known and commonly used technique in attacks. To secure these networks, access control lists (ACLs) are often put in place and can be implemented on both Windows and Linux platforms. The primary function of these ACLs is to restrict access to various IT assets, programs, and objects based on the MAC address of the device connecting to the network. However, even with the implementation of ACLs, MAC address spoofing can bypass these security measures and grant access to attackers. In a MAC address spoofing attack, attackers manipulate the MAC address of their device to match that of an authorized device, thereby bypassing the ACL and gaining network access. This form of attack can have severe consequences, such as the compromise of sensitive information or the ability to launch further attacks.

The detection of falsified RAPs (Rogue Access Points) is paramount in maintaining the security and integrity of wireless networks and their connected devices and systems. Therefore, it is of utmost importance to implement effective measures to detect and prevent MAC address spoofing attacks to safeguard the connected devices and systems in wireless networks.

2.1.5 Access Control List Bypassing

Attackers always attempt to gain unauthorized access to an internal network of an organization by exploiting the constraints of access control lists (ACLs) with the help of MAC address spoofing. MAC address spoofing is a technique in which an attacker modifies a device's MAC address to match that of an authorized device, allowing them to circumvent the ACL restrictions. To execute this type of attack, an attacker can employ various methods to gather a list of authorized MAC addresses, including active and passive sniffing techniques. Once an authorized MAC address list is obtained, the attacker can use it to perform MAC address spoofing and successfully gain access to the network without being detected

2.1.6 Authorized User Credentials

Access to a WLAN is a vital point for an attacker, but it is only one element in a complex series of steps to compromise an organization's data security. The applications that run over the WLAN often contain sensitive data, which can be exploited by an attacker through application vulnerabilities and authorized user access credentials. Therefore, it is crucial to implement effective Rogue Access Point (RAP) detection mechanisms to secure organizational data and prevent unauthorized access. RAPs serve as an important security measure to ensure that organizations can secure their WLAN networks and protect sensitive data from unauthorized access.

2.1.7 Wired Equivalent Privacy (WEP)

To safeguard the privacy of users in WLAN networks, the WEP (Wired Equivalent Privacy) technology is utilized. As with any wireless network, WLANs are vulnerable to attacks that can result in privacy breaches, and the WEP protocol was designed to mitigate this risk. The technology relies on the use of a pre-shared key that is shared among wireless stations, which is then utilized to encrypt data packets transmitted over the network. This makes it difficult for an unauthorized user to decipher the data packets, as they do not possess the pre-shared key. However, if the pre-shared key is poorly constructed, an attacker may be able to deduce it by capturing and analyzing the data packets transmitted over the network.

2.1.8 Wi-Fi Protected Access 2 (WPA2)

The WPA2 algorithm was developed to overcome the security vulnerabilities found in the WEP and WPA technologies used in local area networks operating under IEEE 802.11 standard. Its design employs advanced encryption and authentication mechanisms to offer improved security. To strengthen encryption, it uses the AES algorithm. For authentication, it uses two methods: pre-shared key and IEEE 802.11 standard authentication, to prevent identity theft. The WPA2 algorithm operates in two modes, regular and enterprise. It initially uses pre-shared key authentication in regular mode, and later switches to enterprise mode.

a) WPA-2 Vulnerabilities

Despite its improved security features, WPA2 is not immune to vulnerabilities and attacks. Some of the existing vulnerabilities in the WPA2 technology are as follows:

- The IEEE 802.11 standard only addresses security at the data link layer, leaving the physical layer vulnerable to attacks, which could result in a loss of availability.
- The various frames used in wireless LAN operations, which are responsible for successful configuration and deployment, are vulnerable to various attacks and may reveal important information about the network to an attacker.
- The WPA2 feature of de-authentication, intended to improve security, could also be exploited by an attacker to carry out various spoofing attacks.
- The WPA2 also has a feature called disassociation, which an attacker may use to carry out various authentication attacks.

2.2 Rogue Access Point

A rogue access point (AP) is an unauthorized AP that is not installed by the WLAN administrator. Attackers can set up rogue APs with the same SSID as genuine APs to lure users into connecting to them.

This can enable the attackers to collect personal information from users or conduct a man-in-the-middle (MITM) attack. Attackers can also capture the MAC address information of legitimate APs through passive monitoring, and then modify the MAC address of the rogue AP to masquerade as a legitimate AP and avoid being detected. Rogue APs are low cost and easy to install, which poses a significant security risk to WLANs, especially public WLANs.

The Rogue Access point is a device that pretends to be a legitimate access point in order to direct user traffic to itself (Samra *et al.,* 2015). The goal of this attack is for the malicious attacker to launch additional attacks against the end user. Once connected to the attacker's rogue access point, the end user is vulnerable to whatever action the attacker chooses to take. Interception of traffic, falsification of traffic being sent to the user, and blocking user access.

A Rogue Access Point (RAP) is an unauthorized, unauthenticated access point (AP) that was not created by WLAN administrators (Han, et al., 2018). RAP is frequently configured to look like a legitimate AP in order to trick network users wirelessly into connecting the device to the RAP, thereby classifying it as cybercrime. This RAP is typically configured with an SSID that is similar to, if not identical to, the original AP (SSID and MAC Address). The majority of ordinary users believe that both APs with the same SSID are legitimate APs (Syahrulah *et al.,* 2018). Users of Wi-Fi networks who are stuck on RAP will be easily spied on information privacy or all user activities when using the internet will be known by the author of the RAP attack, causing user data to be leaked and exploitable by the perpetrator. In 2016, Indonesia had the world's second-highest rate of cybercrime, trailing behind Japan. The overall number of cyber-attacks has surpassed 90 million. The illustration depicts a cyber-attack carried out by Indonesian individuals, which also involves RAP attacks (Syafruddin *et al.,* 2016). This RAP attack is a social technique engineering attack in certain current hacking techniques, leveraging the target's weak areas to gather sensitive data that will subsequently be utilized as a first step to perpetrate a larger crime.

Rogue APs are classified into four types by (Liran *et al,* 2018), improperly configured APs, unauthorized APs, phishing APs, and compromised APs. Improperly configured APs are set up as a result of any configuration error, insufficient knowledge to select from encryption schemes and authentication algorithms, and any faulty AP can become a Rogue AP. An unauthorized AP is one that behaves like a legitimate AP and is installed into a secure network without the permission of the server. Phishing AP attempts to obtain credentials, such as usernames and passwords, by impersonating a legitimate AP. An intruder creates a compromised AP by cracking encryption schemes. Once the intruder has obtained the security credentials, he can create an unlimited number of Rogue APs. It is an insider attack, making it more dangerous.

2.2.1 Rogue Access Point Attacks

According to (Wei et al, 2009), the rogue access point is one of the most difficult security breaches to a Wi-Fi network rogue access point. Rogue access point(s) are installed without the explicit permission of a network administrator. An attacker can use a rogue access point to redirect clients to bogus login portals, steal passwords, access credit card information by eavesdropping on communication channels, launch man-in-the-middle attacks, and so on. All these attacks can perform by creating an evil twin of a legitimate access point.

2.2.2 Evil Twin Attack

An attacker creates an evil twin AP to entice clients into connecting to it and redirecting them to fraudulent websites in order to steal client information. To set up the evil twin, the attacker spoofs the MAC address and the Service Set Identifier (SSID) of the genuine AP. When a client views the list of available Wi-Fi APs, it only sees one AP rather than two, because the evil twin AP spoofs both the MAC address and the SSID of the genuine AP. Most modern operating systems (OS) are set up to connect to the AP with the strongest signal if there are multiple APs with the same SSID. In the presence of an evil twin AP, the client(s) are associated with the evil twin AP if the signal strength of the evil twin exceeds the signal strength of the genuine AP. Higher signal strength equals higher throughput and lower frame loss. As a result, a client will always prefer APs with higher signal strength. All modern operating systems display a list of available APs in descending order of signal strength. This type of attack is typically launched near public Wi-Fi hotspots, libraries, coffee shops, hotels, and other popular Wi-Fi locations.

It should be noted that the evil twin must provide Internet access to the clients who connect to it. Normally, the AP provides Internet access to clients. If the evil twin AP does not provide Internet access, clients will disconnect from the evil twin AP and switch to other APs. The evil twin can either bridge the connection using the genuine AP (because the genuine AP is already configured to provide Internet services) or provide a private Internet connection entirely on its own. The attacker's private connection assists it in evading many existing detection methodologies. It was assumed in this work that the attacker who set up the evil twin provides a private connection.

2.3 Rogue Access Detection

The challenge of detecting rogue APs lies in the lack of cooperation from both the rogue AP and the system that is utilizing the rogue AP for malicious purposes. Different approaches will be examined and analyzed to identify the most effective means of detecting rogue APs on the network. Through the evaluation and comparison of various rogue AP detection methods, a comprehensive understanding of the strengths and limitations of each approach will be developed. The ultimate aim is to identify the most efficient and reliable approach that can accurately detect rogue APs and prevent potential security breaches on the network. This research seeks to provide insights into the best approaches to rogue AP detection that can be employed in wireless and wireless local area networks. The findings of this research will be useful to network administrators and security experts in identifying the best methods for mitigating security threats posed by rogue APs.

2.3.1 Necessity for Rogue Access Point Detection

There are four major types of losses that can occur as a result of a network security breach. These losses are as follows:

- Loss of confidentiality
- Loss of availability
- Loss of integrity
- Loss of identity

When there is a breach of confidentiality, the contents of the IT objects are seen by an unauthorized person, resulting in a breach of confidentiality.

Many times, attackers launch an attack on a server to ensure that it cannot function properly. When this occurs, authorized clients will be unable to access the server's services. This type of loss is referred to as a loss of availability.

When data is being transferred over a channel, there are some attacks in which the attacker obtains the data. An attacker then modifies the data obtained in the middle.

The attacker then sends the modified data to the original recipient. There is no way for this receiver to know whether or not data has been modified. This is referred to as a loss of integrity.

In some attacks, the attacker assumes the identity of another user or computer and sends a message to a legitimate user. As a result, the authorized user comes to the incorrect conclusion about the sender's identity. This type of loss is referred to as identity loss.

When RAP is deployed in an IEEE 802.11 wireless LAN, an attacker can launch a variety of attacks, resulting in all of the major losses listed above. Furthermore, if a wireless LAN is linked to a wired LAN, an attacker may gain access to the organization's internal network. Based on these losses, it is clear that the presence of RAP is a major threat to organizational security.

As a result, technologies and methods for detecting the presence of RAP are required.

2.3.2 Rogue Access Point Detection Methods

Approaches to detecting rogue APs are discussed in this section. Client-side, Server-side, and Hybrid methods are the three main classifications. Figure 2 shows the overall classification and techniques for each approach. Every strategy has advantages and disadvantages. With Server-side's Hybrid framework efficient solution can be achieved.

Figure 2. Rogue AP detection methods

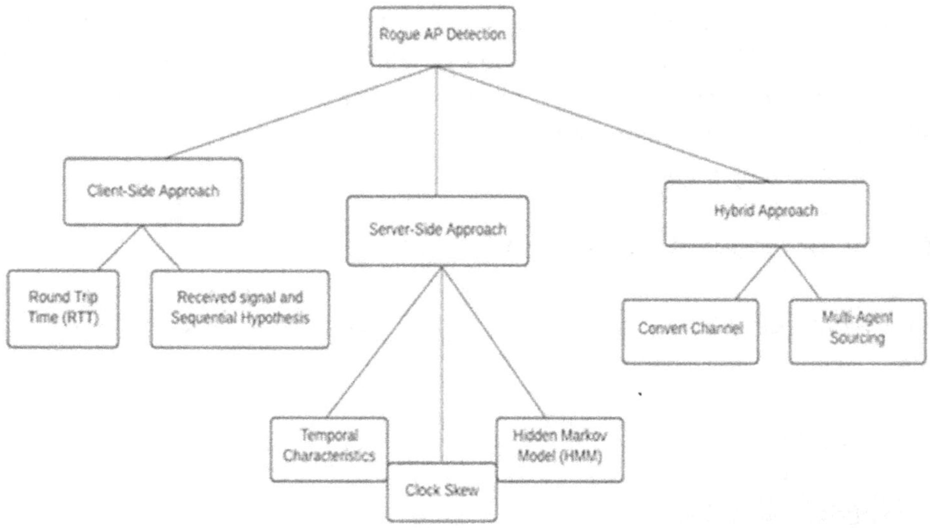

2.4 Related Works

With the proliferation of wireless networks, wireless security has become a critical issue. One of the significant risks to wireless security is the presence of rogue access points (RAPs). Rogue access points are unauthorized access points that are installed without the knowledge or consent of the network administrator, creating an opportunity for attackers to launch attacks. This section provides an overview of RAPs and the types of attacks that can be executed through these access points. The chapter focuses on analyzing different types of RAP attacks and the detection mechanisms used to mitigate them. Additionally, this chapter examines previous works on RAPs, identifying their limitations and suggesting potential solutions. By presenting a comprehensive review of RAPs, this section will contribute to the broader field of network security by enhancing our understanding of RAPs and the challenges they pose to wireless networks.

Figure 3. Rogue AP scenario
Source: Kalitut (2020)

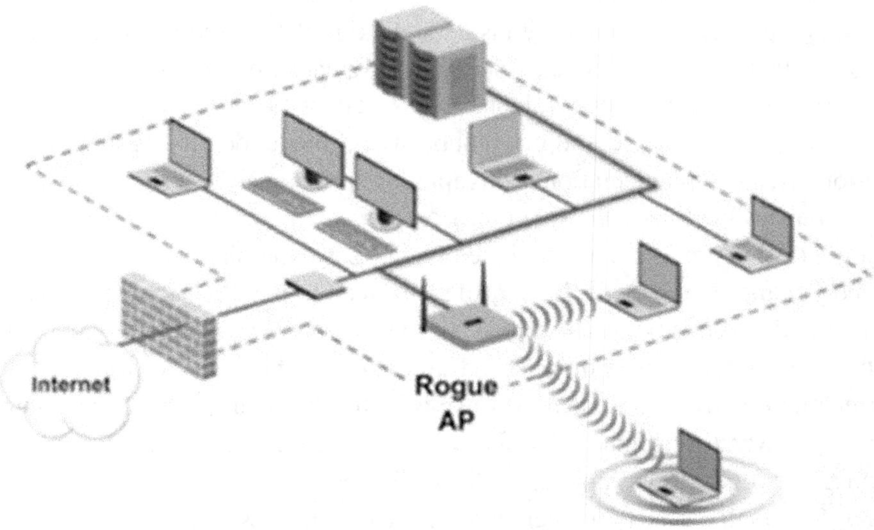

According to (Wei et al, 2009), the rogue access point is one of the most difficult security breaches to a Wi-Fi network rogue access point. Rogue access point(s) are installed without the explicit permission of a network administrator. An attacker can use a rogue access point to redirect clients to bogus login portals, steal passwords, access credit card information by eavesdropping on communication channels, launch man-in-the-middle attacks, and so on. All these attacks can perform by creating an evil twin of a legitimate access point.

Shivraj et al. (2008) developed a server-side detection approach for identifying rogue access points (RAPs) using a Hidden Markov Model (HMM). This method utilizes varying packet inter-arrival time to distinguish between authorized access points and RAPs, achieving an average detection accuracy of up to 85 percent. While the approach is straightforward to manage and maintain and requires minimal effort and expenditure, it has a limitation of requiring a large amount of trained data for detection, which can be a time-consuming process. Furthermore, the approach is only effective in detecting specific types of Denial of Service attacks and may not be suitable for detecting other types of attacks. The proposed model can detect the presence of a RAP within one second with high precision, indicating low false positive and false negative ratios.

Kao et al. (2009) proposed a client-side approach for detecting rogue access points (RAPs) using bottleneck bandwidth analysis based on passive packet analysis. This technique estimates the bandwidth through the use of pair technology and has the advantage of being easy to implement. They also proposed an improved technique called client-side bottleneck bandwidth with sliding window, which enhances detection accuracy. However, this technique has the disadvantage of requiring a reduction in the size of the sliding window, which can affect the accuracy of detection. Furthermore, the technique necessitates the development of a sophisticated algorithm that can be quickly deployed to protect the entire network, which can be a time-consuming process.

Lanier et al., (2011) proposed a novel method to tackle the problem of backdoor rogue devices, which are becoming increasingly prevalent due to the widespread availability of commodity APs. The decrease in the size of APs makes it challenging for network administrators to detect them visually, particularly when attackers use laptops as access points. Unlike typical attacks that come from outside the network, RAP insertion is typically perpetrated by insiders, making it even more challenging to detect. The authors emphasized that the use of rogue devices can have catastrophic consequences since they provide a backdoor entry point into the network, jeopardizing network security. While this approach is effective in detecting backdoor rogue devices, it may not be applicable to identifying other types of rogue access points. Additionally, the implementation of this approach requires significant resources and infrastructure, which may not be feasible for smaller organizations.

Nyathi et al., (2014) presented a technique that utilizes dynamic values to generate time, where the values of y and y change based on the latency of the beacon frame. By utilizing repeaters between clients and repeaters, the difference between APs is expected to increase, leading to a reduction in scalability due to latency. The manipulation of the beacon frame can prevent clients from connecting to rogue access points. This technique can be implemented by using the free bits of any information element to modify the beacon frame. However, this technique's effectiveness may be limited when attackers use more advanced methods to disguise rogue access points. Additionally, the technique's performance may be affected by environmental factors that affect the latency of the beacon frames, such as distance and interference.

Sartid et al., (2017) proposed a novel approach to detecting network intrusions by introducing a distributed intrusion detection system (DIDS). The DIDS employs mobile agent technology combined with network topology design to handle and withstand network attacks. By concealing the network's core resources, the DIDS separates network resources into segments and installs the monitored host on each segment, making the system resistant to all types of attacks. The proposed system also incorporates a variety of security measures, such as the elimination of single points of failure in the design. Furthermore, the shadow agent, in combination with the proxy agent, provides a quick backup and recovery method, while communication between all IDS is encrypted to enhance network security. The proposed DIDS employs public key cryptography to simplify the complexity of the architecture. Although the DIDS offers an efficient and robust method for detecting network intrusions, it may require substantial computing resources due to the deployment of multiple monitored hosts, resulting in high costs. Additionally, the use of mobile agents can introduce security risks due to the possibility of unauthorized access and malicious code execution.

Jang et al., (2020) propose a tool named Powerful Hardware based rogue access point (PrAP)-hunter, which is designed to be a highly accurate detector for determining whether a currently connected access point (AP) is a rogue access point (RAP) or legitimate access point (LAP). The tool is intended for use by network administrators in scenarios where multiple APs are set up with the same Service Set Identifier (SSID) on different channels. PrAP-hunter can also identify the location of APs of interest, even in densely populated and heavily trafficked areas. It is capable of running on both high-performing and low-performing devices, and can be placed on multiple locations to increase detection accuracy. The solution is lightweight, mobile, and easy to use, and requires two Wireless Network Interface Cards (WNICs) on the client device, as well as a Linux operating system. However, a limitation of this tool is that it only works on Linux and Android operating systems, which may not be suitable for all network environments. Additionally, the requirement for two WNICs may limit the use of the tool on certain devices. Finally, while the solution can detect RAPs with high accuracy, it may not provide sophisticated mitigation techniques for dealing with such attacks.

The primary objective of this research is to enhance the security of WLANs by detecting and preventing unauthorized access through rogue access points (RAPs), which pose a significant threat to the network's confidentiality, integrity, and availability. This study aims to overcome the limitations and drawbacks of existing RAP detection techniques, including limited detection accuracy and reduced scalability. To achieve this objective, the research proposes a new approach that utilizes multi-parameter dynamic features to enhance the accuracy, efficiency, and scalability of RAP detection in WLANs. This new approach will provide a reliable and effective solution for RAP detection and prevention, significantly improving the overall security of WLANs.

3.0 METHODOLOGY

3.1 Rogue AP Detection Algorithm

The goal of the rogue access point detection algorithm is to identify access points (APs) that are not authorized to be part of a wireless local area network (WLAN). Rogue APs can be set up by attackers with the intention of passively collecting user personal information or actively conducting a man-in-the-middle (MITM) attack. To detect rogue APs, the algorithm uses a set of parameters that are unique to each AP: the service set identifier (SSID), the basic service set identifier (BSSID), the channel ID, and the media access control (MAC) address list.

The set of all rogue access points is denoted by N, which is initialized as an empty set. To identify rogue APs, the algorithm applies each rule in R to each access point in A(P) and adds any access points that meet at least one of the rules to the set N. This is represented mathematically as:

$$N = \{a\_j \mid a\_j \in A(P), \exists r\_k \in R: r\_k(a\_j)\} \quad 1$$

- The equation $N = \{a\_j \mid a\_j \in A(P), \exists r\_k \in R: r\_k(a\_j)\}$ is a set-builder notation that defines the set N of identified rogue access points.
- The notation $\{a\_j \mid \ldots\}$ means that the set N contains all the elements a_j that satisfy the conditions specified in the following statements.

- The condition a_j ∈ A(P) means that the element a_j is an access point that has been identified in the captured packets set P.
- The condition ∃r_k ∈ R: r_k(a_j) means that there exists at least one rule r_k in the set of rules R such that r_k(a_j) is true. The expression r_k(a_j) means that the rule r_k is applied to the access point a_j, and if it is true, then the access point is identified as rogue.
- Therefore, the overall condition a_j ∈ A(P), ∃r_k ∈ R: r_k(a_j) means that the access point a_j belongs to the set of identified access points A(P), and there exists at least one rule r_k in the set of rules R that identifies it as rogue.

Finally, the algorithm outputs the set N of identified rogue access points. The administrator of the WLAN can then take appropriate action to remove these rogue APs from the network and prevent further security threats.

a) Header Inspection

Header inspection, also known as AP inspection, is a process used to analyze information about access points (APs) on a network. This process involves collecting data about the APs through network scanning, including the AP's SSID (Service Set Identifier), MAC address (Media Access Control address), signal strength, and channel number. The collected data is then analyzed for abnormalities or deviations from expected standards.

b) MAC Address List Matching

The section discusses the Address List Matching process used by the program to identify legitimate access points (APs) on the network and prevent unauthorized access through duplicate APs. The program collects information about the AP's SSID, MAC address, channel number, signal strength, and other relevant data. The AP's data is analyzed to ensure it meets the expected standards and to check for any anomalies or deviations from normal behavior. The program compares the incoming AP's data with the information in the table to identify any potential duplicates or unauthorized APs. If there is a match, the program alerts the system administrator. If there is no match, the AP is added to the list of approved APs and considered a legitimate network device. This process helps ensure the security and integrity of the network.

c) Hashing and Salting

The process of hashing and salting is used to ensure the security and integrity of WLANs. This involves applying a hashing algorithm to the incoming access point's SSID, MAC address, and channel number to generate a unique hash value that represents these characteristics. The hash value is then salted with a nonce to improve security, and the program checks if it is already listed in the approved AP hash values table. If it is present, the program raises an alert and adds the hash value to the table as duplicates. If it is not present, the hash value is added to the list of approved AP hashes and passed on to the database. By generating a unique hash value for each AP and checking for duplicates, this process helps to prevent the addition of unauthorized or duplicate devices to the network, thus protecting it from unauthorized access and malicious activity.

d) File Module/Database

The file module/database is a critical component of the program that stores the approved access points' list, associated information, and unique hash values. The stored information is used as a reference point to validate whether or not an incoming access point is legitimate or malicious. This process helps to ensure the network's security and integrity by comparing each incoming access point's information and hash value against those in the database. When a new access point is detected, the program collects its information and generates a hash value using a hashing algorithm and nonce. The generated hash value is compared to those in the database, and if there is a match, the incoming access point is already approved. If there is no match, the access point is added to the approved list, and its information and hash value are stored in the database. By performing this comparison and verification process, the program can detect and alert the administrator to any potential issues or anomalies on the network, ensuring the security and integrity of the network as a whole.

e) Automation

The program is designed to continuously monitor the network for any changes or updates, particularly the addition or removal of any access points (APs), in order to ensure network security and integrity. By running indefinitely, the program can detect any unauthorized or malicious activity in real-time and alert the administrator or take appropriate action to protect the network from potential threats. The continuous monitoring process is crucial for maintaining network security and reliability.

4.0 RESULT AND DISCUSSION

This comparative analysis results in valuable information about the strengths and weaknesses of different RAP detection methods. With this information, organizations can make informed decisions when selecting the most appropriate approach for their specific needs.

a) Accuracy

This study evaluated the accuracy of different RAP detection methods using metrics such as detection rate, throughput, and latency. The "Rogue Access Point Detection using Multi-Parameter Dynamic Features on WLAN" approach achieved a 98.7% detection rate and 80Mbps average throughput with 20ms latency. In comparison, the "A Client-side Solution for Rogue Access Point Detection based on Received Signal Strength" approach achieved a detection rate of 80% and an average throughput of 60Mbps with 25ms latency. Other approaches were also evaluated, with the "Server-side HMM-based RAP detection approach" having a higher detection rate but lower network throughput and increased latency. The "Hybrid approach for RAP detection in wireless networks" showed promising results with high detection rate and minimal impact on network performance. Overall, the evaluation of RAP detection methods based on detection rate, throughput, and latency provides insight into their suitability for different WLAN environments, and the use of multi-parameter dynamic features offers an effective solution to RAP detection with minimal impact on network performance.

Figure 4. Rogue AP accuracy graph

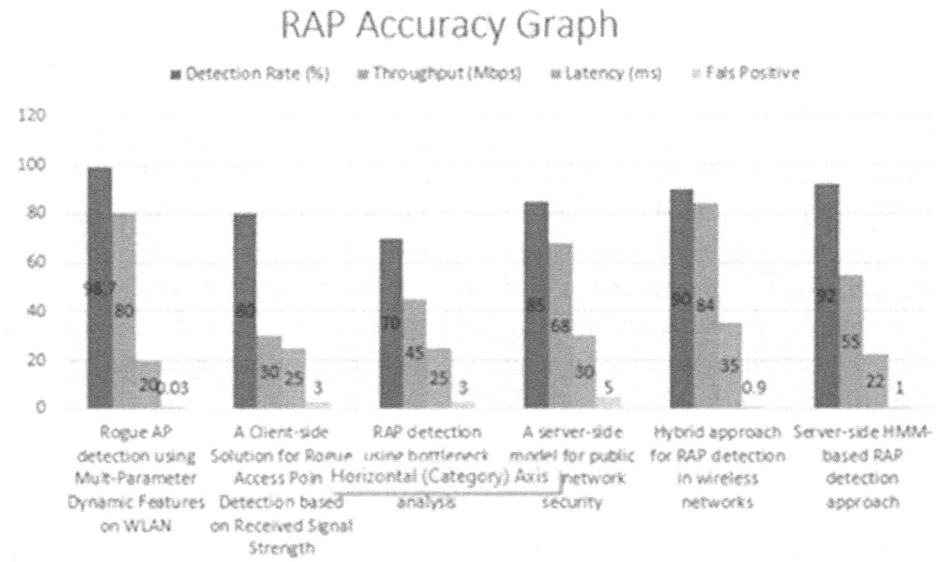

b) Scalability

The scalability of different RAP detection methods was evaluated to determine their effectiveness in large-scale networks. "Rogue Access Point Detection using Multi-Parameter Dynamic Features on WLAN" was found to be a highly scalable method that can be easily integrated with existing WLAN systems. This is due to its ability to use the unique features of Access Points (APs) to detect and monitor rogue APs. In contrast, "Client-side Solution for Rogue Access Point Detection based on Received Signal Strength" may have limited scalability due to its reliance on the signal strength received by client devices. The scalability of a RAP detection method should be evaluated based on the network's specific needs and requirements.

c) Performance

This section examined the performance of four different RAP detection methods. The "Rogue Access Point Detection using Multi-Parameter Dynamic Features on WLAN" approach provides a detailed assessment of each AP's features but can be more resource-intensive and have longer processing times. The "Client-side Solution for Rogue Access Point Detection based on Received Signal Strength" approach is faster but may not assess all AP characteristics comprehensively. The "Hybrid approach for RAP detection in wireless networks" combines client-side and server-side methods for RAP detection but may require more computational resources. The server-side HMM-based RAP detection approach can be effective in active data transmission cases, but not as effective when RAPs are passive and may have longer processing times. Each approach's performance depends on specific use cases and computational resources available. The "Rogue Access Point Detection using Multi-Parameter Dynamic Features on WLAN" approach may provide more dependable AP evaluation and higher accuracy in RAP detection, while other approaches may compromise accuracy or comprehensiveness.

5.0 CONCLUSION AND FUTURE WORKS

This study aimed to detect rogue access points (RAPs) in wireless networks using multi-parameter dynamic features. The proposed method involves scanning available access points and comparing their dynamic features to identify any RAPs, which are then blacklisted in real-time to ensure network security. Results showed that the proposed method effectively detected RAPs and provided continuous real-time protection to the network. This approach is more robust than traditional methods that rely on a single parameter. The success of this project demonstrates the importance of addressing RAPs and provides a basis for further research in wireless network security. This solution can be improved and integrated into existing systems for enhanced security. Future study on rogue access point detection on WLAN utilizing multi-parameter dynamic features could focus on varied environments, such as big corporate networks, public places, or residential networks, to verify its robustness and applicability for different network types. Another interesting area of research might be the application of machine learning techniques to automatically detect rogue access points based on the existing approach's multi-parameter dynamic properties. Incorporating additional characteristics or attributes, such as the location of the access point or the encryption type, may also increase the detection approach's accuracy and robustness. Finally, including the method within network security systems may make it easier to adopt and utilize while also improving overall network security.

REFERENCES

Bshara, M., Orguner, U., Gustafsson, F., & Van Biesen, L. (2010). Fingerprinting Localization in Wireless Networks Based on Received-Signal-Strength Measurements: A Case Study on WiMAX Networks. Vehicular Technology. *IEEE Transactions on Vehicular Technology*, *59*(1), 283–294. doi:10.1109/TVT.2009.2030504

Chandra, R. (2019). Rogue Access Point Detection for Wireless LAN Using Multiparameter Dynamic Feature Analysis (DAIR). Dense Array of Inexpensive Radios that analyze wireless networks of businesses that use desktop technology. *IEEE Transactions on Mobile Computing*, *18*(12), 2123–2134.

Devi, V. B., & Shunmuganathan, K. L. (2017). Neural KDE Based Behaviour Model for Detecting Intrusions in Network Environment. *IAES International Journal of Artificial Intelligence*, *6*(4), 166. doi:10.11591/ijai.v6.i4.pp166-173

Jang, R., Kang, J., Mohaisen, A., & Nyang, D. (2020). Catch Me If You Can: Rogue Access Point Detection Using Intentional Channel Interference. IEEE Transactions on Mobile Computing, 19, 1056-1071. doi:10.1109/TMC.2019.2903052

Kao, F. K., Chen, C. W., Chang, C. J., & Chu, T. H. (2014). An Accurate Fake Access Point Detection Method Based on Deviation of Beacon Time Interval. In *IEEE Eighth International Conference on Software Security and Reliability-Companion* (pp. 1-2). San Francisco, CA: IEEE. 10.1109/SERE-C.2014.13

Kumar, A., & Paul, P. (2016). Security analysis and implementation of a simple method for prevention and detection against Evil Twin attack in IEEE 802.11 wireless LAN. In *2016 International Conference on Computational Techniques in Information and Communication Technologies (ICCTICT)* (pp. 176-181). New Delhi, India: IEEE. 10.1109/ICCTICT.2016.7514574

Li, Y., Liu, B., Shang, Z., & Chen, M. (2019). DDoS attack detection method based on feature extraction of deep belief network. *IOP Conference Series. Earth and Environmental Science*, *252*(3), 032013. Advance online publication. doi:10.1088/1755-1315/252/3/032013

Ma, L., Teymorian, A. Y., & Cheng, X. (2008). A Hybrid Rogue Access Point Protection Framework for Commodity Wi-Fi Networks. In *The 27th Conference on Computer Communications* (pp. 1220-1228). IEEE. 10.1109/INFOCOM.2008.178

Nakhila, O., Amjad, M. F., Dondyk, E., & Zou, C. (2018). Gateway independent user-side wi-fi Evil Twin Attack detection using virtual wireless clients. *Computers & Security*, *74*, 41–54. doi:10.1016/j.cose.2017.12.009

Shivraj, S., & Raghavendra, R. S. (2008). Server-side HMM-based RAP detection approach. In *Proceedings of the International Conference on Wireless Communications, Networking and Mobile Computing* (pp. 1-5). IEEE.

Wang, C., Zheng, X., Chen, Y., & Yang, J. (2017). Locating Rogue Access Point Using Fine-Grained Channel Information. *IEEE Transactions on Mobile Computing, 16*, 2560 - 2573. doi:10.1109/TMC.2016.2629473

Watkins, L., & Singh, S. (2011). Preventing backdoor rogue devices in wireless networks. In *Proceedings of the International Conference on Wireless Communications, Networking and Mobile Computing* (pp. 1-5). IEEE.

Zhang, Z., Hasegawa, H., Yamaguchi, Y., & Shimada, H. (2020). Rogue AP Detection using Similarity of Backbone Delay Fluctuation Histogram. In *2020 International Conference on Information Networking (ICOIN)* (pp. 239-244). Barcelona, Spain: IEEE. 10.1109/ICOIN48656.2020.9016480

Compilation of References

Abaoud, M., Almuqrin, M. A., & Khan, M. F. (2023). Advancing Federated Learning Through Novel Mechanism for Privacy Preservation in Healthcare Applications. *IEEE Access : Practical Innovations, Open Solutions*, *11*, 83562–83579. doi:10.1109/ACCESS.2023.3301162

Abas, N., Dilshad, S., Khalid, A., Saleem, M. S., & Khan, N. (2020). Power quality improvement using dynamic voltage restorer. *IEEE Access : Practical Innovations, Open Solutions*, *8*, 164325–164339. doi:10.1109/ACCESS.2020.3022477

Abdalrdha, Z. K., Al-Qinani, I. H., & Abbas, F. N. (2019). Subject review: Key generation in different cryptography algorithm. *International Journal of Scientific Research in Science, Engineering and Technology*, *6*(5), 230–240. doi:10.32628/IJSRSET196550

Abiodun, M. K., Awotunde, J. B., Ogundokun, R. O., Misra, S., Adeniyi, E. A., Arowolo, M. O., & Jaglan, V. (2021, February). Cloud and big data: A mutual benefit for organization development. *Journal of Physics: Conference Series*, *1767*(1), 012020. doi:10.1088/1742-6596/1767/1/012020

Adee, R., & Mouratidis, H. (2022). A dynamic four-step data security model for data in cloud computing based on cryptography and Steganography. *Sensors (Basel)*, *22*(3), 1109. doi:10.339022031109 PMID:35161853

Adeniyi, E. A., Ogundokun, R. O., & Awotunde, J. B. (2021). IoMT-Based Wearable Body Sensors Network Healthcare Monitoring System. In IoT in Healthcare and Ambient Assisted Living. Studies in Computational Intelligence (vol. 933). Springer. doi:10.1007/978-981-15-9897-5_6

Agarwal. (2014). Virtualization in Cloud Computing. *Information Technology and Software Eng, 4*(2).

Agarwal, V. (2021). Identity theft detection using machine learning. *International Journal for Research in Applied Science and Engineering Technology*, *9*(8), 1943–1946. doi:10.22214/ijraset.2021.37696

Ahmed, T. Y. (2012). Analytic Study of Load Balancing Techniques Using Tool Cloud Analyst. *International Journal of Engineering Research and Applications, 2*(2). www.ijera.com

Al Rubaie, E. M. (2021). Improvement in credit card fraud detection using ensemble classification technique and user data. *International Journal of Nonlinear Analysis and Applications*, *12*(2), 1255–1265.

Alaca, F., & Oorschot, P. C. (2020). Comparative analysis and framework evaluating Web single sign-on systems. *ACM Computing Surveys*, *53*(5), 1–34. doi:10.1145/3409452

Alazizi, A., Habrard, A., Jacquenet, F., He-Guelton, L., & Oblé, F. (2020). Dual sequential variational autoencoders for fraud detection. *Advances in Intelligent Data Analysis XVIII: 18th International Symposium on Intelligent Data Analysis, IDA 2020, Konstanz, Germany, April 27–29, 2020 Proceedings*, *18*, 14–26.

Ali, A., Pasha, M. F., Fang, O. H., Khan, R., Almaiah, M. A., & Al Hwaitat, A. K. (2022). Big Data Based Smart Blockchain for Information Retrieval in Privacy-Preserving Healthcare System. In *Big Data Intelligence for Smart Applications* (pp. 279–296). Springer International Publishing. doi:10.1007/978-3-030-87954-9_13

Ali, M., Khan, S. U., & Vasilakos, A. V. (2015). Security in cloud computing: Opportunities and challenges. *Information Sciences, 305*, 357–383. doi:10.1016/j.ins.2015.01.025

Ali, S., Abdullah, T. P. T. A., Athar, A., Hussain, A., Ali, M., Yaseen, M., Joo, M.-I., & Kim, H.-C. (2023). Metaverse in healthcare integrated with explainable ai and blockchain: Enabling immersiveness, ensuring trust, and providing patient data security. *Sensors (Basel), 23*(2), 565. doi:10.339023020565 PMID:36679361

Alkhatib, K. I.-A. (2021). Credit Card Fraud Detection Based on Deep Neural Network Approach. In *12th International Conference on Information and Communication Systems (ICICS)* (pp. 153-156). IEEE.

Al-Marridi, A. Z., Mohamed, A., & Erbad, A. (2021). Reinforcement learning approaches for efficient and secure blockchain-powered smart health systems. *Computer Networks, 197*, 108279. doi:10.1016/j.comnet.2021.108279

Alphand, O., Amoretti, M., Claeys, T., Dall'Asta, S., Duda, A., Ferrari, G., Rousseau, F., Tourancheau, B., Veltri, L., & Zanichelli, F. (2018). IoTChain: A blockchain security architecture for the Internet of Things. In 2018 IEEE wireless communications and networking conference (WCNC) (pp. 1-6). IEEE. doi:10.1109/WCNC.2018.8377385

Al-Rayis, E., & Kurdi, H. A. (2013). Performance Analysis of Load Balancing Architectures in Cloud Computing. *IEEE Proc. of European Modeling Symposium (EMS),* 520-524. 10.1109/EMS.2013.10

Alzahrani, A. H. (2018). Generation of DDoS Attack Dataset for Effective IDS Development and Evaluation. *Journal of Information Security, 9,* 225-241. doi:10.4236/jis.2018.94016

AlZain, M. A., Pardede, E., Soh, B., & Thom, J. A. (2012). Cloud computing security: from single to multi-clouds. In *2012 45th Hawaii International Conference on System Sciences* (pp. 5490-5499). IEEE. 10.1109/HICSS.2012.153

Amandeep, Yadav, & Mohammad. (2014). Different Strategies for Load Balancing in Cloud Computing Environment: A Critical Study. *International Journal of Scientific Research Engineering & Technology, 3*(1).

Amit & Kariyani. (2013). Allocation Of Virtual Machines In Cloud Computing Using Load Balancing Algorithm. *International Journal of Computer Science and Information Technology & Security, 3*(1).

An, J., & Cho, S. (2015). *Variational Autoencoder based Anomaly Detection using Reconstruction Probability.* SNU Data Mining Center. Retrieved April 26, 2020, from http://dm.snu.ac.kr/static/docs/TR/SNUDM-TR-2015-03.pdf

Angeline, P. J. (1993). *Evolutionary Algorithms and Emergent Intelligence* [Dissertation]. The Ohio State University.

Aniello, L., Baldoni, R., Gaetani, E., Lombardi, F., Margheri, A., & Sassone, V. (2017, September). A prototype evaluation of a tamper-resistant high performance blockchain-based transaction log for a distributed database. In *2017 13th European Dependable Computing Conference (EDCC)* (pp. 151-154). IEEE.

Aono, Y., & Hayashi, T. (2017). *Privacy-preserving deep learning via additively homomorphic encryption.* IEEE TIFS.

Aremu, D. R., & Moses, A. K. (n.d.). Grid, cloud, and big data: Technologies overlaps. *International Journal of Information Processing and Communication.*

Asl, P. F., Monjezi, M., Hamidi, J. K., & Armaghani, D. J. (2018). Optimization of flyrock and rock fragmentation in the Tajareh limestone mine using metaheuristics method of firefly algorithm. *Engineering with Computers, 34*(2), 241–251. doi:10.100700366-017-0535-9

Awotunde, J. B., Jimoh, R. G., Folorunso, S. O., Adeniyi, E. A., Abiodun, K. M., & Banjo, O. O. (2021). Privacy and security concerns in IoT-based healthcare systems. In *The Fusion of Internet of Things, Artificial Intelligence, and Cloud Computing in Health Care* (pp. 105–134). Springer International Publishing. doi:10.1007/978-3-030-75220-0_6

Awujoola, O. J., Ogwueleka, F. N., Irhebhude, M. E., & Misra, S. (2021). Wrapper based approach for network intrusion detection model with combination of dual filtering technique of resample and SMOTE. In *Artificial Intelligence for Cyber Security: Methods, Issues and Possible Horizons or Opportunities* (pp. 139–167). Springer International Publishing. doi:10.1007/978-3-030-72236-4_6

Bagwaiya & Raghuwanshi. (n.d.). *Hybrid approach using Throttled and ESCE Load Balancing Algorithm in Cloud Computing*. Academic Press.

Bahache, A. N. E. (2018). *A Metaheuristic Based Approach for Solving the Index Selection Problem in Data Warehouses* [Doctoral dissertation]. FACULTE Mathématique et Informatique Departement D'Informatique.

Bala, K., Vashist, S., Singh, R., & Singh, G. (2014). A Review of the Load Balancing Techniques. *International Journal of Advances in Computer Science and Communication Engineering*, *2*(I).

Bal, P. K., Mohapatra, S. K., Das, T. K., Srinivasan, K., & Hu, Y. C. (2022). A joint resource allocation, security with efficient task scheduling in cloud computing using hybrid machine learning techniques. *Sensors (Basel)*, *22*(3), 1242. doi:10.339022031242 PMID:35161987

Bannerman, S., & Orasch, A. (2020). Privacy and smart cities: A Canadian survey. *Canadian Journal of Urban Research*, *29*(1), 17–38.

Bao, Y., Hilary, G., & Ke, B. (2022). Artificial intelligence and fraud detection. *Innovative Technology at the Interface of Finance and Operations*, *I*, 223–247. doi:10.1007/978-3-030-75729-8_8

Barsocchi, P., Bartoli, G., Betti, M., Girardi, M., Mammolito, S., Pellegrini, D., & Zini, G. (2020). Wireless Sensor Networks for Continuous Structural Health Monitoring of Historic Masonry Towers. *International Journal of Architectural Heritage*. Advance online publication. doi:10.1080/15583058.2020.1719229

Batra, G., Atluri, V., Vaidya, J., & Sural, S. (2019). Deploying ABAC policies using RBAC Systems. *Journal of Computer Security*, *27*(4), 483–506. doi:10.3233/JCS-191315 PMID:31929684

Bedi, & Singh. (2014). *An Efficient Load Balancing based on Resource Utilization in Cloud Computing*. Computer Science and Engineering Department of Thapar University.

Behnia, R., Ebrahimi, M., & Riasi, A. (2023, July). Efficient Secure Aggregation for Privacy-Preserving Federated. *Machine Learning*, *19*. arXiv2304.03841v4 [cs.CR]

Belchior, R., Vasconcelos, A., Guerreiro, S., & Correia, M. (2021). A survey on blockchain interoperability: Past, present, and future trends. *ACM Computing Surveys*, *54*(8), 1–41. doi:10.1145/3471140

Bellinger, C. D. (2017). Manifold-based synthetic oversampling with manifold conformance estimation. *Machine Learning*.

Benabbou, F. (2015). Load Balancing for Improved Quality of Service in the Cloud. *International Journal of Advanced Computer Science and Applications*, *6*(7).

Bendiab, K., Kolokotronis, N., Shiaeles, S., & Boucherkha, S. (2018, August). WiP: A novel blockchain-based trust model for cloud identity management. In *2018 IEEE 16th Intl Conf on Dependable, Autonomic and Secure Computing, 16th Intl Conf on Pervasive Intelligence and Computing, 4th Intl Conf on Big Data Intelligence and Computing and Cyber Science and Technology Congress (DASC/PiCom/DataCom/CyberSciTech)* (pp. 724-729). IEEE. 10.1109/DASC/PiCom/DataCom/CyberSciTec.2018.00126

Bengio, Y., Lamblin, P., Popovici, D., & Larochelle, H. (2006). Greedy layer-wise training of deep networks. *Advances in Neural Information Processing Systems*, 19.

Berisha, B., Mëziu, E., & Shabani, I. (2022) Big data analytics in Cloud computing: an overview. *Journal of Cloud Computing*, *11*, 24.

Berwa. (2015). *Load Balancing in Cloud Computing.* Department of Computer Science and Application, K.U., Kurukshetra, India.

Berwal & Kant. (2015). Load Balancing in Cloud Computing. *International Journal of Computer Science and Computing, 6*(2).

Bhaskar, Deepu, & Shylaja. (2012). Dynamic Allocation Method For Efficient Load Balancing In Virtual Machines For Cloud Computing Environment. *Advanced Computing: An International Journal, 3*(5).

Bhatawdekar, R. M., Armaghani, D. J., & Azizi, A. (2021). Review of Empirical and Intelligent Techniques for Evaluating Rock Fragmentation Induced by Blasting. In *Environmental Issues of Blasting* (pp. 21–39). Springer. doi:10.1007/978-981-16-8237-7_2

Bhola, J., Soni, S., & Kakarla, J. (2019). A scalable and energy-efficient MAC protocol for sensor and actor networks. *International Journal of Communication Systems*, *32*(13), e4057. doi:10.1002/dac.4057

Bigelow, S. J., Neenan, S., Casey, K., & Earls, A. R. (2023, May 17). *What is public cloud? Everything you need to know.* Cloud Computing. https://www.techtarget.com/searchcloudcomputing/definition/public-cloud

Bikramjit, A. (2017). Survey on Various Load Balancing Techniques in Cloud Computing. *Advances in Computers*, *2*, 28–34.

Blasimme, A., Ferretti, A., & Vayena, E. (2021). Digital contact tracing against COVID-19 in Europe: Current features and ongoing developments. *Frontiers in Digital Health*, *3*, 660823. doi:10.3389/fdgth.2021.660823 PMID:34713135

Bonguet, A., & Bellaiche, M. (2017). A Survey of Denial-of-Service and Distributed Denial of Service Attacks and Defenses in Cloud Computing. *Future Internet*, *9*(3), 43. Advance online publication. doi:10.3390/fi9030043

Brandão, A., Mamede, H. S., & Gonçalves, R. (2018). Systematic review of the literature, research on blockchain technology as support to the trust model proposed applied to smart places. *Trends and Advances in Information Systems and Technologies*, *1*(6), 1163–1174. doi:10.1007/978-3-319-77703-0_113

Braun, T., Fung, B. C., Iqbal, F., & Shah, B. (2018). Security and privacy challenges in smart cities. *Sustainable Cities and Society*, *39*, 499–507. doi:10.1016/j.scs.2018.02.039

Briggs, Z. F., & Andras, P. (2021). *A review of privacy-preserving federated learning for the internet-of-things.* Federated Learning Systems. doi:10.1007/978-3-030-70604-3_2

Britannica. (2023, March 3). Information retrieval. In *Encyclopedia Britannica.* https://www.britannica.com/technology/information-retrieval

Brown, I., & Marsden, C. T. (2023). *Regulating code: Good governance and better regulation in the information age.* MIT Press.

Bshara, M., Orguner, U., Gustafsson, F., & Van Biesen, L. (2010). Fingerprinting Localization in Wireless Networks Based on Received-Signal-Strength Measurements: A Case Study on WiMAX Networks. Vehicular Technology. *IEEE Transactions on Vehicular Technology*, *59*(1), 283–294. doi:10.1109/TVT.2009.2030504

Bughin, J., Chui, M., & Manyika, J. (2010). Clouds, big data, and smart assets: Ten tech-enabled business trends to watch. *The McKinsey Quarterly*, *56*(1), 75–86.

Büyüközkan, G., & Göçer, F. (2018). Digital Supply Chain: Literature review and a proposed framework for future research. *Computers in Industry*, *97*, 157–177. doi:10.1016/j.compind.2018.02.010

Buyya, R., Broberg, J., & Goscinski, A. M. (2010). *Cloud computing: Principles and paradigms*. John Wiley & Sons.

Buyya, R., & Murshed, M. (2002). Gridsim: A toolkit for the modeling and simulation of distributed resource management and scheduling for grid computing. *Concurrency and Computation*, *14*(13-15), 1175–1220. doi:10.1002/cpe.710

Calheiros, Ranjan, De Rose, & Buyya. (2009). *CloudSim: A Novel Framework for Modeling and Simulation of Cloud Computing Infrastructures and Services*. Academic Press.

Cao, X., & Fang, M. (2020). *Fltrust: Byzantine-robust federated learning via trust bootstrapping*. arXiv preprint arXiv:2012.13995.

Carl, D. (2016). Tutorial on Variational AutoencodersCarnegie Mellon UC Berkeley.

Chai, W., & Bigelow, S. J. (2022, November 10). *Cloud computing*. https://www.techtarget.com/searchcloudcomputing/definition/cloud-computing

Chain, K., Chang, K.-H., Kuo, W.-C., & Yang, J.-F. (2015). Enhancement authentication protocol using zero-knowledge proofs and chaotic maps. *International Journal of Communication Systems*, *30*(1), e2945. Advance online publication. doi:10.1002/dac.2945

Chamani, J. G., Wang, Y., Papadopoulos, D., Zhang, M., & Jalili, R. (2022). Multi-User Dynamic Searchable Symmetric Encryption With Corrupted Participants. *IEEE Transactions on Dependable and Secure Computing*, *20*(1), 114–130. doi:10.1109/TDSC.2021.3127546

Chamikara, M. A. P., Bertok, P., Liu, D., Camtepe, S., & Khalil, I. (2018). Efficient data perturbation for privacy preserving and accurate data stream mining. *Pervasive and Mobile Computing*, *48*, 1–19. doi:10.1016/j.pmcj.2018.05.003

Chandra, H., & Bahuguna, H. (2017). A survey of load balancing algorithms in cloud computing. *International Journal of Computer Engineering and Applications*, *11*(12).

Chandra, R. (2019). Rogue Access Point Detection for Wireless LAN Using Multiparameter Dynamic Feature Analysis (DAIR). Dense Array of Inexpensive Radios that analyze wireless networks of businesses that use desktop technology. *IEEE Transactions on Mobile Computing*, *18*(12), 2123–2134.

Chaudhary, D., & Chhillar, R. S. (2013). A New Load Balancing Technique for Virtual Machine Cloud Computing Environment. Department of Computer Science and applications, M.D. University, Rohtak, Haryana, India. doi:10.5120/12114-8498

Chen, W. N., Choquette-Choo, C. A., & Kairouz, P. (n.d.). Communication efficient federated learning with secure aggregation and differential privacy. NeurIPS 2021 Workshop Privacy in Machine Learning.

Chen, K., Liu, L., Chen, K., & Liu, L. (2011). Geometric data perturbation for privacy preserving outsourced data mining. *Knowledge and Information Systems*, *29*(3), 657–695. doi:10.100710115-010-0362-4

Chen, M., Malook, T., Rehman, A. U., Muhammad, Y., Alshehri, M. D., Akbar, A., Bilal, M., & Khan, M. A. (2021). Blockchain-Enabled healthcare system for detection of diabetes. *Journal of Information Security and Applications*, *58*, 102771. doi:10.1016/j.jisa.2021.102771

Cho, Jhunjhunwala, Li, & Smith. (2022). *To federate or not to federate: Incentivizing client participation in federated learning*. arXiv preprint arXiv.

Chong, F., Carraro, G., & Wolter, R. (2006). Multi-tenant data architecture. MSDN Library, Microsoft Corporation.

Choo, K. K. R. (2010). Cloud computing: Challenges and future directions. *Trends and Issues in Crime and Criminal Justice*, (400), 1–6.

Chraibi, A., Alla, S. B., & Ezzati, A. (2022). An efficient cloudlet scheduling via bin packing in cloud computing. *Iranian Journal of Electrical and Computer Engineering*, *12*(3), 3226–3226. doi:10.11591/ijece.v12i3.pp3226-3237

Chuanxin, Zhou, Sun Yi, & W. D. (n.d.). Federated learning with Gaussian differential privacy. *Proceedings of the 2020 2nd International Conference on Robotics, Intelligent Control and Artificial Intelligence*, 296-301.

Church, K. S., Schmidt, P. J., & Ajayi, K. (2020). Forecast Cloudy—Fair or Stormy weather: Cloud computing insights and issues. *Journal of Information Systems*, *34*(2), 23–46. doi:10.2308/isys-18-037

Cingolani, P., & Alcalá, F. J. (2013). jFuzzyLogic: A java library to design fuzzy logic controllers according to the standard for fuzzy control programming. *International Journal of Computational Intelligence Systems*, *6*(1), 61–75. do i:10.1080/18756891.2013.818190

Comer, D. E. (2021). The Cloud Computing. CRC Press.

Cui, Y., Gao, F., Shi, Y., Yin, W., Panaousis, E., & Liang, K. (2020). An Efficient Attribute-Based Multi-Keyword Search Scheme in Encrypted Keyword Generation. *IEEE Access : Practical Innovations, Open Solutions*, *8*, 99024–99036. doi:10.1109/ACCESS.2020.2996940

Cui, Z., Jiang, M., Jeong, K., & Kim, B. (2014, May). A Cloud Database Service Approach to the Management of Sensor Data. *2014 International Conference on Information Science & Applications (ICISA)*. 10.1109/ICISA.2014.6847327

Danezis, G., Domingo-Ferrer, J., Hansen, M., Hoepman, J. H., Metayer, D. L., Tirtea, R., & Schiffner, S. (2015). *Privacy and data protection by design-from policy to engineering*. arXiv preprint arXiv:1501.03726.

Dang, S., Amin, O., Shihada, B., & Alouini, M.-S. (2020). What should 6G be? *Nature Electronics*, *3*(Jan), 20–29. doi:10.103841928-019-0355-6

Darko Galinec, D. M. (2017). Cybersecurity and cyber defence: National level strategic approach. *Journal for Control, Measurement, Electronics, Computing and Communications*.

Daryapurkar, A. (2013). Efficient Load Balancing Algorithm in Cloud Environment. International Journal of Computer Science and Applications, 6(2).

Das, D., & Kalra, S. (2020). *An Efficient LSI Based Multi-keyword Ranked Search Algorithm on Encrypted Data in Cloud Environment*. International Wireless Communications and Mobile Computing. doi:10.1109/IWCMC48107.2020.9148123

Dayan, I., Roth, H. R., Zhong, A., Harouni, A., Gentili, A., Abidin, A. Z., Liu, A., Costa, A. B., Wood, B. J., Tsai, C.-S., Wang, C.-H., Hsu, C.-N., Lee, C. K., Ruan, P., Xu, D., Wu, D., Huang, E., Kitamura, F. C., Lacey, G., ... Li, Q. (2021, September). Zhong. Federated learning for predicting clinical outcomes in patients with COVID-19. *Nature Medicine*, *27*(10), 1735–1743. doi:10.103841591-021-01506-3 PMID:34526699

de Oliveira, B. C. F., Marció, B. S., & Flesch, R. C. C. (2021). Enhanced damage measurement in a metal specimen through the image fusion of tone-burst vibro-acoustography and pulse-echo ultrasound data. *Measurement, 167*. doi:10.1016/j.measurement.2020.108445

Delfs, H., Knebl, H., & Delfs, H. (2015). Symmetric-key cryptography. Introduction to Cryptography: Principles and Applications, 11–48. doi:10.1007/978-3-662-47974-2_2

De, M., & Kundu, A. (2020, October). *Datacenter Selection in Cloud Framework for Efficient Load Distribution Using a Fuzzy Approach. Mexican International Conference on Artificial Intelligence*, Mexico City, Mexico. 10.1007/978-3-030-60884-2_32

Denning, D. E. R. (1982). *Cryptography and data security* (Vol. 112). Addison-Wesley.

Deshmukh, A., Sreenath, N., Tyagi, A. K., & Eswara Abhichandan, U. V. (2022). Blockchain Enabled Cyber Security: A Comprehensive Survey. *2022 International Conference on Computer Communication and Informatics (ICCCI)*, 1-6. 10.1109/ICCCI54379.2022.9740843

Devi, V. B., & Shunmuganathan, K. L. (2017). Neural KDE Based Behaviour Model for Detecting Intrusions in Network Environment. *IAES International Journal of Artificial Intelligence*, *6*(4), 166. doi:10.11591/ijai.v6.i4.pp166-173

Di Chai, L. W., Yang, L., Junxue, Z. J., Chen, K., & Yang, Q. (n.d.). *A Survey for Federated Learning Evaluations: Goals and Measures*. https://www.researchgate.net/publication/373333429_A_Survey_for_Federated_Learning_Evaluations_Goals_and_Measures

Dietrich, D., Heller, B., & Yang, B. (2015). *Data Science & Big Data Analytics: Discovering, Analyzing, Visualizing and Presenting Data*. John Wiley & Sons, Inc.

Distante, C., Fineo, L., Mainetti, L., Manco, L., Taccardi, B., & Vergallo, R. (2022). HF-SCA: Hands-Free Strong Customer Authentication Based on a Memory-Guided Attention Mechanisms. *Journal of Risk and Financial Management*, *15*(8), 342. doi:10.3390/jrfm15080342

Doddini Probhuling, L. (2013). Load Balancing Algorithms In Cloud Computing. *International Journal of Advanced Computer and Mathematical Sciences, 4*.

Doersch, C. (2016, August 13). Tutorial on Variational Autoencoders. https://www.researchgate.net/publication/304163568

Douthwaite, J. A., Lesage, B., Gleirscher, M., Calinescu, R., Aitken, J. M., Alexander, R., & Law, J. (2021). A modular digital twinning framework for safety assurance of collaborative robotics. *Frontiers in Robotics and AI*, *8*(Dec), 758099. doi:10.3389/frobt.2021.758099 PMID:34977162

Du, H., Lv, L., Guo, A., & Wang, H. (2023). AutoEncoder and LightGBM for Credit Card Fraud Detection Problems. *Symmetry*, *15*(4), 870. doi:10.3390ym15040870

Dulla, G. L., Gerardo, B. D., & Medina, R. P. (2019). A unique message encryption technique based on enhanced blowfish algorithm. In *IOP Conference Series: Materials Science and Engineering*. IOP Publishing. 10.1088/1757-899X/482/1/012001

Dutta, P., & Dutta, P. (2019, April 30). Comparative Study of Cloud Services Offered by Amazon, Microsoft and Google. *International Journal of Trend in Scientific Research and Development, 3*(3), 981–985. doi:10.31142/ijtsrd23170

Dutta, S., Das, T., & Jash, S. (2014). A cryptography algorithm using the operations of genetic algorithm & pseudo random sequence generating functions. *International Journal (Toronto, Ont.)*, *3*(5).

Dwivedi, Y. K., Hughes, D. L., Coombs, C., Constantiou, I., Duan, Y., Edwards, J. S., Gupta, B., Lal, B., Misra, S., Prashant, P., Raman, R., Rana, N. P., Sharma, S. K., & Upadhyay, N. (2020). Impact of COVID-19 pandemic on information management research and practice: Transforming education, work and life. *International Journal of Information Management*, *55*, 102211. doi:10.1016/j.ijinfomgt.2020.102211

Ebadifard, F., & Babamir, S. M. (2021). Autonomic task scheduling algorithm for dynamic workloads through a load balancing technique for the cloud-computing environment. *Cluster Computing*, *24*(2), 1075–1101. doi:10.100710586-020-03177-0

El Zaatari, S., Marei, M., Li, W., & Usman, Z. (2019). Cobot programming for collaborative industrial tasks: An overview. *Robotics and Autonomous Systems*, *116*(June), 162–180. doi:10.1016/j.robot.2019.03.003

ElhusseinA.GursoyG. (2023). Privacy-preserving patient clustering for personalized federated learning. arXiv:2307.08847v1 [cs.LG].

Elmi, A. H., Sallehuddin, R., Ibrahim, S., & Zain, A. M. (2014). Classification of SIM Box Fraud Detection Using Support Vector Machine and Artificial Neural Network. *International Journal of Innovative Computing*, 19–27.

Elsayed, M., Le-Khac, N. A., Dev, S., & Jurcut, A. D. (2020, November). Network anomaly detection using LSTM based autoencoder. In *Proceedings of the 16th ACM Symposium on QoS and Security for Wireless and Mobile Networks* (pp. 37-45). 10.1145/3416013.3426457

Enem, T. A., & Awujoola, O. J. (2023). Malware detection and classification Using embedded convolutional neural network and long short-term memory technique. *TheScientificWorldJournal*, *18*(2), 204–211.

Fajardo, A. V. (2018). VOS: A Method for Variational Oversampling of Imbalanced Data. *International Journal of Advanced Computer Science and Applications*, 8.

Fallah, A., Mokhtari, A., & Ozdaglar, A. (2020). *Personalized federated learning: A meta-learning approach.* arXiv preprint arXiv:2002.07948.

Fanai, H., & Abbasimehr, H. (2023). A novel combined approach based on deep Autoencoder and deep classifiers for credit card fraud detection. *Expert Systems with Applications*, *217*, 119562. doi:10.1016/j.eswa.2023.119562

Fang, W., Chen, W., Zhang, W., Pei, J., Gao, W., & Wang, G. (2020). Digital Signature Scheme for information non-repudiation in Blockchain: A state of the art review. *EURASIP Journal on Wireless Communications and Networking*, *2020*(1). doi:10.1186/s13638-020-01665-w

FAR 52.224-3 Privacy Training. (2023). *Acquisition.GOV*. https://www.acquisition.gov/far/52.224-3

Faraahi & Goudarzi. (2014). Effective load balancing in cloud computing. *International Journal of Intelligent Information Systems*.

Fattahi, H., & Hasanipanah, M. (2021). Prediction of blast-induced ground vibration in a mine using relevance vector regression optimized by metaheuristic algorithms. *Natural Resources Research*, *30*(2), 1849–1863. doi:10.100711053-020-09764-7

Feng, Z., Liu, T., Li, H., Lu, H., Shou, L., & Xu, J. (2020). Indoor Top-k Keyword-aware Routing Query. *IEEE 36th International Conference on Data Engineering (ICDE),* 1213-1224. 10.1109/ICDE48307.2020.00109

Feng, Q., He, D., Zeadally, S., Khan, M. K., & Kumar, N. (2019). A survey on privacy protection in blockchain system. *Journal of Network and Computer Applications*, *126*, 45–58. doi:10.1016/j.jnca.2018.10.020

Feng, Q., He, D., Zeadally, S., & Liang, K. (2019). BPAS: Blockchain-assisted privacy-preserving authentication system for vehicular ad hoc networks. *IEEE Transactions on Industrial Informatics*, *16*(6), 4146–4155. doi:10.1109/TII.2019.2948053

Fernandes, D. A., Soares, L. F., Gomes, J. V., Freire, M. M., & Inácio, P. R. (2014). Security issues in cloud environments: A survey. *International Journal of Information Security*, *13*(2), 113–170. doi:10.100710207-013-0208-7

Ficek, J., Wang, W., Chen, H., Dagne, G., & Daley, E. (2021, September). Differential privacy in health research: A scoping review. *Journal of the American Medical Informatics Association : JAMIA*, *28*(10), 2269–2276. doi:10.1093/jamia/ocab135 PMID:34333623

Finlow-Bates, K. (2021). *U.S. Patent No. 10,938,566*. Washington, DC: U.S. Patent and Trademark Office.

Fournier, Q., & Aloise, D. (2019, June). Empirical comparison between autoencoders and traditional dimensionality reduction methods. In *2019 IEEE Second International Conference on Artificial Intelligence and Knowledge Engineering (AIKE)* (pp. 211-214). IEEE. 10.1109/AIKE.2019.00044

Fu, Z. (2022). Computer Cyberspace Security mechanism supported by cloud computing. *PLoS One*, *17*(10), e0271546. Advance online publication. doi:10.1371/journal.pone.0271546 PMID:36206264

Gai, K., Guo, J., Zhu, L., & Yu, S. (2020). Blockchain meets cloud computing: A survey. *IEEE Communications Surveys and Tutorials*, *22*(3), 2009–2030. doi:10.1109/COMST.2020.2989392

Gardie, B., Azezew, K., & Bitew, H. (2021). Hybrid Fuzzy-Genetic Load Balancing Scheme for Cloud Computing. *International Journal of Research in Engineering and Science*, *9*(3), 82–89.

Ghojogh, B., & Crowley, M. (2019). *Linear and Quadratic Discriminant Analysis: Tutorial*. Machine Learning Laboratory, University of Waterloo.

Ghorbel, A., Ghorbel, M., & Jmaiel, M. (2021). Accountable privacy preserving attribute-based access control for cloud services enforced using blockchain. *International Journal of Information Security*, *21*(3), 489–508. doi:10.100710207-021-00565-4

Ghosh & Banerjee. (2016). *Priority Based Modified Throttled Algorithm in Cloud Computing*. Academic Press.

Gnanasundaram & Suresh. (2015). Optimal load balancing in cloud computing by efficient utilization of virtual machines. *International Journal of Advanced Technology in Engineering and Science, 3*(2).

Gorkhali, A., Li, L., & Shrestha, A. (2020). Blockchain: A literature review. *Journal of Management Analytics*, *7*(3), 321–343. doi:10.1080/23270012.2020.1801529

Gradxs, G. P. B., & Rao, N. (2023). Behaviour Based Credit Card Fraud Detection Design And Analysis By Using Deep Stacked Autoencoder Based Harris Grey Wolf (Hgw) Method. *Scandinavian Journal of Information Systems*, *35*(1), 1–8.

Gubbi, J., Buyya, R., Marusic, S., & Palaniswami, M. (2013). Internet of Things (IoT): A vision, architectural elements, and future directions. *Future Generation Computer Systems*, *29*(7), 1645–1660. doi:10.1016/j.future.2013.01.010

GuH.LuoJ.KangY.FanyL.WebankQ. Y. (2023). HKUST, FedPass: Privacy-Preserving Vertical Federated Deep Learning with Adaptive Obfuscation. arXiv:2301.12623v2 [cs.DC].

Guo, C., Chen, X., Jie, Y., Fu, Z., Li, M., & Feng, B. (2020). Dynamic Multi-Phrase Ranked Search over Encrypted Data with Symmetric Searchable Encryption. *IEEE Transactions on Services Computing*, *13*(6), 1034–1044. doi:10.1109/TSC.2017.2768045

Guo, L., Xie, H., & Li, Y. (2020). Data encryption based blockchain and privacy preserving mechanisms towards big data. *Journal of Visual Communication and Image Representation*, *70*, 102741. doi:10.1016/j.jvcir.2019.102741

Guo, Z., & Ye, J. (2020). Improved Algorithm for Management of Outsourced Database. *Neural Computing & Applications*, *33*(2), 647–653. doi:10.100700521-020-05047-7

Gupta, A. (2019). *Generative Image Translation for Data Augmentation of Bone Lesion Pathology. Proceedings of Machine Learning Research, 102, 225–235* .

Gupta, A. K., Govindarajan, V., & Wang, H. (2008). *The quest for global dominance: Transforming global presence into global competitive advantage*. John Wiley & Sons.

Gupta, A., Siddiqui, S. T., Alam, S., & Shuaib, M. (2019). Cloud Computing Security using Blockchain. *International Journal of Emerging Technologies and Innovative Research*, *6*(6), 791–794.

Habib, G., Sharma, S., Ibrahim, S., Ahmad, I., Qureshi, S., & Ishfaq, M. (2022). Blockchain technology: Benefits, challenges, applications, and integration of blockchain technology with cloud computing. *Future Internet*, *14*(11), 341. doi:10.3390/fi14110341

Hady, A. A. (2020). Duty cycling centralized hierarchical routing protocol with content analysis duty cycling mechanism for wireless sensor networks. *Computer Systems Science and Engineering*, *35*(5), 347–355. doi:10.32604/csse.2020.35.347

Hahn, C., Yoon, H., & Hur, J. (2023). Multi-Key Similar Data Search on Encrypted Storage with Secure Pay-Per-Query. *IEEE Transactions on Information Forensics and Security*, *18*, 1169–1181. doi:10.1109/TIFS.2023.3236178

Hakak, S., Khan, W. Z., Gilkar, G. A., Assiri, B., Alazab, M., Bhattacharya, S., & Reddy, G. T. (2021). Recent advances in blockchain technology: A survey on applications and challenges. *International Journal of Ad Hoc and Ubiquitous Computing*, *38*(1-3), 82–100. doi:10.1504/IJAHUC.2021.119089

Halim, Z. (2020). Optimizing the DNA fragment assembly using metaheuristic-based overlap layout consensus approach. *Applied Soft Computing*, *92*, 106256. doi:10.1016/j.asoc.2020.106256

Hamdani, M., & Youcef, A. (2021). Enhanced active VM load balancing algorithm using fuzzy logic and K-means clustering. *Multiagent and Grid Systems*, *17*(1), 59–82. doi:10.3233/MGS-210343

HanB.SchottenH. D. (2022). Multi-sensory HMI for human-centric industrial digital twins: A 6G vision of future industry. doi:10.1109/ISCC55528.2022.9912932

Handa, R., Rama Krishna, C., & Aggarwal, N. (2020). Efficient Privacy-Preserving Scheme Supporting Disjunctive Multi-Keyword Search with Ranking. *Concurrency and Computation*, *32*(2), e5450. doi:10.1002/cpe.5450

Haque, F., Dehghanian, V., Fapojuwo, A. O., & Nielsen, J. (2019, January). A sensor fusion-based framework for floor localization. *IEEE Sensors Journal*, *19*(2), 623–631. doi:10.1109/JSEN.2018.2852494

Hasan, O., Brunie, L., & Bertino, E. (2022). Privacy-preserving reputation systems based on blockchain and other cryptographic building blocks: A survey. *ACM Computing Surveys*, *55*(2), 1–37. doi:10.1145/3490236

Hashem, I. A. T., Yaqoob, I., Anuar, N. B., Mokhtar, S., Gani, A., & Ullah Khan, S. (2015, January). The rise of "big data" on cloud computing: Review and open research issues. *Information Systems*, *47*, 98–115. doi:10.1016/j.is.2014.07.006

Hashizume, K., Rosado, D. G., Fernández-Medina, E., & Fernandez, E. B. (2013). An analysis of security issues for cloud computing. *Journal of Internet Services and Applications*, *4*(1), 1–13. doi:10.1186/1869-0238-4-5

Hassan Ak, S., Shalash, A. F., & Saudy, N. F. (2014). Modifications on rsa cryptosystem using genetic optimization. *International Journal of Research and Reviews in Applied Sciences*, *19*(2), 150.

Hassan, M., Obazu, D., Zmij, K., Azhygulov, K., & Sitaula, S. (2022). Microsoft Azure's Leading Edge in Cloud Computing Services. *IUP Journal of Computer Sciences, 16*(2).

Hassan, J., Shehzad, D., Habib, U., Aftab, M. U., Ahmad, M., Kuleev, R., & Mazzara, M. (2022). The Rise of Cloud Computing: Data Protection, Privacy, and open research challenges—a systematic literature review (SLR). *Computational Intelligence and Neuroscience*, *2022*, 1–26. doi:10.1155/2022/8303504 PMID:35712069

Hassan, M. U., Rehmani, M. H., & Chen, J. (2019). Privacy preservation in blockchain based IoT systems: Integration issues, prospects, challenges, and future research directions. *Future Generation Computer Systems*, *97*, 512–529. doi:10.1016/j.future.2019.02.060

Hatamizadeh, A., Yin, H., Molchanov, P., Myronenko, A., Li, W., Dogra, P., Feng, A., Flores, M. G., Kautz, J., Xu, D., & Roth, H. R. (2023). Do Gradient Inversion Attacks Make Federated Learning Unsafe? *IEEE Transactions on Medical Imaging*, *42*(7), 2044–2056. doi:10.1109/TMI.2023.3239391 PMID:37021996

Hathaliya, J., Sharma, P., Tanwar, S., & Gupta, R. (2019). Blockchain-based remote patient monitoring in healthcare 4.0. In *2019 IEEE 9th international conference on advanced computing (IACC)* (pp. 87-91). IEEE. 10.1109/IACC48062.2019.8971593

Healthcare Cybersecurity Market to Reach USD 27.10 Billion by 2026. (2019). *Reports and Data*.

Hexa-X Deliverable D1.2: Expanded 6G Vision, Use Cases and Societal Values - Including Aspects of Sustainability, Security and Spectrum. (2021). https://hexa-x.eu/wp-content/ uploads/2021/05/Hexa-X_D1.2.pdf

Hind, S. A., & Sanaa, A. S. (2021). Hybrid Load Balancing Approach based on the Integration of QoS and Power Consumption in Cloud Computing. *International Journal of Advanced Trends in Computer Science and Engineering*, *10*(2), 1079–1090. doi:10.30534/ijatcse/2021/841022021

Hofmann, P., & Woods, D. (2010, November). Cloud Computing: The Limits of Public Clouds for Business Applications. *IEEE Internet Computing*, *14*(6), 90–93. doi:10.1109/MIC.2010.136

Huang, J., Asteris, P. G., Manafi Khajeh Pasha, S., Mohammed, A. S., & Hasanipanah, M. (2020). A new auto-tuning model for predicting the rock fragmentation: A cat swarm optimization algorithm. *Engineering with Computers*, 1–12.

Huang, W., Li, T., Wang, D., Du, S., Zhang, J., & Huang, T. (2022, April). Fairness and accuracy in horizontal federated learning. *Information Sciences*, *589*, 170–185. doi:10.1016/j.ins.2021.12.102

Huang, Z., Shen, Y., Li, J., Fey, M., & Brecher, C. (2021, September). A survey on AI-driven digital twins in Industry 4.0: Smart manufacturing and advanced robotics. *Sensors (Basel)*, *21*(19), 6340. doi:10.339021196340 PMID:34640660

Hu, J., Wang, Q., & Yang, K. (2021, February). Energy self-sustainability in full-spectrum 6G. *IEEE Wireless Communications*, *28*(1), 104–111. doi:10.1109/MWC.001.2000156

Hu, R., Guo, Y., Li, H., Pei, Q., & Gong, Y. (2020). Personalized Federated Learning With Differential Privacy. *IEEE Internet of Things Journal*, *7*(10), 9530–9539. doi:10.1109/JIOT.2020.2991416

Hussien, W., Peng, T., & Wang, G. (2015). A Weighted Throttled Load Balancing Approach for Virtual Machines in Cloud Environment. *International Journal on Computer Science and Engineering*, *11*(4).

Ikeda, Y. (2018, December 21). Estimation of Dimensions Contributing to Detected Anomalies with Variational Autoencoders. arXiv:1811.04576v2 [stat.ML].

IMI. (2021, April 22). *Identity and Access Management for Cloud Security*. Identity Management Institute. https://identitymanagementinstitute.org/identity-and-access-management-for-cloud-security/

Internet World Stats. (n.d.). https://www.internetworldstats.com/stats.htm

Iovan, Ş., & Iovan, A. A. (2016). Cloud Computing Security. *Fiability & Durability/Fiabilitate Si Durabilitate*, *1*, 206–212.

Iqbal, A. (2020). Protecting Digital Privacy: Why the United States Should Follow Europe's Lead and Pass Federal Legislation. *Harvard Kennedy School Review*, *20*, 87–91.

Issa, M., & Abd Elaziz, M. (2020). Analyzing COVID-19 virus based on enhanced fragmented biological local aligner using improved ions motion optimization algorithm. *Applied Soft Computing*, *96*, 106683. doi:10.1016/j.asoc.2020.106683 PMID:32901204

Jabbar, S., Lloyd, H., Hammoudeh, M., Adebisi, B., & Raza, U. (2021). Blockchain-enabled supply chain: Analysis, challenges, and future directions. *Multimedia Systems*, *27*(4), 787–806. doi:10.100700530-020-00687-0

Jadeja, Y., & Modi, K. (2012). Cloud Computing - Concepts, Architecture and Challenges. *International Conference on Computing, Electronics and Electrical Technologies (ICCEET),* 877-880. 10.1109/ICCEET.2012.6203873

Jaeger, P. T., Lin, J., & Grimes, J. M. (2008). Cloud computing and information policy: Computing in a policy cloud? *Journal of Information Technology & Politics*, *5*(3), 269–283. doi:10.1080/19331680802425479

Jang, R., Kang, J., Mohaisen, A., & Nyang, D. (2020). Catch Me If You Can: Rogue Access Point Detection Using Intentional Channel Interference. IEEE Transactions on Mobile Computing, 19, 1056-1071. doi:10.1109/TMC.2019.2903052

Jansen, W., & Grance, T. (2011). *Guidelines on security and privacy in public cloud computing*. Academic Press.

Javed, L., Anjum, A., Yakubu, B. M., Iqbal, M., Moqurrab, S. A., & Srivastava, G. (2023). ShareChain: Blockchain-enabled model for sharing patient data using federated learning and differential privacy. *Expert Systems: International Journal of Knowledge Engineering and Neural Networks*, *40*(5), e13131. doi:10.1111/exsy.13131

Jawaid, S., & Jamal, A. (2014). Generating the best fit key in cryptography using genetic algorithm. *International Journal of Computer Applications*, *98*(20), 33–39. doi:10.5120/17301-7767

Jayaprakash, V., & Tyagi, A. K. (2022). Security Optimization of Resource-Constrained Internet of Healthcare Things (IoHT) Devices Using Asymmetric Cryptography for Blockchain Network. In *Proceedings of International Conference on Network Security and Blockchain Technology. ICNSBT 2021. Lecture Notes in Networks and Systems* (vol. 481). Springer. 10.1007/978-981-19-3182-6_18

Jayaprakash, V., & Tyagi, A. K. (n.d.). The Security Optimization of Resource-Constrained Internet of Healthcare Things (IoHT) Devices Using Lightweight Cryptography. Information Security Practices for the Internet of Things, 5G, and Next-Generation Wireless Networks. doi:10.4018/978-1-6684-3921-0.ch009

Jayasinghe, U., Lee, G. M., MacDermott, Á., & Rhee, W. S. (2019). TrustChain: A privacy preserving blockchain with edge computing. *Wireless Communications and Mobile Computing*, *2019*, 2019. doi:10.1155/2019/2014697

Jhingran, R., Thada, V., & Dhaka, S. (2015). A study on cryptography using genetic algorithm. *International Journal of Computer Applications*, *118*(20), 10–14. doi:10.5120/20860-3559

Jiadong, R. J., & Wang, Q. (2019, June 16). Building an Effective Intrusion Detection System by Using Hybrid Data Optimization Based on Machine Learning Algorithms. *Hindawi Security and Communication Networks*, 11.

Jia, J., & Lei, Z. (2021). Article. *Journal of Physics*. Advance online publication. doi:10.1088/1742-6596/1802/3/032021

Jiayu, S. X. (2018). Learning Sparse Representation With Variational Auto-Encoder for Anomaly Detection. *IEEE Open Access Journal*.

JinW.YaoY.HanS.CarleeJ. (2023). *FedML-HE: An Efficient Homomorphic-Encryption-Based Privacy-Preserving Federated Learning System*. arXiv:2303.10837v1 [cs.LG].

Jorge, J. V. (2018). *Proceedings of the 13th International Joint Conference on Computer Vision, Imaging and Computer Graphics Theory and Applications (VISIGRAPP 2018)* - Volume 5 (pp. 96-104). Science and Technology Publications.

Kaliappan, V., Yu, S., Soundararajan, R., Jeon, S., Min, D., & Choi, E. (2022). High-secured data communication for cloud enabled secure Docker image sharing technique using blockchain-based homomorphic encryption. *Energies*, *15*(15), 5544. doi:10.3390/en15155544

Kanter, R. M. (1997). *World class*. Simon and Schuster.

Kao, F. K., Chen, C. W., Chang, C. J., & Chu, T. H. (2014). An Accurate Fake Access Point Detection Method Based on Deviation of Beacon Time Interval. In *IEEE Eighth International Conference on Software Security and Reliability-Companion* (pp. 1-2). San Francisco, CA: IEEE. 10.1109/SERE-C.2014.13

Karagozlu, D., Ajamu, J., & Mbombo, A. B. (2020). Adaptation and effects of cloud computing on small businesses. *Brain. Broad Research in Artificial Intelligence and Neuroscience, 11*(4), 149–167. doi:10.18662/brain/11.4/146

Kashyap & Viradiya. (2014). A Survey of Various Load Balancing Algorithms in Cloud Computing. *International Journal of Scientific & Technology Research, 3*(11).

Kashyap & Viradiya. (2014). A Survey of Various Load Balancing Algorithms In Cloud Computing. *International Journal of Scientific & Technology Research, 3.*

Katoch, S., Chauhan, S. S., & Kumar, V. (2021). A review on genetic algorithm: Past, present, and future. *Multimedia Tools and Applications, 80*(5), 8091–8126. doi:10.100711042-020-10139-6 PMID:33162782

Kaur, J. (2012). Comparison of load balancing algorithms in a Cloud. *International Journal of Engineering Research and Applications.*

Kayworth, T., & Whitten, D. (2010). Effective information security requires a balance of social and technology factors. *MIS Quarterly Executive, 9*(3), 2012–2052.

Kent, K., & Souppaya, M. (2006). *Guide to Computer Security Log Management.* National Institute of Standards and Technology. doi:10.6028/NIST.SP.800-92

Kessler, G.C. (2003). *An overview of cryptography.* Academic Press.

Khan, I., Dewangan, B., Meena, A., & Birthare, M. (2020). Study of Various Cloud Service Providers: A Comparative Analysis. SSRN *Electronic Journal.* doi:10.2139/ssrn.3672950

Khan, R. S. (2019). *An Adaptive Multi-Layer Botnet Detection Technique Using Machine Learning Classifiers.* doi:10.3390/app9112375

Khan, S., Zhang, Z., Zhu, L., Rahim, M. A., Ahmad, S., & Chen, R. (2020). SCM: Secure and accountable TLS Certificate Management. *International Journal of Communication Systems, 33*(15), e4503. Advance online publication. doi:10.1002/dac.4503

Khatoon, A. (2020). A blockchain-based smart contract system for healthcare management. *Electronics (Basel), 9*(1), 94. doi:10.3390/electronics9010094

Khubrani, M. M. (2021). A framework for blockchain-based smart health system. *Turkish Journal of Computer and Mathematics Education, 12*(9), 2609–2614.

Kiennert, C., Bouzefrane, S., & Benkara Mostefa, A. F. (2015). Digital Identity in Cloud Computing. *Digital Identity Management*, 207–244. doi:10.1016/B978-1-78548-004-1.50005-5

Kim, J. (2020, April 1). Botnet Detection Using Recurrent Variational Autoencoder. doi:10.1109/GLOBECOM42002.2020.9348169

Kim, H. M., & Laskowski, M. (2018). Toward an ontology-driven blockchain design for supply-chain provenance. *International Journal of Intelligent Systems in Accounting Finance & Management, 25*(1), 18–27. doi:10.1002/isaf.1424

Kingma, D. W. (2019). An Introduction to Variational Autoencoders. *Foundations and Trends® in Machine Learning, 12*(4), 307-392. doi:10.1561/2200000056

Korkoman, M. J., & Abdullah, M. (2023). Evolutionary algorithms based on oversampling techniques for enhancing the imbalanced credit card fraud detection. *Journal of Intelligent & Fuzzy Systems*, (Preprint), 1-13.

Kosba, A., Miller, A., Shi, E., Wen, Z., & Papamanthou, C. (2016). Hawk: The blockchain model of cryptography and privacy-preserving smart contracts. In 2016 IEEE symposium on security and privacy (SP) (pp. 839-858). IEEE. doi:10.1109/SP.2016.55

Kostiainen. (2012). *On-board credentials: An open credential platform for mobile devices.* Academic Press.

Koteska, B., Karafiloski, E., & Mishev, A. (2017). Blockchain implementation quality challenges: a literature. *SQAMIA: 6th workshop of software quality, analysis, monitoring, improvement, and applications, 1938.*

Kulkarni, G., Chavan, N., Chandorkar, R., Waghmare, R., & Palwe, R. (2012, October). Cloud security challenges. In *2012 7th International Conference on Telecommunication Systems, Services, and Applications (TSSA)* (pp. 88-91). IEEE. 10.1109/TSSA.2012.6366028

Kumar, T., Ramani, V., Ahmad, I., Braeken, A., Harjula, E., & Ylianttila, M. (2018). Blockchain utilization in healthcare: Key requirements and challenges. In *2018 IEEE 20th International conference on e-health networking, applications and services (Healthcom)* (pp. 1-7). IEEE. 10.1109/HealthCom.2018.8531136

Kumar, A., & Chatterjee, K. (2016). An efficient stream cipher using genetic algorithm. *2016 International Conference on Wireless Communications, Signal Processing and Networking (WiSPNET)*, 2322–2326. 10.1109/WiSPNET.2016.7566557

Kumar, A., & Paul, P. (2016). Security analysis and implementation of a simple method for prevention and detection against Evil Twin attack in IEEE 802.11 wireless LAN. In *2016 International Conference on Computational Techniques in Information and Communication Technologies (ICCTICT)* (pp. 176-181). New Delhi, India: IEEE. 10.1109/ICCTICT.2016.7514574

Kumari, K. A., Sangeetha, S., Rajeevan, V., Dharshini, M. D., & Haritha, T. (2023). Trade Management System Using R3 Corda Blockchain BT - Intelligent Systems Design and Applications. Springer Nature Switzerland.

Kumar, R., & Tripathi, R. (2021). DBTP2SF: A deep blockchain-based trustworthy privacy-preserving secured framework in industrial internet of things systems. *Transactions on Emerging Telecommunications Technologies*, *32*(4), e4222. doi:10.1002/ett.4222

Kurien, L. C. (2019, December). An Ameliorated method for Fraud Detection using Complex Generative Model: Variational Autoencoder. *International Journal of Innovative Technology and Exploring Engineering*, *9*(2S).

Kushida, K. E., Murray, J., & Zysman, J. (2011). Diffusing the cloud: Cloud computing and implications for public policy. *Journal of Industry, Competition and Trade*, *11*(3), 209–237. doi:10.100710842-011-0106-5

Ladani & Gupta. (2013). A Framework for Performance Analysis of Computing Clouds. *International Journal of Innovative Technology and Exploring Engineering, 2*(6).

Lahouij, A., Hamel, L., & Graiet, M. (2022). Formal reconfiguration model for cloud resources. *Software & Systems Modeling*, *22*(1), 225–245. doi:10.100710270-022-00990-6

Lashkari, B., & Musilek, P. (2021). A comprehensive review of blockchain consensus mechanisms. *IEEE Access : Practical Innovations, Open Solutions*, *9*, 43620–43652. doi:10.1109/ACCESS.2021.3065880

Lee, C., Kang, C., Ko, H., Woo, J., & Hong, J. W.-K. (2023). A comprehensive and quantitative evaluation method for Blockchain Protocols. *2023 IEEE International Conference on Blockchain and Cryptocurrency (ICBC)*. 10.1109/ICBC56567.2023.10174935

Lee, S. (2012). Database management system as a cloud service. *International Journal of Future Generation Communication and Networking*, *5*(2).

Lemieux, V. L. (2017, November). Blockchain and distributed ledgers as trusted recordkeeping systems. In *Future technologies conference* (Vol. 2017). FTC.

Leonelli, S. (2014). What difference does quantity make? On the epistemology of Big Data in biology. *Big Data & Society*, *1*(1), 2053951714534395. doi:10.1177/2053951714534395 PMID:25729586

Li, B., Liang, R., Di Zhu, W. C., & Lin, Q. (2020). Blockchain-based trust management model for location privacy preserving in VANET. *IEEE Transactions on Intelligent Transportation Systems*, *22*(6), 3765–3775. doi:10.1109/TITS.2020.3035869

Li, F., Ma, J., Miao, Y., Liu, Z., Choo, K.-K. R., Liu, X., & Deng, R. H. (2023). Towards Efficient Verifiable Boolean Search Over Encrypted Cloud Data. *IEEE Transactions on Cloud Computing*, *11*(1), 839–853. doi:10.1109/TCC.2021.3118692

Li, J., Ma, J., Miao, Y., Yang, R., Liu, X., & Choo, K.-K. R. (2022). Practical Multi-Keyword Ranked Search With Access Control Over Encrypted Cloud Data. *IEEE Transactions on Cloud Computing*, *10*(3), 2005–2019. doi:10.1109/TCC.2020.3024226

Li, L., Liu, J., Cheng, L., Qiu, S., Wang, W., Zhang, X., & Zhang, Z. (2018). Creditcoin: A privacy-preserving blockchain-based incentive announcement network for communications of smart vehicles. *IEEE Transactions on Intelligent Transportation Systems*, *19*(7), 2204–2220. doi:10.1109/TITS.2017.2777990

Li, M., Yu, S., Ren, K., & Lou, W. (2010). Securing personal health records in cloud computing: Patient-centric and fine-grained data access control in multi-owner settings. *Security and Privacy in Communication Networks: 6th Iternational ICST Conference, SecureComm 2010, Singapore, September 7-9, 2010 Proceedings*, *6*, 89–106.

Lin, C., He, D., Huang, X., Kumar, N., & Choo, K.-K. R. (2020). BCPPA: A blockchain-based conditional privacy-preserving authentication protocol for vehicular ad hoc networks. *IEEE Transactions on Intelligent Transportation Systems*, *22*(12), 7408–7420. doi:10.1109/TITS.2020.3002096

Lin, T. H., & Jiang, J. R. (2021). Credit card fraud detection with autoencoder and probabilistic random forest. *Mathematics*, *9*(21), 2683. doi:10.3390/math9212683

Lin, Z. W., Cui, H., Li, B., & Wang, C. (2021). Privacy-Preserving Similarity Search With Efficient Updates in Distributed Key-Value Stores. *IEEE Transactions on Parallel and Distributed Systems*, *32*(5), 1072–1084. doi:10.1109/TPDS.2020.3042695

Liu, G., Yang, G., Bai, S., Wang, H., & Xiang, Y. (2022). FASE: A Fast and Accurate Privacy-Preserving Multi-Keyword Top-k Retrieval Scheme Over Encrypted Cloud Data. *IEEE Transactions on Services Computing*, *15*(4), 1855–1867. doi:10.1109/TSC.2020.3023393

Liu, J., Li, X., Ye, L., Zhang, H., Du, X., & Guizani, M. (2018). BPDS: A blockchain based privacy-preserving data sharing for electronic medical records. In *2018 IEEE Global Communications Conference (GLOBECOM)* (pp. 1-6). IEEE. 10.1109/GLOCOM.2018.8647713

Liu, X., Fan, L., Wang, L., & Meng, S. (2016). Multiobjective reliable cloud storage with its particle swarm optimization algorithm. *Mathematical Problems in Engineering*, *2016*, 2016. doi:10.1155/2016/9529526

Liu, X., Huang, H., Xiao, F., & Ma, Z. (2019). A blockchain-based trust management with conditional privacy-preserving announcement scheme for VANETs. *IEEE Internet of Things Journal*, *7*(5), 4101–4112. doi:10.1109/JIOT.2019.2957421

LiuY. (2022). *Vertical Federated Learning*. arXiv:2211.12814v2 [cs.LG].

Liu, Z., Chen, Y., Zhao, Y., Yu, H., Liu, Y., Bao, R., Jiang, J., Nie, Z., Xu, Q., & Yang, Q. (2022). Contribution-aware federated learning for smart healthcare. *Proceedings of the 34th Annual Conference on Innovative Applications of Artificial Intelligence (IAAI-22).*

Li, X. (2022). A blockchain-based verifiable user data access control policy for secured cloud data storage. *Computational Intelligence and Neuroscience*, *2022*, 1–12. doi:10.1155/2022/7498025 PMID:35528363

Li, X., Cheng, L., Sun, C., Lam, K.-Y., Wang, X., & Li, F. (2021). Federated learning- empowered collaborative data sharing for vehicular edge networks. *IEEE Network*, *35*(3), 116–124. doi:10.1109/MNET.011.2000558

Li, X., Tong, Q., Zhao, J., Miao, Y., Ma, S., Weng, J., Ma, J., & Choo, K.-K. R. (2023). Xinghua and Tong, Qiuyun and Zhao, "VRFMS: Verifiable Ranked Fuzzy Multi-Keyword Search Over Encrypted Data". *IEEE Transactions on Services Computing*, *16*(1), 698–710. doi:10.1109/TSC.2021.3140092

Li, Y., Liu, B., Shang, Z., & Chen, M. (2019). DDoS attack detection method based on feature extraction of deep belief network. *IOP Conference Series. Earth and Environmental Science*, *252*(3), 032013. Advance online publication. doi:10.1088/1755-1315/252/3/032013

Li, Y., Ning, J., & Chen, J. (2022). Secure and Practical Wildcard Searchable Encryption System Based on Inner Product. *IEEE Transactions on Services Computing*, •••, 1–14. doi:10.1109/TSC.2022.3207750

Lopez-Martin, M. E. (2018, December). Variational data generative model for intrusion detection. *Knowledge and Information Systems*. Advance online publication. doi:10.100710115-018-1306-7

López-Sorribes, S., Rius-Torrentó, J., & Solsona-Tehàs, F. (2023). A Bibliometric Review of the Evolution of Blockchain Technologies. *Sensors, 23*(6), 3167. . doi:10.3390/s23063167

Lotfi, N. (2019). Data allocation in distributed database systems: A novel hybrid method based on differential evolution and variable neighborhood search. *SN Applied Sciences*, *1*(12), 1–10. doi:10.100742452-019-1787-3

LuoJ.ZhangY.ZhangJ.QinS.WangH.YuY.XuZ. (2023). Practical Privacy-Preserving Gaussian Process Regression via Secret Sharing. arXiv:2306.14498v1 [cs.CR].

Lu, Z., Liu, W., Wang, Q., Qu, G., & Liu, Z. (2018). A privacy-preserving trust model based on blockchain for VANETs. *IEEE Access : Practical Innovations, Open Solutions*, *6*, 45655–45664. doi:10.1109/ACCESS.2018.2864189

Ma, L., Teymorian, A. Y., & Cheng, X. (2008). A Hybrid Rogue Access Point Protection Framework for Commodity Wi-Fi Networks. In *The 27th Conference on Computer Communications* (pp. 1220-1228). IEEE. 10.1109/INFOCOM.2008.178

Macfarlane, R. B. (2015). TFTP DDoS amplification attack. *Computers & Security*. Advance online publication. doi:10.1016/j.cose.2015.09.006

Mahalle, Kaveri, & Chavan. (2013). Load Balancing on Cloud Data Centres. *Advanced Research in Computer Science and Software Engineering, 3*.

Mahalle, S., Kaveri, R., & Chavan, V. (2013). Load Balancing on Cloud Data Centers. *International Journal of Advanced Research in Computer Science and Software Engineering*, 1–4.

Maheswari, J. U., Vijayalakshmi, S., N, R. G., Alzubaidi, L. H., Anvar, K., & Elangovan, R. (2023). Data Privacy and Security in Cloud Computing Environments. *E3S Web of Conferences, 399*, 04040. doi:10.1051/e3sconf/202339904040

Mallick. (2015). A Comparative Study of Load Balancing Algorithms in Cloud Computing. *International Journal of Computer Applications, 117*(24).

Manvi, S. S., & Shyam, G. K. (2014). Resource management for Infrastructure as a Service (IaaS) in cloud computing: A survey. *Journal of Network and Computer Applications*, *41*, 424–440. doi:10.1016/j.jnca.2013.10.004

Manzoor, A., Shah, M. A., Khattak, H. A., Din, I. U., & Khan, M. K. (2019). Multi-tier authentication schemes for Fog computing: Architecture, security perspective, and challenges. *International Journal of Communication Systems*, *35*(12), e4033. Advance online publication. doi:10.1002/dac.4033

Marston, S., Li, Z., Bandyopadhyay, S., Zhang, J., & Ghalsasi, A. (2011). Cloud computing—The business perspective. *Decision Support Systems*, *51*(1), 176–189. doi:10.1016/j.dss.2010.12.006

Mather, T., Kumaraswamy, S., & Latif, S. (2009). *Cloud security and privacy: an enterprise perspective on risks and compliance*. O'Reilly Media, Inc.

Mayuranathan, M. (2019). Best features based intrusion detection system by RBM model for detecting DDoS in cloud environment. *Journal of Ambient Intelligence and Humanized Computing*. Advance online publication. doi:10.100712652-019-01611-9

McCallister, E., Grance, T., & Scarfone, K. (2010, April). *Identifiable information (PII)*. Guide to Protecting the Confidentiality of Personally Identifiable Information (PII). doi:10.6028/NIST.SP.800-122

McGonigle, D., & Mastrian, K. (2021). *Nursing informatics and the foundation of knowledge*. Jones & Bartlett Learning.

Mehrdanesh, A., Monjezi, M., Khandelwal, M., & Bayat, P. (2021). Application of various robust techniques to study and evaluate the role of effective parameters on rock fragmentation. *Engineering with Computers*, 1–11.

Meng, Z., Xie, Y., & Sun, J. (2023). Detecting Credit Card Fraud by Generative Adversarial Networks and Multi-head Attention Neural Networks. *IAENG International Journal of Computer Science*, *50*(2).

Miao, Y., Tong, Q., Deng, R. H., Choo, K.-K. R., Liu, X., & Li, H. (2022). Verifiable Searchable Encryption Framework Against Insider Keyword-Guessing Attack in Cloud Storage. *IEEE Transactions on Cloud Computing*, *10*(2), 835–848. doi:10.1109/TCC.2020.2989296

Miao, Y., Zheng, W., Jia, X., Liu, X., Choo, K.-K. R., & Deng, R. H. (2023). Ranked Keyword Search Over Encrypted Cloud Data Through Machine Learning Method. *IEEE Transactions on Services Computing*, *16*(1), 525–536. doi:10.1109/TSC.2021.3140098

Mikulic, M. (2019). *Projected growth in global healthcare data* (Vol. 2020). Statista.

Minos-Stensrud, M., Haakstad, O. H., Sakseid, O., Westby, B., & Alcocer, A. (2018). Towards automated 3D reconstruction in SME factories and digital twin model generation. *2018 18th International Conference on Control, Automation and Systems (ICCAS)*, 1777-1781.

Mirjalili, S., & Mirjalili, S. (2019). Genetic algorithm. Evolutionary Algorithms and Neural Networks: Theory and Applications, 43–55. doi:10.1007/978-3-319-93025-1_4

Mishra, S., & Bali, S. (2013). Public key cryptography using genetic algorithm. *International Journal of Recent Technology and Engineering*, *2*(2), 150–154.

Misra, S., Thakur, S., Ghosh, M., & Saha, S. K. (2020). An autoencoder based model for detecting fraudulent credit card transaction. *Procedia Computer Science*, *167*, 254–262. doi:10.1016/j.procs.2020.03.219

Mitra, A. (2017, March 2). *What is smurf attack*. Retrieved May 08, 2020, from https://www.thesecuritybuddy.com/dos-ddos-prevention/what-is-smurf-attack/

Mohammed, M. A., & Abed, F. S. (2020). A symmetric-based framework for securing cloud data at rest. *Turkish Journal of Electrical Engineering and Computer Sciences*, *28*(1), 347–361. doi:10.3906/elk-1902-114

Mohanta, B. K., Jena, D., Ramasubbareddy, S., Daneshmand, M., & Gandomi, A. H. (2020). Addressing security and privacy issues of IoT using blockchain technology. *IEEE Internet of Things Journal*, *8*(2), 881–888. doi:10.1109/JIOT.2020.3008906

Mohanta, B. K., Jena, D., Satapathy, U., & Patnaik, S. (2020). Survey on IoT security: Challenges and solution using machine learning, artificial intelligence and blockchain technology. *Internet of Things*, *11*, 100227. doi:10.1016/j.iot.2020.100227

Molina, F., Betarte, G., & Luna, C. (2021). Design principles for constructing GDPR-compliant blockchain solutions. In *2021 IEEE/ACM 4th International Workshop on Emerging Trends in Software Engineering for Blockchain (WETSEB)* (pp. 1-8). IEEE. 10.1109/WETSEB52558.2021.00008

Moqadam, A. N., & Kazemi, R. (2019). A novel triple-band microwave chip-less sensor tag for structural health monitoring applications. *Electromagnetics*, *39*(7), 524–535. doi:10.1080/02726343.2019.1658168

Mougayar, W. (2016). *The business blockchain: promise, practice, and application of the next Internet technology*. John Wiley & Sons.

Mulat, W. W., Mohapatra, S. K., Sathpathy, R., & Dhal, S. K. (2022, May). Improving Throttled Load Balancing Algorithm in Cloud Computing. In *Proceedings of International Joint Conference on Advances in Computational Intelligence: IJCACI 2021* (pp. 369-377). Singapore: Springer Nature Singapore. 10.1007/978-981-19-0332-8_27

Munonye, K., & Péter, M. (2021). Machine learning approach to vulnerability detection in OAUTH 2.0 authentication and authorization flow. *International Journal of Information Security*, *21*(2), 223–237. doi:10.100710207-021-00551-w

Murli, D. J. (2015). Credit card fraud detection using neural networks. International Journal of Students'. *Research Technology Management*, *2*(2), 84–88.

Murlidhar, B. R., Armaghani, D. J., & Mohamad, E. T. (2020). Intelligence prediction of some selected environmental issues of blasting: A review. *The Open Construction & Building Technology Journal*, *14*(1), 298–308. doi:10.2174/1874836802014010298

Myrzashova, R., Alsamhi, S. H., Shvetsov, A. V., Hawbani, A., & Wei, X. (2023). Blockchain Meets Federated Learning in Healthcare: A Systematic Review With Challenges and Opportunities. *IEEE Internet of Things Journal*, *10*(16), 14418–14437. doi:10.1109/JIOT.2023.3263598

Nagde, D., Patel, R., & Kelde, D. (2013). New approach for data encryption using two-way crossover. *International Journal of Computer Science and Information Technologies*, *4*, 58–60.

Nair & Tyagi. (2023). Blockchain technology for next-generation society: current trends and future opportunities for smart era. In *Blockchain Technology for Secure Social Media Computing*. doi:10.1049/PBSE019E_ch11

Nair, M. M., & Tyagi, A. K. (2021). Privacy: History, Statistics, Policy, Laws, Preservation and Threat Analysis. Journal of Information Assurance & Security, 16(1), 24-34.

Nakhila, O., Amjad, M. F., Dondyk, E., & Zou, C. (2018). Gateway independent user-side wi-fi Evil Twin Attack detection using virtual wireless clients. *Computers & Security*, *74*, 41–54. doi:10.1016/j.cose.2017.12.009

Naseri, M., Hayes, J., & De Cristofaro, E. (n.d.). *Toward Robustness and Privacy in Federated Learning: Experimenting with Local and Central Differential Privacy*. Academic Press.

NaseriM.HayesJ.De CristofaroE. (2020). *Local and Central Differential Privacy for Robustness and Privacy in Federated Learning*. https://doi.org/https://doi.org/10.48550/arXiv.2009.03561

Ngai, E. W., Hu, Y., Wong, Y. H., Chen, Y., & Sun, X. (2011). The application of data mining techniques in financial fraud detection: A classification framework and an academic review of literature. *Decision Support Systems*, *50*(3), 559–569. doi:10.1016/j.dss.2010.08.006

Niu, X., Wang, L., & Yang, X. (2019). *A comparison study of credit card fraud detection: Supervised versus unsupervised.* arXiv preprint arXiv:1904.10604.

NK, S., & Pai, G.V. (2009). Design of stream cipher for text encryption using particle swarm optimization based key generation. *Journal of Information Assurance and Security*, 30–41.

Noble, G., & Sujitha, M. (2015). Flow Based Solutions for DoS and DDoS Attack Detection. *International Journal of Advanced Research in Computer Engineering and Technology*.

Nurgalieva, L., O'Callaghan, D., & Doherty, G. (2020). Security and privacy of mHealth applications: A scoping review. *IEEE Access : Practical Innovations, Open Solutions*, *8*, 104247–104268. doi:10.1109/ACCESS.2020.2999934

Nzuva, S. (2019). Smart contracts implementation, applications, benefits, and limitations. *Journal of Information Engineering and Applications*, *9*(5), 63–75.

O. B. (2013). *SATW White Paper Cloud Computing*. Swiss Academy of Engineering Science.

Ohm, P. (2009). Broken promises of privacy: Responding to the surprising failure of anonymization. UCLA l. *Rev.*, *57*, 1701.

Outsideinmarketing. (2012). http://outsideinmarketing.files.wordpress. com/2012/02/cloud_difference_aas.jpg

Oya, S., & Kerschbaum, F. (2021). Hiding the Access Pattern is not enough: Exploiting Search Pattern Leakage in Searchable Encryption. *Proc. 30th USENIX Secur. Symp. (USENIX Secur.),* 127-142.

Padhy, R. (2011). Load Balancing in Cloud Computing Systems. Academic Press.

Palagan, C.A., Gupta, S., & Dhas, A.J. (2022). An IoT scheme based on wireless body area sensors for healthcare applications. *SIViP*. doi:10.1007/s11760-022-02294-0

Pandey, A. A., Fernandez, T. F., Bansal, R., & Tyagi, A. K. (2022). Maintaining Scalability in Blockchain. In A. Abraham, N. Gandhi, T. Hanne, T. P. Hong, T. Nogueira Rios, & W. Ding (Eds.), *Intelligent Systems Design and Applications. ISDA 2021. Lecture Notes in Networks and Systems* (Vol. 418). Springer. doi:10.1007/978-3-030-96308-8_4

Panghal, & S. R. (2015). A Parametric Weighted Approach to Perform Load Balancing in Load Balancing. *IJCSC*, *6*, 45–52.

Panwar. (2015). A Comparative Study of Load Balancing Algorithms in Cloud Computing. *International Journal of Computer Applications, 117*(24).

Pareek, N. K., & Patidar, V. (2016). Medical image protection using genetic algorithm operations. *Soft Computing*, *20*(2), 763–772. doi:10.100700500-014-1539-7

Park, S., Kim, H., & Ryou, J. (2018). Utilizing a lightweight PKI mechanism to guarantee secure service in a cloud environment. *The Journal of Supercomputing*, *74*(12), 6988–7002. doi:10.100711227-018-2506-3

Pasha, & Agarwal. (2014). Round Robin Approach for VM Load Balancing Algorithm in Cloud Computing Environment. *International Journal of Advanced Research in Computer Science and Software Engineering*, *4*(5).

Pavithra, S., Ramya, S., & Prathibha, S. (2019). A survey on cloud security issues and blockchain. *2019 3rd International Conference on Computing and Communications Technologies (ICCCT).* 10.1109/ICCCT2.2019.8824891

Peng, L., Feng, W., Yan, Z., Li, Y., Zhou, X., & Shimizu, S. (2021). Privacy preservation in permissionless blockchain: A survey. *Digital Communications and Networks, 7*(3), 295–307. doi:10.1016/j.dcan.2020.05.008

Pham, H. L., Tran, T. H., & Nakashima, Y. (2018). A secure remote healthcare system for hospital using blockchain smart contract. In 2018 IEEE GLOBECOM workshops (GC Wkshps) (pp. 1-6). IEEE. doi:10.1109/GLOCOMW.2018.8644164

Poohoi, R., Puntusavase, K., & Ohmori, S. (2023). A novel crossover operator for genetic algorithm: Stas crossover. *Decision Science Letters, 12*(3), 515–524. doi:10.5267/j.dsl.2023.4.010

Pramod, A., Naicker, H. S., & Tyagi, A. K. (2020). *Machine Learning and Deep Learning: Open Issues and Future Research Directions for Next Ten Years. In Computational Analysis and Understanding of Deep Learning for Medical Care: Principles, Methods, and Applications.* Wiley Scrivener.

Prattic̀o, F. G., & Lamberti, F. (2021). Towards the adoption of virtual reality training systems for the self-tuition of industrial robot operators: A case study at KUKA. *Computers in Industry, 129*(Aug), 103446. doi:10.1016/j.compind.2021.103446

Prayitno, C.-R. S., Putra, K. T., Chen, H.-C., & Tsai, Y.-Y. (2021, November). A systematic review of federated learning in the healthcare area: From the perspective of data properties and applications. *NATO Adv. Sci. Inst. Ser. E. Applied Sciences (Basel, Switzerland), 11*(23), 11191. doi:10.3390/app112311191

Preethi, B. (2014). Optimization of Resources in Cloud Computing Using Effective Load Balancing Algorithms. International Advanced Research Journal in Science, Engineering and Technology, 1(1).

Quasim, M. T., Algarni, F., Abd Elhamid Radwan, A., & Goram Mufareh, M. A. (2020). A blockchain based secured healthcare framework. In *2020 International Conference on Computational Performance Evaluation (ComPE)* (pp. 386-391). IEEE. 10.1109/ComPE49325.2020.9200024

R. (2015). *An Analytical Model to Efficiently Assess Data Centre Performance and QOS in Cloud.* International Journal of Multidisciplinary Research Development.

Rachur, A., Putman, J., & Fisher, C. (2022). What did the digital age mean for privacy in the United States? *Journal of Business &amp. The Journal of Business and Retail Management Research, 17*(01). Advance online publication. doi:10.24052/JBRMR/V17IS01/ART-08

Radha & Kumar. (2016). Efficient VM Load Balancing Algorithm for Dynamic Allocation of Resources in Cloud Computing Environment. *International Journal of Innovative Research in Computer and Communication Engineering, 4*(6).

Ragavan, M., & Prabu, K. (2022). Evaluation of cryptographic key generation performance using evolutionary algorithm. *International Journal of System Assurance Engineering and Management, 13*(S1, Suppl 1), 481–487. doi:10.100713198-021-01478-0

Ragmani, A., Elomri, A., Abghour, N., Moussaid, K., & Rida, M. (2020). FACO: A hybrid fuzzy ant colony optimization algorithm for virtual machine scheduling in high-performance cloud computing. *Journal of Ambient Intelligence and Humanized Computing, 11*(10), 3975–3987. doi:10.100712652-019-01631-5

Rahmani, M. K. I., Shuaib, M., Alam, S., Siddiqui, S. T., Ahmad, S., Bhatia, S., & Mashat, A. (2022). Blockchain-based trust management framework for cloud computing-based internet of medical things (IoMT): A systematic review. *Computational Intelligence and Neuroscience, 2022*, 2022. doi:10.1155/2022/9766844 PMID:35634070

Raj & Agarwal. (2015). Load Balancing Algorithm in Cloud Computing. *International Journal of Computer Applications, 132*(2).

Ramani, V., Kumar, T., Bracken, A., Liyanage, M., & Ylianttila, M. (2018). Secure and efficient data accessibility in blockchain based healthcare systems. In *2018 IEEE Global Communications Conference (GLOBECOM)* (pp. 206-212). IEEE. 10.1109/GLOCOM.2018.8647221

Ranger, S. (2022, February 25). *What is cloud computing? Everything you need to know about the cloud explained.* ZDNET. https://www.zdnet.com/article/what-is-cloud-computing-everything-you-need-to-know-about-the-cloud/

Rani, M., Guleria, K., & Panda, S. N. (2022). Blockchain technology novel prospective for cloud security. *2022 10th International Conference on Reliability, Infocom Technologies and Optimization (Trends and Future Directions) (ICRITO).* 10.1109/ICRITO56286.2022.9964666

Rastogi, Pasha, & Agarwal. (2014). Round Robin Approach for VM Load Balancing Algorithm in Cloud Computing Environment. *International Journal of Advanced Research in Computer Science and Software Engineering, 4*(5).

Razaque, A., Shaldanbayeva, N., Alotaibi, B., Alotaibi, M., Murat, A., & Alotaibi, A. (2022). Big Data Handling Approach for unauthorized cloud computing access. *Electronics (Basel), 11*(1), 137. doi:10.3390/electronics11010137

Reaves, B., Shernan, E., Bates, A., & Carter, H. (2015). Boxed Out: Blocking Cellular Interconnect Bypass Fraud at the Network Edge. *Proceedings of the 24th USENIX Security Symposium.*

Reddy, S. G., & Reddy, G. R. M. (2014). *Optimal Load Balancing in Cloud Computing By Efficient Utilization of Virtual Machines*. IEEE.

Rezvy, S. P. (2019). Intrusion Detection and Classification with Autoencoded Deep Neural Network. *11th International Conference, SecITC 2018.* 10.1007/978-3-030-12942-2_12

Riaz, U. K., Xiaosong, Z., Rajesh, K., Abubakar, S., A, N. G., & Mamoun, A. (2019). An Adaptive Multi-Layer Botnet Detection Technique Using Machine Learning Classifiers. *Applied Sciences.*

Rodrigo, N. C., Rajiv, R., Anton, B., Cesar, A. F. D., & Rajkumar, B. (2011). CloudSim: A Toolkit for Modeling and Simulation of Cloud Computing Environments and Evaluation of Resource Provisioning Algorithms. *Software, Practice & Experience, 41*(1), 23–50. doi:10.1002pe.995

Rodríguez-Mazahua, N., Rodríguez-Mazahua, L., López-Chau, A., Alor-Hernández, G., & Peláez-Camarena, S. G. (2021). Comparative Analysis of Decision Tree Algorithms for Data Warehouse Fragmentation. In *New Perspectives on Enterprise Decision-Making Applying Artificial Intelligence Techniques* (pp. 337–363). Springer. doi:10.1007/978-3-030-71115-3_15

Roseline, J. F., Naidu, G. B. S. R., & Pandi, V. S. (2022). Autonomous credit card fraud detection using machine learning approach☆. *Computers & Electrical Engineering, 102*, 108132. doi:10.1016/j.compeleceng.2022.108132

Rothstein, M. A., & Tovino, S. A. (2019). California takes the lead on Data Privacy Law. *The Hastings Center Report, 49*(5), 4–5. doi:10.1002/hast.1042 PMID:31581323

Rountree, D., & Castrillo, I. (2014). Introduction to the Cloud. *The Basics of Cloud Computing*, 1–17. doi:10.1016/B978-0-12-405932-0.00001-3

Sagar, S., Ahmed, M., & Husain, M. Y. (2021). Fuzzy Randomized Load Balancing for Cloud Computing. In *Advances on P2P, Parallel, Grid, Cloud and Internet Computing-Proceedings of the 16th International Conference on P2P, Parallel, Grid, Cloud and Internet Computing, PGCIC 2021* (vol. 343, pp. 18-29). Academic Press.

Saha & Ahmad. (n.d.). *Federated Transfer Learning: concept and applications*. Academic Press.

Sai, G. H., Tripathi, K., & Tyagi, A. K. (2023). Internet of Things-Based e-Health Care: Key Challenges and Recommended Solutions for Future. *Proceedings of Third International Conference on Computing, Communications, and Cyber-Security. Lecture Notes in Networks and Systems.* https://doi.org/https://doi.org/10.1007/978-981-19-1142-2_37

Saia, R., & Carta, S. (2019). Evaluating the benefits of using proactive transformed-domain-based techniques in fraud detection tasks. *Future Generation Computer Systems*, *93*, 18–32. doi:10.1016/j.future.2018.10.016

Saif, S., & Wazir, S. (2018). Performance Analysis of Big Data and Cloud Computing Techniques: A Survey. *Procedia Computer Science*, *32*, 118-127, ISSN 1877-0509.

Sallehuddin, R., Ibrahim, S., Mohd Zain, A., & Hussein Elmi, A. (2015, November 26). Detecting SIM Box Fraud by Using Support Vector Machine and Artificial. *Jurnal Teknologi*, *74*(1), 3. doi:10.11113/jt.v74.2649

Salomaa, A. (1996). *Public-key cryptography*. Academic Press.

Sandip Patel. (2015). *CloudAnalyst A Survey of Load Balancing Policies*. Patel Department of Computer Engineering, Charusat University Changa, Gujarat, India.

Sangeetha, S., Kumari, K. A., Shrinika, M., Sujaybharath, P., Varsini, S. M., & Kumar, K. A. (2023). Ensuring Location Privacy in Crowdsensing System Using Blockchain BT - Futuristic Communication and Network Technologies. Springer Nature Singapore.

Sangeetha, S., Sudha Sadasivam, G., Nithesh, V., & Mounish, K. (2022). *Confluence of Cryptography and Differential Privacy: A Hybrid Approach for Privacy Preserving Collaborative Filtering BT - Proceedings of the International Conference on Paradigms of Communication, Computing and Data Sciences*. Springer Singapore. 10.1007/978-981-16-5747-4_29

Sangeetha, S., & Sudha Sadasivam, G. (2019). Privacy of Big Data: A Review. In A. Dehghantanha & K. K. Choo (Eds.), *Handbook of Big Data and IoT Security*. Springer. doi:10.1007/978-3-030-10543-3_2

Sangeetha, S., Sudha Sadasivam, G., & Srikanth, A. (2022). Differentially private model release for healthcare applications. *International Journal of Computers and Applications*, *44*(10), 953–958. doi:10.1080/1206212X.2021.2024958

Sarmah, S. S. (2018). Understanding blockchain technology. *Computing in Science & Engineering*, *8*(2), 23–29.

Schaub, A., Bazin, R., Hasan, O., & Brunie, L. (2016). A trustless privacy-preserving reputation system. In *ICT Systems Security and Privacy Protection: 31st IFIP TC 11 International Conference, SEC 2016, Ghent, Belgium, May 30-June 1, 2016, Proceedings 31* (pp. 398-411). Springer International Publishing.

Selvadurai, N., Kisswani, N., & Khalaileh, Y. (2017). Strengthening data privacy: The obligation of organizations to notify affected individuals of data breaches. *International Review of Law, Computers &amp. Technology*, *33*(3), 271–284. doi:10.1080/13600869.2017.1379368

Selvakumar, S., & Manivannan, S. S. (2021). A spectrum defragmentation algorithm using jellyfish optimization technique in elastic optical network (EON). *Wireless Personal Communications*, •••, 1–19.

Selvaraj, S. (2021, June 1). Utility-Based Differentially Private Recommendation System. *Big Data*, *9*(3), 203–218. Advance online publication. doi:10.1089/big.2020.0038

Selvaraj, S., Sadasivam, G. S., Goutham, D. T., Srikanth, A., & Vinith, J. (2021). Privacy Preserving Bloom Recommender System. *2021 International Conference on Computer Communication and Informatics (ICCCI)*, 1–6. 10.1109/ICCCI50826.2021.9402528

Sezer, B. B., Topal, S., & Nuriyev, U. (2022). TPPSUPPLY: A traceable and privacy-preserving blockchain system architecture for the supply chain. *Journal of Information Security and Applications*, *66*, 103116. doi:10.1016/j.jisa.2022.103116

Sharafaldin, I. L. (2018). Toward Generating a New Intrusion Detection Dataset and Intrusion Traffic Characterization. In *ICISSP 2018 - 4th International Conference on Information Systems Security and Privacy*. SCITEPRESS – Science and Technology Publications, Lda. 10.5220/0006639801080116

Sharma, Sharma, & Sharma. (2012). *Efficient Load Balancing Algorithm in VM Cloud Environment*. Dept. of CSE Sri Sai College of Engineering & Technology, Badhani, Pathankot, Punjab, India.

Sharma, A., Tomar, R., Chilamkurti, N., & Kim, B.-G. (2020). Blockchain based smart contracts for internet of medical things in e-healthcare. *Electronics (Basel)*, *9*(10), 1609. doi:10.3390/electronics9101609

Sharma, P., Jindal, R., & Borah, M. D. (2020). Blockchain technology for Cloud Storage. *ACM Computing Surveys*, *53*(4), 1–32. doi:10.1145/3403954

Sharma, P., Moparthi, N. R., Namasudra, S., Shanmuganathan, V., & Hsu, C.-H. (2022). Blockchain-based IoT architecture to secure healthcare system using identity-based encryption. *Expert Systems: International Journal of Knowledge Engineering and Neural Networks*, *39*(10), e12915. doi:10.1111/exsy.12915

Sharma, V., & Ramamoorthy, S. (2023). A Review on Secure Data access through Multi-Keyword Searching in Cloud Storage. *Third International Conference on Intelligent Communication Technology and Virtual mobile Networks*, 70-73. 10.1109/ICICV50876.2021.9388595

ShayestehTabatabaei. (2020). A novel fault tolerance energy-aware clustering method via social spider optimization (SSO) and fuzzy logic and mobile sink in wireless sensor networks (WSNs). *Computer Systems Science and Engineering*, *35*(6), 477–494. doi:10.32604/csse.2020.35.477

Sheninger, E. (2019). *Digital leadership: Changing paradigms for changing times*. Corwin Press.

Sheth, & Tyagi. (2022). Deep Learning, Blockchain based Multi-layered Authentication and Security Architectures. *2022 International Conference on Applied Artificial Intelligence and Computing (ICAAIC)*, 476-485. 10.1109/ICAAIC53929.2022.9793179

Shi, L., Shu, J., Zhang, W., & Liu, Y. (2021). HFL-DP: Hierarchical Federated Learning with Differential Privacy. *2021 IEEE Global Communications Conference (GLOBECOM)*, 1–7. 10.1109/GLOBECOM46510.2021.9685644

Shivraj, S., & Raghavendra, R. S. (2008). Server-side HMM-based RAP detection approach. In *Proceedings of the International Conference on Wireless Communications, Networking and Mobile Computing* (pp. 1-5). IEEE.

Shobha. (2018). *A Novel Load Balancing Algorithm Based on the Capacity of the Virtual Machine*. Academic Press.

Shrestha, K., Alsadoon, A., Prasad, P. W. C., Maag, A., Thu Hang, P. D., & Elchouemi, A. (2019). Health Monitoring based on Wireless Sensor Networks: A Comprehensive Framework. *2019 11th International Conference on Knowledge and Systems Engineering (KSE)*, 1-6. 10.1109/KSE.2019.8919390

Shreyas Madhav, A. V., Ilavarasi, A. K., & Tyagi, A. K. (2022). (2022). The Heroes and Villains of the Mix Zone: The Preservation and Leaking of User's Privacy in Future Vehicles. *Arunachalam, V., Sivasankaran, K. (Eds) Microelectronic Devices, Circuits and Systems. ICMDCS 2022. Communications in Computer and Information Science*. https://doi.org/https://doi.org/10.1007/978-3-031-23973-1_12

Siddiqui, A. W., & Raza, S. A. (2021). A general ontological timetabling-model driven metaheuristics approach based on elite solutions. *Expert Systems with Applications*, *170*, 114268. doi:10.1016/j.eswa.2020.114268

Sidhu, A. K., & Kinger, S. (2013). Analysis of Load Balancing Techniques in Cloud Computing. *International Journal of Computers and Technology*, *4*(2), 737–741. doi:10.24297/ijct.v4i2C2.4194

Singh, H., Bhasin, A., Kaveri, P. R., & Chavan, V. (n.d.). Cloud Resource Management: Comparative Analysis and Research Issues. *International Journal of Scientific & Technology Research.* www.ijstr.org

Singh, K. S. (2015). A systematic review of IP traceback schemes for denial of service attacks. Punjab: Department of Computer Science and Engineering, S B S State Technical Campus, Punjab 152004, India. doi:10.1016/j.cose.2015.06.007

Singh, A. P., & Choudhary, A. (2021). Approach for Ensuring Fragmentation and Integrity of Data in SEDuLOUS. In *Proceedings of Second International Conference on Computing, Communications, and Cyber-Security* (pp. 857-869). Springer. 10.1007/978-981-16-0733-2_61

Singh, S., Jeong, Y. S., & Park, J. H. (2016). A survey on cloud computing security: Issues, threats, and solutions. *Journal of Network and Computer Applications*, *75*, 200–222. doi:10.1016/j.jnca.2016.09.002

Singh, S., Rathore, S., Alfarraj, O., Tolba, A., & Yoon, B. (2022). A framework for privacy-preservation of IoT healthcare data using Federated Learning and blockchain technology. *Future Generation Computer Systems*, *129*, 380–388. doi:10.1016/j.future.2021.11.028

Snyder, L. (2012). American College of Physicians ethics manual. *Annals of Internal Medicine*, *156*(1_Part_2), 73–104. doi:10.7326/0003-4819-156-1-201201031-00001 PMID:22213573

Soltanisehat, L., Alizadeh, R., Hao, H., & Choo, K.-K. R. (2020). Technical, temporal, and spatial research challenges and opportunities in blockchain-based healthcare: A systematic literature review. *IEEE Transactions on Engineering Management.*

Son, H. X., Le, T. H., Nga, T. T. Q., Hung, N. D. H., Duong-Trung, N., & Luong, H. H. (2021). Toward a blockchain-based technology in dealing with emergencies in patient-centered healthcare systems. In *Mobile, Secure, and Programmable Networking: 6th International Conference, MSPN 2020, Paris, France, October 28–29, 2020, Revised Selected Papers 6* (pp. 44-56). Springer International Publishing. 10.1007/978-3-030-67550-9_4

Soni, A., & Agrawal, S. (2012). Using genetic algorithm for symmetric key generation in image encryption. *International Journal of Advanced Research in Computer Engineering and Technology*, *1*(10), 137–140.

Soumya. (2013). Response Time Minimization of Different Load Balancing Algorithms in Cloud Computing Environment. *Computer Applications, 69*(17).

Sri, P. S. G. A., & Bhaskari, D. L. (2018). A study on blockchain technology. *Int J Eng Technol, 7*(2.7), 418-421.

Srikanth, K., Reddy, S. R., & Swathil, T. (2014, May). Virtualization in cloud. *International Journal of Computer Science and Mobile Computing*, *3*(15), 540–546.

Srivastava, Anshu, Bansal, Soni, & Tyagi. (2023). Blockchain Enabled Internet of Things: Current Scenario and Open Challenges for Future. In Innovations in Bio-Inspired Computing and Applications. IBICA 2022. Lecture Notes in Networks and Systems (vol. 649). Springer. doi:10.1007/978-3-031-27499-2_59

Standardization Council Industrie 4.0. (2020). *German Standardization Roadmap Industrie 4.0, Version 4.* VDE and DKE. Available online: https://www.sci40.com/english/publications/

Stedman, C. (2022, July 26). *What is a cloud database? An in-depth cloud DBMS guide.* Cloud Computing. https://www.techtarget.com/searchcloudcomputing/definition/cloud-database

Subashini, S., & Kavitha, V. (2011). A survey on security issues in service delivery models of cloud computing. *Journal of Network and Computer Applications, 34*(1), 1–11. doi:10.1016/j.jnca.2010.07.006

Sunilkumar, M., & Gopal, S. K. (2021). *Cloud Computing concepts and technologies.* CRC Press.

Sun, L., Qian, J., & Chen, X. (2020). LDP-FL: Practical Private Aggregation in Federated Learning with Local Differential Privacy. *ArXiv. Abs, 2007*, 15789.

Sun, S.-F., Steinfeld, R., Lai, S., Yuan, X., Sakzad, A., Liu, J., Nepal, S., & Gu, D. (2021). Practical Non-Interactive Searchable Encryption with Forward and Backward Privacy. *Proceedings 2021 Network and Distributed System Security Symposium.* 10.14722/ndss.2021.24162

Sun, W., Cai, Z., Li, Y., Liu, F., Fang, S., & Wang, G. (2018). Security and privacy in the medical internet of things: A review. *Security and Communication Networks, 2018*, 1–9. doi:10.1155/2018/5978636

T. S. S. K. S. M. & Ramasubbareddy. (2019). Analysis of Load Balancing Algorithm using Cloud Analyst. *International Journal of Recent Technology and Engineering, 7*(6).

T. W. P.; Ramadhan. (2018). Experimental Model for Load Balancing in Cloud Computing Using Throttled Algorithm. *International Journal of Applied Engineering Research, 13*(2), 1139-1143.

Tabrizchi, H., & Kuchaki Rafsanjani, M. (2020). A survey on security challenges in cloud computing: Issues, threats, and solutions. *The Journal of Supercomputing, 76*(12), 9493–9532. doi:10.100711227-020-03213-1

Takabi, H., Joshi, J. B., & Ahn, G. J. (2010). Security and privacy challenges in cloud computing environments. *IEEE Security and Privacy, 8*(6), 24–31. doi:10.1109/MSP.2010.186

Tan, Z., Yu, H., Cui, L., & Yang, Q. (2022). *Towards personalized federated learning*. IEEE Transactions on Neural Networks and Learning Systems. doi:10.1109/TNNLS.2022.3160699

Tariq, F., Khandaker, M. R. A., Wong, K.-K., Imran, M. A., Bennis, M., & Debbah, M. (2020). A speculative study on 6G. IEEE Wireless Communications Magazine, 27(4), 118-125. doi:10.1109/MWC.001.1900488

Tasnim, R., Mim, A. A., Mim, S. H., & Jabiullah, M. I. (2022). A Comparative Study on Three Selective Cloud Providers. *International Journal on Cybernetics & Informatics.* https://www.ijcionline.com/paper/11/11422ijci13.pdf doi:10.5121/ijci.2022.110413

Taylor. (2015). *Inessential of Cloud Computing*. CRC Press.

Teppler, S. W. (2023). Attorney Cybersecurity and Supply Chain Risk. *The Florida Bar Journal, 97*(3), 14–16.

Tharwat, A. G. (2017). *Linear Discriminant Analysis: A Detailed Tutorial.* dx.doi.org/10.3233/AIC-170729

Thomas, E., Zaigham, M., & Ricardo, P. (2013). *Cloud Computing Concepts, Technology & Architecture.* Prentice Hall/Pearson PTR.

Tiilikka, P. (2013). Access to information as a human right in the case law of the European Court of Human Rights. *Journal of Medicine and Law, 5*(1), 79–103. doi:10.5235/17577632.5.1.79

Tikkinen-Piri, C., Rohunen, A., & Markkula, J. (2018). EU General Data Protection Regulation: Changes and implications for personal data collecting companies. *Computer Law & Security Report, 34*(1), 134–153. doi:10.1016/j.clsr.2017.05.015

Tingfei, H., Guangquan, C., & Kuihua, H. (2020). Using variational auto encoding in credit card fraud detection. *IEEE Access : Practical Innovations, Open Solutions, 8*, 149841–149853. doi:10.1109/ACCESS.2020.3015600

Tiwari & Katare. (2014). Analysis of Public Cloud Load Balancing using Partitioning Method and Game Theory. *International Journal of Advanced Research in Computer Science and Software Engineering, 4*(2), 807-812.

Tripathi, G., Ahad, M. A., & Paiva, S. (2020). S2HS-A blockchain based approach for smart healthcare system. Healthcare, 8(1). doi:10.1016/j.hjdsi.2019.100391

Truong, N. (2021). *Privacy preservation in federated learning: An insightful survey from the GDPR perspective.* Elsevier Ltd. https://creativecommons.org/licenses/by/4.0/

Tseng, J.-H., Liao, Y.-C., Chong, B., & Shih-wei, L. (2018). Governance on the drug supply chain via gcoin blockchain. *International Journal of Environmental Research and Public Health, 15*(6), 1055. doi:10.3390/ijerph15061055 PMID:29882861

Tsui, E., Cheong, R. K., & Sabetzadeh, F. (2011, June). Cloud-Based Personal Knowledge Management as a service (PK-MaaS). *2011 International Conference on Computer Science and Service System (CSSS).* 10.1109/CSSS.2011.5975019

Tyagi, A. K. (2023). Decentralized everything: Practical use of blockchain technology in future applications. In Distributed Computing to Blockchain. Academic Press. doi:10.1016/B978-0-323-96146-2.00010-3

Tyagi, A. K., Nair, M. M., & Niladhuri, S. (2020). Security, Privacy Research issues in Various Computing Platforms: A Survey and the Road Ahead. Journal of Information Assurance & Security, 15(1), 1-16.

Tyagi, Aswathy, & Aghila. (n.d.). *AARIN: Affordable, Accurate, Reliable and INnovative Mechanism to Protect a Medical Cyber-Physical System using Blockchain Technology.* Academic Press.

Tyagi, A. K. (2021). *Analysis of Security and Privacy Aspects of Blockchain Technologies from Smart Era' Perspective: The Challenges and a Way Forward. In Recent Trends in Blockchain for Information Systems Security and Privacy.* CRC Press.

Tyagi, A. K., & Aswathy, S. U. (2021, October). AARIN: Affordable, Accurate, Reliable and INnovative Mechanism to Protect a Medical Cyber-Physical System using Blockchain Technology. *IJIN, 2*, 175–183.

Tyagi, A. K., Chandrasekaran, S., & Sreenath, N. (2022). Blockchain Technology:– A New Technology for Creating Distributed and Trusted Computing Environment. *2022 International Conference on Applied Artificial Intelligence and Computing (ICAAIC),* 1348-1354. 10.1109/ICAAIC53929.2022.9792702

Tyagi, A. K., Dananjayan, S., Agarwal, D., & Thariq Ahmed, H. F. (2023). Blockchain—Internet of Things Applications: Opportunities and Challenges for Industry 4.0 and Society 5.0. *Sensors (Basel), 23*(2), 947. doi:10.339023020947 PMID:36679743

Tyagi, A. K., & Sreenath, N. (2021). Cyber Physical Systems: Analyses, challenges and possible solutions. *Internet of Things and Cyber-Physical Systems, 1*, 22–33. doi:10.1016/j.iotcps.2021.12.002

Van Dijk, M., Nguyen, N. V., Nguyen, T. N., Nguyen, L. M., & Nguyen, P. H. (2020). Asynchronous Federated Learning with Reduced Number of Rounds and with Differential Privacy from Less Aggregated Gaussian Noise. *ArXiv. Abs, 2007*, 09208.

Varsha, R. (2020, January 1). Deep Learning Based Blockchain Solution for Preserving Privacy in Future Vehicles. *International Journal of Hybrid Intelligent Systems, 16*(4), 223–236.

Veetil, A. (2015). An encryption technique using genetic operators. *Int J Sci Technol Res, 4*(7).

Velliangiri, S. (2021). Blockchain based privacy preserving framework for emerging 6G wireless communications. *IEEE Transactions on Industrial Informatics, 18*(7), 4868–4874.

Vermesan, O., & Friess, P. (Eds.). (2013). *Internet of things: converging technologies for smart environments and integrated ecosystems.* River publishers.

VibhoreTyagi & Kumar. (2015). ORT Broker Policy: Reduce Cost and Response time using Throttled Load Balancing Algorithm. *International Conference on Intelligent Computing, Communication ,and Convergence, 48*, 217-221.

Vipin, A. (2018). Analysis and detection of SIM box. *International Journal of Advance Research, Ideas and Innovations in Technology, 4*(3).

Voss, W. G. (2022). Cross-border data flows, the GDPR, and Data Governance. *International Organisations Research Journal, 17*(1), 56–95. doi:10.17323/1996-7845-2022-01-03

Waldo, J. (2018). A hitchhiker's guide to the blockchain universe. *ACM Queue; Tomorrow's Computing Today, 16*(6), 21–35. doi:10.1145/3305263.3305265

Wang, C., Zheng, X., Chen, Y., & Yang, J. (2017). Locating Rogue Access Point Using Fine-Grained Channel Information. *IEEE Transactions on Mobile Computing, 16*, 2560 - 2573. doi:10.1109/TMC.2016.2629473

Wang, D., Zhang, L., Huang, C., & Shen, X. (2021). A privacy-preserving trust management system based on blockchain for vehicular networks. In 2021 IEEE wireless communications and networking conference (WCNC) (pp. 1-6). IEEE. doi:10.1109/WCNC49053.2021.9417492

Wang, W. W. (2018). A HMM-R Approach to Detect L-DDoS Attack Adaptively on SDN Controller. *Future Internet MDPI, 10*(83). doi:10.3390/fi10090083

Wanga, X., Dua, Y., Linb, S., Cuia, P., Shenc, Y., & Yanga, Y. (2019, November 17). adVAE: a Self-adversarial Variational Autoencoder with Gaussian Anomaly Prior Knowledge for Anomaly Detection. arXiv:1903.00904v3.

Wang, D., Jia, X., Wang, C., Yang, K., Fu, S., & Xu, M. (2015). Generalized pattern matching string search on encrypted data in cloud systems. *IEEE Conference on Computer Communications (INFOCOM),* 2101-2109. 10.1109/INFOCOM.2015.7218595

Wang, J., Gao, Y., Yin, X., Li, F., & Kim, H.-J. (2018). An enhanced PEGASIS algorithm with mobile sink support for wireless sensor networks. *Wireless Communications and Mobile Computing, 2018*, 9472075. doi:10.1155/2018/9472075

Wang, J., Ju, C., Gao, Y., Sangaiah, A. K., & Kim, G. J. (2018). A PSO based energy efficient coverage control algorithm for wireless sensor networks. *Computers, Materials & Continua, 56*(3), 433–446.

Wang, T., Li, J., Deng, Y., Wang, C., Snoussi, H., & Tao, F. (2021, May). Digital twin for human-machine interaction with convolutional neural network. *International Journal of Computer Integrated Manufacturing, 34*(7-8), 888–897. do i:10.1080/0951192X.2021.1925966

Wangy, Z. (2017). DDoS Event Forecasting using Twitter Data. *Proceedings of the Twenty-Sixth International Joint Conference on Artificial Intelligence (IJCAI-17).*

Wankhede, P., Talati, M., & Chinchamalatpure, R. (2020, April 2). Comparative study of cloud platforms - microsoft azure, google cloud platform and amazon EC2. *International Journal of Research in Engineering and Applied Sciences, 5*(2).

Warner, K. S., & Wäger, M. (2019). Building dynamic capabilities for digital transformation: An ongoing process of strategic renewal. *Long Range Planning, 52*(3), 326–349. doi:10.1016/j.lrp.2018.12.001

Warner, S. L. (1965). Randomized Response: A Survey Technique for Eliminating Evasive Answer Bias. *Journal of the American Statistical Association, 60*(309), 63–69. doi:10.1080/01621459.1965.10480775 PMID:12261830

Watkins, L., & Singh, S. (2011). Preventing backdoor rogue devices in wireless networks. In *Proceedings of the International Conference on Wireless Communications, Networking and Mobile Computing* (pp. 1-5). IEEE.

Wei, K., Li, J., Ding, M., Ma, C., Yang, H. H., Farokhi, F., Jin, S., Quek, T. Q. S., & Poor, H. V. (2020). Federated Learning With Differential Privacy: Algorithms and Performance Analysis. *IEEE Transactions on Information Forensics and Security, 15*, 3454–3469. doi:10.1109/TIFS.2020.2988575

Wickremasinghe, B. (2009). CloudAnalyst: A CloudSim-based Tool for Modelling and Analysis of Large Scale Cloud Computing Environments. Distributed Computing Project, Csse Dept., University of Melbourne.

Wood, A., Altman, M., Bembenek, A., Bun, M., Gaboardi, M., Honaker, J., & Vadhan, S. (2018). Differential privacy: A primer for a non-technical audience. *SSRN*, *21*, 209. doi:10.2139srn.3338027

Woods, L. (2019). Digital Privacy and Article 12 of the Universal Declaration of Human Rights. *The Political Quarterly*, *90*(3), 422–429. doi:10.1111/1467-923X.12740

Wu, J., Ping, L., Ge, X., Wang, Y., & Fu, J. (2010). Cloud storage as the infrastructure of cloud computing. In *2010 International conference on intelligent computing and cognitive informatics* (pp. 380-383). IEEE. 10.1109/ICICCI.2010.119

Wu, Y., Xing, N., Chen, G., Tien, T. A. D., & Luo, Z. (2023). Falcon: A Privacy-Preserving and Interpretable Vertical Federated Learning System. *Proceedings of the VLDB Endowment, 16*(10). 10.14778/3603581.3603588

Wu, Yang, Luo, & Hang. (2022). Enabling Traceable and Verifiable Multi-user Forward Secure Searchable Encryption in Hybrid Cloud. *IEEE Transactions on Cloud Computing*. . doi:10.1109/TCC.2022.3170362

Wu, E., Cui, H., & Welsch, R. E. (2020). Dual autoencoders generative adversarial network for imbalanced classification problem. *IEEE Access : Practical Innovations, Open Solutions*, *8*, 91265–91275. doi:10.1109/ACCESS.2020.2994327

Wu, G., Wang, S., Ning, Z., & Zhu, B. (2021). Privacy-preserved electronic medical record exchanging and sharing: A blockchain-based smart healthcare system. *IEEE Journal of Biomedical and Health Informatics*, *26*(5), 1917–1927. doi:10.1109/JBHI.2021.3123643 PMID:34714757

Wu, X., Zhang, Y., Shi, M., Li, P., Li, R., & Xiong, N. N. (2022). An adaptive federated learning scheme with differential privacy preserving. *Future Generation Computer Systems*, *127*, 362–372. doi:10.1016/j.future.2021.09.015

Xia, Z., Wang, X., Sun, X., & Wang, Q. (2020). A Secure and Dynamic Multi-Keyword Ranked Search Scheme over Encrypted Cloud Data. *IEEE Transactions on Parallel and Distributed Systems*, *27*(2), 340–352. doi:10.1109/TPDS.2015.2401003

Xie, H., Zhuang, L., & Wang, X. (2022, December). Semi-supervised Learning Enabled Fault Analysis Method for Power Distribution Network Based on LSTM Autoencoder and Attention Mechanism. In *International Conference on Big Data and Security* (pp. 248-261). Singapore: Springer Nature Singapore.

Xie, C., Nguyen, H., Bui, X. N., Choi, Y., Zhou, J., & Nguyen-Trang, T. (2021). Predicting rock size distribution in mine blasting using various novel soft computing models based on meta-heuristics and machine learning algorithms. *Geoscience Frontiers*, *12*(3), 101108. doi:10.1016/j.gsf.2020.11.005

Xie, S., Zheng, Z., Chen, W., Wu, J., Dai, H. N., & Imran, M. (2020). Blockchain for cloud exchange: A survey. *Computers & Electrical Engineering*, *81*, 106526. doi:10.1016/j.compeleceng.2019.106526

XingZ.ZhangZ.LiM.LiuJ.ZhuL.RusselloG.AsgharM. R. (2023). Zero-Knowledge Proof-based Practical Federated Learning on Blockchain. arXiv:2304.05590v2 [cs.CR].

Xiong, P., Chi, Y., Zhu, S., Moon, H. J., Pu, C., & Hacigumus, H. (2011, April). Intelligent management of virtualized resources for database systems in cloud environment. *2011 IEEE 27th International Conference on Data Engineering*. 10.1109/ICDE.2011.5767928

Xue, J., & Shen, B. (2020). A novel swarm intelligence optimization approach: Sparrow search algorithm. *Systems Science & Control Engineering*, *8*(1), 22–34. doi:10.1080/21642583.2019.1708830

Xu, J., Xue, K., Li, S., Tian, H., Hong, J., Hong, P., & Yu, N. (2019). Healthchain: A blockchain-based privacy preserving scheme for large-scale health data. *IEEE Internet of Things Journal*, *6*(5), 8770–8781. doi:10.1109/JIOT.2019.2923525

Xu, L., Li, W., Zhang, F., Cheng, R., & Tang, S. (2020). Authorized Keyword Searches on Public Key Encrypted Data With Time Controlled Keyword Privacy. *IEEE Transactions on Information Forensics and Security*, *15*, 2096–2109. doi:10.1109/TIFS.2019.2957691

Yadav, S. K., Sharma, K., Kumar, C., & Arora, A. (2022). Blockchain-based synergistic solution to current cybersecurity frameworks. *Multimedia Tools and Applications*, *81*(25), 1–22. doi:10.100711042-021-11465-z

Yaga, D., & Mell, P. (2018). *Blockchain Technology Overview*. National Institute of Standards and Technology. doi:10.6028/NIST.IR.8202

Yang, Y. (2019). Improving the Classification Effectiveness of Intrusion Detection by Using Improved Conditional Variational Auto Encoder and Deep Neural Network. *Sensors*, 2.

Yang, C., Huang, Q., Li, Z., Liu, K., & Hu, F. (2017). Big Data and cloud computing: Innovation opportunities and challenges. *International Journal of Digital Earth*, *10*(1), 13–53. doi:10.1080/17538947.2016.1239771

Yang, M., Cheng, H., Chen, F., Liu, X., Wang, M., & Li, X. (2023). Model poisoning attack in differential privacy-based federated learning. *Information Sciences*, *630*, 158–172. doi:10.1016/j.ins.2023.02.025

Yang, W., & Zhu, Y. (2021). A Verifiable Semantic Searching Scheme by Optimal Matching Over Encrypted Data in Public Cloud. *IEEE Transactions on Information Forensics and Security*, *16*, 100–115. doi:10.1109/TIFS.2020.3001728

Yang, Y., Zheng, K., Wu, C., & Yang, Y. (2019, June 2). Improving the Classification Effectiveness of Intrusion Detection by Using Improved Conditional Variational AutoEncoder and Deep Neural Network. *Sensors (Basel)*, *19*(11), 2528. doi:10.339019112528 PMID:31159512

Yavaprabhas, K., Pournader, M., & Seuring, S. (2022). Blockchain as the "trust-building machine" for supply chain management. *Annals of Operations Research*, 1–40. PMID:35967837

Yilmaz, I. M. (2019). Expansion of Cyber Attack Data From Unbalanced Datasets Using Generative Techniques. arXiv:1912.04549v1 [cs.LG].

Yin. (2021, July). A Comprehensive Survey of Privacy-preserving Federated Learning: A Taxonomy, Review, and Future Directions. *ACM Computing Surveys*, *54*(6), 131.

Yli-Huumo, J., Ko, D., Choi, S., Park, S., & Smolander, K. (2016). Where is current research on blockchain technology?—A systematic review. *PLoS One*, *11*(10), e0163477. Advance online publication. doi:10.1371/journal.pone.0163477 PMID:27695049

Younis, H. J. (2015). *Efficient Load Balancing Algorithm in Cloud Computing*. Gaza Deanery of Post Graduate Studies Faculty of Information Technology.

Yulianto, A. S. (2018). Improving AdaBoost-based Intrusion Detection System (IDS) Performance on CIC IDS 2017 Dataset. In *The 2nd International Conference on Data and Information Science*. IOP Publishing. 10.1088/1742-6596/1192/1/012018

Zadeh, L. A. (1965). Fuzzy sets. *Information and Control*, *8*(3), 338–353. doi:10.1016/S0019-9958(65)90241-X

Zafar, S., Hassan, S. F., Mohammad, A., Al-Ahmadi, A. A., & Ullah, N. (2022). Implementation of a distributed framework for permissioned blockchain-based Secure Automotive Supply Chain Management. *Sensors (Basel)*, *22*(19), 7367. doi:10.339022197367 PMID:36236466

Zeng, H., Zhang, C., Yi, X., & Xiong, R. (2021). Heuristic fragmentation-aware scheduling for a multicluster time-sensitive passive optical LAN. *Optical Fiber Technology*, *66*, 102662. doi:10.1016/j.yofte.2021.102662

Zhai, Z., Shen, S., & Mao, Y. (2022). BPKI: A secure and scalable blockchain-based public key infrastructure system for web services. *Journal of Information Security and Applications*, *68*, 103226. doi:10.1016/j.jisa.2022.103226

Zhang, H., Li, G., Zhang, Y., & Gai, K. (n.d.). Blockchain-based privacy-preserving medical data sharing scheme using federated learning. *Knowledge Science, Engineering and Management: 14th International Conference, KSEM 2021, Tokyo, Japan, Proceedings, Springer International Publishing,* 634–646.

Zhang, C. S. (2016). An Imbalanced Data Classification Algorithm of De-noising Auto-Encoder Neural Network Based on SMOTE. *MATEC Web of Conferences, 56*. 10.1051/matecconf/20165601014

Zhang, H., Zhao, S., Guo, Z., Wen, Q., Li, W., & Gao, F. (2023). Scalable Fuzzy Keyword Ranked Search Over Encrypted Data on Hybrid Clouds. *IEEE Transactions on Cloud Computing*, *11*(1), 308–323. doi:10.1109/TCC.2021.3092358

Zhang, M., Chen, Y., & Huang, J. (2021). SE-PPFM: A Searchable Encryption Scheme Supporting Privacy-Preserving Fuzzy Multi keyword in Cloud Systems. *IEEE Systems Journal*, *15*(2), 2980–2988. doi:10.1109/JSYST.2020.2997932

Zhang, N., Liu, D., & Zhang, Y. (2013, November). A research on cloud computing security. In *2013 International Conference on Information Technology and Applications* (pp. 370-373). IEEE.

Zhang, Q., Cheng, L., & Boutaba, R. (2010). Cloud computing: State-of-the-art and research challenges. *Journal of Internet Services and Applications*, *1*(1), 7–18. doi:10.100713174-010-0007-6

Zhang, Y., Li, B., Wu, J., Liu, B., Chen, R., & Chang, J. (2022). Efficient and Privacy-Preserving Blockchain-Based Multifactor Device Authentication Protocol for Cross-Domain IIoT. *IEEE Internet of Things Journal*, *9*(22), 22501–22515. doi:10.1109/JIOT.2022.3176192

Zhang, Z., Hasegawa, H., Yamaguchi, Y., & Shimada, H. (2020). Rogue AP Detection using Similarity of Backbone Delay Fluctuation Histogram. In *2020 International Conference on Information Networking (ICOIN)* (pp. 239-244). Barcelona, Spain: IEEE. 10.1109/ICOIN48656.2020.9016480

Zhou, J., Qiu, Y., Armaghani, D. J., Zhang, W., Li, C., Zhu, S., & Tarinejad, R. (2021). Predicting TBM penetration rate in hard rock condition: A comparative study among six XGB-based metaheuristic techniques. *Geoscience Frontiers*, *12*(3), 101091. doi:10.1016/j.gsf.2020.09.020

Zissis, D., & Lekkas, D. (2012). Addressing cloud computing security issues. *Future Generation Computer Systems*, *28*(3), 583–592. doi:10.1016/j.future.2010.12.006

Zou, J., He, D., Zeadally, S., Kumar, N., Wang, H., & Choo, K. R. (2021). Integrated Blockchain and cloud computing systems: A systematic survey, solutions, and challenges. *ACM Computing Surveys*, *54*(8), 1–36. doi:10.1145/3456628

Zyuzin, V. D., Vdovenko, D. V., Bolshakov, V. N., Busenkov, A. A., & Krivdin, A. D. (2020). Attack on hash functions. *EurAsian Journal of Biosciences*, *14*(1), 907–913.

About the Contributors

Lakshmi D. is presently designated as a Senior Associate Professor in the School of Computing Science and Engineering (SCSE) & Assistant Director, at the Centre for Innovation in Teaching & Learning (CITL) at VIT Bhopal. She has 17 international conference presentations, and 21 international journal papers inclusive of SCOPUS & SCI (cumulative impact factor 31). 3 SCOPUS inee book chapters. A total of 24 patents are in various states and 18 patents have been granted at both national and international levels. One Edited book with Taylor & Francis (SCOPUS Indexed). She has won two Best Paper awards at international conferences, one at the IEEE conference and another one at EAMMIS 2021. She received two awards in the year 2022. She received two awards in the year 2022. She has addressed innumerable guest lectures, acted as a session chair, and was invited as a keynote speaker at several international conferences. She has conducted FDPs that cover approximately ~80,000 plus faculty members including JNTU, TEQIP, SERB, SWAYAM, DST, AICTE, MHRD, ATAL, ISTE, Madhya Pradesh Government-sponsored, and self-financed workshops across India on various titles.

Amit Kumar Tyagi is working as Assistant Professor, at National Institute of Fashion Technology, 110016, New Delhi, India. Previously he has worked as Assistant Professor (Senior Grade 2), and Senior Researcher at Vellore Institute of Technology (VIT), Chennai Campus, 600127, Chennai, Tamilandu, India for the period of 2019-2022. He received his Ph.D. Degree (Full-Time) in 2018 from Pondicherry Central University, 605014, Puducherry, India. About his academic experience, he joined the Lord Krishna College of Engineering, Ghaziabad (LKCE) for the periods of 2009-2010, and 2012-2013. He was an Assistant Professor and Head- Research, Lingaya's Vidyapeeth (formerly known as Lingaya's University), Faridabad, Haryana, India for the period of 2018-2019. His supervision experience includes more than 10 Masters' dissertations and one PhD thesis. He has contributed to several projects such as "AARIN" and "P3- Block" to address some of the open issues related to the privacy breaches in Vehicular Applications (such as Parking) and Medical Cyber Physical Systems (MCPS). He has published over 100 papers in refereed high impact journals, conferences and books.

* * *

Mesfin Abebe is an Assistant professor at the Department of Computer Science and Engineering of Adama Science and Technology University. His research is situated in the field of Smart and Autonomous Systems which integrate Intelligent Systems, Software Engineering and Hardware. Dr. Mesfin teaches several courses for postgraduate students since 2016 such as Machine Learning, NLP, AI, Image Processing, Big Data Analytics, Reinforcement Learning, Deep Learning, Semantic Web, Information Retrieval & Storage, Application of IoT and several Software Engineering course.

Moses Kazeem Abiodun holds a doctoral (Ph.D.) degree in Computer Science from University of Ilorin, an (M.Sc.) degree in Computer Science, also from University of Ilorin, Ilorin, Nigeria and a Bachelor of Science (education) (B.Sc.(ed)) degree in Physics, from University of Lagos, Akoka, Nigeria. He started his working career in teaching in 1993 as a Physics teacher in Zinnia College, Lagos, Programmer at the Buromat Data System Limited, Lagos in 1995. Senior Programmer at Buromat Limited, 1996. Head of ICT at Thomas Adewumi International College, Oko and rose to the position of Vice-Principal/ Director of Studies in 2003. Presently a Lecturer at Landmark University, Omu-Aran, Kwara State, Nigeria. His current research interest are Software Engineering, Artificial Intelligence, Grid Computing, Cloud Computing and Big Data Analytics. He has published some papers in his area of research interest.

Victor Uneojo Akuboh is an IT professional with experience in software engineering, networking and cyber security. He has a first degree in Computer Science from Kogi State University and a Master's degree in Cyber Security from Federal University of Technology, Minna. He has worked with a lot of organizations including banks, notably consulting for the World Bank on social investment program, tech start-ups and other organizations in Nigeria. He is currently a lecturer in the Cyber Security Department of the Nigerian Defence Academy, Kaduna, a premier Military University in West Africa. His research interests include: Machine learning applications in cyber security, network security, intrusion detection, malware detection and analysis, cyber security risk management and cyber-physical systems (IIoT).

Olalekan Awujoola is a seasoned Chief Systems Analyst Programmer for the Nigerian Defence Academy, boasting over two decades of experience. His expertise spans a broad spectrum of skills acquired through dedicated work in the field. His passion for academia knows no bounds, as evidenced by his acquisition of the following degrees: a National Certificate in Education (NCE) in Mathematics/ Physics from the Institute of Education at ABU in Zaria, a Bachelor of Technology (B.Tech) in Mathematics with Computer Science from the Federal University of Technology Minna, a Master of Science (M.Sc) in Computer Science from Ahmadu Bello University in Zaria, a Master of Science (M.Sc) in Nuclear and Radiation Physics from the Nigerian Defence Academy, and a Master of Science (M.Sc) in Information Technology from the National Open University of Nigeria. He is currently on the cusp of completing his PhD in Computer Science, eagerly anticipating the final stages of external assessment. He also lectures Cadets of computer science in the department of computer science. Mr. Awujoola is deeply entrenched in the pragmatic application of machine learning, deep learning, artificial intelligence, the Internet of Things, and computer vision—an enthusiasm that is reflected in his specialization in Python-based machine learning. This dedication is further substantiated by his contributions to an array of research papers and book chapters. In terms of technical proficiency, he excels in developing and implementing machine learning models to tackle real-world challenges. His formidable toolkit includes expertise in Python, R, and Java, complemented by hands-on experience with frameworks such as TensorFlow, PyTorch, and scikit-learn.

G. Balamurugan is working as Assistant Professor in Department of Computing Technologies at SRM Institute of Science and Technology, Kattankulathur Campus, Chengalpattu, Tamilnadu. He is holding 8 years of experience in academics. He received his Doctorate in Philosophy (Computer Science and Engineering) in 2023. He obtained his M.Tech (Computer Science and Engineering) in 2015 with University Rank in Pondicherry University. He received his B.Tech (Information Technology) in 2013 from Pondicherry University. He is holding a life time membership in IAENG and ISTE. His research domain is Video Processing and Computer vision. He has published various research papers in reputed journals like Scopus index and Science citation index. He filled 3 design patents in IPR, 2 Patent publications under IPR, 1 Product Grant in IPR and 1 copyright in Canadian IPR. He has participated in IEEE, Springer Conferences and won best paper awards International Conference on Emerging Innovative Technologies in Engineering -2022 sponsored by AICTE. His area of interest includes Artificial Intelligence, Information Security, IoT, Video Processing, Deep Learning and Computer Vision.

Kiran Bellam holds a Ph.D. in Computer Science from Auburn University and has served as a faculty member at Prairie View A&M University, where she currently holds the position of Associate Dean for the College of Engineering. Dr. Bellam's research has significantly contributed to fields like cloud computing, energy-efficient storage disks, and Engineering education. She secured substantial research grants to support her research. Her work has been widely published and recognized, making her a notable figure in the field of computer science.

Numan Çelebi received his M.Sc. in electrical engineer from Istanbul Technical University, Turkey in 1989. He received his Ph.D. in Industrial Engineering from Sakarya University, Turkey, in 2004. He was in Auburn University, USA in 2009-2011 as a visiting scholar funded by TUBITAK, Turkey. His current research interest in in the area of data mining on rough set theory. In addition Dr. Çelebi is interested in the area of metaheuristic algorithms and their applications in computer science.

Shalbani Das is an ambitious student enrolled at the esteemed Institute of Information Technology, Amity University Kolkata. She is currently pursuing her Master of Computer Applications (MCA) degree, with a projected completion date in 2025. Recognizing her academic excellence, Amity University has bestowed upon her a merit scholarship, acknowledging her outstanding achievements. Shalbani's passion lies in the field of cybersecurity, and she aspires to conduct research in various domains within this rapidly evolving area. Already making strides in her academic journey, she recently presented a paper on Quantum Key Distribution at an esteemed International Conference, showcasing her knowledge and dedication to exploring cutting-edge topics. She has contributed significantly to the academic community, having previously published a chapter with IGI Global, a renowned publisher in the field of information technology and computer science. Her dedication to scholarly pursuits and her contributions to academia exemplify her commitment to expanding the boundaries of knowledge in the realm of cybersecurity.

Tegegn Dita is a graduate of Adama Science and Technology University, Ethiopia in MSc in Software Engineering. He worked for Samara University in teaching and research activity. His research area is related to Cloud Computing and Software Engineering.

Piyush Gidwani is an accomplished Information Technology expert with over two decades of experience in Information Security, Risk Assessment, Regulatory Compliance, Privacy Assessment, and Business Continuity Planning. He has an extensive background in the banking and defense industry. Piyush earned his Master of Science in Information Technology from Sikkim Manipal Institute of Technology and holds notable cybersecurity & privacy certifications including CRISC, CISM, CISA, CIPP/EU, and GIAC-GEVA. Additionally, he is a certified solution and security architect for AWS and Azure.

Jeyalakshmi J. has received B.Tech degree in Information Technology from Kamaraj College of Engineering and Technology affiliated to Anna University, Chennai, India in 2005, and M.Tech degree from Sathyabama University, Chennai, India in 2009. She has obtained Ph.D from Anna University, Chennai, India. She has published in several International Journals and Conferences. Her areas of interest include Data Analysis, Social Media Analysis. She is presently working as a Senior Assistant Professor at Department of Computer Science and Engineering, Amrita School of Computing, Amrita Vishwa Vidhyapeetham, Chennai, India.

Agripah Kandiero (Ph.D.) is the head of the computer science and information systems department at Africa University, a career ICT professional with a passion for positive social change. A problem solver with strong analytics, technical and leadership skills honed in industry, and academia. Worked in the technology industry covering the full lifecycle from project inception through development and testing to post-deployment troubleshooting, stakeholder management, team leadership, and customer support. He holds the following qualifications BSc Computer Science & Statistics double major (University of Zimbabwe); Honours in Information Systems (University of South Africa), MBA (University of Zimbabwe), MSc Computer Science (WIU, USA), Masters in ICTs (University of Cape Town, RSA), Ph.D. Information Technology (University of the Witwatersrand, RSA).

Sanjay Kumar completed his M.Sc. from Gurukula Kangri Vishwavidyalaya Haridwar At present he is a research scholar at National Institute of Technology, Raipur.

Santhiya M. is currently working as Assistant Professor in Rajalakshmi Engineering College, India.

Sudhir Kumar Mohapatra received his PhD degree in Computer Science and Engineering with a specialization in Machine Learning for Software Testing. His research interest includes Application of Machine Learning in Software Testing and in Medical Image Diagnosis. He published research papers on testing, machine learning and cloud computing in reputable journals. He worked in different research projects from AASTU and AICTE. He is a regular reviewer of journal published by IEEE, Springer, Elsevier, Willy, Taylor and Francis, Hindawi.

Krishnaraj N. is working as an Associate Professor, School of Computing, SRM Institute of Science and Technology, Kattankulathur, Tamilnadu, India. He is having 15 years of experience in teaching and research, his research areas are Biometrics, Wireless sensor networks, Internet of Things, Medical image processing. He has completed one funded research project supported by DST, India. He is Cisco certified Routing and switching professional. He has published more than 65 articles in reputed international journals and 15 articles presented in international conferences. He is being serving as a Editorial board member of MAT Journal, IRED and Allied Academic Sciences. He has delivered several special lectures in workshops and seminars. He is a professional society member for ISTE, IEI and IAENG.

Lakshmi Kanthan Narayanan is pursued Ph.D. in CSE from SRM Institute of Science and Technology, Chennai, India. He received his Masters in VLSI Design from Anna University, Chennai In 2013. He is a member of IWA. His research areas include Internet of Things, Machine Learning, Real Time systems, Software Agent based system.

Selvaraj P. is an Associate Professor in the Department of Computing Technologies, SRM Institute of Science and Technology, Kattankulathur 603203, Chennai, Tamil Nadu, India. He has been working in SRMIST for the past 18 years. He published 37 indexed journals in IoT, Bigdata, Computer Vision, and Intelligent Networks. He is constantly involved in research related to artificial intelligence with IoT. He is currently guiding 5 research scholars.

Santhiya Palanisamy is working as Assistant Professor in the Department of Computer Science and Engineering, Builders Engineering College, has about 2+ years of teaching experience. She received her B.E degree in Computer Science and Engineering and M.E. degree in Computer Science and Engineering from Anna University, Chennai and she is doing her research in the area of Machine Learning in the same University. She has published 2 research papers in refereed international journals and various international conferences. Her areas of research include Machine Learning and IIOT.

Nikunj Patel is a student and cybersecurity analyst at the University of Wisconsin - Madison with a strong background in cybersecurity. Nikunj Patel is working towards a B.S. in computer science and hopes to be a part of the ushering of the new age of cybersecurity.

Rahul Patel is a seasoned Cyber / Information Security professional with over 25 years of experience defending the Availability, Confidentiality, and Integrity of information assets in banking industry and government. Rahul Patel holds a PhD from Northcentral University, M.B.A. from DePaul University, M.S. from Illinois Institute of Technology, and Bachelor of Engineering from M. S. University of Baroda.

Srinivas Prasad is Professor in the Department of Computer Science and Engineering, GITAM University, Visakhapatnam A.P., INDIA .He has 31 years of industry, teaching and research experience in India and USA.

Gaythrisri R. is B.E - CSE Student, Department of Computer Technology, Madras Institute of Technology (MIT) Campus, Anna University, Chrompet, Chennai - 600044, India.

Shangeeth R. is B.E - CSE Student, Department of Computer Technology, Madras Institute of Technology (MIT) Campus, Anna University, Chrompet, Chennai - 600044, India.

Yadav Krishna Kumar Rajnath is born in Ghazipur in Uttar Pradesh (India) on 10th July 1988. He migrated to Maharashtra (India) during the childhood and received his schooling from Maharashtra State Board. He obtained Bachelor's in Engineering (B.E.) in Mechanical Engineering from K.J. Somaiya College of Engineering, Vidyavihar (Mumbai) in 2010 with First Class with Distinction and completed the Masters of Technology (M.Tech.) in Mechanical Engineering with specialization on Refrigeration, Air-conditioning and Heat Transfer from the National Institute of Technology (NIT) Patna, Bihar (India) in 2014 with First Class with Distinction. In the following year, Dr. Yadav joined as a Junior Research Fellow (JRF) in a Govt. of India sponsored research project on "Flow control in complex duct using synthetic jets" in the Department of Applied Mechanics at the Motilal Nehru National Institute of Technology (MNNIT) Allahabad, Prayagraj (India) and continued in the project till June 2017. He also joined in the Ph.D. programme in the same department in July 2015 and completed Doctor of Philosophy (Ph.D.) in February 2021.

Anika Lakshmi S. is B.E - CSE Student, Department of Computer Technology, Madras Institute of Technology (MIT) Campus, Anna University, Chrompet, Chennai - 600044, India.

Gobinath S. is working as an Head of the Department in the Department of Computer Science and Engineering, Builders Engineering College, has about 14+ years of teaching experience. He received his B.Tech degree in Information Technology and M.E. degree in Computer Science and Engineering from Anna University, Chennai and he is doing his research in the area of Machine Learning in the same University. He has published 8 research papers in refereed international journals and various international conferences and one patent in his credit. He has completed a certification Redhat Certified System Administrator (RHCSA) from Redhat. His areas of research include Machine Learning, Artificial Intelligence and IOT. He is an active member of ISTE.

Muthurajkumar S. has completed his M.E.and PhD from Anna University, Chennai. Currently he is working as Assistant Professor in Anna University, Chennai. His areas of interest are Cloud Networks, Artificial Intelligence, Wireless Sensor Network and Data Mining.

Soumyajeet Sarkar is a student in the Institute of Information Technology, Amity University Kolkata. Mr. Sarkar is currently pursuing BCA-MCA integrated course (2019-2024) from Amity University. He has been awarded with an on-admission scholarship from Amity University. He has a great interest on the domain of Cloud Computing.

Deepmala Sharma completed her Ph.D. from Indian Institute of Technology Roorkee in the area of Cryptography. After completing her doctorate she joined Birla Institute of Technology and Sciences, Pilani and worked as Assistant Professor for about four and half years. At present she is working as Associate Professor at National Institute of Technology, Raipur. Her research interest is in Cryptology and Biostatistics.

Natnael Tilahun Sinshaw earned a BSc in Computer Science and Information Technology on January 28, 2018, and an MSc in Software Engineering on January 28, 2021, both from Addis Ababa Science and Technology University (AASTU) in Addis Ababa, Ethiopia. He worked as an Academic Research Assistant at AASTU in Addis Ababa, Ethiopia, from September 11, 2018, to September 5, 2020. Subsequently, he served as a Computer Science instructor at CPU College in Addis Ababa, Ethiopia. Additionally, he held the position of department head for Computer Science at the American College of Technology (ACT). Currently, he is working as an instructor in the Department of Software Engineering at Addis Ababa Science and Technology University (AASTU). His research interests include Deep Learning, Machine Learning, Computer Vision, Big Data, and IoT.

Deekshitha Somanahalli Umesh is a passionate Quality Assurance Analyst with over 4 years of experience in the financial and healthcare industries. Deekshitha Somanahalli Umesh holds a Master's degree from Illinois Institute of Technology in Information Technology and Management and a Bachelor of Engineering from Visvevaraya Technological University.

Gulshan Soni is an Associate Professor in the CSE department at MSEIT, MATS University, Raipur, India. He holds a Ph.D. from Pondicherry University, along with a B.Tech. from NIT Raipur and an M.E. from NITTTR Chandigarh. His research interests include wireless sensor networks, wireless body area networks, MAC and routing protocols, and distributed computing. Dr. Soni has published extensively in reputable journals and presented at national and international conferences. With over seven years of teaching experience, he brings valuable expertise to both government and private academic institutions in India.

Priyanga Subbiah received the B.Tech degree in Information Technology from New Prince Shri Bhavani College of Engineering and Technology, Chennai, India, in 2015 and the M.E. degree in Computer Science and Engineering from Thiagarajar College of Engineering, Madurai, in 2020. He is currently pursuing the Ph.D. degree in Computer Science and Engineering at SRM Institute of Science and Technology, Chengalpattu, Tamil Nadu, India. From 2022, she was a Research Scholar with the Computer Science and Engineering. His research interest includes the processing of images and detection of disease in the plant using Artificial Intelligence.

Tarikwa Tesfa Bedane is currently a lecturer in the Department of Software Engineering at Addis Ababa Science and Technology University, Ethiopia. She holds a BSc degree in Computer Science and IT and an MSc degree in Software Engineering from the same university. Tarikwa is a young and passionate educator and researcher. She is committed to helping her students learn the skills and knowledge they need to succeed in the software engineering profession. She is currently engaged in different data science research projects dedicated to advancing the field of data science through stat-of-the-art technologies. Her research interests include data science specifically machine learning and natural language processing (NLP).

Preethiya Thandapani received her B.E. degree from Anna University, Chennai in the year 2007 and M.E. degree from Anna University, Thiruchirapalli, Tamil Nadu, India in the year 2009. She has completed Ph.D from Kalasalingam Academy of Research and Education in the field of Mobile Wireless Sensor Network in the year 2020. Her research primarily centered on improving the energy efficiency of mobile unmanned vehicles engaged in communication, with a specific focus on factors related to their speed while in motion. After completing her Ph.D., her curiosity extended to Data Science, and she seamlessly merged it with her WSN expertise, charting a new research trajectory. With over 11 years of teaching experience, she has authored numerous research papers in the field of WSN and Data Science, particularly in addressing environmental monitoring healthcare challenges.

Ravi Shekhar Tiwari is a Researcher, Innovator, and an Engineer. He has written more than 0.5 billion lines of code that are adding value to people's lives. He has 4+ years of industry experience working as an Artificial Intelligence Engineer, Penetration Tester, and MFDI Engineer in Multinational IT companies as well as start-ups. He also holds a position as a reviewer and editor in reputed journals and as an author in technical magazines with Indian Patents, SCI research papers SCOPUS research papers, Book Chapters SCOPUS indexed, and as an Editor in Book Series titled as 'Futuristic Trend in Artificial Intelligence' and 'Futuristic Trend in IoT''. He has won awards as a Researcher, Contribution to Student Development. Ravi Shekhar Tiwari research domain includes Time Series Analysis, Protein Structure Prediction and Generation, Federated Learning, the Internet of Things, Microcontrollers, Gait Analysis,

AI and Healthcare, XAI, Cloud Computing, Computer Vision, Parallel and Distributed Computing in the cloud. Currently, he is pursuing his Master in Technology in Mahindra University with Specialization Artificial Intelligence and Data Science with Teaching Assistant. As a responsible member, he always tries to enhance and uplift society by teaching students remotely. He has been invited as a guest speaker at 2 international conferences. He is also a teacher and mentor without the border where he teaches students to overcome difficulties and pursue their interests as their careers. He also writes poems and short inspirational stories in periodicals.

Biswajit Tripathy was educated at Utkal University obtained his B.Tech (1991) and M.Tech from FM University (2008) and PhD from Biju Patnaik University of Technology(2018). He is currently working as Professor and Principal in Einstein College of computer application and management, Khurda, Bhubaneswar (India). He is having total 29 years' experience both industries and teaching in the field of Computer Science. His area of interest is E-commerce, Software Engineering, Artificial Intelligence, IOT, Software Project Management and Network Security.

Harish Venu completed his PhD in 2018 and has nearly 2800+ citations and 60+ SCI publications. Currently, he is pursuing Post Doctorate fellowship in Malaysia.

Virendra Kumar Verma is currently working as an assistant professor in Institute of Engineering & Rural Technology (IERT) Prayagraj. His area of interest is Manufacturing Technology, Artificial Intelligence, Optimisation techniques, etc.

Ali Wided was born in Bir el ater, Tebessa, Algeria in 1984. She obtained his magister degree in 2011 from Tebessa University (Algeria). She received her PhD from the University of Biskra (2020). Currently she is an associate Professor class A in Department of science and technology, Echahid Cheikh Larbi Tebessi University., Algeria. Her research work focuses on Distributed systems, Smart systems, Grid and Cloud Computing and Artificial Intelligence.

Index

D

E

F

G

H

S

T

U

V

W

Z

www.ingramcontent.com/pod-product-compliance
Lightning Source LLC
LaVergne TN
LVHW080115011026
849160LV00013B/1107